"The Titanic and the Indifferent Stranger"

By
Dr. Paul Lee

The Complete Story of the Titanic and the Californian

ISBN 978-0-9563015-0-5

Acknowledgements

A book without attributes or acknowledgement is simply a work of conceit; all works should require a dedication as it is the work of countless people who shape the mind and methods of the author. Primarily, I must thank the various teachers and tutors who have "moulded" me over the years. From Darlington's Eastbourne Comprehensive School, then known as possibly the worst school in the North-East of England, my thanks must go to a multitude of teachers, of whom the most notable are; Mr. Robert Anderson, my English teacher, who not only taught his charges how to write, but also how to *think*, and to reason; Mr. Robert Walker, my French teacher, who nurtured an interest in self-development beyond school; Mr. Cliff French, a wonderfully gifted physics teacher; and Mr. Gerard Kivlehan, my form teacher, a gentle and kind soul. The pupils were unanimously regarded as rotten, but the teachers were worth their weight in gold. A clichéd statement, but entirely true.

From the Queen Elizabeth Sixth Form College, my thanks to Mr. Pursey and his late wife who convinced me that University life was an opportunity not to be dismissed; Dr. Denis Kemp, a wonderful physics teacher who injected a sense of joy in the wonders of the micro- and macroverse; and Dr. Roger Partington, a fantastically eccentric Chemistry boffin. The college truly deserves its reputation for excellence.

At Southampton University, I must thank Dr. Malcolm Coe and Dr. Kevin Ross for the chance to study physics with their highly experienced colleagues; and at York University, thanks to Dr. Douglas Watson and Dr. Robert Wadsworth for guiding me through more than 3 years of disillusionment, and finally, triumph. To list every teacher would be an onerous task, and, due to the failing memory of this author, any inadvertent omission might be considered an insult. None was intended. Therefore, to anyone overlooked – thank you.

To my fellow Titanic researchers who provided immeasurable help and permission to quote from their own work, I offer my sincere thanks. These include; Dave Gittins, Samuel Halpern, Dave Billnitzer, George Behe, Rob Ottmers and Parks Stephenson. I would also like to thank Carmal Spreadborough and Phil Marley for their help in proof reading. Additionally, I would like to thank Captain Tom Barnett and Edward de Groot for answering many, seemingly trivial questions. Also thanks to Dr.Ciaran O'Keeffe for his discussion with matters of psychology. Thanks also to Mr. Robert Stone, the grandson of the *Californian's* 2nd Officer, and Steve Robinson, the Senior Administrator of "Sea Breezes" magazine for allowing me to quote from his fine magazine.

From academic and official organisations, a big thank you to the Merseyside Maritime Museum, the National Maritime Museum, the Births, Marriages and Deaths Archives (UK), the National Archives (UK), the National Archives (U.S.A), the Newfoundland Maritime Museum, the Marine Accident

Investigation Branch, Southampton and Liverpool City Archives, the Bodleian Library, the New York Historical Society, the Library and Archives Canada and the Royal Opera House in Covent Garden, London.

A big debt of thanks to Haynes Publishing for allowing me to determine the truth behind the efforts to stifle "*The Ship That Stood Still*." Gratitude is also offered to those individuals and sources who prefer to remain anonymous. Their contributions are hidden under the "Private Information" moniker.

Last, and by no means least, I would like to thank my parents and brother, and a huge debt of gratitude to my wife, Carly, who pestered me and ensured that the project was completed when my own enthusiasm was waning.

All images are either from the author's collection, or are donated thanks to the courtesy of Mr. J.H. Stephens, or are believed to be in the public domain. The exception is the chart of the disaster area as determined by the M.A.I.B., which is reproduced courtesy of Her Majesty's Stationery Office.

About the author:

Dr. Paul Lee was born on Hallowe'en night, 1971 in Apapa, Nigeria, and travelled back to England upon expiration of his father's work visa the following May.

His interest in the *Titanic* started when the wreck was discovered in 1985. The *Californian* incident was one of his first obsessions, and he enjoyed many years correspondence with fellow researchers John C. Carrothers, Leslie Harrison and David Eno. Since the publication of *"The Ship That Stood Still"*, Paul had an epiphany and has become more sceptical on the subject.

Paul's first piece of research into the *Californian* resulted in him not only winning a silver trophy from the Royal Institute of Navigation's annual competition in 1990, but also a trip to sea aboard HMS Broadsword as she escorted the Royal Yacht Britannia from Portsmouth to London as part of HM The Queen Mother's birthday celebrations in August that year. Two of the highlights of the trip were being hoisted from one ship to the other by means of a jackstay, the other being a 12-4am watch on the bridge.

Since then, Paul has acted as a front of house assistant and guide, and unofficial adviser during the 2003 Titanic Artefact Exhibition at London's Science Museum. He also has lectured at the White Swan Hotel in Alnwick, which house a portion of wood panelling from the Titanic's sister, the Olympic, upon her scrapping in the 1930s. He is also due to lecture at the 2012 titanicvoyages.com recreation of the Titanic's maiden voyage.

Paul possesses a 1st Class B.Sc. (Hons) in Physics from Southampton University (1993) and a Doctorate in the field of Nuclear Physics from York University (1997). He now works in the computing industry.

Paul lives in the Midlands with his beloved wife Carly and 13 ravenous guinea pigs.

Contents

Introduction

With the possible exception of the factions of *Titanic* enthusiasts who debate the moralities of salvaging items from the wrecksite, nothing in the story of the supposed 'Unsinkable' White Star passenger liner has provoked more acrimony than the saga of the *Californian*, 'The Ship That Stood Still.' This is surprising as it occupies only a peripheral part of the story of the sinking. Even now, nearly 96 years since the tragedy, the ability of the *Titanic* story to mesmerise us holds strong, and with it, the fate of a little known Leyland Line vessel under the command of Captain Stanley Lord.

For some, the debate as to whether the crew of the *Californian* was indeed guilty, or innocent of ignoring the *Titanic*'s distress signals and failing to act in the rescue, can be likened to the fervour and zeal normally attributed to the behaviour of some religious fundamentalists; people who hold either one of the polarising views are 'right' and to some, it feels like a personal matter, or an obsession. In these circumstances, it is an impossible task to bypass these emotional convictions with reasoned logic or discussion. Some of the arguments, and indeed, some of the protagonists, have been downright nasty, and there are stories of threats and legal action. How could this little-known story possibly rouse so much anger when all the witnesses in the case are now dead, and the *Californian* itself now lies on the sea floor? Seductive personalities on both sides of the argument may be an important issue in this matter, as this text will hopefully demonstrate. It certainly explains why the matter has survived successive attempts to bury the whole tale once and for all. Does the story still matter 96 years later? To some, it obviously does.

While writing this book, this author was advised to focus on just the navigational aspects of the *Californian* incident. But this neglects an important facet of the case; the people involved. How did they interact, and could this have contributed to the tragedy? It is a difficult question to answer. Unlike many parts of the *Titanic* story, the *Californian* saga extends well beyond the halls of the Scottish Drill Hall in 1912, where the presiding judge, Lord Mersey, his assessors, counsel and the public heard the words of Captain Lord and his men. It takes us to the present day, through the numerous appeals, petitions and debates on the case; for the people who inherited the *Californian* incident have extended the controversy beyond a mere discussion of lights seen at night, ships turning in the current, latitude, longitude or the law describing distress signals at sea. It now encompasses the methods undertaken to stifle the mouths of critics, and suppress their works. In the annals of the sea and its multitude of sea farer's yarns and tales, it is difficult to imagine a comparable case that is so complicated – but paradoxically so simple, that is so unutterably hideous to the lay observer.

A word about sources, references and footnotes:

To prevent accusations that evidence has been chosen selectively to support this author's thesis, vast swathes of testimony have been recited verbatim; the tedious repetition of question number and page number from which the questions have been extracted in footnotes and references has been circumvented for this work. But, quotations of the evidence can be found in the Titanic Inquiry transcripts, available on-line and easily searchable. Readers are highly recommended to read through the transcripts, for contained within is not only verification of the extracts presented in this book, but also priceless snippets of information that contradict long held historical beliefs; for instance, the notion that all the *Titanic's* engineers stayed at their posts until the last minute (some actually left their posts long before the final plunge) and that the White Star Line chairman escaped in a serenely deserted boat deck (he actually seemed to be in the midst of a scrum, complete with gunfire from the *Titanic's* officers).

Technical and maritime terms

To understand some of the technical terms mentioned in the book, this following chapter describes some of the common nautical terminology and practises in use in 1912.

To aid navigation, ship's sectors are divided into the areas as denoted below. In addition to port (left hand side) and starboard (right hand side), ahead and astern (behind), the following portions are recognised:

Abeam – left or right of the ship, i.e. starboard and port beam
Astern – immediately behind the vessel
Starboard bow – an area between ahead and the starboard beam (front right)
Starboard quarter – an area between astern and the starboard beam (rear right)
Port beam – an area between ahead and the port beam (front left)
Port quarter – an area between astern and the port beam (rear left)

The term "abaft" is used to described a line of sight behind a reference, either bow, stern or one of the beams. For instance, observing a ship 45° abaft the port beam, means on the port quarter. In the same fashion, the term "forward", or "foreward", means in front of a reference.

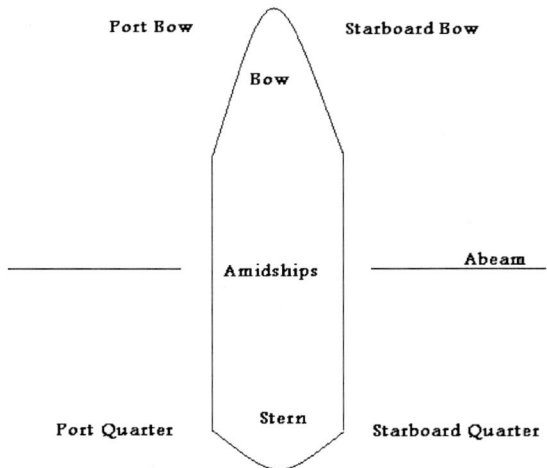

Illustration 1: Ship Sectors

The lighting convention for ships is displayed below. The masthead light can be seen in an arc from ahead to 22.5° abaft the beam on either side, therefore covering an arc of 225° in total. The stern light covers the remaining 135° therefore providing all-round illumination. The coloured side lights indicate to an observer the direction that the ship is heading; red for port, green for starboard. These lights can be seen in an arc ranging from ahead to 22.5° abaft the beam. Both coloured lights can only be observed at the same time from directly ahead.

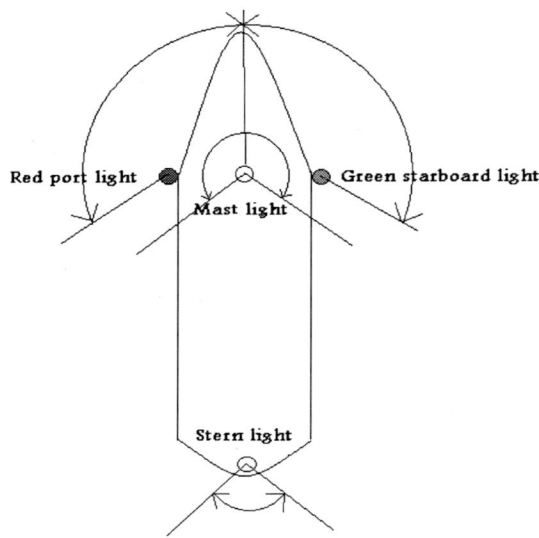

Illustration 2: Ships lights

The term "shut in" is used to describe the condition when a light can no longer be observed. For instance, if an observer were to see the vessel from more than 22.5° abaft the port beam, the red light would no longer be visible; that is, a specially placed screen would obscure the light, and it would be "shut in".

Masthead lights are sometimes called "steaming lights". In 1912, regulations stated that, "A steam vessel when under way may carry an additional white light similar [to the one on the other mast]. These two lights shall be placed in line with the keel that one shall be at least 15 feet higher than the other, and in such a position with reference to each other that the lower light shall be forward of the upper one. The vertical distance between these lights shall be less than the horizontal distance."

In addition to these conventions, the masthead lights of a steamer were required by regulations to show for at least 5 miles, and the sidelights for at least 2 miles[1]. *Californian* carried two lights, on her two forward masts, 70 feet apart.

As well as lighting, shipping companies adopted conventions in order to identify their ships at sea. This meant the display of "house flags", and colour schemes for their funnels. For the main players in our story, these were: White Star Line (*Titanic*) – buff/yellow colour with a black top; Cunard Line (*Carpathia*) – orange/red with two black rings, topped in black ; Leyland Line (*Californian*) – salmon pink with a black top; Canadian Pacific Lines (*Mount Temple*) - yellow with a black top[2].

The points of the compass are displayed in the following schematic. These would be displayed as a "compass rose" on board ship, the most prominent point being North. The other points are self explanatory; from clockwise, North-North-East, North-East, East-North-East etc. In addition, the compass is further divided into "points", each point being 11 ¼ ° to enable more precise bearing and headings to be used. For instance, one might say N 52 W (or N 52° W) indicating an angle of 52° in an anti-clockwise direction from North, or an angle between NW and WNW.

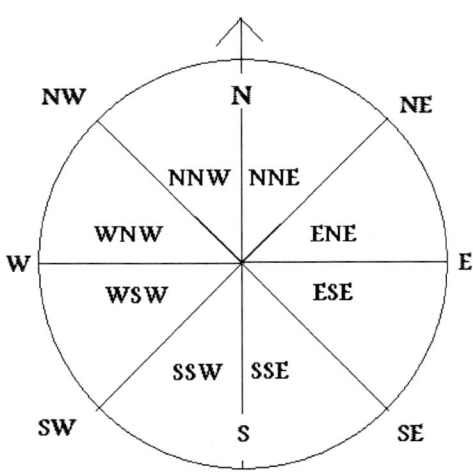

Illustration 3: Compass sectors

---

1   One researcher (Senan Molony) has asserted that these distances are just 5 and 2 miles, without the "at least" qualifier. Obviously, some form of Star Trek-style shield of invisibility descends after that, obscuring visibility. He has also stated that "stars aren't red" (to one person who inquired about star colours being mistaken for ship's lights) and that lights can't be seen beyond the visible horizon (a nonsense comment, as this would mean that the usefulness of lighthouses is severely minimised). The reader will soon realise just how poorly the author's statements are founded in reality.

2   See http://www.geocities.com/samuel_halpern/mypage.html

To confuse matters, True North and Magnetic North are not usually in coincident directions. This discrepancy is termed the "Variation" and alters as one traverses a course. In the following diagram, the variation is 45° West of North. On a ship, one refers to a "True Course", or a course measured from True North (e.g. N 65 W). When actually steering the ship, the course is referenced relative to Magnetic North, as this will be displayed on the compass. In this example, N 20 W (20° being the difference between the course and Magnetic North). Yet another correction has to be made, known as "Deviation". This is the deflection of the compass caused by magnetic materials within the ship itself. In the case of the *Californian*, these deviation values were recorded in a book.

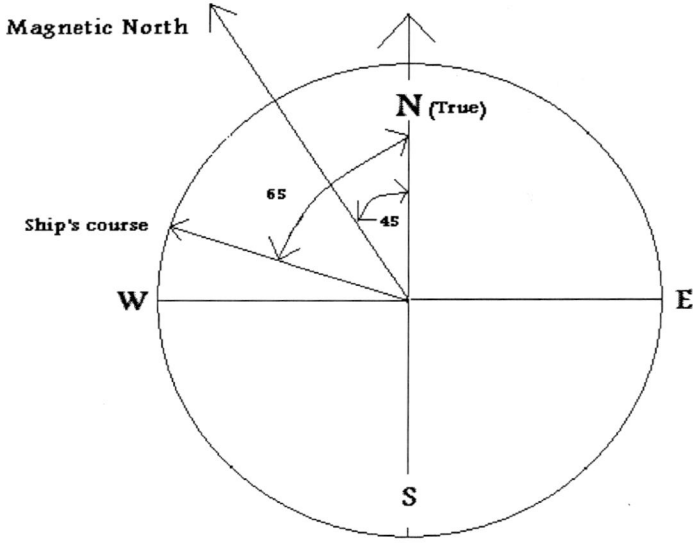

Illustration 4: True and Magnetic North

Derivation of one's position at sea is obtained by one of two methods; the first, and more precise method (before GPS was invented) was to take observations of the Sun, planets or stars at known times. By applying mathematical formulae, one's position could be calculated to a surprising degree of accuracy. This process is known as "Observation". The other process provides only an estimate of one's position and is known as "Dead Reckoning". Simply put, if one knows the direction that a ship is heading, its speed, and the duration since the last position, one extrapolates the ship's movements forward in time. This method does not take into account external forces which serve to deflect a ship from its course, such as current. It can also be skewed by errors in the calculations: for instance, the

Titanic's 4th Officer placed his ship some 13 miles too far west in his calculations, leading to a huge discrepancy between the SOS location and actual wrecksite position.

Co-ordinates at sea are specified in terms of degrees, minutes (1/60th of a degree) and seconds (1/60th of a minute) in latitude (north or south of the equator) or longitude (east or west of the Prime Meridian at Greenwich). One minute of latitude is one nautical mile, or 6080 feet, slightly more than the statute mile of 5280 feet; due to the spherical nature of the Earth, one minute of longitude changes as one approaches the poles. At the *Titanic*'s latitude, 1 minute of longitude is about 4610 feet. One nautical mile per hour is commonly known as 1 knot.

With regard to radio, it should also be noted that not all ships possessed wireless installations, and, of those that did, there were great rivalries between the different types; Marconi, De Forest and Telefunken. Ships and land stations were assigned three letter identifying call signs, with the first letter denoting the type of equipment used: for instance, MGY (Marconi – *Titanic*), MPA (Marconi – *Carpathia*), MWL (Marconi – *Californian*); SBA (De Forest – *Birma*).

To save time, various abbreviations were used when sending messages, for instance:

- CQ (phonetically, "seek you") - 'Calling any stations';
- CQD – 'Calling any stations, this is a distress call';
- GN – 'Good Night';
- TU – 'Thank you';
- OM – 'Old Man';
- DDD – 'Stop Transmitting'.
- 'SOS' is generally taken to mean 'Save Our Souls', but it has no meaning; it was adopted simply because it is recognisable to anyone as 3 dots, 3 dashes and 3 dots.

Wireless operators were expected to maintain a log of their incoming and outgoing messages; the quality and detail of their entries varied from operator to operator. The log of the messages is known as a "PV", or Proces-Verbal.

A 24 hour wireless watch was not mandatory in early 1912. To allow communications for ships not equipped with wireless, pyrotechnics and lighting displays (see Appendix B) were used, as were semaphore, Morse lamps etc.

Watches on board ship were punctuated by a system of bells[3], with officers on watch for 4 hours, and off for 8 hours. The watch on which Stone and Gibson saw the rockets was the "Middle Watch", from midnight till 4am.

Lastly, another aspect of ship's time should be borne in mind. As ships

---

3   See http://en.wikipedia.org/wiki/Ship's_bells and http://en.wikipedia.org/wiki/Watch_system

progressed westward, clocks were routinely set back to compensate for the time zones that had been traversed. This explains why the time kept on ships in different longitudes had different times (usually expressed relative to New York), and different Captains had different practises for retarding their clocks. The RMS[4] *Titanic*, for instance, set her clocks back around midnight so that her on-board time was correct for the longitude at noon the following day; the *Mount Temple*'s clocks were adjusted in the forenoon.

---

4   RMS means "Royal Mail Steamship", a moniker used by vessels licensed to transport Royal Mail. In other cases, the abbreviation SS (for "Screw [Propeller] Ship") is also used.

Chapter 1. April 18th, 1912

For three days she had been the ship of mystery, transmitting nothing but a list of survivors' names to the eager, news-hungry shores of the world. Ignoring all requests for information from the media, the *Carpathia*, under the command of Captain Rostron, was steaming westward toward New York and the baying journalists. The lack of news generated many rumours, most specious, none of them true. Just the bares bones were known; the iceberg and the immense loss of life. And that the mighty *Titanic*, proclaimed "unsinkable" by many authorities was now at the bottom of the Atlantic Ocean.

Upwards of 30,000 New York residents had arrived at Pier 54, North River to watch the homecoming. Pausing briefly to release the Titanic's salvaged lifeboats at the White Star dock, the *Carpathia* was tied up by 9.35pm. To the survivors, the lightning flashes and grumbles of thunder must have reminded them of the useless attempt to summon help with distress rockets three days before.

The 700 survivors marched ashore, their class pedigree preserved: first class first, then second and finally third. The first class had relatives or cars waiting for them...at the other end of the class spectrum, the bewildered third class had finally arrived at their intended homes, many lost and alone, in many instances, their main dependants and guarantees of income now bobbing lifeless in the Atlantic Ocean with some 1500 companions. The pathetic throng were now reliant on human generosity and kindness, and the people of New York provided these in abundance.

The world demanded answers. But those answers only prompted more questions. And the source of the biggest questions of all would arrive in Boston early the next morning.

Illustration 5: The SS Californian of the Leyland Line

The SS *Californian* of Frederick Leyland & Co., Ltd (colloquially known as "The Leyland Line") was a 13 ½ knot tramp steamer: in other words, transporting cargo to whichever port wanted it. She was a vessel of 6223 tons, was 447 feet long and a beam (width) of 53 feet. She possessed a single screw (propeller) powered by a triple expansion engine and dual boiler combination. She was launched on November 26th, 1901. At about this time, the Leyland Line became part of magnate J.Pierpont Morgan's shipping combine, the International Mercantile Marine, or I.M.M.; other members of this conglomerate were the American Line, the Red Star Line, the Atlantic Transport Line and the White Star Line, whose later vessels would include, ironically, the *Titanic* herself. In April 1902, the Dominion Line chartered her for five voyages, which she completed in December of that year.

The *Californian* left London on April 5th and although she was certified to carry up to 47 passengers, on this infamous voyage she carried none. She had a crew of 55 men.

Illustration 6: The Californian officers, from the trip preceding her infamous voyage. Front row, left to right: Captain Lord, Chief Officer Stewart. Back row, left to right: 2nd Officer Stone, 3rd Officer Groves

In command was Stanley Lord, a native of Bolton[5]. He had gone to sea at the age of 13 ½, first finding placement as an Apprentice on board sailing vessels; he had then proceeded rapidly "through the ranks", first in the West India and Pacific Steam Navigation Company, and then in the Leyland Line, after it had absorbed the former company. Lord attained the rank of Captain of the SS *Antillian* in 1906 and for the next 6 years he commanded a variety of Leyland steamers, before taking charge of the *Californian*. Now 35, he was commanding her on his 6th voyage on that ship, which comprised routine trips to American and European ports. During his assignments, he left behind a wife, Mabel, and a three year old son, Stanley Tutton Lord[6].

Lord's Chief Officer was George Frederick Stewart, a 34 year old Liverpudlian. Herbert Stone, 24, from Devon, was the 2nd Officer, and Charles Victor Groves, again 24, and hailing from Cambridge, was the 3rd Officer[7]. The *Californian* had one wireless telegraphist, Cyril Furmston Evans, and one Apprentice, James Gibson.

The media knew that the *Californian* had been in the vicinity of the *Titanic* disaster, as several Marconi messages ("Marconigrams") from other ships had been overheard by shore stations. Roy W. Howard, a passenger on *Titanic*'s sister, *Olympic*, and News Manager of the United Press, issued a message saying that the *Californian* had victim's bodies, to be unloaded at Boston[8].

Now the reporters wanted to know if any survivors or bodies were aboard the ship; the *New York American* asked, 'Have you Astor's[9] body or any others'; the *Boston Globe* enquired, 'Have you any survivors or bodies of *Titanic* victims? Please rush answer at our expense Will repay wireless charges on your arrival in port'; 'How many bodies of *Titanic* victims on board men and women any survivors any bodies identified wireless at our expense,' signalled the *Boston American*; and J. Fitzpatrick of the *Boston Post* had the following message transmitted: 'Send collect any news even if slight and survivors aboard relieve worlds anxiety.'

Lord's reply, published in *The Boston Post* on April 19th, simply stated, "Captain Lord, upon receiving the distress signal [of the *Titanic*], forced the slow-going freighter to the limit of her speed and reached the scene six hours after the *Titanic* had gone to the bottom. According to his message, he cruised around but saw no signs of bodies of the passengers who went down in the whirlpool caused by the suction as the *Titanic*'s massive hulk sank."

---

5   Biographies of Captain Lord can be found in "*A Titanic Myth*" and "*The Ship That Stood Still*".

6   "Tutton" was his wife's maiden name.

7   Although his compatriots had a fairly nondescript history, the *Cambridge Daily News* reports that Groves was in St.Petersburg during the Black Sunday Massacre and also saw the wreck of the Berlin off the Hook of Holland.

8   *Daily Herald* April 18th 1912

9   John Jacob Astor, the richest man on the ship, who had perished.

The Leyland Line itself sent a few dispatches, 'Press reports you were near *Titanic* and have remains victims on board have you anything to report' and then later, 'Understand press representatives on board *Winnissimnet* you may permit them aboard steamer unless in your judgement this is undesirable'.

The *Californian* docked at the Clyde Pier in Boston at 4a.m. on April 19th. No-one could guess the controversy that would ensue, for she was a ship in turmoil, possessing an indignant crew.

The scrutiny of the press was an intrusion that Captain Lord could easily have done without. But even so, although he was within his rights to refuse them admission to his ship, he welcomed the reporters on board to regale them with great tales of courage.

Early the next morning, a throng of relatives and friends of *Titanic* passengers and crew had congregated at the dockside, desperate for news, no matter how faint, and a representative of the shipping firm that owned the *Californian* was willing to allow reporters on board the ship. Before this impromptu press conference could start, Captain Lord had a private meeting with a representative of Leyland's in his cabin.

It was now time to meet the press. What transpired during the sinking of the *Titanic*, the reporters must have wondered?

Although the Marconigram to shore the previous day had sought to allay any hopes that survivors, or bodies were on board, Captain Lord's first pronouncement simply confirmed this news. Several people in the audience, hopeful of better news, left sobbing. The inevitable questions from the press followed.

A typical story, from the *Boston Traveller*, appeared the next day, the headline proclaiming "Leyland Liner Rushed to Scene of *Titanic* Disaster but Found Only Wreckage". The piece said,

"My wireless operator, C.F. Evans, received the SOS message at 5:30 Monday morning when we were 30 miles north of the scene of the frightful disaster. This message was sent from the steamship *Virginian*. I do not know where the *Virginian* was at the time.

Long before we got to the scene we saw the *Carpathia* picking up all the lifeboats from *Titanic*, and were close in when the last of the boats were hauled on board the Cunarder. We steamed as close to the spot as we could, but there was no sign of life about. For three hours I remained steaming about the spot, hoping to be able to pick up something, or recover some body, but we saw nothing.

Running close to the *Carpathia*, the cries and wailings of the women and children could be heard in spite of the fact that they had been taken to the cabins and staterooms, where they were attended by those on board the rescue ship. The ocean was smooth and calm and the weather was fine, but there was a desolate aspect about the place that impressed us all on board the *Californian*. No other ship was in sight but the *Carpathia*. I do not know where the *Virginian* was then.[1011]

At the end of three hours[12], our search having been without result, we put on steam and headed for Boston."

The Boston Globe reported that the *Californian* was "separated from the scene of the catastrophe by great masses of ice, including a number of large bergs and field ice, which in places was two miles wide... We set about reaching the scene of the accident as quickly as possible.

"At best however, it was slow going. At times, nervous and anxious as we were, we hardly seemed to be moving. We had to dodge the big bergs, skirt the massed field ice and plow through the line of least resistance. For three full hours we turned, twisted, doubled on our course - in short, manoeuvred one way or another - through the winding channels of ice.

"Of course the waters were pretty well littered with wreckage, but we were really a bit surprised, considering the size of the wreck, that there wasn't more. We seamen would describe the amount of floating material as 'scant wreckage' but I suppose a landsman would have thought that the waters teemed with floating stuff. The wreckage consisted of cushions, chairs and similar things."

The Boston Advertiser added some more material on the vain and valiant rescue attempt, "I ordered more speed, but owing to the thick ice fields the *Californian* was only able to make about 10 knots, although [she was] a 13 knot vessel. Through the ice she plowed, and it was 8.30am when the *Californian* hove in sight of the scene of the wreck." And *the Boston Herald* added, "it was often necessary to slow down the engines to permit the ship to break her way through [the ice] without ripping off the plates."

Only one puzzle remained. *The Boston Evening Transcript* noted that "...the reporters were requesting what [Captain Lord] termed 'state secrets' and that the information would have to come from the company's office. Ordinarily when a steamer reaches port and has anything to report, figures giving exact positions reckoned in latitude and longitude have always been obtainable from the ship's officers...."

Trying to elicit further information, the *Transcript*'s reporter wanted to

---

10   The *Virginian* was one of the first ships to inform the *Californian* of the *Titanic* disaster.

11   As noted by Leslie Reade in *"The Ship That Stood Still"*, Titanic survivor Beesley and *Carpathia* passenger J.R. Joyce noted that the rescued members of the Titanic seemed stunned, unable to cry or even speak. The weather conditions at about that time had deteriorated; a wind had sprung up and the sea was described as choppy, putting some overloaded lifeboats in peril. Regarding the statement that "no other ship was in sight", it is highly likely that the *Mount Temple* (at least) was visible to the west, or north-west, although Captain Rostron claimed to have never identified her.

12   In *the Boston Globe* on April 26th, Lord was quoted, "We remained [at the wrecksite for] four hours, thinking we might find someone floating on wreckage."

obtain some information from Evans, but "he had nothing to say. So far as was apparent his vocal organs were not impaired."

And that, seemingly, was that. The *Californian*, 30 miles north of the disaster scene, was immobile and, with her wireless set deactivated, unable to hear the desperate pleas for help so very near. When the distress calls were heard shortly after daybreak, the *Californian* raced to the rescue, dodging icebergs and navigating through the icepack, but arriving too late to help in the rescue effort. The story seemed to satisfy the press. It seemed that the *Californian* would simply become a footnote in history, along with ships such as the *Mount Temple*, the *Birma*, the *Virginian* and the *Frankfurt* who "did their best" but ultimately, were too far away to be of any assistance to the survivors of this great maritime disaster.

The minor point about the *Californian's* position overlooked as a seemingly trivial concern, the reporters left Captain Lord and his officers to file their reports for the next editions of their papers.

Chapter 2. "Sailors will tell anything when they are ashore"

April 19th – 25th, 1912

The first intimation that the United States intended to probe the causes of the disaster had come shortly after it was confirmed that the *Titanic* had gone to the bottom. Republican Senator William Alden Smith of Michigan, had telephoned Charles Hilles, Secretary to President Howard Taft and asked what action was to taken, but was told that Taft had no intention of doing anything as he grieved over the loss of his military advisor, Major Archibald Butt on the *Titanic*, as well as being embroiled in a battle for the Republican presidential nomination with Theodore Roosevelt. To Smith, this was clearly unacceptable. Although the *Titanic* was a British ship, she was under the ultimate control of the I.M.M., an American conglomerate. The *Titanic* was carrying many American passengers and was bound for New York and this was sufficient reason for an Inquiry to be ordered as important questions needed to be asked, and if he were the one to do it, so be it. For, by now, scandalous details had emerged of the disaster. Not only had the Titanic lawfully gone to sea with lifeboat coverage for barely half of her incumbents, she had proceeded at full speed into an area studded with ice, a fact that the doomed ship had known. Smith addressed the Senate on April 17th, proposing an Inquiry by a committee. His suggestion was approved, and he and his staff were given powers to subpoena whomever was necessary.

Illustration 7: Senator William Alden Smith

On the same day as the congregation of reporters were told of the *Californian*'s belated heroics in Boston, the U.S. Senate Inquiries into the *Titanic* disaster commenced at 10.30am at the Waldorf-Astoria Hotel in New York.

On this very first day, there were indications that the *Titanic*'s death throes were seen by more than the 2200 passengers and crew stranded in mid-ocean by the useless, fractured hulk of the White Star giant. Bedroom Steward Alfred Crawford testified, "[The Captain] gave us instructions to pull to a light that he saw and then land the ladies and return back to the ship again. It was the light of a vessel in the distance. We pulled and pulled, but we could not reach it." This statement failed to arouse any interest, but later, in response to a question by Senator Smith, Crawford returned to this point of a mystery vessel:
    "[We] kept pulling and trying to make a light, and we could not seem to get any closer to it. We kept pulling and pulling until daybreak. Then we saw the *Carpathia* coming up, and we turned around and came back to her."[13]
    This should have provoked some necessary questions. Was Crawford, and by inference, Captain Smith mistaken? How could a ship that was so close as to be visible, not have come to the *Titanic*? Did she hear the *Titanic*'s wirelessed pleas? If so, had she ignored them? But this tale failed to elicit any curiosity from Senator Smith or his staff.
    The U.S. Inquiry resumed on Monday, April 22, having relocated to the Senate Office Building in Washington, D.C. On that day, *The Washington Post*'s front page reported 1ˢᵗ class passenger The Countess of Rothes as saying that a vessel had been seen 3 miles away from the *Titanic*, and that Captain Smith had ordered her and the incumbents of lifeboat number 8 to row to the vessel and return to the sinking ship. That vessel slowly disappeared. Here was corroboration of Crawford's strange steamer. It is unknown whether Smith or the other senators knew of this detail in the newspapers, but if so, they were circumspect about it, and failed to mention it in their daily sittings. A prudent decision; for rival newspapers were printing a medley of fabricated stories to satisfy the public's thirst for drama, devotion and sacrifice. Not that the public knew that some of their daily intake of tales of woe from the *Titanic* were of dubious origin.
    The *Titanic*'s 4ᵗʰ Officer, Joseph Groves Boxhall, the final Inquiry witness of the day, would contribute new details to the mystery of this neighbouring vessel.
    During the interrogation, Boxhall said that he "was around the bridge most of the time, sending off distress signals and endeavouring to signal to a ship that was ahead of us."
    "How far ahead of you?" inquired Senator Smith, but Boxhall found it hard to provide an opinion;
    " I saw his masthead lights and I saw his side light." Boxhall had observed the lights almost ahead of him, seemingly heading towards, or "meeting" the

---

13   Transcripts of all the testimonies can be found at http://www.titanicinquiry.org

Titanic.

"You say you fired these rockets and other- wise attempted to signal her?" asked Smith.

"Yes, sir," replied Boxhall, "She got close enough, as I thought, to read our electric Morse signal, and I signalled to her; I told her to come at once, we were sinking; and the Captain was standing --"

"This was the signal?" Smith interrupted.

"Yes, sir ... I told the Captain about this ship, and he was with me most of the time when we were signalling."

"Did he also see it?" asked the Senator.

"Yes, sir."

"Did he tell you to do anything else to arrest its attention?"

"I went over and started the Morse signal [lamp]. He said, 'Tell him to come at once, we are sinking.'"

"And did you get any reply?"

Boxhall replied, "I can not say I saw any reply. Some people say she replied to our rockets and our signals, but I did not see them."

"Did you see any signals from this ship at all?"

"No; I can not say that I saw any signals, except her ordinary steaming light. Some people say they saw signals, but I could not."

"In referring to "some people," whom do you mean?"

"People who were around the bridge, " Boxhall said; stewards he thought, and people waiting in the boats.

Senator Smith again asked the question: "From what you saw of that vessel, how far would you think she was from the *Titanic*?"

"I should say approximately the ship would be about 5 miles."

"What lights did you see?"

"The two masthead lights and the red light."

"Were the two masthead lights the first lights that you could see?"

"The first lights, " affirmed Boxhall.

"And what other lights?"

"And then, as she got closer, she showed her side light, her red light."

"So you were quite sure she was coming in your direction?" enquired Smith..

"Quite sure."

"Did they continue up to the time you assisted in clearing the lifeboats?"

"I would signal with the Morse and then go ahead and send off a rocket, and then go back and have a look at the ship, until I was finally sent away," replied Boxhall

"How are the rockets exploded?"

"The rockets are exploded by a firing lanyard."[14]

---

14   The socket signals ("rockets") were small metal cylinders, fired by attaching a

"They shower?"

"They go right up into the air and they throw stars."

Illustration 8: Boxes of socket distress signals of a type as used on the Titanic. This photograph was taken at the Cotton Powder Company base near Favesham in Kent, England in 1915

Boxhall's testimony had obviously disturbed the committee, and the remarks about the unresponsive ship were discussed. Inspector General Uhler, Chief of the Bureau of Steamboat Inspection, was asked his opinion: "The account by 4th Officer Boxhall of a steamer near the *Titanic* the night of the disaster, and her failure to come to the help of the sinking steamship has impressed me. It is a strange story. He gives details that any experienced mariner would expect. He says

---

lanyard to the shell, which, when pulled sharply, ignited the propellant charge forcing the pyrotechnic into the air, where the signals would ignite after a determined time, producing a thunderous explosion and a shower of bright stars.

he saw her lights at the masthead. There were two. He was not clear whether they were both on the foremast, or one on the mainmast as well as the foremast. In the first case it would have indicated that she had a tow. In the other that the lights were used that way as range lights simply ... but it is inconceivable that any vessel that could be seen from the *Titanic* should not have seen the rockets or the Morse signals from the *Titanic*. The rockets can be seen from ten to fifteen miles, and that was, from every account, a calm, clear night."

"I am inclined to think that in the latter fact lies the only sound explanation of the matter. Ordinarily the stars at sea disappear before they set below the horizon. But on a clear, calm, snappy night, like that the stars set in the water, as the old mariners say. I have been many times completely deceived by them and have thought I saw the lights of a vessel."

"I think that Boxhall must have seen two stars very close to the horizon, and their reflection in the still water added to the deception. I have tried to think of some method of discovering what ship could have been in that place at that time, and can think of no way except from the shipping offices in New York."

"But it would seem as if every shred of information available in that way had been brought out, and I have no hope that there will be any confirmation on the steamer. The navy could have none. Only the steamship companies themselves can help, and they have done all they could."[15]

Alden Smith agreed with Uhler that Boxhall and his fellows must have been mistaken about a ship in the vicinity. A vessel – any vessel - would have seen the rockets and assisted the stricken *Titanic*. Boxhall must therefore have been mistaken in his identification of the light. The reporters, their interest aroused by this whole matter, inquired whether Boxhall had seen the *Carpathia*, but Smith disagreed. The *Carpathia* was only seen hours after the Titanic had sunk. "No, the light – if there was a light – was not the *Carpathia*." [16]

The New York Times presented a new theory: that the strange lights seen were from the *Titanic* itself – reflected back from some of the icebergs in the area. The paper reminded readers that some people on the deck thought they saw the lights of the other ship answering the *Titanic* back: "If the iceberg theory is correct, the Captain and the stewards simply deluded themselves in their great anxiety into believing the flashes reflected back from the icebergs to be a sympathetic response to their appeal for help." This hypothesis is similar to that espoused by British Admiral Sir Cyprian Bridge in the paper on April 25th, who remarked that this phenomenon is often seen in the ice regions, and indeed, had seen similar reflections many times himself.

But others were not so certain, and suspicions soon fell on a ship named *Hellig Olav*. She was a passenger steamer of over 10,000 tons plying her trade between New York and Copenhagen, and had docked in New York on April 17th.

---

15   *New York Times*, 24/12/12
16   *"The Titanic: End of a Dream"* page 149

She had the latest Marconi apparatus and one operator. The Liverpool *Daily Echo* wondered about the fate of the strange vessel, and on April 23rd pondered in its pages, "Did she too strike an iceberg and go down?"

The weekend break brought little new information on the story to Senator Smith.

But 400 miles to the North-East of where Smith was conducting his Inquiry, a new name, practically unknown outside Boston and its environs, would emerge. For, on the 23rd, the following headline appeared in *The Clinton Daily Item*: "CALIFORNIA [sic] REFU.S.ED AID - Foreman Carpenter on Board this Boat Says Hundreds Might Have Been Saved FROM THE *Titanic*"

If true, the story would be scandalous, for its contents screamed of purported negligence on the part of a British seafarer.

"According to a story told by the foreman carpenter on board the steamship *California* [sic], that boat was within ten miles of the *Titanic* when that steamship met its fate, and but for the orders of the Captain could have aided the *Titanic* and probably saved hundreds of passengers. This story was told to John H.G. Frazier, but because of a possible outcome of these facts the name of the man is withheld. "

Mr. Frazier's cousin was in Clinton Sunday on a leave of absence from Saturday night until Sunday night while the *California* was docked at Boston. It is said the ship will probably never sail again under the same Captain as a result of his action on the night of the disaster. The story as told to Mr. Frazier is to the effect that the *California*, which belongs to the Leyland Line, which is under the same control as the White Star Line, was within 10 miles of the Titanic when she struck the iceberg. At this time the *California* was sailing just ahead of the *Titanic* but had seen a big field of ice and in order to avoid it turned south and went round the big mass. It is also said that the wireless officer on board the *California* notified the Titanic and all other vessels in that vicinity of the presence of the big ice field.

It was shortly after the *California* had gone by the ice field that the watch saw the rockets which were sent up by the *Titanic* as signals of distress. The officer on watch, it is said, reported this to the boat, but he failed to pay any attention to the signals excepting to tell the watch to keep his eye on the boat. At this time the two boats were about 10 miles apart. It being in the night the wireless operator on board the *California* was asleep at the time.

It is said that those on board the *California* could see the lights of the *Titanic* very plainly, and it is also reported that those on the *Titanic* saw the *California*. Finally the first mate on the *California*, who, with several of the officers had been watching the *Titanic*, decided he would take a hand in the situation and so roused the wireless operator and an attempt was made to communicate with the *Titanic*. It was then too late, as the apparatus on the *Titanic* was out of commission. The operator did, however, catch the word '*Titanic*' which was probably being sent from the *Carpathia* or some other boat, and this information was given to the Captain. He immediately ordered the boat to stop and was very much concerned as to the fate of the *Titanic* after that, but it was far too late. The *California* had by this time continued ahead under full steam and by the time the name of the boat was ascertained it is believed to have been about 20 miles away.

The *California* turned back and started for the scene but it is a very slow boat as compared with the *Carpathia* and several others, and although the *Carpathia* was about 50 miles away when it first learned of the accident it was able to get there much sooner than the *California*. The next morning the *California* learned from the *Carpathia* that it had reached the scene and that the *Titanic* had gone down and that all the survivors had been picked up. According to Mr. Frazier's cousin the Captain of the *California* had the appearance of being 20 years older after the news reached him. The *California* proceeded to Boston.

It is the belief of Mr. Frazier's cousin that the Captain will never be in command of the *California* again and he told Mr. Frazier that he would positively refuse to sail under him again and that all of the officers had the same feeling. Mr. Frazier says according to the story as told him that had the Captain of the *California* turned back when the rockets were first seen hundreds of the *Titanic*'s passengers could have been taken off on that boat."

Despite the slightly incorrect name of the ship, this article marks the genesis of what is called laconically 'The *Californian* Incident.' For, regardless of the other errors contained in the piece (such as describing the *Californian* as moving during the time of the *Titanic* sinking), the accusations are damaging.

The "*New York Herald*" on April 23rd picked up on this lead and reported on the rumours coming out of Clinton, Massachusetts that the *Californian* "was within sight of the *Titanic* and failed to respond to her calls for assistance," Captain Lord was solicited for a quote and responded, "Sailors will tell anything when they are ashore... With the engines stopped, the wireless was of course not working, so we heard nothing of the *Titanic*'s plight until the next morning." [17] It seemed definitive. The *Californian*'s engines were stopped, and not plodding along during the time of the disaster.

The very next day, *The Times* of London, which was not been aware of the insinuations about the *Californian*, reported on its own findings about vessels in the disaster area: "It is even quite gratuitously insinuated that [The indifferent stranger seen by the *Titanic*] may be the German ship *Frankfurt*, which has been accused on rather slender evidence of having ignored the *Titanic*'s calls." But this accusation lacks substance, for it can be proven that the *Frankfurt* was well outside the area of the calamity.

Back to the *New York Times* for more speculation: "Did *Titanic* See The *Californian*?" the paper conjectured: "Only 19 Miles Away, Perhaps Not So Far,

---

17   Actually, the engines and wireless work on separate, independent systems.

and Mast Lights were Well Within Range of Visibility". Pandora's box had been opened and the name of the *Californian* had well and truly escaped.

The article body read "Dispatches from Boston and Portland, Me., last night indicated that the surviving officers and passengers of the *Titanic* who say they saw the lights of another ship nearby when the big liner went down are not mistaken ... From the bridge of the *Titanic*, about 100 feet above the water [sic-60.5 feet], the horizon would be twelve miles away [sic-approximately 9 miles]. Allowing 100 feet for the height of the mast lights of the *Californian* this would extend the view of those on the *Titanic*'s bridge to twenty-four miles.

"Moreover, the Captains fixed the position of the two ships at night by dead reckoning and exact reckoning might bring the *Californian* within fifteen miles of the Titanic so that her lights would be easily visible..."

Although the article relied on inaccurate distances and heights for its speculative piece, it did bring a new candidate for the *Titanic*'s stranger to light; "The freight steamer *Lena*, now at Portland, was also close to the *Titanic* on the night she sank, but being without wireless passed on, unconscious of the peril of the 2,300 persons only a few miles away." The body of the article did not provide a value for the distance at which the Lena was alleged to have passed the *Titanic*, but the headline did; "--Freighter Only 30 Miles Off." The next day, a denial was issued. The *Lena*, from Fowey, England, was indeed 34 miles to the north-east according to Chief Officer Evans Elias. "That one of three other steamers which appeared on the horizon of the *Titanic* is a reasonable deduction. All three of these vessels were bound west, and all three were going so much faster than the *Lena* that it is figured they would have been nearer the scene of the disaster at the time it occurred.

At noon on Sunday, according to Elias, the *Lena* was about 120 miles from the place where the Titanic went down, but the *Lena* was heavily loaded and not speedy. The tramp steamer *Kelvindale*, which passed the *Lena* at 4 o'clock Sunday afternoon[18], was moving about three knots faster and was several miles south. In ten hours to the time the *Titanic* sank the *Kelvindale* would have gained just about thirty miles on the *Lena*. At 8 o'clock Sunday night a four masted passenger ship bound west, passed the *Lena* three miles south. She could have made the distance from that point to the *Titanic* as could a freighter which passed later in the evening."

That there were ships in the area is not in doubt. The Leyland Liner *Etonian*, which docked in New York on the evening of April 16th, "reports that he passed along route taken by *Titanic* and that number of fishing boats were in vicinity of the disaster at the time[19]." This would have been on April 12th, where, at 42°N, 50°W, she passed about 20 icebergs and a field of ice 108 miles in length.

---

18   She actually hove into view three hours earlier. The *Kelvindale* will re-enter our narrative later.

19   http://www.titanicinquiry.org/U.S.Inq2/AmInq15Farrell06.php

The British oil tanker *Balakani* had docked at the City of Port Arthur, Texas, and she "was in the vicinity of the steamship *Titanic* on 15/4/12 and saw a number of vessels[20]."

Also in the 24th April issue of the same newspaper, was an article entitled, "The Conflicting Evidence". In part, it discusses the strange lights, saying that "some have explained that they were the northern lights," before concluding that, "...experienced mariners are often deceived by the strange forms and colours of the aurora borealis."

But not all commentators were convinced that the fleeting lights seen by the desperate passengers or crew were illusory. On April 24th, word reached the Senate Inquiry of a possible solution to the conundrum. Dr. F. C.Quitzman [also variously spelt Quitzrau and Quitzran[21]] sent a report to William Alden Smith alleging that a ship named the *Mount Temple*, which had docked in St. John, New Brunswick on April 18th after travelling from London via Antwerp, was within five miles of the *Titanic* when she sank and "without heeding signals of distress, steamed away." The headlines the next day screamed, "Acting Canadian Premier Gets the Evidence." Quitzman informed Smith that he was willing to appear at the Inquiry.[22]

The Washington Post added to the story, adding that "Quitzman" was coming to Washington to testify and that Senator Smith was arranging to have depositions of the *Mount Temple*'s crew to be taken at St. John. Quitzman's statement read:

"I retired about 9p.m. on Sunday. I was awakened by the sudden stopping of the machinery. I asked what was wrong and was told that the *Titanic* had struck an iceberg and was sinking, and that the lights of her distress signals had been seen. I dressed and coming on deck shortly after daybreak I saw a tramp steamer about half a mile north in the field of ice. She was cruising around evidently trying in an attempt to get out. A Russian boat came alongside, but did not give any word. She made a circle around where the *Titanic* was said to have sunk, as well as around us. A little later, at 6 o'clock, we sighted the *Carpathia* to the south-east. We made a circle around what was said to be the scene of the wreck but did not see any kind of wreckage or bodies. At 8 we got a message from the *Carpathia* that the *Titanic* had struck a 'berg and was at the bottom of the sea. The *Carpathia* said that 700 people had been saved, all the others being lost and that there was no need to stand by."

---

20   The *Balakani* only spoke to the German vessel *Ypiranga* on Monday April 15th, and it was from that vessel that the Captain, F.A.White, learned of the disaster.

21   The most bizarre misspelling of his name was "Quataran" as reported in *"The Northern Echo"* (UK) on April 26th!

22   *New York Times*, April 25th. Note that this report inaccurately says that "Quitzman" was not on the *Mount Temple*. Later inquiries by the Acting Premier of Canada determined that "Quitzman" was a British subject, even though he is described as a Toronto physician.

Captain James Moore of the *Mount Temple*, was highly indignant of the accusation. Via telegram from Montreal, he recounted:

"'We received a wireless message after midnight Sunday from the *Titanic* stating that she had struck an iceberg and to come at once. We turned about at 12.30 o'clock and steamed back to the position given us, arriving there at 4.30 o'clock. We encountered so much ice, however, that we stopped until daylight. We cruised about, but could not see any sign of the ship. About 6 a.m., on the other side of an immense ice field, we saw the *Carpathia*. We also saw the *Californian*, which was to the northward of us, steaming west, then coming down to the southward, and she met us. She did not communicate anything. At 8.46 o'clock, ship's time, we received a general message that the *Carpathia* had picked up twenty boats. We asked if they wanted assistance, but got no reply. Shortly afterwards we received another general message stating, "Nothing more can be done; no need to stand by." We then left the scene and proceeded on our way.[23]"

The report continues, "Captain Moore said that as soon as he turned about he called all hands on deck and immediately put them to work getting boats ready to be lowered, allotting ropes and accommodation ladders in readiness for service. He placed men in crews and had one sailor hoisted to the very top of the mast, instructing him to keep a sharp lookout. When he turned his ship and rushed back, he declared, among immense fields of ice he was doing so at great risk, for he had on board 1461 passengers besides his crew. Nevertheless, he avers that he promptly answered the call for help. Capt. Moore said that when he turned away from the scene to continue on his course the steamers *Carpathia*, *California* [sic], *Birma*, *Frankfurt*, and a tramp were in the vicinity."

"Furthermore," the reporter quotes Moore as saying, "what do the people who were on board my steamer know what I was doing or where I was going? How could they tell in what direction I was sailing? It was past midnight and they were below. The statement is absurd. Leaving humanity out of the question, do you not think that I would have liked to have been the lucky one to pick up those people?"

But the story was not quite as clear as Moore proclaimed, that is, if another newspaper can be believed. On April 25th, the *New York American* bellowed, "'WE WATCHED DISTRESS SIGNALS OF *Titanic* FOR HOURS, BUT DID NOT RESPOND', SAY CANADIAN CREW --- Captain Moore, at St. John N.B. Stoutly Denies This --- Admits Getting Wireless Call --- Asserts He Went to Rescue, But Would Not Enter Ice Field."

"While members of the crew of the Canadian Pacific steamship *Mount Temple* declare that that vessel caught the distress signals of the *Titanic* and deliberately steered away from her, the Captain of the vessel made denial of these grave statements to-day. Minor officers of the ship are silent and refer all inquiries to the Captain ... Sailors and fireman say that they sat on deck for hours on the fatal

---

23   This was also reported in the *Boston Evening Transcript* and the *Boston Herald* on April 25th.

night of the wreck and watched the rockets and red and blue lights[24] sent up from the doomed ship, while their vessel steamed cautiously but steadily away. These statements were brought out to-day, following the declaration from Captain Moore of the *Mount Temple*."

"In any event, we were at least fifty miles from the sinking steamer, and between us was the immense field of ice," Captain Moore is quoted as saying, "I at once sent for my engineer and instructed him to keep a full head of steam, as it would be necessary for us to make all possible haste to the assistance of the disabled vessel. In the meantime , I had our crew prepare the lifeboats. Some of them were made ready for launching, while others were merely loosed so that they could be made ready on short notice. Ropes were dropped from the side, and one of my officers went aloft, remaining there for some hours. We did not enter the ice field; what was the use? We did not know where to go, and I have fifteen hundred passengers aboard. If there had been any definite information, or if we had known the exact location of the *Titanic*, it would have been different, but in the dark and with her position in doubt we might just as well not have been there at all."

"At no time during the night, nor indeed during the whole incident, did I or any of my officers, so as far as I know, see any signals[25]. If we had done so I would have taken every risk even with my passengers, to render whatever assistance was possible."

The newspaper article continued thus with its charges: "The first officer of the *Mount Temple* adds to this statement that on orders of the Captain, he went aloft and remained in the lookout for upward of three hours during which time he was nearly frozen. But he states positively that in this time he never saw any signal of any kind. On the other hand there are members of the crew who are outspoken in their condemnation of the failure of the *Mount Temple* to reach the scene of the wreck. As opposed to the statements given above sailors, firemen and others declare that they sat on deck for hours and watched the *Titanic* sending up rockets and burning red and blue lights until the *Mount Temple* steamed so far away that these signals were lost. One of the sailors, who says he was on watch Sunday night, states that he heard 3rd Officer Notley tell the Captain of the distress message and that instead of the steamer being headed directly to the wreck she steamed away on her own course so the lights were soon lost. An Oiler named Pickard, who was on duty at the time declares that the second engineer came below and asked the men to keep her fired up to the limit as it was a case of life or death. Another engineer adds that when his watch was over that he went on deck and with a lot of others, passengers, and crew, leaned over the rail and saw the almost steady stream of rockets being sent up by the *Titanic*. He adds that in spite of the cold of the night he

---

24   Although some survivors on the *Titanic* mention coloured rockets or lights being shown, the general consensus is that the distress signals were white.
25   In the Liverpool *Weekly Courier* of 27/4/12, Moore qualified this by saying he had seen neither rockets, or red fire, one of the other methods of signalling distress at night.

remained on deck until almost 2 o'clock watching as the signals were tossed by the *Titanic*. His version of the affair is that at the time of the accident the *Mount Temple* was only five and ten miles from the scene. The crew are outspoken in their comments on the affairs. they have no hesitation in telling what they think they know of it, but among the officers a different state of mind prevails."

"2nd Officer Heald says that if he wanted to talk he could tell a lot, but it was not his business to talk and if anyone wanted information, they had to go to the Captain.

Dr. Bailey, the surgeon of the *Mount Temple*, pleads that he is not a navigation officer, and being purely a professional man would not be in a position to say anything. He admits, however, that they were very much further south than had been expected.

The statements of the crew agree with those of the Captain in so far as reports of preparing the lifeboats, etc. are concerned, but the men differ from the officers on the essential point regarding the distance of the *Mount Temple* from the scene of the wreck and also as to whether the rockets and other signals were actually seen. There is a distance of forty or forty-five miles in their computations of the distance."

The article contains many "facts", some of which can be challenged. Captain Moore is quoted as saying "If we had [witnessed any signals] I would have taken every risk even with my passengers, to render whatever assistance was possible", but this contradicts his later statements about not being permitted to enter field ice. It also seems preposterous that Moore would risk his massive crew and passenger roster.

The unnamed engineer's assertions are also problematic. Watches would end at 12.00am and 4.00am. Neither time is consistent with the timings of the Titanic's rockets (roughly 12.45am to 1.45am), allowing for a few minutes difference caused by clock differences, although the reported time of seeing the rockets ("until almost 2 o'clock" is curious). The exact navigational details of the *Mount Temple* are lost, but it does seem incredible that she could be so far off course as to be within 5 or 10 miles of the scene of the wreck at midnight even allowing for the Gulf Stream current which may have pushed her closer to the *Titanic* and the icefield.

Senator Smith sent a telegram to Hon. R. L.Borden, Prime Minister of Canada on April 23rd repeating the allegation that the *Mount Temple* was within five miles of the *Titanic*. As the *Mount Temple* was due to sail from St. John to Halifax the next day, Smith was wondering if the sailing could be stopped so that the Captain could be interrogated "until the rumor [concerning the passenger's statement] can be established as fact or successfully denied." A telegram the next day from G. M. Bosworth, the Vice President of the Canadian Pacific Railway, to George Foster, the Acting Premier of the Canada sent along the bare details of Captain Moore's story, which corroborated his later testimony; this telegram was later forwarded to Smith.

Captain Moore telegrammed another message to Foster; "Not knowing when the *Titanic* sank I cannot say that I was within five miles of her. Not having seen anything of the ship [.] passengers statement cannot be credited." Bosworth suggested that Moore's testimony could be taken in St.John, a solution that for a time seemed to satisfy Smith, but a short while later, a request was made for Moore to proceed to Washington: "this is considered better than the more incomplete way of securing statement by Commission."

Smith was also keen on "Quitzran" appearing before the Senate Committee, but he had made a demand for the advancement of $50, and Smith was unable to offer him anything more than $3 per day, plus railroad transportation etc.

The U.S. Senate Committee received a telegram signed by *Mount Temple* officers J.H.Moore, A.H.Sargent, Chief Officer, H.Heald, 2nd Officer, and J.Durrant, the Marconi operator, practically repeating the information contained in the Premier's message, saying that the *Mount Temple* did not see the *Titanic*'s lights, that the *Carpathia* was sighted at 6.30am and the *Birma* was sighted at 8 o'clock, coming from the southwest.[26]

The Boston Post's headlines on April 24th were now full of the *Californian*: "Leyland Liner Got No Signals Wireless Not Working, though but 20 Miles Away". Captain Lord, the piece said, "stoutly denied that his was the ship which was said by *Titanic* survivors to have passed within five miles of the sinking steamer and ignored distress signals." Captain Lord also said his vessel "had sighted no rockets or other signals of distress. The wireless operator retired about 11 o'clock, and up to the moment of shutting down no message of distress or any signal of distress was received or sighted."

A few further scraps were added to this statement[27]; Captain Lord was emphatic that had he known of the *Titanic*'s plight all the passengers might have been saved. Lord repeated that his calculations place the distance between himself and the White Star Liner was from 17 to 19 miles, and stopped about 10.30pm when he entered an immense ice field. The distress signals were picked up from the *Virginian* in the morning, and then they started for the scene of the disaster.

Finally, a denial of the *Hellig Olav* was received from her owners, the Forenede Dampskibs Selskab. They reported that "it can be proved that at the time of the collision, the *Hellig Olav* was at least 350 nautical miles west of the spot." A

---

26   The gist of this telegram also appeared in *the Buffalo Courier* on April 25th: "the *Mount Temple* did not see the *Titanic's* lights. At 6:30 a.m. the *Mount Temple* sighted the *Carpathia*, and later the *Californian*. At 8 o'clock she sighted the Russian steamer *Birma*, coming from the south and west. The names of the passengers who claimed they saw the lights of the *Titanic*, the message said, were not known" The word 'later' in this context is meaningless. 5 minutes later? An hour later?

27   *The Times* (London) Thursday April 25th 1912

report from New York[28] states that the *Hellig Olav* was on April 13th, at position 41°43'N, 49°51'W, where she passed three large icebergs, and on the same date, at 41°39'N, 50°8'W, encountered one medium sized berg and field ice. By the 14th, she would therefore be well to the west of the ice field that lay between the *Titanic* and New York, and which had caused the *Californian* to stop for the night. This icefield was located at roughly 50°W.

The continued intrigue of the *Mount Temple* et al. surely must have contributed to the following comment in *The Times*, "The statements attributed to the Captain of the *Mount Temple* and the *Californian* both present curious features. The *Mount Temple* is said to have reached the scene of the disaster at 4.30, after apparently taking four hours to cover 50 miles. At 4.30 the *Carpathia* was on the scene picking up the *Titanic*'s boats; other ships arrived soon afterwards; but none has yet mentioned the presence of the *Mount Temple*. It seems necessary to suppose, therefore, if the times given are correct, that the *Mount Temple* had picked up a misleading account of the *Titanic*'s position and went to the wrong spot.

A similar presumption seems to be required in the case of the *Californian*, which, according to her Captain, was only from 17 to 19 miles distant from the *Titanic* at the time of the disaster, but failed to see any of her rockets. Rockets fired from the bridge of the *Titanic* must have risen to a height of at least 300ft [sic]. Above sea-level, and should therefore have been visible on the water-line at a distance of 19 miles. From the bridge of another ship they would be visible at a greater distance still. It would not be surprising if these mysteries are solved by the discovery that the statements attributed to both Captains are not wholly accurate."

In retrospect, it must be said that the *Mount Temple* had indeed "gone to the wrong spot," but this was not doubt to any fault of her navigation, but rather the navigator of the *Titanic*!

The Boston Globe quoted Lord and his crew on April 25th, which ran with the following headline: "Denial on the *Californian*:

One who said he was in the crew of the Leyland steamer *Californian* and who was visiting relatives in Clinton last Sunday night is alleged in a statement printed in *The Daily Item* of that city, to have said that the signals of distress sent up by the *Titanic* were seen by the *Californian* and ignored. The name of the man is not given. According to this unnamed authority, the *Californian* was within 10 miles of the *Titanic* when the accident occurred.

Captain Lord simply ignored the story yesterday. 'Here are some facts and you can see for yourself.' He then gave the position of the *Californian*[29], when he stopped in the icefield, and the position of the *Titanic*, as given by the *Virginian*. This shows that the *Titanic* was 18 miles [sic – 19 miles] due south of us and seven miles west, which would make her 20 miles away.

The first thing picked up by the operator, says First Officer Stewart, was a

---

28   *Lloyd's Weekly Shipping Index*, 2nd May 1912.
29   No longer a "state secret"!

confused message from the *Frankfurt* in which it was made out finally that the *Titanic* was sinking.

None of the crew yesterday would say they had seen any signals of distress or any lights on the night of Sunday, April 14. One of them said he did not believe that anyone else did. The chances, he added, were that anyone on deck that night was not looking for signals of distress but was more likely looking for some warm place in the lee, as it was very cold."

"The story is perfectly absurd," said agent J.H. Thomas of the Leyland Line in Boston. 'Upon Captain Lord's arrival here he reported to me the relative positions of the *Titanic* and the *Californian* ... the vessels were 20 miles apart.'" But if so, why were the positions described as "State secrets" to the press?

By April 25th, the above quotes from the *Californian* not withstanding, attention was focussed on the *Mount Temple*. Had she cruelly abandoned the *Titanic*?

Captain Moore left for Washington D.C. to testify on that date, and to clear his name of the "false and cruel" allegations. After reading a telegram detailing the charges, *The New York Times* on April 26th 1912 mentioned that a "ship's oiler" was his accuser and that the passenger who had been quoted didn't see the lights himself. The reporter obtained a statement from Moore[30]:

"Why, that man, whoever he is, is telling a deliberate lie. He is either looking for notoriety or has some grievance against us and thinks that he is getting even. Do you think that had I seen any signals I would not have gone to the *Titanic*'s assistance?" Moore repeated his earlier statement, with a new inclusion: that he had passed the rescue ship *Carpathia* at 9.30 on Sunday night. He added that he had insisted to his chief engineer, upon receipt of the *Titanic*'s distress call, for his firemen to work harder. Moore said, "As has been stated, the *Titanic* sank at 2.02 o'clock [sic-2.20], and at that time I was ten miles away from her."

The Boston American now had its scoop. For, on April 25th, the front page claimed:

"Says He Saw Titanic's Rockets - Ernest Gill, Donkeyman on the *Californian*, Says His Captain Ignored the Signals"

"I, the undersigned, Ernest Gill, being employed as second donkeyman[31] on

---

30   The oiler was named Pickard, as previously noted. However, the crew agreement for the *Mount Temple* shows that the only person with such a name on board was a "C.Pickard", and he is listed as an assistant steerage steward. Also, unlike his whistle blowing counterpart on the *Californian* who deserted his ship, Pickard signed on board with Captain Moore on 27/3/12 in London and was discharged on 14/5/12, again at London.
31   Gill had actually been promoted from fireman as the 2nd donkeyman had failed to join. A donkeyman had the responsibility of looking after the auxiliaries, generators, donkey 'steam boiler', pumps, ballast and cooing water pumps, and also assisted in the engine room.

the steamer Californian, Capt. Lord, give the following statement of the incidents of Sunday, April 14.

I am 29 years of age[32], native of Yorkshire, single. I was making my third[33] voyage on the *Californian*. On the night of April 14 I was on duty from 8 p.m. until 12 in the engine room. At 11:56 I came on deck. The stars were shining brightly. It was very clear and I could see for a long distance. The ship's engines had been stopped since 10:30 and she was drifting amid floe ice. I looked over the rail on the starboard side and saw the lights of a very large steamer about 10 miles away. I could see her broadside lights. I watched her fully for a minute. They could not have helped but see her from the bridge and lookout.

It was now 12 o'clock and I went to my cabin. I woke my mate, William Thomas. He heard the ice crunching alongside the ship and asked, "Are we in the ice?" I replied, "Yes, but it must be clear off to starboard, for I saw a big vessel going along full speed. She looked as if she might be a big German."

I turned in, but could not sleep. In half an hour I turned out, thinking to smoke a cigarette. Because of the cargo, I could not smoke 'tween decks, so I went on deck again.

I had been on deck about 10 minutes when I saw a white rocket about 10 miles away on the starboard side. I thought it must be a shooting star. In seven or eight minutes I saw distinctly a second rocket in the same place, and I said to myself, "That must be a vessel in distress."

It was not my business to notify the bridge or the lookouts; but they could not have helped but see them.

I turned in immediately after, supposing that the ship would pay attention to the rockets.

I knew no more until I was awakened at 6:40 by the chief engineer, who said, "Turn out to render assistance. The *Titanic* has gone down."

I exclaimed and leaped from my bunk. I went on deck and found the vessel under way and proceeding full speed. She was clear of the field ice, but there were plenty of bergs about.

I went down on watch and heard the second and fourth engineers in conversation. Mr. J. C. Evans is the second and Mr. Wooten [sic- Hooton] is the fourth. The second was telling the fourth that the 3rd Officer had reported rockets had gone up in his watch. I knew then that it must have been the *Titanic* I had seen.

The second engineer added that the Captain had been notified by the Apprentice officer, whose name, I think, is Gibson, of the rockets. The skipper had told him to Morse to the vessel in distress. Mr. Stone, the second navigating officer, was on the bridge at the time, said Mr. Evans.

---

32   Gill's actual age, as confirmed by his birth certificate, was 27.
33   Some sources claim that this says "first," but this was actually Gill's third voyage, as confirmed by the *Californian* crew agreements.

I overheard Mr. Evans say that more lights had been shown and more rockets went up. Then, according to Mr. Evans, Mr. Gibson went to the Captain again and reported more rockets. The skipper told him to continue to Morse until he got a reply. No reply was received.

The next remark I heard the second pass was, "Why in the devil didn't they wake the wireless man up?" The entire crew of the steamer have been talking among themselves about the disregard of the rockets. I personally urged several to join me in protesting against the conduct of the Captain, but they refused, because they feared to lose their jobs.

A day or two before the ship reached port, the skipper called the quartermaster who was on duty at the time the rockets were discharged, into his cabin. They were in conversation three-quarters of an hour. The quartermaster declared he did not see the rockets.

I am quite sure the *Californian* was less than 20 miles from the *Titanic*, which the officers report to have been our position. I could not have seen her if she had been more than 10 miles distant, and I saw her very plainly.

I have no ill will toward the Captain or any officer of the ship, and I am losing a profitable berth by making this statement. I am actuated by the desire that no Captain who refuses or neglects to give aid to a vessel in distress should be able to hush up the men.

Ernest Gill
Sworn and subscribed to me this 24th day of April, 1912
Samuel Putnam, Notary Public

"The *Californian* of the Leyland Line was the ship which was sighted by the *Titanic*, but which refused to respond to her signals of distress. Captain Lord of the *Californian* thought it was some small vessel and refused to risk his ship by sending her through the ice at night to the rescue.
These charges are made in affidavit by Ernest Gill, second donkeyman on board, who is on his way to testify before the Senate Investigating Committee. They were repeated in the presence of four members of the crew and a notary public, and by an officer of the ship, who affirmed them in a confidential communication to *the Boston American*."

The Boston Herald countered this story on the same day. Captain Lord said that he was "perfectly willing to go to Washington and appear before your American investigating committee. I would of course, like to sail as originally planned, but anything I can do I am willing to do."
"Captain Lord's story of the *Californian*'s position and the other occurrences on that night was corroborated by First Officer Stewart, 2nd Officer Stone, and the quartermaster on duty at the time. Stone emphatically denied that he

had notified Capt. Lord of any rockets, as he had seen none, nor had any been reported to him. He also denies that he signed any statement, under compulsion by the Captain, stating that he had seen any signal of distress."

As far as Captain Lord was concerned, Gill's incredible tale was nothing but a mere canard.

And the *Boston Journal* weighed in, *"Californian's* Captain Warned *Titanic* of Iceberg Before Wreck:

The Leyland Liner *Californian*, which is now berthed at East Boston, warned the *Titanic* of the iceberg danger in time to enable the liner to protect herself, according to information which came to the Senate Committee which is investigating the disaster at Washington yesterday.

As a result Capt. Lord and Wireless Operator Evans of the *Californian* have been subpoenaed to appear before it, although the steamer is set to sail Saturday morning.

The summons came after, but apparently had no connection with, the story told yesterday by Ernest Gill, second donkeyman aboard the *Californian*....

Said Lord, "'If I go to Washington, it will not be because of this story in the paper, but to tell the committee why my ship was drifting without the power, while the *Titanic* was rushing under full speed. It will take me about ten minutes to do this,' declared Captain Lord.

Captain Lord said last night the charges which had been printed in an evening paper were all bosh....

Every officer and man of this crew is an Englishman and a white man, and no Englishman will stand by and see anybody or anything in distress without trying to lend assistance."

Mr. Stewart, the first officer, was on the bridge during the times that the signals were supposed to have been seen, and he can tell you himself that nothing of the kind was seen by him, or any of the men who were on watch with him.

Everything had been quiet during the night and no signals of distress or anything else had been seen, and about 5 o'clock in the morning, which is my regular time for getting up, I told Mr. Stewart to wake up 'Wireless' and have him get in touch with some ship and get an idea of what kind of an ice field we had gotten into.'"

It is all foolishness for anybody to say that I, at the point of a revolver, took any man into this room and made him swear to tell any kind of a story. No member of the crew has ever been in this room, and none of them come near the place except to clean up."

If any of you gentlemen is a notary you are at liberty to take my sworn statement for what I have told you, and any other man on the ship will tell you the same story which is the truth."

It seems all the Boston newspapers were keen to obtain quotes from Captain Lord. *The Daily Sketch* said: "Help Near All The Time – *Californian* was in Icefield with *Titanic* – But Wireless Communication Had Been Cut Off:

"We could not have been more than 19 miles distant from the *Titanic* at half past ten on the Sunday night," Lord is quoted as saying. The article continues that, "A telegram from Boston, Mass., states that the vessel whose lights loomed in the eyes of the hundred perishing on board the Titanic was undoubtedly the Leyland Liner *Californian*."

The master, Captain Lord, who was interviewed on the arrival of the steamer, said: - '... We had steamed into an immense icefield, and, in order to insure the safety of the vessel, the engines were shut off and the wireless apparatus being cut off we thus knew nothing of the plight of the *Titanic* until we received wireless messages at daybreak. We saw no signals whatsoever.'"

And later in the same paper, a reporter speculated: "The Mystery of the Lights – Could they have been those of the *Californian* - It will be noted that the Captain of the *Californian* says: "We saw no signals whatsoever". That being the case it is hardly likely that the lights seen on the *Titanic* were those of the *Californian*. If the *Titanic* could see the *Californian*'s lights the *Californian* (it would be natural to assume) would see the *Titanic*'s rockets."

On April 26th, the day after Gill's allegations had been made public, *The Boston Herald* published an interview with his room mate, William Thomas, who was "highly indignant yesterday that his name had been brought into the affidavit. 'I knew nothing about this affidavit,' he said, '...Gill woke me up soon after 12 o'clock that night and I asked him why he was so late. 'Its all right, the engines aren't running,' he answered. 'Then I heard a bumping against the side of the ship, and I asked him if it was ice. He said it was....'

"'I think Gill would have told me if he had seen rockets. I don't believe that he could see a ship ten miles off if there was one, because the change from the engine room to the deck partly blinds a man, and besides that night it would have been easy to take fixed stars for vessels' lights and shooting stars for rockets.'

It seems unlikely that Thomas had read Gill's affidavit. For one thing, he seemed to know nothing of it, so presumably he is not one of the crew members who witnessed the taking and signing of the statement before Samuel Putnam. Thomas was also obviously not in the engine room when Gill was on duty.

Gill's statement was clear that he could see another ship, and not just 'fixed stars'. The same can be said for the rockets/shooting stars. Gill had waited long enough to see a second light before he knew it was a rocket. But Thomas' comment about 'being blinded' is a valid point. Walking along the deck from the engine room hatch aft to his quarters forward would not have enabled Gill to have got his 'night vision in' (to use nautical parlance). His sight, still used to the brightness of the engine room would not have adjusted to the stark blackness of the night, and he would have seen very little out on deck.

With subpoenas issued, it was now time for the men on the *Californian* and the *Mount Temple* to tell their stories to the American public.

Chapter 3. Washington D.C.

April 26th – May 1912

26th April

Gill's affidavit was transmitted to Senator Smith shortly after it was taken. Smith had intended to take testimony from Captain Lord and Wireless Operator Evans due to an ice warning that had been transmitted before the *Titanic* catastrophe, and now he included Gill in his list of witnesses.

Illustration 9: Ernest Gill

As Lord was to tell Smith on April 26th, "As soon as the marshal came to me - he came about half-past 7 last night - I told him I did not like to go without notifying - at least I told him I would not go until my owners gave me permission. We went to the telephone together, and I told the assistant manager what had happened. He said, "All right, I will notify [Leyland agent] Mr. Thomas. Keep handy and I will let you know the result." It was a question of whether or not they would allow me. I do not know what the discussion was. He did not say, 'You are not to go.'" The response was to "hurry up and go"

Gill, having evidently travelled by himself, was the first to arrive, and

Smith delegated the current questioning of a witness to another Senator as he left the chamber to meet Gill. Smith was sure that the story was little more than invention, but Gill, "a rather wild-looking young man with strawberry blonde hair and a shaggy moustache [who was] skittish and fidgety[34]" assured Smith that the story was true. How much had he been paid, asked Smith. '$500', Gill responded, but again repeated that the story was true. 'He couldn't have given out the story unless he'd been paid for it; he fully expected to "get the sack" as soon as the Captain got wind of it, and he'd need the money between his present job and the next,' U.S. Investigation chronicler Wyn Craig Wade would scribe. Smith hurriedly scheduled Gill to take the stand.

Gill was sworn before the committee and his affidavit read out, which Gill confirmed as being true. He had first seen the "pale blue or white" rockets at 12.30am, which coincided with one bell, on the starboard bow of the *Californian*; when first seen, it was not plain and he caught only the tail end as the stars spangled out. He neither saw nor heard anything of the ship firing the rockets at the time. Gill was sure that the ship he had first seen at about midnight[35] was the Titanic. He was doubtful that the *Titanic* was 20 miles away: "I seen the ship, and she had not had time to get 20 miles away by the time I got on deck again."

"Was this ship moving at that time?" Senator Fletcher asked.

"I did not take particular notice of it, sir," Gill replied, "with the rushing to call my mate. I went along the deck. It taken me about a minute going along the deck, to get to the hatch I had to go down, and I could see her as I walked along the deck. Suppose I am going forward, now; I could see her over there, a big ship, and a couple of rows of lights; so that I knew it was not any small craft. It was no tramp. I did not suppose it would be a "Star" boat. I reckoned she must be a German boat. So I dived down the hatch, and as I turned around in the hatch I could not see her, so you can guess the latitude she was in. As I stood on the hatch, with my back turned, I could not see the ship. Then I went and called my mate, and that is the last I saw of it."

"How long after that was it before you saw the rockets go up?"

"About 35 minutes, sir; a little over half an hour."

"Did you observe the rockets go up in the direction this ship was as you first saw her, from where the *Californian* was?"

"It was more abeam, sir; more broadside of the ship," Gill responded.

Gill's interrogation was surprisingly brief. His testimony was simple but at times tended to be nonsensical, for instance:

---

34   "*The Titanic: End of a dream*" page 231
35   Although the transcript says that Gill saw the ship "At four minutes after 12, exactly,", he next describes how he climbed up the ladder to leave the engine room to fetch Mr. Wooten [sic- Hooton] at five to twelve, which would have taken one minute. Presumably, Gill really said "At four minutes afore 12, exactly."

Senator FLETCHER: "Was the *Californian* passed by the *Titanic*, her course being the same as the *Titanic's* course was originally?"

Mr. GILL: "I think she must have passed the *Titanic*. The *Titanic* must have passed us first, because we were floating, and that would take a lot out of our way. We were a slower boat."

Senator FLETCHER: "After the *Titanic* struck the iceberg did the *Californian* pass by the *Titanic*?"

Mr. GILL: "The only way I can account for this, we were stopped in the ocean, and it is not natural for a ship to keep her head all the time. She must have been drifting."

And with that, Gill was gone. Astute readers will recall that Gill repeated his initial allegations to the newspaper "in the presence of four members of the crew ... and by an officer of the ship." Readers may also wonder who these people were and whether they could add anything to the story, but, like much information in this case, one's hopes are in vain. Their identities and any useful anecdotes they may have are now lost to us.

Next to be called was Captain Stanley Lord himself.

The meeting between Lord and Senator Smith was cordial enough. The men talked about the use of binoculars by look-out men, how far lights could be seen at night, the weather at sea, and about ice, which Lord admitted was new to him: "I have not a great deal of experience in ice. This is my first experience amongst an ice field. Previous to this I have seen small bergs, in the North Atlantic, only. I have seen any amount of it around Cape Horn, but that was when I was in a sailing ship."

The testimony inevitably turned to the events of April 14th. At 9.40am, the *Californian* had reached 42°N, 47°W, whereupon she turned to the west for the remainder of her voyage to Boston, steaming at 11 knots. At midday and at a longitude of 47° 25' west, in accordance with normal practise, her clocks were altered: 1 hour and 50 minutes ahead of New York. At 6.30pm the *Californian*, at 42° 5' N 49° 10' W, passed two large icebergs, and 45 minutes later, her log recorded "Passed one large iceberg, and two more in sight to the southward." There is no mention of a position for these icebergs.

Upon getting dark at 8.00pm, Lord doubled the lookouts, based on ice reports he had received previously.

A few hours later, the *Californian* ran into the ice; it was practically on top of them, and was seen only a mile and a half distant. On seeing it, the engine was reversed and put full speed astern, and the action of reversing turned the ship to starboard, leaving her heading about northeast true. During the night, she would slowly turn to starboard.

The *Californian* was stopped in loose ice, a quarter of a mile from the edge of a huge icefield, in a position determined by dead reckoning to 42°5' N 50°7' W, 19 ½ to 19 ¾ miles from the eventual radioed location of the Titanic's on a bearing of S 16° W. It was 10.21pm. The next day, Lord estimated that the ice field was about 26 miles long and from 1 to 2 miles wide, although that night, he never thought the ice was stretching as far down as the *Titanic*'s course.

The prudent thing seemed to be to stop till morning.

With the background to the *Californian*'s voyage established, Senator Smith, with Gill's affidavit and testimony fresh in his memory, cut to the chase; "Captain, did you see any distress signals on Sunday night, either rockets or the Morse signals?"

"No sir; I did not. The officer on watch saw some signals, but he said they were not distress signals."

Readers will no doubt recall the pronouncements to the press in Boston, that *"no signals of distress or anything else had been seen."* Now a different story was slowly emerging.

"They were not distress signals?" repeated Smith.

"Not distress signals."

"But he reported them?"

"To me. I think you had better let me tell you that story," Lord replied.

"I wish you would."

"When I came off the bridge, at half-past 10, I pointed out to the officer that I thought I saw a light coming along, and it was a most peculiar light, and we had been making mistakes all along with the stars, thinking they were signals. We could not distinguish where the sky ended and where the water commenced. You understand, it was a flat calm. He said he thought it was a star, and I did not say anything more. I went down below. I was talking with the engineer about keeping the steam ready[36], and we saw these signals coming along, and I said "There is a steamer passing. Let us go to the wireless and see what the news is." But on our way down I met the operator coming, and I said, "Do you know anything?" He said, "The *Titanic*." So, then, I gave him instructions to let the *Titanic* know. I said, "This is not the *Titanic*; there is no doubt about it." She came and lay at half-past 11, alongside of us until, I suppose, a quarter past, within 4 miles of us. We could see everything on her quite distinctly, see her lights. We signalled her, at half-past 11, with the Morse lamp. She did not take the slightest notice of it. That was between half-past 11 and 20 minutes to 12. We signalled her again at 10 minutes

---

36   Steam was kept up all night. Lord: 'The engines were ready. I gave instructions to the chief engineer and told him I had decided to stay there all night. I did not think it safe to go ahead. I said, "We will keep handy in case some of those big fellows come crunching along and get into it."'

past 12, half-past 12, a quarter to 1 o'clock. We have a very powerful Morse lamp. I suppose you can see that about 10 miles, and she was about 4 miles off, and she did not take the slightest notice of it. When the 2nd Officer came on the bridge, at 12 o'clock ,or 10 minutes past 12, I told him to watch that steamer, which was stopped, and I pointed out the ice to him; told him we were surrounded by ice; to watch the steamer that she did not get any closer to her. At 20 minutes to 1 I whistled up the speaking tube and asked him if she was getting any nearer. He said, "No; she is not taking any notice of us." So, I said "I will go and lie down a bit." At a quarter past he said, "I think she has fired a rocket." He said, "She did not answer the Morse lamp and she has commenced to go away from us." I said, "Call her up and let me know at once what her name is. So, he put the whistle back, and, apparently, he was calling. I could hear him ticking [the Morse lamp] over my head. Then l went to sleep."

"You heard nothing more about it?" asked Smith.

"Nothing more until about something between then and half-past 4, I have a faint recollection of the Apprentice opening the room door; opening it and shutting it. I said "What is it?" He did not answer and I went to sleep again. I believe the boy came down to deliver me the message that this steamer had steamed away from us to the southwest, showing several of these flashes or white rockets; steamed away to the southwest."

The phrase "I believe" is a feeble excuse with which to hide behind. Readers will soon find that Lord had written statements from the men on the bridge detailing exactly what was seen and done.

In later discussion, Lord reported that the strange ship "was stopped until 1 o'clock, and then he started going ahead again; and the 2nd Officer reported he changed from south-southeast to west-southwest, 6 1/2 points; and if he was 4 miles off, the distance he travelled I estimated to be 7 or 7 1/2 miles in that hour."

"Captain, these Morse signals are a sort of language or method by which ships speak to one another?" asked Smith.

"Yes, sir; at night."

"The rockets that are used for the same purpose and are understood, are they not, among mariners?"

"As being distress rockets?" clarified Lord.

"Yes."

"Oh, yes," Lord confidently asserted, "you never mistake a distress rocket."

Senator Smith continued with his questioning. "Suppose the Morse signals and the rockets were displayed and exploded on the *Titanic* continuously for a half to three-quarters of an hour after she struck ice, would you, from the position of your ship on a night like Sunday night, have been able to see those signals?"

"From the positions she was supposed to have been in?"

"Yes."

"We could not have seen her Morse code; that is an utter impossibility," Lord replied.

"Could you have seen rockets?"

"I do not think so. Nineteen and a half miles is a long way. It would have been way down on the horizon. It might have been mistaken for a shooting star or anything at all."

"Was the *Titanic* beyond your range of vision?"

"I should think so. 19 1/2 or 20 miles away."

According to Lord, the watch officer and the Apprentice all concurred with his conclusion that what they were seeing was an ordinary cargo steamer and that Lord had first seen its green light and single mastlight on the *Californian*'s starboard side. Prior to this, at about 10.50 or 11.00 pm, Lord has asked wireless to send a message to the *Titanic* advising her that the *Californian* was stopped and surrounded by ice, but he was told to shut up on account that he was busy with his own transmissions. When Lord passed Evan's cabin at about 12.15am, the light was off, the wireless man having evidently gone to sleep. The *Titanic* had just started to send out desperate calls for help[37]. Lord admitted that had he known of the *Titanic*'s situation, his ship would "most certainly" have gone to assist.

At daylight, Lord was wakened and saw a yellow-funnel steamer to the southwest, beyond where the other ship had supposedly steamed away a few hours before, about 8 miles away. Lord didn't think this was the same ship that he had observed before he retired. The identity of this steamer, and the stranger rocket firer, was never ascertained.

Shortly after 5am, the *Californian* finally received word of the disaster, from the *Frankfurt*. The message was curt: "Ship sunk." The Chief Officer, having been sent down to wake up the wireless operator, came back and reported this information. Lord ordered him to go back and wait until he found out what it is. The officer went back, and about 10 minutes afterwards he came back and gave Lord the startling news that the *Titanic* had sunk after hitting an iceberg." Lord again ordered him back to wireless and find the position as quickly as possible. The Chief Officer obliging trotted off and came back, saying "We have a position here, but it seems a bit doubtful." "You must get me a better position. We do not want to go on a wild goose chase," Lord requested, and while waiting for the location of the casualty, he marked off the position from the tentative position given by the *Frankfurt* in the message, and headed the *Californian* in that direction.

While waiting for official word from the *Frankfurt*, the *Virginian* chimed in at 6am, "*Titanic* struck berg; wants assistance; urgent; ship sinking; passengers in boats. His position 41° 46', longitude 40° 16'." "Great excitement," as Lord put it, gripped the ship. The next message from the *Virginian* was about an hour and a half later, which was, "When you get to the scene of disaster will you please give me

---

37   *Mount Temple* received the first distress call at 10.25pm New York Time, or 12.15 on the *Californian*.

45

particulars of what is happening?"[38]

At six o'clock, proceeding slow, the *Californian* pushed through the thick ice, clearing it at 6.30, and then proceeded at full speed (13 – 13 ½ knots) towards the SOS location. Lord's ship pushed ice aside, and finally stopped close to the *Carpathia* at 8.30am, which was taking the last few people out of the lifeboats. In the water bobbed a small amount of wreckage, a few lifejackets and some abandoned lifeboats. The *Californian* was in communication with the *Carpathia* until 9 o'clock, enquiring about "the particulars of the accident" and then she departed with the *Titanic*'s survivors. Captain Lord "went full speed in circles over a radius - that is, I took a big circle and then came around and around and got back to the boats again, where I had left them." At 11.20, surrounded by icebergs, and having seen no-one, living or dead, Lord left the area and proceeded on his course to Boston.

Cyril Furmston Evans was the next to be examined. Evans had only been a Marconi operator for just over 6 months; he had made one trip on the White Star's *Cedric*, and three on the *Californian*.

Evans provided more information on the 'jamming' issue referred to by Lord moments before: "I went outside of my room just before that, about five minutes before that and we were stopped, and I went to the Captain and I asked him if there was anything the matter. The Captain told me he was going to stop because of the ice, and the Captain asked me if I had any boats, and I said the *Titanic*. He said "Better advise him we are surrounded by ice and stopped." So I went to my cabin, and at 9.05 New York time I called him up. I said "Say, old man, we are stopped and surrounded by ice." He turned around and said "MGY MGY MGY MWL Shut up, shut up, I am busy; I am working [the ground radio station at] Cape Race," and at that I jammed him.' Being closer to the *Titanic* than the ground station at Cape Race, Evans' message must have nearly deafened his counterpart, Phillips, on the *Titanic*. At 11.25 ships time, Evans still heard the *Titanic* transmitting passenger's private messages to Cape Race. Ten minutes later, Evans had removed his headphones, undressed and clambered into bed.

Researcher Dave Gittins has suggested that Evans should have preceded his message with MSG, for "Master Service Gram". By doing so, his message should have been delivered to the bridge and would have taken precedence over passenger related traffic[39]. Even so, the *Californian*'s ice message was irrelevant without a position, and there is no evidence that Evans was ever provided with one.

---

38 Controversy over the *Virginian*'s wireless transmissions will be revisited later in this book.
39 Some PVs show that messages sent to the *Carpathia* and preceded by MSG were refused: for instance, a 3pm MSG sent on 15th April by the SS *Virginian*.

So why bother to transmit a message in the first place? However, Evans said "I was just giving [the "stopped and surrounded by ice" message] as a matter of courtesy, because the Captain requested me to." On the other hand, Lloyd's very comprehensive shipping publications detailing contemporary ships' movements often lists "position unreported" in its "Ships spoken" section, but not in its meteorology and debris reporting sections.

Evans was awakened from his slumber, not by a steward at 7.00am ships time, but by Chief Officer Stewart at about 5.20am. Through repetitive questioning, Evans reported that Steward had said, "There is a ship that has been firing rockets in the night. Please see if there is anything the matter." Evans jumped out of bed, slipped on a pair of trousers and a pair of slippers, and went at once to his Marconi key, starting the motor and gave "C.Q." About a second later he was answered by the *Frankfurt*, "D.K.D., D.F.T." ("D.F.T," is the *Frankfurt*'s call), who said, "Do you know the *Titanic* has sunk during the night, collided with an iceberg?" Evans responded, "No; please give me the latest position." which was provided. He put the position down on a slip of paper, and then acknowledged the message to the operator, and then the *Virginian* started to call. He said, "Do you know the *Titanic* had sunk?" Evans said, "Yes, the *Frankfurt* has just told me." Evans then sent a service message, ("that an operator can always make up if he wants to find out something"), asking, "Please send me official message regarding *Titanic*, giving position."

Before the *Californian* reached the scene of the wreck, Evans found himself in discussion with the ship's Apprentice, Gibson, who had been on the bridge during the night and had seen the rockets for himself. The ship that he had been watching had ignored the *Californian*'s Morse lamp. During the watch, the Captain had been roused three times.

It is interesting to compare this story, even though it was not first hand evidence, with Lord's statement. Lord version had only remarked on two occasions when he had communicated with the bridge officers; the first via voice tube when he was awake, the second when Gibson had visited the chart room personally, where Lord was sleeping on the settee. Lord had no recollection of this visit other than the door opening and closing and asking the Apprentice "What is it?" He claimed that he received no reply. Also recall Lord's statement to the Boston press about the reason why Evans had been awakened; "I told Mr. Stewart to wake up `Wireless' and have him get in touch with some ship and get an idea of what kind of an ice field we had gotten into.'" If this was the case – and Evans had perjured himself during his testimony - why the urgent need to wake him over an hour and a half earlier than he would normally have risen?

Lord's statements about the *Titanic* disaster, and how it arrived, rouses one's scepticism, as he describes three different trips to the wireless office by Stewart. On the first occasion, Stewart reports back that a ship had sunk; the next time, he reports that it is the *Titanic*; and on the third, he gets a position. Evans reports that he got all this information – albeit unofficially – at the same time. If Lord is right, one must assume that Stewart rushed off to report to the him once he had been told a ship had sunk, without waiting to hear the rest of the message! And then there is the matter of timing. The *Californian* started on her mission to the rescue at 6.00am. Evans knew of the *Titanic* disaster a few minutes after 5.20am. What was going on for the next 40 minutes? Other ships reacted much more promptly to the initial distress calls. Why the concern over going on "a wild goose chase"?

After leaving the wrecksite, according to Evans, the ship was full of discussion about the rockets and the Captain having been called on three occasions. Some people had seen the pyrotechnics, and there was much speculation about them; they did not know what rockets they were, and some thought they were from the *Titanic*. None of these discussions were in the presence of the Captain. Evans mentioned that he may have heard Gill's story.

It was whilst in Boston, on the night of April 24th, that Evans encountered Gill at one of the train stations. Gill asked if he "was not going back any more", presumably a reference to rejoining the *Californian* on the return leg of her voyage. Gill said he had told the newspaper his story, and remarked that "I think we[40] will make about $500 out of it."

This raises a few points. Gill had evidently been thinking of deserting the *Californian*. Obviously, his public statement must have made him feel that staying on board was untenable. Gill then says that he had given his affidavit to a paper, but that he was not sure about how much money he would make! The use of the word "we" is interesting. Does this refer to the (unnamed) compatriots? Was he going to "split" the money? To Evans' credit, he informed the Senate Inquiry that he would not attempt to make any money from the tragedy, as he did not think it was "right" to do so, in contrast to the Titanic's junior wireless operator, Harold Bride, who had been paid a massive sum by *The New York Times* for his account of the disaster.

And thus was the Inquiry into the *Californian* and her activities concluded. One would have thought that given the tantalising evidence provided, Smith would have ordered more members of the crew to provide testimony, particularly Gibson and Stewart. They may have provided mere repetition of information to be given in London in a few weeks time; or Smith may have called crew members whose stories are now lost to history. But these three witnesses provided the sum total of information gathered on the *Californian* incident during the U.S. Senate Inquiry. A wasted opportunity[41].

---

40   In another part of his testimony, Evans reports that Gill had merely said "I think I will make about $500 out of it."
41   *The Times* (London) noted on 27th April that "The most interesting part [was played by] the wireless operator ... Gill's evidence should be treated with reserve."

Over a week later, U.S. Navy Captain John J. Knapp, the hydrographer for the U.S. Bureau of Navigation, testified regarding ice reports collated by his office, and submitted charts and memoranda detailing the position of ships and ice. The conversation turned to Captain Lord and his ship:

"Captain, can you think of anything else that you desire to say that will tend to throw any light upon the Inquiry being made by the committee into the causes leading up to this wreck, and subsequent events, including any memorandum or data bearing upon the position of the steamship *Californian* on the night of this accident?" asked Senator Smith.

Referring to the second chart (reproduced below) that he had produced for the Inquiry, Knapp replied, "I invited especial attention to that part of the memorandum referring to the hypothetical position of the *Californian*, as shown on that chart, and, in connection therewith, it is desirable to explain that the arcs of circles drawn about the position of the steamship *Titanic* and about the position of the steamship *Californian* were drawn to graphically illustrate the testimony of certain witnesses before your committee ... The outer arc around each ship is drawn with a radius of 16 miles, which is approximately the farthest distance at which the curvature of the earth would have permitted the side lights of the *Titanic* to be seen by a person at the height of the side lights of the *Californian*, or at which the side lights of the *Californian* could have been seen by a person at the height of the side lights of the *Titanic*. The inner circle around each ship is drawn with a radius of 7 miles. This is approximately the distance after reaching which the curvature of the earth would have shut out the side lights of the *Californian* from the view of one in a lifeboat in the water[42]. It appears, therefore, that if the *Titanic's* position at the time of the accident was as fixed by the testimony and if it was the side light of the *Californian* that was seen from the boat deck of the *Titanic*, the *Californian* was somewhere inside of the arc of the 16-mile circle drawn about the *Titanic*. It further appears that if the above hypothesis be correct and if the side light of the other steamer could not be seen, as is testified to, from one of the lifeboats of the *Titanic* after being lowered, the *Californian* was somewhere outside of the circle with the 7-mile radius drawn about the *Titanic*."

"In the case of the *Californian*, if the steamer which in the testimony given by members of the crew of the *Californian*, including the Captain and the donkey engine-man and others, is said to have been seen by them, was the *Titanic*, she must have been somewhere inside of the circle with the 16-mile radius drawn around the *Californian*. If that be the case, as the *Californian's* side light was shut out by the curvature of the earth from the view of anyone in a lifeboat of the *Titanic* after being lowered into the water, then the *Titanic* must have been outside of the circle drawn with the 7-mile [sic] radius around the *Californian*," Knapp

---

42   This is hopelessly wrong. This figure describes a line of sight at an altitude of zero feet above the water! If we include the height that a person's eye-line would be above the water (3-4 feet), it extends this distance by over 2 miles.

continued.

"Further reference to this chart will show plotted a hypothetical position of the *Californian*. On the hypothesis that the *Californian* was in this position, a dotted line is drawn on the chart on the bearing given by the Captain of the *Californian* as that on which the steamer was sighted. This bearing is drawn on the chart to intersect the track of the *Titanic*. Another dotted line is drawn parallel thereto from a point on the course of the *Titanic* where she apparently was at 10:06 P.M., New York time, April 14, that being 11:56 P.M. of that date of the *Californian's* time, at which Ernest Gill stated that the large steamer was seen by him. If the *Californian* was in the hypothetical position shown on the chart, the *Titanic* could have been seen by the officers and crew of the *Californian* at the time mentioned."

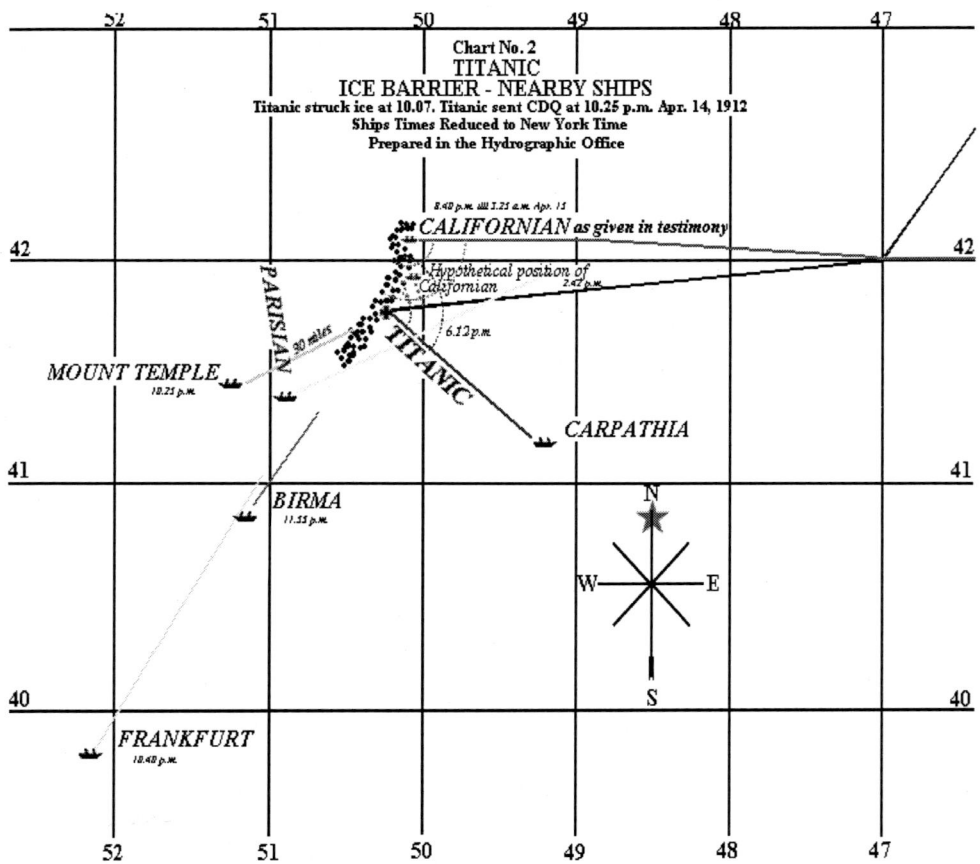

Illustration 10: Captain Knapp's map of the North Atlantic, with locations of the Californian marked

Smith asked, "Captain, are you able to state to the committee whether there was any vessel between the position of the *Titanic* just preceding and following the accident and the position of the *Californian* at that time?"

"From being present at hearings before your committee and from reading the printed testimony of witnesses examined by the committee I am led to the conclusion that if there was any vessel between the *Californian* and the *Titanic* at the time referred to she does not seem to have been seen by any of the ships near there on the following morning, nor have there been any reports submitted to the Hydrographic Office which would indicate that there was any such steamer in that locality. The evidence does not indicate to me that there was any such third steamer in those waters, especially in view of the fact that no such steamer was seen by other steamers or by those in the lifeboats the following morning, and as the ice barrier, from all reports, between the reported position of the *Californian* and that of the *Titanic* was impassable to a vessel proceeding to the westward, and there is no testimony to show that if such a steamer was between the *Californian* and the *Titanic* she proceeded to the eastward, the Captain of the *Californian*, having testified that he last saw the said steamer proceeding to the westward and being on a bearing to the westward of the *Californian*. Nothing appears in the testimony to show that the steamer so seen reversed its course and proceeded to the eastward."

Although Knapp's computations showed that it was possible for the *Californian* to see the *Titanic* and vice-versa, he did not explain how Captain Lord's vessel could find herself so far south of her expected track. His chart also contains a few errors: the SS *Birma* is too far east, and the *Mount Temple*'s determination of the longitude of the western edge of the icefield (see below) is ignored, allowing the *Titanic* to sink east of the ice, which is consistent with eyewitness accounts, but not with the navigational details. The *Mount Temple*'s longitude is noticeably absent from Knapp's memorandum of ships and their movements, which he had supplied to Senator Smith.

27ᵗʰ April

A veteran of 32 years at sea, 27 of them on the North Atlantic, Captain James Henry Moore testified on April 27ᵗʰ. Whilst he and the Inquiry committee conversed, his other officers resumed the *Mount Temple*'s voyage to Halifax.

What ensued during the cross-examination was a convivial, but general discussion between Smith and Moore, starting with the subject of ice, before turning to the events on board ship during the time the Titanic was foundering. Moore was steaming on a course heading for St.John, and was aiming to reach 42° N 47° W, but due to ice reports, he steered down to pass 50° W in 41° 15' N, that is, giving the ice 10 miles. This proved beneficial: he saw no ice whatsoever.

At 12.30am ship's time on April 15ᵗʰ, the *Mount Temple* was located at 41° 25' north and 51° 41' west when her operator picked up the distress call. Moore was awakened from his slumber and the ship was turned around. Moore plotted the course to the *Titanic*'s location: north 65° east true, about 49 miles away. The wireless operator had picked up the initial dispatch from the *Titanic* (41° 44' north, longitude 50° 24' west) but had now received a corrected location – the famous position of 41° 46' north, 50° 14' west.[43]

As Moore said, "After I was sufficiently dressed I went down to the chief engineer and I told him that the *Titanic* was sending out messages for help, and I said 'Go down and try to shake up the fireman, and, if necessary, even give him a tot of rum if you think he can do any more.' I believe this was carried out. I also told him to inform the fireman that we wanted to get back as fast as we possibly could." Moore estimated that his ship was making 11 ½ knots, or perhaps a little more with the Gulf Stream helping her, pushing her towards the east-north-east. The ship was readied for a possible rescue, her boats swung out, and ladders and lifebelts were prepared.

At about 3am, the *Mount Temple* started to encounter heavy ice. The engines were immediately put on stand by, and the lookout doubled. At 3.25am, the ship had coasted to a stop. At this point, by Moore's reckoning, he was still 14 miles from the *Titanic*. There then followed a peculiar episode: "[Shortly after 3am] I want to say that I met a schooner or some small craft, and I had to get out of the way of that vessel, and the light of that vessel seemed to go out ... When this light was on my bow, a green light, I starboarded my helm [so that the *Mount Temple*'s green light would be facing this other green light]." To Moore, the light was between him and the *Titanic*, and he could not discern her mastlights. The ship was not moving very fast.

"I should say this light could not have been more than a mile or a mile and a half away, because I immediately put my helm hard astarboard [2 points], because I saw the light, and after I got the light on the starboard bow then the light seemed to suddenly go out. I kept on and then the quartermaster must have let her come up toward the east again, because I heard the foghorn[44] on this schooner. He

---

43   This is a mistake in the transcript. Despite Moore reading his 12.30am DR position from a memorandum, this should be 41° 25' north and 51° 14' west, which yields 50 miles, covered in 4 1/3 hours. This latter position is referenced in *The New York Times* on April 27th. This position raises another question: it is well to the west of a possible course to St.John, and hence further away from the *Titanic*. There is no reason for Moore to continue heading west, or placing his ship on a wrong heading after reaching 41° 15' N, 50° W. If we take the distance that the *Mount Temple* had travelled between this "corner" and the 12.30 position, but place her on this "correct course", she can be placed at 41° 38' north and 51° 9' west, a distance of 42 miles to the SOS location. Conversely, Moore told Senator Smith that, had there been no ice, he would have headed for 42° N, 47° W, and then headed for Cape Sable. If he did this at his new "turning point", then his 12.30am location is only a short distance away from the course for Cape Sable.

44   The 1900 *Rules of the Road* for ships at sea remarks (in Article 5) that sailing ships are only allowed red and green lights at sea; Article 28 mentions that one short blast (duration of one second) on a foghorn for a vessel in sight means "I am directing my course

blew his foghorn, and we immediately put the helm hard astarboard, and I ordered full speed astern and took the way off the boat," Moore recounted. After the schooner had got out of the way, the *Mount Temple* was put on her way again.

Senator Smith asked, "What I am trying to get at is this: One or two of the ship's officers of the *Titanic* say that after the collision with the iceberg they used the Morse signals and rockets for the purpose of attracting help, and that while they were using these rockets, and displaying the Morse signals they saw lights ahead, or saw lights, that could not have been over 5 miles from the *Titanic*. What I am seeking to develop is the question as to what light that was they saw."

"Well, it may have been the light of the tramp steamer that was ahead of us, because when I turned there was a steamer on my port bow ... [going] almost in the same direction. As he went ahead, he gradually crossed our bow until he got on the starboard bow, sir"

This stranger ship was a 4-5000 ton tramp and although he was never close enough to determine her name, Moore was sure she was not an English ship because she did not show her Ensign. The funnel was black, with some device in a band near the top. This ship was visible until after 9am and followed Moore along the perimeter of the ice pack : "I think he was under the impression that I was going to the eastward, that I was bound to the eastward, and I think when I turned back after we both stopped, when we found the ice too heavy, he followed me, because when I turned around, after finding the ice too heavy to the southward, after I went to the southward later on in the morning, when it got daylight, and I went down to where he was, thinking he perhaps had gotten into a thin spot, when I got there he had stopped, he had found the ice too heavy. I went a little farther, and I turned around because it was getting far too heavy to put the ship through. But that would be about 5, or perhaps half past 5, in the morning, sir. "

After 3.25am, she proceeded slowly and eventually reached the vicinity of the *Titanic*'s distress location at 4.30am in the morning. By this time, the tramp was a little to the southward and ahead of Moore. At this point, Moore's journey was interrupted by a massive ice pack right in his track, about 5 or 6 miles wide and extending north and south as far as could be seen.

Moore's testimony is interesting: we know that after the *Titanic* sank, 4th Officer Boxhall was firing green flares from lifeboat 2, and these would have been visible up to 10 miles away. Since the green lights of a steamer are supposed to cover an arc of angles from straight ahead to two points abaft the beam, it is telling that Moore and his officers did not see the white mast lights of the ship seen after 3am which should have been visible at the same time; indeed, none of the ship with

---

to starboard." But if the unknown schooner turned to starboard, she would not have shut her green light in, and indeed, may have shown her red light. Incidentally, since the wind picked up only towards daybreak – at about 4am – this ship was presumably without motive power. Where did she go and how did no-one else see her? Perhaps Moore only assumed that this ship was a sailing vessel because of the lack of steaming lights?

this green light was seen either. Moore estimated that the ship was moving very slowly, yet with sunrise imminent, this ship was never seen again – by anyone. It is tempting to speculate that the *Mount Temple* saw Boxhall's flares, which would indicate that he was closer to the wrecksite than expected – and indeed, to the east of the SOS location. We do not know the bearing of this green light from the *Mount Temple*, except to say that it must have been on the port bow, as Moore turned his ship to ensure "green to green". No other witness reports hearing a fog horn.

Moore also reported that the *Carpathia*'s rockets were not seen, rockets that were fired to placate *Titanic*'s survivors that help was on the way. Two feeble explanations may be that, with his ship running north-east at the time, and the *Carpathia* well off to the south-west, he and his officers may not have been looking in the right direction, which would have been near their starboard beam; or that the rockets may have been eclipsed by the large icebergs in the nearby ice field. The rockets would have been very low down on the horizon and may have been obscured.

Or it may be that the *Mount Temple* was, as her master asserted, too far away. The entry in the PV for 10.40pm New York Time says "M.G.Y. still calling C.Q.D. Our Captain reverses ship. We are about 50 miles off." Well before Moore had a motive to concoct a false position and alibi, here he was confirming that he was well away from the disaster. But is this entry an accurate one? It seems that the "50 miles off" line is not contemporary and was added later as a scribbled addendum in the margin:

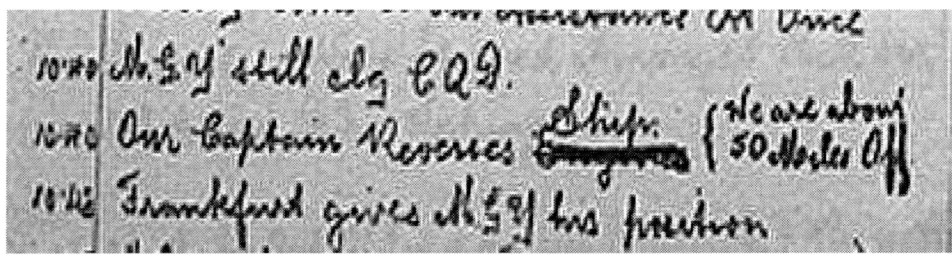

Illustration 11: Extract from the Mount Temple's wireless log

The *Carpathia*'s rockets were probably of a similar design to the *Titanic*'s. Her last rocket was fired at 1.45am, when the *Carpathia* was still 2 ½ hours away from the wrecksite. She would therefore have been some 36 miles away. From the bridge of the *Carpathia*, with a line of sight about 49 feet above the water, the rockets would have to have been seen from a total distance of about 44 miles, or from the crow's nest, some 20 feet higher, we get 46 miles. The theoretical maximum distance that rockets could be seen, irrespective of the luminosity of the detonation would be 41 miles, so it is consistent with the *Carpathia* not seeing the rockets.

So, rockets fired and seen from elevation were not seen from this distance. We can apply this to the *Mount Temple* and get a rough estimate of how far off she would have to be at 3.15am <u>not</u> to have seen the *Carpathia*'s rockets.

The two scenarios can be explored by simple sketch maps (see below). In the first diagram, we have points A (*Mount Temple* at 3.00am), B (*Carpathia* when she was firing rockets), C (*Titanic*'s SOS location), D (*Titanic*'s actual wrecksite) and G (the *Mount Temple*'s start position).

Knowing the approximate speed and headings of the *Carpathia* and wrecksite, we can deduce that the former ship was at about 41°34'N, 49°48'W when she was firing rockets. The *Mount Temple* would be at approximately 41°36'N, 50°43'W. The distance between these two points would be 41 miles. From these values, no rockets or lights from the *Carpathia* would be seen at all, confirmation of Moore's navigation.

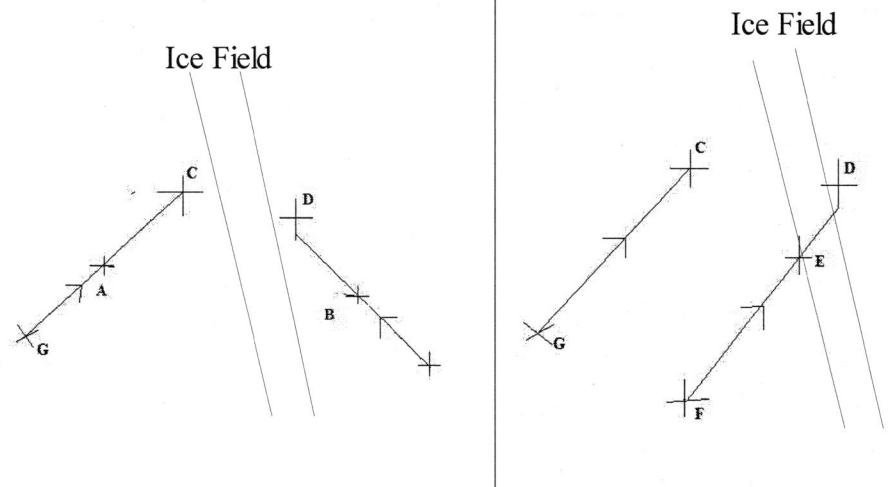

Illustration 12: Sketches displaying two possible Mount Temple routes: (left) the Mount Temple's course while the Carpathia fires her rockets; (right) the Mount Temple sights Boxhall's flares, near the wreck site. Sketches are not to scale. The notation is described in the text.

What of the other suggestion, that Moore saw Boxhall's flares? The second sketch shows this possibility: the line G-C is the original path of the *Mount Temple*, F-D is the hypothesised route, with E being 3.00am, when the "green light" was seen. For this to have been a flare, the distance would have to be a maximum of 10 miles. And, if the *Mount Temple* was showing her red light, or at the least, bow on, as Moore's testimony implies, then his ship would have to be on the line or to the south-east of it. If we take these conditions at face value, and allowing for a southern drift of Boxhall's boat, the *Mount Temple* would have to be about 41°39'N, 50°10'W. This longitude is right in the vicinity of the ice field – and just about where Moore said he started to encounter ice[45].

Where would the *Mount Temple* have to be at 12.30am to end up at this position? If we use Moore's estimates, the distance travelled would be 35 miles in 2 ½ hours, this gives 41°24'N, 50°52'W, or 16 miles, almost due east from his DR estimate. It is hard to envisage a current causing such a strong displacement of location, though the direction is consistent with an easterly Gulf Stream. It would also mean that the *Carpathia*'s rockets would be visible.

Either of these two situations is plausible, but they are inconsistent with each other.

But, if the *Californian* was 19 miles to the north-east of the *Titanic*, as Captain Lord claimed, the watch officers would have seen the *Carpathia*'s rockets when she was less than 14 miles from the wrecksite at 3.15am. Could the *Californian* have seen the *Carpathia*'s rockets? The answer, as will be detailed soon, is 'yes'.

The *Mount Temple* was supposed to be stopped at 3.25am, 14 miles from the SOS position and then proceeded slowly, reaching the location at 4.30am. This would indicate a speed of 11.2 knots, hardly consistent with his recollection of a "slow" speed.

Then there is the problem of the ice field. The only field in the vicinity of the *Titanic* was about 3 ½ miles to the east of the SOS position, as we will see presently. Evidently, the *Mount Temple* was much further east than her 12.30am DR position indicated.

We return to Moore's testimony: at 4.30am, he could see no wreckage or boats or any indication that the *Titanic* had ever been there. The PV, indicating New York time and kept by Marconi operator Durrant corroborated this:

3.00. All quiet. We are stopped amongst pack ice.
3.20. *Birma* and *Frankfurt* working. We back out of ice and cruise around. Large bergs about.

These messages would be timed at 4.46 and 5.06am local time respectively.

The *Mount Temple* searched for a way to proceed through the ice, but not finding a route, Moore " steered away to the south-southeast true, because [he] thought the ice appeared thinner down there. When [he] got down, [he] got within about a mile or so of this other [tramp] ship, which had already stopped, finding the ice was too strong for it to go through." Following instructions from the Canadian

---

45   On the other hand, a belated ice report by Captain Lord said that the western edge of the ice field was at 50°42 W; since this is far to the west of the *Mount Temple*'s own longitude shortly after sunset of the western perimeter of the field, it is safe to assume that Captain Lord may have referred to loose field surrounding the heavier pack ice.

Pacific Line that their vessels were not to enter field ice under the circumstances, the *Mount Temple* stopped and turned around. She proceeded north along the eastern edge of the icefield, and at about 6am the *Carpathia* was sighted.

Smith bluntly asked Moore, "Some passengers on your vessel, Sunday night about midnight, claim to have seen these rockets from the decks of the *Titanic*. Have you heard anything about that?" to which Moore replied "I have read it in the papers, sir; but as a matter of fact, I do not believe there was a passenger on deck at 12 o'clock at night. I am positive, because they would not know anything at all about this, and you may be sure that they would be in their beds. I know the steward tells me there was nobody on deck; that is, the night watchman at the aft end. At the forward end there was nobody on deck. The man in what we call the permanent steerage that passes under the bridge deck - we have a permanent steerage there, and the other, of course, is a portable one we can take down - and nobody saw a passenger on deck, sir."

"Do you wish to be understood as saying that you did not see, on Sunday night or Monday morning, any signal lights from the *Titanic*?"

"I can solemnly swear that I saw no signal lights, nor did my officers on the bridge see any signal lights."

"Let me ask you right there, did you see the rockets from the *Carpathia*?"

"I never saw any rockets whatever, sir."

"Is it possible that this passenger from Toronto, who claims to have seen rockets, may have seen the rockets from the *Carpathia* at that time?"

"I do not think it possible, sir, because if the *Carpathia* was farther away it is not likely you would see her rockets. But you see, this ship says she is sending rockets up. So it is possible that other ships may have seen them. I do not know. I thought of sending rockets up, but I thought it far better to let it alone, because if other ships - they thought they saw them - might be coming to me, and I had not seen anything of the *Titanic* and did not know exactly where she was; because I think, after all, the *Titanic* was farther east than she gave her position, or, in fact, I am certain she was."

Moore explained that he was confident that the *Titanic* was at least 8 miles to the east of the SOS position. When asked to clarify, he said, "Because when I got the position in the morning I got a prime vertical sight; that is a sight taken when the sun is bearing due east. That position gave me 50° 91/2' west. I got two observations. I took one before the prime vertical and on the prime vertical[46]. We were steering north at the time, steering north to go around this pack again, to look out, to see if we could find a hole through the ice, and we took these two positions, and they both came within a quarter of a mile of each other; so that the *Titanic* must have been on the other side of that field of ice, and then her position was not right which she gave."

---

46   The other sighting was of 50° 9 ¾' W. Astronomy programs demonstrate that this would be about 7.00am on April 15th.

Mention of the *Californian* being unable to find anything at the SOS position either led to Moore to volunteer, "I saw the *Californian* myself cruising around there, sir ... She was there shortly after me, because when I came to this great pack of ice, sir, as I remarked, I went to the southeast to try to get around them because I realized that if he was not in that position - I had come from the westward - he must be somewhere to the eastward of me still ... This pack of ice between us and the *Carpathia*, it was between 5 and 6 miles. She did not communicate with me at all. When we sighted her she must have sighted us ... The *Californian* was to the north, sir. She was to the north of the *Carpathia* and steaming to the westward ... As I was going to the north the *Californian* was passing from east to west ... He was then north of the *Carpathia*, and he must have been, I suppose, about the same distance to the north of the *Carpathia* as I was to the westward of her ... I understand he is cruising, because after we go up toward him he goes to the south and misses us, passes about a mile off, and then he gets where we came from. Then we go over the ground, and we have not seen anything of the ship, and we think we must cruise on farther. "

This important passage laboured the point that, with the *Carpathia* at the wreck site, the *Californian* was only 5 or 6 miles to the northward.

And that was it, other than relating that Evans of the *Californian* had swamped the airwaves with incessant chatter and jamming other stations, leaving Marconi Inspector Balfour on the SS *Baltic*, to tell him to "stand by"; that is, to shut up.

The next day, although Moore's evidence had successfully demolished the charges against his ship, another accusation appeared in *The New York Times*. From Nelson, New Brunswick, a statement emerged from a Mr. W.H. Kenervost[47], another passenger on the *Mount Temple*, who also stated that the ship was within 5 miles of the *Titanic* half an hour before the ship went down.

"Kenervost declared he saw the lights of the *Titanic* and although Capt. Moore ... had received wireless messages that the White Star liner was sinking ... he hove to his ship in spite of the entreaties of his officers to rush to the aid of the *Titanic*.

"He said that the other officers ... had urged Capt. Moore to make an attempt to reach the Titanic, but that Capt. Moore had replied that it was too dangerous and he would not risk the lives of his own passengers."

Kenervost said that he had gained information as to the wireless message received by the *Mount Temple* and also as to Capt. Moore's orders to his officers through a friend of the Marconi operator on board.

It may be speculated that Senator Smith might have been more conducive towards investigating the *Mount Temple* more thoroughly if he had received this, and other similar reports. However, neither now, nor a few weeks later in London at the British Inquiry, was the matter of the *Mount Temple*'s possible proximity ever

47   Also spelt "Kennervost" in some newspaper reports.

58

explored publicly.

29th April

Smith had dispatched one of his assistants ("Ab" Carroll) to Toronto to take Dr. Quitzrau's deposition, which read:

"Dr. F. C. Quitzrau; being first duly sworn, deposes and says that he was a passenger, travelling second class, on steamer *Mount Temple*, which left Antwerp April 3, 1912; that about midnight Sunday, April 14, New York time, he was awakened by the sudden stopping of the engines; that he immediately went to the cabin, where were already gathered several of the stewards and passengers, who informed him that word had been received by wireless from the *Titanic* that the *Titanic* had struck an iceberg and was calling for help.

Orders were immediately given and the *Mount Temple* course changed, heading straight for the *Titanic*. About 3 o'clock New York time, 2 o'clock ship's time, the *Titanic* was sighted by some of the officers and crew; that as soon as the *Titanic* was seen all lights on the *Mount Temple* were put out and the engines stopped and the boat lay dead for about two hours; that as soon as day broke the engines were started and the *Mount Temple* circled the *Titanic's* position, the officers insisting that this be done, although the Captain had given orders that the boat proceed on its journey. While encircling the *Titanic's* position we sighted the *Frankfurt* to the northwest of us, the *Birma* to the south, speaking to both of these by wireless, the latter asking if we were in distress; that about 6 o'clock we saw the *Carpathia*, from which we had previously received a message that the *Titanic* had gone down; that about 8.30 the *Carpathia* wirelessed that it had picked up 20 lifeboats and about 720 passengers all told, and that there was no need for the *Mount Temple* to stand by, as the remainder of those on board were drowned."

Evidently, Quitzrau had seen no lights for himself, and his information amounted to little more than a repetition of rumours and stories that had been circulating. The affidavit curiously places New York time ahead of apparent ship's time and this makes it difficult to know what time the "*Titanic*" was supposed to have been sighted; was it 2 o'clock ship's time, or 4.46 (3 am New York Time + 1 hour 46 time difference)? Regardless of the correct time, the *Titanic's* mystery ship had been seen fairly early on in the sinking, possibly about midnight. Quitzrau's description of the *Frankfurt* is also wrong; that ship approached from the southwest, not the northwest.

As Wyn Craig Wade, the 'biographer' of the U.S. Senate Inquiry, wrote,

"Dr.Quitzrau apparently was quite upset that he hadn't been taken to Washington and complained to the vice-consul at Toronto 'who appealed to [Senator] Smith, who invited the doctor's useless affidavit as a matter of diplomatic tact.'"[48]

But, taken in isolation, why would Quitzrau fabricate such a damaging report? The answer may be due to an incident during the voyage that may have humiliated Quitzrau. He held a steerage ticket, but because of overcrowding, his cabin was upgraded 2nd class. However, when he was found on the Saloon deck and was challenged over the type of ticket he held, he was removed from the deck when he replied "steerage"; evidently the crew member who queried Quitzrau felt that he was nothing more than a gate-crasher[49]

Smith's suspicions were focussed on the *Californian* as being the *Titanic's* mystery ship, but there seemed to be no shortage of other possibilities. A promising report was published in *The Daily Sketch* on Friday 3rd May 1912, which screamed "The Mystery Ship. Reported Statement by British Captain. ' Heard Passengers Voices' – PARIS, Thursday" It read, "A telegram from Algiers to Le Journal suggests that the mysterious ship seen from the *Titanic* might have been the British steamer *Kura* which arrived yesterday at Algiers from New York. The Captain of the *Kura* remembers having had a glimpse of a large liner through the fog and having heard the voices of passengers; but the dense mist prevented him from discovering anything abnormal concerning the liner. He concentrated his attention upon avoiding the icebergs. He did not hear of the catastrophe until he arrived at Algiers. The *Kura* left in the evening for Genoa".

But a simple check on newspapers of the era quashes this story. The *Kura* was tied up in New York on April 14th and was reported to be quite likely to be laid up for a while as she was damaged by ice during her voyage. The fog conditions were also not encountered by the *Titanic* at the time of the accident[50]. A shadow of doubt hangs over this, as *Lloyd's Weekly Shipping Index* notes that she left New York for Genoa on April 13th, and passed Gibraltar on the 29th of that month. Whatever, she could not have reached the disaster area in time.

Eventually, accusations of lax Captains evaporated, leaving the *Californian* as the sole candidate for the *Titanic's* indifferent stranger.

---

48   *"The Titanic: End of a dream"* page 228
49   *"The Ship That Stood Still"* page 276
50   *The New York Times* April 15th 1912

Chapter 4. "Hostile! At Once!"[51]

May 1912

The United Kingdom would also seek its own answers. As Dave Gittins writes[52], "The disaster was obviously too significant to be handled by the routine Board of Trade Inquiry normally made into shipping accidents. Short of a full-scale Royal Commission, only the convening of a Wreck Commissioner's Court would suffice. This move was supported by the leader of the Conservative Party, Andrew Bonar Law. The government moved quickly and on 23 April, the Lord High Chancellor, Robert Threshie, Earl Loreburn, appointed the distinguished barrister and judge, the Right Honourable John Charles Bigham, Lord Mersey, to be a Wreck Commissioner for the United Kingdom," thus beginning Mersey's connection with high-profile shipping disasters, for he would later preside over the investigations launched following the sinking of the *Empress of Ireland* (1914) and the *Lusitania* (1915). A year after the sinking of the *Titanic*, he would chair the first SOLAS (Safety Of Life At Sea) conference.

Illustration 13: Lord Mersey

It may be providential to dispel one myth repeated in *Titanic* circles for decades, that the British Inquiry was conducted by the Board of Trade. Although it was ordered by the Board of Trade, it was conducted by an <u>independent</u> Wreck Commissioner (Lord Mersey) assisted by technical assessors appointed by the

---

51   This is Captain Lord's later (1961) opinion of Lord Mersey.
52   An excellent summary of the British Inquiry is contained in his e-book.

Home Secretary.

The Investigation commenced at the Royal Scottish Regiment Drill Hall in Buckingham Gate, London on May 2nd, despite its abysmal acoustic properties. Lord Mersey and his assessors sat on a raised dais at the far end, the witness box situated to their right. Behind this box was an enormous half model of the *Titanic*, loaned from the ship's builders (Harland and Wolff); the hall also sported a large map of the North Atlantic, showing the doomed liner's route. In front of Mersey sat reserved areas for the legal teams and representatives of various bodies and unions, the press, and members of the public. Sylvia Lightoller, the wife of the *Titanic*'s surviving 2nd Officer, is reported to have been present in the public gallery during each and every one of the 36 days the Inquiry was in existence.

Illustration 14: Lord Mersey and his assessors (The Daily Sketch, May 3rd, 1912)

Counsel on behalf of the Board of Trade were Sir John Simon (the 'Solicitor General') , Butler Aspinall, and Sir Rufus Isaacs (the 'Attorney General'). This trio was assisted by a more junior team, comprising of Sydney Rowlatt and Raymond Asquith, the Prime Minister's son.

The Inquiry was charged with determining the answer to some 22 questions, all set by the Board of Trade, which had reserved the right to amend, or add to these basic queries as necessary. As the reader will soon learn, this was indeed done, to the detriment of the *Californian*.

The questions covered both the construction and seaworthiness of the *Titanic*, but also its life saving provisions, how they were utilised (or under utilised in many cases), the number of passengers and crew carried by the liner – and how many were saved. The remainder of the comprehensive list queried the ice warnings received by the *Titanic*, how the ship sank, messages transmitted in an effort to elicit help, whether binoculars were provided to the look-out men etc. etc. None of the questions covered any laxity on the part of other ships to provide assistance to the *Titanic*. Yet.

Illustration 15: The Court of the British Investigation (The Daily Sketch, May 3rd, 1912)

The *Californian* arrived at the Huskisson Dock in Liverpool on May 10[th,] minus two crew members; for Ernest Gill had indeed deserted the ship in Boston[53]. Lord and his officers visited the Leyland Line's Liverpool office and spoke to its Marine Superintendent, Captain Fry, and it was during this meeting, 3rd Officer Groves ventured his opinion that the ship he had seen while they had been stopped in ice had been the *Titanic*. Lord was surprised at this, and told Fry that this was the first time he had heard this. Subsequent to this, various members of the crew gave written depositions (or 'proofs') to the Receiver of Wrecks, E.J.M. Bates, to assess who, if any, would be called to give evidence at the British Investigation. Proofs were also obtained by the Leyland Line for use by its legal representative in London, Robertson Dunlop.

At some point Lord was allegedly shown a report from a crew member on board another Leyland ship, the SS *Almerian* which had been bound from Mobile,

---

53   The other absent crew member was a fireman, William Kennerdale, who had died in Boston after spitting blood. This fact, recorded in the ship's official log, is not mentioned by Captain Lord's chief defender, Leslie Harrison.

Alabama to Liverpool and had recently docked, but was now underway again, to Barbados. The report was copied by Lord, but we are unsure of its actual source, or the reason why it was written. It may have been written by the master of the *Almerian,* Captain Thomas, or Lord may have received it from a sympathetic crew member of that ship. We simply don't know. Incidentally, the *Almerian* was not equipped with wireless and hence had no knowledge of the disaster until she reached port unless she gathered the information via Morse lamp communications with other steamers whilst at sea.

The report is as follows:

"April 15. at 3 a.m. Approx. I was informed there was ice alongside. I at once ordered the ship stopped. There was a steamer on the port quarter. I asked the 2nd Officer, Mr. Havard, if he had communicated with her. He said he had endeavoured to but could not
understand his signals, only "...ount...".

At daylight (about 4 a.m.) we could see ice extending as far to the north-east and southward as we could see, field ice and icebergs.

I proceeded at various speeds in a northerly direction on the western extremity of the icefield with the object of finding a way to clear water in the east. The vessel which at 3 o'clock was on the port quarter and stopped was also steering in a northerly direction and as we thought endeavouring to find a passage through the icefield to the east. Later we saw apparently at the eastern extremity of the ice-field about 6 or 6 ½ miles off a large four masted steamer. With the aid of a telescope we saw she had derricks up at No. 1. We could not distinguish her funnel. Shortly (after), we sighted smoke ahead which on nearer approach turned out to be a Leyland liner. At this time the vessel which had stopped at 3 o'clock on our port quarter and since had been steering to the north ahead of us suddenly turned northwest. This surprised me at the time (since) up to this point I (had) thought she was an east-bound ship. As we approached and before we got up to her the Leyland liner commenced steaming through the ice in the direction of the other four-masted steamer we could see east of the icefield.

I continued in a northerly direction, not having communication with any vessel. To my astonishment she (the first ship) which had been in sight the whole time headed to the East and approached so that with the aid of the glasses I made out her name (*Mount Temple*). After reading her name she again steamed NW.

I continued north until about 9.50am when I steamed slowly through the icefield which I cleared at 10.30am. I did not see any more of the vessels mentioned.

April 15:	3.5	stopped	41.20 N, 50.24 W
	10. 30	cleared ice	41.48 N, 50.24 W
	Noon		41.51 N, 50.00 (?) W

(*Mount Temple*'s position at 0.25am – 41.25 N, 51.14 W)"

A number of anomalies are apparent. The "Leyland liner" seen by the *Almerian* was identified by Captain Lord as the *Californian*; the ship seen on the other side of the ice-field obviously being the *Carpathia*. At the British Inquiry, on May 14th, Lord testified to seeing this Leyland steamer:

7400. Was there another vessel near the "*Mount Temple*"?
- There was a, two-masted steamer, pink funnel, black top, steering north down to the north-west.

However, no other person called by either Inquiry mentioned this pink and black funnelled ship. Lord did not mention it to Senator Smith. The strange ship seen by Captain Moore of the *Mount Temple*, unidentified to this day, had a black and white funnel; furthermore, he made no mention of using the Morse lamp to communicate with any vessel, or of turning back to the east to allow this new stranger a convenient look at his ship's name, when his true course was to Canada, to the North-West[54]. Also, the time given for daylight is suspicious. In that area of

---

54   David Gittins has performed considerable research on this matter, and as he points out on his website http://users.senet.com.au/~gittins/Almerian.html that the *Almerian*'s navigation details are suspect. Gittins notes that the *Almerian* should have been nowhere near the scene of the accident, but we simply do not know her course. She may have travelled up the Eastern U.S. coastline before heading east at some point enabling her to reach the vicinity of the *Titanic*. We also know now from the *Titanic*'s correct distress location, 13 miles to the East South East of her reported position, that the *Almerian* would not have been able to see the *Carpathia* from her stated co-ordinates, but she would have been had the *Titanic*'s reported location been correct. A simple explanation is that the *Almerian*'s stated position on the report may have been due to sloppily deduced – and highly coincidental - dead reckoning calculations. The navigation details also include the *Mount Temple*'s position at 12.25 a.m on April 15th. Why was this included? It could have been obtained from the U.S. Inquiry (April 27th) or the British Inquiry (May 15th). It may have been used to concoct the *Almerian*'s navigation, but if so it ignored the *Mount Temple*'s U.S. testimony that the *Titanic* must have stopped many miles east of its supposed location. However, in 1912, it was a foolish individual to question the validity of the *Titanic*'s reported location. Moore was one such "fool" - but brave. And correct. Even Captain Lord, before he was called to the U.S. Inquiry, told two newspapers (*The Boston Globe*, April 25th and *The Boston Journal*, April 26th) that he considered the Titanic's position to be correct

the North Atlantic, nautical twilight started at 4.37am, civil twilight at 5.11am, and sunrise at 5.40am[55].

Taking a brief break from this chronology, the UK Authorities had been diligent in contacting U.S. and European shipping companies and ports to try to determine the identity of Captain Moore's black-and-white funnelled ship. Although many suggestions were provided, few were investigated, and only a handful of reports and logs from Captains were obtained. One of the shipping companies which was asked about the potential proximity of its vessels to the *Titanic* was the Leyland Line itself. They replied on June 7th 1912 that only the *Californian* and another vessel of their line, the *Antillian*, were reported to be in the area. The latter ship, as far as Leyland's could ascertain, was "outside the ice region, saw no ice, and had clear weather" - that is, nowhere near the wreck. From the *Shipping Gazette and Lloyd's List*, we learn that the *Antillian* was reported to be 70 miles west of Brow Head, Ireland at 3.24pm on April 21st. At a steady run of 11 knots, she may have been able to reach the vicinity of the wreck site.

In response to a query from the UK Board of Trade, the Leyland line also provided instructions it gave to commanders of its vessels:

"Commanders must run no risk which might by any possibility result in an accident to their ships. It is to be hoped that they will ever bear in mind that the safety of the lives and property entrusted to their care is the ruling principle that should govern them in the navigation of their vessels, and that no supposed gain in expedition or saving of time on the voyage is to be purchased at the risk of accident. The company desires to maintain for its vessels a reputation for safety, and only looks for such speed on the various voyages as is consistent with safe and prudent navigation.

Commanders are reminded that the steamers are to a great extent uninsured, and that their own livelihood as well as the Company's success, depends upon immunity from accident; no precaution which ensures safe navigation is to be considered excessive."

These words no doubt filtered through Captain Lord's mind when he
_____
even though he later recanted this opinion and pushed the *Titanic*'s wreck many miles to the south. Regarding the suspect course of the *Almerian*, this author has performed research which showed that many ships which steamed to or from ports in the Gulf of Mexico also encountered ice in the area of the Titanic. Were these ships off-course too? This research is at http://www.paullee.com/titanic/ice.html

55   Between nautical and civil twilight, the glimmerings of the sun are apparent, but it it is still dark enough to see stars to perform navigation: stellar observations by both the *Titanic* and *Californian* at 7.30pm on April 14th were performed under such conditions. Outlines of objects can be discerned. During nautical twilight, the horizon is indistinct. Before nautical twilight, sky illumination is so faint that it is practically imperceptible. Please note that the actual time as recorded on the ships may vary by a few minutes due to ship's actual time difference between local time and Greenwich Mean Time.

decided to stop the *Californian* on April 14th, rather than risk unsafe passage through ice at night. This was after all his first time navigating in such conditions. But had these instructions prevented him from attempting a rescue of the passengers and crew of the *Titanic*? It did not concern him on April 15th, when he entered the ice on three separate occasions – but then, he could see what he was doing during daylight. It may explain why, despite being called from the chart room at about 4.30am, the *Californian* did not start moving until 5.15am, and the first CQ call sent about this time. At this point, the sun was peering over the edge of the horizon. Lord later wrote, on August 14th, to various papers, including the Mercantile Marine Service Association (a seafaring union of which he was member) the following, "I did not hear of the disaster until daylight, and that only after it was deemed safe for my steamer to proceed[56]." Groves would later comment on this when interviewed four decades later.

As we will see[57] the suggestion that *Almerian* was close by was not universally accepted by Lord in 1912, although he did waver on this point, and his counsel during the British Inquiry did not mention her at all, though he must have been familiar with the movement of Leyland line ships (the only such ship referenced by Captain Lord's council was the *Memphian*).

The *Almerian* was to materialise again many decades later. A 1980 letter addressed to Lord's main advocate, Mr. Leslie Harrison, came from a Mr. Havard, whose father, Essex Havard, was the 2nd Officer on board the *Almerian*, and had sailed with Captain Lord on Leyland's S.S. *William Cliff* on its 15th August and 31st October, 1910 voyages. Essex told his son that "many years ago, he believed it was possible that the *Almerion* [sic] was the mystery ship at the time of the *Titanic*'s sinking. He said that on that night they were in an ice field and thought they could see a ship in the far distance. They fired some rockets thinking that if the ship was in trouble they would answer with a distress flare. There was no reply."

If the *Almerian* did fire rockets, why did no-one on the *Titanic* see them? If the story has a grain of truth, it could be – feebly – argued that all eyes in the vicinity were, with few exceptions, firmly set on the *Titanic* and not on the surrounding waters until after she had sunk, when hundreds of eyes scanned the horizon for first inklings of any rescuing vessels[58]. And, if the dubious navigation

---

56   Perhaps another contributing factor can be found in an interview between Lord and his chief advocate Leslie Harrison in February 1961, when the latter asked, "Well, the temptation of the salvage.." "was everything," concluded Lord.

57   And as can be seen on Dave Gittin's website

58   There is one intriguing story, reproduced in Michael Davie's book "*The Titanic-The Full Story of a Tragedy*". Reproduced in that book is a letter from Marian Thayer in which she writes, "While still on the boat deck I saw, on the port side, what appeared to be the hull of a ship, and quite near us (perhaps a mile away) from which rockets were being sent up. I am certain of this, for later, on reaching the water, I was disappointed to find she had disappeared. The impression I had received was that the vessel was less than half the

is to be believed, the *Almerian* would be well to the south of the *Titanic*; Boxhall – and many people were intently looking at the strange ship on the northern horizon, hoping for a response- this ship being in the opposite direction to the supposed *Almerian*. But was there a precedent for using rockets as methods of communication? Indeed yes, and it comes from Captain Lord himself. When he served as Chief Officer aboard the West India Company's *Darien* c.1901, Lord was instructed by Captain Myles to fire a distress rocket to greet a ship of the same line, the *Atlantian*, as she passed. The *Atlantian* responded in kind[59].

Harrison was interested, but neglected to use this information in the book that he was preparing on Captain Lord. He wrote to Mr. Havard that "it seems to me [the Leyland Line management] deliberately withheld from the Board of Trade the fact that the *Almerian* had been so close to the scene of the disaster." Regarding the rough draft of his book on the *Californian*, which was then in preparation, Harrison referred to a section which he deleted in later revisions, where he mentioned that "there appears to be a successful operation to suppress the truth about the *Mount Temple*'s part in the affair," and that, "having seen just how badly Captain Lord was being treated, [Leyland] decided not to expose Captain Thomas to the same treatment!"

It may also be worth remarking that none of the other ships mentioned in evidence (e.g. Lord's yellow funnelled 4 masted steamer seen at 4 a.m, or other ships seen by Captains Rostron or Moore) were investigated at all: as mentioned above, on May 21st, the British Consulate asked U.S. ports about recently docked or departed vessels[60]; all the testimony regarding mystery ships had been given in evidence by then. Information obtained from other sources was checked, if possible. For instance, one letter, which was sent to Lord Mersey by a person named W. Monk, alleged that the Canadian Pacific Line's *Lake Michigan* was in the vicinity. A quick check proved otherwise. "The vessel," an internal memo stated, "was well over 200 miles to the E [sic] and N" away from the *Titanic* at the

_____

size of the [SS] *Cedric*, and higher out of the water at her bow than the *Carpathia*." It is difficult to ascertain where she was when this was said, or in which direction she was looking – on the port bow, where the well attested mystery light was seen by dozens, or on the port quarter, where the *Almerian* (if she was there) would be. By her account, Mrs. Thayer reached the water in lifeboat no.4 at 1.40a.m, which corresponds nicely with the findings of the British Inquiry, and the work of Bill Wormstedt, Tad Fitch and George Behe at http://home.comcast.net/%7Ebwormst/Titanic/revised.html Of course, Mrs. Thayer could be mistaken and/or the *Almerian* story could be bunkum.

59   *A Titanic Myth* page 33

60   The request from the Consulate seems to be a confabulation between evidence from the *Californian* and the *Mount Temple*, as it asked for information on a ship with "one black funnel with a white band and some device which was undecipherable, which vessel might have been showing 2 mast-head lights in the vicinity ... on or about 1.30am and 4.00am [in the area of the wreck]."

time of the casualty[61]. The report concludes that the ship had a yellow funnel with a black top, black hull with the exception on the midships bridge plating which was painted buff; hence she did not match the black and white funnel ship. Other ships that had been suggested by foreign ports were seemingly never investigated at all; the files at the UK Public Records Office are full of such suggested 'mystery ships.'

The black and white funnel ship remains unidentified to this day, although several suggestions have been made by researchers. One was the SS *Saturnia*[62] of the Donaldson Line, which sailed from Glasgow to St.John, New Brunswick on April 6th, arriving on April 18th. The identification of the *Saturnia* is based on information provided by two passengers bound for Glasgow aboard the ship, who state that the ship was only 5 miles away from the *Titanic* and stopped on account of the ice. Researcher George Behe informs me that her master, Captain Taylor, proved that the ship was actually 350 miles west of the wreck site at the time of the disaster.

Trautenfels and *Lindenfels* have also been suggested. Both these ships, petroleum carriers belonging to the Hansa Line in Bremen, had one black funnel each with a white band, around which were red hoops; the *Lindenfels* also had a Maltese cross in the middle of the white band. Both ships lacked wireless and had two masts.

However, George Behe notes the following on these ships: "*Trautenfels*: At 8 a.m. on April 14th the *Trautenfels* was already west of long. 50° W. Captain Huper said his vessel was 100 miles southwest of the *Titanic* by the time the disaster took place. *Lindenfels*: The sole reference to this vessel I've been able to find was in a letter from the Treasury Dept. to the Commissioner of Navigation that was quoted in the Senate Inquiry: "The *Trautenfels* of that line arrived at this port [Boston] early in the morning on 18th April, and the *Lindenfels* on 20th April. As I am informed that the voyage from the locality mentioned by the Bureau to this port is from three to five days, according to the speed of the steamer, the *Trautenfels* would probably not have been in that locality on 15th April." Also, *The Shipping Gazette and Lloyd's List* reports: "*Boston 18th April* - German Steamer *Trautenfels* from Hamburg reports:- April 14th, 5.40am in lat 42° 01 long 49° 53 sighted two icebergs fully 200 feet long and 50 feet high: soon after heavy field ice was encountered which extended for a distance of 30 miles and made it necessary for the steamer to run in a south-westerly direction for 25 miles to clear it; in the field ice Captain Huper counted 30 bergs, some of which were very large; off to the southward no clear water was seen, so that the Captain estimated that the ice in that direction must have extended fully 30 miles."

---

61   Actually her positions, as determined from her log by the Board of Trade are given as follows: Noon 14/4/12 43°21 N 62°36 W Noon 15/4/12 44°17 N 56°28 W placing her well to the west of the *Titanic*

62   "*Titanic: Triumph and Tragedy*" p.174

Obviously, by the time the *Titanic* struck, *Trautenfels* would not have been in the vicinity, unless the Captain suffered some form of aberration which caused him to turn around and remain nearby. One little puzzle does remain. The *Trautenfels* was bound towards Boston. After clearing the ice field she would have presumably turned back to the north-west, so how does she wind up "100 miles southwest" of the *Titanic* at the time of the accident? Also, the 100 miles, even if it is an approximation, seems too small: her position at 5.40am is about 17 miles north-north-east of the wrecksite. To cover a total of 117 miles in 18 hours would entail an average speed of 6.5 knots, a surprisingly slow speed. These reports must be a mistake and indeed, recent research has confirmed this; the *Trautenfels* was actually collecting weather data and recorded her noon position in a log which was later stored in a German archive. This log showed that at 12.00pm on April 14th, she was slightly north of the wreck, but west to the west. She was even further advanced to the west by noon the next day, the 15th.

Finally, the *Trautenfels* and *Lindenfels* were heading west to Boston, and could not have been Moore's unknown vessel, which was travelling to the east.

On day 7 of the British Inquiry, a brief respite occurred in the questioning of *Titanic* survivors, for it was now time for the crew of the *Californian* to present their stories to the public. Their sailing schedules had prevented them from appearing previously. Public interest during this session was high, as it was believed that J. Bruce Ismay himself would be in attendance: he was vilified in some sections of the press because not only had he survived the disaster, but he was the head of the White Star Line and some people had roundly proclaimed that he should have gone to the bottom with his creation. Also due to attend was Lord and Lady Duff-Gordon and the promise of salacious gossip[63] also must have help to boost the attendance figures; in the event, they were delayed on their travels and couldn't attend, the spectators having to settle for a seemingly dull story of a freighter trapped in the ice. The body of the hall and the galleries were well filled, the seats being occupied chiefly by women[64].

Robertson Dunlop rose and asked the court, "Will your Lordship allow me to appear on behalf of the Leyland Line - the owners, Master and Officers from the *Californian*, who are to be examined today?[65]"

---

63   The Duff-Gordons faced the accusation of having bribed the crew of their lifeboat (which despite a maximum capacity of 40 people, only held 12) not to return to rescue dying swimmers after the Titanic had sunk.

64   *The New York Times*, May 15th, 1912.

65   Strangely, the Allan Line (owners of the SS *Virginian*) and the Canadian Pacific Railway Company (The *Mount Temple*), then in early stages of a merger, had instructed Member of Parliament Hamar Greenwood to watch proceedings on their behalf. Why? Were these shipping lines concerned about attacks on their Captains too? None of the

The Attorney-General responded, "Of course, this question of the *Californian* raises an issue between the Master and Officers of the *Californian*, and, certainly, one man who was employed as a donkeyman or as an assistant donkeyman. The question substantially is this: The *Californian* is said by this donkeyman to have seen the distress rockets fired from a vessel which, according to this man, was the *Titanic*, and to have taken no notice of those distress rockets. There is no doubt, as I understand the evidence, that rockets were seen on this night and that the *Californian* was not at a very great distance from the *Titanic*, but whether it was the *Titanic* that she saw or not is a matter which can only be determined after we have heard the evidence. It is a little difficult again to say that that has a very direct bearing upon the particular questions which have been submitted so far for your Lordship's consideration. Some of the evidence undoubtedly will be material on these questions as to the position, what was seen and what precautions were taken by the *Californian*, and the wireless messages that were sent and received, and they will be undoubtedly important matters for your consideration. This question, as between the donkeyman and the Master is a different matter, but it does seem to me that in view of the statements which have been made and the evidence that has already been given elsewhere about it, it would be desirable that your Lordship should hear what there is to be said. I propose therefore to ask them a few questions. I do not propose to go into it at any length, but to ask them on such as would be essential, so that your Lordship will be enabled to form some opinion as to whether or not this story told by the donkeyman is right."

"I cannot deal with your application at present, Mr. Dunlop. If anything is said which I think requires explanation from your clients I will take care to let you know," the Wreck Commissioner replied, which seemed to satisfy Dunlop, and then went on to say that he could watch the proceedings, "and, if you find any attack is made upon your clients, then you can ask me to allow them to go into the box." The Attorney-General remarked that the allegations about the *Californian* "cannot affect the owners, I think; it may affect the Master if the story were true."

Now it was time for the *Californian*'s insouciance to be examined.

Captain Lord took the stand and his evidence was essentially the same as given in America; travelling S 89 W (true), the *Californian* had encountered the ice field, stretching north and south as far as could be seen. Lord ordered his ship stopped, and she swung to starboard, eventually heading towards the north east; close upon 11pm[66], he casually observed a steamer's light approaching from the east on the starboard side, about six or seven miles away. Lord then went to Evans

_____

testimony refers to malfeasance on the part of any Captain other than Stanley Lord.

66   Lord would write (in a statement typed up on 21st May 1912) that, as he was leaving the bridge [at 10.30pm], he "pointed out to [the] 3rd Officer what [he] thought was a light to [the] East, he said he thought it was a star, I then left the bridge." Groves would later contradict this account.

room and asked what ships he had[67]. "Nothing, only the *Titanic*," Evans replied. Lord's testimony indicates that he remarked at the time that the ship approaching them was not the *Titanic* judging by her size and illuminated condition, and he instructed Evans, as a matter of courtesy, to send a message to the *Titanic* telling them that they were stopped and surrounded by ice. In his opinion, the ship approaching them did not have wireless at all[68].

As Lord watched the ship approaching, he could make out her green sidelight, a single masthead light and one or two deck lights. He continued to watch her till about 11.30, when she seemed to stop. To Lord, the other ship was a medium sized steamer, "something like [the *Californian*]." He could see Groves, the 3rd Officer vainly trying to communicate with the ship by Morse lamp from the bridge, and at 12.10, Groves was replaced on watch by the 2nd Officer. Lord gave him instructions to let him know if the ship altered her bearings or got any closer to the *Californian*. Five minutes later, Lord went to the chart room, just below the bridge.

Let us pause to interject an important point. Lord was now clear on the point that 2nd Officer Herbert Stone was on the bridge. Recall that a newspaper interview in Boston yielded the following quote from the Captain: "'Mr. Stewart, the first officer, was on the bridge during the times that the signals were supposed to have been seen, and he can tell you himself that nothing of the kind was seen by him, or any of the men who were on watch with him.

At 12.40, Lord whistled up the voice pipe, and asked Stone if the other vessel had remained the same, to which the 2nd Officer replied that she had, and had ignored his attempt to communicate with her with the Morse lamp. Lord informed Stone that he was going to lie down on the chart room settee, which he did, fully clothed. At 1.15, Stone whistled down the voice pipe, and Lord got up, went to his cabin next door and picked up the tube. He was informed that the other ship had fired a white rocket and, at 12.50 had started to alter her bearing from the south east, moving to the south west. As we shall see, Stone had by now seen five rockets, so why did he not report all of them to the Captain? Perhaps one explanation lies in the regulations regarding the means to summon assistance from a vessel in distress, the relevant one being ,"Rockets or shells, throwing stars of any colour or description, used one at a time at short intervals." Obviously this rule is meant to apply to a steady barrage of rockets or shells. By just admitting to have been told of one – or being cognisant of just the one - a defence could be

---

67   A trivial difference with the evidence in America; Lord had reported talking to the Chief Engineer, when Evans approached him; Evans corroborated this fact - that he had gone to speak to Lord, rather than the Captain coming to his cabin.
68   Lord explained, "This steamer had been in sight, the one that fired the rocket, when we sent the last message to the *Titanic*, and I was certain that the steamer was not the *Titanic*, and the operator said he had not [got] any other steamers, so I drew my conclusion that she had not got any wireless."

constructed by stating that, "Only one rocket is not a signal of distress; more are needed to remove ambiguity."

Whatever vestiges of impartiality Lord Mersey may have had were submerged by his next proclamation; "What is in my brain at the present time is this, that what they saw was the *Titanic* ... That is in my brain, and I want to see whether I am right or not."

The Attorney-General asked Lord, "Can you tell us whether you saw one or two masthead lights?" to which he was told that he had only seen one, but volunteered the fact that the 3rd Officer had said he saw two.

One can imagine the ears of the Attorney-General pricking up; "Now that is important," he remarked. Mersey agreed, "That is very important, because the *Titanic* would have two."

In fact research has shown that the *Titanic* only ever had one mast light, and this was affixed to the forward most mast of the two she had. How and why Mersey and the Attorney-General had gained an opinion that the *Titanic* had two is unknown; presumably from newspaper reports. Whatever the source of this misleading 'fact', it only added to their certainty that it was the *Titanic* herself that was visible.

But Mersey was not happy. "I am sorry to interrupt you, but it is not satisfactory to me. When was it the 3rd Officer said he saw two lights? The 3rd Officer by this time was below; I do not know what you are talking about now."

Sir Rufus Isaacs attempted to clarify: "When was it the 3rd Officer told you he had seen the two lights?"

"Before 12 o'clock."

"Before 12 o'clock?" Lord was queried.

"Before midnight. At the time I saw one, he saw two."

"Were you on deck when he told you this?"

"He told me the following day, I think; I do not think it was mentioned that night."

"He told you next day he had seen two white lights when on deck about 12 o'clock?" asked the Attorney General. Yes, two masthead lights, Lord replied.

One can understand now why critics are sceptical of Lord's testimony in witness box. Some commentators have labelled his performance as "inept" and "contradictory", and the above passage is a perfect example of this.

The questioning continued:

"Why did you ask him how many there were?"

"Well, I was curious about this *Titanic* accident. I was trying to locate the ship that was supposed to be between us and the *Titanic*."

"Were you in doubt as to whether you had seen one or two lights?" asked Isaacs. Lord replied that he wasn't.

The Commissioner chimed in, "Then I cannot understand why you should ask him how many lights he had seen if you yourself had no doubt whatever about it."

"If he did see two lights it must have been the *Titanic*, must it not?"

"It does not follow," a perfectly sensible reply by Lord.

"Do you know any other vessel it could have been?"

"Any amount."

"Which - I mean, at this particular time, you know, and at this particular spot. Can you suggest any other vessel it could have been?"

"Well, I do not know," Lord replied.

Mersey and the rest of the counsel were familiar with Groves' formal statement made upon arrival in Liverpool. They now sought to compare Lord's version of events with Groves'.

"Has the 3rd Officer ever expressed any opinion to you that it was the *Titanic* he saw?"

"No, my Lord," forgetting that Groves had stated his opinion to Captain Fry in Liverpool just a few days earlier.

"I must put this to you. Do you remember about a quarter-past 11 on that night, that is the night of the 14th, his telling you that he had noticed a steamer - that is, the 3rd Officer, Mr. Groves?"

"No, I do not."

"A steamer about three points abaft the starboard beam, 10 to 12 miles away?"

"No, I do not."

"Did you ask about her lights?"

"Not then."

"At any time?"

"No. A quarter to 12 was the first time I ever mentioned anything to him about the steamer, that I recollect."

"Did he say to you that she was evidently a passenger steamer?"

"No."

"And did you say to him, "The only passenger steamer near us is the *Titanic*?"

"I might have said that with regard to the steamer, but he did not say the steamer was a passenger steamer."

"You might have said what?"

"The *Titanic*."

"What about the *Titanic*?"

"The *Titanic* we were in communication with."

Isaacs must have been getting frustrated, "That is not what I put, you know." The Commissioner agreed, "No, and it is not what he said." "It is a very different thing," Isaacs replied.

"You said, according to your statement, "The *Titanic* is the only passenger steamer near us." You said that to him?"

"She was," said Lord, but admitted that he could not recollect saying it.

After continuing in this manner for a few more minutes, Mersey grumbled, "You do not give answers that please me at present," and it is easy to see why. Lord could not recollect what he had said about nearby passenger steamers. He denied seeing the lights of the other steamer going out, or Groves mentioning this to him.

The questioning now focussed on Apprentice Gibson and his purported report to the Captain, who, had a "recollection" of him opening and closing the chart room door some time between half-past 1 and half-past 4. In accordance with his American testimony, Lord stated that he had said "What is it?" and that Gibson had closed the door. Apparently, the Captain only learned that Gibson had been told to report by 2nd Officer Stone at 7am the next morning. The report would have been that 8 rockets in total had been fired and the other had steamed away.

The Captain had been woken up at 4.30 by the Chief Officer. It was now breaking day, and Stewart reported that the ship, a yellow-funnelled vessel, that had fired "the rocket" was to the south of them. Lord claimed that he did not know a number of rockets had been fired. The two men tramped up to the bridge. As Lord said, "Well, I was conversing with him about the probability of pushing through the ice, to commence with. I was undecided whether to go through it or to turn round and go back, and we decided to go on, so I told him to put the engines on and stand by. He did so. Then he said, "Will you go down to look at this steamer to the southward?" I asked him, "Why, what is the matter with it?" He said, "He might have lost his rudder." But I said, "Why? He has not got any signals up." "No, but," he said, "the 2nd Officer in his watch said he fired several rockets." I said, "Go and call the wireless operator." Lord had run the engines ahead for a few minutes, stopping them when Stewart returned after 15 or 20 minutes with the news that a ship had sunk. Stewart then traipsed back to the wireless cabin, and returned with the news that it was the *Titanic* that had gone to the bottom. Following this shattering information, Lord himself went to wireless.

Nothing was said about the rockets, the ship seen the night before, or the possibility of it having been the *Titanic*. The only thing that crossed Lord's mind was whether the *Titanic*'s signals or distress rockets could be seen at 19 miles distance. It seemed possible, he thought, but he never, he claimed, thought that the steamer that the *Californian* had seen sending up rockets was the *Titanic* because it is an "utter impossibility" to mistake a ship like that. For one thing, he was certain he would have heard the report as the rocket detonated. But Lord could suggest no other passenger vessels, or indeed rocket firing ships, that were in the vicinity that night. To this author, this seems reasonable. Why should Lord be expected to possess this information? He did not carry shipping schedules for all vessels in his head.

Following the *Virginian*'s wireless message at 6am, which provided the *Titanic*'s distress location, the *Californian* proceeded, heading between south and south west between then and 6.30am through about 3 miles of ice, endeavouring to make as close to S. 16° W as possible. At 7.30am, the *Mount Temple* was passed, and the *Californian* stopped too[69]. Near the *Mount Temple* was "a two-masted steamer, pink funnel, black top, steering north down to the north-west." About this time, a message was received that the *Carpathia* was standing by the Titanic, asking that the *Californian* have her boats and lifebelts ready. The *Californian*, now evidently underway again, passed the reported location of the *Titanic*'s foundering at 7.30am, but saw no wreckage, and eventually viewed the *Carpathia*, where he did see flotsam and jetsam from the lost liner. The *Californian* was now proceeding south, or south by east (true) along the western edge of the ice field at 13 knots. She steamed on her course until 8am, and then turned to the north-east at full speed: at 8.30, she reached the *Carpathia*. At 11.15, Lord and his crew left the debris in a position of 41°33'N. and 50°1'W, pushing slowly through the ice again.

This position is well to the south and east of the *Titanic*'s SOS location, and this is where Lord considered the disaster to have taken place. He obtained this location by sun sights taken at noon, which put her in a longitude of 50 °9' W and then extrapolated backwards; this gives a speed of 6 knots.

It is also apparent that from this evidence that the self-aggrandizing stories spun by Lord in Boston about his attempts to reach the *Carpathia* were also bogus. All that can be said is that, in fairness, Lord may have been guilty of exaggerating the situation, and the *Californian*'s performance, on the morning of April 15th.

Dodging back and forth between topics, the interrogation focussed at one point on the exchange between Stone and Lord at 1.15 in which "the rocket" was first mentioned. Despite knowing, as he admitted, that there was danger to a moving steamer, Lord had remained in the chart room. He asked the 2nd Officer if the rocket was a company's signal, but Stone did not know. This did not satisfy Lord, but he claimed he had no reason to think that it was anything different. His impression "right along" was that the other ship was acknowledging the *Californian*'s Morse lamp: "A good many steamers do not use the Morse lamp." He asked Stone to continue Morsing and to send Gibson down with any reply from the steamer. But no reply came. And Lord went back to sleep.

"If it was not a company's signal, must it not have been a distress signal?" asked Isaacs.

"If it had been a distress signal the Officer on watch would have told me," countered Lord.

"I say, if it was not a company's signal, must it not have been a distress signal?"

"Well, I do not know of any other signals but distress signals that are used at sea," Lord admitted.

---

69   This was the first and only time Captain Lord described his ship as stopping. If so, why did she stop? Was she considering whether to risk a passage through the ice? Or had the crew become confused between seeing the *Carpathia* picking up survivors, and yet there was nothing at the official distress site and were debating what to do?

"You do not expect at sea, where you were, to see a rocket unless it is a distress signal, do you?"

"We sometimes get these company's signals which resemble rockets; they do not shoot as high and they do not explode."

"You have already told us that you were not satisfied that was a company's signal. You have told us that?" inquired Isaacs.

"I asked the Officer, was it a company's signal."

"And he did not know?" interjected Mersey.

"He did not know," confirmed Captain Lord.

"That you were not satisfied it was a company's signal. You did not think it was a company's signal?"

"I inquired, was it a company's signal."

"But you had been told that he did not know?"

"[Stone] said he did not know."

"Very well, that did not satisfy you?" Lord replied that it had not.

"Then if it was not that, it might have been a distress signal?"

"It might have been."

"And you remained in the chart room?"

"I remained in the chart room."

"Expecting Gibson, the Apprentice, to come down and report to you?"

"Yes."

The Attorney General proceeded. "That is rather important, you see - that is the message which the boy was supposed to have delivered to you which you heard next day?"

"Yes."

"I want to put this to you. Did not the boy deliver the message to you, and did not you inquire whether they were all white rockets?"

"I do not know; I was asleep," insisted Lord.

"Think. This is a very important matter, " said Isaacs, in a classic of understatement, and obviously highly sceptical of the story emerging.

"It is a very important matter. I recognise that."

"It is much better to tell us what happened, Captain?"

"He came to the door, I understand. I have spoken to him very closely since. He said, I opened my eyes and said, "What is it"? and he gave the message; and I said, "What time is it"? and he told me, and then I think he said I asked him whether there were any colours in the light."

"Just think. You say you do not doubt it for a moment. Do you see what that means. That means that the boy did go to the chart room to you. He did tell you about the rockets from the ship and you asked whether they were white rockets, and told him that he was to report if anything further occurred?"

"So he said. That is what he said."

"Have you any reason to doubt that is true?"

"No; I was asleep."

"Then do you mean you said this in your sleep to him, that he was to report?"

"I very likely was half awake. I have no recollection of this Apprentice saying anything to me at all that morning."

"Why did you ask whether they were white rockets?"

"I suppose this was on account of the first question they asked, whether they were Company's signals."

"Do just think!"

"Company signals usually have some colours in them."

"So that if they were white it would make it quite plain to you they were distress signals?"

"No, I understand some companies have white."

"Do really try and do yourself justice," an exasperated Sir Rufus Isaacs sighed.

"I am trying to do my best."

"Think you know. Mr. Lord, allow me to suggest you are not doing yourself justice. You are explaining, first of all, that you asked if they were white rockets, because companies' signals are coloured. I am asking you whether the point of your asking whether they were all white rockets was not in order to know whether they were distress signals? Was not that the object of your question, if you put it?"

"I really do not know what was the object of my question."

"And you think that is why you asked about it?"

"I think that is why I asked about it."

But there was one more instance when Lord had been called and had no recollection. Mentioned by Evans in America, but "forgotten" by the Captain during his questioning, details now emerged for the first time:

"I must ask you something more. Do you remember Mr. Stone reporting at twenty minutes to three to you that morning through the tube?" Lord claimed ignorance of this message.

Evidently referring to Stone's proof, Isaacs continued, "Listen to this - he reported to you at twenty minutes to three through the tube and told you that the steamer had disappeared bearing south-west half west. Do you remember that?"

But Lord would not budge. "I do not remember it. He has told me that since."

"Listen to this: - "The Captain again asked me if I was sure there were no colours in the lights that had been seen." Do you remember that?" Again, Lord replied in the negative.

""And that he" - Mr. Stone - "assured you that they were white lights"?"

"He has told me all about this since, but I have not the slightest recollection that anything happened that way."

"This is what he says: "I assured him that they were white lights, and he" - that is you - "said 'All right.'" Have you no recollection of that conversation?"

"I have no recollection of any conversation between half-past one and half-past four that I had with the 2nd Officer."

Thus, Lord had denied any knowledge of more than one rocket being fired: it was only the next day that he learned of this message, and that Stone had seen the stern light of the other ship faintly through his binoculars. It may be that Lord had slept soundly, or was not awake sufficiently to absorb the information imparted to him. But he was sufficiently awake to raise himself from his settee, walk to the adjacent cabin, answer the voice pipe, and then walk back to his makeshift bed.

Cross-examined by Mr. Thomas Lewis, representative of the British Seafarers' Union, Lord was asked if he considered it reasonable, seeing that the Captain had very little experience of ice, to go below to the chart room and lie there. Lord thought he was perfectly justified when a ship was stopped.

"Do you consider it reasonable, in view of the fact that you had been in communication with other ships that your wireless operator should have gone off duty at 11 o'clock?" Lord agreed.

"Under those circumstances, seeing that there was a possibility of the boat being near, do you consider it reasonable that you should go off duty?"

"Perfectly reasonable. I was looking after my own ship."

The Commissioner demurred again, "These are answers that do not do you the least good, and they are not the answers that you want."

Only Robertson Dunlop, who represented the Leyland Line, offered Lord any respite from the barrage of questions, but even he was subject to interruptions from Lord Mersey.

"Assuming that she sank somewhere between 2 and 3, could you, in fact, if you had known at 1.15 a.m. in the morning that the *Titanic* was in distress to the southward and westward of you, have reached her before, say, 3 a.m.?" asked Dunlop. Lord replied not.

"Could you have navigated with any degree of safety to your vessel at night through the ice that you, in fact, encountered?"

"It would have been most dangerous."

Mersey intervened. "Am I to understand that this is what you mean to say, that if he had known that the vessel was the *Titanic* he would have made no attempt whatever to reach it?"

"No, my Lord. I do not suggest that, " Dunlop said, and then, turning to Lord, he asked, "What would you have done? No doubt you would have made an attempt?"

"Most certainly I would have made every effort to go down to her," Lord vacillated.

"Would the attempt from what you now know in fact have succeeded?"

"I do not think we would have got there before the *Carpathia* did, if we

79

would have got there as soon."

If the ship under surveillance from the *Californian* was indeed the *Titanic*, then Lord could have got there, depending on whatever speed was deemed prudent in the icy conditions, possibly before the *Carpathia* did, at about 4.15am. In the morning, it had taken Lord and his cohorts 2 ½ hours to reach the wrecksite. But a more direct, line-of-sight route would have taken a lot less time, especially if the distances estimated in the court were accurate. Moreover, a law passed the previous year noted that "...the Master of person in charge of a vessel shall, so far as he can do so without serious danger to his own vessel, render assistance to every person." It was therefore up to the Captain to judge the situation before deciding on a possible rescue mission.

But, as critics point out, Lord hadn't even gone up on deck to view the rockets being sent up.

"Did you question your 2nd Officer as to why you had not been called?"
"I did."
"What was his explanation to you?"
"He said that he had sent down and called me; he had sent Gibson down, and Gibson had told him I was awake and I had said, "All right, let me know if anything is wanted." I was surprised at him not getting me out, considering rockets had been fired. He said if they had been distress rockets he would most certainly have come down and called me himself, but he was not a little bit worried about it at all.[70]"

Here Gibson is reporting that Captain Lord was awake at the time this crucial information was being imparted!

"If they had been distress rockets he would have called you?"
"He would have come down and insisted upon my getting up."
"And was it his view that they were not distress rockets?"
"That was apparently his view."

Two final matters remained. In Boston, after the allegations by Gill but before giving evidence, Lord drew a rough sketch of the movements of his ship between 6.30 and 8.30am, with the positions of the ice field marked, and a long, detailed statement on the back. He did it because, "after the statement that this man Gill made in the papers that we were supposed to have ignored the *Titanic* signals I knew at once there would be an Inquiry over it." If he collated his notes to answer the charges against him, why did he not provide it to Senator Smith?

---

70   Indeed, in an interview with Captain Lord in 1961, he was asked "And if there'd been any urgency you'd have been out like a shot?" Lord predictably replied, "Of course I would."

The second matter relates to the ship's log, written up by the Chief Officer, with each section initialled by each officer at the end of their watch. It contained nothing about the strange ship or equally strange rockets. "If we had realised they were distress rockets we would have entered them," was the Captain's explanation to the court.

The map and statement were handed to Lord Mersey, and this concluded Stanley Lord's ordeal.

Illustration 16: The crew from the Californian during a recess. From left to right, Fireman George Glenn, Greaser William Thomas, Wireless Operator Cyril Evans, Apprentice James Gibson, 2nd Officer Herbert Stone, Seaman William Ross, 3rd Officer Charles Groves, Chief Officer George Stewart

The next witness was the *Californian*'s Apprentice, James Gibson. Recounting his story to the court, he told them that he had joined the watch officer on the bridge at about 12.15 a.m. and asked Stone if there were any steamers around. Stone pointed out the other ship on the starboard beam.

Gibson could clearly see a white masthead light, and through binoculars, the red sidelight. He seemed unsure as to whether he could see a second mastlight, but later admitted in the questioning that he had only seen one and couldn't have missed a second light if it had been there. He could also see a faint glare of white lights on the ship's afterdeck.

For Gibson to have seen the red light, the other ship must have been pointing to the northward of N.N.W, as he agreed later, otherwise her green light would be seen[71]. The bow was therefore pointing to the right of the *Californian*, similar to the situation reported on the *Titanic*.

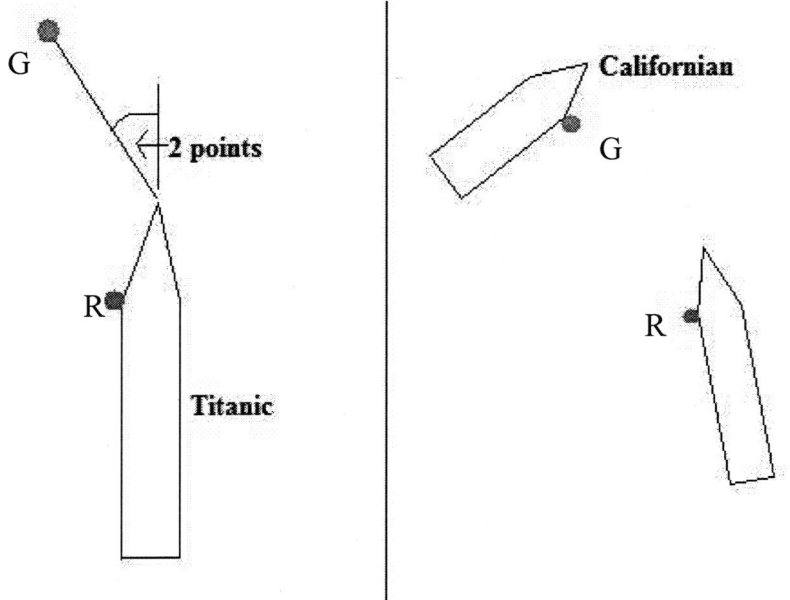

Illustration 17: Comparison of observations as seen from the Titanic (left) and Californian (right) at about 12.30am April 15th 1912. Although the Titanic diagram shows 2 points, witness statements describe an off-bow bearing of ½, 2 or 4 points. 'R' and 'G' indicate the red and green side lights respectively.

Gibson noticed that the light was flickering, and thought that a Morse lamp was being used. Gibson signalled back, but could not discern any reply. Through

71   Stone later agreed that, when he first saw the other ship, she would have been heading in the same direction as the *Californian*; that is, to the north-east, or more broadside than Gibson had intimated.

binoculars, he decided that it was just the mast light of the other ship flickering. The ship seemed to be a tramp steamer, stopped directly abeam, 4 to 7 miles away. Stone agreed with Gibson's assessment; the stranger seemed to be burning oil lamps, hence the flickering.

At 12.25, Gibson went below to attend to his chores. Returning to the bridge about half an hour later, Gibson noticed that the other ship was now 2 ½ points before the starboard beam, causing by the *Californian*'s slow clockwise turn during the night.

Gibson was informed by Stone that the ship had fired 5 rockets, and that he had reported to the Captain, who had instructed him to keep signalling with the Morse lamp, but without success.

Stone ordered Gibson to try the Morse lamp; he called her up for three minutes and then focussed his binoculars on the other ship.

Then she fired another rocket, which burst into white stars. He saw two more, with the naked eye. He heard no explosion.

Despite being a mere Apprentice, Gibson knew the meaning of rockets at sea.

Thomas Scanlan, Counsel on behalf of the National Sailors' and Firemen's Union of Great Britain and Ireland, wanted to know more about the rockets.

"Did you know when the rockets were being sent up that they were being sent up as danger signals?"

"No."

"What did you think they were sent up for?"

"I thought they were some private signals."

"Who told you they were private signals?"

"Nobody told me."

"Had you ever seen private signals of that kind?"

"No."

"And never heard of private signals of that kind?"

"I have heard of private rockets, private signal rockets."

Questioned by Mr. Harbinson, counsel for the third class passengers[72], Gibson was asked, "As a matter of fact is not there a code of rockets for use at sea? Do you know as a matter of fact whether there is or is not?"

"I know now there are only distress rockets used at sea and private signals used near the shore," Gibson replied

"And what colour are distress rockets?"

"White – any colour at all."

Mr. Laing, appearing as counsel for the White Star Line, pursued this point: "Do you know that a distress signal, the regulation distress signal, is a rocket throwing stars?"

"Yes."

---

72   Not one of whom were called to testify!

"You knew that?"

"Yes."

And following a question by Lord Mersey, Gibson admitted that he knew it at the time he saw the rockets.

"And each of those rockets which you saw, which you have described as white rockets, were they throwing stars?"

"All throwing stars."

The *Californian* continued with her slow turn to the south, and when the other ship passed from the starboard to the port bow, the red light disappeared. The white light on the ship was still visible, but not as brightly as before.

At 1.20am, Stone remarked that the other ship was slowly steaming away to the south west.

During all this time, Gibson was signalling continuously, but when asked if he could see the ship steaming away, he testified, "No. The 2nd Officer was taking bearings of her all the time."

"What had you noticed between one o'clock and twenty minutes past one, looking at her through your glasses?" enquired Isaacs.

"The 2nd Officer remarked to me, "Look at her now; she looks very queer out of the water; her lights look queer.""

"You are sure that is what he said - "She looks very queer out of the water"?"

"Yes."

"Did he say what he meant?"

"I looked at her through the glasses after that, and her lights did not seem to be natural."

"He made this observation to you. Did you look at her then through your glasses?"

"Yes," said Gibson. It seemed as if she had a heavy list to starboard. Her lights did not look the same as they did when he first saw them. Her sidelight and lights from the afterdeck seemed to be higher than before, but try as he might, Gibson was unable to describe what he had seen whilst in the witness box. He could recollect saying to Stone, "She looks rather to have a big side out of the water," and the 2nd Officer agreed.

Immediately after the *Titanic* sustained her mortal wound, her list was to starboard. For the remainder of the evening, until she sank, she had a list to port which may have been as much as 10° at the end. How then did Gibson see a list to starboard? One witness at the British Inquiry was a stoker named Frederick Barrett; he had actually been in a boiler room when water rushed in as the ship contacted the iceberg. He had then relocated to a second boiler room, and this too, flooded, before making his way to the boat deck. He left the ship in lifeboat number 13, which launched at about 1.35am. The inquisition in London revolved partially around his observation of a list to *starboard* before he boarded the boat. Indirectly, his testimony can be supported by comparing his testimony with passenger Lawrence Beesley, also in the same boat. As no.13 was lowered, a discharge vent issuing massive amounts of water forced the boat aft, actually under the lowering boat 15, threatening to crush Barrett, Beesley and everyone else. Boat 13 escaped just in time. About half an hour later, the occupants of boat 'C', on the same side of the *Titanic*, but forward of, boat 13, described how the list to port was so great that the boat rubbed against the rivets of the hull. As boat 13 descended, she would have experienced the same problem, and would have actually been swamped by the discharge at the water line. The fact that this didn't happen indicates that the boat must have been hanging some distance from the side of the ship, perhaps by a list to starboard. Thereafter, there would be a list to port.

"I should like you to tell me what were you saying to each other?" Isaacs asked.

"He remarked to me that a ship was not going to fire rockets at sea for nothing." And Gibson agreed with Stone.

The Commissioner then asked a series of questions. "Then do I understand from you that the 2nd Officer came to the conclusion that this was a ship in distress?"

"No, Sir, not exactly."

"What do you mean by "not exactly"? The 2nd Officer said to you, "A ship does not fire up rockets for nothing"?"

"Yes, Sir."

"Did not that convey to you that the ship was, in his opinion, in distress?"

"Not exactly in distress, sir."

"What then?"

"That everything was not all right with her."

"In trouble of some sort?" asked Isaacs.

"Yes, Sir."

Mr. Harbinson pressed this point. "Did you say anything to the 2nd Officer, Mr. Stone, or did he say anything to you, with reference to these rockets that were repeatedly sent up?"

"Yes."

"Did not you think it very curious that so many rockets should be sent up so close to one another?" Gibson agreed.

"Did you say anything to him about going to see the Captain and saying this seemed to be a serious matter?"

"No, he told me he had reported it to the Captain and the Captain had told him to keep calling her up."

"Did Mr. Stone say this vessel seemed to be in distress?"

"No; he said there must be something the matter with her."

"Did he make any remarks to you as to the Captain taking no action? Did he say anything to you at the time?"

85

"No."

"Are you sure?"

"Yes."

"Did you say anything to yourself about it?" asked Mersey.

"I only thought the same that he thought."

"What was that?"

"That a ship is not going to fire rockets at sea for nothing, and there must be something the matter with her."

"Then you thought it was a case of some kind of distress?"

"Yes."

The 2nd Officer instructed the Apprentice to deliver a message to Lord, "Call the Captain and tell him that that ship has disappeared in the South-West; that we are heading West-South-West, and that she has fired altogether eight rockets." The other ship last seen a little on the *Californian*'s port bow.[73] Gibson had never seen the ship turn round, never seen her stern light and had her mastlight under observation until the time she disappeared. If the other ship had steamed off, she must have backed off, in reverse[74]. So, here was a vessel – steaming slowly into the south west (or "disappearing"), with a heavy list to starboard, firing rockets and unwilling to respond to repeated Morse hails. Since the regulations for the use of rockets on the high seas were dictated by international convention, they should have been taken as distress signals, but why should such a crazy vessel steam away from help when the *Californian* was only a few miles to the north?

Gibson walked down the stairs, opened the chart room door, and finding the Captain awake, delivered Stone's message. Lord asked if there were any colours in the rockets. Gibson said no, and the Captain asked what the time was. "2.05" by the wheelhouse clock was his reply (there was no clock on the upper bridge). Gibson returned to the bridge. Why the Captain asked what time it was is another minor mystery, as there was a clock mounted to the rear wall of the chart room, mere feet away, which could also be observed from the flying bridge through the skylight. The clock that Gibson referred to was in the unused wheelhouse, just forward of the chart room in which Lord was resting. Could he not see these clocks, in easy visible range? And just what did Gibson mean by "awake?" Captain Lord later told his supporters that he was lying down on the settee, with his peaked cap over his eyes to shield them from the light; did Gibson mean that Lord was up, awake, and *compos mentis*?

The verbiage used intrigued Isaacs. "You say you were told to report that the ship had disappeared. What did you understand by "disappeared"?"

---

73   Gibson also testified that the *Californian* was heading WSW. If the other ship had indeed disappeared "a little on the port bow", then she was bearing somewhere in the south-west. When seen, she was originally in the south-east.

74   Leslie Harrison later (c.1989) wrote to me and said that this would be a most unseamanlike activity, as it exposed her vital rudder and propeller to damage by ice.

"We could not see anything more of her."

Lord Mersey was equally as intrigued, "Did it convey to you, and did the man who was speaking to you, in your opinion, intend to convey that the ship had gone down? That is what I understand by disappearing. Did you understand him to mean that?"

"No, my Lord," replied Gibson.

"What did you understand him to mean that she had steamed away through the ice?"

"That she had gone out of sight."

"Oh, yes. A ship goes out of sight when she goes down to the bottom," sneered Mersey. "What did you understand by the word "disappeared"?"

"That is all I could understand about it."

"A ship that had been sending up rockets; then you are told to go to the Captain and say, "That ship which has been sending up rockets has disappeared." What did you understand the 2nd Officer to mean? Did not you understand him to mean that she had gone to the bottom?"

"No"

"Then what did you understand, that she had steamed away through the ice?"

But from the witness box came only silence.

At about 3.40am, Stone again whistled down to the Captain, but Gibson did not hear what was said. Shortly after this, Gibson observed another rocket, and he pointing this out to Stone. Two more followed, but Stone did not report these to the Captain. These white rockets were right on the horizon. Gibson raised his binoculars to his eyes, but could see nothing – no mast or side lights – of the ship firing them.

It was about this time that the *Carpathia* was sending up rockets to inform the *Titanic*'s survivors that help was imminent. The British Inquiry failed to appreciate this, and seemed to equate these rockets with the green flares sent up by Boxhall. Wherever the *Titanic* had been, the *Carpathia* was still well to the south and east of the wrecksite, that is, further away from the *Californian*.

An eventful night over, Gibson went off watch at 3.45am.

Gibson departed from the box, his place being taken by Herbert Stone.

Stone went on watch shortly after 12 midnight, he told the court, and conversed with the Captain. The 2nd Officer was told that the *Californian* was stopped and surrounded by ice, and the other ship to the south was pointed out to him, noting that the 3rd officer had tried to contact her by Morse lamp but with no reply. He could see one masthead light and a red sidelight and two or three small indistinct lights, about 5 miles away to the south-south-east. To Stone, it looked like a smallish steamer. Lord gave instructions to tell him if the bearing of the steamer altered or if she got any closer to them. Stone left Lord and went to the bridge, where he relieved Groves, who confirmed that he had received no reply and that it had stopped at about one bell.

Under examination, Stone corroborated Lord's account of being informed at about 1.10 by the speaking tube. Except in this case, Stone uses the word "rockets", and not "rocket". The 2nd Officer had first been distracted while walking up and down the bridge when he saw a white flash above the other steamer, perhaps a shooting star he thought. He viewed the ship through binoculars and saw four more white flashes, at an interval of about three or four minutes. He was now sure that they were rockets.

"What do you think they meant?" asked Isaacs.

"I thought that perhaps the ship was in communication with some other ship, or possibly she was signalling to us to tell us she had big icebergs around her."

"Possibly, what else?"

"Possibly she was communicating with some other steamer at a greater distance than ourselves."

"What was she communicating?" inquired Mersey.

"I do not know."

"Is that the way in which steamers communicate with each other?" inquired Isaacs.

"No, not usually."

"Then you cannot have thought that. Just attend to the question[75]," retorted Lord Mersey.

Isaacs continued. "You had been keeping this vessel under close observation and saw five rockets go up in fairly quick succession. What did you think at the time they, meant? You applied your mind to the matter, did you not?" Stone reported that he had, but would only admit that the rockets were signals "of some sort."

"Signals of what sort did you think?"

"I did not know at the time."

"Now try to be frank," upbraided Mersey.

"I am."

"If you try, you will succeed. What did you think these rockets were going up at intervals of three or four minutes for?"

"I just took them as white rockets, and informed the Master and left him to judge."

"Do you mean to say you did not think for yourself? I thought you told us

---

75   One commentator on the case has suggested that the ship may have been using the flares/rockets to illuminate her way through the icefield, in much the same way that a battlefield is lit up at night.

just now that you did think." Stone gave no answer. One can only feel sorry for this young man, floundering in the dock.

"You know they were not being sent up for fun, were they?" asked Butler Aspinall, counsel for the Board of Trade.

"No."

"You know, you do not make a good impression upon me at present," objurgated Mersey.

"Did you think that they were distress signals?" asked Aspinall. Stone replied no, and that it did not occur to him at the time. Only later, after he heard that the *Titanic* had gone down did the thought cross his mind. But he did not think they were necessarily from the *Titanic*, as the ship he was watching was not that vessel.

Having informed Lord of the rocket, or rockets, Stone was asked if they were company's signals. Stone did not know, simply reporting that they were "white rockets" and that no reply to his Morse lamp signalling had arrived. Lord told him to carry on morsing and to send Gibson down with any information. At the time the first rocket was fired, the other ship seemed to be steaming away, from her position in the south-south-east to the south-west.

A short time later Gibson arrived on the bridge, having returned from an errand to get ready a fresh patent log, and Stone informed him of the white rockets and his contact with the Captain. Gibson immediately went to the Morse lamp and called the other ship up, but with no response. Stone denied that he and Gibson discussed the meanings of the rockets at the time: "[Gibson] remarked to me once that he did not think they were being sent up for fun, and I quite agreed with him."

"Did either you suggest to Gibson or did Gibson suggest to you that that ship over there is probably in trouble and wants assistance?"

"No."

"Are you sure?"

"I made no remark about that at all, about the ship being in distress, the whole time."

"Did it never occur to you?"

"It did not occur to me after what the Captain said," Stone asserted.

"But what had the Captain told you which would force your mind to the conclusion that that is a vessel which is not in distress?"

"He emphasised the fact about company's signals."

"But you knew they were not company's signals, did you not?"

"I said I did not think so ... I had never seen company's signals like them before."

"What did you think?" asked Isaacs.

"I just thought they were white rockets, that is all."

"That you know because your eyes told you of it, but what did you think they were being sent up for?"

"Naturally, the first thought that crossed my mind was that the ship might be in trouble, but subsequent events showed that the ship steamed away from us; there was nothing to confirm that; there was nothing to confirm that the rockets came from that ship, in the direction of that ship. That is all I observed."

So, what did Stone think of the rockets? Under questioning from the Attorney General, he now offered a new theory: that the rockets seemed to come from a greater distance <u>past</u> the other ship. He had discussed this theory with the Captain, and with the chief and 3ʳᵈ officer on the journey to Boston.

"Tell me what you said to the Chief Officer."

"I have remarked at different times that these rockets did not appear to go very high; they were very low lying; they were only about half the height of the steamer's masthead light[76] and I thought rockets would go higher than that."

"Well, anything else?"

"But that I could not understand why if the rockets came from a steamer beyond this one, when the steamer altered her bearing the rockets should also alter their bearings."

"That pointed to this, that the rockets did come from this steamer?"

"It does, although I saw no actual evidence of their being fired from the deck of the steamer except in one case," this being one of the last three, observed by himself and Gibson. This rocket seemed to be brighter than the others. One can cynically wonder if this was the same rocket that Gibson had seen, with the aid of binoculars, fired from the deck. If Gibson had not stated his observation, would Stone have told the court that the rocket had come from the other steamer's decks? Or would he have clung to his "fired from beyond the ship" defence?

"And you had further confirmation in the fact as you have told my Lord, that when the navigation lights altered their bearing, the rockets altered their bearings in a corresponding manner?"

"Yes."

"That would tell you as a sailor that it was almost certain that those rockets were being fired from that steamer which was showing you those navigation lights?"

"Almost certain, yes."

"I suppose, at any rate, now you have not any doubt but that that ship which was showing you the navigation lights was the ship which was showing you these series of rockets?"

"Except, as I say, that they were very low; they did not appear to go high enough to me."

As we now know, the distance between the *Californian's* dead reckoning position and the actual location of the *Titanic* wrecksite is some 21 miles. For a rocket reaching an altitude of 660-860 feet, simple trigonometry can show that the

---

76   It is a great pity that Gibson was not asked how far he thought he saw the rockets ascend.

angle that a viewer would see such a projectile rising above the horizon would be between 0.3 and 0.4°. Compare this with the angular width of the moon of about 0.5°. Rockets from 21 miles distance would indeed be seen very low down on the horizon, but even if Stone's uncooperative rocket emitter was firing signals, those fired from the *Titanic* would still be visible, rising well into the sky. So what on earth was Stone looking at? If his story was right, he would have seen rockets coming not only from the strange ship, but also from over the horizon!

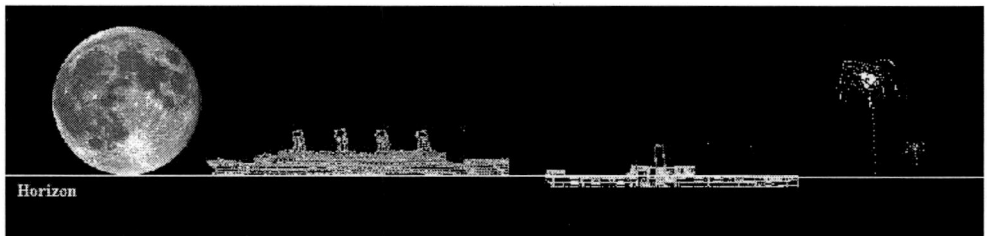

Illustration 18: Picture showing the size of the moon, the Titanic on the horizon, the Californian at 5 miles (as an example of a "medium sized tramp steamer"), and the height a rocket explosion from 21 miles would be seen to reach: the fainter explosion, to the far right, is what a Carpathia socket signal would look like from a distance of about 31 - 35 miles; this would be the rough distance the Carpathia would be at about 3.15am in the morning. Note that the first explosion is well above the heights of the mast lights (the faint dots above the forward decks of the ships), and that the "tramp" seems to be the same size as the Titanic at about 8 miles.

The last rocket had been seen at about 1.40am, Stone keeping the ship under observation constantly with binoculars, and about twenty minutes later, Gibson was sent down to report to the Captain.

"During that 20 minutes did you notice anything which you would call funny or odd about her light?"

"Yes."

"What did you notice?"

"On one occasion I noticed the lights looked rather unnatural, as if some were being shut in and others being opened out; the lights appeared to be changing their position - the deck lights."

"Her deck lights?"

"Yes, and I lost sight of her red sidelight."

"That would be consistent with her altering her heading?"

"Yes."

"What was there funny about it?"

"Merely that some lights were being shut in and others exposed and I remarked to Gibson that the lights looked peculiar, unnatural, but when I took the glasses and brought her under close observation I took it to be due to the fact that very likely she was porting for some iceberg close at hand and was coming back on her course again, showing her other lights, the original lights."

"Is this right, that during this 20 minutes Gibson said this to you: "Look at her red light; is not there something funny about it"? Did anything of that sort happen?"

"Not her red light that I remember."

"Gibson has been here, and he told us that he directed your attention to the red light. If you do not remember it, say so?"

"I do not remember his saying anything about her red sidelight at all."

"Did anything of that sort pass? Did you say something of this sort to Gibson: "A ship is not going to fire rockets at sea for nothing"?"

"Yes, I may possibly have passed that expression to him."

"Did you say this to Gibson, "Have a look at her now; it looks queer; she looks to have a big side out of the water"?"

"No, I did not say she had a big side out of the water; he remarked it to me."

"He remarked that to you?"

"Yes."

"Did you say, "Have a look at her now; it looks queer"?"

"That is at the time when I told him the lights appeared to be altering their position with regard to one another. Yes."

"Did you think it looked queer?"

"I merely thought it was a funny change of her lights, that was all. That was before I had looked at her through the binoculars."

"In view of the fact that this vessel had been sending up rockets, and in view of the fact that you said it looks queer, did not you think at the time that that ship was in distress?"

"No."

"Are you sure?"

"I did not think the ship was in distress at the time."

"It never occurred to you?"

"It did not occur to me because if there had been any grounds for supposing the ship would have been in distress the Captain would have expressed it to me."

The Commissioner again spoke up: "You want me to believe, do you, that, notwithstanding these rockets, neither you nor Gibson thought there was anything wrong on board that ship; you want me to understand that?"

"Yes."Stone told Gibson to go down to the Master "and be sure and wake him up and tell him that altogether we had seen eight of these white lights like white rockets in the direction of this other steamer; that this steamer was disappearing in the S.W., that we had called her up repeatedly on the Morse lamp and received no information whatsoever." Gibson provided the master with this report, who asked if there were any colours in the rockets and what time it was. He was told that they were all white, and then returned to the bridge.

"And after Gibson had returned did you continue to keep this ship under observation?"

"Until she disappeared, yes."

"What did you see of her which disappeared?"

"A gradual disappearing of all her lights, which would be perfectly natural with a ship steaming away from us."

"What do you mean by all her lights?" Mersey asked.

"The deck lights, which were in view. The masthead light would be shut in except for a slight flickering, the glare of it, and the red sidelight would be shut in altogether. The lights I would see would be the lights at the end of the alleyway or engine room skylight, and the stern light."

"Did the stern light that you speak of as disappearing, suddenly become black or
gradually fade away as if it was going away?" asked Aspinall.

"It gradually faded as if the steamer was steaming away from us."

"Did it have the appearance of being a light on a ship which had suddenly foundered?"

"Not by any means."

"Did you say to Gibson "Tell the Captain she is disappearing," or did you say "Tell the
Captain she has disappeared," which did you say?" Lord Mersey sought to clarify.

"I could not have said that she had disappeared, because I could still see her stern light. I saw this light for 20 minutes after that ... About 2.40 ... I blew down again to, the Master; he came and answered it, and asked what it was. I told him the ship from the direction of which we had seen the rockets coming had disappeared, bearing S.W. to half W. the last I had seen of the light."

"In view of the fact that when you saw her stern light last you thought nothing had happened to her, why did you make this report to the Captain?"

"Simply because I had had the steamer under observation all the watch, and that I had made reports to the Captain concerning her, and I thought it my duty when the ship went away from us altogether to tell him."

At about 3.20 Gibson reported that he had seen a white light in the sky to the southward of them, just about on the port beam. The *Californian*, slowly turning clockwise, was heading about west at the time. Stone crossed over to the port wing of the bridge and watched its direction with his binoculars. Shortly after, he saw a white light in the sky right dead on the beam. The white lights were at "such a distance that if it had been much further I should have seen no light at all, merely a faint flash," he told the court. Because it was on a different bearing, he did not think it could have come from the steamer under vigilance shortly before.

"And were these lights rockets?" asked Mersey.

"I think not," replied Stone.

The strange tale of the Middle Watch continued: "Just after 4 o'clock - a few minutes possibly ... the Chief Officer relieved me. I gave him a full report of everything I had seen and everything I had reported to the Master, his instructions, when the steamer disappeared, and the way she was bearing - the whole information regarding the watch. He looked over on the port beam, and he remarked to me, "There she is; there is that steamer; she is all right." I looked at the steamer through the glasses, and I remarked to him "That is not the same steamer; she has two masthead lights." I saw a steamer then just abaft the port beam showing two masthead lights apparently heading much in the same direction as ourselves."

The merciless interrogation continued, but now focussed on the issue of the rockets. Stone admitted that he knew the prescribed methods of signalling for help, one of which was "rockets or shells, throwing stars of any colour or description, fired one at a time at short intervals."

"And is not that exactly what was happening?" asked Mersey. Scanlan repeated: "That was what was happening?" Stone replied simply, "yes."

"The very thing was happening that you knew indicated distress?"

"If that steamer had stayed on the same bearing after showing these rockets - " Stone started.

"No, do not give a long answer of that kind," Mersey interrupted, "Is it not the fact that the very thing was happening which you had been taught indicated distress?"

"Yes."

"You knew it meant distress?" Scanlan queried.

"I knew that rockets shown at short intervals, one at a time, meant distress signals, yes."

"Do not speak generally," Scanlan admonished Stone, "On that very night when you saw those rockets being sent up you knew, did you not, that those rockets were signals of distress?"

"No," Stone stubbornly replied.

This was too much for Mersey. "Now do think about what you are saying. You have just told me that what you saw from that steamer was exactly what you had been taught to understand were signals of distress. You told me so?"

"Yes."

"Well is it true?"

"It is true that similar lights are distress signals, yes."

"Then you had seen them from this steamer?"

"A steamer that is in distress does not steam away from you, my Lord."

"You saw these before this steamer steamed away from you?"

Stone insisted, "I saw them at the same time the ship started to alter her bearings."

Mr. Scanlan resumed his questioning, "But for a long time while this ship was stationary like your own, you noticed at frequent intervals that she was sending up rocket after rocket?"

"No."

And in further questions, Stone repeated that the ship was altering her bearings from the time she showed her first rocket.

It was now time for Harbinson to tackle Stone.

"Did you notice [if] this ship had a list?"

"No, I did not."

"Are you sure?"

"Yes."

"Did you tell Gibson to look through his glasses, and that the ship had a list?"

"No; he remarked to me that it looked as if she had a list to starboard."

"Did you look?"

"I looked."

"Did you notice it?" asked Mersey.

"I did not. I remarked to him that it was owing very probably to her bearing and her lights were changing possibly. She had no list as far as I could see."

Mr. Laing took over, querying Stone about various headings, sidelights seen etc. One question, posed by Lord Mersey during this session, is of interest.

"She must have shown her green light, you know?"

"We are heading west-south-west. and the steamer's stern was south-west, ahead of us. All we would see is her stern light. I did not see any sidelight at all after she started to steam away."

Now Stone is saying that the sidelight vanished at the same time that the ship started to move – that is, about the time that the first rocket was sent up. From his testimony, Stone was clear that the red light was shut in, but this is inconsistent Gibson's testimony, which stated that the red light was visible until much later on, until the 7th rocket had been fired[77].

Dunlop was next to question the 2nd Officer. He focussed on the situation at 4am, when yet another steamer was seen.

"And there was another steamer which you say was there the next morning?"

"I saw three steamers the next morning."[78]

---

77   See also Stone and Gibson's "secret statements", released in 1958, and reproduced in chapter 7.

78   It is a pity that Stone was not asked about the other two steamers. After being

95

Regarding the mysterious rocket firing vessel, Stone was asked how long had he had her stern light under observation.

"From just about 1 o'clock to the time I lost her, I should say. The last light I saw must have been her stern light. It may have been the light at the end of an alleyway, or some bright light on deck."

"About how long do you think she was showing her stern light?"

"About an hour."

A ship cannot show both its red light and stern light to an observer at the same time. Again, Stone's answers contradict the evidence that the red light was being shown until fairly late. Asked by Rufus Isaacs, Stone told the court that he took the brightest light he could see to be the stern light. At about this time, Gibson observed the ship's mastlight, an impossibility given Stone's "stern light" statement. It could be argued that, a mastlight could be mistaken for a stern light if the ships headings were correct, but since a mastlight is (obviously) placed quite high, and a stern one much lower (usually at the rear of the poop deck), such a difference in height would be obvious, even if the ship was "down at the head", as the *Titanic* was at the time, making the mast light seem closer to the waterline. Even Gibson, Apprentice though he was, would have known the difference between a stern lamp, placed at, or below the level of any lights on amidships superstructure, and a mast light, situated well above it.

Stone was excused and the court adjourned until the following day.

Upon the resumption of proceedings the next day, if Captain Lord thought that the court alone was being overly hostile to him and the conduct of his crew, he was mistaken, for a surprising foe would appear. From his own ranks, no less.

Groves testimony must have been a surprise to Lord, as the 3rd Officer disagreed with just about every piece of evidence his commanding officer had provided. If Lord was expecting loyalty from all his officers, he must have been disappointed.

Groves story commenced as follows: the *Californian*, in his view, stopped at 10.26pm, and the Captain stayed there for another 9 or so minutes, asking the 3rd Officer to report to him if any ships approached. The stars were showing right down to the horizon; "it was very difficult at first to distinguish between the stars

---

woken when the *Californian* had cleared the ice field, he was placed in the crow's nest and may have been witness to vital navigational information from his high perch. Although he had been denied his full eight hour's sleep (4am – 12pm), he was on duty at midday to obtain navigational information. If he was awake and on watch during that timeframe, he would have seen more than three ships: the *Mount Temple*, the *Carpathia*, the *Frankfurt*, the pink/black or black/white funnelled unidentified vessels in the area and possibly the *Birma* too.

and a light, they were so low down ... I made out a steamer coming up a little bit abaft our starboard beam," he told the court. He first saw her at about 11.10, ten to twelve miles away; about five minutes later the ship had caught his full attention, but he did not take note exactly when this was, having last set his own watch by the ship's chronometer at 6.00pm. When he first saw her, he would estimate that the ship was 3 ½ points abaft the starboard beam, but again, he took no precise measurements.

"What lights did you see?" Groves was asked by the Attorney-General.

"At first I just saw what I took to be one light, one white light, but, of course, when I saw her first I did not pay particular attention to her, because I thought it might have been a star rising."

A star rising implies that he first saw the light to the east. But this does not seem to be the case, as we shall soon see. And 3 ½ points "abaft the beam", even if this was a rough estimate, is not "a little bit abaft the starboard beam."

By about 11.25, he could make out two white mast lights, but no others sources of illumination on the ship. The ship seemed to be getting closer, her lights now over the horizon and getting clearer. If it was the *Titanic* he saw, to have seen the "mastlights" [sic] but not the deck lights, the distance between the two ships would be between 17 ½ and 22 miles.

"Was she changing her bearing?"

"Slowly."

"Coming round more to the south and west?"

"More on our beam, yes, more to the south and west, but very little."

Coming "more on the beam" from the south implies a ship heading to the east, not to the south and west. The situation is summarised in the following diagram:

97

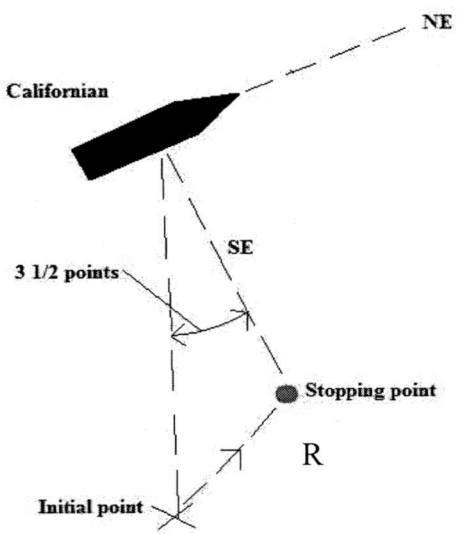

Illustration 19: The movements of the other ship, according to 3rd Officer Groves and 2nd Officer Stone. 'R' indicates the red, port light.

Groves left the bridge at about 11.30 to report personally to the Captain in the chart room that there was a steamer approaching on the starboard quarter ("coming up obliquely ... perhaps at an angle of 45° to us ... coming up astern" he would say in London). Lord asked if Groves could make out anything of her lights, and was informed "Yes, she is evidently a passenger steamer." "I told him that I could see her deck lights and that made me pass the remark that she was evidently a passenger steamer," he later elaborated. There was no doubt that the ship was a passenger steamer, in his opinion, judging by the amount of light she was showing. Later in his evidence, Groves recounted that, after Lord had left the bridge at 10.35, he was left alone on the bridge. To leave the bridge empty, for whatever reason, could be interpreted as dereliction of duty.

Lord told Groves to call the ship up on the Morse lamp, and see if he could get any reply. Groves returned to the bridge and rigged up the lamp and started tapping away. At first confident that he was getting a reply, he continued signalling but soon dismissed the flickering he could see when he viewed the ship through binoculars as anything meaningful. Captain Lord came back on the bridge to find a solitary Groves at the Morse key. Lord saw the flickering light and remarked to Groves that the vessel was replying. But Lord was wrong; he too have been deceived by the light.

"After that was done, did you have any more conversation with the Captain about the steamer?""

"When he came up on the bridge he said to me, "That does not look like a passenger steamer." I said, "It is, Sir. When she stopped her lights seemed to go out, and I suppose they have been put out for the night.""

"Now, what about putting out the lights?"

"I said she put out her lights as she stopped."

"Was anything said at any time about the *Titanic*?"

"After the Captain came on the bridge."

"Was that before the lights appeared to go out?"

"No, that was after," Groves replied.

"You said something about the lights of the ship going out. When did they go out?" asked Mersey.

"At 11.40."

"Was the Captain standing with you?"

"No, my Lord."

"Had he gone away?"

"He had not been on the bridge again since about 10.35."

"Now you said something about the lights going out; what was it?"

"Well he said to me, "It does not look like a passenger steamer." I said, 'Well, she put her lights out at 11.40' - a few minutes ago that was."

"Then had she put her lights out before the Captain came on the bridge?"

"Yes, my Lord."

"When did she put her lights out?"

"At 11.40."

"And you told the Captain this, did you?"

"Yes."

"What did he say to that; did he say anything?"

"When I remarked about the passenger steamer he said: 'The only passenger steamer near us is the *Titanic*.'[79]"

"He said that, did he?"

"Yes, my Lord."

"What makes you fix the time 11.40 for her lights going out?" Asked Mr. Rowlatt.

"Because that is the time we struck one bell to call the middle watch."

Lord himself had said that he had seen the other ship stop at 11.30. Cynics of Groves' story may argue, quite accurately, that the collision time between the *Titanic* and iceberg of 11.40pm had been widely reported in the papers, and Groves may well have known this fact. There are other obvious problems reconciling Lord and Groves' story. Lord says that he watched the other ship after he had left Evans'

---

79   "*A Titanic Myth*" page 183, states that Groves' reply, reported in the press, was actually "When I remarked about the passenger steamer's lights, he said: "The only passenger steamer near us is the *Titanic*"."

cabin, saw her stop, and that he had seen Groves signalling with the Morse lamp. Groves, on the other hand, says that Lord was in the chart room during this time. But, with Groves on the bridge, how would he have known where Lord was at any one time? Lord may only just have temporarily returned to the chart room.

The other ship was now stopped, five to seven miles away.

"Do you remember that bell was struck at that time?"

"Most certainly."

"Did the steamer continue on her course after that?"

"No, not so far as I could see."

"She stopped?"

"She stopped."

"Was that at the time when her lights appeared to go out?"

"That was at the time that her lights appeared to go out."

"Were the lights you saw on her port side or her starboard side?"

"Port side."

"I want to ask you a question. Supposing the steamer whose lights you saw turned two points to port at 11.40, would that account to you for her lights ceasing to be visible to you?"

"I quite think it would."

An important matter needed to be reminded to Mr. Rowlatt by Mersey, "... at 11.40 the engines were stopped on the *Titanic*."

Mr. Rowlatt took up the questioning, "Did you say 'would' or 'might'? I do not want to put it too high?"

"In my own private opinion it would," affirmed Groves.

"You are speaking of deck lights?"

"Yes."

"Lights from the ports and windows?"

"Yes."

"Did you continue to see the masthead lights?"

"Yes."

"Did you see any navigation lights - sidelights?"

"I saw the red port light."

Mersey was quite right, but Groves' description of the vessel coming up obliquely from the south, and to stop in the south and east do not match the movements of the *Titanic*, which was heading almost due west at the time of the collision. Although Groves did not take great notice of the time that he first saw his strange steamer, his 11.15 time is also a problem; again, the *Titanic* was heading to the west at that time.

Is there any evidence that the *Titanic* altered her heading in such a radical manner, going from west to north? Directly and indirectly, the answer is 'yes'.

100

First, let us consider the testimony of Alfred Oliver, Quartermaster[80] on the *Titanic*. He was on the compass platform between the second and third funnels and heard three clangs of the look-out's bell from ahead. Knowing that this meant an obstruction directly ahead, he looked up but couldn't see anything. He left and went forward, and entered the bridge not only in time to see the tip of the iceberg disappearing astern, but also to hear and fear the shock of the glancing collision.

Oliver heard the order to run hard-aport[81], and saw 6th Officer Moody supervising Quartermaster Hichens at the wheel as the order was carried out. This instruction would have swung the *Titanic*'s head to starboard. The engine room telegraph was then rung half-speed ahead. Seaman Scarrott confirmed that, as the berg passed astern, the *Titanic* seemed to be under port helm, dodging around the iceberg.

What Oliver did not see or hear, was that very soon after the lookouts had telephoned the iceberg warning, the order "hard-astarboard" was given, turning the ship 2 points to port, and "full speed astern." Estimates of the time from sighting to collision were approximately half a minute, perhaps a little more, all the time the *Titanic* slowing. If the wheel was left hard-aport, the ship would continue to swing to starboard, bringing the ship from a westerly heading to somewhere west or north-west. Oliver provided his recollections in Washington, but did not testify in London. Both Boxhall, heading towards the bridge at the time of the collision, and Hichens did testify in both locations, but neither recalled the hard-aport order. Oliver was clear on this point in America.

Steward Alfred Crawford provided valuable evidence in America[82]:

Senator FLETCHER. If the *Titanic* was moving west you moved southwest?

Mr. CRAWFORD. Probably so.

Senator FLETCHER. Toward the light?

Mr. CRAWFORD. Yes, sir.

Senator FLETCHER. And then the *Carpathia* appeared in what direction?

Mr. CRAWFORD. She came right up around and started to pick up the boats.

Senator FLETCHER. She came from the northeast from you, then?

Mr. CRAWFORD. Probably so.

Senator FLETCHER. Assuming you had been going southwest?

Mr. CRAWFORD. Yes, sir.

---

80   A Quartermaster (Q.M.) is a member of the crew who is directly responsible for manning the helm of a ship, relays messages to other parts of the ship, and assists officers with shipboard activities.

81   'Hard-aport' indicates that the bow was turned to starboard, in compliance with the direction that the tiller of a ship would be turned, not the bow of a ship.

82   http://home.earthlink.net/~dnitzer/NorthernLights/North.html

Here, Crawford was talking about his lifeboat rowing towards the lights of the vessel on the horizon. Then, after hours of failing to reach the light, and with the *Carpathia* in sight, the lifeboat was turned around and headed towards this new source of salvation. Crawford's initial recollections do corroborate a *Titanic* that had remained on a westerly heading. But careful analysis of his words suggest what he really meant. For the *Carpathia* had actually approached the wrecksite from the south-east, and he had turn round to reach her. To Crawford, he was going southwest, and the *Carpathia* had appeared to the northeast; in other words, in the same direction to the way his own lifeboat was heading. Therefore, this implies that the light, which was seen on the *Titanic*'s bow, must have been heading in the same direction as the *Carpathia*. Namely, in a north-westerly direction. Crawford was obviously using headings relative to the way that he believed that the *Titanic* was still heading.

Stewart Hart also remarked seeing the lights of the other ship, albeit on the starboard bow: "I should take [the mastlights] bearing North."

Bedroom Steward Etches provided more clues as to the *Titanic*'s heading. Between 4 and 5 o'clock in the morning, he noticed "a very large ice floe of flat ice" from his lifeboat. When asked in which direction this ice was, he told Senator Smith, "I should say it would have been well over on the port side of the *Titanic*, in the position she was going. I should say, by the way we pulled, it must have been on the port side of the *Titanic*." The ice floe was ahead of the *Titanic* when she struck, and lay to the west, in a roughly north-south orientation. Etches' testimony showed that the *Titanic* had been heading to the north when she sank. The lay of the icefield also indirectly supports a northward-heading *Titanic*. We know from the *Mount Temple* and the *Californian* herself that the eastern edge of the icefield in the approximate longitude of the disaster was about 50°2'W. This is just under 4 miles from the wrecksite. Lifeboats that had been ordered to, or found themselves rowing towards the mystery light would have either found themselves rowing into this icefield, or being within visual range of it within a few miles and a short space of time – if the *Titanic* had been pointing west, and they had been rowing to a light virtually ahead of them. But by obliquely rowing towards the ice field rather than head-on, the time taken to reach the ice would have been increased.

Q.M. George Thomas Rowe was another witness. He had been on the after bridge on the poop deck, at the very stern of the ship. He had watched the iceberg drift by the starboard side and waited and watched as his relief (Q.M. Bright) appeared, then saw lifeboats and finally rockets being fired. When he saw a lifeboat in the water, he telephoned the bridge and a surprised Boxhall instructed him to report to him with rockets. In London, he had the following exchange with Mr. Butler Aspinall.

17667[83]. When you saw this light did you notice whether the head of the

---

83   The British Inquiry numbered their questions. These have been omitted when reconstructing the exchange of Counsel with witnesses for the sake of readability; only

Titanic was altering either to port or starboard?
Yes.

17668. You did notice?
Yes.

17669. Was your vessel's head swinging at the time you saw this light of this other vessel?
I put it down that her stern was swinging.

17670. Which way was her stern swinging?
Practically dead south, I believe, then.

17671. Do you mean her head was facing south?
No, her head was facing north. She was coming round to starboard.

17672. The stern was swung to the south?
Yes.

17673. And at that time you saw this white light?
Yes.

17674. How was it bearing from you?
When I first saw it it was half a point on the port bow, and roughly about two points when I left the bridge.

So, here was one witness who *did* notice the heading of the *Titanic* and explicitly said so. The ship was heading to the north when he saw the lights of the other vessel, which would have been shortly after he arrived on the bridge. In addition, Rowe also noticed that the *Titanic's* head was slowly swinging to starboard, bringing her head more to the north. And, as we shall see in forthcoming chapters, Rowe's observations of a "planet" on the starboard quarter much later on in the sinking also indicate a northerly pointing *Titanic*.

5th Officer Lowe was another one who felt that the light on the port bow was to the north. In a statement to the British Consulate General in New York in May 1912, Lowe indicated that the other ship was to the north, on the port bow. For the light to be on the port bow, the *Titanic* would have to have been pointing somewhere to the north; that is, towards the *Californian's* direction. Why should he give a heading that is so different from the *Titanic's* course to New York unless he knew that it was right?

2nd class passenger Lawrence Beesley wrote a book on his observations during the sinking soon after the *Carpathia* landed in New York, and he says the following: "Almost immediately after leaving the *Titanic* we saw what we all said was a ship's lights down on the horizon on the *Titanic's* port side: two lights, one above the other, and plainly not one of our boats; we even rowed in that direction

---

out of context sequences, or sequences not presented in chronological order retain their numbers in this text.

for some time…In the absence of any plan of action, we rowed slowly forward – or what we thought was forward, for it was in the direction the *Titanic's* bows were pointing before she sank. I see now we must have been pointing northwest, for we presently saw the Northern Lights on the starboard, and again, when the *Carpathia* came up from the south, we saw her from behind us on the southeast, and turned our boat around to get to her." And shortly afterwards, Beesley notes that "Towards 3 a.m., we saw a faint glow in the sky ahead on the starboard quarter." This glow turned out to be the Northern Lights. Aside from his contradictory statement that he saw this glow 'ahead' and 'on the starboard quarter' [i.e. The rear of the boat], this could be an indication that the lights were actually on the starboard bow, and the boat was facing north-west. After all, Beesley was a landlubber; he may have got his nautical terminology confused.

Criticisms have been levelled at this account. If the Northern Lights appeared to the starboard, then Beesley and his fellow survivors must have been heading west? Beesley would have known that the *Titanic* was heading towards New York; it would have been just as easy for him to explicitly say that the ship was heading west? Perhaps it is more plausible that Beesley meant that he saw the Northern Lights on the starboard bow[84]?

The occupants of lifeboat 6, with the panicking helmsman Hichens at the tiller, gave more evidence on a northward facing *Titanic* and one of these was Major Arthur Peuchen. He described the following situation in Washington:

> Senator FLETCHER. After you took to the lifeboat you proceeded to row in the direction in which the ship had been moving, westward?
>
> Maj. PEUCHEN. No; we started right off from the port side of the boat directly straight off from her about amidships, on the port side, right directly north, I think it would be, because the northern lights appeared where this light we had been looking at in that direction appeared shortly afterwards.

Helen Candee also told the investigators in Washington, "[Hichens] said we did not even know the direction in which we were rowing. I corrected him by pointing to the North Star immediately over our bow." Hichens remembered that his orders were to "pull for that light."

A lifeboat that steered for a light, with the North Star over the bow, and the northern lights in the direction of the strange ship, can only have been pointing towards the north.

The only other witness to describe the northern lights was Able Seaman Edward Buley, who, despite his somewhat self congratulatory (and impossible

---

84   A later defender of Captain Lord (Leslie Harrison) was so keen for the *Titanic* to have been heading west after the collision with the iceberg that he wrote (and told me in correspondence c.1989) that Beesley had said in his account that the ship was heading west. The reader will soon learn that this is but one example of Captain Lord's legion being somewhat economical with the truth.

statement) that he could see 21 miles, said, "[The other ship] was stationary there for about three hours, I think, off our port, there, and when we were in the boat we all made for her, and she went by us. The northern lights are just like a searchlight, but she disappeared. That was astern of where the ship went down (i.e. his own lifeboat, number 10, was astern of the *Titanic*)." Sadly, it is difficult to understand what Buley meant and he his evidence was never clarified. If Buley meant that the northern lights, low down on the horizon, were like a searchlight, providing illumination to see the other ship which then "disappeared," it may imply a ship lying to the northwards. But such an inference is incredibly flimsy.

In America, Seaman George Moore said the following under examination;
Senator NEWLANDS.
How far do you think you pulled from the point where the ship went down?
Mr. MOORE.
I could hardly say.

Senator NEWLANDS.
Do you suppose you pulled as far as 10 miles?

Mr. MOORE.
No, sir. We were going against the current.

Senator NEWLANDS.
Was there a current?

Mr. MOORE.
I should say so, sir. We kept the boat's head to the wind. We kept going toward this white light.

Moore was in boat 3, pulling for the light on the horizon. Both the current, and the wind that emerged close to dawn, came from the north.

But one person who doubted that the *Titanic* was on anything other than a westerly heading was 4th Officer Boxhall himself. He gave the following information in America:
Senator FLETCHER.
Apparently that ship came within 4 or 5 miles of the *Titanic*, and then turned and went away in what direction, westward or southward?
Mr. BOXHALL.
I do not know whether it was southwestward. I should say it was westerly.

Senator FLETCHER.
In westerly direction; almost in the direction which she had come?

Mr. BOXHALL.
Yes, sir.
Senator SMITH.
On the same course, apparently?

Mr. BOXHALL.
No; oh, no.

Senator SMITH.
On the same general course?

Mr. BOXHALL.
By the way she was heading she seemed to be meeting us.

Senator FLETCHER.
In which direction?

Mr. BOXHALL.
She was headed toward us, meeting us.

Senator FLETCHER.
Was she a little toward your port bow?

Mr. BOXHALL.
Just about half a point off our port bow[85].

Senator FLETCHER.
And apparently coming toward you?

Mr. BOXHALL.
Yes

On the face of it, this destroys the observations of the first set of witnesses discussed here: for, if the other ship was meeting the *Titanic* head-on, and was nearly dead ahead, and had come from the west, then the *Titanic* must also have been heading west too. But there are indications that Boxhall was mistaken in his statements. Straight after the crash, he went down into the forward bowels of the ship to inspect the vessel for any signs of damage but could not find any. He returned to the bridge to report this happy news to the Captain who told him to find the carpenter to sound the ship for any intake of water. As he left the bridge, Boxhall encountered the carpenter who breathlessly told him that the *Titanic* was making water. As the carpenter reported to the Captain, Boxhall rushed down again, and was told that the mail room was flooding, which he saw for himself.

It is obvious that Boxhall was only on the bridge for a brief while after the collision. How long did his incursions below decks take? 10 minutes? We do not know. But whilst he was away, the bridge rang various orders down to the engine room, which mainly comprised of stop and "slow astern" instructions. These orders have never been explained, and their exact number and timings cannot be reconciled[86]. Boxhall was asked about the movements of the *Titanic*:

---

85   The same as Q.M. Rowe, when he first saw the ship.
86   A good summary of these instructions can be found in "*The Night Lives On*" pages

15419. Do you know at all whether the *Titanic* was swinging at this time?
No, I do not see how it was possible for the *Titanic* to be swinging after the engines were stopped. I forget when it was I noticed the engines were stopped, but I did notice it; and there was absolutely nothing to cause the *Titanic* to swing.

The *Titanic* was doomed, and immediate assistance was required. Boxhall helped to uncover the lifeboats and proceeded to the chart room, where he worked out the location of the ship. He seemed to be remarkably insular in his task. He used a set of stellar observations at 7.30pm and extrapolated a course based on the *Titanic*'s course and speed. But here he does something strange; he guesses that the time of collision, and hence the "stopping point" was at 11.46, and the ship's speed was 22 knots. He consulted no-one about these values, and both are at odds with the accepted time (11.40) and speed (22.5 knots). He also did not mention in testimony the *Titanic*'s movements after the collision, which he likely did not witness, which may also have affected his calculations. It seems safe to reason that Boxhall was below when the ship was steaming on, and he may not have known in which direction.

It is likely that he knew nothing of the orders rung down on the telegraphs while he was away inspecting the damage. He would ultimately make an error of more than 13 miles in his DR computations. If this is the case, is it possible that he did not go to a convenient binnacle and check the *Titanic*'s heading on the compass? Could it be that Boxhall assumed that the *Titanic* was heading west, and based the easterly heading of the other ship on this assumption because he saw the other ship almost head-on?

Reconciling all this evidence leads to the following rough schematic illustrating a possible trajectory for the *Titanic*. The actual heading of the White Star giant upon stopping is not known, but "the other ship" is known to have been seen on the port bow. If Rowe's evidence is right, then the *Titanic* would have been slowly swinging, bringing the light ultimately closer to the *Titanic*'s starboard bow[87].

242-245.
87   Only Ismay recollected the light as being a little on the starboard bow. Given the weight of the other evidence, it is possible he was simply mistaken. Q.M. Bright, who was in charge of a port side lifeboat launched minutes after Ismay's, remarked that he saw the light on the port bow.

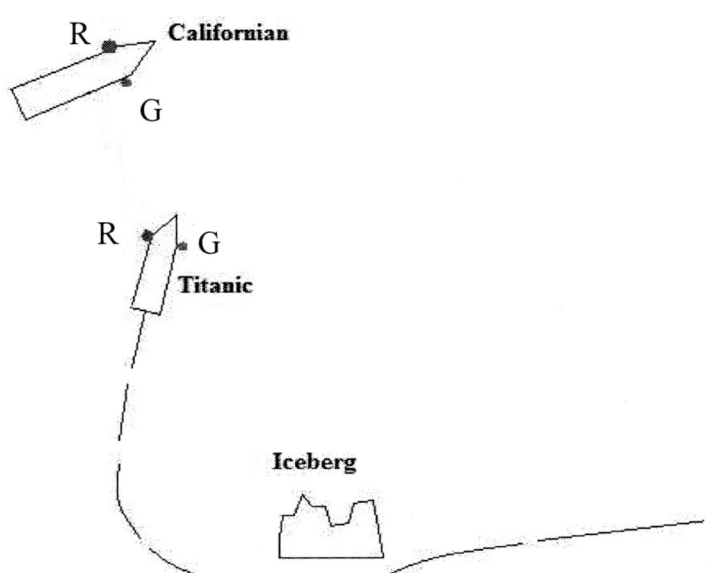

Illustration 20: Hypothesised movements of the Titanic before, during and after the collision with the iceberg (not to scale). 'R' and 'G' denote the red and green sidelights.

Groves' mention of seeing the red (port) sidelight tallies exactly with the statements of Stone and Gibson, who saw it a little while later. At this point, all three witnesses describe a ship, showing its port side to the *Californian*, and pointing in a direction somewhere to the east of them. But let us recall the words of Captain Lord, who had seen the ship stop at about 11.30: he had seen a green light on this other ship between 11 and 11.30, and when questioned about the heading of the vessel, the following exchange took place:

6778. Can you tell us at all how this ship was heading?
She was heading to the westward, that is all I can tell you.

Once again, a chasm exists in the recollections of Groves and his commanding officer, but here the evidence seems to favour the multitude of witnesses (Groves, Gibson and Stone) who saw a red light on the other ship, indicating a vessel turned somewhere to the north-east. We shall shortly see how this detail confounds even Groves.

"When did you see [the red light]?" asked Mersey.

"As soon as her deck lights disappeared from my view."

Mr. Rowlatt: "Did it strike you that going out of the glare of the other lights could show up the port light? Is that what you mean?"

"Yes, it would do."

"I mean, you are not suggesting that the port light was opened, having been shut in before?"

"Oh, no."

"I only want to understand. You cannot see a red light in the midst of the glare of the deck lights. That is what you mean?"

"Yes, because of the blaze of the white lights."

"Was that at 11.40?"

"Yes."

"It was after this that you had a conversation with the Captain about the *Titanic*?"

"Yes."

"It was after you had seen those white lights disappear that you had a conversation with him in which he said to you "the only passenger steamer is the *Titanic*"?"

"That is so."

"Did you have any further conversation with the Captain?"

"I did not."

"Did he stay on the bridge or go down again?"

"I do not think he would have been up there for more than three minutes at the outside with me."

"Then he went down again?"

"He did."

"Did you stop on the bridge?"

"I stopped on the bridge."

"Did you continue to observe the steamer?"

"After I had tried ineffectually to Morse her I did not pay any particular attention to her."

"Did you not notice her or did you notice her?"

"Oh, I noticed her certainly."

"Was she keeping her same position?"

"The same position, yes. We were swinging slowly to port [sic], very slowly."

"Did you not take her bearing by the compass?"

"Not that steamer's bearing, no."

"How long did you stay on the bridge?"

"I stayed on the bridge till something between 12.10 and 12.15."

This late departure from the bridge, necessitated by 2nd Officer Stone's late arrival, is taken by some to mean that the *Californian*'s clocks had been set back at midnight, and indeed they may have been. However, Stone was delayed arriving on the bridge, he wrote later, by Captain Lord who informed him of the other ship, implying a time change (if there was one) of a much lesser clock retardation than 10 or 15 minutes.

"Did you point out the steamer to Mr. Stone?"

"Yes."

"Did you tell him what you thought she was?"

"Yes."

"What did you say?"

"I pointed out the steamer to him and said, "She has been stopped since 11.40"; and I said, "She is a passenger steamer. At about the moment she stopped she put her lights out.""

"Wait a moment: "I pointed the steamer out to Stone and said, 'She is a passenger steamer.
She put her light out.'" Do you mean by that she shut her light out?" asked Mersey.

"She shut her lights out, my Lord."

Was Lord Mersey putting words in Groves' mouth? The *Titanic*'s lights did not go out until a few minutes before she foundered.

"To get it quite clear, at that time was it your impression she had put her lights out or shut
them out?"

"At that time it was my impression she had shut them out, but I remember distinctly remarking to him that she had put them out."

"That means that she had shut them out?"

"Yes."

"That is what you intended to convey?"

"Yes."

"By changing her position?" asked Mersey and Groves agreed.

"Did you say that you thought she had put her lights out because of the time of night?"

"I did say that, I think, my Lord."

"Then which is it to be, that she shut them out because she was changing her position, or that she had put them out because, in your opinion it was bed-time on board the ship?"

"Well, at the time the lights disappeared I thought in my own mind she had put them out because in the ships I was accustomed to before I joined this company[88] it was the custom to put all the deck lights out, some at 11, some at 11.30, and some at midnight - all the deck lights except those absolutely necessary to show the way along the different decks. But when I saw the ice I came to the conclusion that she had starboarded to escape some ice," elaborated Groves.

"You came to the conclusion then, did you, while you were on the bridge?"

"Yes, my Lord."

Using data gleaned from research conducted for Appendix C, one can construct a picture of what the *Titanic* would have looked like, seen obliquely: depending on the distances involved, many of the pools of light would merge into one or more regions of light, and no discreet, individual sources of light would be discernible. Most of the sources of illumination would be doused, as many passengers would be in bed at such an hour, and many lights in public areas would be turned off. The following images display such a possible image.

Illustration 21: Model of the Titanic, from a vantage point of two points on the port bow, the bearing of her mystery ship.

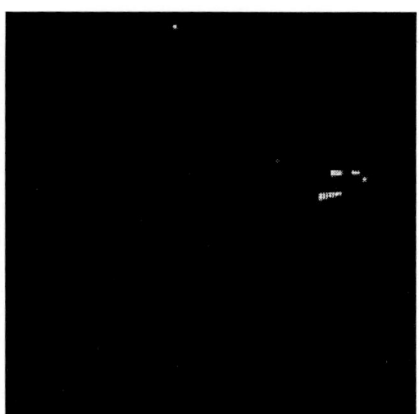

Illustration 22: The Titanic at night, showing all sources of illumination as at 11.40pm. Recall that Gibson had agreed in London that "the glare of light that you saw on the afterpart of [the ship] seem to be a pretty considerable distance from the masthead light."

From bow to stern, such a view of the *Titanic* would cover approximately 0.6°, 0.3° and 0.2° at 5, 10 and 15 miles respectively. A U.S., or UK penny held at arms length would cover 1.8°. *Titanic*, mighty as she was, would be seen as a

---

88   The Peninsular & Oriental Steam Navigation Company   ("The P&O Line")

sparse collection of lights at these distances.

Mersey and Rowlatt conversed for a while, and were in agreement that it was only the relative motion, or heading of the other ship that had given the illusion that the lights have gone out; they have merely been obscured as the ship turned.

"Would a change of two points such as we know took place on the *Titanic* cause the two white masthead lights to alter their relative positions?"

Mr. Rowlatt thought so and sought confirmation from the witness.

"Yes, it would, but I do not think at that distance the difference would be perceptible."

"It would bring them a little nearer together?"

"Yes, a little nearer together."

"Did you notice anything of that sort?"

"No, I did not."

Groves would be right on this point: a change of heading of two points would bring the mastlights closer together, but this would be hard to observe even with binoculars given the power of the lights, and their distance. However, Stone was sure that the other ship only had one mast light, whereas Gibson seemed unsure and would waver on this point. The *Titanic* would only have one, but was widely believed to have two; even today, paintings of the ship show two lamps affixed to the masts. Finally, Mersey, Rowlatt and Groves seem to be at cross purposes. Groves referred to a possible change of two points when the other ship was already heading to the north-east, but, on the *Titanic*, such a course change was reported straight after the collision, when the ship was still heading in a westerly direction. The *Titanic* would thus be heading to the south-west. There is no discussion of the *Titanic* heading in a huge arc to the north.

His watch over, Groves wandered off to Evans' cabin. Evans, colloquially known as "Sparks" was in bed, asleep. The 3rd Officer woke him and asked "What ships have you got, Sparks?" "Only the *Titanic*," came the tired reply.

"Did you take his instruments and put them to your ears?"

"Yes."

"Could you read a message if you heard one?"

"If it is sent slowly - yes."

"Did you hear anything?"

"Nothing at all."

"How long did you listen?"

"I do not suppose it would be more than 15 seconds at the outside - well, 15 to 30 seconds," Groves estimated. "I did it almost mechanically.".

"Did you do anything more before you turned in?"

"I may have said a few more words to him, but I have no recollection, but when I left his house I went straight to my cabin."

"And went to bed?"

"And went to bed."

"What time was it you were talking to this man whom you call Sparks?" asked Mersey.

"As near as I can judge it would be between 12.15 and 12.20."

"What time did you turn out again in the morning?"

"About 6.40; I did not notice the time particularly."

"Were you woke up by the Chief Officer?"

"Yes."

"Did he come to your room?"

"Yes."

"Did he tell you, you were wanted on the bridge?"

"He did."

"Did he say why?"

"Yes. He said, "The *Titanic* has sunk, and the passengers are all in the lifeboats in the water ahead of us," or words to that effect."

A fascinating statement. If this is taken literally, "the passengers are all in the lifeboats in the water ahead of us" could mean that the lifeboats could be seen already.

"Did you see Mr. Stone?"

"I saw Mr. Stone almost immediately after the Chief Officer left my room."

"Where was he?"

"He was in his room."

"Is that close to yours?"

"Yes, two or three yards away, that is all; diagonally opposite."

"Do you mean you went out of your room before you dressed and saw him?"

"Yes, I jumped straight out of my bunk and I went to his room."

"Now, did he tell you anything had happened in his watch?"

"Yes, he told me he had seen rockets."

"Did he say where the rockets were, or what sort of rockets, or anything of that sort?"

"As far as my recollection goes all he said was he had seen rockets in his watch, but at that time I did not pay particular attention to what he said, except that he had mentioned rockets."

"You do not remember more than that he mentioned rockets?"

"No, nothing more."

"You do not remember anything more passing with him at that time?"

"Well, I went to his room for the purpose of asking him if he was right about the *Titanic*, and he said, 'Yes, old chap, I saw rockets in my watch,' and I went straight back to my cabin."

"You had just heard that [the *Titanic*] had gone down?"

"Yes."

113

"Now try to recollect what the conversation you had with Stone was?"

"I went only to his door; he was just getting dressed himself then, and I said, 'Is this right, Mr. Stone, about the *Titanic*?' I told him what the Chief Officer had said. He said, 'Yes, that is right; hurry up and get dressed; we shall be wanted in the boats.' He said, 'I saw rockets in my watch.'"

"That conveys to me the notion that when he said he saw rockets in his watch he was referring to the rockets which he believed had come from the *Titanic*. Did he give you that impression?"

"Well, it is rather difficult for me to say what impression I got then because I was rather excited, but I have told you what he said to me and what I said to him."

Recall Gill's affidavit: after being awakened at 6.40am and reporting to the engine room, he overheard the 2nd Engineer tell the 4th that the 3rd Officer [sic] "had reported rockets going up in his watch." If the time is right, Stone was not afraid to let it be known, now that he had just been awakened, of the events of the Middle Watch.

Leaving Stone in his cabin, Groves rushed back to his cabin, got dressed and hurried to the bridge. The ship was making good speed at the time, bumping against the ice that surrounded the *Californian*. The lifeboats were being swung out for a possible rescue.

"Now it is getting on for 7?"

"I suppose by the time I got on the bridge it would be 6.50; but you understand the time is only approximate."

"I quite understand that. Were there any other vessels in sight?"

"Yes."

"What were they?"

"There was a four-masted steamer abeam on our port side."

"What steamer was that?"

"I did not know at the time, but I knew afterwards she was the *Carpathia*."

"How far off was she?"

"I should think she would be about 5 miles - possibly more, possibly less, but about five."

"Did you look at her with the glass?"

"I did."

"Who asked you to do that, anybody?"

"The Captain."

"Did you make out anything about her?"

"After I had been looking at her I made out she had her house flag half-mast. She had a red funnel with a black top."

"She had what half-mast?" asked Mersey.

"Her house flag."

"Is there any significance in its being half-mast?"

"It is half-masted for death, my Lord."

"What did your vessel do then?"

"We continued on our course for a little time after I had told the Captain she had a red funnel with a black top and the house flag half-masted, and the next thing that was done we starboarded."

The *Californian* had completed her slow south/south-westerly crawl through the ice and was now heading south. As Groves says, his timing of seeing the *Carpathia*, is only an estimate - but he places it significantly sooner than Lord does (viz. after leaving the *Mount Temple* at about 7.30, Lord sees the *Carpathia* many miles to the south-east[89]). By 6.50, if Groves is right, the *Carpathia* is already in sight to the east. If the Cunarder was now picking up survivors from the wrecksite, this obviously places the *Californian* extremely close to the *Titanic* during the night. This does roughly accord with Captain Moore's comments in the United States about seeing the *Californian* earlier than Captain Lord would admit to.

"You made straight for her?"

"We made practically straight for her," Groves repeated.

"Did you see any other vessel?"

"Yes, I saw two other vessels."

"At this time?"

"Yes. I fancy one of them was in sight at the same time as I noticed this four-master."

"Do you know what they were?" asked Mersey.

"I know what one of them was."

"What was it?"

"The *Mount Temple*."

"Where was she?"

"She was ahead, a little on our starboard side when I saw her first."

"Before you changed your course?"

"Before we headed for the *Carpathia*."

"How far off was she, do you think?"

"Well, when I noticed her first - I had been paying particular attention to this other steamer - I should think she would be perhaps a mile and a half away from us."

"Nearer than the *Carpathia*?

"Much nearer than the *Carpathia*," confirmed Groves.

"Was she stopped?"

---

89   If the *Californian* maintained a speed of 13.5 knots from 6.30 to 8.30, then we can estimate when the *Carpathia* would be abeam the *Californian*. Rostron said that he saw the *Californian* at 8.00am, 5 or 6 miles to the WSW. Simple trigonometry yields a time of approximately 7.50am. At 7.30, the *Californian* would be another 4.5 miles north. The distance between the two ships at this time, using Lord's timings, would be 7.4 miles

"Stopped."

"In the ice?"

"In the ice[90]."

"Did you see any other vessel?"

"I saw another vessel a little on our port bow; she was coming down almost end on."

"You do not know her name?"

"I do not, but as far as I remember she had a black funnel. She was a small steamer."

"Did you reach the *Carpathia*?"

"We did."

"What time did you reach the *Carpathia*?"

"I think it would be about 7.45."

Groves had seen the *Carpathia* 5 miles to the east at 6.50; she reached her at 7.45. In this time, the *Californian* would have travelled over 12 miles. Given later evidence from Rostron, that he first saw the *Californian* at 8.00am to the south west 5 or so miles away, this is a huge hurdle in Groves' evidence. It also means that there is a problem with the distances and directions travelled too.

"Did she signal to you first?"

"Yes."

"That the *Titanic* had struck an iceberg?"

"Not at first. The first signal shown was fixed on the jumper stay. That is a signal that she wanted to semaphore."

"Did she signal to you by semaphore?"

"Yes."

"What did she tell you?"

"I think the first question she asked was had we any survivors on board, survivors or people, I do not know which she said."

"Did you answer by semaphore?"

"We did."

"You said, No?"

"We said, No."

"Did she say anything more?"

"Yes; I think the next thing which happened was, I fancy, we asked him if we could be of any assistance, and he said, No."

"Were you personally signalling?"

"No, I was not, but I was reading it."

"Anything more - any more messages?"

"He told us the *Titanic* had struck an iceberg at 12 o'clock and had sunk at 3, and they had 800 or 700 - I am not sure which - people on board, including Mr.

---

90   Obviously in the loose ice surrounding the main pack ice, given the standing instructions to the officers of the Canadian Pacific Railway fleet.

Bruce Ismay. When we asked him if we could be of any assistance they said, no. And then Captain Lord suggested that we should search down to leeward."

"Did you search to leeward?"

"Yes."

"Did you find anything?"

"Only boats and wreckage."

"Empty boats?"

"Boats with no people in."

"At about 9 a.m. did the *Carpathia* steam off?"

"Yes, almost exactly at 9 a.m., because I heard her bell strike."

So, now we are expected to believe that the *Californian* met the *Carpathia* at 7.45, but that the two ships remained in situ for well over an hour exchanging semaphore messages – an hour that could have more productively spent searching for survivors clinging to the floating wreckage or even picking up the shivering people from the lifeboats?

"Did you search longer?"

"Yes, we searched longer."

"Till about 10.40?"

"Ten-forty exactly. That is when we resumed our course."

"After that did you see much more ice?"

"After 10.40?"

"Yes?"

"Yes, we saw a lot of ice; we passed a big field; we passed through a particularly long field about half a mile wide, and we had to absolutely force our way through it."

"Was that further south than the wreckage you had seen from the *Titanic*?"

"I think it was about the same latitude, roughly, within a mile or so. But I never said we saw the *Titanic*; I said we saw the wreckage."

The 10.40 time is in contrast to the time of 11.20 given in evidence by others; Groves is not asked how he could be so sure of his timings.

The main sources of discrepancy are the times. Either Groves is right, or Lord and his supporting officers are right. Indeed, Groves timings are used to support the contention that the *Californian* was close to the sinking *Titanic*, and authors with that thesis in mind are supportive of his evidence. But given the deviations between Lord and Groves, one could say that the former is lying to protect his reputation and future, and/or the latter is telling the truth, or is so indignant at his ship's inactivity in the face of rockets being sent up, that he decided to manufacture a story that would make Lord's life as hard as possible. Certainly, there seems to be no way to reconcile the two sets of evidence.

One other point must be made about the problems with the timings. Groves is certain of times when external devices (that is, bells) summon his attention; one bell being struck on the *Californian* at 11.40pm, and the 9.00am ringing of the bell on the *Carpathia*: these times are fixed and incontrovertible in the *Titanic* timeline. But all other times that do not have any such external associations or sources are controversial. It is unclear what this means. Were his estimates of times deliberately or accidentally wrong? Or, flippantly, was there a problem with his watch? He had last set it to ship's time at 6pm the previous night, and he remarked that his ship had stopped at 10.26pm – a small, five minute discrepancy with the accepted time of 10.21. Small, but significant perhaps? But this is of little help to us, as Groves' later times were before the times stated by Lord et al.

But, at least Groves differentiated between the location where the *Titanic* had sunk, and where the wreckage was left; something that Captain Lord did not do.

"At the time you left the bridge was it a clear night?" asked Scanlan.

"Quite clear."

"Was it so clear that your Captain could have picked his way, even through that ice-field to the ship which you saw?"

"He could have picked his way through there, but it certainly would not have been a particularly safe proceeding. There is no doubt he could have done it."

The questioning was resumed by Harbinson, "When you saw this steamer, at any time had you any doubt about its being a passenger steamer?"

"No doubt whatsoever."

"And you for your part never considered it was a tramp steamer?"

"No, I did not."

"And you told the Captain, you have told us, that you believed it was a passenger steamer?"

"Yes, I told the Captain that."

"And that you could see the two masthead lights?"

"I do not think I told him that I could see two masthead lights."

"What did the Captain say when you told him it was a passenger steamer? - Do you remember?"

"Yes, I do. He said to me, "The only passenger steamer near us is the *Titanic*.""[91]

"The question I propose to follow that up with is this: Did the Captain make any observation
as to the distance at that time the *Titanic* should be away? Did the Captain say at what distance the *Titanic* would be away at that time?"

"No."

"He said nothing?"

"Nothing."

Now, Robertson Dunlop had his chance to challenge Groves' version of

---

91   If Groves is right, then how did Lord know this? There might have been any number of passenger ships nearby. Possibly Lord had formed his opinion from his conversation with Evans, who said that the Titanic was "near us."

events that had been so damaging to his client.

"In the logbook it is stated that when you stopped your ship in the ice the position of the ship was 42° 5' N. and longitude 50° 7' W. Is that accurate?"

"Well, it is bound to be accurate if the Captain put it in."

"This witness would not know, would he?" objected Isaacs.

Dunlop continued, "Did you take part in ascertaining the position of your ship at noon on the 15th?"

"Yes."

"Did you get good sights?"

"Perfectly good sights."

"And the position which you found was 41° 33' N.; and the longitude, do you remember what it was?"

"No."

"50° 9' W," Dunlop reminded Groves. "Do you know how far it was you had steamed between noon and the time you left the wreckage?"

"On the Sunday or Monday?"

"On the 15th, on the Monday. You take your position at noon on the Monday shortly after leaving the wreckage, and I want you to help me to fix the position of this wreckage?"

"In reference to our noon position?"

"Yes; you have the noon position. How far do you think you had travelled from the time that you got on your way after searching round the wreckage until your noon position? Do you think it would be about five miles?"

"No, more than that; about 11. That is in distance, " Groves said.

"You would be in the same latitude then as the wreckage was found?"

"That I could not say."

"If the *Titanic* was in latitude 41° 33', which is the position she has given, and the position in which the wreckage was found, and your vessel was, as stated in the log, in latitude 42° 5', the *Titanic* would be some 33 miles to the southward of the position where you were lying stopped?"

"If she stopped in 41° 33' and we were in 42° 5'."

"Yes?"

"Yes, about 30 miles."

"And if the *Titanic* was 30 miles to the southward of the position where you were stopped, I do not suppose you could see any navigation lights at that distance?"

"No, none whatsoever."

"Nor indeed any rockets at that distance?"

"I could not say about rockets, but I should not think it was likely."

"If this vessel which you did see was only some 4 or 5 miles to the southward of you, do you think she could have been the *Titanic*?"

"That is a question I want this Witness to answer," interrupted Mersey.

"Speaking as an experienced seaman and knowing what you do know now, do you think that steamer that you know was throwing up rockets, and that you say was a passenger steamer, was the *Titanic?*" the Commissioner asked Groves.

"Do I think it?"

"Yes?" edged on Mersey.

"From what I have heard subsequently?"

"Yes?"

"Most decidedly I do, but I do not put myself as being an experienced man."

"But that is your opinion as far as your experience goes?"

"Yes it is my Lord."

Captain Lord was sitting in the public gallery of the court, and would later indicate that he heard Lord Mersey concur with Grove's opinion, that the *Californian* had seen the *Titanic*. This was struck from the record.

"That would indicate that the *Titanic* was only 4 or 5 miles to the southward of the position in which you were when stopped," remarked Dunlop.

"If his judgement on the matter is true it shows that those figures, latitudes and longitudes that you are referring to are not accurate. That is all it shows," said Mersey.

"The accuracy we will deal with, my Lord," replied Dunlop.

"I mean to say, if what he says is right, it follows that the figures must be wrong."

Dunlop continued in his examination of the 3rd Officer, "You will appreciate, Mr. Groves, that if the latitudes are right it follows that your opinion must be wrong?"

"f the latitudes are right, then of course I am wrong," conceded Groves.

"If the latitude of your ship and that of the "Titanic" are anything approximately right, it follows that the vessel which you saw could not have been the *Titanic?*"

"Certainly not."

Questioning now returned to the ship seen by Groves on the night of April 14th.

"What, apart from the masthead lights, was there to indicate to you that this was a large passenger steamer?"

"The number of deck lights she was showing."

"So that the deck lights would not indicate to you the probable length of the steamer showing them?"

"Well, no."

"They would be all bunched up?"

"They would be bunched up together."

"That being so, how did those deck lights communicate to you that this was a large passenger steamer?"

"Well, as I said before, by the number of her lights; there was such a glare from them."

"You mean from the brilliance of the lights?"

"Yes, from the brilliance of the lights."

"But I suppose a small passenger steamer might have brilliant light?"

"She would have brilliant light, but they would not show the light I saw from this steamer."

"Has any small passenger steamer been heard of in this locality at this time?" inquired Mersey.

"You have told us that you did see on the following morning a steamer whose name you do not know?" Dunlop asked Groves.

"A small steamer, yes."

"Was she a passenger steamer?"

"That I could not say."

"Have you tried to find out her name?"

"No, I have not; I took no further interest in her."

"What size boat was she?" Mersey asked.

"I never saw her broadside; I only saw her end-on."

"You told me it was a very small boat?"

"It was a small boat. I judged that from her end-on view."

"Was it much smaller than the boat the lights of which you had seen the night before?"

"I should judge so."

"Was she a vessel about your own size?" Dunlop asked, resuming his interrogation.

"No, in my opinion she was considerably smaller."

"Before the vessel which you saw stopped, on what course did she seem to you to be steering?"

"Do you mean the steamer I had seen at 11.40?"

"Yes, before she stopped at 11.40 you had had her under observation for some time, noticing her movements?"

"Yes, but I took no notice of the course she was making except that she was coming up obliquely to us."

"Was she making to the westward or to the eastward?"

"She would be bound to be going to westward."

Thus begins the most confusing part of Groves' evidence. He had seen the ship on the starboard quarter, well to the stern, heading towards them at an angle, eventually seeing her red light. The ship would therefore be heading, if not east, at least north-east. But Groves knows that the *Titanic* would be heading to the west. The evidence from this point on seems to confound Dunlop, perhaps deliberately, as Groves confuses what he saw (the ship heading east) and what he knows (the

121

Titanic's heading). A deliberate case of bafflegab?

"Was she?"

"She was bound to."

"Did you see her going to westward?"

"Well, I saw her red light."

"If she was going to the westward and was to the southward of you, you ought to have seen her green light?"

"Not necessarily."

"Just follow me for a moment. She is coming up on your starboard quarter, you told us?"

"On our starboard quarter."

"Heading to the westward?"

"I did not say she was heading to the westward."

"Proceeding to the westward?"

"Yes."

"Then the side nearest to you must have been her starboard side, must it not?"

"Not necessarily. If she is going anything from N. to W. you would see her port side. At the time I left the bridge we were heading E.N.E. by compass."

"Never mind about your heading. I am only dealing with her bearings. She is bearing S.S.E. of you - south-easterly?"

"About south."

"She is south of you and apparently proceeding to the westward?"

"Yes, some course to the westward."

"Does it follow from that that the side which she was showing to you at that time must have been her starboard side?"

"No it does not follow at all. If she is steering a direct west course, yes."

"Did you see her green light at all?"

"Never."

Groves would not yield, and Dunlop gave up this line of questioning.

"And then the Captain at some time looked at her and said, "That does not look like a passenger steamer"?"

"That was about 11.45 on the bridge."

"What lights was she then showing?"

"Two masthead lights and a side light, and a few minor lights."

"Some deck lights?"

"A few deck light, yes; that is what I could see."

"Is that before or after you say the deck lights had gone out?"

"That was after the deck lights went out."

"What were those deck lights that you saw when the Captain came on the bridge?"

"I do not think that then I could see more than 3 or 4."

"You have told us the deck lights had gone out?"

"Yes; when I say that the deck lights had gone out I mean that they disappeared from my view."

"They disappeared from your view, and then apparently some of them again came into view?"

"Yes."

"Was that indicating that the vessel was swinging?"

"Well, it might do."

"Turning her head in the ice as you were?"

"It might do."

"But was, like yourselves, stopped in the ice?"

"That is so."

"The Captain states that he was on the bridge at 11 o'clock and was there till 11.30?"

"I say he was not."

"You say he was not?"

"Most emphatically."

"There must be a mistake somewhere?"

"Well, it naturally follows, does it not?"

The matter of the scrap and formal log was now raised by Dunlop.

"You were the officer of the watch, as I understand, from 8 p.m. till midnight. Would you then be keeping the scrap log?"

"I was keeping the scrap log."

"Is the scrap log here?"

"No, it is not kept."

"Is it destroyed from time to time?" asked Mersey. Groves agreed, "There is one log always kept, of course, but the scrap log is destroyed from time to time."

"I want to know a little about this. Before the scrap log is destroyed in what sort
of a book is it kept?"

"It is copied from the scrap log into the printed log."

"Into this fair copy - this book which I have here?"

"Yes," and, in forthcoming questions, Groves said that the scrap log was a book, thinner than the more formal record.

"How much thinner? How many weeks will it take?"

"It is my duty to rule that book up myself. It all depends. If we want a piece of paper on the bridge we occasionally tear a piece out of it; and whenever we take occasional observations we work them on the back."

"I want you to give me an idea how big a book is the book in which the scrap log is kept?"

"I do not think it would take more than 25 days."

"There is only one in use?"

"Yes."

"You would know this book was the book which contained the real record for the 14th April?"

"Of course I knew that."

"And by that time, of course, you, and others on your ship, knew quite well there was a very serious Inquiry being made as to the position of your ship and what she was doing on the 14th April?"

"Certainly."

"And by that time you knew that there was some discussion as to whether the ship which you had seen was the *Titanic* or some other ship?"

"That was a discussion amongst ourselves."

"When did you write up the log book - I do not mean the scrap log book, but the log book. When did you write it up?"

"I do not write it up at all."

"When was it written up on board your steamer?"

"That I cannot say. The Chief Officer writes that up."

"Would he write it up every day or once every two days?" inquired Mersey.

"I fancy he writes it up every day."

"I do not know whether your recollection will enable you to tell me, but I had better ask you. As you were making entries in the scrap log book from 8 to 12 that night, do you know whether you made any entry as to any ship that you saw?"

"No, no entry whatsoever relating to any ship."

"You must have seen the scrap log book the next day when you came on duty; do you know whether it contains any entry of rockets being seen?"

"I saw none myself."

"Did you look to see if there was any reference as to rockets?"

"No my Lord, I did not."

"Then you must be careful how you answer."

Perhaps a case of Groves going too far in telling the court what they wanted to hear?

"Then when would you come on duty and be the officer on the watch and have to keep the scrap log?"

"It is my duty between 8 and 12 under ordinary conditions."

"By that time you had heard the news about the *Titanic*?"

"Yes."

"Knowing that, did not you look back in the scrap log and see what entries had been made by your colleague between midnight and 4 a.m.?"

"No, I did not."

"It would be on the very next page, would it not? You turn over the page I suppose when you get to midnight?"

"Yes, we finish a page when we get to midnight."

124

"You would have only to turn back one page and see the record made by the officer of the watch from midnight to 4 a.m. as to what he had seen?"

"Yes."

"And you did not do it?"

"No, I did not do it."

So, Groves, despite later learning about rockets in the middle watch, is so seemingly unconcerned that he doesn't even look in the scrap log book!

"If you had been on the bridge instead of from 8 to half-past 12, from 12 to 4, and had been keeping the scrap log book and had seen a succession of white rockets with stars going up from this vessel which you speak of or from the direction of this vessel, would you in the ordinary course of things have made a record of the fact in your scrap log?"

"Most decidedly, that is what the log book is for."

"So I should have thought. Then it would have been the business of the man who had charge of this book to record those facts?"

"I think so, my Lord."

"And, therefore, if Mr. Stone did what you think was his duty, this scrap log book which was thrown away, or which, at all events, cannot be found, would contain a record of these rockets having been seen?"

"Yes, my Lord, but it is not my duty to criticise a senior officer, though."

"I am asking what is the ordinary practice," Mersey placated Groves.

Chief Officer Stewart was the next to take the stand. He went off watch at 8pm on April 14th, and turned in at 9.30, leaving the 3rd Officer to take over for the 8-12 watch. Stewart came back on duty at 4am, relieving Stone, who reported on the night's events, saying that he had seen a ship four or five miles away when he first came on deck and had seen some white rockets at 1 o'clock.

At the moment the rockets started, the ship started to steam away, Stone told the Chief Officer.

"I ask you, as an experienced Officer, when you were told this ship which was in the ice had been throwing up white rockets at night, what did you suppose she was throwing up her rockets for?" Isaacs asked.

"I thought what had really happened was she had seen a ship firing rockets to the southward, and was replying to them."

"Replying? Do you reply to another ship by firing rockets?"

"Well, my Lord, [Stone] told me he had called him up repeatedly by the Morse lamp and the ship did not answer," replied Stewart.

"But I do not understand this replying by means of rockets. Did you ever hear of such a thing?"

"Well, I never heard of such a thing, but he might have replied to let them

125

know he had seen them."

"You are supposing now something you have never heard of happening before," said Mersey.

"Let me follow," said Isaacs, "Did it not enter your head when you heard this, that those might be distress signals?"

"Yes."

"What made you think they might be distress signals?"

"Because they were rockets," was Stewart's simple answer.

"They were from the description just what you would expect if they were distress signals?"

"They were white rockets."

"And did Mr. Stone tell you he had reported to the Captain?"

"He told me he had reported to the Captain, yes."

At 4 o'clock, it still being dark, Stewart took up the binoculars and scanned the surrounding water, seeing a steamer to the southward. She had two white mastlights and a few[92] lights amidships. Stewart asked Stone whether this steamer was the one he had seen before, but the 2nd Officer remarked that he had not seen it before and did not think it was the ship that had fired the rockets a few hours earlier.

About half an hour later, Stewart called the Captain, telling him that Stone had informed him that he had seen rockets in the middle watch.

"Not a rocket, but rockets?"

"Rockets."

"What did the Captain say to you when you said that?"

"He said: "Oh, yes; I know.""

"Is that all he said?" asked Mersey.

"He said. "Yes, I know, he has been telling me.""

"Did the Captain come on the bridge?"

"At once."

The two men walked up the steps to the bridge, and talked about the possibility of going through the ice and proceeding on their voyage. Stewart asked Lord if he was going to the southward to see what the ship was. The Captain said, "No, I do not think so; she is not making any signals now."

"Did you tell the Captain that Mr. Stone, who had been on watch, thought this was not the ship that had thrown up the signals?"

"No."

"If Mr. Stone, who was on the watch when it happened, was right, there

---

92   Stewart's proof had said that this ship had "a lot of lights" and that "[Stone said that he] called the Captain, and the latter asked him whether they were company's signals. Stone replied he did not know. I asked him during our own talk were they distress signals, and he said he did not think they were. He said he had informed the Captain on three occasions at intervals."

was no comfort to be got from the fact that that steamer looked all right?"

"He told me the steamer that had fired rockets had steamed away to the South-West, and he last saw her about two o'clock, just faintly with glasses; she steamed away from him."

"Then did you suppose that the steamer which you could see at 4.30 was the same steamer?"

"I thought she might have drifted back - that she had found that she could not get through the ice."

This did not satisfy Lord Mersey, "Now, think about what you are saying. Do you want me to understand that you thought it was possible that the ship which had steamed away after throwing up the rockets had drifted back and was there before your eyes ... do you want me to believe that?"

"I thought she might have come back, or she might have known something about the other ship."

"Have you ever made that suggestion to a living soul until now?"

"I do not believe so," conceded Stewart.

"It comes out for the first time in the last minute?"

"I thought all the time that that ship had something to do with it or knew something about it."

"But you never told anybody so until now?"

"No."

Isaacs resumed his questions, "On that day you thought she might have drifted back?"

"Or go back."

"Did you say drifted?"

"Yes, but I did not mean it in that sense of the word."

"You did not mean drifted back?"

"No."

"What did you mean?" inquired Mersey.

"That she had come back."

"She had steamed back?"

"Yes."

"Did you ever say to Stone afterwards, "Why, that is the steamer of last night, and it has
drifted back"?" asked Mersey.

"No."

"It was a little later than that that your wireless people heard that the *Titanic* had sunk?"

"Yes."

"When you heard that did it occur to you that the steamer that had been sending up distress rockets might have been the *Titanic*?"

"Not the steamer we saw."

"That is not what I asked you. I will put the question again, if I may. When you heard that the "Titanic" had sunk that night, did it occur to you that that steamer which you had heard had been sending up rockets, might have been the *Titanic*?"

There was an awkward silence.

"Now, come; answer that question!" roared Mersey.

"No, I did not think it could have been the *Titanic*."

Leaving the issue of rockets and mysterious ships aside for the time being, the court enquired about the practise of keeping and maintaining a log on board the ship. Stewart confirmed that the scrap logbook was "all bits that are torn out and destroyed. The logbook is written up every day and the Officer signs it." At the end of day when the log entries have been copied from the scrap log, the page is torn out of the scrap version and destroyed. Only one log is kept, as per instructions from the Leyland Line itself.

"Now let me tell you at once why I press you about this. While you have been out of this room we have had in that box the 3rd Officer, and I have been asking the 3rd Officer why he did not turn back in the scrap logbook and read what was written for the previous day. He did not suggest to me that it would probably be torn out you know. Now do you suggest it is torn out day by day?"

"Yes."

"Always?"

"Always," confirmed Stewart.

"Who made the calculation to find out what her latitude was when she stopped?"

"The Captain gave the position at 10.21."

"Was there any reason that you know of why between noon on the 14th of April and the time when she stopped, she should have altered her course and ceased to go on more to the south?"

"No."

"I would like to understand as I go along. Do your questions suggest this log has been doctored," asked Mersey.

"What I want to know is, how they arrived at the latitude which is put down, I

presume, by dead reckoning at 10.20. I am right; it would be by dead reckoning you would get it?" Isaacs posed.

"Not only that; I had the Pole Star at half-past ten." [sic]

"Could you tell me when you changed your course? Look at the log and tell me. Start from noon on the 14th April, Sunday. Can you tell me from your log when you changed your course?"

"N. 61° W. at noon."

"Is that altered at noon?"

"Yes."

"It altered at 9.40 and 9.55," added Robertson Dunlop.

"Would that keep you on the same latitude?"

"Yes."

"Now, I should like to follow this. As far as your memory serves you, did you enter into that logbook everything that you found on the scrap log sheet?"

"Yes."

"You observe there is nothing at all in your logbook about seeing distress signals?"

"Yes."

"Is there anything?"

"No, nothing."

"Nothing at all?"

"No."

"No reference to any of these events of the night at all?"

"No."

"Does that convey to you that there was no reference to those events in the scrap log?" Mersey said.

"Yes, my Lord."

"Give us your views," said Isaacs. "Supposing you were keeping the scrap log on a watch when you were in ice, and supposing you saw a few miles to the southward a ship sending up what appeared to you to be distress signals, would not you enter that in the log?"

"Yes," Stewart said, but immediately became uncertain, "I do not know."

"Oh, yes you do!" Mersey thundered.

"Yes, I daresay I should have entered it, but it was not in our scrap logbook."

Isaacs must have been getting frustrated at the evasions he was encountering. "That is not what I asked you. What I asked you was - apply your mind to it - supposing you had been keeping the scrap log in those circumstances and you saw distress signals being sent up by a ship a few miles from you, is that, or is not that, a thing you would enter in the log?"

"Yes."

"How do you account for it not being there?" Mersey said.

"I do not know, my Lord."

"It was careless not to put it in, was it not?"

"Or forgetful."

"Forgetful?" spat Mersey. "Do you think that a careful man is likely to forget the fact that distress signals have been going on from a neighbouring steamer?"

"No, my Lord."

"Then do not talk to me about forgetfulness."

But Stewart was clear on one point. The scrap log was generally written up at the end of the watch, and Stewart was going to take charge of the same sheet of paper.

"Did not it occur to you that it was odd that there was nothing entered on the scrap logbook?"

"I did not notice the scrap logbook at that time."

"You made entries on the same sheet of paper between four and eight o'clock, did not you?"

"Not till eight o'clock."

"At eight then?"

"Yes."

"Did not you notice it then?"

"I noticed there was nothing on it then."

"But by that time you had had the message that the *Titanic* had sunk?"

"Yes."

"Did not you notice it then?"

"I noticed there was nothing there."

"You did notice it?"

"Yes."

"Then you did at eight o'clock notice there was nothing in the scrap logbook about what had happened between midnight and four?"

"Yes."

"This piece of paper, whatever it was in the scrap logbook for 15th April, would be used
until midnight on the 15th, would not it?"

"Yes."

"When you destroyed [the scrap log page] did you notice then there was no record on it about these distress signals, did not you notice that?"

"No, I just copied it off as it was."

And Stewart had not discussed the omission of the rockets from the scrap log with anyone, not even the Captain or the 2nd Officer.

"There is just one other question I must put to you because we are going to call the Marconi operator. You have told us that during your watch between four and eight, you went in to see the Marconi operator, did not you?"

"Yes."

"Try and remember what it was that you told him?"

"I told him to get out and see what the ship was to the southward."

"I want you to be as accurate as you can. Do you think that is all you said to him?"

"I think so."

" I must just put it to you. Did not you go to his room and did not you say to him that rockets had been seen during the night?"

"I do not think so, Sir."

"And did not you ask him whether he could find out with his Marconi apparatus whether anything was amiss?"

"I told him to call up and see what that ship was to the southward. I remember that distinctly, Sir."

"Did you at that time think that anything was amiss?"

"I thought something had happened, yes."

"But you do not think you said that?"

"I do not think so, Sir."

One is reminded how different this account is to Evan's story in Washington, which he was to repeat in London in a few minutes time. Next to interview Stewart was Clement Edwards M.P., on behalf of the Dock, Wharf, and Riverside Workers' Union.

"What time did you start moving?"

"5.15."

One must wonder what was going on between 4.30, when the Captain was wakened, and 5.15. By now, the sun would be creeping above the horizon, and navigation through the ice would be a lot safer than during the night. But what happened between 5.15 and the waking of Evans, some 20 minutes later? What conversations transpired? What changed the mood to urgently wake Evans?

"At that time you were surrounded by a considerable lot of ice?"

"Yes."

Once the news of the *Titanic* had been received, and the *Californian* moved to effect whatever rescue was possible, she was going "very, very slowly" for the first three or four miles ("just crawling through the ice"), but Stewart was unable to quantify this as he was not very much on the bridge after that time.

Dunlop took up the questioning, and commenced by asking Stewart when he wrote up the formal copy of the log. He wrote up the log entry of 14th April just after noon the next day, Stewart told him.

"I see that at 9.40 on the 14th April the course was altered to north 60° west, and again at 9.55 to north 59° west?"

"Yes."

"At 6.30 your log, if you look at it, records passing two large icebergs, and gives the latitude and longitude [of your ship]?"

"Yes."

"When did you get the observation of the pole star that enabled you to fix your position?"

"About half-past 7."

"Assuming the position given to the Marconi operator was latitude 42°3' north, I
find in your log latitude 42°5' north?"

"Yes."

131

"What is the explanation of the two degrees' difference of latitude?"

"Two miles on account of observation."

"Two minutes of difference - is that your explanation?"

"I had the star then. I thought the star was more accurate."

This is a curious admission to make. Knowing that, at 7.30am, the DR latitude is wrong, he either goes to the scrap log and changes it, or alters the formal log. Why such retrospective alterations? And how far back did these alterations go? And if Stewart was happy with the 7.30 Pole Star fix, why did he not change his obtained 6.30pm latitude to 42°05 ½ N, and not 42°05 N? There is another example of retrospective alteration of the evidence. At 5.20 p.m. New York time on April 15th, a message was sent to the *Olympic*: "*Californian* sends through following ice report: Icebergs and field ice at 42°3' north 49°9' west; 41°33' north, 50°09' west. He tells us he is 200 miles out of his course." If Stewart altered the previous latitudes in the scrap log, then why was the ice message with an incorrect 42°03' N value, sent more than a day after the ice report, not corrected and given to Evans? It is also suspicious that Stewart did not expend a little more effort and obtain more star sights to obtain longitude values too, as this would help to obtain a correct, not deduced value for the current. Cynics might say that only a latitude sight was needed, as it would show a cessation in southerly movement.

How did Lord get from a latitude of 42°05 ½ N at 7.30 to one of 42°05 N at 10.21? His affidavit 47 years later, based on notes made in late May 1912, would provide illumination on this point: he thought that a current of about one knot was setting to the WNW: the course of S 89° W steered during the day had almost compensated for this current, yielding a course of almost due west, which by luck or whatever reason, had arrested the *Californian*'s movement south – and towards the *Titanic*. But this current would seem to be inconsistent with a southerly current from the Labrador Current, and an ENE set further south (The North Atlantic Drift). It would also seem that, if Lord intended to steer to reach 42°N, 51°W as he stated, then he gave up this plan when the pole star observation was computed.

"Is the explanation this: That at 6.30 the latitude given to the Marconi operator was latitude by dead reckoning from your noon position?"

"Yes."

"Is there any room for doubt about the accuracy of that position [of the Pole Star] there?"

"No."

It may be an opportune moment to sidestep the narrative briefly and discuss the track of the *Californian* in the afternoon and evening prior to encountering the ice field.

Captain Lord, in his discussion with Senator Smith, had the following exchange:

Senator SMITH: What other entries have you in the log, of your position on that date [14th April]?

Mr. LORD: At 6.30.

Senator SMITH: 6.30 p.m.?

Mr. LORD: Yes; we had, 42° 5' and 49° 10', as having passed two large icebergs.

Senator SMITH: What is the next entry?

Mr. LORD: There is no position given there. The next entry was 7.15 o'clock. "Passed one large iceberg, and two more in sight to the southward."

Senator SMITH:Where were you at that time?

Mr. LORD:No position entered here, sir.

Captain Lord was clear on this, having read the data from his logbook. In London, probably from memory, we now see this exchange, regarding an ice warning sent to another Leyland vessel, the *Antillian*:

6693. (The Attorney-General.) It was a message sent to the *Antillian* ... giving the position of three large icebergs, was it?
  Yes.
6694. Would you tell me the position that you gave him?
Forty-two deg. five min and 49 deg. 9 min.
6695. Forty-two deg 5 min N and 49 deg 9 min W?
– Yes.
6696. The three icebergs were reported five miles to the southward of you?
Yes.

So, the iceberg sighting is now 1 degree more east, and the message now describes three bergs rather than two. 1 degree east at this latitude is about ¾s of a mile, and may be due to faulty memory. The actual message sent to the *Antillian* is as follows;

"*Californian* Office. Sent 5.35 p.m., 14th April. by C. F. Evans addressed to Captain '*Antillian*,' 6.30 p.m. apparent ship's time; lat. 42° 3' N., long. 49° 9' W. Three large bergs five miles to southward of us. Regards. Signed Lord"

This confirms the "three icebergs five miles south" account, but the latitude is wrong, albeit by only 2°, or 2 miles, south. The *Antillian* may have scribbled down the wrong co-ordinates, except for one thing: this message was overheard and noted by Operator Bride on the *Titanic*, confirming that "42° 3' N" was indeed sent by Evans, given to him by an Officer on the ship.

In later years, Stanley Lord helped to draft an affidavit, in which it is written "on 14th April, the noon position by observation was 42° 5' N., 47° 25' W." Obviously, taken with Evan's message, this indicated that the *Californian* was now on a course slightly south of due west. But, in the absence of other evidence, the 6.30 message would be a dead reckoning position. If this is the case, then how was the "42° 3' N" latitude arrived at? A possible clue may be gleaned from the

133

remainder of Lord's affidavit: " ... and [the] course was altered to North 61° West (magnetic) to make due West (true). I steered this course to make longitude 51° West in latitude 42° North on account of ice reports[93] which had been received." These statements are incompatible with each other. By steering due west, the *Californian* would eventually have reached 42° 5' N., 51° W. Only steering slightly to the south of due west could the *Californian* have reached 42° N, 51° West longitude ... but Lord and his crew found themselves heading, if anything, slightly north of due west, getting further away from where the *Titanic* would find herself in desperate trouble in just a few hours.

The U.S. Hydrographic Department rather tardily reported the following message from the *Californian*, on April 23rd; "April 14, 6:30pm, latitude 42°05 N., longitude 49°10 W., sighted two large icebergs 5 miles south of the above position. At 7:15pm, latitude 42°05 N., longitude 49°20 W., two bergs, and 7:30pm two bergs. At 10:20pm, latitude 42°05 N., longitude 50°07 W., encountered heavy packed field ice, extending north and south as far as the eye could see and about 5 miles wide; also numerous bergs could be seen. From above position until April 15, 2:30pm, latitude 41°33 N., longitude 50°42 W., almost continuously in field ice. At the last position sighted two bergs and cleared the field ice."

This is a curious hybrid message. It contains the 'right' 6.30pm latitude of 42° 5' N, but now the number of icebergs has again reduced to two. The 7.15pm message now has a set of co-ordinates, in contrast to Lord's recitation of his log in Washington where he said that no position has been entered. Recall Lord telling Smith, "Passed one large iceberg, and two more in sight to the southward," for the 7.15 report, but now the message has mutated into just two bergs. And we have two bergs, seen at 7.30pm, which Lord did not mention at all. Although these discrepancies could be due to honest mistakes, in total they make it easy to view the *Californian*'s navigational data as highly suspect.

Of perhaps more concern is why the ice report took so long to reach the Hydrographic department. Indeed, it notes "Received in branch hydrographic office, Boston Mass., April 22." This is three days after the *Californian* had docked in Boston! Given the differences in the 6.30pm ice warning latitudes, perhaps time was needed to doctor the navigation?

Or, as Dave Gittins says, this could be an example of "rubbery navigation."

"Then at 10.21 there is an entry that the ship was stopped in latitude 42°5 north and longitude 50°7 west?" Dunlop inquired.

"Yes."

---

93   These ice reports were: "From MHB To MWL 'Ice field reported 4 April in 43.20 N 49 long extending as far to NNE horizon as visible'," received on April 9th and "West bound steamers report Bergs growlers and field ice in 42N from 49 to 51 West April 12th," received on April 13th from Captain Barr of the SS *Caronia*. MHB is the *Nieuw Amsterdam* of the Holland America Line. A growler is the name given to a small piece of ice that rests on top of the water.

"Do you know who took that position?"

"The Captain gave us that position."

"Did you or not subsequently verify this position?"

"Yes."

"When did you verify it?"

"The next day."

"And did you find this position to be accurate?"

"Yes."

One wonders how the 10.21pm position was verified. Neither Lord nor Stewart mentioned taking observations the next morning to fix the ship's position. And if this wasn't done, there was no way to be sure of the *Californian*'s location. The first opportunity to find out their position was to take sun sights, once it had risen well above the horizon, which would be about 7.00am, which was when the *Mount Temple* took a prime vertical sight. No one recalled this being done on Lord's ship. The only other way to verify a position would result in an approximation; from a final point on a map, and taking account of steaming times, directions and speeds, one can work backwards to find a starting point. However, without accurate knowledge of the currents affecting a ship, this can only ever lead to a rough result. The courses and speeds taken by the *Californian* between 6 and 6.30am were only known very roughly, and Stewart admitted that he wasn't on the bridge very much at about this time, so he would have had to rely on others for the values for his reverse computations. The straight line distance between where Stewart said the *Titanic*'s wreckage was found, and the *Californian*'s 10.21pm position was 32 miles. Between leaving the ice at 6.30 and re-entering it at about 8.00, the *Californian* would have travelled approximately 20.25 miles, in a roughly north-south direction. Allowing for the *Californian* to have stopped for an unknown length of time at 7.30, as per Lord's evidence, this still leaves a huge discrepancy between the actual distance and the traversed distance, and one wonders where fabrication of navigational evidence, or drift, or both is to blame.

Incidentally, if Stewart is correct, and he verified the *Californian*'s overnight location, then how did he determine the drift? And what value and direction did he use? Working backwards would give 42.5 North, 50.7 West, plus contributions from drift. From a knowledge of the *Titanic*'s actual location, we know that she was affected by a SW current. The *Carpathia* was probably influenced by an east-north-easterly current, and the *Mount Temple* may have been similarly deflected too. The *Californian* was the "odd one out." Lord never once considered that his ship was vulnerable to drift and current whilst stopped. The upshot is this: Stewart's statement about his ship's position being verified should not be merely accepted. Dunlop Robertson was naturally seeking to make the Leyland Line, and its employees look as blameless as possible. It is a wonder that Mersey, Isaacs or any of the other inquisitors did not question this.

"At noon on the 15th did you take observations to fix your position?"

Dunlop continued.

"Yes."

"Who was taking part in these observations?"

"All the Officers took them."

"Did you get good sights?"

"Very good sights."

"Did the sights taken by the various Officers agree?"

"They all agreed."

"And was the position as ascertained by those sights latitude 41°33? Can you tell me?"

"Yes, 41°3 N., 50°9 W."

"Are you able from working back from that noon position to fix accurately the position of the wreckage which you came up to at 8.30?"

"Yes."

"How many miles had you travelled between the time you proceeded on your course and when you took this position?"

"About four or five miles," Stewart replied, contradicting Groves.

"And between 11.20 and noon you say you travelled some four or five miles?"

"Yes."

"Were you encountering ice at the time?"

"Yes."

"Is the position stated in your log as the position in which you were searching for the boats of the *Titanic* accurate or not - latitude 41°33 north and longitude 50°1 west?"

"Yes."

"Was that the latitude and longitude in which you found the wreckage?"

"Yes."

Note that Groves had said there was a distance of 11 miles between the noon position and the location in which the wreckage was left, but then, he did state that the *Californian* had resumed her voyage at 10.30 or 10.40am. 11 miles due east from 41°33 N, 50°9 W is 41°33 N, 49°54 W.

Stewart did not think the *Titanic's* rockets could be seen by the *Californian* from such a latitude, but Mersey was not impressed, "It all proceeds upon the assumption that all these figures are right. The other evidence to my mind is of vastly more importance. However, I do not want to shut you out from it, you know."

"You have heard my Lord's observation. Have you any reason to doubt the accuracy of these latitudes?" Dunlop asked Stewart.

"No, Sir."

But Mersey was not finished.

"The previous Officer told me, in answer to a question, that I think you yourself suggested, that he was satisfied that it was the *Titanic*, and at present I do not mind telling you that is my attitude of mind. You may perhaps change it," he said referring to Stewart

Stewart admitted that he had been thinking about the matter a great deal and had been discussing it with Officers and others, but he was steadfast that he did not think the vessel firing rockets seen from the *Californian* was the *Titanic*.

"Does it surprise you that you have not been able to find out the name of the steamer that was firing rockets at midnight?"

"Well, we never knew what ship that was that we saw to the southward," Stewart replied.

Mersey was sceptical: "Do not you think that if there had been a steamer firing rockets at that time we should have heard something about her by this time?"

"Your Lordship may yet," replied Dunlop.

"I know; but we have not so far, and you see it is a month since this happened," Mersey stated.

"Did you ask [the 2nd Officer] whether [the rockets] were distress signals?"

"Yes, I asked if he thought they were distress signals."

"And what did he reply to you?"

"He said, No, he did not think they were; they did not make any report."

Dunlop turned to Stewart, "Did he give you any reason for thinking that they were not distress signals?"

"He said he thought they might have been replying to somebody else to the southward."

"Did you ask him what kind of rockets they were - whether they made any report or anything of that kind?"

"Yes, Sir."

"What did he say?"

"He said, No, they did not make any report, and they did not leave any trail in the sky, and they did not seem to go any higher than the masthead lights."

"And did he mention these matters as reasons for thinking that they were not distress signals?"

"Yes."

"But signals made by way of communication with some other vessel to the southward?"

"Yes."

"Did you ask, or not, what he thought this vessel had been firing rockets for?"

"Yes, Sir."

"Did he state any opinion to you?"

"He said he thought she was answering to somebody else."

"Were you able to proceed direct to the position of the *Titanic* given by the

Virginian, or had you to skirt the edge of the ice-field?"

"We went along the edge of the ice-field, I remember that."

"Did you see what kind of ice there was to the South-West of the position where you were?"

"It was thick field ice."

Lord had testified to a "T" shaped ice field, with thick ice separating the *Californian* from the location of the *Titanic's* wreckage. We will return to this issue presently.

"Did [Stone] say what happened to her lights, and what he saw of them?"

"He said he saw a stern light as she was going out of sight, and it got very faint, so faint that he had to use the binoculars to get the bearing of it."

"Was there any report made of the lights having disappeared in the sense of a vessel having foundered?"

"Not at 4 o'clock."

"Or anything of that kind?"

"No."

"Was that the impression which his report created on your mind?"

"No."

"Did you ask him whether he had seen anything else?"

"He said he thought there was a light to southward about 20 minutes to 4."

"And when he stated that, what did you do, if anything?"

"I looked and I could see a light to the southward."

Mr. Edwards now took his turn to ask questions about the strange arrival on the scene at 4am, which had been overlooked by Stone.

"May I suggest that your Lordship asks this Witness this question: How many funnels the *Carpathia* has?"

"Can you tell us how many funnels the *Carpathia* has?" Mersey asked Stewart.

"One funnel, my Lord."

"How many masts has the *Carpathia* got?"

"Four masts."

This combination of funnels and masts matching the ship that Stewart had seen, the inevitable question was raised: "Is it in your mind at all that it was the *Carpathia* you saw?"

"No; I thought it was a yellow funnel boat when the sun was up."

"How long after you had got to the Marconi House did you find out that the *Titanic* had sunk?"

"I could not exactly say how long it was - the time I took to get the operator out and to his machine."

"Did the Marconi operator tell you where he had got the information from?"

"He said he had the *Frankfurt*."

"Would it not have been the right thing, I ask you, as Chief Officer, assuming that you saw these lights in close proximity to the ice and rockets also going up - would it not have been the right thing to have gone immediately to the operator, and asked him to get into communication if possible with this ship?"

"Yes, I think so now."

"But would not you do it as your duty?"

"I saw a ship to the southward there, but she would not answer."

"But assuming that you could not get any definite reply from her, would it not have been the best thing to have gone and got the Marconi instrument into operation to see if you could get into touch with her?"

"Yes, now I think so."

Stewart's turn in the box was finished, but there was one last matter to resolve before a new witness was called. As Isaacs said, "What we propose to do, subject to your Lordship's approval, is to recall the 3rd Officer and the 2nd Officer just on this one point about the log, so that your Lordship may have the evidence about it, and then we propose to call the Marconi operator."

Groves re-entered the box, but Stone was not asked to. This is odd, as he was responsible for the scrap log during his watch. Failure to fill in the necessary details would mean obvious laxity on his part, and yet he was not recalled. Why?

"I want to ask you one or two questions about the waste logbook to clear up something," the Attorney General asked Groves, "I understood you to tell us that the waste logbook, as a book, was destroyed. Is that so?

"Not as a book, no, Sir," corrected Groves.

"How is it destroyed?"

"Page by page."

"Every day?"

"Not necessarily every day. I do not think it is done at any stated intervals, but I do not have anything to do with the destroying of it."

"Perhaps you can tell us this. On April 15th, when you came on duty, had the page before been destroyed?"

"That I could not say, but I hardly think it would be."

"You could not tell as to any particular days when they were destroyed?"

"No."

Mersey seemed satisfied. "I think you have got the evidence now about the logbook and the scrap logbook."

"Your Lordship does not care about having the other Officer again?" asked Isaacs.

"No, I do not think so. I may tell you that the effect of these things on my mind is this - That it is the practice to tear out the sheets of the scrap log from time to time and destroy them. But, you know, that does not get over my difficulty that apparently, if this evidence is true that has been given in the box, there was no entry of any kind in that scrap log of these rockets having been seen."

The final *Californian* witness of the day was Cyril Evans. His evidence was mostly a repetition of what he had recounted in America. He ran through the familiar story: the wireless message to the *Antillian* at 5.35pm ship's time, the "keep out!" exchange with the *Titanic*, and retiring for bed shortly afterwards, at 11.30pm. But now, the time difference between his ship and New York was reported to be 1 hour and 55 minutes.

Evans had his wireless logbook with him; apart from a brief appearance during the testimony of *Titanic*'s junior Marconi Officer Harold Bride a few days hence, it would not be seen in public again.

After the *Californian* had stopped for the night, Evans had left his cabin and found Captain Lord and the Chief Engineer in discussion.

"And then did the Captain make a communication to you and ask you to do something?" asked Isaacs.

"Well, Sir, he was talking about the ice then; he was talking to the Chief Officer [sic]. I asked him if anything was the matter, and if he wanted me. A little after that he came along to my cabin to talk to me."

"What did he want to know?"

"He asked me what ships I had got."

"What did you say?"

"I said, "I think the *Titanic* is near us. I have got her.""

"Did you say "I think the *Titanic* is near us" or "is nearest"?"

"Near us."

""Nearer" is it you are saying?" queried Mersey.

"She was "near us,"" clarified Evans.

This was about 10.55pm. Evans did not know of any ship with Marconi apparatus that was closer than the *Titanic*, although he did not know where she was at the time. There then followed the brush-off by the *Titanic*, but Evans did not take it as an insult. Shortly afterwards, he heard Phillips on the White Star liner calling up Cape Race to resume relaying passenger's messages. During this time, the *Titanic*'s signals had become much better in strength.

Half an hour later, Evans hung up his headphones and the clockwork detector ran down, preventing the reception of any more messages.

"Do you recollect the 2nd Officer [sic], Mr. Groves, coming into your room a little later?"

"Yes, I have a faint recollection of it," replied Evans.

"Can you give me any idea as to what sort of time it was?"

"About a quarter-past 12, I think."

"Mr. Groves' watch ended at midnight, you know?"

"Yes."

"And he came in you say at about a quarter-past 12?"

"He stopped up on the bridge, I think, for 10 minutes until 10 minutes past 12 with the other Officer to get his eyes in[94]."

"When Mr. Groves came into your room, what did he do?"

"He asked me what ships I had got; if I had got any news."

"Yes, what did you tell him?"

"I told him I had got the *Titanic*. I said, "You know, the new boat on its maiden voyage. I got it this afternoon," said Evans

"You got it this afternoon. Had you got the *Titanic* earlier than half-past 7?"

"No."

"When you said "This afternoon," you mean at half-past 7"?"

"Yes, Sir, that was right."

"Did anything more happen then?"

"I do not remember Mr. Groves picking the 'phones up, but Mr. Groves says so."

"That he picked them up and put them into his ears?"

"Yes; of course, I was half asleep," said Evans. And who can blame him? He had been on duty since 7am, allowing for meal breaks and rest times.

"Did he tell you, as far as you recollect, then at a quarter-past twelve of anything that he had seen since the ship had stopped?"

"No."

"He only came in and asked what ships you had got?"

"Yes. He generally comes in my room and has a talk."

"And then, I think, you went to sleep?"

"Then I went to sleep. He switched out the light and shut the door."

At 3.40, or 3.45 New York Time, Evans was awakened by Stewart. It was just after dawn.

"Just tell us carefully, if you will, what it was he said?"

"He said: "There's a ship been firing rockets. Will you see if you can find out whether there is anything the matter?""

"Did you ask him any more about the rockets?" asked Mersey.

"No, I jumped out of my bunk and took up the 'phones at once."

"You took up the 'phones immediately?"

"Yes."

"If you had been asked to do that at any time in the night you could have done it, could not you?"

"I could have done it."

"And would have done it, of course?"

"Yes."

"When you get hold of your instrument you send out a call don't you?"

---

94   That is, time to allow his eyes to adjust to the darkness.

"I listened at first to see if anybody was working."

"You listened first?"

"Yes."

"But you did not hear anything?"

"No."

Evans sent out a CQ call to any ships listening. The *Mount Temple* replied first with the message, "Do you know the *Titanic* has struck an iceberg, and she is sinking?" giving out the position of the *Titanic*. The *Frankfurt* jumped into the communication, with the same message and position. Evans scribbled down the position and gave it to the Chief Officer, who rushed off to the Captain. It was now about 5.45am ship's time, or 3.50 in New York. Whilst Stewart was absent, Evans got in touch with the *Virginian* and asked for an official statement on the current predicament, which he obtained as follows, "*Titanic* struck berg; wants assistance; urgent; passengers in boats; ship sinking. His position, 41.46 North, 50.14 West. - Gamble [sic], Commander." Ten or fifteen minutes later, the *Californian* got underway.

Evans had no knowledge of Stewart waking him and asking him to find out about the ship to the southward.

"When you approached the *Carpathia* did you find any difficulty in getting into communication with her?"

"Yes."

"You tried to communicate did you?"

"Yes, but I heard him say this; he said that he had picked up twenty boat loads, I think it was."

"Did they tell you the same thing as the other boat did, to shut up? I understand you did not think it was rude, but on another occasion another boat told you to shut up. He told you to do the same?"

"Yes."

"How soon did you get into touch with the *Carpathia*?"

"I did not get her until I got nearly alongside of her."

"What time was that?"

"About half-past 8, I think," said Evans.

During questioning, Evans admitted to a rivalry between the Marconi Company and that of De Forest; although they had worked together in the case of the emergency, they were not supposed to interact at all. Indeed, the SS *Birma* had received a "Shut up" message from the *Carpathia* once the *Titanic*'s survivors had been rescued.

The Solicitor General, Sir J. Simon only had a few minor points to raise following Evans' statements: "From the *Californian* there is this Donkeyman Gill, who is not here at present, and who gave evidence in America. I have three or four other *Californian* witnesses, but it does not appear to me they would add anything."

142

Mersey replied, "Of course, I do not know what they have got to say; you must exercise your discretion."

"I have done my best to decide whether they would, from any point of view, add anything, and I do not think so, and therefore we do not propose to call any more unless Mr. Dunlop wants them."

"Do you want any more, Mr. Dunlop?" asked Mersey

"No, my Lord, I do not think they add anything," replied Sir Robert Finlay, counsel for the White Star Line.

"What should the *Californian* witnesses do?" asked Simon.

"As far as I am concerned, they may go," responded Mersey. "I do not want them. I do not suppose anyone else does."

And with the information that they were due to sail on Saturday, the witnesses, both called and uncalled, were dismissed.

Author Leslie Reade would later trace these witnesses from the witnesses expenses document for the British Inquiry[95]: William Ross, Able Bodied Seaman, George Glenn, Fireman and William Thomas, Greaser.

Thomas had already been interviewed for *The Boston Herald*, where he denied that his bunkmate Gill had said anything about seeing another ship close to midnight. Reade, sadly, made no attempt to trace him.

Ross and Glenn had passed away by the time of Reade's researches in the 1960s[96]. He traced their descendants and got interesting bequeathed tales. Glenn's eldest son recounted what he could recall, as his fathers papers had been destroyed in the Second World War. Glenn had apparently been on deck with another fireman and saw rockets fired from another ship. George Glenn, Jr., wrote "My father drew the attention of the Officer of the Watch to the rockets."

William Ross's son could add little too: his father had told him that, whilst walking on deck, "he could see flares on the horizon which were interpreted as some kind of distress signal."

The day's witnesses concluded with Captain Moore of the *Mount Temple*. His testimony is essentially the same as given in Washington, with a few differences, one of which is a stark deviation from his previous story.

Now, he had decided to steer his ship for 42° W, 49° 20 N (rather than 49° 15N as stated in America) before heading north-west for St. John. This is only a minor difference of 5 miles north, but he had still seen no ice. He had still met heavy ice at 3.25 but had encountered scattered ice before then. He was now 15 or

---

95   Reade might have saved himself some trouble in identifying these uncalled witnesses, as they were named in a caption of *Californian* witnesses in *The Daily Sketch* on May 15th 1912.

96   *"The Ship That Stood Still"*, pages 302-304

16 miles from the *Titanic*'s location (c.f 14 miles in Washington)

Now, when asked the question, "And I think shortly before 8 a.m. you came in sight of the *Carpathia* and the *Californian*?" Moore replies yes. A very different story from the one he gave in Washington, where he saw the *Californian* somewhat earlier than this.

The schooner that had displayed the green light was seen shortly after 3am, but Moore could not say it was a small or a large schooner- it was "simply the green light of a sailing vessel."

He was asked about the other ship he had seen.

"Later on did you see a light or lights of any other vessel?"

"I had seen the lights of a vessel proceeding the same way, but steering a little more to the southward than mine; I could see a stern light."

"At what time was that?"

"Shortly after we turned round."

"That is earlier than this. About what time was that?"

"Say one - between one and half-past one," Moore replied.

"You only saw a stern light?"

"We saw a stern light, and then the masthead lights as she was crossing our bows to the southward."

"Beyond that you know nothing of her?"

"I saw her afterwards in the morning, when it was daylight. She was a foreign vessel - at least, I took her to be a foreign vessel. She had a black funnel with a white band with some device upon it, but I did not ascertain her name."

"How are you able to say that the vessel that was showing you a stern light was the vessel you saw at daylight?"

"We saw her all the time."

"You kept her under observation?"

"Yes."

"Was she going west?"

"She was going east," corrected Moore.

And Moore's official part in the saga finished. If doubts still remained about him and his ship, it did not affect his employment with the Canadian Pacific Railway Line; he remained as master of the *Mount Temple* until January 1914 when he was transferred to another vessel of the line. If his employers ever had any doubt about him, it is not displayed in his service record, for he was allowed to continue with them even after the *Mount Temple* was grounded in Montreal Harbour on 24th September 1913.

It had been over a week since the majority of the *Californian* witnesses had provided evidence in London, and only one crewman remained to tell his tale:

Ernest Gill.

"Your Lordship will remember this was the assistant donkeyman of the *Californian*, with regard to whom some statement was made by the other Witnesses of the *Californian*," Isaacs informed the court. "The only point was he was referred to as a deserter at Boston. The suggestion at one time was that he had made a statement which was not true in America about the distress signals having been sent up, and there was a suggestion at one time made that in consequence of a story which he had put forward, which would not bear examination, he had deserted the vessel at Boston. It is no longer necessary to clear that up, because Mr. Gill's story, as told in America, has - I do not want to say more than this - been very much confirmed by the evidence which we have put before the Court of the various officers - your Lordship will remember we called a number of them - and also of Gibson, the Apprentice; so that it is not necessary now to go into his story, whatever it may be, as your Lordship will see the substance of it is no longer in dispute, and he was fully justified in what he said in America. The Officers have now borne out the substance of his statement."

The majority of Gill's story is essentially the same as the one he told to the newspapers and to Senator Smith. He still maintained that he saw a passenger steamer just before midnight: "It could not have been anything but a passenger boat - she was too large. I could see two rows of lights which I took to be porthole lights, and several groups of lights which I took to be saloon and deck lights. I knew it was a passenger boat. That is all I saw of the ship:" in later examination, he claimed to see two mastlights and lots of illumination from her broadside lights, but could not see the red or green side lamps. A criticism is that, at the distance claimed by Gill, how he could see two rows of lights, as any discreet sources of illumination would "fuse into one enormous glow," as one critic would say decades later.

"Did you notice whether she appeared to be moving?" asked Isaacs.

"I did not stand to look at the ship, but I supposed she would be moving. I did not expect a ship to be lit up like she was and stationary, and nothing to stop her, because I could see the edge of the ice flow, the edge of the field of ice; it appeared to be 4 or 5 miles away."

"Could you see the edge?"

"Yes."

"Between you and the ship?"

"Yes, what appeared to be the edge."

Gill claimed that he could discern the edge of the ice field as it seemed to be darker; the ice field, he confirmed to Lord Mersey, was between him, the starboard side of the *Californian*, and the large vessel. But we know that the *Californian* was headed to the north-east at the time, and the ice field was half a mile off to the west, extending north and south. Although Gill was correct in his description of the surrounding ice, he is very mistaken in the direction and extent of the ice field. Then there is the obvious problem of Gill having seen a big vessel going along at full speed just before midnight, when Lord and Groves, despite the obvious differences in their stories, both stated that the ship had stopped at 11.30, or 11.40 respectively. And how Gill could determine that a vessel was proceeding at full speed after viewing her for only a minute is never explained.

The ex-Donkeyman led the court through his story, about how he had risen from his bunk because the noise of the ice grinding against the ship's hull had kept him awake and had gone on deck for a smoke, when he saw two rockets after "one bell"- that is, after 12.30am. Again, he had seen no sign of the ship firing the rockets.

"Now can you tell me whether that was in the same direction from you as the steamer had been that you had seen?"

"It was slightly astern of where I had seen the steamer," Gill replied. "The steamer was more than ahead of us, just on our quarter, as we say, and the light was more astern. It was more abeam of our ship."

This statement deserves closer examination. Since the nautical term "quarter" refers to the rear portion of a vessel, it is incompatible with the steamer being observed "more than ahead of us."

The statements by the officers of the *Californian* place the steamer exactly abeam at this time, and not forward or astern. In Washington, he had described how he had seen the rockets on the starboard bow, and seconds later related how they were more abeam of where the other ship had been. This is identical to his proclamations in London, were it not for the fact that the *Californian*, swinging to starboard during the night, would have resulted in the rockets being seen, relatively speaking, more to the bow of Gill's ship. Indeed, when he returned to the bridge at about 12.55am, Gibson noticed that the other ship was now 3 ½ points on the starboard bow, and not abeam, where he had seen it some little time before.

So, now we have Ernest Gill, unable to sleep, and on deck in freezing weather conditions, smoking cigarettes, observing rockets and wearing "a thin flannel suit". Many spectators opine disbelief that this is credible, but one critic of Captain Lord glibly suggested that, for Gill to act in such a matter, there must have been something worth watching!

In an address to a meeting of the Titanic Historical Society (T.H.S) in September 1988, retired engineer John C. Carrothers (who will play a more prominent role later on) informed the attendees in a paper that "Without exception, when smoking is prohibited because of a dangerous cargo, the living quarters where Gill was in bed are never affected. Whereas the open deck where he allegedly went to smoke because of the cargo is always the first place to be declared 'off limits' for smoking for the simple reason that a live spark finding its way down a ventilator shaft and into the cargo could spell instant disaster. It does seem strange that no effort was made to find out what this dangerous cargo was at

146

the official Inquiry."

The most obvious contradiction between Gill in London and Gill in America can be found in his opinion of the rockets. Gill's newspaper affidavit contained the line, "That must be a vessel in distress."

Dunlop asked, "You did not attach much importance at the time apparently to what you say you had seen?"

"No, not any importance. It was a signal, and other people on the ship, the proper people would attend to that. It was nothing to do with me."

"And it was not till after you had heard of the loss of the *Titanic* that it occurred to you that this signal that you had seen might have been of some importance?"

"Yes," agreed Gill.

"What I am suggesting is that neither you nor anyone who saw those signals attached at the time any importance to them?"

"I do not know whether anybody else did who saw them, but I did not."

"What he said was, "It was nothing to do with me."" reported Isaacs.

Following the rockets, Gill went back to his bunk and was woken by the Chief Engineer with the news that the *Titanic* was now at the bottom of the Ocean. Gill's story continues as before, and his timing of 6.40 when he was awakened is similar to the time that Groves was roused, and shortly after the time when Stone was roused from his bunk. Having had the news that the *Titanic* had foundered for over an hour, why wait so long so muster the extra crew? Coincidentally, or not, the *Californian* had just cleared the western edge of the ice field.

What else could Gill tell the court about the ship he had seen? Was it, as he said in his affidavit, moving at full speed? Finlay, had a few questions.

"Was the vessel that carried these lights moving?"

"Well, I did not stay long enough to see whether she was moving or in what direction she was going. She was there; she was a ship passing; and I had no interest in her, Merely that she was a ship. She was a big ship, I could see that at a glance; in fact, I did not think she was a British ship; I thought probably she would be a German boat, and I made that remark to my mate as I woke him up."

"You could not make out whether she was moving or not?"

"No."

Mr. Dunlop had a few more questions. "When you saw the lights of this steamer, how was she heading with reference to you; was she heading in the same direction as you were at that time?"

"That I could not say; I did not stay long enough to observe which way she was going. No doubt if I had stayed another minute I could have been sure of the direction."

"But you have, have you not, stated what the heading of this vessel was when you first saw her?"

"Yes, but, of course, they said was she moving. I did not think the ship would be standing still with nothing to stop her."

"Have you ever stated that the vessel you saw was heading in the same direction as the *Californian*?"

"Yes, I have made that remark[97]."

"Is that right or wrong? Do you want to correct it?"

"Well, I am not sure whether she was going in that direction or not. On second thoughts I cannot be sure."

"On second thoughts you appreciate now that if that other vessel was heading in the same direction as you were she was heading towards Europe?"

"Well, I do not know."

"Do you think she was heading towards Europe or towards New York?"

"I do not know about that. I am not a sailor. I do not know anything about the latitude or longitude. My compass is the steam gauge."

Finally, Gill had denied that he had no intention of deserting the *Californian*, but that he had been served a subpoena and this was the reason he did not get back to Captain Lord's ship. But Lord and Evans had managed to return to the *Californian* in time for her journey back to Liverpool; also, Evans' Washington testimony strongly hint that Gill had already decided to abandon the *Californian* when they met at a railway station in Boston.

The Attorney-General, agreeing that Gill was justified in what he had said in America had one more thing to say, "I am not going to ask questions, My Lord, in detail about it because your Lordship has the evidence of the *Californian* before you; but I want to say this, so that my friend, Mr. Dunlop, may understand the contention, that I disagree entirely with his observation that, according to the evidence, nobody paid any attention to these rockets. I have the evidence."

Mersey agreed.

"It is not in accordance with my recollection."

"Nor with mine. I only say it so that my friend may not think I am passing it because I admit the statement; I differ entirely from it," said Isaacs.

The evidence was now concluded; but the legal jousting had barely begun.

---

97   It may be pointed out that, in Washington, Gill was unaware that the *Californian* was now heading north-east; assuming that she was still heading west, the *Titanic* would indeed have been heading in that direction. Had Gill found out the truth and did not want to offer any opinion that would destroy his credibility?

Chapter 5 "Superseded"

May 1912 - 1958

Captain Lord fully expected to return to his command; indeed, he even signed on the *Californian* on May 16th. However, the next day, he had been removed. His signing out details on the crew agreement list his departure simply as "superseded" and a new Captain installed in his place – William Masters. Stone and Gibson remained on board.

On May 21st, and with nothing better to do, Captain Lord sat down and wrote a statement of the movements and observations of the *Californian*. When he was happy with his recollections, he typed up his notes.

Most of the statement follows his testimony at the two inquiries, with few salient additions.

At 4.30a.m., it is written that "The Chief Officer reported that it was breaking day and that the steamer was still to the starboard that fired the rocket. I replied 'Yes, the second mate said something about a rocket' I then went on the bridge," thus reigniting the debate about whether Lord had been told of "a rocket" or "rockets." After arriving on the bridge, Lord reports seeing the yellow funnel steamer bearing SSE. In Washington, he had said this new arrival was to the south-west. After instructing Stewart to wake up Evans, "there was a considerable delay before we received a proper message [about the disaster]."

The most interesting entry is for "6.30 a.m. Cleared field ice. Full speed (70 revolutions) about 7.30 passed *Mount Temple* stopped, Chief Officer remarked to me that she hadn't any boats ready, as there wasn't any sign of disaster about, I proceeded further south, shortly after passing one funnel two masted steamer, bound North (this steamer resembled S.S. "*Albanian*"[98]) a little later I sighted a four masted steamer SSE of us on East side of ice field[99] , & verbal message from operator that "*Carpathia*" was at scene of disaster steered to South until steamer was nearly abeam, I then steered through ice field heading for the four masted steamer and stopped alongside the "*Carpathia*" at about 8.30 a.m."

As well as confusing the distance between himself, the *Titanic*, and the *Mount Temple*, Lord was now content to move the position of the *Carpathia* to whatever location suited him. Captain Moore was quite sure that the *Carpathia* was due east of him, but now Lord placed Rostron's ship well to the south east.

---

98   Another Leyland vessel, of similar size to the *Almerian*. Why Lord did not name this ship as the "*Almerian*" may be either because he did not consider the *Almerian*'s report credible, or this summary was written before he received the information about the *Almerian*. If the former case, he certainly made good use of the ship's supposed association with the *Titanic* in an affidavit made many years later.
99   Lord's rough draft puts the *Carpathia* SSE at a distance of 9 miles; his fair copy says "sighted 4 masted steamer to the south and east of us"

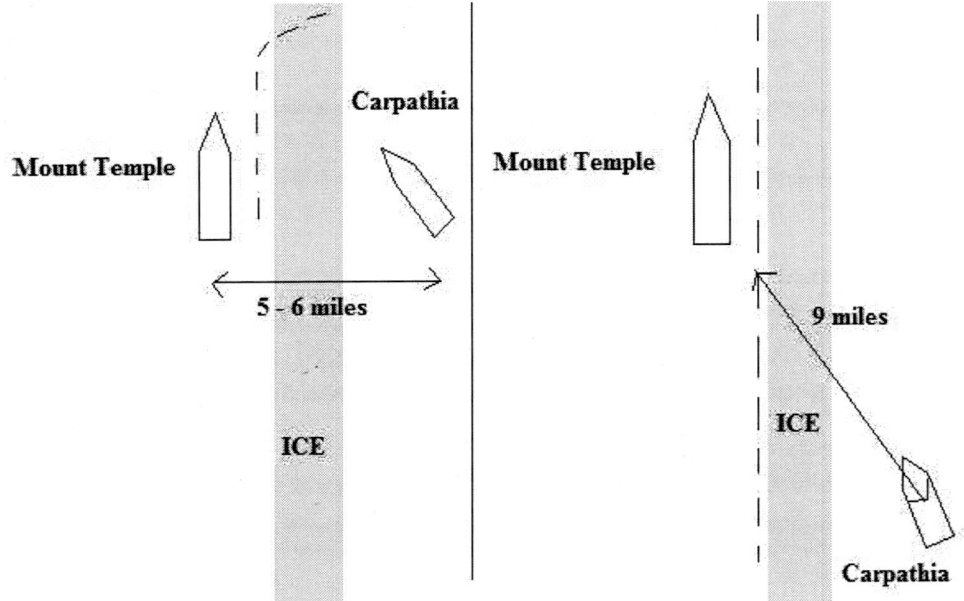

Illustration 23: The locations of the Carpathia relative to the Californian; (left) according to Moore in Washington and (right) according to Lord. The dashed line indicates the route of the Californian.

Interestingly, Lord had indicated that Stewart had noted at 7.30 that the *Mount Temple*'s boats were not ready. But it wasn't yet confirmed that the *Carpathia* had picked up all the boats and survivors; it is safe to assume that had the *Mount Temple* been able to pick a route through the ice field, she would have helped in the rescue operation with any apparatus to hand, including lifeboats, so why would Stewart have said what he did about the *Mount Temple*'s boats? Moore had already testified that, "We had the gangway ready for lowering, and we had ladders ready to put over the side; we had ropes with riggings in the ends to lower over; we had lifeboats and lifebelts and everybody was on hand and everything was all made ready along the deck."

Senator Smith's own Inquiry had finally concluded, and on May 28th, he recited his report to the U.S. Senate.

In his speech, encased in typical florid verbiage, Smith blamed his namesake, the master of the *Titanic*, for "his indifference to danger ... [and his] overconfidence and neglect to heed the oft-repeated warnings of his friends" for the disaster." The ship's high speed was attributed to "the presence of Mr. Ismay and

150

Mr. Andrews [the *Titanic*'s designer] stimulated the ship to greater speed than it would have made under ordinary conditions, although I cannot fairly ascribe to either of them any instructions to this effect." The Michigan Senator condemned the "indifferent" way the radioed ice warnings had been treated.

Smith was highly critical of the organisation immediately after the disaster; "No general alarm was given, no ship's officers formally assembled, no orderly routine was attempted or organized system of safety begun. Haphazard, they rushed by one another on staircase and in hallway, while men of self-control gathered here and there about the decks, helplessly staring at one another or giving encouragement to those less courageous than themselves." The lifeboats "were manned so badly that, in the absence of prompt relief, they would have fallen easy victims to the advancing ice floe ... The lifeboats were filled so indifferently and lowered so quickly that, according to the uncontradicted evidence, nearly 500 people were needlessly sacrificed to want of orderly discipline in loading the few that were provided ... And yet it is said by some well-meaning persons that the best of discipline prevailed. If this is discipline, what would have been disorder?"

Once the alarm had been raised, "Some of the men, to whom had been entrusted the care of passengers, never reported to their official stations, and quickly deserted the ship with a recklessness and indifference to the responsibilities of their positions as culpable and amazing as it is impossible to believe. And some of these men say that they 'laid by' in their partially filled lifeboats and listened to the cries of distress 'until the noise quieted down'."

Smith dealt with Captain Lord's version of the night of April 14th by rejecting it outright. By doing so, he could have been risking criticism; Gill's story, in spite of his assurances that it was true, could be labelled as a fabrication with the intention of making money. Evan's testimony regarding rockets could have been dismissed as hearsay and rumour, and it is surprising that more witnesses from the *Californian* were not subpoenaed immediately. By doing so, the inconsistencies in Gill's evidence and affidavit, now so obvious in retrospect, would have been challenged. How much, if any, of the London *Californian* evidence Smith had followed is not known.

Before providing a summary of the events on board the *Californian*, Smith gave an indication of his feelings towards Lord and his ship; "The steamship *Californian* was within easy reach of [the *Titanic*] for nearly four hours after all the facts were known to Operator Cottam [of the *Carpathia*]."

"Why did the *Californian* display its Morse signal lamp from the moment of the collision continuously for nearly two hours if they saw nothing? And the signals which were visible to Mr. Gill at 12.30 and afterwards, and which were also seen by the Captain and officer of the watch[100], should have excited more solicitude than was displayed by the officers of that vessel, and the failure of Capt. Lord to

---

100   Recall that Lord had seen no signals himself, and no officers were called from the *Californian* to confirm Gill's statement that "they must have seen them."

arouse the wireless operator on his ship, who could have easily ascertained the name of the vessel in distress and reached her in time to avert loss of life, places a tremendous responsibility upon this officer from which it will be very difficult for him to escape. Had he been as vigilant in the movement of his vessel as he as he was active in displaying his own signal lamp, there is a very strong probability that every human life that was sacrificed through this disaster could have been saved. The dictates of humanity should have prompted vigilance under such conditions"

Smith told his audience that both Great Britain, and, since April 18th, the United States, had regulations placed in law which compelled the master in charge of a vessel to afford assistance, "so far as he can do so without serious danger to his own vessel, her crew, and passengers (if any)[101]."

"I am well aware from the testimony of the Captain of the *Californian* that he deluded himself with the idea that there was a ship between the *Titanic* and the *Californian*, but there was no ship seen there at daybreak and no intervening rockets were seen by anyone on the *Titanic*, although they were looking longingly for such a sign and only saw the white light of the *Californian*, which was flashed the moment the ship struck and taken down when the vessel sank. A ship would not have been held there if it had been eastbound, and she could not have gone west without passing the *Californian* on the north or the *Titanic* on the south. That ice floe held but two ships - the *Titanic* and the *Californian*. The conduct of the Captain of the *Californian* calls for drastic action by the Government of England and by the owners of that vessel, who were the same owners as those of the ill-fated ship ... The committee is forced to the inevitable conclusion that the *Californian*, controlled by the same company, was nearer the *Titanic* than the 19 miles reported by her Captain, and that her officers and crew saw the distress signals of the *Titanic* and failed to respond to them in accordance with the dictates of humanity, international usage, and the requirements of law. The only reply to the distress signals was a counter signal from a large white light which was flashed for nearly two hours from the mast [sic] of the *Californian*. In our opinion such conduct, whether arising from indifference or gross carelessness, is most reprehensible, and places upon the commander the *Californian* a grave responsibility. The wireless operator of the *Californian* was not aroused until 3.30

---

101   *Lloyd's Weekly Shipping Index* (July 4th, 1912) reported that, Senator Nelson, Chairman of the Commercial Committee simultaneously introduced a bill in the Senate identically to the one passed in the house, regarding changes to shipping rules after the *Titanic*. Section 16, referring to "Assistance at sea", reads "That the master or person in charge of any vessel of the United States shall, so far as he can do without serious damage to his own vessel, crew or passengers, render assistance to every person who is found at sea in danger of being lost, and if he fails to do so he shall, upon conviction, be liable to a penalty of not exceeding $1000 or imprisonment for a term not exceeding two years, or both." This is very similar to the law as it stood in England, with the proviso that the term of imprisonment may be with, or without hard labour.

a.m., New York time, on the morning of the 15th, after considerable conversation between officers and members of the crew had taken place aboard that ship regarding these distress signals or rockets[102], and was directed by the Chief Officer to see there was anything the matter, as a ship had been firing rockets during the night. The Inquiry thus set on foot immediately disclosed the fact that the *Titanic* had sunk. Had assistance been promptly proffered, or had wireless operator of the *Californian* remained a few minutes longer at his post on Sunday evening, that ship might have had the proud distinction of rescuing the lives of the passengers and crew of the *Titanic*."

It was now about a month since the majority of the evidence from the *Californian* witnesses had been gathered, and day 24 of the British Inquiry re-introduced Lord's vessel into the proceedings. Dunlop, the *Californian's* representative, was not in court.

For, on that date, without Dunlop's or Lord's knowledge, a discussion ensued that aimed to add a question relating to the *Californian* into the Inquiry and its report. Mersey agreed with Isaac's opinion, and asked if he had jurisdiction over Captain Lord's certificate, but Isaacs noted that this would only be the case in a collision between two vessels.

"Assume that I take a view adverse to the conduct of the Captain of the *Californian*, all I can do is to express an opinion about it?" asked Mersey.

"Yes," responded Isaacs, "What we were going to ask your Lordship to do was to express your view upon the evidence which you have heard, and to give us the benefit of your Lordship's conclusions of fact."

"Quite," replied Mersey.

"And then we shall be able to consider it," concluded Isaacs.

The issue of amending or altering the Inquiry's questions was revisited five days later, when Isaacs told Mersey of his intention to revise question 24, which said, "What was the cause of the loss of the '*Titanic*', and of the loss of life which thereby ensued or occurred?" To this, the Attorney-General proposed to add the following: "What vessel had the opportunity of rendering assistance to the "*Titanic*," and, if any, how was it that assistance did not reach the '*Titanic*' before the '*Carpathia*' arrived?"

"That question will cover the "*Californian*."" concluded Isaacs.

Dunlop does not appear to have been in court, and therefore this proposal was accepted unopposed.

Urging of Mersey to pronounce against the *Californian* and its conduct was made on June 21st by Clement Edwards; "One point I was coming to immediately

---

102   How did Smith know that "considerable conversation" had taken place between the officers and crew before Evans was awakened?

yesterday, but which I do not propose to deal with very fully, is the matter of the *Californian*. As the case has now presented itself I shall submit that there is really no substantial element of doubt that the lights which were unquestionably seen from the deck of the *Californian* were the lights of the *Titanic*, and that the explanation of the Captain of the *Californian*, Captain Lord, that he thought possibly they might have been private signals cannot be treated otherwise than the merest idle excuse. There is not a particle of justification in his evidence for his suggestion that they might possibly have been private signals. Your Lordship will perhaps bear in mind in this connection that a question was asked, I think by myself, of Mr. Sanderson[103], as to whether the International Mercantile Marine Company controlling the Leyland line did issue to the Leyland line a copy of these Sailing Instructions. In these Sailing Instructions on page 23, there are these particulars given as to distress signals: "The following signals numbered 1, 2 and 3 when used or displayed together or separately shall be deemed to be signals of distress at night (1.) a gun fired at intervals of about a minute. (2.) Flames on the ship as from a burning tar barrel, oil barrel, etc. (3.) Rockets or shells of any colour or description fired one at a time at short intervals[104]."

I will tell you what I think the *Californian* will attempt to say that having regard to the bearings these lights cannot have been the lights of the *Titanic*. I expect you are not prepared to deal with that," commented Mersey.

"Yes, my Lord, I was, but it is perfectly clear that the learned Attorney-General must deal pretty fully with the matter. But what I was coming to was this, and it was rather from that point of view, that so far as the question may arise as to whether those were the signals of distress of the *Titanic* in fact, or whether they were the signals of distress of another ship, so far as the personal conduct of the responsible Captain of the *Californian* is concerned, his conduct, I shall submit, is equally reprehensible."

"I think, you know, he is going to say, or it will be said on his behalf, rather, that these signals were not distress signals at all, necessarily; that they were ship's signals."

"That, of course, my Lord, is what he has already endeavoured to say in evidence; but I think, in face of the two main facts, the first that the Officer Groves, in reply to your Lordship, did say in specific terms that in the light of all the facts he had not the slightest doubt that the signals which were seen were the signals of the *Titanic* -"

"I do not want to stop you," interrupted Mersey, "but I think the onus of proof in this matter is upon the *Californian*. I think for myself - I do not speak with absolute certainty for my colleagues - that it will be for the *Californian* to satisfy us that those were not the signals of the *Titanic*; whether they will succeed I cannot say, but I think you may leave it.

---

103   A director of the White Star Line.

104   See Appendix B for more information on distress signals.

On June 28th, Dunlop at last had a chance to try and convince Mersey that the *Californian* had not seen the *Titanic's* lights, a task he felt would take "about two hours." Although, as Dunlop had rarely been present at the Inquiry, he was told by his friends who had attended that his position, as advocate for the *Californian*, was not a enviable one. Dunlop started by apologising that the *Californian* had not been in a position to afford any assistance to the *Titanic*, but, he hoped that his discussion of points of evidence (times, lights, bearings, rockets etc.) might satisfy Mersey that the *Titanic* and the *Californian* were not visible to each other at any point that night.

The navigational data were the first items to be debated. Dunlop had prepared a sketch map that detailed Lord's course during the time of the *Titanic* disaster. Mersey was sceptical; he had been told by an assessor "that the information to be obtained from the log does not enable anyone to lay down that track [on the map]." What was needed was the *Californian's* compass deviation book to convert a compass course to a true course, but this was not available. There were assurances that the book would be sent down from Liverpool.

"There is no record in the log of any alteration of course between 7.30 and the time when she stopped, nor is there any suggestion that she did alter her course, between these times. My Lord, these were recorded at the time in the scrap log according to the evidence and copied into the log from the scrap log. They appeared in the scrap log long before the *Titanic* was lost - several hours before the *Titanic* was lost and, therefore, before there was any inducement whatever to those on board the *Californian* to make their log appear as if their vessel was further North than she in fact was. It was not suggested to the Master or the Officers of the *Californian*, nor are there any grounds for the suggestion, that the log before your Lordship has been 'cooked.' The log on the face of it appears to be a perfectly genuine log," Dunlop informed the court.

"I think you are putting that too high - you say there is no suggestion," grumbled Isaacs.

"No question was put, my Lord, to the Master ... From the 7.30 position, running as they say they were running at nearly full speed takes them at 10.21 to the place where they stopped - into the position which is recorded in the log as 42.5 North and 50.7 West. My Lord, I submit that the Master of the *Californian*, if he is to be judged at all, must get the benefit of his logbook, which, after all, is not his log. It is the log kept by the Chief Officer, a person whose conduct is not in any way the object of this Inquiry and who is not concerned in the result of what your Lordship's views may be. We are dealing now with the Master, and I submit the Master is entitled to have his conduct judged, amongst other things, in the light of what is recorded in the Chief Officer's log. But that is further confirmed by what appears in the entries on the following morning. If you test it, my Lord, by the distance which he ran from 6 o'clock in the morning, when he heard of the *Titanic's* loss, until 8.30, when he came up to the *Titanic*'s position, your Lordship will see that he must have run a distance very considerably over 20 miles."

Following a short discussion about the lack of information in the logbook about the *Californian*'s headings and speeds between 6 and 8.30am on April 14th, Dunlop confidently asserted that "making allowance for the fact that he was not able to proceed direct to the *Titanic*'s position, but had to go round the edge of the ice-field, it confirms the statement in my submission that he was at least 20 miles to the northward of the *Titanic*'s position ... if there is one point on which all the evidence agrees it is this, that as soon as they did hear of the *Titanic*'s loss they with all speed went to her assistance. They went in the direction reported [sic] by the *Carpathia*, and did so at full speed. If you allow for 2 hours at full speed and 30 minutes at slow, and her full speed is something like 13 knots or 13 ½ knots, I submit, my Lord, it follows that the position recorded in the log as the place where the *Californian* was stopped must be approximately accurate ... That also, my Lord, is corroborated by the distance which you would ordinarily expect to find between vessels bound respectively to New York, as the *Titanic* was, and to Boston, as the *Californian* was, at the 50th Meridian of longitude. You would expect to find them at about 20 to 30 miles apart, if they were both steering the course to the port to which each was respectively bound. If the log is approximately right, it follows that neither vessel could possibly have been at any time in sight of the other. They were separated by so great a distance and so great an interval of time that the *Californian* could not possibly have been of any assistance had she steamed to the *Titanic* as soon as the *Titanic* struck the iceberg. So much, my Lord, for the log," which was true, if one only considers Lord's statements about his navigation, and not Groves, or Moore's U.S. comments (which were not repeated, and never considered in London). This 30 mile value does not take into account overnight drift, or the fact that the *Californian* had undertaken a "dog-leg" course to proceed through the ice for the second time, this time to the *Carpathia*.

Dunlop conceded that "certain signals" were seen, but refuted that they were signals of distress: "if they were distress signals they were not signals from a vessel herself in distress; or if they were distress signals from a vessel in distress that vessel that vessel was not the *Titanic*." They were "private night signals."

"The evidence is all against that," remarked Isaacs.

Mersey was not happy with Dunlop's suggestion either; "You will have a great deal of difficulty in persuading me of that. If they were distress signals, whether they came from the *Titanic* or not, [the *Californian*] ought to have made for them."

Dunlop's address was to attempt to demolish the various issues one by one that pointed to the "guilt" of the *Californian*. Issues that, despite a hiatus between 1913 and 1958, would still be argued to this day, usually by applying a generous amount of spin, and selective quotation of evidence to argue whatever point matches the current whims of authors and researchers.

The *Californian*'s ex-donkeyman was an obvious target for Dunlop's demolitions of the accusation against his charge. Dunlop was to say, "But even Gill, the donkeyman, with his imagination stimulated by what had taken place in New York, could not and did not say that she was the *Titanic*. He judged her to be a passenger steamer because of the glare of lights - her saloon lights and her port lights""; In summary, since he had seen a moving steamer shortly after [sic] midnight, and since Groves had seen ship stop at 11.40, this led to the obvious conclusion: "If Groves is right Gill must be wrong, and if Gill is right Groves cannot be right. So much, my Lord, for Gill."

Groves' damaging insinuations also had to be countered. "Up to that moment [of questioning] ... [Groves] had not the courage to say that she was the *Titanic*, but, thus stimulated, he said this: "From what I have heard subsequently I do, but I do not put myself forward as an experienced man." That was the best answer, my Lord, he was able to give .. My Lord, it is perfectly clear, I submit, that Groves did not think so at the time, because at the end of his watch he went to have his usual chat with the Marconi operator, who was a kind of "Evening News" to him. He went there to find what vessels there were and what news there was, and, according to the operator's version of the conversation which took place at the end of Groves' watch, not a word was said about the steamer which Groves described in the witness-box. He did not mention her - nothing about seeing a large passenger steamer and her lights going out at 11.40. He did not ask: "Is this vessel the *Titanic*"? or anything of the kind. My Lord, that appears in the Marconi operator's evidence at Questions 9034 to 9050, where the Marconi operator told your Lordship that there was no reference at all by Groves to the steamer which he had seen, and both went off to bed. Groves attached no importance at the time to the vessel which he had seen, and he attached no importance at all to any of the incidents which he described when here in the witness-box; and I submit that his evidence was largely the result of imagination stimulated by vanity."

The discussion of witnesses seeing red or green lights teetered on the point of lunacy at points.

"The effect of starboarding[105] would not be to open the red light to any vessel to the northward of the *Titanic*'s position. Therefore, both before the *Titanic* struck the berg and after, if she had been within sight of the *Californian*, it is the green light and not the red light which the Witnesses
from the *Californian* would have seen," Dunlop tells the court, and then, logically, says that Captain Lord must have been mistaken seeing a green light, as "the weight of the evidence is that it was the red light or different vessels."

"Or the *Titanic* swinging?" observed Mersey.

"No, it could not be the *Titanic* swinging, because Captain Lord is referring

---

105   That is, turning the head of the ship to port, according to the shipping
conventions of the day.

to a period before the *Titanic* struck the iceberg."

"He said about half-past 11, did he not?"

"He says here at 11 o'clock; he keeps her in view until she stops, about 11.30. During the time she is approaching him she is showing a green light; that is his evidence. The evidence of the others is that she was not showing her green light, but was showing her red light."

"She would show her green light, I suppose, before the collision?"

"Yes."

"But after the collision we cannot tell what she showed."

"Yes, my Lord, according to the evidence; the evidence is she starboarded two points for the iceberg."

"Yes, but you do not know what happened to her after that?" and then followed this question with details on Boxhall's statements (who denied that the *Titanic* was swinging) and Rowe's comments (who had noted the ship's stern settling to the south, bringing the bow north).

"After that time the alteration of heading was to port, under a starboard helm, an alteration which could not possibly open the red light to any vessel to the northward of her. But I am not so much concerned with the sidelight seen after the *Titanic* struck the iceberg as the sidelight which was seen before 11.40, while the vessel which they describe came up and stopped in the ice; because that is the time when we know that the *Titanic* was steering West and would, if she was in sight, be showing to the *Californian* her green light. At that time the body of the evidence is that she was showing her red light," said Dunlop, forgetting, or perhaps not knowing, that Boxhall had said he had seen the masthead lights and the green light first to Senator Smith.

Mersey said, "What Groves says at Question 8228 is this: "Did you see any navigation lights?" He has just said, you know, that he saw two masthead lights. "Did you see any navigation lights - sidelights? - (A.) I saw the red port light. (The Commissioner.) When did you see that? - (A.) As soon as her deck light disappeared from my view." That would be possible, I should say probable, when her helm was being starboarded."

This is perfectly asinine. If the *Titanic* was headed slightly south of due west (S 86 W was the course) and starboarded two points (that is, turned to port 22 ½ degrees), then the green light might be shut in. Her stern light would be observable, but the red light would not be visible. The *Titanic*'s deck lights might also be diminished in intensity, but the ship would still be more-or-less broadside to the *Californian*. Mersey was quite prepared to posit lunatic suggestions to force the *Titanic* to show a red light. As we have seen above, the majority of the evidence, which has been discussed above, and showing that this was possible, was available to Mersey but he had forgotten it or had failed to grasp its importance.

Dunlop could see that Mersey was 'clutching at straws', "But, my Lord, she could not open her red light," insisted Dunlop.

"But you do not know," scolded Mersey, "Her deck lights would disappear very likely, she might be pointing stern on towards the *Californian*," thereby also forgetting that Groves, Stone and Gibson had remarked seeing the mast light(s) after the other vessel had stopped, but not the stern light. The only one to notice the stern light was Stone as he watched his mysterious stranger 'steam away.' And you cannot see a stern light and mastlight(s)/red/green lights at the same time.

So what did the *Californian* witnesses see? "What [they] saw was a vessel coming up from the field ice and then stopping, and apparently they see a vessel which is bound, not to America, as the *Titanic* was, but bound to some European port, and, therefore, showing to them her red light, and, apparently, to the 3rd Officer, steering about N.E. And that is also what Gill, the donkeyman, described, because, although his glimpse was only a momentary one, what he saw of the vessel was a vessel apparently heading in the same way as the *Californian* was, and the evidence from the *Californian* is that at that time she was heading about N.N.E. by the compass, which would be about N.E. true. The vessel, therefore, which Gill saw would not be the *Titanic*, but heading in the opposite direction. There is no evidence that the *Titanic* turned round before she sank and headed in the direction of Europe."

So, despite disposing of Gill's and Groves' evidence, here Dunlop uses their statements as proof that the ship under observation was not the *Titanic*. And there is no mention of Captain Lord's green light. That too had been ditched.

"Gill appears to have thought that the steamer that was visible was out of the field ice. That is so, is it not? He says he looked and he could see the edge of the field ice, in which they were, about five miles away," commented Mersey.

"Yes."

"And the steamer that he saw was five miles further away and, therefore, would be in open water."

"My Lord, I should have thought that evidence was extremely unreliable; the evidence of a donkeyman going forward to call his mate at midnight. He would not in the ordinary course of things notice how far the ice extended and whether the vessel that he saw was navigating in clear water or not."

"Gill did not give me the impression of a man who wanted to make a case against his ship."

"My Lord, he may not have given your Lordship that impression, but - "

"Do you suggest he came here with a desire, I will not say with an intention to deceive, but with a desire to make out that it was the *Titanic* they did see?" interrupted Mersey.

"Yes, my Lord, I think he did, and I think he did for this reason. This donkeyman hearing of the loss of the *Titanic* the next morning, a few days later arrived in New York [sic], interviewed by New York [sic] reporters, giving evidence at the American Inquiry, his imagination got fired by all this excitement and he began to imagine that the steamer of which he had a momentary glimpse

159

was in fact the *Titanic*. I submit that from whatever point of view you test the evidence of the *Californian*, either as regards the class of vessels seen, the lights seen, the movements which they describe as having seen, they all point to the same conclusion that the vessel which they saw was not and could not have been the *Titanic*."

But this hardly explains why Gill was backed up when making his initial affidavit in Boston by "four members of the crew ... and by an officer of the ship, who affirmed them," but this does not seem to be a detail that Dunlop knew, nor do the comments which appeared in the *Clinton Daily Item*, coming second hand from Lord's carpenter on his ship. It seems that many people had their imagination fired by the *Titanic*'s foundering!

And what of the *Titanic*? What was seen on that ship?

"The evidence from the *Titanic* also shows that the *Californian* was not in sight at any time. Before 11.40 your Lordship has the evidence of the look-out men who were in the crow's-nest, Lee and Fleet. Neither of those men at any time between 10 and 12, when they were in the crow's-nest, saw the lights of any steamer, and if the *Californian* had then been 10 or 5 miles, or whatever distance, the witnesses from the *Californian* have stated the vessel which they saw was, they could not have helped seeing the lights of the *Californian*. But neither of them saw anything of the kind. Hogg relieved Fleet and Lee at midnight, and went into the crow's-nest, and was there until he was called out of the crow's-nest and went away in one of the boats. During the time he was in the crow's-nest, and no doubt anxiously looking for lights, he did not see any lights; he did not see the *Californian*'s lights, nor did he see the Morse signals of the *Californian*, which would, of course,
show a greater distance than the ordinary navigation lights ... So that up to the time when the *Titanic* struck the berg, the *Californian* was not in sight of the *Titanic*."

This obviously deserves comment. While it is true that both Fleet and Lee, stationed in the crows nest at the time the *Titanic* struck and shortly afterwards, denied having seen any lights from their perch, there are some indications that they were wrong.

The earliest witness to the other ship that we know of, was seaman Buley, who said in America that he had seen the light, "When we started turning the boats out. That was about 10 minutes after she struck." We can disregard his statement that the ship "was there when [the *Titanic*] struck, and she passed right by us. We thought she was coming to us; and if she had come to us, everyone could have boarded her. You could see she was a steamer. She had her steamer lights burning," as he was below at the time, reading in the mess, before being called in by 1st Officer Murdoch to help turn the boats out. If he was right, Buley would have seen this ship during Fleet and Lee's 8-12am watch. Fleet had said that the light was reported by "the other lookout"; but his relief was never questioned on this matter.

Boxhall too had heard of a light seen off the bow while unlacing the

160

lifeboat covers on the port side and wanted to see this stranger for himself. However, before he did so, Boxhall attended to another of his duties: ascertaining the position of the ship from the navigational data collected during the evening. We know now that his position was transmitted at 12.25am. Therefore the time that he saw the light would be about this time, or some 35 minutes after Buley's claim.

Was Buley right about his timing? Lookout Symons arrived on the boat deck about midnight, with orders to assist in preparing the boats for lowering. Passenger Lawrence Beesley had ventured out on deck immediately after he felt the shudder of the collision, and seeing nothing went below for a while, where he conversed with people in the smoking room before retiring back to his cabin. After reading for a while, he dressed and returned to the boat deck where he noticed that the *Titanic* was moving slowly forward again. He observed the cover of lifeboat 16 being thrown off. This vivid and detailed account corroborates Buley's – that the preparation of the lifeboats began soon after the collision. We do not know how long Beesley stayed below before returning and seeing boat 16 readied, but, by inference, it cannot have been long. He specifically notes the ship moving on again, and it is known that she was stationary when Boxhall had performed his position calculations. It was possibly about midnight, but Buley's statement stands: he noticed the light while he was assisting in swinging out the boats[106]. And the lookouts had seen nothing.

So, how did two trained lookouts (who, it must be said, had nearly missing seeing the fatal iceberg!) not see any lights directly in front of them? One is impressed by the arguments put forward by a later author[107] who sought a professional consensus from nautical experts who would say that "they would expect the stopped, comparatively small, comparatively sparsely lit *Californian* to see the huge, fast-moving, brilliantly-lit *Titanic* before the latter saw the *Californian*, and in fact long before the *Titanic* did so ... the *Titanic* did not see the *Californian*, not because she was not there, but merely because the multitudinous stars acted as effective, although temporary, camouflage."

The residue of Dunlop's discussion on the light observed from the *Titanic* was concerned with what was seen, and her actions. He dismissed those statements that seemed to refer to lights from fishing vessels, from lifeboats or from the *Carpathia*, although how a witness was expected to be able to identify fishing vessels from their lights alone is not explained. The most important witnesses were Boxhall, Lucas and Hart, who had described a steamer, which moved, approached and then moved off. "They are the only Witnesses who mentioned seeing a steamer at all, and that was not until some time between 1 and 2," Dunlop pointed out. But

106   This is in contrast to comments made by Captain Lord's followers in later decades. Leslie Harrison aimed to put Boxhall's first sighting of the other ship as close to 1am as he could, and John Carrothers wrote that people on the *Titanic* watched as the vessel came over the horizon. Neither of which is true.

107   Leslie Reade in "*The Ship That Stood Still*", page 312

Boxhall had seen the ship for the first time at about 12.25am; Hart saw the lights before and after he escaped, in boat 8, which left, according to Mersey's later timescale at approximately 1.10am. Only seaman Lucas describes seeing the other ship once he was in the water (boat 12, 1.25am), but his descriptions do not seem to match what the others had seen. He refers to seeing a red light and a mastlight, but, not ahead, on the port or starboard bow, but on the starboard quarter – that is, the right rear. Lucas' use of nautical terminology seems sloppy as he agrees that it would be "broad on the starboard side" - that is, abeam. So much for an able bodied seaman!

And although many witnesses in the U.S. and England mentioned that the other ship was moving off, others mention that she was there all night, or that they had rowed for her for hours without making any headway, and that, as daylight came up, the chase was abandoned and the lifeboat turned around for the *Carpathia* – which was in view as the same time as the mysterious vessel.

"Is there any evidence to show that the *Californian* saw this steamer or the vessel or the lights that the Witnesses from the *Titanic* say they saw?" Mersey asked.

"I do not know whether this steamer which Boxhall is referring to is or is not the steamer which the Chief Officer of the *Californian* saw at four o'clock, a vessel which had been steaming to the S.W. and afterwards was seen steaming to the N.E. or steaming in a Northerly and Easterly direction. That is the only evidence which seems to connect the vessel which Boxhall saw with any vessel which the *Californian* saw."

One wonders where Dunlop obtained his "steaming to the N.E." information from. The vessel that was seen from the *Californian* after 4am was heading in the same direction as she was – to the north-west. Was he confabulating Grove's steamer, which moved in a south-west to north-east direction with Boxhall's steamer, that he was sure had come from the west and moved back in the same direction?

Dunlop concluded this section of his submission thus, "I submit to your Lordship that the conclusion of the whole evidence, the *Titanic*'s evidence, the *Carpathia*'s evidence, and the *Californian*'s evidence, all point to the same conclusion that they were never in sight of each other. If that is so, then the whole foundation of the charge against Captain Lord disappears. The whole significance of what is described as the *Californian* incident at once vanishes if the vessels were never in fact in sight of each other. In that case the rockets seen could not possibly have been the rockets of the *Titanic*, but must have been the rockets of another vessel which we have not, unfortunately, got before the Court."

Mersey asked if Dunlop had attempted to ascertain the identity of the unknown steamers, but his sources of information had been limited to five issues of *Lloyd's Weekly Shipping Index* from April and early May; despite this, a few possibilities had become apparent, "but, of course, it would ill become the Leyland

Line to endeavour to ascertain the name of a steamer which may have seen the *Titanic's* rockets and did not in fact go to her assistance; it is no part of my purpose. It would ill become the Leyland Line to make enquiries from the Masters or owners of other vessels with a view to showing that there was a vessel nearer to the *Titanic* than the *Californian* herself was, and, therefore, we have made no effort."

"Why would it ill become them?" asked an intrigued Mersey.

"I submit that for them to bring evidence with a view to showing that there was a vessel nearer to the *Titanic* than the *Californian* was, which we know did not in fact go to the *Titanic's* assistance, or did not in fact render any effective assistance, would only be to involve some other vessel in the criticisms which have been made in the course of this Inquiry."

"I think it would be your duty to do it."

"Well, my Lord, the view which my clients have taken, and I respectfully agree with them, is that for one shipowner to endeavour to throw blame upon a steamer belonging to some other owner is not what I should have thought would be the loyalty owed by one shipowner to another. It is no part of my purpose and certainly no part of theirs to attempt to throw blame upon any other vessel."

"This is a very high sense of duty; I do not appreciate it at all."

Dunlop remarked that the evidence regarding other steamers in the vicinity was incomplete, and that the only reason that a list of other ships had been collated was because of their use of the Marconi apparatus. There must be, Dunlop reasoned, other vessels which did not use this equipment and which were unknown. But Dunlop was mistaken on one point; he accused the Board of Trade of not inquiring about ships that might have been in the area. In fact, the Board had contacted various foreign ports as early as May 21st asking for departures and arrivals that matched the funnel colours of a ship seen by the *Mount Temple*. Such a ship was apparently, Dunlop said, "a vessel which was apparently bound to Europe, which appeared to be a tramp steamer, which was not provided with Marconi apparatus, and apparently did not use or did not understand Morse signalling ... The circumstances of the *Californian* are such as I think would rather induce Masters to keep away from the Court; they have excellent reasons for keeping away rather than for coming here to say that they were in the vicinity and had an opportunity of rendering assistance, but for some reason or another they were not, in fact, able to do so. The steamers seen by the *Californian* or the *Titanic* may have been either of the two which are mentioned in the deposition[108] of the Master of the *Carpathia*. ... Further, the evidence from the *Californian* shows that there were three, or possibly four, other steamers in this neighbourhood whose names we do not know. The Master described at Question 7400 a vessel which he says - a two-masted steamer with a pink funnel and a black top, apparently steering to the North-West. Stone, the Chief Officer, at Question 8017, saw, just after 4 o'clock, a steamer with two

---

108   See later.

masthead lights heading to the Eastward or North-East [sic]. Groves, at Question 650, saw a four-masted steamer which he thought afterwards was the *Carpathia*, but he must be wrong about that because, according to the *Carpathia*, the *Carpathia* and the *Californian* were not in sight of each other until 8 o'clock in the morning. Therefore the steamer that he saw was probably not the *Carpathia*. At Question 8339 he says he saw two other vessels. That is Groves, my Lord."

These "two other vessels" were the *Mount Temple* and the unknown steamer. Notice also how Dunlop disposes of Groves' evidence that he had seen the *Carpathia* at 6.50a.m.; but Groves claimed that this ship was the Cunarder as he was on the bridge when the *Californian* turned to port and approached her!

The *Trautenfels* was the first candidate from Dunlop's perusal of the Lloyd's journals, and has been described previously. Mersey asked what time the *Trautenfels* had come across the massive ice field, but Dunlop did not know what time this was noted.

"It may not have been the vessel which [the *Californian*] saw. I cannot put it as high as that, because we do not know at what time she was in this latitude. All we do know is she was there at some time on the 14th April, and she did what the Witnesses from the *Californian* described the vessel which they saw did. They saw a vessel encounter ice and then run in a S.W. direction until she went out of sight."

All very well and good, but another Lloyd's publication ("*The Shipping Gazette and Lloyd's List*") puts the time that the *Trautenfels* encountered the ice as being at 5.40am on April 14th. She could not be the *Californian*'s mystery ship.

Mersey asked if Dunlop had contacted the Hansa Line, owners of the *Trautenfels*. Dunlop replied that he hadn't.

"Was that because you did not want to know what they would say?"

"No, my Lord."

"Then, why did you not communicate with them?"

"Because it is no part of our purpose; it is no part of the object with which we are here to say the *Trautenfels* did anything wrong, and I do not want to suggest that *Trautenfels* failed to render assistance or had any opportunity of rendering assistance."

"She would not be likely, I agree, to assist you if that was your object."

"No, and it would be unfair to approach them."

"I do not agree with you about being unfair at all, but I do agree to this, that if she knew what you were about she would not be likely to help you."

"No, my Lord, and we could not have asked them without telling them what our object was."

"At all events you have not attempted to get any information from her."

Isaacs had new information for the court. "I think I ought to tell your Lordship - I did not know it till this moment - that we have been making some inquiries with reference to it. There is a reference to the *Trautenfels* in consequence of the funnels - the colour of the funnels and description - we traced that it might

164

be one of the Hansa line, and we have been in communication about it to see if we could ascertain. The letter that I have is from the Treasury Department of the United States Customs Service at the Port of Boston, to which the *Trautenfels* was bound, a letter of the 23rd May. I will read it so that your Lordship may have such information as we have got ... The letter is from the Treasury Department, United States Customs Service Boston, to the Commissioner of Navigation at Washington, dated 23rd May, 1912. "In reply to Bureau letter (62052.), dated 21st instant, I beg to report that the only steamships known to this office which have a funnel resembling the one described in Bureau letter are those of the Hansa Line. The *Trautenfels* of that line arrived at this port early in the morning on 18th April, and the *Lindenfels* on 20th April. As I am informed that the voyage from the locality mentioned by the Bureau to this port is from three to five days, according to the speed of the steamer, the *Trautenfels* would probably not have been in that locality on 15th April. The steamers of this line do not clear foreign from this port, but proceed to New York with residue of cargo. The s.s. *Inverclyde*, sailing on the American and Oriental Line arrived 22nd April. I have been unable to obtain a description of her funnel. I presume that it can be obtained from the agents in New York. No vessel having a funnel like that described by the Bureau cleared foreign from this port within a period of two weeks prior to 15th April."

And there the matter of the *Trautenfels* rested, although Dunlop tried to associate her "one black funnel each with a white band, around which were red hoops" identification with the pink funnel/black topped steamer seen by Captain Lord between 6.30 and 7.30am. A "remarkable resemblance," as Mersey was told, one can imagine with tongue firmly in cheek.

A remarkable exchange then occurred.

Mersey asked, "What question is expressly directed to the conduct of the *Californian?*"

"Well, I think it is 24," Isaacs replied.

"It is wide enough to cover the *Trautenfels?*" asked Dunlop. Here he was trying to implicate another ship!

"That is not the one," Mersey replied, ignoring Dunlop.

Isaacs stood corrected: "It is the one that covers the *Californian*; that is, if your Lordship has the amended question."

"I am afraid I have not," an apologetic Mersey replied.

"I amended it so as to include the *Californian*," Isaacs informed the Wreck Commissioner.

Dunlop's appeal to the court, not to implicate his client, was proceeding, and yet here was Sir Rufus Isaacs admitting that he had already amended a question to cover the *Californian*'s conduct. Why do this unless they had already decided on the Leyland Line's ship's 'guilt'?

"Then, my Lord, there is the steamship *Paula*. She is the petroleum steamer," continued Dunlop.

"Have you given us the best one?" asked Mersey.

"Yes, the *Trautenfels* is the best, because she steams to the S.W."

"The *Trautenfels* is the best you have got, you say?"

"Yes; the *Paula* is very good."

"Are they all very good?"

"These are the two best, my Lord, because these are the only two which gave us their position on the 14th April."

"Have you a description of the *Paula*?" inquired Isaacs.

"Yes. The *Paula* is a three masted oil tank steamer of 2,748 tons gross with ... a black funnel with yellow and a red R on the yellow, and she belongs to the Deutscher-Americana Petroleum Company of Hamburg."

"She is not likely to look like a passenger boat?"

"No, she would look more like what the Master and 2nd Officer and Gibson say, a medium-sized vessel, apparently a tramp, not having the appearance of a passenger steamer."

"Again, my Lord, we are not told the times; we only know those were the positions which she reported as having been in at some time on the 14th of April. There, again, your Lordship will see a steamer going to the Westward and then apparently steaming a South-Westerly direction in order to avoid the ice-field. In addition to these vessels there are some others, the *Memphian*, the *Campanillo*, and the *President Lincoln*."

Mersey asked if the Leyland liner *Memphian* had been placed on Dunlop's chart of putative mystery ships.

"Yes, I think so. I do not know anything about the *Memphian*. She is not in Lloyd's Register. I am told the *Paula*, and the *Trautenfels*, are both in Lloyd's Register, but the *Memphian* is not. I ought to say that the *Campanillo* and the *President Lincoln* both had Marconi apparatus."

Isaacs piped up. "I have some information about the *Paula*, if it is of any use. Enquiries have been made of a very extensive character for the purpose of dealing with this point. This has gone through the Board of Trade to the Foreign Office to America to make enquiries. This is the answer on May 27th, from the Treasury Department of the United States Customs Service, Port of Arthur, Texas: "I have the honour to reply to your letter 62052-N of May 21st, 1912, relative to a vessel in the vicinity of the *Titanic* disaster, and to say that I am unable to find any vessel with a black funnel and white band that has entered here since the disaster that would have been in the vicinity at or about the time of the disaster. The German steamer *Paula* (oil tank), Rieke, Master, and owned by the Deutscher-Americana Petroleum Gesellschaft, of Hamburg, W. T. Worden, 26, Broadway, New York, American agent, arrived at the Port of Sabine, this district, on April 29th, and the Master stated that he passed through the ice-field on Sunday a few hours before the *Titanic*, and that, finding the ice getting worse, he changed course directly to the South for 25 or more miles. It may be possible that Captain Rieke may have seen the vessel of which you request information. The *Paula* cleared hence for Ozelosund, Sweden," I do not think it helps very much."

It is possible, using contemporary records, to extend our knowledge of the movements of these ships, and our data *nearly* eliminates them all as contenders for the position of the unknown strangers: the *Paula* passed Dunnet Head April 3rd and arrived in Norfolk (Va.) Apr 20, according to *Lloyd's Weekly Shipping Index*. The U.S. Hydrographer Captain Knapp had already given data to Senator Smith about the movements of this petroleum tanker; "April 14, 11:40 A.M., latitude 41° 54' N., longitude 40° 32' W., one large iceberg. April 14, 11:40 A.M., latitude 41° 50' N., longitude 49° 33' W., one large iceberg. April 14, noon, latitude 41 53' N., longitude 49 36' W., one large iceberg. April 14, forenoon, from latitude 41° 58' longitude 49° 30' W., till 41° 56', 49' 52', heavy pack ice (one field). April 14, 5:30 P.M., from latitude 41° 55', longitude 50° 13', till latitude 41° 40', longitude 50° 30' heavy pack ice and 30 large icebergs in one field." At the time of the *Titanic* disaster, the *Paula* would be well to the west of the collision point.

The Leyland Line ship *Memphian* left Liverpool April 7th, passed Tuskar April 7th and arrived in Boston on April 20. She was in pack ice from 4pm on April 15th to 2am on April 16th; between positions 42° N 48° W to 50° W she steamed through a field of broken ice and icebergs. At longitude 49° 25 W she ran into field ice which was cleared in 50° W. Again, this information is derived from *Lloyds Weekly Shipping Index*, dated 9/5/12. Incidentally, another Leyland ship, the *Louisianian* (one of Stanley Lord's old commands), reached the ice field on April 15th, at 41° 26'N, 49° 36'W, described as being about 17 miles long and interspersed with 30 bergs of various sizes.

Leyland had told the Board of Trade that, at the time of the *Titanic* disaster, another one of their steamers (the *Antillian*) has been in the area. Since they did not mention the *Memphian* or *Louisianian*, we can presume that the *Antillian* had been closer to the wreck. But we do not know where.

The *Campanello* (spelt *Campanillo* in the British Inquiry transcripts) left New York on April 12, heading to Rotterdam, and was reported as being 140 miles west of Brow Head on Apr 23. The 27/4/12 issue of "*The Shipping Gazette and Lloyd's List*" mentions that, between April 14th and 15th, she encountered heavy pack ice, large bergs and field ice, in position 41° 10 N to 42° N, 49° W to 50° 16 W, drifting south. She *may* have been in the wreck's vicinity. She had one funnel, 4 masts but with a top speed of 13 knots, it would have taken her well over three days to reach the *Titanic*, not allowing for any contributions from the North Atlantic Drift which may have assisted her progress eastward. This is an interesting discrepancy with her ice positions reported above. In 1912, the *Campanello* was being operated by the Uranium Line, and would have had a black funnel. Her reported gross tonnage of 9001 tons would be inconsistent with Captain Moore's estimate of the 4,000 - 5,000 ton vessel he had seen close by on April 15th.

The *President Lincoln* will be mentioned again in forthcoming pages, where she will be exposed as another wild goose chase.

But why had a steamer displayed rockets, if they did not mean distress? Dunlop tackled this question too.

"Nobody has been called from the steamer and therefore we can only speculate as to why it was that this steamer which the *Californian* witnesses describe was seen exhibiting rockets. They have given their explanation and put forward their theories, and I want to mention the theories which have been put forward to your Lordship, because I submit that the theories of the men who were on the spot, who not only saw the rockets, but also saw the movements and the class of vessel that was exhibiting the rockets, is very much more likely to be right than the opinion of people who like ourselves were not there. The explanation of these rockets in the first place may be that they were answering rockets, that they were rockets fired by a vessel which was between the *Californian* and the *Titanic*, fired in answer to some other vessel which may have been in distress; or, it may be that the vessel which fired the rockets had sustained the kind of damage which a vessel is likely to sustain in field ice; she may have broken a blade or two of her propeller or damaged her rudder and wanted a tow in daylight. She may have been signalling to the *Californian* to stand by till daylight with a view to towing her if she required towage in the morning."

"I do not know; do people signal by means of rockets in such a way as to indicate a request to stand by?"

"It is the only means."

"I thought the signals were "Come to our assistance," not to stand by."

"My Lord, there is no other signal to the eye, if you exclude Morse signalling, than rockets."

"Would rockets mean, or may they mean, "We are foundering"?"

"It may mean that and it may mean a great deal less than that."

"You do not stand by at a distance of 10 miles for that ... You go to the vessel, at least, I should think so. What is the use of standing by ... when a vessel is going down to the bottom? I do not know."

"No, my Lord, but supposing this vessel was not going down to the bottom?"

"We do not know whether she was or was not."

"No," conceded Dunlop.

"Are you going to stand off 6 miles away and trust to chance and say to yourselves "She may be going down to the bottom or she may not, so we will stay here"?"

"What these [*Californian*] witnesses saw was this," Dunlop hypothesised, "they saw a vessel steaming through field ice and then stopping, and they had this vessel under observation. It may well have been that this steamer stopped because owing to moving in field ice she had damaged her propeller or her rudder, stops for the purpose of making an examination, discovers on examination that she has damaged her rudder or propeller, sees a vessel some five or six miles away which she may want to tow her when towage is possible, and signals to her for that purpose."

If this so, one may ask, how, and why does such a damaged steamer move away? And reversing into an icefield would only expose such damaged areas to even more risk!

"She has no other means of conveying to that other vessel the request that that other vessel shall stand by her. At least, I know of no other signal. If she has wireless telegraphy she may do it by wireless or she may use Morse signals, but this vessel was not in fact using Morse signals while she was under observation. Eliminating wireless telegraphy and Morse signalling she was using the only means of communication that would be at her disposal.

The first theory, namely, that these signals were not signals of distress in the sense of not being signals from a vessel which was herself in distress, was the theory of the witnesses from the *Californian*, the witnesses who saw the rockets. It is the view which they say they formed at the time; it is the view which they stated in the witness-box here.

Ridicule was thrown at the time on this suggestion that a vessel would fire distress rockets as a means of answering some other vessel, but this theory obtained remarkable confirmation a day or two after the *Californian* witnesses left the witness-box, when we got the evidence from the *Carpathia*. The *Carpathia* sent up rockets in order to indicate to those in the *Titanic* that the *Titanic*'s distress signals had been recognised and that the *Carpathia* was going to her assistance. I should have thought it was the only means at night if a vessel sees another sending up distress rockets, and wishes to acknowledge that she has seen them and is going to act upon them."

"Then why did not [the *Californian*] send up rockets?"

"[They] were Morse signalling to her, and [they] were standing by, so that the theory of the witnesses themselves is supported by what the *Carpathia* is said to have done; in other words, to sum it up, those rockets were not signals from a vessel in distress; they were answering signals, signals of reply, and not signals of request for assistance. That is their theory. If the 2nd Officer, who was the only Officer who saw the rockets, had thought they were signals from a vessel herself in distress, what would his conduct have been?"

"That is what I wondered," said Mersey, perhaps not without a hint of sarcasm.

"In the first place, I submit he would have reported to the Master that he saw a ship in distress and signalling for assistance. He made no such report; he stopped and discussed whether they were private night signals, or whether they were signals of distress."

"He should not have stopped to discuss anything about it; he should have gone to the Master at once."

"He did not do so, my Lord, because he did not think that they were signals from a vessel herself in distress. That is his view. His view may have been wrong or it may have been right, but he was there."

"Was he the man who said "I do not suppose that ship is sending up those signals for nothing"?"

"I think there was some discussion of that kind with Gibson, the Apprentice, or Gibson said so. What I wish to point out is that the conduct of the 2nd Officer at the time is quite inconsistent with the conduct of a man who has seen rockets which he thinks to be signals from a vessel herself in distress."

"I agree with you there - it is."

"And therefore one has to look in order to ascertain what it really was they saw, one has to test it by what they did at the time, by their conduct, and their conduct at the time is the best indication in my submission, of what it really was that they saw, what impression was conveyed to their minds by the rocket which they saw, and the movements of the steamer which they saw. In the second place he would take effective measures to call the Master and get him to come on deck if for no other higher motive than that of shifting the responsibility for inaction from his own shoulders to that of the Master. He was quite content to remain during that watch with the knowledge that the Master was sleeping in the chart room alone, and he made no attempt to bring the Master on to the deck. I say he would certainly have called the Master on deck and communicated with him and taken measures to see that the Master did come on deck if he had for one moment thought there was a vessel in distress and wanting assistance. He would also have called the Marconi operator. It would have been no trouble for him to do so; he would have done that, and not remained content with signalling to her by Morse signals."

"Distress rockets may, according to the Rules, be anything?" queried Mersey.

"Yes, they may be any colour."

"They are generally white."

"I expect they are generally white because most rockets are white. My Lord, he did not call the Marconi operator; he was content to go on signalling to this vessel by Morse signals and getting no reply. That I submit he would not have done had he thought this vessel was a vessel in distress and wanted assistance. He would not have been content with the steps he took to get into communication with her. And lastly, if they had been distress rockets, you would have found those signals entered in the scrap log. According to the evidence they were not entered there."

"We have never seen the scrap log."

"No, my Lord, and the 3rd Officer, Groves, who had no responsibility in the matter at all because at all material times he was below, was asked if he saw the scrap log on the following morning and he said he did. He was asked was there any entry in the scrap log of those signals."

"I have forgotten what your explanation is, or was, of the fact that rockets are not referred to in the log at all. What is the explanation?"

"The explanation is because they did not think that the rockets were signals of distress. They thought they were what they call private night signals."

"They did the next morning when they knew what had happened to the *Titanic*."

"Not the Officers."

"Oh, yes," Mersey snorted.

"They still in the witness-box denied that they were distress rockets in the sense of being rockets from a vessel in distress. The whole of their evidence is to the effect that they were not. In one sense distress rockets, true, because they are rockets which show a white light, but in the sense of being rockets from a vessel in distress their answer is no, and there is no evidence to the contrary."

"How many rockets did you see?"

"I think, my Lord, the evidence is about eight."

"How many rockets did the *Titanic* send up?" After a brief discussion, where *Titanic* witness recollections of anything up to a dozen rockets were sent up was reviewed, the number of eight was reached.

"And the witnesses from the *Californian* describe seeing rockets a considerable time after the *Titanic* had ceased to exhibit rockets. They saw rockets till nearly 4 o'clock in the morning."

"It is suggested they came from the boats," remarked Isaacs.

"The *Carpathia* was sending up rockets then, was she not?" asked Mersey.

Dunlop responded, "The *Carpathia* was a long way off, steaming up towards the *Californian* at that time. I do not think it was suggested that the rockets which were seen about 4 in the morning were the *Carpathia*'s rockets."

"At all events, does not it come to this, that the *Titanic* was sending out white rockets and [the *Californian*] saw white rockets; that the *Titanic* sent up about eight rockets, and [the *Californian*] saw about eight rockets?"

"Yes, it is a coincidence."

"Yes, it is a coincidence," repeated Mersey.

"As to the colour, it is not of importance, because that is the colour of rocket you would expect if a rocket was sent up at all. The number, again, my Lord, is purely guesswork on the part of the Officer who was firing them, because he was not counting them. What he said was, "I was sending up rockets during the course of an hour.""

"And did not you see the rockets just at the same time that the *Titanic* was sending her rockets up ... you see the same colour that the *Titanic* sent up; the same number that the *Titanic* sent up, and you see them just about the same time that the *Titanic* is sending them up."

"Yes," admitted Dunlop.

"Those are all coincidences."

"Is not that perfectly consistent with the view that the vessel firing rockets was firing answering rockets? If so, the numbers and the colours would coincide."

"I was on a different point. I was on the question as to whether [the *Californian*] saw the *Titanic*'s rockets."

"Yes, and I submit not. The fact that we saw eight and saw white rockets does not show they were the *Titanic*'s rockets because that happens to be the number which her Witnesses say they sent up, or the colour which they sent up, because if they were answering rockets as is the theory of the Witnesses from the *Californian*, you would expect to find precisely the same coincidence; or you might find the same coincidence. For every rocket on the *Californian* sent up there was one sent up in reply from the intermediate steamer."

"But you do not signal at night by means of rockets in the same way that you would signal in the daytime by means of flags, do you?"

"Oh, no."

"I mean you do not carry on conversations by means of rockets."

"No, but if rockets are sent from a vessel herself in distress and the steamer seeing them wishes to acknowledge them, if she has not got the means of acknowledging them in any other way she will or may very likely fire rockets. At any rate that is the theory of the witnesses from the *Californian*. That is the view they formed at the time. It may be now that we know what, in fact, was happening that their theory was wrong, but we are now dealing with the conduct of the men at the time, and we must judge that conduct, I submit, by the views that they formed at the time. Their theory is, I submit, quite consistent with the colour of the rockets and the number of the rockets, if, as they say, these were rockets fired in answer to rockets from a vessel herself in distress. It may be the vessel which the *Californian* saw firing these rockets, being between the *Californian* and the *Titanic*, was herself seeing the rockets from the *Titanic* and taking that means of acknowledging that she had seen them."

Dunlop continued: "Those men have their conversation. Both said to each other, and said when they came here, that they were not signals from a vessel in distress. True, they made that observation that they were not sending them up for fun, and I do not suggest that she was. On their theory, it was far from fun she was indulging in, but this vessel was sending up rockets in answer, as they thought, to some other vessel which may have been in distress. So satisfied were Stone, the 2nd Officer, and Gibson, the Apprentice, that the vessel whose rockets they were seeing was not in distress that although after five minutes past two they saw two or three more rockets, according to their evidence, they thought there was no need to tell the Master, much less to call him. I submit that is very significant that they should have seen two or three more, knowing that the Master was remaining below, and should not have reported these additional rockets to him. That only shows that what they were seeing did not at the time convey to their minds that the rockets were rockets from a vessel in distress.

It is easy for critics who were not there, speaking with the knowledge that comes after the event, to say that these men ought to have attached importance to them at the time. It is very easy to say that, but one must remember that these men were watching the steamer herself. They saw what her movements were, and what she was doing, and the rockets, taken in conjunction with what they saw led them to think that the steamer which they saw was not in distress. And the opinion of men on the spot is generally more reliable and more accurate than the opinion of persons who were not.

The steamer they saw disappearing in the distance as she steamed away to the South-West may or may not have been the steamer which the 4th Officer of the *Titanic* said he saw approaching not answering his Morse signals, and afterwards steaming away. It is significant that the same Witnesses who described the firing of these rockets say that as soon as the vessel which they saw began to fire rockets she at the same time began to steam away to the South-West and steamed away until gradually her lights were lost sight of in the distance. That is the evidence, and the reports made at the time by the 2nd Officer and by Gibson. If that is true the vessel that was firing these rockets cannot have been the *Titanic*, because the *Titanic* at this time was lying stopped, and the fact that they saw this vessel steaming away at the same time as they saw the rockets no doubt was the factor which led them to suppose that the vessel that they saw was not herself in distress, but was going off in answer to some other vessel which was away to the Southward of her."

If that were the case, then where was she in the morning?

It was all a brave and valiant spectacle, and Dunlop's finale dispensed with the discussion of nautical matters, and what was seen, to what the court could legally do with Lord and his fellows. For the previous parts of the address, Mersey and Isaacs had frequently interrupted Dunlop, but these interjections had grown fewer and fewer, and now Lord's representative recounted the possible legal stance in silence. His magniloquent ensued thus:

"Now, my Lord, I want to deal, if I may quite shortly, with the case on the assumption that the vessel which was seen, and whose rockets were seen was the *Titanic*. I am going to ask your Lordship to judge of Captain Lord's conduct by the circumstances as they were present to his mind at the time these events happened ... As a Captain, his first care and duty was the safety of his own vessel, [but] he was not unmindful of the safety of other vessels"; indeed, he had sent his own wireless warnings to ships.

At this point there is a conflict of evidence as to whether the Master was asleep, as he says he was, or was awake, as Gibson says he was. The truth probably lies between the two; the man was half asleep, and in that condition the Master repeated the question which he had put earlier in the evening to the 2nd Officer as to the colour of the rockets ... I am going to submit he put that question because he

could not understand how the steamer which he himself had seen and which was then reported to him to be steaming away to the South-West could be wanting assistance, and the description of her movements, therefore, created a doubt in his mind as to whether they were signals of distress or not, and, therefore, he enquired as to the colour of the rockets. He also asked
what o'clock it was. I venture to think he asked that question because he wanted to know how long
it was before daybreak, in case assistance might be wanted.

The attitude of his mind was this: "If she is steaming away to the South-West, then these are not distress signals and she is not in need of my assistance. If she is lying stopped she may have sustained some damage to her propeller or her rudder. I can do nothing for her until daylight; I am stopped here in the ice and so is she. I will wait till daylight." That appears to have been the attitude of his mind as the result of the communications made to him by the 2nd Officer and by the Apprentice Gibson. In any case, he was entitled to rely on the watch on deck sending for him if they thought there was any need for him to be on deck. They were the judges of the situation, and he was entitled to rely, and did rely, on their judgement.

He was relying upon the 2nd Officer and Gibson, and if any erroneous impression was drawn by these men who were on watch, it was not Captain Lord's fault. He was entitled to rely upon them, and he was lulled into a state of security and unsuspicion by the reports that he got and the way in which those reports were made. He is allowed to continue his sleep and is called at daybreak, in accordance with the orders he had given the night before.

The conduct of Captain Lord that morning was not the conduct of a man who was callous or indifferent to the duties which he owes to humanity. I submit that his inaction was purely the result of ignorance of the conditions that were actually existing some two or three miles away from him on this particular night. He was entirely ignorant of what was going on during the time he was resting in the chart-house. Had he only known, he would have rushed to the *Titanic's* assistance, and no one regrets more than he does that he did not do so, but the remorse for his apparent inactivity during these fatal hours of midnight is relieved by the knowledge that if he had gone to this vessel's assistance when called by Gibson at five minutes past two he could not by any possibility have got to her before the *Carpathia* had herself arrived upon the scene.

There are reasons why, in my submission your Lordship, even although you may take an unfavourable view of Captain Lord's conduct, ought to refrain in your report from censuring him. There are three grounds on which I submit that your Lordship, even although you think that his conduct merits rebuke, ought in your report to refrain from rebuking him. The first ground is, I venture to think, the ground of public policy. I submit it would be a grave mistake to introduce into your report a topic which cannot but affect the prestige of the British Mercantile Marine

174

if the topic is introduced for the purpose of censuring the conduct of Captain Lord. Your Lordship's report will have an international interest and importance. It will be circulated by the press in all foreign countries, or in most foreign countries, and if it contains any censure of the *Californian*, it will put into the hands of foreign critics a weapon of attack on the reputation of the British Mercantile Marine, of which we are very justly proud and jealous. I mention this in order that your Lordship may have present to your mind this aspect of the case, and consider whether it is in the public interest that publicity and advertisement should be given to what has been called the
Californian incident.

"...The Commission was not appointed to enquire into his conduct at all. His conduct had absolutely nothing to do with the objects of this Inquiry as stated by the Attorney-General in his opening speech. There was no jurisdiction to hold any Inquiry into Captain Lord's conduct. Under the Merchant Shipping Act an Inquiry may be held into the conduct of a Master who, after being in collision with another ship unreasonably fails to stand by her or give her his name. But apart from that section there is no power to hold an Inquiry into the conduct of a Master who, after being in unreasonably withheld assistance from a vessel in distress. It is admitted that there is no jurisdiction here to suspend or cancel Captain Lord's certificate. If it has not that jurisdiction, it has no jurisdiction to censure him, because censure is merely ancillary to the jurisdiction which the Court possesses if it has jurisdiction of cancelling or suspending his certificate. Censure is frequently an alternative to the power which the Court has of suspending or cancelling a certificate in a fit case. But if the Court has no jurisdiction to deal with his certificate it cannot have a jurisdiction to express censure on his conduct. Whatever we may think, they are merely opinions which ought not to have the sanction which your Lordship's report would give to the opinions which your Lordship may possibly hold. If the Board of Trade had power to order an Inquiry into Captain Lord's conduct, it did not exercise the power, and it cannot now treat the Inquiry, which was not into his conduct, as if it had been.

Under the Rules which regulate proceedings at these enquiries, if a charge is made against a Master, he must be told what the charge is. That is required by the Merchant Shipping Act, and is also required by the Rules which govern the procedure on these enquiries. The Rules are set out at page 723, and under Rule 3 he must, when an Inquiry is ordered, be served by the Board of Trade with a notice in the form which your Lordship will find on page 729, containing a statement of the questions which, on the information then in possession of the Board of Trade, they intend to raise on the hearing of the investigation, and service of this notice is essential in order to make a Master a party to an Inquiry.

No such notice was given to the Master of the *Californian*.

On the 14th of May, Captain Lord attended here and gave his evidence ... I asked on that occasion to be allowed to appear on behalf of the *Californian* and the

175

Master, and my application was very properly resisted by the Attorney-General and objected to by your Lordship. My application was resisted or certainly not assented to by the Attorney-General, who properly explained that although the evidence showed that rockets were seen by the *Californian*, and the evidence showed that the *Titanic* was not very far from the *Californian*, it was very difficult to say that that evidence had any bearing upon the questions submitted to your Lordship, and, therefore, as the *Californian* was sailing, he proposed to put a few questions to the witnesses. That is, on the 14th of May after the Board of Trade had all the information which they now have bearing on the *Californian* incident. No charge at that time was made against Captain Lord, no intimation was made that any charge would be made, and he was not made a party to the Inquiry. He appeared here in no other capacity than as a Witness to give to the Court such assistance as he could in answering questions which had then been submitted by the Board of Trade for your Lordship to answer. And the capacity in which I appeared is properly stated on the front page of the various records of the day's proceedings "as having watched the proceedings on behalf of the owners and Officers of the *Californian*, as distinct from "appearing on behalf of the *Californian*," which are the words I see opposite more distinguished names. It is not until the 14th of June, a month after Captain Lord has left the witness-box, that an intimation is given that the Board of Trade propose to formulate a question[109] relating to the *Californian*, which would give the Court an opportunity of censuring Captain Lord. It is not my province nor my purpose to criticise the procedure which has been adopted with relation to the *Californian*, but it is manifest from the statement of facts as I have stated them, that Captain Lord has been treated here in a way which is absolutely contrary to the principles on which justice is usually administered, or on which these enquiries are generally conducted.

I respectfully urge the Attorney-General to consider whether this question ought really to be put at all ... it is stated that the object of this question is that the Law Officers of the Crown should get from your Lordship a finding of the facts relating to the *Californian* incident in order to enable them to make up their minds whether, in the public interest, they ought to institute criminal proceedings which may be instituted under Section 6 of the Maritime Convention Act. If that is the object of the question, I submit it is a wholly unfair object. If this man may be prosecuted hereafter, he ought to have had notice of this question before he entered the witness-box; he ought to have known precisely what the charge made against him was, and he ought to have had an opportunity of hearing the evidence given by the other Witnesses before he himself had to give his own evidence.

If you deal with this question, my Lord, and find the facts against Captain Lord, what chance would he have of a fair and impartial trial before a jury which

---

109   Namely, "What vessel had the opportunity of rendering assistance to the "*Titanic*," and, if any, how was it that assistance did not reach the '*Titanic*' before the '*Carpathia*' arrived?"

had read your Lordship's report? If that is the object, my Lord, of this Question, this invitation to your Lordship to find the facts with regard to the *Californian* incident, if the object is with a view to future proceedings, I respectfully and strongly urge that it is a most unfair object. If that is not the object, then I do not know what the object of the question is. If it is not in the public interest that Captain Lord should be charged with a failure to render assistance, then the question ought not to be raised so publicly here in the form of the question which has been submitted to you.

Captain Lord has already been sorely and severely punished for his apparent inactivity during these fatal midnight hours. That inactivity, whichever view your Lordship may take of the facts, is, I venture to submit, an inactivity due to mere thoughtlessness or error of judgement and not to any wilful disregard of duty. He may have relied too much on his 2nd Officer and Gibson, the Apprentice; he may have erroneously drawn a wrong inference from the reports which they made to him. Whatever his conduct was it was conduct due to a want of appreciation of what the real circumstances at that time were, and not to any wilful disregard of duty.

The ordeal of public criticism and public censure, through which he has already passed, will, without further censure, be a sufficient warning to him and to other Masters of the strict duty that lies upon those who go down to the sea in ships of rendering assistance if they can to other vessels in distress. It requires no further rebuke to impress upon Master Mariners the importance of that duty. That counsel should have to appear here to vindicate his reputation and defend his honour is not the least humiliation that this man has had to undergo.

For all the reasons that I have urged, I do ask your Lordship not to pass any censure upon this man, and I venture to think that if your Lordship does not censure him then truth and justice and mercy will meet together in your Lordship's report."

And still the dry legal arguments trundled on. Three days later, they were still being debated during the final sessions of the Inquiry. However, Mersey seemed unclear what his position was with regard to the *Californian* and asked Isaacs to clarify it.

"First of all the view which I take of it is that so far from being desirous of bringing home to the Captain of the *Californian*, or to any of the Officers of the *Californian*, that they saw distress signals and that they took no step after they had seen them, I am most anxious, and have been throughout, to find some possible excuse, for the inaction on the part of the *Californian*. It is not a case of desiring to bring home to them that they did not do their duty; our anxiety and your Lordship's anxiety would be, if possible, to find some reason to explain the failure by them to take any steps when they had seen distress signals. I can only say that to me it is a matter of extreme regret that I have come to the conclusion that the submission I must make to you, is that there is no excuse. Whether I am right or wrong in that is, of course, for your Lordship's consideration ... May I just call your Lordship's attention to the Rules. My submission with regard to it is that by appearing he becomes a party [to the proceedings]. I am not asking your Lordship in any way to deal with this matter, except to state the conclusion of fact to which you arrive."

"Have I any jurisdiction to do more?" asked Mersey.

"I think not. If your Lordship will remember, you put this question to me at an early stage of the *Californian* Inquiry, and the view I took then was the view I take now, and that I submit to you that all we are asking your Lordship to deal with is the conflict of fact that arises upon the evidence, and nothing more ... The facts alleged on the one hand are these, that the *Californian* saw distress signals. As to that there is no conflict. To be quite accurate with regard to it I think one might say that the Captain does not admit that they were distress signals, but he admits that they might have been. That is the exact position. I will show that by reference to one question. Further, that those distress signals came from a vessel in the direction in which the *Titanic* was. That there is no dispute about. The further point is that, having seen the distress signals, the *Californian* took no steps, except to attempt to do Morse signalling with a light. I think that is the position. The comment I make upon it is that for the Master of a British vessel to see distress signals, whether they came from a passenger steamer or not, and whether from a passenger steamer of the size of the *Titanic* or not, is a very serious matter, and because it is a serious matter we have enquired into it very carefully during the course of this investigation; but, having regard to the Inquiry, I think all that your Lordship is asked to do, certainly all that I am asking you to do, is to give the view of the facts which you have formed after hearing all the evidence. I mean by that that suppose your Lordship came to the conclusion that we were right in saying that she did see distress signals and that they were the signals of a passenger steamer of the *Titanic*, and took no steps, that is a finding of fact which I should ask your Lordship to give in the Report which you may make. I do not ask you to do anything more. In point of fact Captain Lord is not summoned before you to answer some attack upon his certificate. That is not the position of matters."

"Let me put it quite plainly: If Captain Lord saw these distress signals and neglected a reasonable opportunity, which he had of going to the relief of the vessel in distress, it may very well be that he is guilty of a misdemeanor. That is so, is it not?"

"Yes, under the Merchant Shipping Act, 1906."

"Am I to try that question?"

"Certainly not."

"I think not."

"Certainly not, my Lord. I never asked and could not ask your Lordship to try that question, but, nevertheless, the facts, which you are asked to find, whether they reflect upon him or not, are material to the Inquiry."

"The facts I can find, but I do not want, unless I am obliged to do it, to find a man guilty of a
crime."

"No, my Lord."

"I do not think I have tried him for any such purpose."

"I agree."

"And, moreover, as you know perfectly well, he might, if he had had any idea that he was going to be tried for a crime, have said when he was in the Witness-box: "I refuse to answer these questions because they may incriminate me.""

"Yes."

"But he did not do that, you know."

If this is the case, then Dunlop had certainly failed to appraise Captain Lord of the gravity of the charges against him and his shipmates, and that answers to the questions posed during the Inquiry may damage his case; but then, he, and the Leyland Line, do not seem to have known of the unfolding hostility levelled at Lord et al. It is not known when Lord knew that he faced questions about his involvement in the *Titanic* matter when he arrived back home in England. He may certainly have known that Gill's story had caused ructions and he might be asked for an explanation when he docked in Liverpool. After arriving at port in England, Lord and his crew (Gill excepted) had just four days before they would attend Mersey's court. There is no reference to Dunlop appraising them of the severity of matters in this time frame: he certainly had not seen the original logbook of the *Californian*. It seems likely that, as Lord's champions would later repeat, the crew of the Californian appeared as witnesses, not as defendants. In this respect, Dunlop seems to have failed. Dunlop's attendance rate was quite poor; he could have posed questions to witnesses on the *Titanic*, *Carpathia* and *Mount Temple* to determine whether certain unidentified lights or steamers were moving or not. This failure culminated when Mersey and Isaacs proposed to introduce a question covering the *Californian* affair into the Inquiry's formal questions. Whether Dunlop could have persuaded Mersey and Isaacs not to do so seems doubtful.

But, if the Leyland Line thought that Lord would not be accused of ignoring a vessel in distress, then why have someone present to represent the *Californian* witnesses? Captain Moore had faced similar accusations in America, but the Canadian Pacific Railway Line did not see fit to providing legal counsel during his London interrogation, which was quite brief. They did ask a Member of Parliament to sit and watch the proceedings, though.

"Different considerations apply, I think," Isaacs continued, "when you are determining whether a crime has been committed, and your Lordship would have to go into questions which certainly, it appears to me, it is unnecessary to find in this case, and which I am not asking you to find in order to determine whether a crime was committed. I will give an indication of what I mean. Supposing he came to a mistaken conclusion with regard to what he saw, clearly there is no crime. Supposing he was careless in coming to that conclusion, there is no crime; but, nevertheless, if you were sitting on another tribunal dealing with the matter from other points of view, you might say, "Well, he ought to have come to the conclusion that these were distress signals from a passenger steamer, and he ought to have gone to the rescue of that vessel." Suppose he, the Captain of the *Californian*, thought that these rockets were distress signals, and that they came from a vessel in distress, apart altogether from whether she was a passenger steamer or not, then you have to consider whether he has any excuse for not going to the assistance of this vessel. Of course there are a number of considerations which you would have to take into account then: Whether he thought he could safely reach her; whether he thought he was running a risk; whether, owing to the fact that he was among ice, and, apparently, according to his evidence, for the first time, that may have formed some explanation of why he did not at once proceed to the assistance of this vessel. All those are questions which no doubt would be very relevant indeed when you are considering whether or not a misdemeanor has been committed. I am not going to ask you to find that at all ... Now, the evidence, which is voluminous, is undoubtedly to some extent very conflicting on some points.

I am not sure that it is possible to reconcile some of these statements that are made, from whatever aspect you look at them. But upon the material points, I submit there is not any real difficulty. The material points are first of all whether the *Californian* saw distress signals. One answer of the Captain it seems to me quite disposes of that."

I do not know whether it will relieve you at all in the trouble you are taking, but I think we are all of opinion that the distress rockets that were seen from the *Californian* were the distress signals of the *Titanic*." replied Mersey, disposing of any pretence of impartiality once and for all.

Isaacs led Mersey through the various points made and testimony given, before reaching his coup de grace: "...After a series of questions we get eventually to Question 6943. "(Q.) Very well, that did not satisfy you? - (A.) It did not satisfy me. (Q.) Then if it was not that, it might have been a distress signal? - (A.) It might have been. (Q.) And you remained in the chart room? - (A.) I remained in the chart room."

Now, my Lord, that establishes quite clearly this, that he thought it might have been, and the moment a man thinks it might have been a distress signal and does not know what else it could be, I should have thought it really means that he knew - I will not say he was quite certain - but he knew at any rate this, that there was a serious possibility of some vessel being in urgent need of assistance close by. It is very difficult to understand. I find it very difficult to understand in reading through all this evidence why it was that in those circumstances he remained in the chart room and took no step. Your Lordship will see what he does. He says he remained there expecting Gibson, the

180

Apprentice, to come down and report. I want to make this comment upon that evidence. It is very
unfortunate, to say the least of it, that there is no entry made in the log of these distress signals."

"It is a most extraordinary thing that no attempt was made to communicate with the *Titanic,*" commented Mersey.

"Quite, the more extraordinary inasmuch as I have certainly understood as the Rule which everybody who goes to sea would never fail to observe, that if you see a vessel in distress you must do your utmost to get to it. I have always understood, certainly amongst sailors, not only in this country, but elsewhere, that that is a Rule of honour from which they do not depart, although they may commit other errors. In this particular case I am unable to find any possible explanation of what happened, except it may be that the Captain of the vessel was in ice for the first time, and would not take the risk of going to the rescue of another vessel which might have got into trouble, as he thought, from proceeding through ice when he himself had stopped. But even that does not explain why they did not call up the wireless operator to ascertain what the condition of things was. We have heard no explanation of it. I think your Lordship is left absolutely in the dark with reference to it. One can only conjecture, and I do not know that it is perhaps quite safe to speculate upon the reasons that made Captain Lord neither come out of his chart room to see what was happening, nor to take any step [to] communicate with the vessel in distress, even such a very slight effort as to have the wireless operator called up.

So far as it throws any light upon this Inquiry I do submit that the answer is to be found in the evidence to which I have already called attention, and that really we get very little assistance by going further into it. That this vessel, the *Californian,* could have got to the *Titanic* and might have got to the *Titanic* in time to save the passengers is, I am afraid, the irresistible conclusion from this evidence. If she was at this distance of 5 to 7 miles, and she could steam 11 knots an hour;
she did steam 11 - she could, in fact, do as much as 13 - even allowing for her having to deviate so as to avoid the ice-field, there still would have been a very considerable opportunity for her to have got there in time, more especially, I think, if you take into account that there must have been some discrepancy between the clocks, or anyhow, the time as given of these events by the Witnesses for the *Californian* ... it still gave her ample time to get there. Of course, the Captain says he was 19 ½ miles away. No human being would suggest that the *Californian* could have seen the sidelights of the *Titanic*, either her red light or her green light at a distance of 19 ½ miles. She must have been within an easy distance in order that her masthead lights and her sidelights were seen, as they were, by the *Californian*.

And, my Lord, I would add to that that the *Californian* is shown to have been seen by the *Titanic*; that in any event the light that was seen so far as we know, according to all enquiries made and according to all the evidence put before you, was the light of the *Californian*. I will not say that all the evidence points irresistibly to that, but I do say this, that if you compare the *Titanic* evidence with the *Californian* it is abundantly plain that the distance between them must have been comparatively small, that is to say certainly within five to seven miles, and could not have been 19 to 20 miles as the Captain of the *Californian* suggests."

Lord Mersey's judgement on the disaster was delivered on July 31[110].

Compared to Senator Smith's oration – labelled by some as 'grotesque' - Lord Mersey's report was issued in simpler, much more restrained language; he too found that the excessive speed of the *Titanic* had contributed to the disaster, and that extra lookouts should have been placed at the stem of the ship; whereas Smith had recommended the use of searchlights, Mersey simply noted that "[they] may at times be of service. The evidence before the Court does not allow of a more precise answer." Differing with his counterpart in the United States, the British Wreck Commissioner found that proper discipline had been maintained during the sinking. Regarding the lifeboats, he determined that "some of them were possibly undermanned. The evidence on this point was unsatisfactory. The total number of crew taken on board the *Carpathia* exceeded the number which would be required for manning the boats." He also concurred with the Senator; "if the boats had been kept a little longer before being lowered, or if the after gangway doors had been opened, more passengers might have been induced to enter the boats. And if women could not be induced to enter the boats, the boats ought to then to have been filled up with men. It is difficult to account for so many of the lifeboats being sent from the sinking ship, in a smooth sea, far from full. These boats left behind them many hundreds of lives to perish. I do not, however, desire these observations to be read as casting any reflection on the officers of the ship or on the crew who were working on the boat deck. They all worked admirably, but I think that if there had been better organisation the results would have been more satisfactory "

Mersey found that Captain Smith had not been negligent (even if the ice warnings had played no major part in the navigation of his ship) as running a ship at speed into an ice infested area was common practise. Reliance on a good look-out had enabled danger to be avoided, and this had resulted in no casualties. At least until April 15th, 1912. Mersey reported, "What was a mistake in the case of the *Titanic* would without doubt be negligence in any similar case in the future."

What both Senator Smith and Lord Mersey *did* agree upon was that the total boat capacity should reflect the number of people carried, and not upon the

---

110   Ironically, Captain Lord's greatest ally, Leslie Harrison was born on this same day!

size of the ship.

Another matter that both men agreed upon was the *Californian*.

Mersey's pronouncements on Lord and his crew were unsurprising as they simply reflected his opinions that he interjected during the process of gathering testimony. In his report, Mersey summarised the *Californian* incident based on the mass of evidence he had heard. But when it came to the overnight position of the *Californian*, Mersey could do no more than issue the blunt, and very bald, statement, "I am satisfied that this position is not accurate," with no hint of justification. He also omitted Stone and Gibson's evidence of seeing rockets after 3a.m. This in itself is a puzzle as he could have gained further capital at Captain Lord's expense by noting that the *Carpathia*'s rockets, fired at about this time, were emitted from a further, and lower base, and that the *Californian* watch officers had done nothing about these new rockets either – they certainly had not roused their Captain from his slumber.

Mersey told the court, "There are contradictions and inconsistencies in the story as told by the different witnesses. But the truth of the matter is plain. The *Titanic* collided with the berg at 11.40. The vessel seen by the *Californian* stopped at this time. The rockets sent up from the *Titanic* were distress signals. The *Californian* saw distress signals. The number sent up by the *Titanic* was about eight. The *Californian* saw eight. The time over which the rockets from the *Titanic* were sent up was from about 12.45 to 1.45 o'clock. It was about this time that the *Californian* saw the rockets. At 2.40 Mr. Stone called to the Master that the ship from which he'd seen the rockets had disappeared.[111]

At 2.20 a.m. the *Titanic* had foundered. It was suggested that the rockets seen by the *Californian* were from some other ship, not the *Titanic*. But no other ship to fit this theory has ever been heard of.

These circumstances convince me that the ship seen by the *Californian* was the *Titanic*, and if so, according to Captain Lord, the two vessels were about five miles apart at the time of the disaster. The evidence from the *Titanic* corroborates this estimate, but I am advised that the distance was probably greater, though not more than eight to ten miles. The ice by which the *Californian* was surrounded was loose ice extending for a distance of not more than two or three miles in the direction of the *Titanic*.[112] The night was clear and the sea was smooth. When she first saw the rockets the *Californian* could have pushed through the ice to the open water without any serious risk and so have come to the assistance of the *Titanic*.

---

111   This is a simplification of the evidence. The witnesses who saw the rockets did not describe them as distress rockets; Mersey and Isaacs were the ones who added the 'distress' qualifier. And the *Californian*, if one combines the statements of Stone and Gibson, actually saw eleven rockets, albeit the last three could only have come from the *Carpathia*.

112   How did he know this? It contradicts evidence given by the witnesses, and, though he could not have known it at the time, a statement that Stone made to Lord on April 18th, was to resurface nearly five decades later.

Had she done so she might have saved many if not all of the lives that were lost."

Mersey had two further points to make. His list of questions, amended to include any neglect on the part of any vessels, was answered:

"24. (a.)What was the cause of the loss of the *Titanic*, and of the loss of life which thereby ensued or occurred? (b.) What vessels had the opportunity of rendering assistance to the *Titanic* and, if any, how was it that assistance did not reach the *Titanic* before the ss. *Carpathia* arrived? (c.) Was the construction of the vessel and its arrangements such as to make it difficult for any class of passenger or any portion of the crew to take full advantage of any the existing provisions for safety?

Answer:

(a.) Collision with an iceberg and the subsequent foundering of the ship.

(b.) The *Californian*. She could have reached the *Titanic* if she had made the attempt when she saw the first rocket. She made no attempt.

(c.) No."

And his list of recommendations also dealt with ships in distress;

"22. That the attention of Masters of vessels should be drawn by the Board of Trade to the effect that under the Maritime Conventions Act, 1911, it is a misdemeanor not to go to the relief of a vessel in distress when possible to do so."

This recommendation was issued as handbill no.310, which was issued to the Masters of vessels, reminding them that "if they fail in carrying out their duty [in attempting a rescue] they render themselves liable ... to punishment ... by fine or imprisonment for two years with or without hard labour."

The day after Mersey's pronounced his verdict, Sydney Buxton, the President of the Board of Trade issued a memorandum to his staff asking whether "it is desirable, or practicable, to institute proceedings against Captain Lord."

The Board's Solicitor, Sir R. Ellis Cunliffe replied immediately that "Captain Lord gave his version of what happened in the Witness box here and in America, he might have taken the objection that he declined to reply lest he should incriminate himself; he did not do so and though the Wreck Commissioner did not accept his views explanation or excuses I would not advise a prosecution of Captn. Lord under Sec 6 of the above Act [the 1911 Maritime Conventions Act] under the circumstance. I need hardly add that his punishment is already very great. Moreover he was in ice and stopped by the Ice to a certain extent for I believe the 1st time."

Now information favourable to Lord was forthcoming, for Captain Rostron had sworn an affidavit in New York on 4th June detailing what he had seen. He was

184

asked about this at the British Inquiry:

Q 25551: Did you say then: "I approached the position of the *Titanic* 41.46N 50.14W on a course substantially N 52 W (true) reaching the first boat shortly after 4:00 am. It was daylight at about 4:20 am. At 5 o'clock it was light enough to see all around the horizon. We then saw two steamships to the northwards, perhaps seven or eight miles distant. Neither of them was the *Californian*. One of them was a four-masted steamer with one funnel, and the other a two-masted steamer with one funnel. I never saw the *Mount Temple* to identify her. The first time that I saw the *Californian* was at about eight o'clock on the morning of 15th April. She was then about five to six miles distant, bearing WSW true, and steaming towards the *Carpathia*. The *Carpathia* was then in substantially the position of the *Titanic* at the time of the disaster as given to us by wireless. I consider the position of the Titanic as given to us by her officers, to be correct." You swore to that? - Yes.

Obviously this aroused Lord's interest. Replying to a letter from him, a sympathetic Rostron wrote, on September 5th, 1912: "I'm sorry I cannot give you any detailed description of the two steamers seen by me. All I know – one, a four-masted one funnel steamer dodging about, I suppose amongst the ice to the north; the other, two masts and one funnel coming from W to E straight on his course[113]. I did not see the colour of the funnels, or notice anything which might distinguish either. You can imagine, I was quite busy enough.

Can't you get your position when stopped and get approx courses you steered, with speed, to where we met? I'll do what I can, but you know I can only say what I know and what I saw, and 'pon my word, it isn't much and I'm sorry too. If you can suggest anything I should be happy to help you, but you see I know so little and have said all I really do know, too"

Sadly, Lord's reply does not seem to have survived, but Rostron wrote back to Lord on November 6th. Part of his letter dealt with the actions of the *Mount Temple*: "Could you find out if he was dodging about somewhere about 5.30 or 6am – I certainly saw '*the*' [emphasis in original] steamer turning and dodging about that time, and if a 2 masted one funnel steamer passed them about 6 to 6.30a.m coming from the westward." Rostron suggested putting the allegations to Captain Moore: "I certainly would 'clear' myself if I were you – even at the expense of [the] *Mount Temple* man – who doesn't seem to have behaved very nicely."

Diverting from our narrative temporarily, on August 10th, Captain Lord

---

113   This ship is marked on the Foweraker chart (see later). However, Groves, who noticed the black and white funnel ship, observed that she was beyond the *Mount Temple*, that is, to the south of her, and not to the west as Rostron declares in this letter.

wrote to Sir Walter J. Howell, Assistant Secretary of the Marine Department of the Board of Trade. Lord's situation had deteriorated. Until now, he had been on paid leave with monthly bonus, and he reported each day at noon to Leyland's head office, "as was the custom among unattached masters."

But on, or about August 2nd, Lord was informed by Captain Fry that Mr. Roper, the managing director of Leyland, could not give him another ship. This was a shock to Lord, as he had "been given" to understand that he would be given command of the Californian again. Despite the short notice, Lord was allowed to see Roper, who said, "Its none of our doing – it's been taken out of our hands altogether. It's strongly against my wishes. Our intention was to put you back in the ship, but the directors in London have decided that public opinion is against you and you must resign. We have no say in the matter."

It transpired that Sir Miles Walker Mattinson, KC, one of the Leyland Line's Board of Directors had been the one opponent to Lord's reinstatement, as he had threatened to resign if Lord remained in the company. Mattinson was a powerful figure in British shipping, and his ultimatum forced Leyland's hand.

Lord's letter to the Board read:

"With reference to Lord Mersey's report on the *Titanic* disaster, he states that the *Californian* was 8 to 10 miles from the scene of the disaster.

I respectfully request you will allow my as Master of the *Californian* to give you a few facts which proves she was the distance away that I gave of 17 to 19 miles. April 14, 6:30 pm, I sent my position to the *Antillian* and *Titanic*, this gives me 17 miles away, and you will see it was sent some hours before the disaster. April 15 about 6:30 am gave my position to S.S *Virginian* before I heard where the *Titanic* sunk, that also gave me 17[114] away. I understand the Marconigrams were in Court.

The evidence of Mr. Boxhall of the *Titanic* who was watching the steamer had in [his] view, states that she approached them between one and two am [sic], the *Californian* was stopped from 10:30 pm to 5:15 am [the] next day.

The steamer seen from the *Californian* was plainly in view from 11:30 pm [sic] the one seen by the Titanic was not, according to her lookout men [sic] seen until 00:30 am.

Capt. Rostron of the *Carpathia* states when at the scene of the disaster: "It was daylight at 4:30 am I could see all around the horizon, about 8 miles North of me (this was the direction the *Californian* was) there were two steamers, neither of these was the *Californian*." Had the *Californian* been within 10 miles from the Titanic she would have been in sight at this time from the *Carpathia*, as she was in the same position[115] as when stopped at 10:30 pm the previous evening.

---

114   Readers will presently note that, at about this time in the morning, another ship (the *Birma*) placed her 15 miles away. In Washington, Lord placed this wireless message at 6a.m. The *Virginian's* messages will be discussed in due course.

115   Again, Lord is neglecting to mention drift.

With regard to my own conduct on the night in question, I should like to add a little more. I had taken every precaution for the safety of my own ship, and left her in charge of a responsible officer at 00:40 am with instructions to call me if he wanted anything, and I lay down fully dressed. At 1:15 am (25 minutes after he had seen the first signal) the officer on watch reported the steamer we had in sight was altering her bearing, in other words was steaming away, and had fired a rocket. I did not anticipate any disaster to a vessel that had been stopped nearly for an hour, and had ignored my Morse signals, and was then steaming away. I asked him was it a Company's signal, and to signal her and let me know the result. It is a matter of great regret to me that I did not go on deck myself at this time, but I didn't think it possible for any seaman to mistake a Company's signal for a distress signal, so I relied on the officer on watch. Although further signals were seen between 1:15 am and 2:00 am, I was not notified until 2:00 am, and then I had fallen into a sound sleep, and whatever message was sent to me then, I was not sufficiently awake to understand, and it was sufficient indication to anyone that I had not realized the message, by the fact that I still remained below, curiosity to see a vessel pushing through the ice would have taken me on deck. The message sent to me at 2:00 am was, I heard later, to the effect that the steamer we had in sight at 11:30 pm, had altered her bearing from SSE to SW ½ W (to do this she must have steamed at least 8 miles, the *Titanic* did not move after midnight) and had fired eight rockets, and was then out of sight.

The question of 'drink' has been raised as the reason I could not be roused. I don't drink, and never have done.

Further signals were seen after 2:00 am, but the officer was so little concerned about them, that he did not think it necessary to notify me. I was called by the Chief Officer at 4:20 am, and in conversation he referred to the rockets seen by the 2nd Officer. I immediately had the wireless operator called, heard of the disaster, and proceeded at once, pushing through field ice to the scene, and I would have done the same earlier had I understood, as I had everything to gain and nothing to lose[116].

There is the conversation between the 2nd Officer and the Apprentice while watching the vessel, that they thought she was a tramp steamer, this is their opinion at the time, which is most likely the correct one.

My employers, the Leyland Line, although their nautical advisers are convinced we did not see the *Titanic*, or the *Titanic* see the *Californian*, say they have the utmost confidence in me, and do not blame me in any way, but owing to Lord Mersey's decision and public opinion caused by this report, they are reluctantly compelled to ask for my resignation, after 14 ½ years' service without a hitch of any description, and if I could clear myself of this charge, would willingly reconsider their decision.

---

116   Perhaps salvage rights, or the personal glory of effecting a rescue of the *Titanic* survivors?

If you consider there was any laxity aboard the *Californian* the night in question, I respectfully draw your attention to the information given here, which was given in evidence, which also proves it was not on my part[117].

I am told that at the Inquiry I was a very poor witness, this I don't dispute, but I fail to see why I should have to put up with all the public odium, through no fault or neglect on my part, and I respectfully request you will be able to do something to put my conduct on the night in question, in a more favourable light, to my employers and the general public."

And, in further communication with the Board, Captain Lord also provided copies of the letters from Rostron to the Board of Trade as he battled to clear his name.

In an effort, one feels, to garner support from his fellow seafarers, Lord also wrote to the seafarer's union, the M.M.S.A. (Mercantile Marine Service Association) of which he had been a member for 15 years. His letter, dated August 14th, appeared in their '*Reporter*' magazine and repeats essentially the same information as his letter to the Board of Trade. The letter opens, " The issue of the Report of the Court, presided over by Lord Mersey, to inquire into the loss of the *Titanic*, ends a compulsory silence on my part on points raised in the course of the proceedings which affect me as the last Master of the steamer *Californian*, and it is a duty I owe to myself and my reputation as a British shipmaster, to do what I have hitherto been prevented from doing, for obvious reasons, in giving publicity to circumstances which the Inquiry failed to elicit, and at the same time to show that the deductions which have been drawn, reflecting upon my personal character as a seaman, are entirely unfounded."

Lord reiterates that he had "no recollection of receiving, and subsequent events were not regarded by the officers so seriously as to induce them to take energetic means of ensuring my cognizance of happenings, which should, and would, most assuredly have had my most earnest attention. I did not hear of the disaster until daylight, <u>and that only after it was deemed safe for my steamer to proceed</u>." [This author's emphasis].

"The evidence is conclusive that none of the responsible officers of the *Californian* were aware of the serious calamity which had taken place. That any seaman would wilfully neglect signals of distress is preposterous and unthinkable – there was everything to gain and nothing to lose. The failure to adopt energetic means of making me aware of the gravity of the signals is conclusive of the fact that my officers did not attach any significance to their appearance.

The absence of any reply to the succession of Morse signals made from the bridge of the *Californian* is further evidence which is entitled to some consideration.

When I asked the 2nd Officer the next day why he had not used more

---

117   As master of the vessel, surely Lord should have accepted responsibility for the conduct of his crew? Was he trying to "pass the buck" onto Stone?

energy in calling me, and insisted on my coming on deck at once, he replied, "If the signals had been distress signals, he would have done so, but as the steamer was steaming away, he concluded there was not much wrong with her." He was the man on the spot – the only officer who saw the signals, so I think I was justified in relying upon his judgement, which ought to carry some weight.

My position at the Inquiry was that of a witness only, and a nautical man rarely makes a good witness.

I trust this lengthy explanation, which I ought to have made earlier, but for various reasons could not, will be the means of removing the undeserved stigma which rests upon me, and through me, upon an honourable profession."

Following the receipt of Captain Lord's letter by the Board, an initial thought to send a copy to Lord Mersey was vetoed. Howell wrote to Buxton, then on holiday, that "Lord Mersey and his court have delivered their judgement, and there is an end of the matter as far as they are concerned. I think if you communicated anything now, whether from Capt. Lord or anyone else concerned, it might be misunderstood, and would create a bad precedent." Buxton concurred. On August 29th, Lord received a reply: "...all the circumstances attending the casualty have formed the subject of a searching investigation by a Court of Inquiry, the Board of Trade would not feel justified in taking any steps with regard to our present statement."

Hypothetically, if Captain Lord had managed to re-open the Inquiry, perhaps by invoking Rostron's affidavit as "new and important evidence," then his problems would not have dematerialised. The Merchant Shipping Act 1894 (475) (2) states that "The Board of Trade may order the case to be re-heard, either by the court or authority by whom the case was heard in the first instance, or by the wreck commissioner, or in England or Ireland by the High Court." This could have meant facing Lord Mersey, and his immovable opinion, again!

Captain Young, the Professional Member of the Board of Trade's Marine Department agreed that no further action against Lord was necessary. But 16 days later, he circulated another note, in which he stated that he "was not aware until the 13th ultimo that it had been decided not to proceed against Capt. Lord, but I have had the opinion from the first that a special Inquiry should have been ordered not only as to his neglect to answer to Distress signals, but also as a consequence of such almost inexplicable neglect, into his competency to continue to act as a master of a British ship." But since the President of the Board have decided not to proceed in the matter, Captain Young felt that he could offer no further observations. The consensus was that Lord's "fault carried its own punishment" which was "already real and very heavy."

Under the Merchant Shipping Act 1894 470 (1), the Board of Trade could cancel or suspend the certificate of a master, mate or engineer "if the court find that the loss or abandonment of, or serious damage to, any ship, or loss of life, has been caused by his wrongful act or default, provided that, if the court holding a formal investigation is a court of summary jurisdiction, that court shall not cancel or suspend a certificate unless one at least of the assessors concurs in the finding of the court" or "[if a court finds] that he is incompetent, or has been guilty of any gross act of misconduct, drunkenness, or tyranny." Section 471 (1) also remarks that "If the Board of Trade, either on the report of a local marine board or otherwise, have reason to believe that any master, officer, mate, or certificated engineer is from incompetency or misconduct unfit to discharge his duties ... the Board may cause an Inquiry to he held." Clearly, this could be a description of Mersey's investigation, but for two things: contrary to 470 (1), the Inquiry was not "a court of summary jurisdiction" and hence lacked the power to suspend or cancel Captain Lord's certificate – or anyone else's for that matter. Secondly, and more importantly, 470 (3)(c) says that "[Where the Inquiry is held by a local marine board, or by a person appointed by the Board of Trade, that board or person they] shall give any master, mate, or engineer against whom a charge is made an opportunity of making his defence either in person or otherwise, and may summon him to appear." This contradicts the treatment that Captain Lord was afforded in London[118].

Could Captain Lord have been prosecuted? Certainly, as his (in)action was covered by the Maritime Conventions Act 1911, that a master must assist a vessel in distress if it is deemed safe to do so. At a subsequent Inquiry, Lord could have argued that the ice field made it impossible for him to afford an attempted rescue of any vessel. He could, ironically, have cited the *Titanic* herself as an example of the danger of ice in the proximity. He could also have mentioned ships such as the *Niagara* and the Leyland Line's own *Armenian* as vessels that had put in port suffering damage by the floes. Or, he could refer to the *Kildonan* and the *Kamfjord*, lost at sea and never seen again, suspected victims of the ice. But could Lord claim these in his defence retrospectively? Without the evidence of the *Californian*'s PV, we shall never know whether he received any reports of damaged or lost vessels which may have affected his opinion not to cross the ice at night, or indeed, move until morning. Lord certainly never mentioned such reports in his testimonies. As such, any information gathered 'after the fact' could be rendered moot. The ice might have made it too difficult to proceed on any putative rescue mission, but Lord did not even attempt to do so. He did not even come on deck to espy the rockets.

But could – or should - Lord be prosecuted either for "gross act of misconduct" or should his master's certificate be forfeited because of "incompetence or misconduct unfit to discharge his duties"? The Board seemed to be worried of a public outcry if Lord was allowed to go "scot free", and if they were later seen to act in far less certain cases. The Assistant Solicitor of the Board, Mr. E. Potter, was asked for his views: "The most that the Court could find that was that lives might have been saved if the *Californian* had gone to the rescue earlier.

---

118   This point has been made many times; see chapter 8 for instance.

They could not find as a certainty that lives would have been saved. The Inquiry was into the loss of the *Titanic* and loss of life from her. The Court could not find that the loss of the *Titanic* and the loss of life from her was caused by 'the wrongful act or default' of Captain Lord ... and there was therefore in my opinion no power to deal with his certificate. It seems to me to be very doubtful whether the conduct of Captain Lord comes within the contemplated meaning of the words 'misconduct rendering him unfit to discharge his duties' ... but apart from that to prove that Captain Lord had been guilty of 'a gross act of misconduct' it would be necessary to show that he had knowledge of the events, was a free agent, and notwithstanding this, acted or refrained from acting deliberately, and I do not think this could be done on the evidence given at the Inquiry before the Wreck Commissioner."

From a reading of Potter's memo, it seems – to this author anyway – that the Board was weary of the whole *Titanic* matter, and seemed disinclined to dredge up the matter again, for a prosecution could have been possible, if one bears in mind the internationally agreed usage of distress signals at night, they matched exactly what Stone and Gibson had informed the Captain.. Such a prosecution could have determined definitely whether any lives could have been saved. But, as one writer notes many years later, "the general opinion leaned towards mercy." Captain Lord, his heavy punishment being the weight of public opinion and the fact that his employers had freed themselves of him, was let off "scot free." And there the matter rested.

There is another reason why such a prosecution might have failed and was not attempted. Lord's censure in the final report, the barbed comments by Mersey, and the modification of the original Board of Trade questions to cover the *Californian* (where neither the Captain nor his counsel were informed of such a decision), were done in a way that was hardly compatible with the law at the time, which provided some measure of protection to a witness. At any subsequent trial or Inquiry, Stanley Lord's counsel could have argued that Mersey's report could be prejudicial to a fair trial; as such, any legal attack on Lord could have been quashed. This would have no doubt resulted in some rebuke against Lord Mersey by any presiding trial judge – much to the embarrassment of not only Mersey but also the Board of Trade, and perhaps the British Government. But this is conjecture.

To their (belated) credit, there is one matter that the Board did judge firmly upon. The ever-helpful *"Lloyd's Weekly Shipping Index"* reports, in its 12th September 1912 issue that "[the Board has announced] that private signals containing rockets [involving] a possibility of confusion with the distress signal rockets [and that the Board has] arranged for the discontinuance of the only private signals containing rockets at present registered by them..." The companies that had agreed to alter their night-time communication signals (all of which were registered to be used only near the UK or Irish coast) were the Allan Line, the Cunard Line and the International Navigation Company Ltd. Presumably this ruling was later imposed upon other rocket firers; for instance, the White Star Line itself.

But Captain Lord was unaware of the legal discussions behind closed doors. He regarded Captain Rostron's affidavit and letters as proof that his ship was nowhere near the wreck site; the navigational details contained in Rostron's documents are admittedly fascinating. In New York Rostron mentioned noticing these two steamers at 5.00am, but later on moves the time to 6.00am. This latter time is interesting, as it was when the *Californian* started moving through the ice. It has been asserted[119] that the two masted steamer was the *Almerian*, and the four masted one was the *Mount Temple*. But there is one important aspect that is overlooked: Rostron saw the four masted steamer dodging about in the ice. The *Mount Temple* never entered the ice field. Indeed, Captain Moore stated in Washington, "We are not to enter field ice under any conditions," although admittedly Groves did first notice the *Mount Temple* "in the ice", although this was in loose ice to the west of the main field. Sam Halpern, in part 2 of his excellent "*Lights On The Horizon*"[120] suggests that this 4 masted steamer "dodging about" is the *Mount Temple* because at 3.25am New York Time (5.11am local time on the *Mount Temple*), Captain Moore had stopped his ship – 14 miles away from the Titanic's (incorrect) CQD location if his estimate is correct. Moore then "went slowly to avoid the ice, because it was too dark to proceed full speed on account of the ice," reaching the Titanic's incorrect position at 4.30 am. Wireless operator Durrant writes in his log "3.00. All quiet. We are stopped amongst pack ice ... 3.20. *Birma* and *Frankfurt* working. We back out of ice and cruise around. Large bergs about. " The local times of these events would be 4.46 and 5.04am. It seems unlikely that a ship that stopped, reversed and then steamed slowly on could be mistaken for a ship that was "turning and dodging". Furthermore, if Moore's estimate of distance is correct, then at 3.25am, he was 14 miles to the south-west of the CQD, and the *Carpathia* would be some 13 miles to the east further still of this location, roughly where the *Titanic* did indeed sink. The distance between these two ships would be so great as to prevent either ship noticing the other. In the sketch map (below), if these estimates are correct, at 5.11 am *Mount Temple* time, the distance would be about 18 miles. The *Mount Temple* would be to the west, not the north.

---

119   For example, in "*A Titanic Myth*"
120   *Titanic Historical Society Commutator,* issue 178

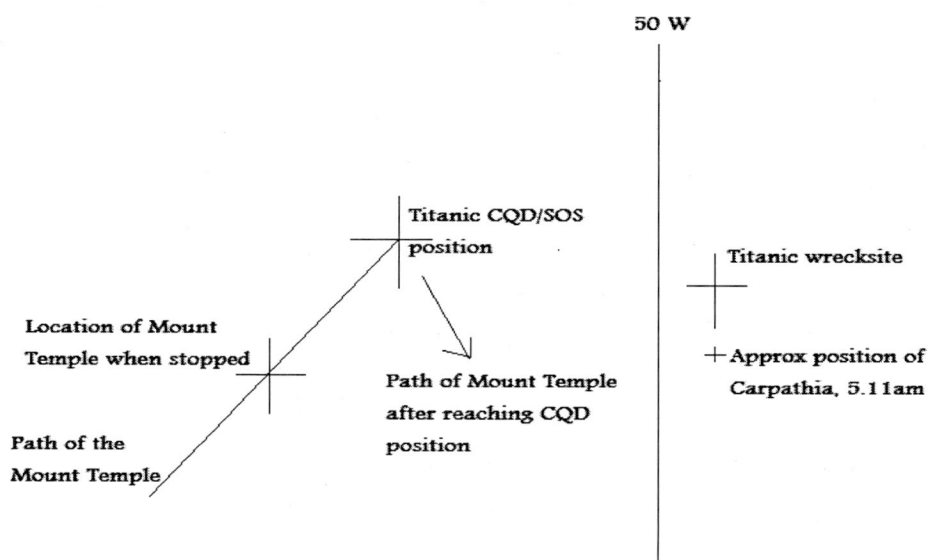

50 W

Titanic CQD/SOS position

Titanic wrecksite

Location of Mount Temple when stopped

Path of Mount Temple after reaching CQD position

+Approx position of Carpathia, 5.11am

Path of the Mount Temple

Illustration 24: The Mount Temple's Movements based on the Testimony of Captain Moore

After reaching the SOS position at about 4.30a.m, the *Mount Temple* proceeded to the SSE looking for clear passage to the east. Not finding it, she turned around at about 5 or 5.30am and headed north along the eastern edge of the ice field. If she was at the *Titanic*'s longitude at 4.30am, then she must have been further south when she turned around. In other words, heading the wrong way and getting further away at 4.30am. The *Californian*'s yellow-funnel ship was in sight at all times between the time of Stewart relieving Stone and the *Californian* receiving the first news of the *Titanic*. Then, she seems to fade from the story. If the *Californian*'s officers were viewing the *Mount Temple* at 5.15am, or earlier, then she must have seen the *Carpathia,* which would have been somewhere to the South-East at the time.

Also, if commentators of this case are correct and the *Mount Temple* was the ship seen 8 miles to the South-West at 4.30 am, then the *Californian*, based on simple geometry, would only have been 13 miles to the North-West of the *Carpathia.* She would be easily seen; most of the hull, superstructure, funnels, masts, smoke, and all her lights lit. Why was she not seen? The simple explanation is that this yellow funnel ship at 4.30 was not the *Mount Temple.*

Captain Lord indirectly agreed with this identification. He gave an interview to *The Savannah Morning News* in 1914 which repeated most of his observations two years earlier, with one interesting addition: "While proceeding in [a southerly direction down the western edge of the icefield] we passed the 4

193

masted steamer with yellow funnel across the ice field to the east of us, considerably nearer the *Titanic*'s position than we had been all night. Passing this steamer and proceeding south, we next passed the steamer *Mount Temple*, lying stopped on the western edge of the icefield in sight of the *Carpathia*, also the small Leyland Line steamer *Almerian* which had no wireless and had just arrived on the scene." It is clear that Lord regarded the yellow funnel vessel and the *Mount Temple* to be two separate ships. No other ship in the area reported this strange yellow funnel ship. Robertson Dunlop's closing remarks in London may also be pertinent here: "At 7.30 [Lord] passed a vessel blocked in the ice. He thought at the time it was the *Mount Temple*. It is quite clear now, from the evidence given by the Master of the *Mount Temple*, that the *Mount Temple* was a good deal further to the Southward, and, therefore, the vessel he saw stopped in the ice must have been some vessel other than the *Mount Temple*. But that is what he sees at 7.30, a vessel which although comparatively near the scene of the tragedy is herself so involved in ice that she is unable to force a passage through it. " Another mystery ship that no-one else noticed? Or was this the yellow-funnel ship? It seems unlikely as Lord never mentioned this fact in the aforementioned newspaper interview. Then there is the problem of where Lord saw this ship. In Washington, it was described as being in the south-west; in London, it was more southerly; and in his 1959 Affidavit, it was SSE[121]. One cannot help but feel that the location of this ship was placed wherever was convenient. Then, how does one reconcile Lord's "8 miles to the south-west" description with the other ship being on the eastern side of the icefield? The following sketch may be instructive, showing the *Californian* half a mile from the ice field, with a thickness of some three miles which was traversed between 6 and 6.30am:

The other ship can appear on the eastern side of the ice if it followed a south-westerly direction too. But no-one else reported such a configuration of the field. It also does not relate very well to Captain Moore's longitude of the *Mount Temple* at about 7.00am, when he was on the western side of the ice. According to the sketch, he would have been well to the east of it, unless the field had a peculiar dog-leg that took it back towards the south east: a feature not reported by anyone. Proponents of Lord's navigation may argue that, between 4.30am and 7.00am, the ice field may have drifted to the east, moving the yellow funnel steamer from the south west to about south, and enabling the *Mount Temple* to be on the west of the ice. But again, there is no evidence to back up such a relatively strong easterly current.

Then there is the problem of heading. In London, Stone testified that, although he couldn't see the "yellow funnel ship's" sidelights, he could tell she was heading in the same direction as the *Californian* – that is, roughly westerly, perhaps north-westerly. He probably managed this by looking at the relative heights of the mast lights on the other ship. Although Stone was obviously not the most diligent

---

121   See http://home.earthlink.net/~dnitzer/6Affidavits/YellowFunnelBoat.html

watch officer (he missed this new arrival on the scene until Stewart pointed it out to him[122]), if his observation of the other ship's heading was correct, then this rules out the *Mount Temple*, which was heading north-east, and then south east at about this time. The only ship in the area which was heading in a westerly direction was the *Carpathia*. And if this is the case, then the *Californian* had been within spitting distance of the *Titanic* disaster at all times. It also means that the Stewart lied when he gave testimony about seeing a yellow funnel.

This makes the identification of the *Mount Temple* as the yellow-funnel ship hazy, and as already demonstrated, the *Almerian's* presence in the area is hardly definite. Finally, does "to the north" mean exactly north, or north-westerly?

Regarding Rostron's statement that "[neither of the steamers] was the *Californian*," we shall return to this later. We must bear in mind that the "dodging and turning" movements witnessed by Rostron fit the *Californian's* movements at this time perfectly.

If we dismiss the *Almerian's* evidence, then this leaves the two masted steamer, seen by Rostron. When Groves saw a black funnelled ship, at apparently 6.50am according to his evidence, he remarked that it "was coming down almost end on", not coming from the westward but from nearly ahead: that is to the south, beyond the *Mount Temple*. There is no mention of how many masts this ship had. It is likely that this ship was the mystery vessel under observation by Moore for hours.

Mention of the *Mount Temple* brings us to conveniently to another interesting point in this story. In August, Captain Lord received a letter from W.H. Baker, who had written from on board the Canadian Pacific Liner *Empress of Britain*, at Quebec. Although Baker was a stranger to Lord, the writer was sure he had met the Captain on the HMS *Conway*, a training ship, a detail that is incorrect.

W.H. Baker was sorry for how Lord had suffered because of the *Titanic*, but had valuable information that might help his case:

"I came home in the *Mount Temple* from Halifax that voyage [i.e. Immediately after the *Titanic* disaster], having been taken out of the Empress at ten minutes' notice to fill up a vacancy, as one of her officers had been given a shore billet on her arrival in Halifax, homeward bound. The officers and others told me what they had seen on the eventful night when the *Titanic* went down, and from what they said, they were from ten to fourteen miles away from her when they saw her signals. I gather from what was told me that the Captain seemed afraid to go through the ice, although it was not so very thick. They told me that they not only saw her decklights but several green lights between them and what they thought was the *Titanic*. There were two loud reports heard, which they said must have been the 'finale' of the *Titanic*; this was sometime after sighting her, I gathered. The Captain said at the Inquiry in Washington that he was 49 miles away – but the officers state that he was no more than fourteen miles off. I must tell you that these

---

122   Or possibly the ship had just arrived on the scene, like the *Carpathia* had

men were fearfully indignant that they were not then called upon to give evidence at the time, for they were greatly incensed at the Captain's behaviour in the matter. The doctor had made all preparations and rooms were turned into hospitals, etc., and the crew were standing by ready to help, on deck, watching her lights and what they said were the green lights burnt in the boats. On our arrival at Gravesend the Captain and Marconi operator were sent for, also the two logs books, scrap and Chief Officer's. What they wanted with the scrap log I cannot understand, for there was only about a line and a half within of what occurred during the four hours, and quite half a page in the chief's book! I saw this myself. These fellows must feel sorry for you, knowing that you could not, in the face of this, have been the mystery ship."

If this letter were indeed true, what can we make of it? We know that green flares were not fired from the lifeboats until after the *Titanic* had sunk. Captain Moore had testified to seeing one green light, but he thought this was on a schooner, and was seen well after the *Titanic* had sunk. Could the 'two loud reports' be the sound of the rockets, either the *Titanic*'s or the *Carpathia*'s, detonating? Doubtful, as the report of the rockets was not heard by everyone in the lifeboats, which were obviously closer to the source of detonation than the *Mount Temple*. Or could the sounds be the loud reports of the *Titanic* breaking apart, mistaken by many survivors as boiler explosions?

How should Captain Lord respond to this information? He informed the secretary of the M.M.S.A., C.P. Grylls who replied that Lord should send it to the Board of Trade. This was done, in a letter marked 'private and confidential' in late August. Grylls' letter submitted to the Board suggested that there were "strong grounds" for concluding that the lights seen from the *Titanic* were those of the *Mount Temple*, and recommended that statements be taken from Chief Officer Seargent [sic], 2nd Officer Heild [sic], 4th Officer Thompson, Chief Officer Gillette and Dr. Roberts (surgeon) and any other witnesses when they arrived back in London: "The only witnesses called from the *Mount Temple* were the Captain and the Marconi Operator. Had the officers of that vessel been called we are informed that they would have given some remarkable evidence as to having seen the distress signals, the lights of the boats of the *Titanic* and the ship herself. Knowing by wireless the *Titanic*'s predicament, the officers were exceedingly anxious to go to her assistance, and this feeling against the Master of the ship because he could not do so at once was very strong, so much so that it is stated they refused to sit at the head of the dining table with him... I am told that one of the officers was so outspoken in his condemnation of the inaction of the Captain, that he has been transferred to an appointment in the Owner's service in Canada."

Grylls' letter contains a wealth of detail not found in Baker's letter. Had Grylls been performing some independent inquiries? We shall probably never know.

A week later the Board replied that it could hardly take action on a letter marked 'private and confidential' with the information contained therein given in strict confidence. Their letter noted that any persons who considered themselves to be in a situation whereby they could shed light on the circumstances revolving around the *Titanic* disaster should have considered it their duty to inform the Board. If anything was to be done by the Board, the person concerned should communicate directly with them, "as it is open to them to do so even now, and perhaps you would suggest this to them."

A.H. Notley[123], the *Mount Temple*'s ex-4th Officer, who had been relieved by Baker in Halifax, met Lord after the Board's reply to the M.M.S.A., and he was introduced to Baker. Lord and Notley had a discussion over lunch one day, and the 4th Officer told Lord that he would willingly provide any information that he was asked for, but he would not volunteer information to the Board of trade in case it hindered his career in the Canadian Pacific Railway. Lord sympathised and let his communication with Notley lapse, but Lord considered the matter to be so important that he couldn't let it drop. Consequently, both Lord and Baker wrote to Dr. W.A. Bailey, who had been on the *Mount Temple* during its controversial voyage. Baker's letter, dated September 15th, is interesting: "if only you fellows had been called upon at the time, to give evidence, the whole thing would have come out and that old 'swine' Moore would have been placed in the position that my friend Captain Lord is now in which as you know Moore fully deserves."

Bailey had since transferred to the P & O Company, and both Lord and Baker had stressed that he might be more willing to help now that he was in a different company. But Bailey's reply to Baker was just a repetition of the information he had given to *The New York American* newspaper in April: "As your letter is practically full of appeal on behalf of Captain Lord, what value would an unprofessional and worthless expression of details as to what occurred on the *Mount Temple* be in face of what has been found? It is clearly Captain Lord's best plan to seek his evidence from Notley at Montreal and the officers who were on the ship at the time who saw certain things and freely discussed matters together; why come to ask me, who doesn't know the blunt from the sharp end of a ship?" Bailey's reply to Lord was similar: not being a navigating officer, the doctor felt that any information he could provide would not be of any use.

Captain Lord's final attempt to contact Dr. Bailey was disappointing. Lord called on Bailey's brother, Matthias, who was also a doctor and practising in Liverpool, but he was out at the time. When he did meet him, Lord was informed

---

123   In "*A Titanic Myth*" (page 135), Lord's advocate, Leslie Harrison, misrepresents Notley's longitude sights of April 15th by saying that his observations "conclusively demonstrated that, at the time, the *Titanic*'s wreckage and lifeboats were some eleven miles to the south-east of the position of the disaster as sent out by wireless, and as Lord had maintained at the inquiries." The observations taken by Notley on the *Mount Temple* show that the *Carpathia* – and by inference, the *Titanic*'s wreckage was 8 miles to the east of the SOS position, and not to the south-east.

that due to family differences, he could not help him get in contact with his brother. Matthias' letter did contain one very interesting piece of information: "I can say this: I have been told by an officer on the *Mount Temple* that distress signals were observed and preparations made, etc. I may be mistaken, they were ten to fourteen miles away, you were twenty-five."

Astute readers will recall that Lord provided a map and statement to the British Court. These elements, drawn up in Boston about April 25th have fascinating details that are found nowhere else in the record. Robert E. Cunliffe provided an analysis and comparison with Lord's evidence[124], and his letters and information that the Captain had recently received about the *Mount Temple*.

"Now as regards the *Mount Temple* it apparently is suggested by Captain Lord that the *Mount Temple* was the ship whose lights were seen by the *Titanic* and so far as I can gather that the *Mount Temple* was between the *Californian* and the *Titanic* on the night of the 14th or at all events in the morning of the 15th April. Further that the *Mount Temple* was equally to blame for not getting fast enough to the assistance of the *Titanic*. What help Captain Lord will get from the mere contention that there was something blameworthy on the part or the Captain of the *Mount Temple* I cannot at present see.

Now unless the evidence of the Captain of the *Mount Temple* and that of the Marconi operator on board her is a tissue of lies, and I must say that the evidence given by them in England was in effect the same as that given by them in America, it would be utterly impossible for the *Mount Temple* at any time while the *Californian* had in sight the vessel that she saw sending up rockets, to have been between the *Californian* and that vessel, and this is borne out by a chart or plan which was drawn out by the Captain of the *Californian* when he arrived in Boston for by it he shows where his ship was stopped during the night and shows the course he took after he heard of the *Titanic*'s disaster to get round to her wreckage and it will be seen that about 6:30 a.m. he passed the *Mount Temple* stopped to the West of where he eventually found wreckage from the Titanic. In the plan in question he shows a vessel to the North of the place where wreckage was seen and Captain Lord might possibly claim that that was the vessel that he saw on the night and not the *Titanic*. He was not able to state the name of the vessel, but that there was such a vessel there when day broke on the 15th of April is corroborated by Captain Rostron of the *Carpathia* who states that at 8 a.m. on the morning of April 15th he saw two steamers to the Northwards of where he was and neither was the *Californian* and that he saw the masthead lights of another steamer between his ship and the *Titanic*'s at about 3.15 a.m. but when these ships got into these positions there is no evidence to show. One would have thought that Captain Lord would, when on the spot, have been anxious to satisfy himself on the question of the identity of this vessel and the best thing he could have done would have been to

---

124   The full text of the analysis can be found at
http://home.earthlink.net/~dnitzer/6Affidavits/YellowFunnelBoat.html

speak to her, but this he did not do. If the wreckage from the *Titanic* drifted South from the place where the *Titanic* sank, as appears to be the case, the spot at which the *Mount Temple* stopped (and apparently she did not stop on her N.E. run until about 3.30) would be almost to the immediate West of the place where the *Titanic* struck and the *Mount Temple* would assuming she is properly placed in the plan[125] be as far away from the *Californian* as the *Titanic* was and not heading West as the vessel was which the *Californian* saw, for the *Mount Temple* had come back on her tracks on a N.E. course. [this author's emphasis]

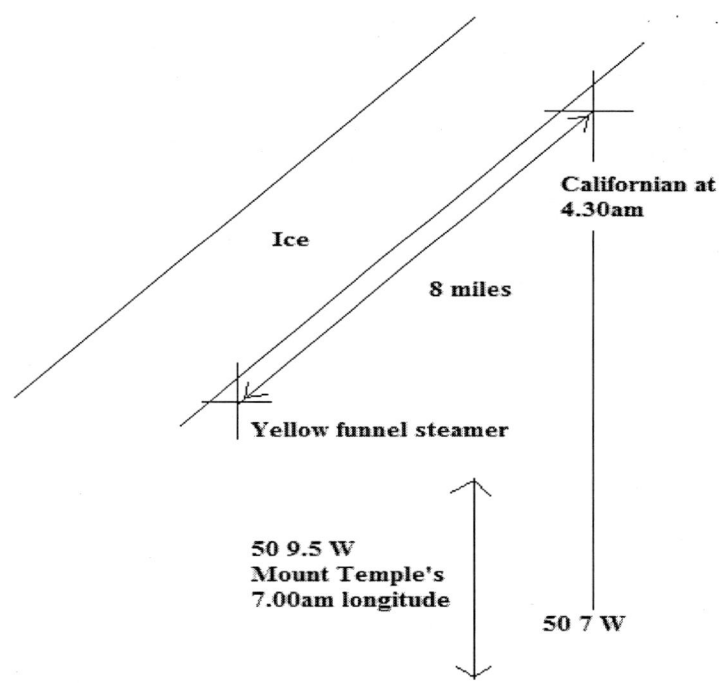

Illustration 25: The Yellow Funnelled Steamer's Position; east or west of the ice?

Moreover if a vessel had been between the *Californian* and the *Titanic* on the night of the disaster then assuming she was the vessel with a yellow funnel and 4 masts shown on Captain Lord's plan, she cannot have been the *Mount Temple* and would probably have easily been seen by those on board the Titanic if she had been there during the night.

---

125   In fact, Lord had already told the Inquiry in London that his map was not to scale.

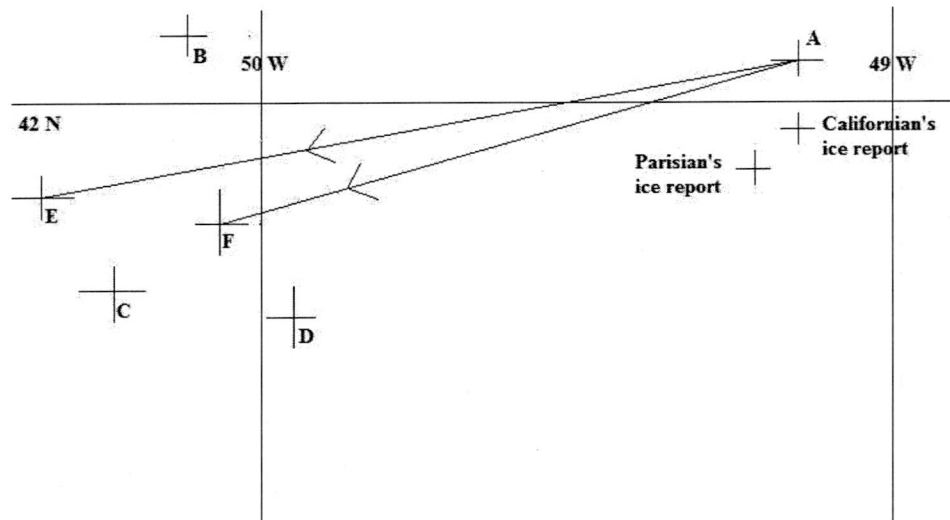

Illustration 26: Possible courses of the Californian: DR position at 6.30 (A); Californian's DR position at 10.21 (B); Titanic's CQD location (C); Titanic's actual location (D); and the Californian's position 10 miles north-west of the CQD position (E) and the actual sinking location (F)

Now as I have stated before whatever may be said against the Captain of the *Mount Temple* by those on board, and there are rumours that people on board seemed to think that at some time she saw lights (probably the flares from the boats in the water) and that she did not do all she could to get to the *Titanic* as I am not able to agree that the vessel that the *Californian* saw was the *Mount Temple*, whether the Captain of the *Mount Temple* did or omitted to do something that he ought not to have done or should have done (and according to his evidence and that of the Marconi operate, he did everything he could) may be a matter for further Inquiry, but so far as I can see does not help Captain Lord.

There was I notice from the remarks made by Counsel for Captain Lord a suggestion that he might have mistaken the place where the *Mount Temple* was stopped but no evidence was given to correct the plan put in.

As regards the Captain of the *Mount Temple*, those on board must have known full well what evidence he and his Marconi operator gave in America, and must have guessed that he and the Marconi operator would be called again as witnesses as the *Titanic* Inquiry in England, and if there were any allegations which persons on board desired to make against the Captain or any evidence which they thought ought to be before the Court in England they clearly ought to have volunteered to come forward as witnesses on the subject. There was nothing in the papers before the Board of Trade to suggest that the Captain of the *Mount Temple* had omitted to do anything that he ought to have done. If the *Mount Temple* could have been the ship which the *Californian* saw on the night of the disaster, I think the Owners of the Leyland Line should have produced evidence to this effect, and if they have reason to suppose that the Captain of the *Mount Temple* has not told the truth, the Owners could produce this evidence. The Leyland Company's shares are owned by the combine who own the greater number of the White Star Line shares and they would be anxious to get at the truth.

It seems to me that it is for Captain Lord to obtain evidence from any source to show why the findings of the Court are wrong so far as he is concerned; it is not enough to suggest that someone else may also have been guilty of conduct that was blameworthy.

We have already told the Solicitors to the Leyland Line that if they will forward any statements from persons who contradict the evidence of the Captain of the *Mount Temple* they will be carefully considered, but whether this would help Captain Lord is as I have said very doubtful and even assuming such evidence to be forthcoming I should have to lay the further facts as disclosed before the Counsel who conducted the Inquiry on behalf of the Board of Trade to know whether under the circumstances any further action is necessary on the part of the Board.

I forward the Log of the *Californian* and the plan and notes prepared by Captain Lord, which should be taken great care of, and should be returned."

Returned to whom? If this meant Captain Lord, it is not in his surviving papers today. Or, if it meant another official within the Board, then one can only sadly presume that the map and statement have been mislaid.[126]

The mention of the rendezvous with the *Mount Temple* at "about 6.30" may pose a problem for the Californian's officers and their supporters[127]. It is roughly in line with Groves' evidence, and may be used as confirmation of Captain Moore's recollections in Washington, especially the remark about the *Mount Temple* – *Californian* – *Titanic* distance: Captain Lord must have known this this was damaging to his own case, but, as Cunliffe says, "no evidence was given to correct the plan put [into evidence]". It may be that Lord was mistaken about the time and distance, but then, he and his crew did seem to make more than an inordinate number of errors and contradictions in England and the United States. But if the two ships did meet at 6.30, how did it take so long (two hours) to reach the *Carpathia*, just a short distance away on the other side of the ice? A clue lies in Lord's London testimony. He admitted stopping at about the time he saw the *Mount*

---

126   This is not the only example of the Board of Trade's papers going astray. The UK TV documentary "*Titanic – A Question of Murder*" (1983) remarks that some files relating to the provisioning of lifeboats on the Titanic and Olympic are missing.
127   Astonishingly, only one writer has grasped the implication of this timing; Dave Billnitzer, a researcher opposed to Captain Lord and his antics.

Temple, although he did not give any duration. He also moved the rendezvous time to 7.30am.

Of importance is the fact that Lord made no mention of the *Mount Temple* in America, and he certainly did not give the time of intercept. Lord's timing of this issue was only made in London a few weeks later. Therefore, his map and statement are the first contemporaneous evidence he made which included navigational details, not including his press conferences which seem to be full of inaccuracies.

Interestingly, the remainder of Cunliffe's note gave hints as to why the *Californian*'s navigational data had been rejected by the Inquiry: "....but Captain Lord was not able to satisfy the Court that the position given in his Log Book was correct and the compass deviation book though asked for on the hearing was not put before the court to enable them to check the navigation prior and up to the time when the engines of the *Californian* were stopped."

The deviation book was eventually provided and "the court came to their decision with the information contained in the book before them," wrote Cunliffe. With the course mentioned in the log book, it might have been able to determine any discrepancies in the *Californian*'s navigation. Today, the deviation book is missing.

But a deviation book can only provide clues as to the direction that a ship may have traversed, and not on distances. An accusation against Captain Lord is that his navigation was a sham, manufactured after the disaster. Therefore, his last publicly admitted position (the "three iceberg" message sent at 6.30pm on April 14th) was his last genuine location, heard by outside stations well before any opportunity to fabricate navigation could be attempted, even if this was just a DR estimate. An ice report by the SS *Parisian* places 3 icebergs within a few miles of those seen by the *Californian* at 6.30pm, and it has been argued that these are one and the same. This may be taken as "proof" that Lord and his crew were north of 42 N at 6.30pm. Or maybe not. Any DR position is an estimate and takes no account of offset caused by drift, which naturally accumulates from the time of the last observational sighting. The location could easily be off by a few miles.

Mersey, Senator Smith, and many spectators regarded the *Titanic*'s CQD location as accurate and sacrosanct, a myth finally foundered [pun intended] when expeditions started searching for the wreck (although Captain Moore's U.S. testimony indicated that the *Titanic* had not sunk where nearly everyone thought she had). Mersey and his assessors had simply placed the *Californian* between 5 and 10 miles north, or north-west of the *Titanic*, regardless of any problems this would pose for the navigation. To do so, from the 6.30pm DR location, the *Californian* would have to have "steered in error at least ten degrees to port of her anticipated course; to have averaged a speed of at least 14.7 knots, over three knots in excess of the speed at which she was cruising; and to have passed completely through the icefield which ran north and south across her track. It is most unlikely that any one of those hypothetical errors could have passed unnoticed, and inconceivable that a combination of all three could have occurred[128]."

There are no other indications why Mersey rejected Captain Lord's navigation. The former's surviving papers on the disaster simply include a copy of the final report and a series of notes that he made on each witness and their testimony, replete with doodles of ships and icebergs.

It is also unlikely that Groves would have overlooked the *Californian* steaming at full speed (actually, in excess of her maximum speed!) through pack ice during his watch! At any rate, he would have mentioned it to Mersey. It is clear that the *Californian* did not pass through the field ice, which was localised roughly north-south at 50° West longitude.

Now, we know the location of the *Titanic* wreck with accuracy. At least in this case, consulting the diagram below, the *Californian* would have remained approximately in the vicinity of the ice field; but it still requires a speed 11.1 knots of and a deviation of greater than 10 degrees to port. This also seems unlikely, unless one also invokes some content of drift between 6.30 and 10.21pm. These navigational matters did not concern Mersey or his staff; and, as we shall see, during the 1960s, an internal UK memorandum implied that Mersey's position for the *Californian* was worked out simply by considering observational data; this is lights, rockets, bearings and headings. Calculated positions had no influence on Mersey's opinion at all.

If Cunliffe's note is correct, the deviation book may have provided a hint that Lord's steering was not as accurate as he believed.

But Cunliffe was right on an important issue. Regardless of what the *Mount Temple* may have done – or may not have done – it does not absolve the *Californian* of its responsibilities. To accuse a fellow shipmaster in the hope that it will get his own conduct "off the hook" makes Captain Lord's accusations, despite Rostron's recommendations, disingenuous. The matter of the *Mount Temple* remains unresolved.

Most accounts of this time after Lord Mersey's judgement necessarily revolve around Captain Lord and his quest for justice. But what about his fellow officers? How did they fare immediately afterwards? Little is known of the attitude of the other *Californian* officers after their appearance at the London Inquiry. There are a few pointers about their attitudes. Groves, in a return trip to Boston on board the *Californian* in June 1912, allegedly visited the offices of the *Boston Herald*, but they wouldn't see him[129]. Stone, in conversation with the mother of 9 year old

---

128   "*A Titanic* Myth" pages176-177
129   This story, related in a pro-Lord book as an example of Groves' evidence being the result of imagination stimulated by vanity," cannot be right. The *Californian*

Sydney Gorrell, repeated the story that the rockets he saw in the sky were low down on the horizon. This information was particularly impressed upon the young mind of Sydney who was present at the meeting between Lord and his mother and who thought pyrotechnics would be much more spectacular[130].

Despite disappointments and rejections from the Board of Trade, Captain Lord had at least one champion: a solicitor by the name of A.M. Foweraker, a solicitor living in Carbis Bay, Cornwall. Through a series of letters, Foweraker's detailed analysis of the evidence given at the two inquiries and a perusal of Lloyds publication, convinced him that more than two ships were confined to the area of the icefield the night the *Titanic* went down. His analysis eventually filled two A4 notebooks. In reply, Lord sent him copies of statements by Stone and Gibson[131], his information on the *Almerian* and various other pieces of information.

His map, used by proponents of Captain Lord and reproduced here, shows several errors, possibly because, as it says, it is based on his testimony in London, and incorporates a deduced (and wrong) position for the collision point. It is speculated that the map is based on the (now missing) map that Lord drew in Boston and submitted in London. The *Mount Temple* is shown too far west; she obtained a Prime Vertical Sight at about 7.00am, which puts her on the vertical line superimposed on the chart. The *Californian* passed to the east of the *Mount Temple* at about this time, at the edge of the ice field, thus casting serious doubt on the supposed route on the map. The known longitude of the *Mount Temple*, and the *Californian*'s route at about this time are placed firmly within the icefield.

---

steamed from Boston on May 18th and docked in Boston on June 1st, departing 7 days later and arriving back in Liverpool on June 21st. During this voyage, Groves was not on board.

130   This information comes 65 years later when Gorrell wrote to Leslie Harrison. He also said that "Mr. Stone recounted how he went to the Master's cabin and reported what he and the Apprentice had seen, but Captain Lord had suggested that they were only signals between passing ships and to ignore them ... Mr. Stone, when the Chief Officer relieved him, told the latter about the events of the watch and inferred that the Captain was drunk, but what the C.O's subsequent action was I cannot recall, my mind revolving around rockets which were not very spectacular" It should be pointed out that Captain Lord is widely reported as being teetotal. However the only source of this information are the Harrison-Captain Lord clique, and Groves, who only sailed with the Captain for a handful of voyages. The rest of Stone's account, via Gorrell, corresponds reasonably well with evidence given in London.

131   These statements will be discussed presently. They would not be made public for many decades.

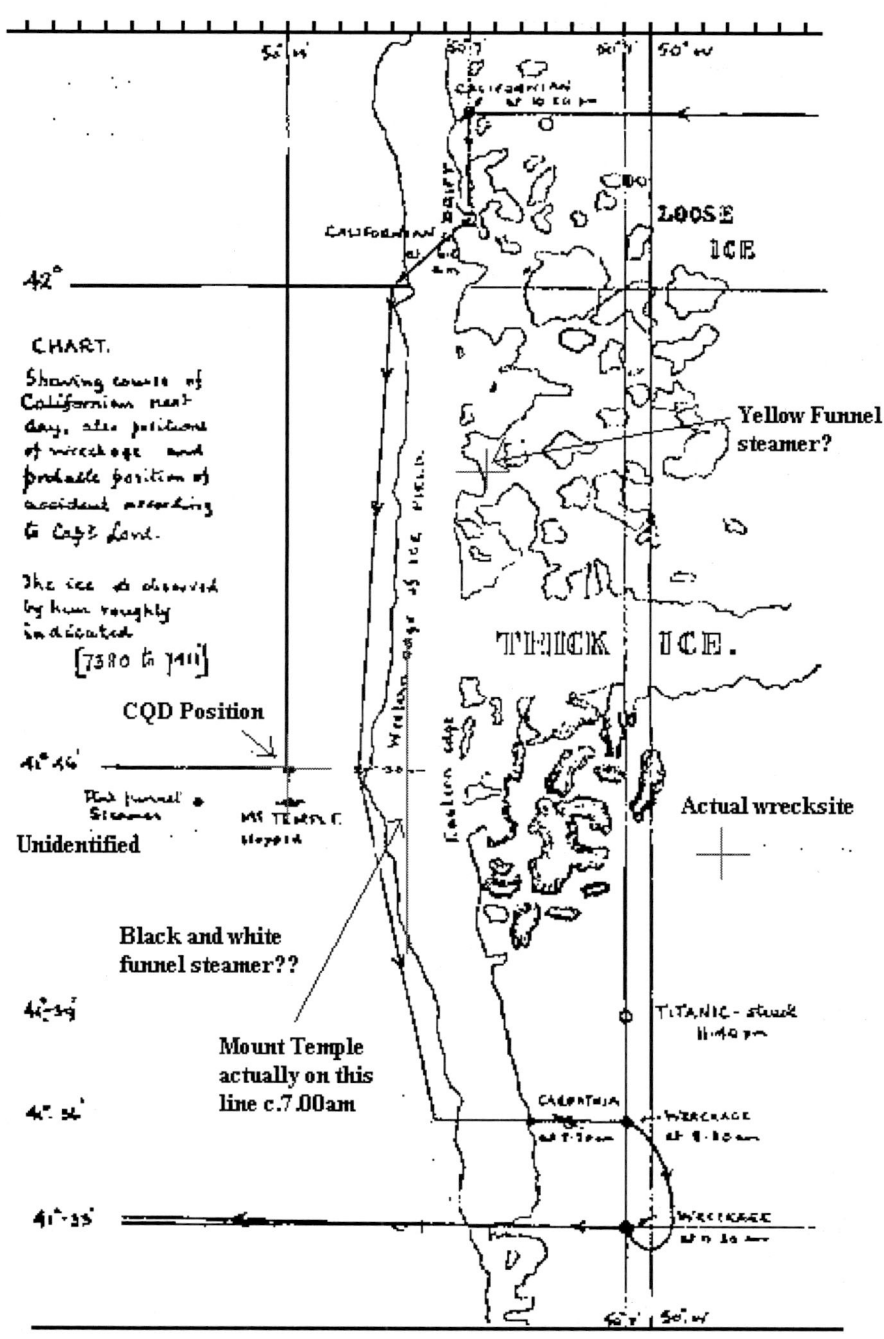

Illustration 27: Foweraker's Diagram. Annotations added by the author

The map alters the *Californian*'s final route towards the *Carpathia*, which was ENE. The "yellow funnel" steamer is missing, but Captain Lord's pink funnel ship[132] is included, although it is unknown how Foweraker placed it there, as all Lord said of it was that it was "steering north down to the north-west", and the *Almerian* report simply says that she was on the western extremity of the icefield: the map places her about 5 miles to the west, and nowhere near her northward traversing meridian of 50°24'W . Finally, the "thick ice" at about 41°50' North, dismissed as fiction by writers critical of the *Californian*, is consistent with Lord's testimony, but is a convenient barrier which would have prevented him from attempting a rescue at the location of the *Titanic* wreck site if she were to move in a direct, straight-line path. No other Captain, or reports in *Lloyd's List*, mentions such a peculiar T-shaped icefield. So-called "secret" statements of Stone and Gibson, released to the public decades later, do refer to a dense, or thick ice field to the south. However, it can be debated as to how far ice, perhaps only showing faint reflections of starlight, can be seen in the dark. Lord himself admitted in America that he saw no icebergs during the night, just field ice. However, consider that, if the eastern edge of the ice field at the *Californian*'s stopped location ran to the south-east, then anyone looking south would see this stretching away from them into the distance. Without more information it is impossible to say with any certainty[133].

  And so 1912 ended in disaster for Lord: one of his last efforts that year to rouse indignation as to his treatment was a letter to his Member of Parliament, Mr. A.H. Gill: "As I mentioned to you in Bolton some time ago, I admit there was a certain amount of 'slackness' aboard the *Californian* the night in question, but I strongly maintain that the position I gave at the Inquiry was correct, and there hasn't been any evidence produced to prove the contrary, and until such evidence is produced, or proof of my log book being 'cooked,' I am entitled to the benefit of that document.".

  With no income, no job and public obloquy heaped upon him, the future, as the saying goes, looked bleak. But on January 19th of the following year, Lord's prospects seemed to improve, for, on that date, he received a letter from Lawther Latta, a London firm which managed the Nitrate Producers Steam Ship Company. It transpired that Mr. Latta was in receipt of a letter from Frank Strachan, a U.S. agent for Leyland's, enquiring whether any opportunities existed in his company as "he apparently considers that [Lord] had been subjected in the recent well-known conflict to unfair treatment." Strachan, who was a "very old friend" of Latta's had spoken very highly of Captain Lord, and on the basis of this recommendation, invited Lord to an interview in London.

---

132   If Captain Lord did indeed provide copies of his Almerian information, why did Foweraker not note it on his chart?

133   More discussion of this map can be found in Dave Gittins' book, "Titanic – Monument and Warning."

Lord was low on funds and was wary about the expense of a, possibly wasted, trip to London; furthermore, Lord also informed Latta of the reasons why he had been dismissed from the Leyland Line. Accordingly, he informed Latta of this and told them that he had no plans to visit London.

Latta's reply heartened Lord; "We have to acknowledge receipt of your straightforward and frank letter of yesterday, the tone of which we appreciate, and naturally we observe it is possible that you may not have had a proper opportunity of setting out your case. So far as our recollection of the examination goes, the chief point against you was not so much as to whether it was your command that was nearest the *Titanic*, but the alleged fact that rockets were seen by your officers, that you were called, but remained callous to the call. Be that so or not, the circumstances were altogether exceptional, and not such as it appears to us sufficiently serious to condemn the reputation of any man."

The letter concluded with the welcome news that Lord would be reimbursed his travel costs in the event that he not be employed by the firm. The ensuing interview lasted an hour and concluded with an offer of employment subject to a reference from Leyland, which was duly provided by Mr. Roper. Captain Lord was offered the command of the SS *Anglo Saxon*, with a salary of £20 per month, with a bonus of £5 per month if everything proved satisfactory. He accepted, and took command of her on 7th March. Upon completion of this first voyage in August of that year, Lord reported his satisfaction to Latta and returned home to enjoy a period of leave, where he found an article discussing the *Californian* case in the M.M.S.A.'s monthly '*Reporter*' magazine. Entitled 'Pushed under the Wheels of Juggernaut' by 69 year-old Captain John d'Arcy Morton, who concluded that Lord's watchkeepers had indeed seen the *Titanic*'s rockets, but that another ship in direct visual line of sight between the *Californian* and the White Star giant had made Stone believe that the rockets that were seen only went to half the height of the mast of this other vessel; as he writes, "it would not take much imagination on the part of an experienced seaman or officer to conclude that she was firing the rockets". The *Californian*'s overnight position is "incontestable, and cannot be shaken."

Subsequent editions of the magazine saw the return of Foweraker, who proposed the two mystery ship solution. Foweraker would also write features for the *Nautical Magazine*, under the banner: 'A Miscarriage of Justice'. In these articles, he criticised Lord Mersey for rejecting the *Californian*'s navigation, blindly accepting the *Titanic*'s position, which put her well to the west of the ice field, and that the *Titanic* had started sending up rockets half an hour before Stone saw any signals. "If there is any error of judgement," Foweraker writes, "it is surely on the part of those responsible for an ambiguous regulation [regarding rockets and private signals]."

Favourable reviews of these articles appeared in, among others, "*Saturday Review*" and "*Review of Reviews*." But one writer, to "*The Nautical Magazine*" was sceptical. Master Mariner (Retired) held the opinion that it was "a mere matter of detail whether those on board the *Californian* saw the *Titanic* or they did not. They evidently saw a vessel of some sort firing rockets, a signal of distress. It was the duty of the *Californian* to have gone to her assistance. They did nothing! They might not have been able to get near her on account of the ice, but they might have tried." But another correspondent disagreed, and writing under the pseudonym 'Blue Light', he reminded readers that "private signals of Atlantic steamship companies are so like rockets that it is impossible to differentiate ... Captain Lord was penalised in quite an unlawful way, for not attempting to go to the rescue of the *Titanic*, which foundered nineteen miles from him. It may be possible, on a very clear night and by the use of extremely powerful glasses, to see rockets nineteen miles away, but it would be impossible at such a distance to say whether they were private signals or distress rockets."

This letter is riddled with error. No vessels had rockets as part of their Transatlantic signalling make-up in 1912. Stone and Gibson certainly knew the difference between private signals and rockets, if their testimonies are anything to go by. Finally, they saw the *Carpathia*'s rockets with the naked eye, at a range much greater than the *Titanic* had ever been.

Foweraker responded to 'Master Mariner' by stating that, if the *Californian* had indeed seen distress rockets, then they should have tried to assist.

Lord had also taken receipt of a reference from the Leyland Line: "We have always found Captain Lord a sober, industrious and careful officer, good officer and disciplinarian, and whilst he has been in command of our steamers, they have run free from accident."

With these testimonials and refreshed public interest, Lord once again appealed to the Board of Trade to reconsider its censure of him. Referring to the recent articles, Lord wanted to draw attention to Mersey's biased opinion on the *Californian*, "before he had heard the whole of the evidence ... A further hearing by an independent court, on the evidence already submitted at the former Inquiry, is all I ask for." The Board rejected this request a month later, having "carefully considered the statements [that Lord had referred to]."

Lord was naturally disappointed, but with a new job, and the confidence of men like Latta, this failure to re-open the Inquiry did not affect him personally or professionally. Frank Strachan was one such proponent of Captain Lord and his abilities; as he told Stanley when the *Anglo Chilean* (his current ship) visited Brunswick, "They wanted a bloody goat, Lord, and they got you!"

And then World War 1 started. Like many other mariners, Lord and his ship were requisitioned to help in the war effort, and he spent the first few months transporting horses from America to France, and the United States Department of Agriculture and the French Authorities congratulated him for the care he had taken of his live cargo. In July 1915, Lord was transferred to another Latta vessel, the SS *Anglo Patagonian*, at very short notice; a command that he held until August 1916, when Lord took a short break from his seagoing life, and thence to supervise completion of company's new ship, the SS *Anglo Chilean*.

One particularly favourable diversion from the war occurred c.1916, when Lord, on a trip to Liverpool during a break in the completion on his new command. For on that day, Lord encountered his ex-Chief Officer Stewart, and the two shared a very amicable meeting over coffee. Inevitably, the spectre of the *Californian* was raised[134].

"What ship did you think the *Titanic* saw?" Lord asked

"I don't know. I don't think there's any question it wasn't us. But what the devil did Stone see? I've never been able to gather what he did see," Stewart replied.

Assuming this anecdote is true and is reported accurately (coming as it does from Lord and reported via his chief apologist), one can only wonder what Stewart meant by impugning Stone. Stone, let us not forget, testified to a ship steaming off. This obviously couldn't be the *Titanic*. He also told Mersey that "a ship that is in distress does not steam away from you." Stone was actually providing evidence that could be used to exonerate his master and his ship mates and ran contrary to Mersey's hypothesis that the *Titanic* and the *Californian* were in sight of each other. For Stewart to cast doubt on such evidence seems somewhat ungrateful.

The *Anglo Chilean* was finally completed after a delay caused by deficiencies found during her trial voyage. She put to sea in March 1917, and two months later she engaged a German submarine in the Mediterranean. In November of that year, she acted as the lead vessel in a convoy from New York to England, with Captain W.H.Owen, RNR acting as commodore of the flotilla.

The remainder of Lord's war service passed uneventfully and he continued at Latta's as the Captain of the *Anglo Chilean*.

In November 1920, during a voyage to New York, Lord declared his intention to the Department of Labor to renounce his status a citizen of Great Britain and to become a citizen of the United States. He completed a form at the Supreme Court of Kings County, New York, stating that he apparently arrived in New York on ("or about") May 20th, 1915. However, like many things in Lord's life, various discrepancies become apparent under analysis. The listed Brooklyn address does not include Lord, or his wife, as an inhabitant in either the 1915 street directory or the 1920 U.S. Census and the people listed at the address have no obvious connection with Lord[135]. Lord also did not "arrive" in New York at the specified date, but had, in fact, just left St.Nazaire on the *Anglo Patagonian*.

There is no record of Stanley or Mabel Lord ever applying for a U.S. passport, but, with two exceptions, U.S. citizens were not required to have a

---

134   "*A Titanic Myth*" page 154
135   Information courtesy of the U.S. National Archives and the New York Historical Society

passport for travel abroad until 1941, the two exceptions were during short periods in the U.S. Civil War (August 19, 1861-March 17, 1862) and shortly after World War 1 (1918-1921).

Whether this application has any relevance to the *Californian* story is unknown; it certainly seems unlikely as Lord had given up debating his part in the *Titanic* disaster seven years earlier. Certainly, Lord did not emigrate to America upon his retirement although he had the financial means to do so.

One voyage, in early 1925, took him and his ship from the Tyne to Sydney, where they were joined by other vessels at anchor, waiting for loading instructions: this delay extended to five weeks, and each day a launch would collect each Captain and take them ashore to attend to routine matters. On one occasion, the Captain of the *Sheaf Mount* dropped some letters as he clambered into the smaller launch. Lord assisted in their retrieval, and the two men chatted sociably. Lord slowly realised that his companion was none other than Charles Victor Groves, the ex-3rd Officer on the *Californian*. Neither of them mentioned the *Californian*, but a day or so later, "as Lord was walking along the quay after disembarking from the launch, Groves, accompanied by another man, came towards him. Groves' companion addressed him.

'Are you, Lord, of the *Californian*,' he enquired.

Lord's reaction was instinctive.

'What of it?' he snapped.

'Oh, nothing,' the other replied, and the pair of them walked away. On reflection, Lord rather regretted his negative response, for it occurred to him that he and Groves might have had a very interesting discussion[136]."

But one incident, where the ship's cook became seriously ill and had to be transshipped to another vessel, had a disturbing effect as it reminded Lord of his own mortality, especially outside while at sea and outside the range of medical assistance. He occasionally suffered from inexplicable stomach pains and indifferent eyesight. Following medical advice, and an assessment of his finances, Stanley Lord decided to retire, and he informed John Latta of his decision in July 1928. A glowing testimonial from Latta followed, which stated that Lord had had their "entire confidence" and they regarded him as one of the "most capable commanders [they] had ever had."

And so Lord, his wife and son settled down to life in Wallasey, on the mouth of the river Mersey. The retired Captain played golf each day and avidly read fiction and biography. The *Titanic* and the *Californian* seemed like a distant, and very happily forgotten, memory. And with the commencement of World War 2,

---

136   When Captain Groves was interviewed by author Walter Lord in the 1950s, he said that, at one point, presumably during the 'dropped letters' episode, he actually said "Good morning, Captain Lord." Lord's response to this greeting is not discernible, due to Walter Lord's poor handwriting (!) However, the reader will soon learn that significant doubts exist over Groves' recollections.

and yet more escalating body counts, interest in the 1500 victims of the North Atlantic that frigid night some three decades earlier, seemed to fade. Lord's life continued unencumbered by such handicaps, although marred by sadness when his wife died in 1957.

With sufficient savings to provide a comfortable lifestyle, Lord and his son were now happy. But a grim reminder of 1912 was about to be resurrected and an old wound was about to be re-opened.

Chapter 6. A Night Best Forgotten?

1955-1958

In 1955, a Manhattan copy editor, with a degree in law from Yale, decided that his lifelong interest in the *Titanic* had been gestating long enough, and resolved to write a book on the last night of the floating city. Tracing as many survivors as he could, he entered into correspondence with over 60 of them, many of whom he maintained contact with for decades.

His name was Walter Lord (no relation to the Captain) and his book would become "*A Night To Remember.*"

Illustration 28: Walter Lord, 1917 - 2002

Lord the author was blessed with many valuable sources and correspondents, from officers on the *Titanic* to 3rd class emigrants. But Lord was determined to tell not only the last night of the White Star leviathan, but peripheral vessels too. Alas, he had little luck finding sources from the *Carpathia*, and found fewer from the *Californian*. Despite contacting UK shipping unions, he was unable to contact Captain Lord; nor did the Captain see any of Walter's adverts in the UK press appealing for those connected with the *Titanic* disaster to get in contact. He later admitted that had he been able to contact Captain Lord, he would not have changed his mind about the validity of the 1912 inquiries.

The *Californian* incident had lain dormant since 1913, when Captain Lord had given up his appeal, and apart from an interview in the *Savannah Morning News* in 1914, the only references to him and his ex-ship were in the 1935 autobiography of the *Titanic*'s 2nd Officer, Charles Herbert Lightoller, (where he reversed the 1912 goodwill he extended towards Lord and now held the opinion that the *Californian* had indeed ignored their call for help) and in a 1943 Nazi propaganda film, where Lord is actually shown, in an apocryphal scene, coming to the bridge and telling his watch-keepers, "...those are white rockets. Not emergency signals. You should know better than to wake me up for that ... that must be the *Titanic* on her maiden voyage, from her position. Maybe they are having a party to celebrate their early arrival in New York tomorrow. Let them have their fun. We are staying on course. Now, good night."

There were a few TV dramatisations in which the *Californian* affair was mentioned: both U.S. and German television networks produced dramatisations of the sleepy rocket ignoring vessel; these were written by a certain Leslie Reade, of whom more later. And other than these, there was nothing. The *Titanic* had been forgotten. Walter Lord's book would reignite interest in the disaster and, unwittingly, stimulate the debate about Captain Lord's conduct from dormancy into vibrant life.

Among Walter Lord's many correspondents was Mr. A. Brian Mainwaring[137]. Mainwaring related his working life on the sea, including 3 years on *Titanic's* sister, *Olympic* and 4 years on another White Star line vessel, the *Majestic*. He personally knew many of the individuals involved in the tragedy, including Herbert Stone, who he had met once during World War 1. Mainwaring wrote, "It was a well-known fact and quoted by him to his friends that Captain Lord of the *Californian* was an insufferable SOB. That after Stone had tried to get him to come up on the bridge, he turned to the Apprentice and said, 'Well, let the bastard sleep.'"

George Thomas Rowe was also forthcoming. As one of the Quartermasters, and one who assisted in the firing the rockets, his information was particularly interesting. One point he notes was that, while Collapsible lifeboat C was being readied (i.e. before 2.00 a.m.) he saw a light on the *Titanic*'s starboard quarter and thought it was a ship. But Captain Smith, looking at the light through binoculars reassured Rowe that it was merely a planet[138]. Using an astronomical programme[139] it can be shown that the only planet that had risen at the time was Jupiter, and she would be in the SSE. Since the starboard quarter is the rear right of a vessel, this implies a northward pointing *Titanic*[140].

---

137   Not Brian Manning, as he is called in Dr. Charles Pellegrino's book *"Ghosts of the Titanic"*. Manning was another Walter Lord correspondent, but he has no connection with the *Californian*.

138   Rowe also confirmed this detail to Leslie Harrison in 1963. While it is true that some of Rowe's accounts mention a "star or a planet", his earliest account, to Walter Lord in 1955, merely mentions a planet.

139   http://www.fourmilab.ch/yoursky/

140   http://users.senet.com.au/~gittins/stars.html includes an anecdote from Rowe's

The most noteworthy correspondent was Captain Charles Groves. He wrote that he stood by his testimony in London, saying that "[he] pointed her out to Captain Lord when he came up on the bridge he remarked "That will be the "*Titanic*" on her maiden voyage." ... Captain Lord certainly did not watch that ship from 11-0 P.M. onwards for he spent practically all hour in his cabin."

With regard to the other ship "coming up on [his] starboard quarter in a blaze of deck lights" and dousing her lamps at 11.40pm, Groves informed Lord that "What however had actually happened was that the iceberg had been sighted on the liner's starboard bow and she had immediately turned to port and then foreshortened her view and accordingly shut out most if not all of her deck lights." There are problems with this interpretation, and although Walter Lord initially accepted this explanation, he later on questioned it.

In 1958, Groves wrote a short memoir of his time on the *Californian* for Walter Lord, entitled "*The Middle Watch*"[141] Although this document is interesting, the first-hand details from Groves read like a simple repeat, almost verbatim, of his evidence in London. Perhaps he had refreshed his memory before writing it? There are a few interesting details: Captain Lord is described as "an austere type, utterly devoid of humour and even more reserved than is usual with those who occupy similar positions." Stone was "a stolid, unimaginative type and possessed little self confidence." The rockets are described as commencing "at 1.10 am", or about half an hour too late. When Groves asked Stone about the rockets upon waking, he was told "Yes, I saw her firing rockets in my watch" - "her" being the *Titanic*.

As she was leaving the wrecksite, Groves writes that "The *Californian* now made one complete turn to starboard followed by one to port and then resumed her passage to Boston passing the Canadian Pacific steamship *Mount Temple*, and another steamship of unknown nationality," a detail that is inaccurate.

Of most interest are the following lines, "All that middle watch the *Californian* remained stationary for news of the rockets being seen did not stir her Captain into action, Mr. Stone lacked the necessary initiative to insist upon his coming to the bridge to investigate things for himself, and it did not occur to him to call the Chief Officer when he realised the apathy of the Captain, who apparently slept peacefully whilst this drama was being enacted about them ... Mr. Stone knew without a shadow of a doubt that there was trouble aboard the vessel from which the distress signals had been fired, but he failed to convince his Captain. But did Captain Lord need any convincing? Was Mr. Stone afraid that if he was too insistent he would arouse the wrath of his superior? Why did Captain Lord take no efficient steps to render assistance before 6 o'clock? Did he consider problematical

grandson. It seems that Rowe was adamant that what he had seen was the light of a ship receding from the *Titanic*. Since Jupiter was well above the horizon, it seems impossible to believe that Rowe could mistake this for a ship.

141   http://home.earthlink.net/~dnitzer/9Testimony/Midwatch.html

damage to his ship was of more importance than the saving of lives? ... Does an experienced shipmaster lay down fully- clothed and in such circumstances sleep so heavily as he said he did on that night? Surely, surely, that is open to the very gravest of doubts."

"The whole unfortunate occurrence was a combination of circumstances the like of which may never again be seen, and a middle watch which will not soon be forgotten," the document concludes.

The previous year, Lord had interviewed Groves and the notes of that meeting show that some of the ex-3rd Officer's unprompted, spontaneous remarks nicely supplement his comments in *The Middle Watch*", but others contradict his 1912 statements: Stone "was always prompt but otherwise he was hopeless: lazy, fat, afraid of Lord. A man who never did anything with living, except lie in his cabin snoozing between watches. How did he get this far in the company? Well, he was from Devon, and they always looked after Devon men." Captain Lord was described as being "a stern, domineering man with a high opinion of himself, a man who hardly will speak to anybody even when spoken to." Evans is described as "a nice enough fellow who'll never set the Thames on fire."

Groves remarked to author Lord that Captain Lord was scared to go the rescue, and Stone was too weak to force the issues.

Most of the interview is similar to "The Middle Watch" and his 1912 recollections, and only significant differences are mentioned here.

After stopping his ship, Lord asks the Quartermaster to bring up some coal. The Q.M. is incredulous and is asked again. Groves nods the Q.M. on, who returns with some coal. Lord takes it and throws it over the side to see how thick the ice is. Satisfied that its too thick to run through, he decides to stop for the night. Groves reveals how, soon after 11 o'clock, he saw a large ship coming up from the east, south of him. He called the Captain who takes a look saying "That'll be the *Titanic* on its maiden voyage," and leaves the bridge again. At 11.40 the ship stops. Groves calls Lord again, who reappears, takes a look at the vessel and says that its not the same ship. Groves said that it was.

This is a gross contradiction of Groves' earlier comments, which has Lord leaving the bridge at 10.35, and only coming back after being told about the other ship coming up astern (not "from the east and south"), which was after she had allegedly stopped at 11.40. If Groves earlier version is true, this was Lord's first view of the stranger. How then could he comment that "it was not the same ship"?

Upon waking, Groves goes to Stone's cabin, who now says either, "The *Titanic* has sunk – I saw her go down" or just simply later in the interview, when asked about the *Titanic*, "I saw her go down."

After coming up to the bridge, Groves tells Author Lord that the Captain is now reported as being so upset he tells the 3rd Officer to "shoot the sun" (a term referring to obtaining data from a solar observation using a sextant to gather navigational data) before the sun was up. The *Californian* finally gets to the wrecksite around 8.15-8.30 just as the *Carpathia* is picking up the last two boats. Groves is the only one who can read the *Carpathia*'s semaphore signals. The *Carpathia* leaves shortly afterwards, and within 15 minutes is gone, "disappeared behind the ice." The *Californian* performs a "perfunctory search – a sort of figure 8," consistent with his 'complete turn to starboard, then a turn to port' in his written account *'The Middle Watch.'*

When Walter Lord suggested to Groves that Captain Lord should have reacted to the news of the rockets immediately, he was told "not necessarily." Stone, Groves stressed, "was the man on the spot. It was up to him to drive home the urgency of the moment to a Captain below. If the Captain seemed reluctant to act, it was up to the man on the bridge to drive all the harder – to make him do something." To Groves, Stone was just as culpable as Lord.

One very important point not covered in the interview, but mentioned to Walter Lord in subsequent letters, was that, sometime during the post-*Titanic* voyage of the *Californian*, Groves' rough calculations on the position of the his ship had been stolen from his bureau drawer. This was not mentioned in *"The Middle Watch"* and one can only wonder why. From the time the *Californian* stopped on April 14th till going off duty shortly after 12am, apart from a brief visit to the Chart room, Groves was on the bridge, before briefly visiting Evans, and then retiring for the night. By the time he woke, the ship's position was already calculated and the *Californian* was en route to the disaster site. So, when did Groves calculate the ship's overnight position? Groves had been asked the following in London:

> 8506. Who would make a dead reckoning and find out where she was at 10.20?
> Well, the Captain; he would work it. I never work it.

If Groves did do any calculations of his own, it must have been after Lord's determination of 50 07 W, 42 05 N; that is, at some point after Stewart had wakened him. One can speculate that, if it did happen, Groves did not mention this "theft" as it might have been one accusation too much for the Inquiry. Another alternative is that the "rough calculation" refer to the noon position of the *Californian* on April 15th.

Walter Lord did not use any of this interview material in his *Titanic* books. Why? It may be because he trusted Grove's 1912 testimony rather than his recollections from 40+ years after. Walter Lord must have evidently known that there were significant differences between the stories imparted by the former 3rd Officer. So, why was Groves' story in *"The Middle Watch"* a recap of his 1912 information? Groves may have simply wanted to refresh his memory. On the other hand, he now had a professional status and had sat as an assessor on some 25 inquiries. He may have wanted to protect his reputation by repudiating, or correcting any erroneous information he had given to Lord in 1957. Whatever, Groves' interview, full of interesting contradictions, was not seen again until this author found it in the late Walter Lord's cache of bequeathed papers in 2005.

"*A Night To Remember*" was published by R & W Holt in December 1955 and was a success; a British edition was released by Longman's the following year. Captain Lord's 'guilt' is taken for granted, but on the whole, the book follows the transcripts of the 1912 enquiries very closely. Ironically, the book was serialized in a local Liverpool newspaper, but Captain Lord had neither been impressed by a quick scan through the editions, nor did he notice any references to the *Californian*.

With the success of the book, and following a two hour live adaptation of the book in America by the Kraft Television Theater, a film seemed inevitable, and this was a task allotted to the British J. Arthur Rank Organisation. They allocated a budget of some $1.7 million for the film, and secured Kenneth More as its top billing artist, portraying 2nd Officer Lightoller. Advance publicity for the film consisted of the customary theatre lobby displays, photographs and pamphlets[142]. This latter item mentioned the *Californian* thus: "The Ship That Watched – Ten miles away, the crew of the cargo ship *Californian* saw the lights of *Titanic*. They saw her stop -'for safety', they thought, for *Californian* herself had stopped because of field ice ahead. They watched the distress rockets arc into the sky. 'Company signals,' they decided. Her Captain [sic] tried to contact the liner with lamp signals. There was no reply. And so, throughout the night, *Californian* watched, unknowing, the greatest peace-time sea disaster of the century. It was not until dawn that she knew, and then it was too late to help."

The 2 hour long black and white film was released on July 3rd, 1958. At its London première was Walter Lord, William MacQuitty (the producer), and various *Titanic* survivors including 3rd Officer Pitman and 4th Officer Boxhall, the latter of whom had served as a technical advisor to the producers. The film would later win a U.S. Golden Globe award, for the Best English Language Foreign Film. It is still regarded today as the most historically accurate[143] of the various *Titanic* films.

Captain Lord was oblivious to all this. Attending screenings of films did not seem to accord with his interests. It must therefore have been something of a shock when he opened his weekend quota of his favourite newspapers, *The Sunday Times*, *The Observer* and *The Sunday Express*. For, contained within were reviews of an ambitious black and white British film that featured a sinking Leviathan

---

142   See "*Titanic Memories – the making of A Night To Remember*" by William MacQuitty

143   The only major errors in the film, as regards the *Californian*, are that it depicts Captain Lord tucked up in bed with the lights off; a reference to non-existent passengers on the ship; and the *Californian* watch keepers viewing the Titanic's broadside, whereas from the Titanic's viewpoint, the *Californian's* light (seen, incorrectly, amongst a sea of churning, choppy water) is visible off the bow. Other researchers have noted that actor Geoffrey Bayldon, aged 34 at the time, is far too old to play the 20 year old Cyril Evans.

while another ship watched her vainly sending up rockets. 'The other ship' being the *Californian*, commanded by an aloof and cold Captain, who had expressed more interested in extra sugar in his tea, than in attending to distress rockets being sent aloft later on that day.

Captain Lord endeavoured to act. The next day, and without telling his son, he took the ferry over to Liverpool, and then walked the short distance to Nautilus House, the home of the M.M.S.A., a union of which he been a member without interruption since 1897.

And so it was, that on July 7th, 1958, Stanley Lord entered the office of Leslie Harrison, the General Secretary of the M.M.S.A., and introduced himself.

"I'm Lord, of the *Californian*."

Chapter 7. "I'm Lord of the Californian"[144]

1958-1962

Walter Leslie Stringer Harrison was born in 1912. After school, he entered the Merchant Navy as a cadet. For a few years during the 1930s, he was based ashore with the Marconi Company. He returned to the sea in 1936, and, during the Second World War, he acted as a master mariner for the Royal Air Force, first as a navigational instructor and then as a navigator in Coastal Command. Following his demobilisation, he became the Secretary of the Officers (Merchant Navy) Federation, and became the General Secretary of the M.M.S.A. in 1956, where he became responsible for "arranging the protection of members involved in courts of Inquiry and for representing shipmasters on a number of official committees."

Illustration 29: Captain Lord's son (left) and Leslie Harrison in 1968

---

144   The majority of quotes and information in this chapter comes from "*A Titanic Myth part 2: Defending Captain Lord.*"

Harrison invited the elderly gentleman to sit down. The General Secretary's initial reaction was one of confusion, as neither 'Lord' nor '*Californian*' meant anything to him, but within minutes, Harrison was sitting listening to Lord's story of his ship's alleged proximity to the *Titanic* and the accusation that he and his crew's inactivity had doomed 1500 people. Stanley Lord had been heartened by the M.M.S.A. support of him in 1912, and was wondering if he could still count on its help? He hoped that the *Californian* matter might be resurrected to counter the damaging depiction of "*A Night To Remember*", but his initial hope – to peruse the M.M.S.A.'s files from the time of the *Titanic* disaster – was quickly dashed, as they had been mislaid or destroyed, presumably during the Luftwaffe's bombing campaign in World War 2.

Upon Lord's departure from his office, Harrison first consulted Herbert Allen, the M.M.S.A.'s solicitor to discuss Lord's case and what could be done about the filmed version of "*A Night To Remember*." The response was discouraging, as the only suggestion was that a case for libel be launched, but Captain Lord was dismissive of this as he desired no publicity. The only alternative was, as Harrison said later, "a public relations exercise," to educate the public about the truth of the *Californian* affair. A letter to the Rank Organisation was written, expressing concern on behalf of Captain Lord about how the matter of the *Californian* had been treated. "Unfortunately," Harrison related, "it had to be emphasised in the letter that, as Captain Lord was now over 80 years of age, no risks had to be run likely to cause him serious concern or to place too great a strain on his health ... The Rank Organisation's reaction ... was predictable. They obviously knew they had nothing to fear by way of legal action from an eighty-year old in poor health, so they could simply claim, as they did, that the film was based on the book, which in turn was based on the findings of the official 1912 Inquiry." The Organisation remarked that it was "a pity" that Captain Lord had not seen any of Walter Lord's newspaper appeals for survivors to get in contact with the author.

The process to educate the public of the 'truth' was initiated. Granted access to Captain Lord's private papers, Harrison quickly became convinced that his client had indeed been the victim of a monstrous injustice. Among the cache of documents were statements made by Stone and Gibson – statements never made available to the public[145]:

---

145 During a meeting with Groves in the 1960s, author Leslie Reade showed these statements to the ex-3rd Officer, who was astonished that these statements existed.

S.S. *Californian,* At Sea,
(18 April, 1912)
Captain Lord,
Dear Sir,

At your request I make the following report of the incidents witnessed by me during my Watch on the Bridge of this Steamer from midnight April 14th - 4 a.m. of the 15th.

On going up to the bridge I was stopped by yourself at the wheelhouse door, and you gave me verbal orders for the Watch. You showed me a steamer a little abaft of our Star-beam and informed me she was stopped. You also showed me the loose field ice all around the ship and a dense icefield to the southward. You told me to watch the other steamer and report if she came any nearer and that you were going to lie down on the chartroom settee. I went on the bridge about 8 minutes past 12, and took over the Watch from the 3rd Officer, Mr. Groves, who also pointed out ice and steamer and said our head was E.N.E. and we were swinging. On looking at the compass I saw this was correct and observed the other steamer S.S.E dead abeam and showing one masthead light, her red side-light and one or two small indistinct lights around the deck which looked like portholes or open doors. I judged her to be a small tramp steamer and about five miles distant.

The 3rd Officer then left the bridge and I at once called the steamer up but got no reply. Gibson, the Apprentice, then came up with the coffee at about 12:15. I told him I called the steamer up and the result. Gibson thought at first he was answering, but it was only his masthead lamps flickering a little. I then sent Gibson by your orders to get the gear all ready for streaming a new log line when we got under weigh again. At 12:35 you whistled up the speaking tube and asked if the other steamer had moved. I replied "No" and that she was on the same bearing and also reported I had called him up and the result.

At about 12:45, I observed a flash of light in the sky just above that steamer. I thought nothing of it as there were several shooting stars about, the night being fine and clear with light airs and calms. Shortly after I observed another distinctly over the steamer which I made out to be a white rocket though I observed no flash on the deck or any indication that it had come from that steamer, in fact, it appeared to come from a good distance beyond her. Between then and about 1:15 I observed three more the same as before, and all white in colour. I, at once, whistled down the speaking tube and you came from the chartroom into your own room and answered. I reported seeing these lights in the sky in the direction of the other steamer which appeared to me to be white rockets. You then gave me orders to call her up with the Morse lamp and try and get some information from her. You also asked me if they were private signals and I replied, "I do not know but they were all white." You then said: "When you get an answer let me know by Gibson." Gibson and I observed three more at intervals and kept calling them up on our Morse lamps but got no reply whatsoever. The other steamer meanwhile had shut

221

in her red side light and showed us her stern light and her masthead's glow was just visible[146]. I observed the steamer to be steaming away to the S.W. and altering her bearing fast. We were also swinging slowly all the time through S. and at 1:50 were heading about W.S.W. and the other steamer bearing S. W. x W. At 2:00 a.m. the vessel was steaming away fast and only just her stern light was visible and bearing S.W . ½ W. I sent Gibson down to you and told him to wake you and tell you we had seen altogether eight white rockets and that the steamer had gone out of sight to the S.W. Also that we were heading W.S.W. When he came back he reported he had told you we had called him up repeatedly and got no answer, and you replied: "All right, are you sure there were no colours in them," and Gibson replied, "No, they were all white." At 2:45 I again whistled down again and told you we had seen no more lights and that the steamer had steamed away to the S.W. and was now out of sight, also that the rockets were all white and had no colours whatever.

We saw nothing further until about 3:20 when we thought we observed two faint lights in the sky about S.S.W. and a little distance apart. At 3:40 I sent Gibson down to see all was ready for me to prepare the new log at eight bells. The Chief Officer, Mr. Stewart, came on the bridge at 4 a.m., and I gave him a full report of what I had seen and my reports and replies from you, and pointed out where I thought I had observed these faint lights at 3:20. He picked up the binoculars and said after a few moments: "There she is then, she's all right, she is a four-master." I said, "Then that isn't the steamer I saw first," took up the glasses and just made out a four-masted steamer with two masthead lights a little abaft our port beam, and bearing about S., we were heading about W.N.W. Mr. Stewart then took over the Watch and I went off the bridge.
Yours respectfully,

(signed) Herbert Stone
2nd Officer

Likewise, Gibson's affidavit is as follows:

Thursday, April 18th, 1912
Captain Lord,
Dear Sir,

In compliance with your wishes, I hereby make the following statement as to what I saw on the morning of April 15th, 1912:

It being my watch on deck from 12 o'clock, I went on the bridge at about

---

146   In communication with this author, Harrison interprets this as meaning that,
"Stone associated the last three 'rockets' with a moving vessel which was changing her bearings." Recall Stone's evidence in London:
"Q. Was the steamer altering her bearing to your vessel during that period of time?
A. Yes, from the time I saw the <u>first</u> rocket." [This author's emphasis].

15 minutes after twelve and saw that the ship was stopped and that she was surrounded with light field ice and thick field-ice to the Southward. While the 2nd Officer and I were having coffee, a few minutes later, I asked him if there were any more ships around us. He said that there was one on the Starboard beam, and looking over the weather cloth, I saw a white light flickering, which I took to be a Morse light calling us up. I then went over to the keyboard and gave one long flash in answer, and still seeing this light flickering. I gave her the calling up sign. The light on the other ship, however, was still the same, so I looked at her through the binoculars and found it was her masthead light flickering. I also observed her port sidelight and a faint glare of lights on her afterdeck. I then went over to the 2nd Officer and remarked she looked like a tramp steamer. He said that most probably she was, and was burning oil lights. This ship was then right abeam.

At about 25 minutes after twelve I went down off the bridge to get a new log out and not being able to find it, I went on the bridge again to see if the 2nd Officer knew anything about it. I then noticed that this other ship was about one and a half points before the beam. I then went down again and was down until about five minutes to one. Arriving on the bridge again at that time, the 2nd Officer told me that the other ship, which was then about 3 ½ points on the Starboard bow, had fired five rockets and he also remarked that after seeing the second one to make sure that he was not mistaken, he had told the Captain, through the speaking tube, and that the Captain had told him to watch her and keep calling her up on the Morse light. I then watched her for some time and then went over to the keyboard and called her up continuously for about three minutes. I then got the binoculars and had just got them focused on the vessel when I observed a white flash apparently on her deck, followed by a faint streak towards the sky which then burst into white stars. Nothing then happened until the other ship was about two points on the Starboard bow when she fired another rocket.

Shortly after that, I observed that her sidelight had disappeared, but her masthead light was just visible, and the 2nd Officer remarked after taking another bearing of her, that she was slowly steering away towards the S.W. Between one point on the Starboard bow and one point on the Port bow I called her up on the Morse lamp but received no answer. When about one point on the Port bow she fired another rocket which like the others burst into white stars. Just after two o'clock she was then about two points on the Port bow, she disappeared from sight and nothing was seen of her again. The 2nd Officer then said, "Call the Captain and tell him that the ship has disappeared in the S.W., that we are heading W.S.W. and that altogether she has fired eight rockets." I then went down below to the chartroom and called the Captain and told him and he asked me if there were any colours in the rockets. I told him that they were all white. He then asked me what time it was and I went on the bridge and told the 2nd Officer what the Captain had said. At about 2:45 he whistled down to the Captain again but I did not hear what was said.

At about 3:20 looking over the weather cloth, I observed a rocket about two points before the beam (Port), which I reported to the 2nd Officer. About three minutes later I saw another rocket right abeam which was followed later by another one about two points before the beam. I saw nothing else and when one bell went, I went below to get the log gear ready for the 2nd Officer at eight bells.
Yours respectfully,

(Signed) James Gibson,
Apprentice

Quite why Stanley Lord kept these statements secret for more than 46 years is a matter ripe for conjecture. Why he asked for them in the first place is also unknown. It is possible that, had "*A Night To Remember*" not been published, these statements would never have become public[147]: it is therefore fortunate that they contain little that was not mentioned in London, although some of the timings are slightly off (for instance, Gibson mentions coming back to the bridge after preparing the new log line at 12.55am, when five rockets had been fired, but Stone puts this at about 1.15am. This possibly unimportant; in London, Gibson stresses the word "about" when describing times. It is clear he was not keeping an eye on the time, except when asked for it by the Captain, who is told "2.05 by the wheelhouse clock.").

Of interest is Stone's mention of informing the Captain after seeing five rockets, but Gibson remembering that the 2nd Officer "remarked that after seeing the second one to make sure that he was not mistaken, he had told the Captain." It is, of course, damaging to Stone that he did not bother to report to the captain after seeing the second rocket, when he would have been sure that what he was seeing conforms to the internationally agreed description of distress rockets at sea. Stone may have told Gibson that he waited till after the second rocket to prevent his sullied reputation being further tarnished. Why wait till 5 had been sent up? But let us give the 2nd Officer the benefit of the doubt. If Stone is correct about informing the Captain after seeing two rockets, then he would have told his superior of seeing these, and not just the one that Lord claimed. Why would Stone only mention seeing one, when he had in fact seen two?

It is up to the reader to decide whether Stone's statement about a flash "observed another distinctly over the [other] steamer" is consistent with him claiming to see a rocket rising no higher than half the height of the mastlight. Also worthy of note is that Stone's account mentions, at about 1.15, and having seen five rockets, that he reports to Lord, "I reported seeing these lights in the sky ... which appeared to me to be white rockets." Note that this refers to rocket<u>s</u> – that, is,

---

147   Copies of these statements had been made available to the Board of Trade prior to 1961, as Captain Quick's report (see later) makes reference to the contents of Stone's declaration.

plural. Lord's evidence refers to only being told of a single rocket by Stone at this time. Gibson's account says that Stone whistled down to Lord after seeing the first two rockets. But Stone's account does corroborate his earlier assertion – that the red light was shut in towards the end of the rocket firing sequence, and not upon commencement of the pyrotechnics.

Recall, too, Stewart's account of Stone's brief report of the rockets seen "at 1.00am" as the Chief Officer said in London. Stone had said at 4 o'clock that the rockets did not seem to go any higher than the masthead lights, and that "they did not leave a trail in the sky." Both Stone and Gibson observed the rockets through binoculars and yet the apprentice did see "a faint streak towards the sky." In London, Stewart had also reported that the light seen at 3.40am, which Gibson had reported as being another set of rockets, thought belonged to the new yellow funnelled arrival on the scene, which had been observed after Gibson had left the bridge at about this time, but before Stewart's arrival. Stone had pointed out the direction in which these "faint lights" were seen, and Stewart spotted the new arrival on the scene. This is exactly the behaviour of the *Carpathia*; with a bearing of the *Titanic* from the *Californian* of S 45° E, the *Carpathia* would be on an approximate bearing of S 52° E beyond the *Titanic* – or a near straight line with the three ships lying on this line (see Appendix D). The *Carpathia* then would be seen in the same direction as the strange rockets seen after 3.00am. The same can't be said of the *Mount Temple*, the leading candidate for the so-called "yellow" funnel steamer, as she didn't fire any rockets.

The question remained: could Captain Lord rely on support from the M.M.S.A.? Its President, Captain George Ayre, was damning of Lord: "By rights Captain Lord should be dead by now, and this matter would be ancient history," he told Harrison over tea, who was aghast. The following afternoon, both men met at a routine meeting of the M.M.S.A. Finance Committee, where Harrison asked for permission "to incur any necessary expenditure in pursuing Captain Lord's case." It was during this meeting that eight of his colleagues remarked that they shared Ayre's opinion, and after long debate on this "extraordinary" case, £100 was apportioned to the matter. The Executive Council agreed the with Finance Committee's action.

Harrison relished his new responsibility and approached slurs on Lord's character with zest It might even be said that he acted in a supererogatory manner. For instance, in May 1959, the *Nautical Magazine* published an account of the *Titanic* disaster by her 4th Officer Boxhall, which partially read, "The ship ... on the port bow was now clearly visible, with portholes brightly shining, and contrary to her master's later given evidence was still moving slowly. And when this ship, the *Californian*, arrived in port, the master decided not to make any report on the night's happenings, and if it had not been for a donkeyman who left her upon arrival, it is doubtful if she would ever have been identified." With an accusation that the *Californian* was moving, and that Lord had committed perjury under oath, Harrison acted speedily and contacted the magazine's editor and a correction and apology was published in the next issue.

An obvious source of information would be the other officers on the *Californian*. Sadly, Stewart had lost his life in World War 2. Gibson had died some 6 month before Harrison could locate him, in August 1963. Fortunately, Groves was still alive, and he was traced in 1959. Letters and a meeting ensued. Apart from refusing to discuss the navigational matters of the case, he was friendly and helpful. Harrison would later write[148] that Groves would not give any indication whether he had changed his mind regarding his original opinion. In fact, Groves had already told him and others that he stood by what he had said in 1912. Harrison also asked if Groves had felt pressured during his appearance at Mersey's court when his evidence, particularly his assertion that the vessel that he had seen was the *Titanic*, damned his commanding officer. Groves was astonished by the accusation and replied that he had felt no pressure at all.

What was Captain Lord's opinion of his fellow crew members? As related in his later book, Harrison tells us that Lord felt his crew were not liars and were trustworthy. In a 1961 interview, Lord had told his champion that he harboured no resentment or animus towards either Groves or Gill.

Only one slight mystery remained. Harrison would later write in his 1986 book that he "made no attempt to trace Stone. By 1963 he would have been in his 70's; having regard to the demonstrably false accusation reliably attributed to him, that Captain Lord was under the influence of drink on the night of the *Titanic* disaster, I had no wish to become involved in any sort of controversy with him."

This is a huge pity; if Harrison had tried to find Stone as soon as Lord appealed for the help of the M.M.S.A., he no doubt would have found him, living but a few miles away in the Waterloo area of Liverpool. Stone had died in late 1959 and there was more than enough time to locate him.

What "demonstrably false accusation" does Harrison allude to? One scours his book for clues, but only source is provided.

"*"A Night to Remember*" ... reveals only some of the minor blunders relating to the tragedy, while brazenly omitting or kissing off the most shocking scandals of all! These scandals, never exposed before, are four-fold. ... The Captain of a nearby ship who could have saved everybody aboard the *Titanic* lay stinking drunk in his cabin while 1,500 died in agony. ... Add to the list of seaborne murderers the name of Captain John [sic] Lord, master of the steamship *Californian*. This ship was only ten short miles away from the *Titanic*--close enough to see its lights--yet didn't show up at the disaster scene until it was too

---

148   "*A Titanic Myth*" page 240.

late. John Lord said he was asleep when the collision occurred, and that his radio operator had gone off duty ten minutes before the SOS was flashed from the luxury liner. Members of his crew saw a spectacular display of rockets fired as signals of distress from the *Titanic*, but according to Lord they didn't realise what the signals meant. Lord's testimony was completely disproved by a statement by 2nd Officer Stone--a statement that never got into print. He had gone to the Captain's cabin to report on the distress rockets and to get orders to rush to the *Titanic's* help. The Captain never gave such orders and for a good reason--he was too drunk to realise what his officer was telling him. Instead he ordered Stone in his best whiskey voice to "Forget thish whole thing and lemme sleep.""

This is from a story written by John Gregory, for a magazine called "Inside Story", published by the American Periodicals Corporation of New York. It is undated, but is obviously contemporaneous with "*A Night to Remember*", so it can be placed about 1958. Why Harrison should consider that the information in the article can be "reliably attributed" to Stone is unknown. Certainly, it is telling that the author of the piece got Captain Lord's first name wrong! And, with the story of the *Titanic* having been resurrected by Walter Lord, it is astonishing that such assertions by "Stone" did not receive greater press coverage, which could have yielded a public comment from Stone himself.

Another alternative for the source of the "drunk on duty" charge comes from Captain Gorrell, whose letter to Harrison has already been quoted. But this information, plus a conversation with Gorrell in 1966 regarding Stone, cannot be the source of Harrison's misgivings regarding Stone, for these recollections occur after 1963, although an annotated copy of Harrison's 1986 book lists Gorrell as the source. Gorrell's comments are not mentioned in Harrison's book. What we are being asked to believe is, between 1958 and 1966, Harrison did not lift a finger to find Stone. Are there any other sources of Stone's public dissatisfaction with Lord? Indeed. In 1962, a gentleman by the name of Ivan Thompson was now President of the M.M.S.A., and his attitude to Lord was hostile as will soon be seen; additionally, he had heard second-hand information that Stone had always thought that what he saw fired from the other ship were indeed distress rockets, and it is possible that he told Harrison this story.

It may be that Harrison did not try to contact Stone for the same reason that Lord Mersey had suggested that Robertson Dunlop did not write to owners of a possible Mystery Ship in 1912, "Was that because you did not want to know what [he] would say?" Simply put, the lack of effort trying to contact Stone is unforgivable, in this author's opinion. It would have been better to hear Stone's own version of events rather than Gorrell's story, which he had heard as an impressionable 9 year old.

Additionally, Harrison had been pleading with Walter Lord and his publishers and indeed, had had some success with the characterisation of the

Californian in the novelization of "*A Night To Remember*". Out of compassion for the Captain, Walter offered – and performed – modifications to three passages in his book. But contrary to this conciliatory approach, the M.M.S.A. interpreted this gesture as "a wholesale confession of error."

Other authors were now prepared to discharge their broadsides at Captain Lord.

In 1960, Commodore Sir James Bisset published the second volume of his memoirs, entitled "*Tramps and Ladies*": it partially covered his time as 2nd Officer on the *Carpathia* when she rescued the *Titanic*'s survivors. He was very critical of the *Californian*, but wrote that there was no wilful neglect on [the officer's] part, "but rather a deficiency of seaman-like reaction in extremely unusual circumstances."

The critical part of Bisset's memoirs reads:

"While we had been picking up the survivors, in the slowly increasing daylight after 4:30 a.m., we had sighted the smoke of a steamer on the fringe of the pack ice, ten miles away from us to the northwards. She was making no signals, and we paid little attention to her, for we were occupied with more urgent matters, but at 6 a.m., we had noticed that she was under way and slowly coming towards us. When I took over the watch on the bridge of the *Carpathia* at 8 a.m., the stranger was little more than a mile from us, and flying her signals of identification. She was the Leyland Line cargo steamer *Californian*, which had been stopped overnight blocked by ice."

There is a problem with this account. At 6.00 a.m., the *Californian* was indeed under way, but she wasn't heading directly towards the *Carpathia*: on the contrary, she was heading between south and south-west to the official distress position. However, Bisset may have glanced up occasionally between his more pressing duties and seen the ship heading his way as the *Californian* proceeded on a southerly course at that time. Other sections of Bisset's volume raise eyebrows too; for instance, the mention of non-existent ice warnings wirelessed to the *Carpathia*, and the mention that the *Californian* saw the *Titanic* stern on at the time she sank.

Bisset wrote, regarding Lord's question "Are they company signals?": "This was one of the most tragic moments on that fateful night. Rockets were the well-known signals of distress, but some of the big shipping companies were in the habit of using Roman candles-combinations of coloured fireworks, which resemble rockets -as signals of identification for their ships, especially when approaching Light Vessels or shore signal stations or the entrances to ports, but also at sea when passing other ships at night-time, at a distance beyond easy visual range for Morse lamp signalling.

This was a practise which should never have been allowed, especially after all big ships were equipped with wireless. The use of fireworks should have been restricted to signals of distress."[149]

One recent writer, ignorant in many matters, has questioned Bisset's sighting of smoke from the steamer to the north, saying that, if it was the *Californian,* she would not have been emitting at the time of sunrise. This is completely inaccurate. Civil twilight was at 5.11 a.m[150].; at this time, the eastern horizon would be showing daylight: indeed the sun rose almost directly due east. All other horizons would still be dark, but gradually showing more illumination as the Earth rotated. We know that Captain Lord "moved the engines first at 5.15 on the 15th of April, full ahead". She stopped for a while before proceeding to the rescue, at 6.00am. The *Californian* would therefore be showing smoke from her funnel. Furthermore, Lord had ordered Chief Engineer Mahan to keep steam up during the night in case they required the engines. To keep the steam up, the boilers would have to be stoked and refuelled, albeit not necessarily in a continual basis as one would expect on a mobile ship; coal's combustion products would have to be expelled – hence smoke from the funnel. There is footage of an immobile *Titanic* in dock at Belfast, with little smoke issuing from one of her funnels, to maintain electrical power. Is it not reasonable to assume that the *Californian* did the same?

Illustration 30: Lifeboat 14 towing boat 'D' to the Carpathia

This same author, desperate to present any evidence in favour of Captain Lord, no matter how poorly researched or presented, also asks, if the *Californian*

---

149   See Appendix B
150   These values may differ slightly from calculations provided by other authors: this author has assumed a 2 hour time difference between the wrecksite and New York Time, for simplicity.

was only 10 miles north of the *Carpathia* in the morning, why does she not appear in the numerous photographs of ice and lifeboats taken during the rescue by the Cunard vessel on April 15th? A little thought would solve this mystery. With a few exceptions, we do not know exactly when the pictures were taken, although they are obviously after sunrise, as the sky is not dark. Of the lifeboats shown, numbers 14, 6 and collapsible D can be identified. The photos are obviously taken looking in a northerly direction, as boat 14 has her sails billowing caused by wind from the north that morning. Daisy Minahan, in boat 14, wrote in an affidavit to the U.S. Inquiry, "It was just 4 o'clock when we sighted the *Carpathia*, and we were three hours getting to her" In London, the Attorney General remarked, during the testimony of Able Bodied Seaman Joseph Scarrott, that boat 14 reached the *Carpathia* between 7 and 8 a.m. Boat D, being towed by 14, would have reached the *Carpathia* at about this time, too.

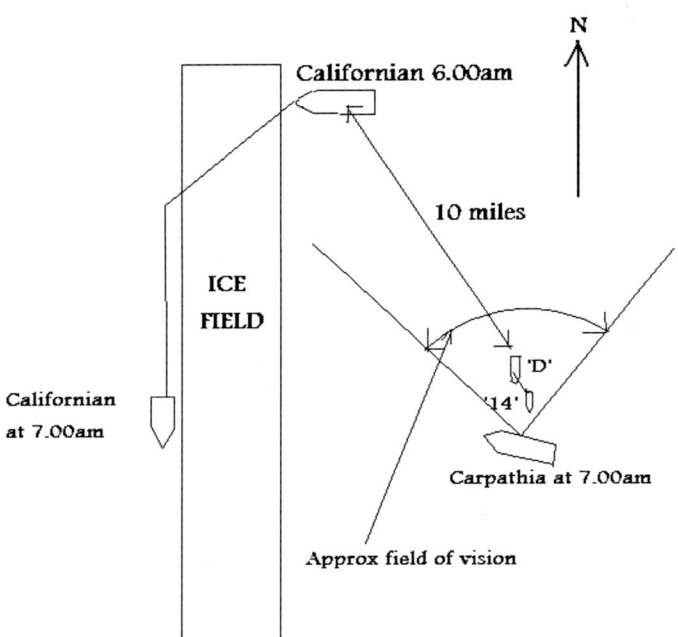

Illustration 31: The Californian, ten miles north of the Carpathia, and visible at sunrise.

As for boat 6, Major Arthur Peuchen noted that "It was after 8 o'clock that I looked at my watch; it was something after 8 o'clock that we got on [the *Carpathia*]." So, the first photo that can be timestamped with reasonable confidence was taken at about 7.00am. Where would the *Californian* be at the time? Between 6 and 6am, she was pushing through the ice field, dodging between south and south-west in an overall heading of S 16 W. She was crawling through the ice for the first half hour, perhaps covering 3 or so miles, then proceeding at full speed south, down the western side of the ice field. A simple sketch shows that the *Californian* would have been to the west of the *Carpathia*, and hence outside the field of vision of the cameras.

The same argument can be applied to any other ship or feature on the ocean. Why don't we seen the *Mount Temple*, the *Almerian* (if she was there at all), the black and white funnelled ship, or indeed, the yellow funnelled steamer seen by the *Californian* crew? Why don't we see their smoke? Why don't we see the floating debris from the *Titanic*? Why don't we see the "thick ice" displayed so prominently on Foweraker's map? Why don't we see <u>any</u> ice? The answer seems simple: the clarity and resolution of the photographs are not adequate for detailed analysis, especially for features at a distance.

Bisset's book containing an attitude critical towards Lord had to be dealt with. Harrison wrote to the publishers, who accepted Captain Lord's story and promised that the chapter dealing with the *Californian* incident would not be published in any reprint without "sweeping changes" to be drafted by Harrison himself. *The Liverpool Daily Post* was running Bisset's book in a serialised form and also gave assurances that anything referring to the *Californian* would not be included.

Captain Lord's health, meanwhile, had deteriorated drastically and he was admitted to hospital for protracted periods of time, first for a cataract removal, then pneumonia, before having an emergency operation for a strangulated hernia. Because of Lord's increasing frailty, the M.M.S.A. council gave Harrison "complete discretion to take such action [that he] considered might be required by the particular circumstances at any time to protect Captain Lord's reputation and to rectify the adverse effects of the [1912 inquiries]." In February 1961 Harrison interviewed Lord on tape, and it gave a permanent record, along with an affidavit[151] drawn up two years previously, of the Captain's opinions and recollections of that night in April 1912.

In May 1961, former Cunard Commodore Sir Ivan Thompson took over from Ayre as President of the M.M.S.A., and he shared his predecessors views. Indeed, Thompson had visited Sir James Bisset during the latter's retirement in Manly, near Sydney, and the two men discussed their anti-*Californian* sentiments. Harrison was concerned that Thompson's new position would have a damaging effect on the campaign to clear Lord's name, and suggested, in a letter that he and Thompson should meet, as Harrison thought that this might be able to clarify some of the "sincerely held views" which the M.M.S.A. General Secretary felt may have been based on "misconceptions." As we shall see, Thompson's scepticism of Lord's case was born at the time of the *Titanic* disaster; he was on the sea at the time and had had a chance to discuss the case with those familiar – and involved – in the matter, unlike Harrison who had not become familiar with the *Titanic* disaster until

---

151   See http://home.earthlink.net/~dnitzer/6Affidavits/Lord_1959.html

many years after.

The meeting between Harrison and Thompson was fruitless. The ex-Cunard Commodore simply reiterated his views that the *Californian's* middle watch was defective and that all the lives lost when the *Titanic* foundered could have been saved[152]. A formal letter from Harrison to Thompson noted that "...your present holding of office as President makes it quite impossible for me to take any such action or to make any statements which conflict with your own personal views ... There is one other point which I should like to make perfectly clear, and that is the fact that any recommendation I have made to the Council are *not* based solely on Captain Lord's side of the story. As General Secretary, I automatically regard any member's side of the case he puts to me as being biased to some degree, so that it consequently becomes my duty to ferret out everything which might be held against him[153]."

Just before Captain Lord's death, Leslie Harrison arranged for Liverpool *Journal of Commerce* reporter C.H. Milsom to meet him. The interview was "off the record" as "it was felt that publicity would only draw attention to the fact that he was still alive and would bring a horde of Fleet Street reporters to his door[154].

The meeting had two purposes, Milsom wrote later; "Firstly, that there should be at least one completely independent witness who could testify, if necessary, to Captain Lord's character and personality ... and secondly, that there should be someone on the staff of the *Journal of Commerce* who had an understanding of the case."

Milsom displayed some misgivings at first, as Lord "had a reputation for arrogance, a reputation, incidentally, which was totally undeserved." But apparently Lord was courteous and hospitable.

Lord repeated his simplistic defence of the *Californian*- "The ship seen by the *Titanic* was moving, so that couldn't have been us because we were stopped. The ship we saw was moving so that couldn't have been the *Titanic* because she was stopped."

By November 1961, "there were clear indications that the editorial staff of a number of leading maritime publications were becoming increasingly aware of Captain Lord's story; and there was an indication that even in official circles doubts were beginning to be felt as to the complete validity of the 1912 Inquiry findings." Now, Harrison hoped to publish a feature entitled, "*The Californian Incident – an*

---

152   See the Epilogue for a discussion on this matter.
153   Interestingly, the concluding paragraph of this letter displays Harrison's opinion of the *Titanic-Californian* matter: he talks of the independent evidence "which appears to demonstrate that the *Californian, although seeing the distant rocket signals from the Titanic,* was too far away to have reached her in time to render any effective assistance [this author's emphasis]." Readers should compare and contrast this with Harrison's later conclusions.
154   *Sea Breezes* Vol. 61, 1987. pp 125-127

Echo of the Titanic Disaster" in the April 1962 edition of the *Merchant Navy Journal*.

There was hostility to this proposal at the next M.M.S.A. Executive Council meeting. Thompson remarked that "his strongly held personal views had extinguished any latent inclination to observe the conventional neutrality of a chairman." If Harrison's later account of this meeting is accurate, Thompson effectively dominated the whole proceedings, interrupting members and labelling the whole *Californian* matter as a waste of time. Harrison's suggestion for a sub-committee to determine why he had been given *carte blanche* to act in any manner that might preserve Lord's reputation, was rejected by ten votes to two, with one abstention. Harrison suddenly felt the support the Council had afforded both him, and Captain Lord, ebbing away. But the Council made one concession: that Harrison could prepare and circulate a document, for later discussion, that would give the facts of the case as he saw them. But a disillusioned Harrison, sickened by the *volte-face* of the committee was now prepared to resign and he organised a meeting with four senior council members to discuss his intentions. Before this could take place, Ivan Thompson told him that he had changed his mind and had no intention of taking part in a meeting: in his opinion, "any authority [Harrison] might once have had to act in Captain Lord's case had been revoked by the Council and matters must now rest until their next meeting in January. Equally bluntly, I stated that if the Council at that meeting were to seek to prevent me from helping Captain Lord, now in the 64th year of his continuous membership of the M.M.S.A., I would have to disobey their instructions."

Sir Ivan's next action surprised Harrison. It appeared that a Council minute dating from 1941 enabled a General Secretary to override the decisions of the Council, and he intended to have it expunged at the next meeting in January. Harrison was unaware of this minute, and, although dis- quietened by the exchange with Thompson, he settled down to work on his document setting out his version of events.

On January 24th, 1962, Captain Lord died, aged 84. His son requested no publicity until after the funeral, which Harrison attended. A few days later the M.M.S.A. Council convened.

Chapter 8. "The facile pen of Mr. Harrison"

1962 – 1968

"Let's get down to this Lord case. Why weren't we told of his death? The Council have got to settle the General Secretary's challenge to the council at the Finance Committee," Thompson said. Harrison replied that his challenge was not aimed at the committee, but to individual members of the Council. The meeting become more and more inflammatory, and Harrison ultimately informed the rest of the members that they would have his written account of the *Californian* affair in two days time. He also formally reported Captain Lord's death. Thompson was ultimately defeated on the abolition of the 1941 'override' clause that could have been invoked by the General Secretary because it only referred to the evacuation of elderly residents from M.M.S.A. property during the Second World War, and was not a mechanism for any secretary to take unilateral action, devoid of Council intervention. Surprisingly, a vote of confidence in the General Secretary was passed.

A few days hence, Harrison dispatched copies of his essay to his fellow Council members. With the paper, he enclosed a ballot paper, which asked two questions. The first was "whether or not, on the facts of the case, Council members considered that there had been a miscarriage of justice ... the second question was a simpler one: should the article be published in *The Merchant Navy Journal*?"

To the first question, six thought no, 24 said yes and two abstained. Regarding the second, 7 said no, 25 said yes. At the February meeting, a more formal vote was taken of the 18 members present. 14 were in favour of publication, four against. Harrison was allowed to publicise the article and was granted an extra £150 from Association funds: "On the issue of the 'full powers' minute of 1941, the Council unanimously agreed that no further action was required."

The article was published, together with a pamphlet which incorporated Lord's affidavit, Stone's and Gibson's statements, and 1912 letters to and from Lord to Rostron, Lightoller, the M.M.S.A. etc. Also included in the set of articles was a reproduction of Lord Mersey's pronouncement on the *Californian*, and a 1962 opinion on the 1912 legality of the British Inquiry's treatment of Captain Lord.

Harrison wrote, in 1996[155], that the only mistake that he appeared to make in his "Echo..." article was his comment that, "It is impossible to escape the conclusion that some, or all of the rockets they saw originated from the *Titanic*." Indeed, he continues by discussing that a line extending from the *Californian* some 25 miles to the south-east would lead to their originating source; the *Titanic*. "On reflection," Harrison sighed in his book, "I now realise that I would have done

---

155   "*A Titanic Myth part 2*" page 38. Ironically, Harrison had failed to notice that he had said the *Titanic* disaster had occurred in February 1912 in one paragraph of '*The Californian Incident.*'

better to qualify this reference, for inevitably it was picked up by my critics and often quoted against me."In subsequent articles, interviews and petitions, he would ascribe the rockets as coming from another, separate ship.

Harrison was evidently extremely generous with his self-critical comments. The *Carpathia*'s account of its final approach to the *Titanic* lifeboats is described as a "zig-zag" course. This is inconsistent with Rostron's testimony. Why did the M.M.S.A. General Secretary describe it so unfaithfully? His logic, in part, is reasonable. The *Carpathia* couldn't have steamed through the ice field on its way to its intended destination, the SOS location. Therefore, she must have been closer to the actual wreck than the 1912 inquiries would speculate. This reduced distance, would, in the words of the "Echo..." article "reduce not only the full speed[156] but the actual distance made good and there can be no doubt that the *Carpathia* actually encountered the lifeboats at least ten, and more probably 18 miles to the south-eastward of the dead reckoning position given by the *Titanic*." There is no discussion as to how the 10, or 18 mile value has been calculated. Of course, it would be consistent with Captain Lord's insistence that the *Titanic* sank 16 miles to the south-east of her SOS location.

Boxhall's testimony had now been transformed, such that he initially saw the masthead light of a ship approaching from hull down (that is, with the hull partially obscured by the rim of the horizon) ..." later her red side light and deck lights were seen ... [finally she] shows her stern light, which receded." On a dark night, it would be impossible to see the hull of a ship, regardless of whether she was coming over the horizon or not. There is no mention of seeing a green light. The stern light receding is not consistent with other information from the lifeboats; some describe the stern light as being visible until daybreak, when the *Carpathia* was seen. The only other 'witness' to be mentioned in the document is Lawrence Beesley.

With regard to what was seen by the *Californian*, Lord's "green light/ship coming from the east" is now ignored in favour of Groves "red light/ship coming from the south-west". Lord's story of being told of a "rocket", and not "rockets" after 1 a.m. is mentioned. There is no reference to the rockets seen after 3 a.m.

Now, with his name eternally linked with the *Californian*, Leslie Harrison was being seen as the bellwether of the Captain Lord campaign.

The article was published, and comment was invited on, or after Friday, 16th March 1962. A press cutting agency was employed to monitor the resultant publicity. On this same day, Ivan Thompson posted his resignation of the M.M.S.A. Presidency to the Vice-president, Captain C.P. Vaughan[157]. Thompson was quoted

---

156   The 17 knot speed attributed to the *Carpathia* the night the *Titanic* went down is a mechanical impossibility; a figure closer to its maximum speed of 14 knots is more likely.

157   Vaughan received the resignation on Monday, 19th March. According to Harrison, Thompson, with Captains Ayre and Vaughan had visited Herbert Allen; the

as telling the press hordes, "I have no wish to be associated with the M.M.S.A.'s report. I do not agree with it. The *Titanic* sinking was the blackest thing that ever happened to British shipping. Everybody connected with shipping in this country considers *Titanic* a nasty word. They hate the idea of it being brought up again. My resignation is a direct protest against this publication ... I deplore the fact that the *Titanic* disaster has been dragged up again. This new account can't do Captain Lord or anybody else connected with British shipping any good. I think the whole things is as dead as cold mutton."

On Monday, Harrison and Thompson faced each other in a debate for a television programme in Manchester. Now, when asked why he had resigned, Thompson told the interviewer, that it was because "Mr. Harrison was attempting to drag into the *Titanic* controversy another British ship, the *Mount Temple*, and another British shipmaster, Captain Moore... I just wondered why he had done it."

Harrison disputed this, pointing out that in his foreword to Captain Lord's affidavit (which had been included in the article), he had mentioned that, navigationally, the *Mount Temple* couldn't have been the ship seen from the *Titanic*."[Captain Moore] is not being dragged in ... and I am amazed that Sir Ivan should have made such a suggestion," responded Harrison.

"It's in your book [sic - pamphlet]," Sir Ivan replied.

"It's not in my book [sic]" Harrison replied, equally assertively.

Harrison is partially correct. In the introduction to the pamphlet containing Lord's affidavit, he provides the reader with a "cautionary comment addressed to anyone who approaches this with a fresh mind. I consider that the most likely explanation of such lights seen [from the *Mount Temple*] is that they were signals exchanged at the last moment between the approaching *Carpathia* and those in the *Titanic*'s lifeboats, but confirmation of this point will probably never be possible," thus leaving readers with an element of doubt on this point.

Let us pause to consider this. While Harrison does take measures to assure his readers that the *Mount Temple* was not the mystery ship, and had not been close to the *Titanic* when she sank, the pamphlet does contain the letters of W.H. Baker, Grylls etc., and their accusations regarding Captain Moore's ship. Any reader who feels inclined to ignore the introduction would be left with the impression that there was indeed sufficient evidence against the *Mount Temple* for the M.M.S.A. to become involved in 1912. Why include these in the first place?

One more point. Harrison also writes in his introduction that "[he] would like to point out that Captain Lord never at any stage attempted to incriminate any other shipmaster." The reader need only peruse the correspondence contained within that very document (!) and the narrative in this book to judge how accurate this comment is.

---

meeting centred on Thompson's conduct, during which he said "Well, I suppose I'd better resign." Which he did later the same day. We can only take Harrison's word on this.

The third document in the M.M.S.A./Captain Lord dispatch was a reprint of Lord Mersey's statement about the *Californian*, and "Some legal aspects of the official British Inquiry 1912 (A 1962 Legal Opinion)." The Inquiry," it states, "was held under the provision of the Merchant Shipping Act, 1894, Section 466 (11)[158]; 'every formal investigation into a shipping casualty shall be conducted in such a manner that if a charge is made against any person, that person shall have an opportunity of making a defence.'" The M.M.S.A. document clarifies the legal language that a 'charge' applies to any imputation of fault which might be made against a person during the course of the proceedings. The only text book dealing with marine inquiries (McMillan's '*Shipping Courts and Inquests*') states "Such charges as are substantiated may have serious consequences for the persons concerned. An express duty is therefore hard on the Court to ensure that the persons charged shall have an opportunity of making a defence, and express provision is made throughout the Act and throughout the rules of procedure for its observation."

The M.M.S.A. document considers the charges against Captain Lord to be unfair for the following reasons:

1. "Captain Lord was called as a witness ... no notice of investigation was served upon him";
2. "[Lord's] Counsel made it quite clear that on certain matters, such as making enquiries as to the possibilities of other ships being in the vicinity, the owners [of the *Californian*] had decided that it was neither proper, nor their duty to do so";
3. "Before Captain Lord was called to give evidence, [Dunlop] made an application to the Court to be made a party – an application which was in any case only a general one ... had the court acceded to their application, and Captain Lord thereupon been made a party, he would have voluntarily subjected himself to the jurisdiction of the Court in the same manner as if a notice of investigation had been served on him. But the Court in its wisdom did not accede to Counsel's request and for the remaining period of the Inquiry, the Counsel concerned only held a watching brief. It is submitted that the Court, by refusing this application, itself deliberately excluded such jurisdiction as it may have thought concerning Captain Lord";

---

158   Subsection 6 of this same area of the Act specifies that "The court after hearing the case shall make a report to the Board of Trade containing a full statement of the case and of the opinion of the court thereon, accompanied by such report of, or extracts from, the evidence, and such observations as the court think fit." Astonishingly, the M.M.S.A. did not pounce on the word "opinion" and declare that the adverse findings against Captain Lord was simply based on the whims of Lord Mersey and his assessors.

4. The officers of the *Californian* were released and not present after the 8ᵗʰ day of the Inquiry;

5. "After this, it must have been apparent from the questions put to the witnesses that the Board of Trade had the information which made it possible to give notice there and then to Captain Lord of their intention to add a question. Consequently it can only be submitted that it was a very serious error of judgement on the part of the Board of Trade and the Court to permit Captain Lord ... to return to his home, where it must have been in their minds at the close of the Californian evidence that further questions might arise."

6. "It is a surprising fact that the inclusion of the question [on the 27ᵗʰ day when Captain Lord was not present] was not bitterly contested, and this fact can apparently only be accounted for by the absence from the Court of Counsel holding only a watching brief [i.e. Dunlop]";

7. "On the 33ʳᵈ day, Counsel made it clear that he had been present very little during the course of the Inquiry";

8. "Despite Counsel's protest on behalf of Captain Lord that he [i.e. Lord] had not been served a notice of investigation and that he, Counsel, was only holding a watching brief, the Court apparently decided that, as Counsel had been present representing Captain Lord it was open for the Court to consider the question relating to Captain Lord. This, on the face of it, appears to be an extremely irregular attitude to have adopted."

In view of the manifest unfairness of the position, it seems strange that further efforts were not made to try to have the proceedings quashed in so far as Captain Lord was concerned ... it is quite evident that no proper case was prepared, or indeed could have been prepared, which fairly represented Captain Lord's position and adequately protested his interests."

Meanwhile, international distribution of Harrison's article had resulted in good publicity for the late Captain Lord and his cause, and the M.M.S.A. took heart that "no attempt had been made by anyone to answer the detailed questions it posed, or to challenge the reasons given in support of the claim that there had been a gross miscarriage of justice in Captain Lord's case."

But could the M.M.S.A. spearhead a parliamentary campaign for Captain Lord's posthumous exoneration? On this matter, there seems to have been some confusion within the M.M.S.A. ranks, and Thompson's resignation can't have helped. On March 19ᵗʰ 1962, Cuthbert Bridgwater, who was 17 when the *Titanic* went down, wrote to Leslie Harrison, saying that he had met Captain Lord "several times when he was master of the *Californian*, and like my father, Superintendant of the Leyland Line in his day, never believed him negligent, slackness being so foreign to his nature. Captain Lord was a fine character." In light of Lord's death, would that part of the *Titanic* Inquiry that censured him be reopened? Would he find a champion in the M.M.S.A.? A fortnight later, Harrison replied: "after an exhaustive Inquiry ... we are convinced that no useful purpose could be served in calling for the re-opening of the *Titanic* Inquiry in so far as it affects Captain Lord." This attitude changed radically. By July, "the Council is now unified in its decision to institute a formal approach to the Ministry of Transport intending to secure a reversal of the 1912 Inquiry findings."

So, what could have happened between March and July that re-energised the campaign to clear Lord's name? Apart from now having a President who was more leniently disposed towards Lord's case, there is only one answer.

On April 16th 1962, a television programme entitled *"The Sinking of the Titanic"* was shown by the Norwegian Broadcasting Corporation. In this show, it was alleged that a Norway sealer, the *Samson*, had been in the vicinity of the *Titanic* and had seen her rockets, but because she was involved in illegal sealing operations, she had sailed away thinking that the pyrotechnics were an indication to stop and be searched. It wasn't until the *Samson* arrived at an Icelandic port that the consul told the crew of the tragedy, and then the connection was made. The source of this report was the Chief Officer of the *Samson*, Mr. Henrik Naess. The story had been known about since 1912, and had been referred to in print once before, in the *Trondhjem Arbeideravisa* on June 9th, 1928.

Illustration 32: The Samson

The broadcast came to the immediate attention of Leslie Harrison. In an address to the A.G.M. of the M.M.S.A. on 4th May, he remarked that he had received confirmation of the report but had not yet been able to check it in every detail. "But," he says, "to me it seems to be absolutely authentic." Harrison had at last found his *deus ex machina* to solve the *Titanic* mystery.

Kjell Arnljot Wig, the producer in charge of the *Samson* segment recounted "after the broadcast ... he had given his oath not to reveal more than he had already done in his TV programme. All available facts, including what Henrik Naess said just before dying, Mr. Wig had turned over to the M.M.S.A ... there are no members of the Samson crew still alive, as far as I have found out." Both men who allegedly saw the rockets were now dead.

"The confidential report filed with the Norwegian consul in Reykjavik is at present in the possession of a Norwegian scientist who received a copy from the Captain of the *Samson*, but this scientist, the name of whom Kjell A. Wig has given his oath not to reveal, has promised not to publish the report until the near relatives of Henrik Naess and other members of the *Samson* crew are dead." Mr. Wig would later say that there were "somewhat delicate circumstances" which prevented him from borrowing the report for a second time in order to help the M.M.S.A clear Captain Lord's name.

*Illustration 33: First
Officer Naess*

A London newspaper reporter informed Leslie Harrison and the M.M.S.A. in 1963 that Naess's will contained a provision that references to the *Samson* and *Titanic* were not to be made until after the death of his near relatives[159]. But Harrison was diligently following other leads and thought that the Seal Fishery Act, 1875 supported the *Samson*'s story. He believed that it had international

159   Strange, as Henrik Naess's son was reportedly alive in 1976

application, and it called for "close time" in seal taking for areas between 67° and 75° North, 5° and 17° West[160]. Unfortunately, all "communal papers" and documents from which verification of the *Samson*'s call to Icelandic ports were destroyed by fire in 1924, he discovered.

Publicity from the *Samson* story, the M.M.S.A campaign, and Harrison's pamphlets resulted in some fascinating information for Harrison. He received a letter from the widow of James Urquhart, who had died four years previously. In 1912, he was an Apprentice on the SS *Baron Ardrossan*, which left Barry Dock for New York on April 5th. From conversations she had had with her husband, she remembered being told that the log book revealed that the Baron was in the area of the casualty: "they were just disappearing over the horizon when the tragedy was happening, and they did not see the distress signals." The ship had no wireless, and was delayed by pack ice and a malfunction of some of the Baron's machinery. Reverend Millar Ogilvie, who knew James Urquhart, provided some more details; it was ascertained that, during the afternoon of that day, Urquhart of the Baron had seen two or three "gleaming specks" on the horizon and was told that they were icebergs. The weather was very clear, and that evening, the ship ran into fog. The speed of the ship was reduced and the fog horn was sounded. While on the 8-12 watch, Captain Reid instructed the watch to keep a look out on the portside at intervals. Urquhart was sent down to the engine room to ascertain the ambient temperature, which was dropping, and it eventually reached freezing point. Shortly afterwards, the lookout on the f'ocsle[161] reported that the ship was entering ice. After a minute or two, the engines were stopped temporarily. During that night, and the next day, the Baron kept encountering ice but eventually left the floes behind, battling through heavy gales, which resulted in the ship being blown off course to the South-West and resulting in an overdue arrival at New York. Reverend Ogilvie had no recollection of any ship having been seen. Finally, the widow of the Baron's 3rd Officer reported that she had been told that the Baron had passed through the area the day after the *Titanic*'s sinking. From the meteorological date (wind and fog references), Harrison determined that the Baron was, indeed, not in the area during the disaster. Sadly, Urquhart's widow was not as convinced, and remained convinced that the Baron was involved. The correspondence between her and Harrison continued for quite a while, with neither side capitulating to the other[162].

Another possible candidate for "the mystery ship" was the SS *Port Pirie*, later renamed the *Kelvinbrae*. She had left Middlesbrough on April 3rd, but a quick check showed that she was still near the UK coast on 18th-20th April. She could not

---

160   This reference was made in February 1972. As we shall see Harrison's research wasn't quite so clear on this point.
161   An abbreviation for 'forecastle'; the head of the ship.
162   Lloyd's publications show that the Baron did not pass near the Titanic's location until April 17 when, at position 41.56 N 50.04 W, she was forced to stop due to heavy field ice.

have made it to the *Titanic* wreck and back.

A copy of *The Western Daily Press* from March 1946 yielded another vessel's name: the *Madawaska*, owned by Hogans of Liverpool and under the command of Captain Carey. The *Madawaska* had a yellow funnel with a black top, but she was not a four masted ship. Despite Harrison determining that the ship was to the south of the *Titanic*, her tale was fascinating, according to Carey in the paper: "We were on the way from Boston to Ceylon with a load of rice when my lookouts saw what he thought was a display of shooting stars in the distance. The next day I was met by an American patrol boat and informed that the *Titanic* had foundered on a 'berg. We could only have been ten miles south of her at the time, and if we had had wireless to inform us of the tragedy we could doubtless have rescued many of the passengers. The 'shooting stars' were evidently distress signals sent up by the distressed vessel." Carey's widow informed Harrison that "if he had been on the bridge at the time he would have realised what the 'shooting stars' were and taken appropriate action. I am unable to believe those on duty would have mistaken normal distress signals for shooting stars."[163]

Harrison's attempts to contact *Titanic* survivors was mostly successful. His communications with Quartermaster Rowe are interesting as they confirm that rockets were being fired before he left the aft docking bridge, that he fired most of the rockets and that he did not know where Boxhall was after the first two rockets had been fired. However, lookout Fred Fleet could not understand what Harrison was saying to him. Harrison shot back: "[my documents] have been circulated all over the world and I am glad to say that not only has no one attempted to dispute the conclusions reached, but it is generally agreed that no future historian can disregard the points I made." Harrison's pomposity had been generated by the M.M.S.A. circulating his documents, including '*The Californian Incident – An Echo of the Titanic disaster*' to various nautical institutions around the world. Harrison would later claim that none of them got back in touch to dispute his evidence or conclusions. Another alternative reason is that the institutions were too apathetic to reply.

---

163   Other ships alleged to have been in the area include the *President Lincoln* (Mrs.Chester H. Cox wrote to the Titanic Historical Society of 3rd May 1977 that her parents and herself were returning [to the U.S.] from Germany and Captain Magin told the passengers they could not go to help as they were surrounded by icebergs.), and the *Premier*, a Gloucester Vessel under the command of Billy Morrison (in *The Patriot Ledger*, on 15th April 1966, it was noted that "it was not until 2 or 3 days later that they had been sailing in the vicinity ... they had seen debris in the water but had paid no attention to it"). Although this current author was unable to find out anything about the *Premier*, Lloyd's publications reveal that the *President Lincoln* left Hamburg on April 3rd and arrived in New York about April 15th according to the *New York Times* on April 17th 1912. She had passed through ice on the 13th between 41 52 N, 50 40 W, and 41 50 N, 50 20 W. Thus she cannot have been in the vicinity of the *Titanic's* location.

Boxhall of the *Titanic* was another of Harrison's contacts. As a retired seafarer, Boxhall had already been in touch regarding financial assistance from the M.M.S.A. But Harrison was not averse to a subtle form of menace in his dealing with the ex-4th Officer. For instance, in 1963, the M.M.S.A. Secretary was assisting the BBC in a radio dramatisation of the *Californian* incident. Realising that the press might pester survivors of the disaster, he wrote to Boxhall, "I am quite prepared to tell [the press] that so far as you are concerned personally, you have never gone deeply into the technical questions which may or may not prove that the *Californian* was the ship involved, and consequently that you have an open mind on the subject. Further, I would add that you have nothing more to say about the incident than is contained in the evidence you gave at the American and British inquiries, and that you wish to be spared any further strain, having regard to your advancing years and ill-health. If you feel that the above accurately represents your attitude towards [the *Californian*], then I am prepared to give you my personal assurance that I will do everything possible to divert unwelcome attention from you." Harrison also offered to send him copies of some of his documents "for [Boxhall's] private use [and which are not] intended as material which might influence you to express support for our efforts."

Boxhall's anti-*Californian* sentiments were well known, but he replied, as he always did, in a cheery, acquiescent manner. One can only imagine what would have happened if Boxhall had disagreed with Harrison and made public statements against Captain Lord!

A much more interesting piece of correspondence – sadly squandered by Leslie Harrison – came from retired Able Bodied Seaman John Cargill[164], who was the helmsman of the *Carpathia* during her rush to the *Titanic*. A newspaper article led Harrison to write to Cargill, who wrote that "There was a ship on the skyline and at the first of day it was about 8 miles away." Harrison, of course, indignantly claimed that this could not be the *Californian*, enclosing a copy of Rostron's affidavit where he mentioned seeing ships at dawn, and writing, "contrary to your own views, the *Californian* was not one of the two ships [Rostron sighted] at daybreak." Cargill responded, "I do no[t] know whether [the *Californian*] got the S.O.S or not but do know that [she] was there at daybreak." Harrison also told Cargill that "you will be interested to learn that, primarily as the result of new information received from a surviving Q.M. of the *Titanic*, it now seems certain that the *Titanic* was heading west after the accident." It is unknown which Q.M. Harrison was talking about. The only surviving one that Harrison was in communication with, according to his records, was George Rowe, and he only got in contact with him a year later, and never discussed the heading of the *Titanic*. As we have discussed, at the British Inquiry, Rowe had said that the *Titanic* was heading north. Why was Harrison so liberal with the truth? If the *Titanic* pointed

---

164   Presumably, Cargill was at the helm during the 4-8am watch.

west, and its mystery ship was off the port bow, then she must have been to the west too – the *Californian* was definitely to the North during the sinking and thus was not "the mystery ship."

But sadly, further valuable historic information from Mr. Cargill was lost forever as the above correspondence marked the end of their communication.

A meeting with *Titanic* survivor Lawrence Beesley was much more profitable. In attendance at the meeting with the 2nd class *Titanic* survivor was Beesley's daughter, Laurien Wade[165] and a BBC producer with whom Harrison was collaborating to create the radio dramatisation (mentioned above). Beesley confirmed that he had seen no rockets fired from the *Titanic* after his boat – number 13 – had reached the water. He also agreed to sign an affidavit swearing to this fact. But Beesley asked that nothing be done that might cause him "emotional stress or physical strain" and Harrison agreed.

There is reason to doubt Beesley's 50 year-old memory. Fellow lifeboat 13 occupant look-out Reginald Lee was asked about the rockets in London:

2582. (*The Attorney-General.*) Did you see any rockets sent up from the *Titanic*?
Yes, Sir.
2583. Before you left the vessel?
Before and after.

And later:

2680. Was it before or after the lowering of your boat that you saw the rockets first go up?
They were sending them up before the boat was lowered into the water.

This accords well with Boxhall's evidence, that he continued firing rockets until he left in lifeboat no. 2, launched some ten minutes after boat 13 at about 1.45a.m[166].

The letters and pieces of data continued to trickle into Harrison's office, but not every piece of correspondence was flattering towards Captain Lord and his

---

165   Mrs. Wade would later write about a fanatical man (unnamed) who had pressurised her father into signing an affidavit regarding the *Titanic* and the *Californian*.
166   Leslie Reade notes this in his posthumous book. This author also informed Harrison in 1989 that there were other witnesses who contradicted Beesley's five decade old assertions; Harrison replied, in a diversionary answer that "The timings of the lifeboat launchings suffer from a degree of uncertainty". This may be true when placing boat 2 and 13 in a chronology, but it doesn't explain how a fellow member of the boat 13 contingent contradicts Beesley, especially when that contradictory information is more contemporary to the Titanic disaster than Beesley's, and hence less prone to the inevitable confusion that time brings to one's memory.

service record. A letter, signed "J.B", and posted from Sandown on the Isle of Wight on 1st July 1962, was scathing:

"I served for many years in the Leyland Line as an officer and master, and sailed with Captain Lord for two voyages. I found him to be a very disagreeable man, a martinet and a bully to anyone that feared him. At the end of my second voyage, I saw the marine superintendant and got a transfer along with the second and 3rd Officers who also refused to sail with him ... Captain Lord was dismissed from the Leyland Line and went to Lawther Latta's and was greatly disliked by all who had the misfortune to sail with him in that firm too."

However, documentation suggests otherwise. Whether by miracle, or oversight, every crew agreement for every voyage of Lord's Leyland Line career[167] as a Captain has survived, allowing a researcher to determine who sailed with who, and when. These were duly obtained, at considerable expense. None of the voyages list anyone with the initials "J.B" as an officer, and the crew agreements show nothing more than the usual migratory patterns of officers and crew between vessels. Nothing sinister can be inferred; in fact, the opposite case could be argued. If the crew agreements suggest anything, it is that the crews expressed loyalty towards Captain Lord. For instance, Leyland Line employees Atkinson, Rollerson and Wickham sailed with Lord as Chief, 2nd and 3rd Officers respectively on no fewer than 7 voyages. It seems likely that "J.B." was nothing more than a hoaxer, trying to derail Harrison's campaign for mischievous reasons[168]

Two new characters now enter our narrative.

The posthumous campaign to clear Captain Lord's name received a boost when Peter Padfield[169], an ex-Merchant Navy Officer, intended to write a book on the seagoing disasters, but this mutated into a book specifically about the *Titanic* and the *Californian*. Like Harrison, Padfield was keen to utilise the Inquiry transcripts and any other source of information (for instance, the internal Board of Trade papers from 1912 which had not yet been released to the public). But one attempt to use such a source met with an angry rebuff. Following Captain Groves' death, Harrison wrote to his brother and asked for access to his private papers. Mr. C.L.D. Groves shot back, "Under no circumstances would I allow you or Padfield to have anything to do with my late Brothers papers. Why? Don't the pair of you let the dead rest in peace." [punctuation as in the original letter]

---

167   *The Ship That Stood Still* appendix I
168   A definitive answer about Captain Lord's demeanour cannot be ascertained. The papers of Captain Lord, his son, and Harrison's research, currently held at the Merseyside Maritime Museum are incomplete.
169   More information can be found at
http://www.guypadfield.com/ppadfield/peterpadfield.html

Padfield soldiered on and was determined to inspect the 'secret' Government *Titanic* files. His quest was not proceeding very happily, as Harrison later related:

"Padfield had been hampered when preparing his book by an unhelpful action on the part of the Ministry of Transport. In January 1964 they refused his request for access to the *Titanic* files and he completed his book without the assistance which reference to those files might have afforded him. Six months later, however, the files were released to the Public Record Office at the insistence of a member of Parliament acting for another author not so well disposed towards Captain Lord as Padfield was."[170]

The unnamed author alluded to by Harrison was Leslie Reade.

Reade's letter to his close friend Walter Lord revealed what had happened the day the *Titanic* files were opened to public inspection: Reade had made an appointment to view the documents, indeed he was the first to be blessed with access. When he arrived, he found Padfield already there, rifling through the papers. Reade was upset, but the two agreed to work together. Within a short space of time, Reade unearthed a very valuable document, for it showed how the Board of Trade had been "tipped off" about the *Californian* and her role in the *Titanic* disaster. The letter was written on April 29th, 1912 by Gerard J.G. Jensen, a civil engineer specialising in sewage and drainage. He had seen a letter originating in America and was sufficiently enraged to ask the Board of Trade to act accordingly:

"I think I am discharging a public duty in bringing to the following matter to your notice and to suggest that at the forthcoming Inquiry witnesses should be called and closely examined from the Leyland Co's S.S. '*Californian*'. My information is from a letter written by the carpenter of the '*Californian*'[171] to a friend of his but I should be obliged if you would consider the source of your information as confidential.

Briefly stated the facts are :-
1. That while the *Californian* was lying in ice with engines stopped, the *Titanic*'s signals of distress were seen by various members of the crew.
2. That the matter was reported to the Capt. of the *Californian* on at least three occasions.
3. That the *Californian*'s Captain took no notice of the matter.
4. That the signals were reported to the First Officer when he relieved the Captain in the ordinary course [sic]
5. That the First Officer then set his Marconi operator to work and got in touch with the '*Titanic*' [sic] – but that it was too late to be of service.

---

170   "*A Titanic Myth*" page 203
171   W.F. McGregor, the source of the story in *The Clinton Daily Item*.

6. That the *Californian* was within 10 miles of the *Titanic* and could have saved every soul, had her Captain responded to the call for help.
7. That Newfoundland fishing boats are occasionally run down by the *Californian* and other liners and no attempt is made to save the lives of the fishermen in the endeavour to keep time in crossing the Atlantic."

Reade showed this document to Padfield, whose response was a massive surprise; "Ha ha! What a great fake!"

Padfield aside, this letter shows that it was Jensen, and not Gill, whose "whistle-blowing' antics precipitated the Board of Trade's action against the *Californian*. A simple check of the crew agreements would reveal the name of the carpenter and it is a surprise that he wasn't called to give evidence at the Inquiry. Maybe he wasn't because his 'proof' would have revealed his story as simple, although incendiary, hear-say. Be that as it may, McGregor, his relatives and friends had effectively scuppered Captain Lord through their public pronouncements. McGregor never sailed with Lord again.

Reade was an Oxford-trained barrister and writer, born in 1904[172]. From a very early age he held a fascination with the *Titanic* and the *Californian*, and wrote the West German TV Production dramatisation of "Die Letzte Nacht Der *Titanic*" ('The Last Night of the *Titanic*'), which featured Captain Lord and his crew, and was broadcast on 13th April 1955. That same year, Reade wrote *"Atlantic Night"* for the Anglo/American "Douglas Fairbanks, Jr. Presents" anthology series for U.S. Television[173], which was shown on 19th September. However, possibly for legal reasons, the names of the crew were changed: we now had Captain Arthur Welch, Chief Officer Fraser etc.[174] . In contrast to Reade's later views, "Lord/Welch" is now shown to be companionable and friendly with his crew, and they all show great remorse when they realise, at the conclusion of the dramatisation, that they had missed the *Titanic's* SOS calls. Reade had already undertaken research into the *"Californian's* mysterious role in the *Titanic* disaster"* and worked on a manuscript entitled *"The Ninth Rocket"*, which he later renamed *"The Ship That Stood Still."* At some point between 1955 and 1965, Reade's attitude towards the *Californian* became markedly more hostile.

For a time, Reade was in contact with Leslie Harrison, and the two seemed to tolerate an uneasy peace[175], although Reade was content to grumble to Walter

---

172   A biography can be found in *"The Ship That Stood Still"* page 342
173   Information from Dick Fiddy of the British Film Institute
174   The only crewman on the *Californian* to retain his own name was Ernest Gill!
175   In *"A Titanic Myth part 2"*, Leslie Harrison indicates that the two established contact after an article, written by Judith Ashe (Reade's wife) had been published in the

Lord about the M.M.S.A.'s – and Harrison's – attitude to the *Californian*. Reade was quite convinced that Stanley Lord had ignored distress rockets, but had he known that there was the prospect of salvage, Reade suspected that the Captain would have immediately reacted; this seems to based on the Captain's response in his 1961 taped interview that the thought of salvage was "everything." Walter Lord likened his namesake's lack of response to behaviour he had witnessed many times in New York City, where onlookers felt loathe to offer help to people in dire situations (such as mugging) hoping that someone else would provide assistance. The late author Douglas Adams would later term this phenomena an S.E.P (Somebody Else's Problem).

The two rivals, Harrison and Reade, even shared a four hour long dinner engagement together on October 29th, 1964 at the Great Eastern Hotel in London, after which Harrison told Reade that "I would very much like to think that you would leave such a meeting convinced of the *Californian*'s innocence and that this may lead you to join with us in seeking to undo so much of the damage that has been done by your publications in the past in so far as Captain Lord's reputation is concerned. Walter Lord, Geoffrey Bennett, Dr. Marcus and others have refused to examine the evidence in the *Californian*'s favour properly; my hope is that you may be influenced to become the first hitherto anti-*Californian* to swing over to the defence of Captain Lord." Such a hope was in vain, but one can see the immense propaganda value this would have. In the end, Harrison got his wish – but from a writer on the other side of the Atlantic.

Harrison seemed wary of Reade and told him, "In general, I am reluctant to try to influence you in your treatment of Captain Lord's case – on the other hand I am equally reluctant to see anyone embarrassed as the result of the publication of a book containing gross inaccuracies or conclusions in which it would be my duty to comment critically <u>after</u> publication." [Harrison's emphasis].

Harrison claimed that Reade replied two days later with the following, "I note ... your thoughtful caution to me about the 'embarrassment' you evidently anticipate I shall suffer from the publication of my book, and your reckless, and

London "*Evening News*" on 8th March 1957 on the Californian matter. Reade had provided the data used in that article, which was entitled "*Ship Stood Still as Titanic went down*," and was number 408 (second series) of the paper's daily "World's Strangest Stories" series. The article contains a number of factual errors; whether introduced by Reade or Ashe (to enhance the story's controversy), it is now not possible to say. Examples include; the mention that Captain Lord, referred to as "a careful navigator and efficient seaman" thought that the other ship that stopped at 11.40pm was 10 or 12 miles away; a paragraph saying that "...Finally, 2.20, the moment when Stone and Gibson saw the strange ship 'disappear,' the Titanic had sunk"; and, following his arousal and before they got to the *Carpathia*, Evans "learned that at 11.40 the previous night at exactly the time when [Groves] had seen the strange steamer 'stop' the Titanic had struck an iceberg." The first two of these references are inaccurate; it is impossible to know for sure if Evans ascertained the time of collision on the morning of April 15th.

insulting assumption that it will contain 'gross inaccuracies'. I have never knowingly published anything, which, if challenged, has not been entirely vindicated. Indeed, my standards of care in such matters are apparently somewhat higher than those which have resulted in the most reckless charges of dishonesty against some of the leading figures in this case. And I say that as one who in all probability had far less respect for authority, or, to use the current word, the 'Establishment' than anybody on Captain Lord's side. I not only believe, but know, from experience that authority is capable of infamy; but I have not discovered a scintilla of anything remotely justifying a doubt about the *bona fides* of those who have been attacked. As I have previously said, I believe I am the most suitable person to set forth my view of this case; and I am presently engaged on that task. When it is completed, it will I hope, present also an objective narrative, with facts fairly recorded, so far as they are known."

Harrison replied: "Unfortunately it seems impossible for me to put points to you without creating misunderstandings, in which case I think it better to refrain from further comment on the individual matters to which you refer. I am particularly sorry that you have not found it possible to set out in simple terms your basic 'philosophy' on the *Californian* case on the lines of my attempt to do so."

This was not the end of their correspondence; for example, Harrison gave (loaned?) a copy of a photograph of himself to Reade in 1971 for the latter's book.

Reade enjoyed a long and fruitful friendship with Holland-based maritime writer Edward de Groot. Reade died in January 1989, his book complete. Under agreement from Reade's estate, de Groot started work on editing the manuscript in early December 1990, and the book was announced at a press conference at Lloyd's of London on March 31st, 1993, where it was available to the throngs of the media. Also in attendance was *Titanic* survivor Eva Hart, who had agreed to write a foreword for the book. "*The Ship That Stood Still*" was released to the public 6 days later.

Padfield wrote about the genesis of his book in its foreword: he had an open mind when starting his project, which was to have been a general book about collisions at sea. The *Titanic* would occupy perhaps two chapters at most, but "the idea was soon shelved. The *Titanic* became all-engrossing." Padfield devoured the Inquiry transcripts, and found himself astonished that Captain Lord was censured based on the "half-cock" evidence he had before him. But as he read, he experienced anger, "not manufactured, literary anger, but the real blood-bubbling bile. This book was begun in anger ... [the evidence and report] pointed to a 'rigged' Inquiry." How could Captain Lord be called as a witness, and then a question concerning his crews' conduct be placed in the official Inquiry record in his absence and without his knowledge, and then he not be prosecuted in the aftermath of the Inquiry? This lack of due course in British law, "which demands that a man must be charged before being found guilty, and must be given every chance to defend himself," indicated but one conclusion – that Lord was sacrificed so "that the public had someone on whom to vent their anger."

But Harrison could not share Padfield's theory of the 'rigged' Inquiry and the (then retired) M.M.S.A. Secretary informed his readers, "For one thing, I am confident that had the Board of Trade actually decided to frame the Inquiry and to condemn the *Californian*, then they would most certainly have set at least one technically qualified official on to the task of investigating the practical points involved. Such a concentrated study of the case must inevitably have revealed the obvious flaws in the superficial case against the *Californian* ... [the Board's files] reveal that, so far from there being a systematic attempt to frame Captain Lord, a very confused state of affairs appears to have existed. Captain Lord was condemned simply because of Lord Mersey's conviction, formed at a very early stage in the proceedings – a conviction shared by others in a position of authority who considered it unnecessary to look any further – that the *Californian* was the guilty ship. Thereafter, as one official actually minuted: 'The Board of Trade cannot well undertake to consider the matter after Lord Mersey has pronounced upon it.'"

The text of the resultant book, "The *Titanic* and the *Californian*," discusses the relevant sections of the inquiries, emphasising the contradictions that exist and the evidence in Lord's favour – evidence that Padfield claimed had been ignored in the court's desire to find a scapegoat. But there are examples of suppression by Padfield himself[176]. And on several issues, Padfield asserts one thing, and then a short time later, presents evidence or an opinion that destroys his original statement[177]. For instance, on page 197, he writes that "[Lord] then went to sleep. He did not receive any message from the Apprentice, Gibson." But proceeding just a few lines, readers find Padfield discussing Gibson's visit to the chart room to

---

176   See, for example http://home.earthlink.net/~dnitzer/Updates/Masters.html It is worthwhile pointing out that Captain Moore's vital evidence was ignored by writers until 1993.

177   A good example can be seen at http://home.earthlink.com/~dnitzer/Updates/Padfield.html where it stated, on page 209 of Padfield's book that Stone "at no time [admitted] that [the rockets could have been distress signals. But four pages on, Stone's exchange with Isaacs is recounted:

"Q. Did you think they were distress signals?

A. No.

Q. Did not that occur to you?

A. It did not occur to me at the time.

Q. When did it occur to you?

A. After I had heard about the *Titanic* going down."

Padfield concludes: "Pressed as to whether, when he had heard about the *Titanic*, he had then thought they were distress signals which he had seen, he said he thought they might have been."

250

deliver Stone's report. Perhaps Padfield had used Lord's alleged somnambulism to confirm his comment that the Captain "did not receive any message"? But Lord had received it, regardless of whether he was asleep at the time or, as Gibson had described the master's state, awake.

Padfield writes, "It is now too far distant in time to make any categorical assertions about the meaning or nature of these rockets which were seen by Stone, Gibson and Gill," but only four pages later, Padfield has changed his mind; "The most likely explanation about the rockets is that they *were* [emphasis in original] the *Titanic*'s rockets seen by a strange coincidence over the deck lights, but below the masthead lights, of the other ship, which lay to the South of the *Californian*." The meaning or nature of the rockets is clear, with Padfield's admission; they were distress signals[178]. And then, two paragraphs later, Padfield casts doubt on his own conclusion, "Whatever the rockets or flares were or were not ..." And there we have the uncertainty reinforced: 'flares'.

If rockets fired from beyond the horizon and seen to reach half the height of the light affixed to the mast, what can we deduce? A sketch depicting the purported geometry of *Titanic* – mystery ship – *Californian* is below.

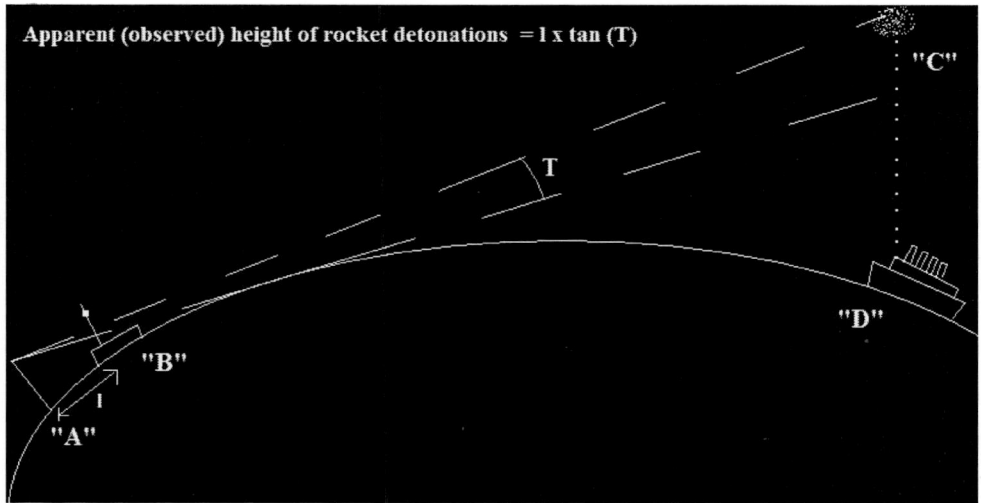

Apparent (observed) height of rocket detonations = l x tan (T)

Illustration 34: How high would the rockets be seen at point "A", fired from the Titanic ("D"), detonating at "C" and seen over the mystery ship "B"? The angle that the rockets rise above the horizon is denoted by "T". The diagram is not to scale.

---

178   Reade had also noticed this, as he told Walter Lord: "After all that tirade, after all that laboured attempt to show that the two sets of rockets were fired at different times, [Padfield] now says that the rockets were the same."

A rigorous mathematical treatment in Appendix E shows that the angle that the rockets would make with the horizon would be about 0.4°. From a distance of 5 miles, the rockets would be seen to ascend 191 feet. We do not know from where Stone claimed he saw the rockets fired, whether it was from the forecastle, or superstructure.

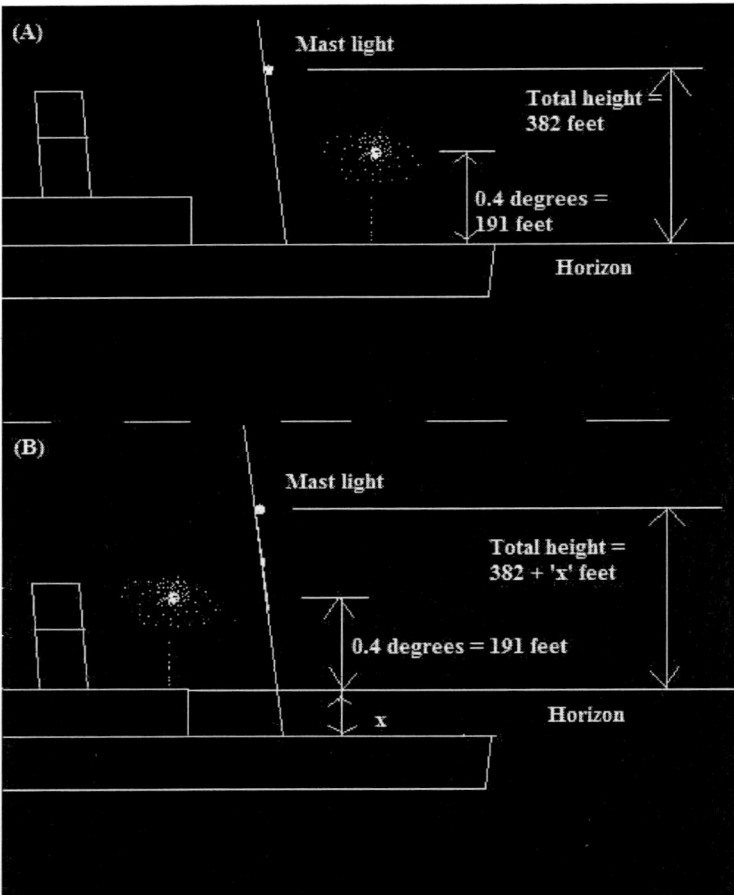

Illustration 35: Stone's claimed rockets, rising to half the mastlight height, seemingly 'fired' from either (a) the forecastle or (b) the superstructure of the other ship.

This gives a minimum height of nearly 400 feet[179] for the height of the light above the deck. The actual top of the mast would be some distance above even this! How does this compare to the mast of the *Titanic*, the largest ship in the world? We know that the distance from waterline to light is some 145 feet. The

179   If the rockets reached their "minimum" height of 660 feet, the apparent height of the mastlight would still be about 300 feet!

distance from the base of the mast to the waterline is some 40 feet, thus giving a height of the mastlight above the deck of about 100 feet, allowing for approximations. Compare this with Stone's 'medium-sized tramp steamer' and its grossly oversized masts and one can see just how precarious the 2nd Officer's tale becomes.

If we can invert the argument, we can construct a scenario that would fit Stone's observations, but far does a rocket ascending to half the height of a mast ascend? 30 feet? 40 feet? When one churns the mathematical handle, such small differences do not matter, as long as one accepts that a medium sized tramp was seen. Then, we can define the situation as follows. The mystery ship would have to be floating in mid-air, well above the horizon.

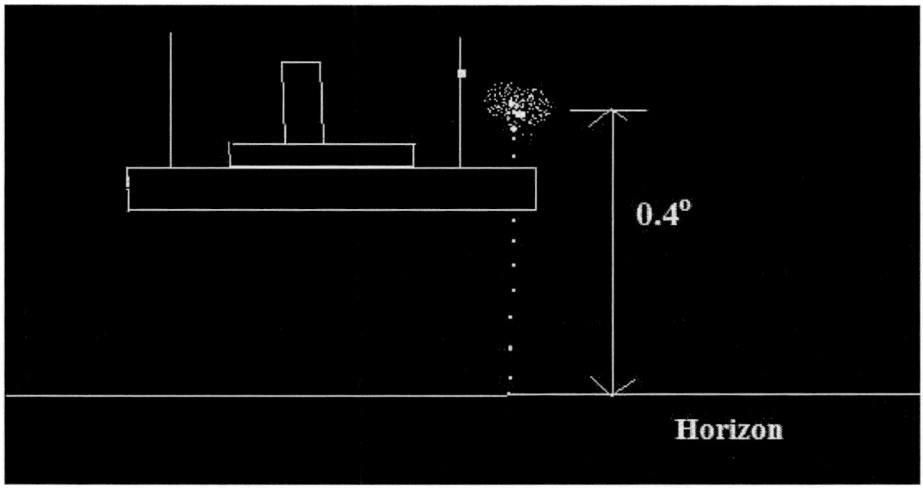

Illustration 36: With the rocket from the Titanic rising well above the horizon, where would the mystery ship have to be for the signals to be seen ascending to half a mast height?

Such analysis aside, things seemed to be proceeding nicely for the pro-Lord lobby. In addition to Padfield's book and the petition, some promising news had at last been gleaned on the *Samson* story. Superficially, it seemed to hold the key to the vessel seen by the *Titanic*. But analysed forensically, the story had many flaws which only managed to destroy its credibility.

In May 1965, the aforementioned Mr. Wig finally released a copy of an extract of Henrik Naess's report on the 14th-15th April 1912. The letter noted that the "present copy is taken from a manuscript confided to the Arctic Explorer [Professor] Adolf Hoel[180], who has authorised its identity with his signature." The report is undated.

---

180   Presumably the "Norwegian scientist" alluded to earlier?

So, why was the document released now? Perhaps significantly, Hoel had died the previous year.

Naess writes that he had given up the *"Munroe"* and worked as a bosun on a coastal vessel for a short while. He suffered from an ear ailment which forced him to stay ashore without work sometime during the winter; indeed, at one time, he was "quite deaf."

After Christmas 1912, he received two good offers of work. One was as a skipper of a small boat from Kristiansund plying the herring trade. The other was a job as a mate on a large sealing vessel belong to the Trondheim group. Naess chose the latter; that vessel, the *Samson*, was a large bark rigged ship with a powerful engine and six, or maybe eight boats (account differ). She was bound for Newfoundland on a sealing expedition, and started her journey from Tonsberg.

From Tonsberg, the *Samson* proceeded to Oslo where she docked and was painted under the waterline. She then returned to Tonsberg, where she was coaled, and departed again on 8th February, passing Tonsberg Tonne and proceeded south along the shore. At Lindesnes, a course was set to the north of the Orkneys. The wind was northwesterly, and the engine was used. Naess writes that there were 45 men on board, and the Master, Captain Ring, "was every inch a seaman. He was also an Arctic expert."

After the Orkneys had been passed, the course was altered to the west, and they approached Newfoundland. The sea water temperature was taken every hour, and when it had dropped to 0°C, it was taken every half hour. This was done because the fog was so dense that they were unable to see anything. Then they entered so-called fishball ice; ice which the sea has broken to bits against the floes; half an hour later, the actual icefloe was reached, which was quite compact and impossible to penetrate; however, this was not Ring's intention as no seals were expected to be found there. They turned towards the southwest and proceeded on that course until the next day.

Naess writes, "By then, our dead reckoning and noon observations showed our position to be on a level with Cape <u>Hatteras</u> and indeed we saw the cape too. [emphasis in original]. The whole afternoon we continued southwest until dusk. Then we entered the ice and stopped for the night. The weather was now quite clear and calm, the stars were shining, and there was a slight swell."

There were 6 hour watches on board the *Samson*, with four seal gunners on each watch. Two of them were on watch on the bridge, one on either side. Naess was on duty that evening, but was sitting with Captain Ring in his cabin, "having a rum toddy and an evening pipe." A little before midnight, Naess went up on deck waiting to be relieved, and whilst walking on deck, he noticed "two big stars" hanging in the sky to the south.

The lights seemed low, he said to the watchman on the bridge, and ordered him to climb to the crow's nest to see what the "stars" might be. Naess thought it might be American sealers lying at the edge of the ice. The watchman turned his telescope towards the stars. "They are not stars," he called out, "They are lights. And I see lots of lights."

"A moment passed, then suddenly some rockets shot up. Then just as suddenly, all the lights went out and it was dark. We could no longer see anything."

"Now our position was such that we were scared that we might be caught violating the territorial limit. The lights out there meant that the Americans were close, and when the lights were put out we immediately thought that they had perhaps observed us and would try to catch us. The rockets were probably signals to other vessels further away. We therefore turned about and started to manoeuvre northwards in order to get out of sight. When dawn came we were quite a distance away and could not see any ships nor any sign that there had been any ships nearby. We passed a lot of big icebergs, some of them enormous, up to 200 feet high. They passed us like great floating islands."

The matter was soon forgotten, and the *Samson* proceeded North; their catch was poor[181] and the crew were feeling downhearted because the lack of seals would affect each man's profit. The *Samson* spent eight days in that location, and then proceeded up the Denmark Strait to try and snare some crested seals. They turned east, got a good wind and after four days of sailing, ice was encountered inside the Davis Strait. But the *Samson* crew had little luck here too.

"Finally the ice began to settle round us. We discussed whether we should go out or remain fast in the ice – we decided on the latter course. We stayed there for a while, but as the ice refused to break up again we had to butt our way out.

We had the wind and sea straight against the edge of the ice, and the ship received many heavy blows. But that did not matter because Samson was one of the strongest and largest of Norway's Arctic vessels."

The ice was moving violently in the sea, and the *Samson* broke out, but collided with an icefloe which was thrust at the ship by the swell. The *Samson* sustained damage, and the crew decided that the prudent course of action was to put into port in Iceland for refuge and repairs.

Captain Ring contacted the *Samson*'s owners and they were ordered to return home and call at Kristiansund for further orders. While waiting for high tide to refloat the ship, Ring and Naess were invited for supper at the home of the local consul.

"Have you heard the last bad news?" asked the consul.

No, Naess and Ring said. The consul informed them of the tragedy of the *Titanic*. Naess asked when this was; "something was beginning to dawn on me," he wrote. The consul told them the date and found a newspaper with the details of the

---

181   Coincidentally, *Lloyd's Weekly Shipping Index* on April 11th reports that the "Newfoundland Sealing Fleet" had also reported that seal catch was poor and that only one of the first five returning vessels (out of 23) had a full catch, the others reporting that "the total kill is not likely to reach 2/3rds of the normal catch."

disaster. Naess took the paper and compared its details with the *Samson*'s log. "The date, hour and position corresponded exactly with our own entries."

"Now, " wrote Naess, "we understood why we had seen the lights and the rockets. We had been 10 nautical miles away from the '*Titanic*' when she went down. There we had been lying with our big ship and eight fine sealing boats – in fair, calm weather. Imagine what we could have done to save lives – if only we had had the slightest idea of what was happening just in front of us. Had we only had a radio, for instance ...."

The document is fascinating for all the wrong reasons. Firstly, it mentions seeing the *Titanic* in the vicinity of Cape Hatteras, North Carolina whereas she sank closer to Cape Race, Newfoundland[182] several hundred miles away, and that shortly afterwards, they proceeded south west; in other words, heading even further away from the *Titanic*'s location. Secondly, no country had dominion over the seas in the area of the *Titanic*; certainly no ship had need to worry about "illegal" seal hunting hundreds of miles from the nearest shore, and territorial waters only extended a few miles from a country's shoreline. Thirdly, if the *Samson* had sailed north away from the ailing *Titanic*, why didn't she see the *Californian*, or vice versa? Fourthly, the ship allegedly seen by the *Samson* fired rockets and then turned its lights out, making Naess wary about nearby Americans. Why should a ship warn every vessel in the vicinity of its proximity with rockets, and then turn out its lights? Next, the navigational details, which initially sound credible, start to veer into fantasy. After the 'encounter' with the *Titanic*, the Samson heads north to the Denmark Strait, which is the channel of water between Iceland and Greenland. That is, to the east of Greenland. The *Samson* then turns east, and then encounters the ice within the <u>Davis Strait</u>. This is located to the <u>west</u> of Greenland. Furthermore, given the distance between the two Straits, it is highly unlikely, if not impossible for the *Samson* to cover this distance in just four days. Then, the manuscript asserts that Naess is offered the post on the *Samson* after Christmas 1912. The *Titanic* sank in April of that year.

Finally, Norwegian mariners would have been familiar with the use of rockets at sea. They had subscribed to an international convention on rockets many years earlier (see Appendix B) and would not have assumed that they were signals to "heave to and be searched," or communications with vessels further away.

One interesting point not made in the manuscript is that Captain Naess wrote to Professor Hoel on 18/11/39 about the *Samson*. Naess remarks that his ship was lying in slack ice with shielded lights at the time. With shielded lights, nothing of her would be seen. 4th Officer Boxhall on the *Titanic* testified that he had seen the "beautiful lights" of the unknown stranger, an obvious and striking

---

182   Lieutenant Commander Craig McLean, National Oceanographic and Atmospheric Administration and David Eno, supporters of the *Samson* story, would later write in the "*Naval History*" journal, Spring 1992, Vol 6 No.1 that "It's possible that [Naess] confused these similar sounding names" (!)

contradiction with Naess's assertions, riddled as they are with holes.

A final fact remains about the *Samson* and her supposed "beautiful lights". Lloyd's Register issues for 1912 to 1920 reveals that she did not have electric lights. She was fitted with oil burning lamps. In fairness, it should be pointed out that some of the *Californian* witnesses thought that the ship they were watching had oil lamps.

Confirmation of the *Samson's* presence near the *Titanic* would be a major boost for the petition to clear Lord's name, which was then in preparation. Harrison sought expert opinion on the *Samson*, and wrote to Captain F.W. Berchem, the Marine Superintendant of Messrs. H.Hogarth and Sons Ltd., a man with more knowledge about handling ships near ice, and the legality of operating sealing vessels. Berchem was less than impressed by the *Samson* story, and remarked that "no vessels [were ever] operated by the Newfoundland Government to prevent the illegal taking of skins." He admitted to being perplexed by the location of the *Titanic*, and was puzzled by the *Samson* "returning home – but from where? If she had been sealing amongst the ice fields of Newfoundland what was she doing in this position? I can form no other conclusion than it is safe to say [that the story is] unreliable." So, here was one expert who did deride the whole story.

But Harrison was not yet finished. In July that year, he wrote to Berchem again with a copy of Naess' report. Again, Berchem was not impressed: "From the outset those responsible on board [the *Samson*] would appear to have very little idea of their whereabouts on the ocean or for that matter any great knowledge of seal hunting. Naess speaks of approaching Newfoundland, then encountering the ice-fields and turning away south west because 'we could not expect to find any seals there'. This actually would have been the very area in which to commence operations and to haul away south-west would take the ships away from the sealing grounds. Having done so the vessel within 24 hours is in a position off Cape Hatteras and thereafter goes on to say that the vessel continued south-west and entered the ice and stopped. This latter is too absurd for comment, firstly there is no ice or sealing grounds off Cape Hatteras, secondly the *Titanic* was nowhere near any such position when she struck the iceberg so how could Mr. Naess or any other member have seen anything whatsoever of the incident. The remainder of his story is equally fantastic, one minute the vessel is bound for the Denmark Straits and the next she is in the middle of Davis Straits, the latter a sheer impossibility at that season of the year in a vessel such as the 'Samson'. I am more than ever convinced that the 'Samson' was never in any way connected with the 'Titanic' and that the whole story is a good 'dog watch yarn' with not a shred of truth to be found in it and as such I would disregard it completely."

Harrison replied, "I entirely accept your contentions that taken literally the statement is nonsensical. However, the fact remains that there are points of detail in [Naess's] statement which are corroborated by the entirely independent information I have received from the Chairman of the Icelandic Shipmasters' Association and

257

bearing in mind that Mr. Naess was probably quite elderly when this manuscript was drafted, our legal advisors in London and Oslo do not consider that we would be justified in dismissing it out of hand as you suggest." Harrison also knew about the problem with Cape Hatteras and the issue of "territorial waters"; he had informed Leslie Reade in 1964 that this was due to a mistranslation. Reade was no fool; he had seen exactly the same source material as Harrison and knew that these troublesome words were in the original, untranslated document.

However, the only information that came from the Icelandic Shipmasters Association refers to the big riot in Isafjord during the *Samson's* stay there in May 1912. There is no reference to the *Samson*'s involvement in the *Titanic* at all. A year later, Harrison would write to a solicitor that "I must confess I have never regarded the '*Samson*' report as being of such significance and importance that it was essential to have evidence from her."

But, at last, the petition to clear Captain Lord's name was ready. The M.M.S.A. unveiled it to the press aboard HQS Wellington on 5th February 1965. Present at Leslie Harrison's invitation, was Leslie Reade. Harrison had perhaps overplayed the importance of Lord's "miscarriage of justice." It warranted just a few tiny mentions in the press, with the bulk of the UK shipping newspapers and journals ignoring the petition completely, as far as this author can ascertain.

Harrison admitted that the petition contained no new information and that its submission had been timed to coincide with Padfield's book. In questions from journalists, Harrison declared that the U.S. Inquiry was "farcical" and that its findings bore no relation to the evidence.

One journalist asked if the M.M.S.A. council members were unanimous in their support of the petition. Harrison replied "yes."

Wasn't it true that a man on the *Californian* had a different opinion to Lord's, asked another. Yes, he was told, 3rd Officer Groves (no mention of Gill). Had his opinion changed? Harrison did not know. Harrison knew that Groves had passed away four years before.

How many witnesses from the *Californian* and the *Titanic* were available to give information? None, replied Harrison, but they were not needed. All the information needed was in the record, particularly concerning the rockets ("flares really," Harrison told the throng).

In response to enquiries about unknown ships, Harrison asserted that there were no organised attempts to ascertain their identities. However, the reader will know that the Board of Trade files reveal that dozens of ships were suggested by foreign ports and many were investigated and eliminated.

Someone in the press remembered the *Samson*. A press release issued by the M.M.S.A. in 1963 had been definitive: "[they now believed] that the ship seen from the sinking *Titanic* was the Norwegian sealer *Samson*, the *Californian* herself being over twenty miles away." How would the petition deal with this vessel? Harrison replied that they couldn't do anything with her; "much too speculative!"

And indeed, there is no mention of the *Samson* in the petition. This did not, as we shall see, prevent Harrison from secretly submitting his *Samson* dossier to the Board of Trade.

The petition, as prepared by Leslie Harrison, reads like a defence brief of the *Californian* and its conduct. There is no explanation, or even an attempt to explain *away* Stone and Gibson's conversation as they watched the rockets; indeed, it is not mentioned. The pamphlet describes two additional ships in the area of the disaster; one seen by the *Titanic*, and one seen by the *Californian*, the latter one of which was firing off rockets/flares. Neither are identified. The *Carpathia*'s rockets, as mentioned by Lawrence Beesley in his 1912 book, are used as evidence that they had a large audible range and that since the *Californian* witnesses heard nothing, this indicated a large separation distance; but there is no mention of the rockets seen by the *Californian* after 3am – rockets which could only have come from the *Carpathia*, and which were fired from a much further range than the ones on the *Titanic*[183]. The *Titanic's* rockets themselves are described as ascending 200 to 300 feet; less than half the height they actually reached. There is no reference to any drift encountered on April 14th/15th 1912 (not even the supposedly north-westerly current that offset the *Californian* before 7.30pm); Captain Lord's navigation is represented as unequivocal, accurate and sacrosanct. The ship seen from the *Californian* is described as approaching "'slowly and obliquely' from the southward to stop at 2150 [New York Time – 23:40 ship's time] only 4 to 5 miles away." This obviously favours Groves' description of the other ship, and not Captain Lord's, which describes a vessel coming from the east, and is self-incriminatory.

The rockets had now, in the words of Harrison, become "rockets or flares", and, to confuse the timeline, they were described as being fired from the *Titanic* 15 minutes before any were seen from the *Californian*; the *Californian* saw her last rocket some time after the last one had been fired from the *Titanic*, therefore there must have been two rocket-firing ships in a small area of the North Atlantic that night, other than the *Carpathia*. The petition labours the point that, "As the rockets, or flares seen by the *Californian's* 2nd Officer and Apprentice did not explode, and as they came from a ship which was steaming away from them, they could not have been distress signals and could not have been from the sinking *Titanic*." Of course, Gibson did not refer to the other ship steaming away, and although he does not use the word "explode", he did refer to the rockets (not flares) bursting into stars. The petition makes great use of Stone's observations.

The thin pamphlet is so full of (apparently deliberate) omissions of data[184] and has such twists of logic that its worth is minimal. It could be argued

---

183   Harrison wrote, in 1964 that "it seems quite likely, however, that [the *Californian*] saw some of the *Carpathia's* distress socket signals and the Titanic's lifeboat flares."
184   One such example is as follows: "One of the Q.M.'s who was on the poop at the time [of the collision] spoke of his impression that, after the impact, her stern swung south.

that, by supporting such a poorly researched document, whose "research" could easily be disproved by reading the 1912 Inquiry transcripts, the M.M.S.A. left itself wide open for criticism that could have damaged its reputation.

The Board worked fast[185]. Alan Kent of the Treasury Solicitor's Department noted four days after the submission that "It appears clear that Mr. Harrison has abandoned his attempt to produce 'new and important' evidence": he re-iterated this point six days later. Mr. Bellamy of the Board offered his personal view that he recommended some form of action, not necessarily a reopening of the 1912 Inquiry, "simply in order to allay rumour and suspicion."

By 24th March, the first signs of impatience had been detected by the Board of Trade. Three questions about the petition had already been raised in Parliament, and Liverpool West Derby Member of Parliament Eric Ogden had also asked a question for answer on April 15th, the anniversary of the *Titanic's* sinking. It was noted that Mr. Kent had given his reasons why, despite the conflicting evidence, the 1912 court was justified in coming to the conclusions that it did[186]. Mr. Kent wrote "in the circumstances, there is no ground for suspecting a miscarriage of justice," and that, "the petition is more a crusade by a particular sectional interest."

Bellamy agreed. On 8th April, he wrote a memorandum circulated to the rest of his staff. He could see no useful purpose after such a length of time, in reopening the Inquiry. There were two choices, as he could see it; the first, which he supported, was to decline the appeal; or appoint someone to carry out an independent Inquiry. Probably with reference to the "rigged Inquiry" thrust of Padfield's book, he further remarked that despite allegations in the press, the suggestion that there was a effort to find a scapegoat for the Board's lapses in 1912 were "absurd" and that there was "certainly no evidence of collusion in any of the [1912] papers we have seen." Additionally, an argument was proffered saying, "How can any lawyer justifiably disagree with the findings of fact 50 years after the event without having seen the witnesses and documents the court saw?"

The Attorney General of the Board also agreed with Bellamy's suggestion not to reopen the Inquiry[187].

This is what might be suggested if the *Titanic's* initial turn to port had been checked and she was swinging back to her original course." Quartermaster Rowe's statements in London explicitly pointed to the *Titanic* heading north and <u>not</u> on her original course, with her bows being in a suitable orientation to see the *Californian*. Thus, Rowe's evidence was cleverly reworded to remove this reference.

185   The minutes of the various personnel can be found at the UK Public Record Office BT 239/785 Also included is a letter from a compatriot of Captain Lord, who served with him aboard the *Anglo Chilean* for 11 months in 1913. In the words of the author, Lord was "one of the most efficient Captains I have ever sailed with, he was a real gentleman and most worthy to be Captain of any ship."

186   These reasons are not recorded in the file; presumably they were verbal and no minutes were taken; a curious lapse.

187   Part 6 of the UK Merchant Shipping Act 1894, section 475/2 required that any

It seems very clear that, by the beginning of June, or perhaps earlier, the Board was not impressed sufficiently by the arguments within the M.M.S.A.'s pamphlet to warrant a reconsidering of the case. Mainly, there was no "new and important" evidence required to allow the matter to proceed. Whether Leslie Harrison knew this is not known. But by the middle of May, he had, typically importunate, already written to the Board, mentioning the *Samson* story, and suggesting an approach to the Norwegian authorities to verify the story. He had also secretly supplied the Board with Beesley's declarations regarding the timing of the rockets. Perhaps Harrison felt that some official muscle may elicit new information about the troublesome little sealer from Norway[188].

A Mr. Bullmore at the Board was not impressed: "Harrison seems to want us to check up with the Norwegian Government before we give a discussion on the petition in case we find we were wrong to turn it down – assuming that we do turn it down!"

Mr. Kent likewise agreed: "Re: *Samson*. The evidence seems to be nebulous in the extreme and I would recommend that you indicate to Mr. Harrison that you are not prepared to raise the matter with the Norwegian Government."[189]. Further discussion within the Board was less restrained as more detail had been gratuitously provided by Harrison, perhaps in an attempt to sway the feelings amongst those considering the petition: "Mr. Harrison's follow-up on this informal reply to a full scale petition is quite unreasonable. If he included the additional information in the petition that the Norwegian Government be approached it could have been different. To give you informally the testimony of Mr. Lawrence Beesley, with its background and a reluctance to give publicity to it is equally absurd. They must either be part of the petition or not."

Whether the M.M.S.A. knew that Harrison had submitted the *Samson* and Beesley stories to the Board is not known.

---

appeal, rehearing etc. could only be heard by a court. When the case was re-examined in 1990-92, The Merchant Shipping (Accident Investigation) Regulations 1989 had overtaken this antiquated law allowing the Marine Accident Investigation Branch to perform the Inquiry. It could not have been performed under the old 1894 Act as it did not allow any individual to perform a rehearing.

188   Quite what Harrison expected the British Government to learn is a matter for debate. Although port documents had long since been lost in a fire, the *Samson's* arrival in Isafjord was still remembered. Captain Jon Errikson, chairman of the Association of Icelandic Shipmakers in Reykjavik wrote to Harrison that "there had been a big riot between the crew of the *Samson* and the local men, who had to guard and protect their womenfolk. The crew had bought all the spirits they could get hold of, and made the place unsafe and had to be brought on board by force." This was apparently early in May 1912.

189   Harrison's introduction of the *Samson* evidence at this point is probably due to the letter received from the Norwegian Broadcasting Corporation on May 21st, 1965

Beesley's evidence was to be submitted formally to the board 3 years later. Harrison had agreed not to make his statement public (at least during Beesley's life) to prevent anything that might cause him "emotional stress or physical strain."[190] The *Samson* evidence could not be obtained in a legally admissible form – either now or later. But by the summer, Harrison was frustrated and asked what the delay was. He was told, "One of the reasons why the Inquiry is taking so long is the conflict of evidence. The navigational aspects are receiving particular attention."

The Board wrote back to Harrison mentioning a possible delay to the petition if it was to be re-worked to include the *Samson* and Beesley "evidence", but this was declined and Harrison asked for the petition to proceed in its "present" form.

A paucity of analysis was delivered by the Marine Division to those considering the petition in mid August: they remarked that "the [1912] court seem to have considered that even if the *Californian* had gone to the assistance of the *Titanic* at 12.45 perhaps not all the lives would have been saved. These findings seem to be justified"

"As the 3rd Officer [sic] remarked to the Apprentice, 'A ship is not going to fire rockets at sea for nothing.' Why then should a ship which is not in distress do so?" the report mentions, before concluding, "*Californian's* position was rejected based on what was actually seen by the witnesses and not on calculations which might have been right or wrong."

The Minister of State for Shipping summed the matter up on 24th August: "I have read all the documentation with interest and while I am of the opinion that Captain Lord did not get a square deal[191], I do not see any way at this time how this could be rectified. If new evidence is to be submitted are we going to go through all this again? Is there no way this could be short circuited and dealt with once and for all?"

Bellamy had sympathies for this viewpoint, but pointed out that they did need to examine new evidence.

There then followed the long and tedious game of bureaucratic tennis between the various personnel, agreeing the exact language of the formal rejection, which was announced publicly on 8th September 1965. As Bellamy wrote to his peers the next day "I agree with a former Parliamentary Secretary of the Ministry of Transport who said 'Surely these events have now passed into history?' I think we have already clearly devoted more than enough effort to this piece of historical research."

The petition was enough to generate indignation. For Peter Padfield, it was because it had been rejected. For Mrs. Sylvia Lightoller, the widow of the *Titanic's*

---

190   *A Titanic Myth* page 212
191   Indeed, many people within the Board mentioned that they felt that it was a pity that Lord was not told of the charges against him and that he should have been informed

2nd Officer, it was simply because it had been presented! In a belated approach, on 7th October 1965, she asked her MP, Roger Greshem Cooke to contact Roy Mason, the Minister of State (Shipping). Sylvia was prepared to signing an affidavit swearing that, not only had she mingled with the *Californian* witnesses (not the Captain) during a recess in the 1912 British Inquiry and that they had said that "[Lord] would not come from his bunk and maintained that they must be having high jinks on the *Titanic* because of its first voyage", but also that her husband was absolutely clear that the ship he had seen "ten miles away was a 3 masted ship of considerable size ... all lit-up" as the *Titanic* sank.

Both of these allegations would seem to be untrue. The "high jinks" statement does not vie with the rest of the evidence. The second allegation is even easier to disprove. First of all, the *Californian* had four masts, not three. Secondly, in Washington, Commander Lightoller had told Senator Smith that he had seen but one light, two points off the port bow, about 3-5 miles away, while the lifeboats were being readied. In London, he repeated this point, stating that he saw this stationary light for about half-an-hour. Thirdly, before he became an opponent of Captain Lord, Lightoller offered his support, and wrote to Lord. On December 15th 1912 from the White Star Liner *Majestic*, he simply re-iterates his prior evidence and reports that he could not say whether it was 1 or 2 masthead lights or the stern light. It is obvious that he was affording this "light" little attention.

Why Sylvia Lightoller should be willing to swear to false accusations is unknown. She may have acquired false memories, or could be so angry at the attention lavished on someone who lay asleep while her husband struggled for life, that she felt the desire to act by sabotaging the petition.

But that was scarcely the conclusion of the petition. On December 1st, Eric Ogden MP mentioned a possible meeting between the M.M.S.A. and the Minister to discuss the petition. Internal resistance was such that this meeting never occurred. And Mr. Mann, the Minister of State wrote on February 14th the next year that Ogden "has told the Minister that the Master Mariner's Association[192] is building up pressure over the '*Titanic*' Inquiry. The Association has approached the Rt. Hon. Ernest Marples MP who according to Mr. Ogden has shown some interest."

But Mr. Marples interest had apparently been overstated, following inquiries by the Board. The Board were therefore "off the hook". For the time being anyway.

Leslie Reade was particularly incandescent in his summary of the M.M.S.A. and its petition. In an essay entitled "*Those Inescapable Rockets*", Reade writes that Captain Lord's admission that the single rocket he admitted being told about "might have been" a signal of distress "make it hard to accept the oft-repeated allegation of Mr. W. L. S. Harrison, the General, and perhaps over-enthusiastic, Secretary of the Mercantile Marine Service Association that the

---

192   The M.M.S.A.?

verdict on Captain Lord made him 'the victim of the grossest miscarriage of justice in the history of British marine inquiries.'

It should never be forgotten that whether the distance between the *Californian* and the *Titanic* – whether it was 5, 10, 19 ½ or even 30 miles, each of which figures has a place in the story – the *Californian* was much closer to the stricken giant than any other known vessel. The *Carpathia*, which thanks to the superb seamanship and determination of Captain Rostron, rescued all the survivors of the *Titanic*, was fifty-eight miles away.

No stress is laid on this matter either in the petition or in Mr. Peter Padfield's book, 'The *Titanic* and the *Californian*,' published simultaneously and arguing the case for Captain Lord on much the same lines. Petition and book have received general public approval. Nor is this surprising. The material which refutes and in the end utterly destroys the case for Captain Lord is to be found mostly only in the transcripts of evidence given at the American and British enquiries. One of the volumes resembles the Bible in bulk; the other is perhaps longer than the First Folio; and both are hard to obtain. It is improbable that the writers who have declared enthusiastically for Captain Lord have ever read a word of either volume, which comment applies equally to the 2600 seagoing and 1500 retired members of the M.M.S.A.

The M.M.S.A. itself, which in this matter means Mr. Harrison, has never in its campaign shown more than what may be called a <u>selective</u> respect for the evidence. That which supports Captain Lord's case is quoted; the rest, if it can't be suppressed, is often ignored or even slightly but significantly altered. Thus, the witnesses in the *Californian* reported the ship they were watching fired 'rockets'; this is changed to 'rockets or flares'. Again, the strange ship was said to have 'disappeared'; the petition prefers to soften this to 'disappeared over the horizon'. The testimony on Lord's side is 'evidence', that on the other is 'personal opinion' – and treated with contempt. It is difficult not to question the integrity of a document which craves in aid such transparent subterfuge, nor to wonder whether they must not in the end recoil.

One flagrant example of the treatment of so-called 'personal opinion' is in the case of the late Captain C.V. Groves ... he declared at the time, and maintained to the end of his life, that he was positive that the ship the *Californian* saw was the *Titanic*. He has therefore been held up to public ridicule and private vilification. Groves was a man of considerable cultivation; but in addition, of all the officers of the *Californian*, he alone in later life attained a high position in his profession, and was widely regarded as a man of exceptional technical knowledge and personal integrity. It is interesting that this reputation is in accord with the impression Groves made, as a young man, at the Mersey Inquiry.

But Groves is only one of the targets of the M.M.S.A. ... the M.M.S.A. professes its eagerness by vindicating [Lord] to remove the slur on the British merchant navy caused by his condemnation. Yet, in this attempt, it does not hesitate to blacken, for one reason or another, the reputation of a large number of other, at least equally skilled and honourable, British seaman, living or dead [viz. Lightoller, Rostron, Boxhall and Bisset]. In fact ... it was not the lawyers [at the Inquiry] who were hostile to [Lord], but some of his own fellow seamen, the men who best understood the case.

The M.M.S.A. takes quite a simple position; all those against Lord, seamen or lawyers, authors or officials, alive dead, in America or Britain, were or are wrong; Lord alone was right.

Anybody who has followed the gestation of the petition must have noted the cynicism with which one new and 'unanswerable' argument after another was abandoned with bewildering rapidity in favour of the next and yet more 'unanswerable' ... Mr. Harrison calmly and with unusual accuracy, announces that the petition contains nothing new at all. Despite its apparent complexities, Captain Lord's case, as will be seen, now stands or falls on one point alone.

'The issue,' says Mr. Harrison, 'can be decided in one hour.[193]'

If the evidence is ignored altogether, instead of only partially, Captain Lord can be vindicated in even less time than that.

Three years ago, the M.M.S.A. propounded their 'Three Ship' case, in which the *Titanic* and *Californian* both saw an unknown ship, but never each other. This third ship was hesitantly identified as the *Mount Temple* [i.e. in *'The Californian Incident: An Echo of the Titanic Disaster'*]. Then, unexpectedly, the 'unknown' was transformed into a mysterious Norwegian sealer called the *Samson*, which although of some 600 gross tons was somehow confused with the *Titanic* of 46,000. Aided by the BBC, an impudent 'documentary' was then foisted on an unknowing (and of course, approving) public, and this broadcast – there were in fact three of them – according to Mr. Harrison, 'marked the turning of the tide.'

With well-founded faith in public forgetfulness, the petition coolly dismisses the 'Three Ship' theory, the *Mount Temple*, the *Samson* and the BBC's 'turning of the tide' without a single word of explanation, or even farewell for all of them together. Instead ... the gravamen of the case for Captain Lord is now a 'Four Ship' theory ... the *Titanic* saw an unknown ship which she mistook for the *Californian*; and the *Californian* saw another unknown ship which she cleverly didn't mistake for the *Titanic* (except, of course, for Groves and two others), even though the *Californian's* 'unknown' ship stopped, threw up altogether eight rockets and disappeared, all of which things the *Titanic* most undoubtedly did. Both of these 'unknown' ships, of course, have left no trace of their identities in any registry, port, document or human memory from the night of their debut and sole appearance until the present time[194]. Not one of the dozens or scores of men, who,

---

193   Somewhat similar to Harrison's comment in *The Sunday Times* on May 25th, 1969: "The case for the *Californian* rests on the 2nd officer's simple statement that 'a steamer that is in distress does not steam away from you.'

194   Dave Gittins, in his excellent e-book, notes that compared to the *Californian*,

as a minimum, must have been aboard them has ever been found; none has ever uttered a single word about his singular adventure."

The remainder of Reade's tirade dismisses the 'Four Ship Theory' as rubbish, questions the time that the *Titanic* and the *Californian* saw their respective 'mystery ships' stating that the White Star giant, much larger than the smaller tramp would be seen sooner than the reverse situation. Witnesses on the *Titanic* who saw the other ship shortly after the collision, and those who disagree with Boxhall's observations of a moving ship are ignored by the M.M.S.A. Reade mentions that Groves seeing the other ship stopping at one bell (11.40pm) "destroys the alleged ten minute difference" between *Titanic* and *Californian*.

Reade continues, "The petition also makes some typically positive assumptions about the identity of certain unnamed witnesses[195] from the *Californian* who were present [at the British Inquiry] but not called. 'They must have included at least one engineer officer,' we are informed, '...in addition, there can be little doubt that the witness included the quartermasters and lookouts.'

All of this has the authentic ring of probability, and the only things that can be said against it is, it happens to be untrue.

Further, as the petition assumes that the Attorney-General was not honestly concerned with finding out the truth, but rather with unscrupulously fixing blame on the innocent shoulders of Captain Lord, '...it is certain (sic)', the petition continues, that had the evidence of these unnamed witnesses 'conflicted' with Captain Lord's, the Attorney-General would have called them.' This is a much less probable guess than the first, but it too is wrong.

For half a century and more no amount of ingenuity or disingenuousness has been able to avoid those inescapable rockets. Mr. Harrison, like a Stalinist rewriting history, insinuatingly and consistently now prefers to call them 'rockets or flares' – a much less disturbing description...we know, of course why the *Titanic* fired her rockets, but neither the M.M.S.A. nor any previous exponent of Captain Lord has ever put forward a cogent reason why the *Titanic* did not see those other rockets, nor why they were fired by this hypothetical 'mirror' ship...it is worth emphasising yet again, and especially as the petition very prudently does not emphasise it, the key factor in the decision must be those deadly rockets, unanswered in 1912 and unanswerable today. It is therefore worth recalling some words that appeared in 1962, the year of the M.M.S.A.'s 'Three Ship' Theory:

'It is impossible to escape the conclusion that some, or all, of the rockets [Stone and Gibson] saw originated from the *Titanic*.'

---

whose crewmembers were anything but quiet, 'whistleblowers' on these unknown vessels have been anything but talkative. Even passengers and crew on the *Mount Temple* were eager to talk to the press in 1912.

195   Their identities, and memories passed from father to son, have already been discussed.

That opinion, by the way, also emanated from the facile pen of Mr. Harrison."

The case of Captain Lord had evidently prompted more discussion in Parliament than had been obvious. For one thing, the Merchant Shipping Act faced yet another revision. From the 1967 final report of "The Court of Inquiry into certain matters concerning the shipping industry", under the chairmanship of the Rt.Hon. Lord Pearson, part 2 dealt with "Proposals for Revision of the Merchant Shipping Act (2)(iii) – Courts' powers in relation to Officers and their certificates". Paragraph 197 states, "In the discussions a complaint was made that in a past investigation or Inquiry a report was made severely criticising an officer, who had been a witness in the Inquiry, although no charge had been made against him and he had not been warned that any adverse criticism was contemplated and he had not been given any or any sufficient opportunity of explaining his conduct that was criticised. We appreciate the hardships of a case of that kind, and we think a court should try to avoid inflicting such hardship on a witness – should whenever possible give him an opportunity of answering what may be said against him – but such hardship is not always avoidable, and we do not think the subject could suitably be dealt with by any legislation or regulation."

This is tacit agreement, as discussed in the internal discussions during the 1965 petition, that Mersey's treatment of Captain Lord was unfair.

In the halls of the M.M.S.A., the campaign for Captain Lord was far from over.

Chapter 9. "A Guilt-Ridden Incompetent Coward"

1968-1987

Lawrence Beesley's death on February 14th, 1967 meant that his "new and important evidence" could now be included in a re-submitted petition. Harrison had agreed not to include this evidence during Beesley's life; now, he could. Cynics could argue that, with Beesley dead, the method of obtaining this "evidence" could no longer be questioned, or the methods used to extract it. This would prove to be of significant importance in the forthcoming decades.

The second petition was formally delivered to the Board of Trade on March 4th, 1968.

Once again, Lord's navigation is regarded as accurate; there is no mention of drift, or the *Carpathia's* rockets being seen from the *Californian*. Harrison is now under the impression that, when first seen, the ships seen from the *Californian* and *Titanic* were showing their red lights – an utterly untrue statement. There is mention of the timing and frequency of the rockets by *Titanic* crewmen Pitman, Lowe, Bright, Symons and Lightoller, but it is Beesley's evidence that is definitive: "The significance of Mr. Beesley's evidence is that in his view the sending up of distress rockets from the *Titanic* had ceased by about 12.45am." This time is from Beesley's 1912 book, and relevant sections of it were included in the petition. Harrison considers that the first rocket was fired at 12.35am[196].

So, in ten minutes, the *Titanic* had fired eight rockets and Boxhall et al. had decided that it was no use sending up any more. What Boxhall and Rowe did in the next hour before they were sent away in lifeboats 4 and C respectively is anyone's guess. It also means that their 1912 testimonies were fabrications. After all, they both described sending up rockets until they were ordered to evacuate the *Titanic*. It also meant that Boxhall's description of "the other ship" turning around "slowly" was also wrong. In ten minutes, she had gone from showing her green (or as Harrison would put it, her red) light, to showing her stern light. Without knowing the other ship's exact orientation, due to the fact that navigation and steaming lights covered a range of angles, it is difficult to quantify the rate of revolution, but it is possible that she turned a maximum angle of 112.5° in ten minutes. Hardly a "slow" turn.

It would not be incorrect to say that Harrison would rely on any information, no matter how dubious or bogus in his moral crusade to clear Captain Lord.

The files at the Public Records Office[197] reveal surprisingly little about the internal deliberations of the Board of Trade. The most salient document is dated March 19th and states, "...little, if any, new evidence of importance" had been

---

196   *"A Titanic Myth"* page 171
197   BT 239/786

unearthed, and that the experience of those who investigate casualties show that "evidence in regard to the time of events is frequently unreliable." However, the memorandum did mention the retardation of clocks and that "this makes comparison of times difficult ... a comparison of times indicate that the times [regarding the firing of rockets] do not appear to vary by more than about 20 minutes."

The memo concluded "It is interesting to see on page 25 of the petition that Mr. Beesley's book says 'Anybody knows what rockets at sea mean'."

The petition was, like its predecessor three years previously, rejected, and one feels that there was a sense of *ennui* within the Board. Leslie Harrison writes, "[The President of the Board of Trade, Anthony Crossland's] decision was given to Parliament in a way which clearly indicated the [Board's] intention to do everything possible to sweep the whole *Californian* business under the carpet. Crossland's statement was made in the form of a written reply to a question, on which a minister cannot be pressed to comment in the House of Commons. That question had been tabled by Hugh D. Brown, member of Parliament for Glasgow, Provan, who could not be traced then – or afterwards – as ever having displayed the slightest interest in the *Californian* case. The reply was issued on a Friday afternoon, on the very last day of a session, just as Parliament rose for the long summer recess. As a final dismissive gesture, the Board of Trade's official confirmation of the reply, first noted in press reports, was sent by the way of the normal postal service, which meant that it was not received in the M.M.S.A.'s head office until the following Monday. All too obviously the Board of Trade hoped that the lapse of time before Parliament re-assembled, and pressure of business as the new session began, would ensure that little, if anything, more would be heard of that petition in the House of Commons. It was a measure of the importance attached by the Board of Captain Lord's case that they should feel compelled to employ a Parliamentary tactic rarely used and only in cases where a government department is extremely apprehensive – and usually with good reason – of public reaction to a minister's decision[198]."

Two submissions of a petition, and two rejections. Matters were looking somewhat bleak, and would prove to deteriorate, for, in 1969, a book written by Geoffrey Jules Marcus, entitled *"The Maiden Voyage"* was released.

The book is segmented into various vignettes, covering different elements of the *Titanic* story, and, naturally, the *Californian* incident is described in lascivious detail. The book is readable and superficially seems well researched, but there are items that are simply untrue, and all to Captain Lord's – and his crew's –

---

198   Indeed, the original annotations and footnotes for Harrison's 1986 book remarks that this "tactic" had also been used when Parliament were debating a hugely unpopular rise in the UK Television license fee. Then, as with the M.M.S.A.'s 1968 petition, debate was left till the last minute to prevent any more publicity on the matter before the summer vacation.

detriment. Witness: "It is necessary at this stage to emphasize the fact that, despite all that was afterwards said to the contrary by Captain Lord, Evans should have remained on watch [during the night]. The custom of the Marconi Marine service required an operator to remain at his post when anything like emergency conditions prevailed – as they assuredly did on the night of the 14th – for fear of missing an important message. The ice-report which the Master of the *Californian* had just sent to the *Titanic* proves the point. The huge ice-field which had stopped their own ship was a manifest danger to navigation."

The source of this information comes from the singularly uninformative phrase, "Private information." A more reliable source may be found in the regulations of the Postmaster-General, which simply states that "Signals of Distress and Admiralty messages will have precedence over all other traffic." There is nothing that describes the manning of a station during emergency situations. Another section, entitled, "Duration of Service" relates that the actual hours of service at each station will be found...[in the] International Radiotelegraph Bureau." Manning requirements are not addressed at all. It is possible that regulations specific to the Leyland, or other IMM vessels may have said differently.

Marcus' next paragraph is also questionable. "It has also been suggested that, since [Captain Lord's] engines were stopped, the Master should have shown 'two red lights vertical and no side lights' (for a steamship not under command), which might conceivably have put other ships in the vicinity on the alert." The source of this is Captain McMillan in *The Journal of Commerce*, March 16th, 1968. But the actual requirement, quoted in *Knights Modern Seamanship* and *The Rules of the Road*, state that, "A vessel which from any accident is not under command shall carry ... two red lights, in a vertical line one over the other, not less than 6 feet apart, and of such a character as to be visible all around the horizon at a distance of at least 2 miles; and shall by day carry in a vertical line one over the other, not less than 6 feet apart, where they can best be seen, two black balls or shapes, each 2 feet in diameter. " The operative words here are "from any accident." This regulation should actually have applied to the disabled *Titanic*, and not the *Californian*!

"*The Maiden Voyage*" laboriously takes the reader through Stone and Gibson's watch, the other strange ship, Evans learning of the disaster (no mention of the *Carpathia's* rockets though) and then resumes in London, where Gill is incorrectly described as being in court during the testimony of his crew mates.

The book proceeds in its description of the British Inquiry: "In court, his officers had done their best for Captain Lord. Outside, in the luncheon interval, however, they were a good deal less reticent about the commander's responsibility for what had happened: and presently, in response to the angry reproaches of the wife of one of the *Titanic's* officer's, they frankly admitted that distress signals had been seen that night from the *Californian*: but they said they had been unable to get Captain Lord to bestir himself; in fact they were unmistakably afraid of him." The 'wife' is obviously Sylvia Lightoller, who has already been discussed. This section of the book particularly roused Leslie Harrison's ire: he remarks that the 'officers' were so 'afraid' of Lord that Groves had the audacity to dispute major points of his commanding officer's evidence, practically labelling Lord as a liar. This is a valid point. The reference to 'fear' of Lord is new, and may have come from Mrs. Lightoller herself, whom Marcus credits as a source in his acknowledgements section. It is of some note that Marcus did not trouble himself mentioning Mrs. Lightoller's demonstrably false statement in the wake of the 1965 petition.

Marcus expresses severe doubt about Captain Lord's performance after the *Carpathia* left for New York, insinuating a half-hearted rescue effort. He writes, "According to the master of the *Californian*, no bodies could be found and after an hour or so he resumed his voyage [to Boston]. It is to be observed that he could not have searched very effectively; for there were in fact hundreds of corpses, drifting to and fro on the face of the waters."

While it is true that, days afterwards, the White Star line had chartered vessels to recover bodies, these were some distance from the position at which Captain Lord searched. With one exception, no-one reported seeing any bodies from the *Carpathia* and the *Californian*, the exception being Captain Rostron who gave evidence that he only ever saw one body during the rescue. Major Arthur Peuchen was indeed surprised to see not one of these "floating corpses" as described by Marcus.

But, aside from the evidence of the Captains of the *Carpathia* and *Californian*, is there anything else that supports the notion that, by some mechanism of drift, the bodies and wreckage had become decoupled? Indeed, there is. In the *Worcester Telegram* on April 17th, 1912, it was reported that, "16/4/12 - [SS] *Parisian* steamed through much ice looking for survivors. No life rafts or bodies were spotted among the floating wreckage which covered a wide area[199]."

---

199   A conflicting report comes *The Boston Globe:* Monday morning when Capt Hains learned what had happened he instructed Mr. Sutherland to keep him fully posted as to wireless messages. Here came again the confusion of messages, is apparent, for Mr. Sutherland picked out of the air indications that succor had reached the *Titanic*. As he got it, both the *Carpathia* and *Californian* were standing by. At that time he got no information that would lead him to believe that his services would be required. So he kept to his course. Being west of the scene of the accident, he had no cause to change his mind. As the day wore on and additional messages were flashing along he got some idea of what had really happened. Then it was too late to put about." With the *Californian* and the *Carpathia* at the scene, the timing of this part of the report (if it is true!) can be placed at about 8.30pm local time. But, in this report, the *Parisian* next turned back for the *Titanic's* location. How, then can the earlier *Worcester Telegram* be right in its statement that the bodies could not be found at the location of the disaster? Any layman would have questioned this, and information from the *Carpathia* and the *Californian* that they had seen no bodies, corroborating the *Parisian*, had not yet reached shore. A strange coincidence.

The SS *Parisian* missed the initial distress call as her wireless operator, Mr. Sutherland, had retired for the night. He picked up the news at about 8am on April 15th, and the *Parisian* turned around, but sadly the *Parisian's* PV is useless to gather timings on this matter. We do not know when she arrived at the wrecksite, but given the specifics of the ship[200] the *Parisian* probably arrived at the location of the wreckage in the later part of the afternoon. This is consistent with her docking at Halifax, Nova Scotia at 7pm on April 17th. So, less than a day and a half after the *Titanic* foundered, already the bodies and wreckage were no longer drifting in unison.

On other points, Marcus makes staggering errors. Although this book is limited to a discussion of the *Californian* incident, a matter peripheral to this is relevant for Marcus tells the readers that "Incidentally a rather intriguing point has come to light in connection with the inquiries that were made about 'wireless and other messages received' respecting the proximity of ice in the North Atlantic. The owners of the vessel that had sent the warning by Morse lamp to the *Titanic* shortly before the collision, Messrs. Furness, Withy and Company, actually informed the Board of Trade [during their search for vessels that had been in the area of the *Titanic*]: 'We beg to advise you that we had no vessels in the vicinity when the disaster occurred.'; and the acting Master of this vessel, the *Rappahannock*, who had himself sent the warning of the icefield ahead, was never called to give evidence at the Inquiry. The explanation may possibly lie in one of the *Titanic* files at the Board of Trade which are still inaccessible to the historian.'

No such inaccessible files from 1912 existed at the time Marcus wrote these words. 'The explanation' is familiar: poor research. On 11th April, the *Rappahannock* passed through an ice field, well to the north and east of the wreck location. Research[201] has shown that the ice warning transmitted by Morse lamp may have occurred on the 13th April, and not the 14th, consistent with a vessel travelling to the east. By the time of the casualty, the *Rappahannock* would have been well away from the *Titanic*. The caption in the book implies that a picture of the *Rappahannock* passing through an ice field was the one that the *Titanic* was heading towards. But this is not the case: the 11th April navigation through the ice was during heavy fog. The picture's caption cannot therefore be accurate.

Concluding his discussion, Marcus tells his readers that the crucial point are the rockets. "The whole matter of discrepancies regarding bearings and timings, which was perfectly well known at the time of the disaster, pales into insignificance compared with the damning evidence of the distress signals ... if one endeavours conscientiously to follow the deeply involved and complicated reasoning of the pamphlet published by the M.M.S.A., one's head begins to reel. And small wonder. After all, it is only necessary to study the logs of the vessels

---

200   See http://www.TitanicInquiry.org/U.S.Inq/AmInq17KnappMemo03.php
201   See http://users.senet.com.au/~gittins/rappahannock.html

engaged in certain naval operations of the past to realize how little dependence can sometimes be placed on the accuracy of times, distances and bearings. If ever there was a case of not seeing the wood for trees, of failing to draw the inescapable conclusions from the evidence, of rejecting the essential for the inessential, we have it here. The author of [the 1965 and 1968 petitions] ought to be a Don ... To clear Captain Lord of the heavy charges brought against him many people would have to be proved wrong. That, indeed, is what has been averred. The Official Inquiries were wrong, declare the Lordites[202], so were the Hydrographer of the Navy Department and his staff, so was Captain Rostron, so were Lightoller, Boxhall and Beesley, so was the 3rd Officer of the *Californian*, the Apprentice Gibson, and Gill, the donkeyman and also were Bisset and the other officers of the *Carpathia*. Everyone, it would appear, is out of step but the Master of the *Californian* ...”

This is absurd. Of course the Lordites dispute the findings of the 1912 Inquiries. The U.S. Naval Department, under the command of Captain Knapp, simply presented a hypothesis that the *Californian* was closer to the *Titanic* than had been given in evidence; this is not 'proof'. Captain Rostron was indeed mistaken about the 'splendid' SOS location he had driven his ship towards, although this was indeed misrepresented by Harrison and the M.M.S.A. to push the *Titanic* wrecksite as far south as possible from Lord et al. Lightoller, although critical of Lord in his autobiography, was full of support in his 1912 letters. Boxhall's testimony actually supports the pro-Lord cause, describing a moving ship. Beesley's book had helped to shape the 1968 petition. And while it is true that aspects of the evidence of Gibson, Groves and Gill, and Bisset's book, did influence public opinion in a way damaging to Lord, there is no mention of what the "other officers of the *Carpathia*" had seen or done. Indeed, Bisset's early sighting of the *Californian* in *"Tramps and Ladies"* is nowhere to be found. Having constructed a 'straw man', Marcus now wastes no time in demolishing it with specious logic.

---

202   'Lordites' is the term used to describe those sympathetic to Captain Lord's plight; 'Anti-Lordites' take the opposing stance.

Illustration 37: Captain Lord on his way to the British Investigation. This is one of the photographs upon which Marcus based his character assessment.

Regarding a suggestion in a periodical about his officers being somewhat nervous of Captain Lord (an assertion given without proof), Marcus has this to say, "There is always a natural inclination to keep on the right side of an autocratic and overbearing master; and if the Master in question were not both autocratic and overbearing it is to be surmised that his photographs, as well as the evidence, do him a grave injustice. It is possible that Captain Lord never encouraged his subordinates to speak their minds freely and openly," and Marcus also tells the reader that "what Stone would sometimes say in private was very different from what Stone said in public." And no source, or evidence for any of these statements is offered; this latter observation may come from another of his 'acknowledgements', a certain Ivan Thompson. And it does seem ridiculous to base an opinion of one's character on photographs, one of which is reproduced here, showing Stanley Lord's eyes glowing devilishly peering from beneath a bowler hat, as he clutches his ship's log.

There is but one more point to make on Marcus' book. In a later edition of *"The Maiden Voyage"*, Marcus included a new foreword in which he reported that an important document regarding the *Californian* was missing from the UK Public Records Office. Ever vigilant, Walter Lord picked up on this and wrote to his friend Marcus asking for clarification. There is no record of a reply in Lord's voluminous documentation, but this was shortly before Marcus passed away and he may not have been able to respond. The identity of this missing document is, thus, unknown, but this author speculates that it is the map and statement that Captain Lord prepared in Boston in late April 1912. Regardless, this important statement is still missing.

The Maiden Voyage proved to be another book that Harrison could not stifle, either through polite means, or by legal manoeuvrings from the M.M.S.A. This did not stop him from trying though.

As the 1960s concluded there was one minor postscript to Harrison's campaign. He had determined that, living at the M.M.S.A. residential accommodation for retired seamen (Mariners Park) was Benjamin Kirk. He was a 22 year old Able Bodied Seaman on the *Californian* in 1912. He eventually agreed to give a statement to Harrison in late 1968:

"I was on lookout 10 to 12 on the night she stopped, surrounded by field ice. I was on the fo'c'sle head. There was a glare of light from another ship on the starboard beam. I cannot remember when I first saw it but I did not report it as an approaching ship so think it must have come up from astern. It was still there when I went off watch at twelve o'clock. I came on watch again at four in the morning. There were no icebergs in sight. Later the Chief Officer asked me to go up in a coal basket shackled to a mainmast stay and hoisted by a gantline to look for survivors or wreckage or boats from the *Titanic*. I could see nothing. I remember very plainly first seeing the *Mount Temple* on the port bow and then the *Carpathia*. There were no boats or wreckage in the water, which was calm, but the *Carpathia* had boats on her foredeck. She steamed away and I came down. When the *Californian* docked in Liverpool no one questioned me about what had happened. I did not go down to the Inquiry."

In photographs of the *Californian* taken from the *Carpathia*, Kirk identified himself as being in a dark 'blob' next to the main mast[203].

His statement is curious, but contains dubious contents. His recollection about 'the other ship' coming up astern ties in with Groves' account. Kirk went off duty at midnight and came back on watch at 4am. Now, assuming that his timing is accurate, this is a surprisingly short amount of time to go off watch; normally, it would be on watch for 4 hours, off watch for 8. His comment about there being no icebergs in sight is a surprise, considering the proximity of the *Californian* to the

---

203   Leslie Reade identified this as the Leyland Line house flag at half mast.

ice field: Groves noticed that there was ice all round his ship and icebergs, when he arrived on the bridge at 6.50am, and Gill confirms this. Kirk also does not mention the yellow funnelled ship seen by Stone and Stewart at 4am. Kirk also claims that, from his high vantage point, he could see neither survivors, wreckage nor boats. Even when he sees the *Carpathia*, he can see no wreckage, which must have been floating nearby, or lifeboats in the water (not even the 7 that were cast adrift). There are suspicions that this affidavit was ghost-written by Leslie Harrison himself[204].

Harrison loaned his copy of '*The Maiden Voyage*' to Kirk and this prompted a letter to The *Nautical Magazine*, in November 1969:

"Sir – I have read [Marcus' book]. I do not agree with these passages, having always found Captain Lord very understanding and a good master to serve under." The rest of the letter is an almost verbatim copy of Kirk's affidavit but one with exception. He did not mention the "glare of light from another ship on the starboard beam" which he presumes came up from astern. Why this is omitted is another one in the long list of curiosities of the whole *Californian* case.

Leslie Reade knew of Kirk's affidavit of course, and attempted to contact the retired seaman, writing to him at Mariners Park. Harrison sent the letter back to Reade, noting to the matron, Mrs. Penn, that "from my knowledge of Mr. Reade, [this] would not necessarily put an end to his efforts to see Mr. Kirk but may possibly have that effect."

Many years later, Reade would write that he had endeavoured to trace Kirk, as there was "no guarantee that a letter addressed to him in care of the M.M.S.A. would reach him." Finally, a suitable intermediate agency agreed to forward a sealed letter to Kirk. The letter was eventually returned to Reade, with a typed postcard, devoid of signature or address: "7th February 1969; Mr. Benjamin Kirk thanks Mr. Reade for his approach but greatly regrets that owing to his present state of health he is not able to become involved in any discussions relating to the *Californian*."

Mr. Kirk, Reade informs his readers, was 78 years old, and still a resident of the seaman's colony [at Mariners Park], the head of which, the "Captain", as he was called, "was one time Chief Officer W.L.S. Harrison."

Reade strongly hints that, because of past differences, Harrison had prevented Reade from gaining access to Kirk.

But Leslie Harrison remembered matters differently[205]; "One potential interviewee who fortunately escaped Mr. Reade's net was Benjamin Kirk ... Mr. Reade implies that, as the administrator of Mariners Park, I hindered him in his attempt in 1969 to establish contact with Kirk ... Mr. Reade's threatening intention towards the 78 year old man are revealed in his own words: 'He could have been

---

204   See http://home.earthlink.net/~dnitzer/Kirk/The%20Man%20in%20the %20Coal%20Basket.html

205   "*A Titanic Myth part 2*", page 160

assured ... of being cross-examined in 1969 much more than thoroughly than would have been possible in 1912.' Kirk spared himself the ordeal, however. Incidentally, Mr. Reade was not the only one to find him elusive. Kirk was very much his own man, and on one occasion in particular simply went to ground when a BBC team visiting Mariner's Park were foiled in their attempt to record his story for their archives."

Fortunately, the 1969 letter to Mrs. Penn has survived and one can compare these two accounts to see which one is more accurate. The "threatening intention" mentioned by Harrison was nothing of the kind; it was simply in response to Kirk's bewilderment, and regret at not having been called for cross-examination in 1912.

Benjamin Kirk aside, Harrison continued in his quest to prove the *Samson's* provenance as the "Mystery Ship". He wrote to Fred Ellis of the Hamilton Shipping Company of Hamilton Ontario, for his opinions on possible ships in or near the ice fields in 1912. Harrison wrote that the ship seen from the *Titanic* "stopped and later went back through the ice," and was wondering if Ellis could confirm that "she was a ship used to navigating in such conditions, and on a mission similar to that of a sealing or fishing vessel?" Ellis' reply was not very encouraging: in his knowledge, very few ships were working as sealers in April 1912 as they were getting short of [coal] bunkers. Some did manage to stay out until the end of April but not many. The only information he could give was that the black and white funnelled ship seen by Captain Moore and Groves matched the colour configuration of the Donaldson line ships. Harrison, in further letters, mentioned that the reason why the *Californian's* "mystery ship" was firing roman candle type flares [sic] "could be the same as the *Carpathia* in order to inform the *Titanic* that he was on the way to the scene". Ellis' replies to other points was simply a repeat of what was already known; that the *Samson* had no need to worry regarding sealing outside the three mile [territorial] limit, as there were no licenses required for such a task at the time: "The *Samson* people were worrying quite needlessly."

But still Harrison would not drop the matter. He had reached the "firm conclusion from documentary evidence from Norway – that the *Titanic* must have seen the *Samson*" and that despite the "unsatisfactory nature of the present documentation which I have, she is most likely to have been the third ship." Ellis' views on the *Samson* were "in line with other views I have had expressed to me." Harrison also told Captain Meadows, the Executive Secretary-Treasurer of the Canadian Merchant Service Guild that "the ship seen from the *Titanic* would seem to be the Norwegian sealing vessel '*Samson*'." And to Captain Gronsond, the director of the Norwegian Shipmasters Association, "... to my mind, there is substance to the [*Samson's*] claim ... [I have] not made any progress in securing legally admissible evidence."

Meanwhile, Leslie Reade's had completed his research and was compiling his notes into a book. By 1973, it was nearing completion, but it seems his publishers were not happy, as they requested that his work be toned done for fear of upsetting "the pro-Lord factions." To placate his publishers, Reade wrote to his MP, Kenneth Baker that year, asking for access to the working papers regarding the 1965 and 68 petitions. Without waiting for a reply, he wrote again, asking for interviews with the personnel involved with the decisions to reject the campaigns. Baker informed Reade that, under the provisions of the "30 Year Act" (whereupon the working papers would be sealed from public inspection until 1995 and 98 respectively), the contents of the files could not be opened. Also, since the Board of Trade had refused requests for an interview with the M.M.S.A. to discuss the petitions, it would be "awkward" if Reade was allowed.

Reade's research would be a hindrance to the pro-Lord publicity that Harrison had spent the last decade manufacturing. Harrison and Captain Lucas, Harrison's successor as General Secretary of the M.M.S.A. had previously provided Reade with a large list[206] of "copyrighted" materials for which prior permission was needed before reproduction. This effectively scuppered his book as Harrison was unlikely to provide clearance of any work of his that was to be used in a work critical of Captain Lord. Harrison wrote to Lord's son that the "intended publishers have halted all action and are unlikely to resume the project." Even though Harrison had retired from the M.M.S.A. in 1975, he was still able to count on its support; for one thing, he was allowed to take the dossier of papers he had accumulated on the *Californian* case during his stint at the M.M.S.A. home with him. No-one else seemed to want them.

Harrison contacted Henrik Naess's son, Harold, in November 1976, informing him that "another [author] may be intending to [refer to sections of the *Samson* manuscript] in critical terms ... The author in question [i.e. Leslie Reade] however has already admitted attempting to use without prior permission copyrighted material owned by me and the possibility of his attempting to do the same with your [father's] manuscript has to be accepted." Harrison asked whether a request had been made to enquire about the use of copyrighted material; if not, and should the M.M.S.A. succeed in an endeavour to check Reade's manuscript before publication, then a check would be made for breaches of copyright.[207]

We shall discuss Reade's book in due course, and the alleged copyright breaches.

From 1975 until c.1985, the matter of the *Californian* seemed to be in limbo; other than mentions in *Titanic* research circles, chapters in books such as

---

206   Presumably, Reade had located copies of some of these items (published openly, and hence quotable, in the 1965 and 1968 petitions for instance), as the only thing that seriously hindered his book were transcripts of the Harrison/Lord tape recorded interview in 1961.

207   There is no record of Harold Naess's reply, if any, in Harrison's surviving papers. Incidentally, Reade's book had come to naught in 1975, so that even a year later, Harrison was sustaining his vendetta against his nemesis.

"*Titanic – End of a Dream*," and remarks in newspapers when "*A Night To Remember*" was repeated on television or released on videotape, one could detect nothing but silence.

But in the mid 1980s, the foe of the Lordites, Walter Lord himself, decided to revisit the *Titanic*. Since his first novel, he had acquired a hallowed status and had been in contact with many hitherto uncontacted survivors of the disaster. He had accumulated a large and unique collection of material related to the *Titanic*, and the time seemed right for a sequel to his earlier work. With the discovery of the wreck in 1985, the public's interest in the ship was now approaching fanatical proportions. Walter Lord's new book, entitled "*The Night Lives On*," was to be a collection of essays on aspects of the disaster – the band playing till the last moment, the rumoured suicide of an officer, the lack of lifeboats ... and the *Californian* incident. He busied himself in extra research. As he revealed in his letters, he had spent more time on the *Californian* that any other single aspect of the *Titanic* disaster.

The large gap between "*A Night To Remember*" and "*The Night Lives On*" (in 1986) seems to have intensified Walter Lord's criticisms of his namesake and his officers, and he did not feel inclined to confine his comments to the *Californian's* crew; he was now willing to launch scathing attacks upon her supporters too: "They come across as energetic, resourceful – and highly selective in presenting their evidence. They play up the testimony that the ship seen from the *Californian* looked like a freighter, but brush off 3rd Officer Groves, who always thought she was a passenger liner. Since the *Californian* was stopped for the night, they parade the witnesses who said the light seen from the *Titanic* was moving, but ignore the witnesses who always thought the lights were stationary. As for the devastating conversation between Stone and Gibson while the rockets were going up, it is seldom mentioned."

Many comfortable "facts" about the *Californian* incident were challenged, such as the acoustic properties of the rockets which "(we are assured) went off with a tremendous bang, easily audible for upward of ten miles. Actually, nobody knows how far the *Titanic's* rockets could be heard. A professional ballistics expert I have consulted says maybe two or three miles." At the time, this author felt that Walter Lord had fed "ballistics expert" Jac Weller false information about the rockets and their audible range; after all, Lord had described their detonation in "*A Night To Remember*" as "muffled" and "distant", and even the filmed version of his book shows the rockets exploding with little more than a pop. However, from perusing the Lord-Weller correspondence, it is clear that, even though neither party knew anything about the exact manufacture of the socket signals, Weller extrapolated the explosive properties from his knowledge of 12 lb mortars. Weller was well suited to such a task: he was an authority on pyrotechnics used in the Vietnam War, and had also acquired first-hand experience of rockets during his time in the U.S. Army. He is not simply, as Lordite author Rob Kamps would later state, "an authority on

279

the Napoleonic Peninsula War"; Weller's expertise extended far beyond that, and stemmed from practical experience.

The chapter contains other statements that can be challenged, most of which are minor. But in one matter, there was a surprising slip by Walter Lord: his reliance on the accuracy of U.S. Hydrographer Captain Knapp's map (reproduced earlier in this book) is misplaced, but yet again it prompts another swipe at Captain Lord's friends, who, it is written "... offer a map, full of authoritative-looking squiggles, showing that the position given by the *Titanic* lay on the far side of an impenetrable ice field ... [Knapp's map] depicts the ice field as lying more from the northeast to the southwest, putting the Titanic's reported position on the near side of the icefield, where of course she belongs. The exact lay of the ice field is, in fact, a subject for endless speculation." In fact, Knapp's map is wrong, as previously stated, because he incorporated ice reports from the *Trautenfels*, which described a SW-NE lay of the field early in the morning of the 14th and ignored evidence from the ships on the scene of the disaster on April 15th which described the SOS location as being to the west of the field. These numerous reports also help to determine an approximate shape and layout of the ice field, which is far from Walter Lord's confident dismissal of its position and boundaries as being the subject of "endless speculation."

As for Groves' inconsistent statements in the 1950s, there is no mention.

Walter Lord soon reaches his *sine qua non*, stating that "The one element that lifts the night of April 14-15 out of the realm of the imponderable is the hard, incontrovertible fact of the rockets – what they were like, what they meant, and what people did about them. And it is here, I think, where the arguments of the *Californian's* defenders really break down," before concluding with a comment that he would use time and again in letters to his friends, "They can say what they like, but they can't get away from those rockets."

The real value of the *Californian* chapter is the first public airing of Leslie Reade's research on the *Samson* story, which Walter Lord had been given permission to quote,. Annoyingly, despite this fable being debunked[208] in 1986, the *Samson* would still be mentioned as a "perennial candidate" well into the 21st century[209].

So, what was the reason for Captain Lord's failure to act and to determine the nature of the rockets for himself? Author Lord was impressed that the Captain was in ice for the first time: "When he made up his mind to stay put, Captain Lord had no inkling that the world's most famous sea disaster was about to occur. He only knew there was a lot of ice out there, and the safe thing to do was to stop for the night. This was the right decision – provided nothing happened. But something

---

208   Some of the data used to debunk the *Samson* has already been discussed; further evidence will be debated shortly.

209   In 1989, this author asked Leslie Harrison about the Norwegian sealer and was told "I have an open mind regarding the *Samson* question."

did happen, and Captain Lord's failure was his inability or unwillingness to adjust to an entirely new situation. True, he had his own ship and crew to think about, but that was no excuse for doing nothing. What was good seamanship before the rockets became a woeful lack of enterprise afterward."

Even after he had been roused by Stewart, it still took these two men about 50 minutes to wake Evans. What was the reason for the delay? Author Lord speculates on the information exchanged during this time. "What changed [Lord's] mind [to wake up Evans]? My hunch is that it was not Stewart's logic or eloquence, but a complete change of circumstances. An entirely new and reassuring element had entered the picture: daylight ... It was at last safe for a prudent man to act."

Leslie Harrison responded with venom[210] . He replied to the publication of *"The Night Lives On"* by repeating that the *Californian's* mystery ship came from the west, as per Groves, and that evidence given in London contradicted Walter Lord's assertion that Groves "thought [that the *Californian* resumed her voyage to Boston] at around 10.40, after the most cursory of examination. Harrison also took umbrage at the statement that the Captain was an "austere autocrat". Another statement that raised the ire was "The [*Californian's*] light that glimmered most of the night on the horizon ... a tantalising lure, always just out of reach", to which Harrison responded that, if this was the case, "more than eight 'socket signals in lieu of guns' would have been fired. As it was, the ship whose attention they were trying to attract did not come into sight until nearly an hour after the liner had stopped. Both of these statements can easily be challenged: only about eight socket signals were fired not, as Harrison told this author, because the other ship was steaming away, but because the crew members firing them were ordered away by Captain Smith; and the assertion that the other ship was not seen until an hour had elapsed can be disproven by witnesses on the *Titanic*.

In summary, Harrison writes, "In '*The Night Lives On*', [Walter Lord] creates an impression, wittingly or unwittingly, that Captain Lord was a guilt ridden incompetent coward."

But the chapter on the *Californian* incident in *"The Night Lives On"* revealed a schism within pro-Lord camps. Harrison would be satisfied with nothing less than a total exoneration of Captain Lord; this his ship was too far away to be of help; that the *Titanic* and the *Californian* were never in view of each other; that the *Californian's* watch officers and Captain were justified in not waking up the wireless operator and for not treating the rockets with more alarm; and that the *Titanic's* rockets were never seen.

In 1962 Retired Marine Engineer John C. Carrothers wrote an article for the *U.S. Naval Proceedings* magazine in which he repeated the charges against Captain Lord. But, shortly afterwards, as Carrothers noted in the Titanic Historical Society Commutator[211] Supplement No.1 (1987) "[he obtained] the irrefutable

210   Titanic Historical Society (T.H.S.) Commutator Supplement No.2 (1987)
211   The Commutator is the official journal of the Titanic Historical Society

evidence concerning the *Californian* [from] Harrison and Padfield". In 1962, Carrothers "depended totally on the newspaper reports of the Mersey Inquiry, and when [he] saw the word 'rockets', [he] went no further", believing that all but Captain Lord had identified the unknown ship as a large passenger liner. In 1968, he wrote "Lord of the *Californian*", a defence of the late Captain, a position he held till the end of his life[212].

Carrother's "*Lord of the Californian*" paper is, if one is unfamiliar with the evidence, a convincing summary of the case for Lord and his cohorts. However, like all the other literature, it omits the "A ship does not fire rockets at sea for nothing" conversation, Captain Moore's observations of the *Californian* and *Carpathia* the morning after the disaster and several other key matters. The light seen from the decks of the *Titanic* appears "about an hour after the collision ... [coming from] over the horizon," a declaration that can be found nowhere in the evidence. Stone and Gibson's evidence is mistreated to make it sound as if they both agreed in "low lying rockets", and ignores the fact that both men agreed that the rockets did indeed come from the other ship. Thus Carrothers argues that that the *Californian* had seen the *Titanic's* rockets, but due to a happy – and coincidental happenstance of events, another ship lay on the exact bearing between Captain Lord and the stricken White Star giant. Carrothers writes that the known capability of the rockets was that they "burst from 2-300 [sic] feet up with an explosion." Rockets rising from the deck of the *Titanic* at a height of "70 [sic] feet", rising to 300 feet would be seen at a distance of better than 22 miles. "Under the ideal weather conditions" that night, the *Californian* could have observed the *Titanic's* rockets at a distance of more than 30 miles.

This "ship in between" hypothesis had been addressed in London in 1912, where sufficient evidence was garnered to disprove it. But this is the theory that Carrothers adopted in 1968, and he repeated it nearly two decades later. Other authors have taken the same stance too.

In 1987, Carrothers wrote a scathing riposte ('*Lord verses Lord*') against Walter Lord's book, saying that, "In no way do we pretend to offer any excuse or alibi for [Captain Lord] not responding to the rockets when reported to him. Our only purpose is to present our conviction that the circumstantial and documentary evidence proves conclusively that the *Californian* lay trapped in the ice fields 19 ½ miles away from the sinking *Titanic* and not five miles as claimed by Lord Mersey." There were other points that Carrothers was at variance with Harrison over, the most significant being that the former felt that the *Titanic's* rockets had been seen by Stone et al. Carrothers also felt that "Lordites believe that if anyone should [have been] censured it should have been the 2nd officer and not Captain Lord."

(T.H.S), originally called the Titanic Enthusiasts of America (T.E.A)

212   Reactions to this 1968 article can be found at
http://home.earthlink.net/~dnitzer/Updates/Letter.html

In his article, Carrothers continues, "With [the *Titanic's* and the *Californian's* mystery ships] established: How come no-one on board the *Californian* recognised the *Titanic* ablaze with lights all during the sinking? How come no one on the *Californian* ever saw the *Titanic's* powerful blinker [Morse] light flashing for help? How come no one on the *Titanic* ever saw the *Californian's* Morse blinker light asking the ship with a few lights stopped about five miles away for identification? For years we have tried to get Walter Lord to reconcile these irrefutable facts concerning the Morse blinker lights. However, he has consistently ignored the issue as though it never existed. Another point that he refuses to recognise is the mystery ship that sailed up to within five miles of the *Titanic* before turning around and slowly sailing away ... Walter Lord's technique is clear – facts that do not fit in the story – ignore them.[213] The ranks of Captain Lord's defenders ... are growing. And, in spite of Walter Lord's cheap shot against us, we fully intend to continue in our efforts in the belief that truth and justice will eventually prevail."

Coincidentally, at almost the exact time that Walter Lord's book appeared, a pro-*Californian* tome was published, for Leslie Harrison himself had decided many years previously that his version of history should be released to the public. A proposal for his inchoated book was submitted to Captain Lord while he was alive, and Harrison laboured on the manuscript between April 1976 and late 1977. After a period of editing, the book, titled "*A Titanic Myth – The Californian Incident*" was submitted to nearly 40 publishers, all of whom rejected it. Harrison seemed to be resigned to the fact that his book was never going to be published, even after he had offered to forego his royalties fees in one case if it would expedite the release of his book. "Then," Harrison later wrote, "came salvation from a most unlikely source – that of the *Titanic* herself." The wreck had been found in late 1985 and the resultant publicity spurred the former M.M.S.A. secretary to approach his first choice of publisher – William Kimber, who agreed in January 1986, to publish the book later that year[214].

The manuscript was submitted to a barrister to be checked for potential libel and copyright matters. Counsel's opinion "devastated" Harrison: "My overall impression is that [the author] considers those who decline to share his beliefs to be either hypocritical and actuated by malice or suffering from culpable delusions

---

213   Ironically, this same statement could be said about Carrothers. This author was friendly with Carrothers in the last three years of his life, and once visited him at his home in Connecticut, and finds criticising him a difficult task. While I do acknowledge that Carrothers played a huge role in marine safety and justice (most notably the *Andrea Doria/Stockholm* collision), it is clear that he is as "guilty" of the sin of omission of evidence as Walter Lord was accused of being.

214   The entire episode is recounted in "*A Titanic Myth part 2: Defending Captain Lord*"

caused by obsession or prejudice."

Harrison was given only five days to respond to Counsel's recommendations, which amounted to thirty items which could have exposed William Kimber and Harrison to possible future legal action. Harrison responded as best he could, and despite interminable reminders from Kimbers about the impending deadline, lest the project be cancelled and Harrison be charged for "any expenses so incurred," the project proceeded under an unhappy cloud. The book was eventually released on November 24th, 1986. Of the initial print-run of 1720 copies, over 900 had been sold by April the next year, and the book eventually went out of print in 1989.

But there is one more sour incident during the production of "*A Titanic Myth*". Walter Lord had acquired a copy of Harrison's manuscript, which had been deposited with long-time mutual friend Edward Kamuda of the Titanic Historical Society. Despite their disagreements, Walter Lord and Harrison maintained a cordial, polite correspondence until "*The Night Lives On,*" when their contact ceased. However, Walter wouldn't debate technical points with Harrison – in fact, he ignored them totally, and Lord seemed to gather an immense feeling of glee in doing so.

Lord informed Harrison that he had acquired a copy of his book which he hoped to use as background research for '*The Night Lives On*'. Harrison wrote back and told Walter that his publisher had pointed out difficulties which could arise depending on the extent of the use of the material contained in his book which Walter Lord wished to make. Harrison requested that Lord inform him if he was considering a formal approach to quote extracts from his manuscript. But, barely two weeks later, Harrison wrote again refusing permission for any material to be reproduced. Walter Lord had already decided that "if you are going to start putting conditions, I think it is better if I don't look at it at all," lest he inadvertently infringe on copyrights, including what Harrison seemed to consider his crowning glory – his schedule of events on board the *Titanic* and the *Californian*. Walter Lord returned the manuscript unread, telling Harrison that he hadn't planned to use any of his material anyway. To this author, this sounds very similar to the successful attempt to derail Reade's book a decade earlier, by agreeing – and then withdrawing – permission to use material from his collection, the resulting legal hassles causing any publishing endeavour to founder. Then, Harrison had been successful, but this time, he wasn't so "lucky".[215]

Harrison's semi-biographical hagiography of Captain Lord is divided into two portions. The first ('The Fact') describes Lord's life up to the time he approached the M.M.S.A. for help in 1958 and is told from his point of view. The concluding part ('The Legend') discusses the efforts taken to analyse the

---

215   Astonishingly, in January 1987, Harrison wrote to a Mr. Mahan, c/o The Editor of *The Irish Times* saying that "Walter Lord refused my offer to let him read the [manuscript] of my own book before completing his."

Californian matter and submit the petitions, and concludes about 1975 (when Harrison started to write the book). Lord's personality is genial and accommodating; a man of total integrity with an incredibly clear memory. The basic thesis of the book is that the ice field held two more ships on the night the *Titanic* went down, one of which was also firing rockets or flares. It is speculated that the *Samson* might also have been in the area, but "none of the evidence relating to [her] alleged involvement in the *Titanic* disaster could be obtained in a legally admissible form," though, of course Harrison knew about the severe reservations his nautical friends and contacts had about the story.

Now it is possible to objectively judge "*A Titanic Myth*" against the research material that Harrison had spent 28 years accumulating, only some of which was accepted into his final manuscript. Here are some examples of Harrison's omissions: he knew that Captain Lord had lied to the press in Boston about Stewart being on the bridge during the middle watch on April 15th 1912. Harrison knew about Cunliffe's internal memo in 1912 in which Lord's map was discussed, and which placed the *Californian/Mount Temple* rendezvous time at about 6.30am, an hour before Lord had claimed[216].

Harrison must also have known about Captain Moore's statement in America that he saw the *Californian* and the *Carpathia* at the same time; although there is no verbatim extract of his testimony in the book, references to the *Mount Temple* indicate that he was familiar with Moore's story. Like Padfield's book, this topic would be too much of a hot potato.

Harrison uses the total steaming time on 15th April from her overnight position to the Carpathia – 2 ½ hours – as evidence that the *Californian* was a suitably large distance away from the *Titanic*, thus ignoring the contrary evidence that exists, but also that this timing refers to the circuitous route around the edge of the ice field, and not a straight-line path, which would have taken less time.

The recollections of Harrison's client – Captain Lord himself – have now been modified, so that the first sighting of a white light from over the eastern horizon, and the subsequent green light are now described as "mistaken." Lord was sure that he had seen them in his 1912 London declarations. Harrison now takes the testimony of Groves and his initial sighting of a ship to the south, heading towards the *Californian's* stern, "coming up obliquely" and stopping heading somewhere to the south and east of him. How can this ship be the *Titanic*, Harrison asks? What about Captain Lord's observations of a ship coming from the east, ask those familiar with the evidence? Why is that suddenly a "mistaken" impression?

The biographical aspect of his work omits Lord's determination to renounce his British citizenship in 1920 in favour of life in the United States. This is curious, as the remainder of Harrison's information about Lord's is quite detailed.

---

216   Indeed, a later writer (Senan Molony) knew about this Cunliffe memo as he published a photocopied extract of it in his pamphlet about the *Mount Temple*. But when it came to writing his own Pro-Lord book, this memo is not mentioned.

Maybe it has no bearing on the *Californian*. But, more likely, it is possible that Harrison did not know of it, for it is included in the second set of documents bequeathed to the Liverpool Maritime Museum upon Stanley Tutton Lord's death, and not the first set, which Harrison had relied upon for his book. If Harrison did not know of this, why did Lord Jnr. withhold it? Another striking deletion from Harrison's record of Lord's life is that his ship, the *Anglo Patagonian,* was damaged in a collision in Hampton Roads on June 15th, 1915. Likely the incident had no impact on Lord's employment with Lawther Latta; he still captained the ship on its next voyage on September 12th. But a Captain is always responsible for his vessel. And the incident *was* significant enough to be recorded on Lloyd's Captains' Register. Did Lord with-hold this information from his friend, or did Harrison ignore it altogether? As recounted in Harrison's book, one gains the impression that Lord's life until 1958 was impeccable and trouble free.

But Harrison' book is notable in one respect, for it features the first time since 1912 that the notion of drift was applied to the overnight position of the *Californian*. A sketch map in the book uses a distance of about 3 miles, possibly derived from Foweraker's sketch, which is reproduced in Harrison's tome.

And what of the strange rockets seen after 3a.m. by Stone and Gibson? They are mentioned in the transcript of their so-called 'secret statements'. There is no mention of them elsewhere in the book; although there is some discussion of the *Carpathia's* use of rockets at about this time, there is no attempt to link these two events. The *Carpathia's* rockets were fired from a much greater distance than the *Titanic's*; if the *Californian* had seen the *Carpathia's* rockets, then she must have undoubtedly have seen the *Titanic's*.

Stewart's evidence that he asked Evans to find out about the ship to the south, and not because of the rockets fired during the night, is not mentioned. Harrison is also very generous when he describes Groves' evidence "Groves then described what he saw when he reached the bridge at about 6.50. The boats were being swung out and the ship had a good speed on her. They passed the *Mount Temple*, and he saw another, smaller, vessel with a black funnel coming down almost end on, a little on their port bow. The reached the *Carpathia* about 7.45, he thought..." The testimony that Groves saw the *Carpathia* abeam on the port side at 6.50, with her house flag at half mast, is ignored.

The matter of the meeting with Lawrence Beesley, and the subsequent affidavit, is recounted in detail in the book, and Harrison repeats that Beesley was sure that the last rocket had been fired by the time he had left the sinking liner, in boat 13. But when was this? Would Harrison still claim that it was 12.45a.m., as he had in the 1968 petition?

"[Beesley's book gives an] indication of what time [the last rocket might have been fired]:

'At about 2.15 a.m., I think we were any distance from a mile to two miles away [from the *Titanic*]. It is difficult for a landsman to calculate distances at sea but we had been afloat an hour and a half.'

Even if Beesley was as much as half an hour out in his estimate, this meant that the last distress signals must have been fired from the *Titanic* before 1.15 a.m. If his estimate were in any way accurate then it confirmed that the last of the distress signals fired from the *Titanic* had been sent up by 1 a.m. [supposed *Californian* time]"

This supposition uses Harrison's own deduced time difference between the *Californian* (taken as 1 hour 50 minutes ahead of New York Time, even though Evans said 1 hour 55 in London) and the *Titanic* (whose noon position, according to Harrison, was 2 hours and 2 minutes ahead of New York) of 12 minutes; he has adopted a 1 a.m. time rather than 1.03 a.m. for simplicity. But Harrison is wrong on this matter: if Beesley's estimate, either 12.45 or 1.15 (and one wonders how this figure was obtained!) is inaccurate, then it renders the 1968 finding about the timing of the final rocket as completely void.

Harrison also omits to tell the reader that he told the Board of Trade about Beesley's affidavit in 1965; whether this breaks Harrison's assurance to Beesley to protect him from emotional stress or physical strain, is perhaps a matter of semantics.

After describing Gill's evidence in London, Harrison refers to another witness called at the Inquiry: "Earlier that day, another witness had given evidence which both Lord Mersey and the Attorney-General evidently considered to be of significance so far as the case against the *Californian* was concerned." It was given by Alfred Crawford, who has already appeared in our narrative. From a reading of Harrison's text, Crawford's testimony confirmed his U.S. evidence: that he had been ordered by Captain Smith to row for the distant lights, deposit their passengers and return to the *Titanic*. An impossibility surely, even if the lights were only a few miles away. But, desperate men do desperate things.

Crawford's tale of how he and his comrades rowed all night for the lights about 5 to 7 miles away and then abandoned the chase upon sunrise was interrupted by Lord Mersey; "Does five to seven miles agree with the information from the *Californian* as to the position she took up when she anchored [sic]?"

Mersey was told that it was "widely different." Harrison obviously wants the reader to think that Mersey had already made his made up that what Crawford had seen was the *Californian*, but Mersey had assumed this from almost the time that Captain Lord had taken the witness stand. Other than this, it would seem that Harrison is trying to put across that possibility that the cross-examination was haphazard, prone to interruption and arguments about semantics (for instance, the exact form of Captain Smith's order was either "Go to the light, put your passengers off, and come back to this place" verses "come back to this ship" - does it really matter?)

But a reading of Crawford's full testimony, side-by-side with Harrison's summary shows massive gaps. And one cannot think that they were anything other than deliberate. For example:

Harrison's text says that Crawford had recalled that "the vessel was turning round and leaving us." But the remainder of his testimony shows a much different story, for Crawford had, at various times said that "[the other ship] seemed to be stationary there," confirming to Robertson Dunlop, in one of his few appearances in court, that "at no time" was she steaming towards Crawford. And then later, when asked "Did [the lights of the steamer] appear to get any nearer?", Crawford said simply, "No," and then opined that he thought the lights were drifting away from him. What on earth was Crawford describing[217]? A ship that may, or may not have moved, but drifting away? Perhaps, whatever he was seeing, was not moving much, if at all, subject to the irregular ebb and flow of an oceanic current?

On one other matter, Harrison relates that, "The Attorney-General submitted that the *Carpathia's* bearing from the lifeboat would be almost exactly south-east," but neglects to relate this to the movements of Crawford and his diligent crew who had been rowing patiently for three hours towards the mystery lights. For Isaacs enquired of Crawford, "At any rate, in the way you were heading in your boat, the *Carpathia* was astern of you?"

"No, she was on the quarter."

"And then you turned round and went to her?"

"Yes"

The "quarter" of any boat, as had been repeated many times, is to the rear; for the *Carpathia* to have appeared in this segment, the lifeboat would have had to have been pointing somewhere towards the north-west. This point is not discussed by Harrison, who simply repeats Boxhall's and Beesley's impression of a westerly heading *Titanic*, with the light(s) off the bows, even though Beesley had said that the White Star behemoth was heading north-westerly when she went down.

In fact, when it comes to the other ship, Boxhall is the only one who is dealt with in any great detail, and he seems to hold majesty over all other accounts. Of course, Boxhall is a prime witness to Lordite writers, for he talked of a moving ship, albeit not moving very fast. Such a ship could not be the *Californian*, stopped all night long. No references to any witness describing a moving, or stationary ship are made in the book.

The book also omits Harrison's contact with Leslie Reade (perhaps as a results of Counsel's proof-reading of the manuscript); and also fails to tell its readers exactly <u>why</u> Harrison thought that Sir James Bisset's chapter on the *Californian* in *"Tramps and Ladies"* had been "embellished with a wealth of

---

217   This is not the only instance of conflicting statements from Crawford. In America, he had said he had seen no sidelight from the other ship. In London, he described them vividly.

imaginative detail" (Harrison neglects to tell uninformed readers that Bisset had seen the *Californian* 10 miles north of the *Carpathia* on the morning of April 15th while picking up survivors from the lifeboats).

Harrison speculates, as did Dunlop seven decades earlier, about the mysterious rocket firing vessel seen by Stone et al.; he hypothesises that the "watchkeepers on the other vessel saw the *Titanic's* rockets low down on the horizon and signalled their intention [to the *Californian*] to go down and investigate, notifying their intention by sending up rockets. If so where was she in the morning?" This explanation does not seem credible. Why send up signals and then not actually go and investigate? Why head off in the wrong direction – to the west – rather than roughly south, or south east to where the Titanic was? This whole theory also relies on the bogus supposition that the *Titanic's* rockets were seen by the other ship but not by Stone and Gibson. Harrison has stated in many publications that the socket signals/rockets/flares rose to an altitude of anywhere between 150 and 300 feet. Lightoller was asked about the rockets in London:

"How are they discharged; are they discharged from a socket?"

Lightoller replied, "In the first place, the charge is no more and no less than what you would use in a 12-pounder or something like that. In the rail is a gunmetal socket. In the base of this cartridge, you may call it, is a black powder charge. The hole down through the centre of the remainder is blocked up with a peg. You insert the cartridge in this socket; a brass detonator, which reaches from the top of the signal into the charge at the base, is then inserted in this hole. There is a wire running through this detonator, and the pulling of this wire fires that, and that, in turn, fires the charge at the base of the cartridge. That, exploding, throws the shell to a height of several hundred feet, which is nothing more or less than a time shell and explodes by time in the air."

Harrison took this 'several hundred feet' testimony from Lightoller as the basis for his height estimate, but his eventual guess was underestimated, as the socket signals were actually designed to reach an altitude of 600-800 feet. Harrison's 150-300 feet altitude amounts to a visible range of between 14 and 20 miles, and he was sure, before the *Titanic* wreck was located, that she and the *Californian* were "never nearer than 25 miles[218]." In Harrison's view, even rockets reaching 300 feet would never be seen by Stone or Gibson, but he never considered – or told his readers – that observers above the waterline could see beyond this visible range, effectively over the horizon, as it were. This means that the watchkeepers on the *Californian* could possibly see rockets fired from between 22 and 28 miles away, bringing the *Titanic's* signals into (possible) visibility.

From his research material, we can now say that Harrison definitely knew that the socket signals used by the *Titanic* and *Carpathia* went up 600-800 feet. We must ask why he kept this fact from his readers. Obviously, rockets detonating lower would have a much lower visible range, concreting the claim that the

---

218   Letter from Harrison to Walter Lord, 8th August 1962

Californian crew never saw the *Titanic's* signals. It is as if readers were being taken firmly by the hand and led unknowingly up the garden path[219].

It may be an instructive exercise for readers to estimate how far rockets reach when standing directly underneath the explosions at a fireworks display, and then comparing their guess with a value provided by an expert. The difference may surprise the reader. Bear in mind that this is what Lightoller was doing. By observing the detonations from directly below them, it is difficult to form any accurate opinion of their altitude.

As for Harrison's other question ("Where was [the other ship] in the morning?"), readers of his book are forced to guess.

...and so the list of (almost certainly) willful distortions, faulty logic and omissions of evidence continues. More than ten years after his death, we can finally see how Harrison worked.

As a biographical exercise, or a description of a defence brief prepared for Captain Lord, "*A Titanic Myth*" has its merits. But as an objective book, it is far from valuable.

---

219   Harrison was also dishonest about other established nautical rules or testimony. In 1989, he told me that he believed that the socket signals were discharged vertically to reach maximum altitude, and that they were fired from the port side of the *Titanic's* bridge. This ignores regulations which stipulated that the rockets be fired at an angle of 20° to the vertical to prevent debris from the detonation from showering the decks. It also ignores 5th Officer Lowe, and his own correspondence with Q.M. Rowe, both of whom place the socket signal firing tube near lifeboat no.1; that is, on the starboard side. In his dotage, Harrison had become an iconoclast of long-held fact.

Chapter 10. "New and Important Evidence"

1987-1992

    The lack of movement on the *Californian* matter was proving to be disheartening for its greatest champion. Despite a Titanic Historical Society poll that showed that a majority of respondents wanted the Lord case re-opened, Leslie Harrison told this author in 1989 that he had long since given up actively debating and campaigning over the *Californian* incident, and had resorted to a simpler strategy; reducing the evidence for Captain Lord to its simplest, basic form. These consisted of photocopies of sections of the inquires[220]. Strangely enough, that very year, he wrote to (then) President Bush of the United States regarding Lord's case. Also in 1989, Harrison and Stanley T. Lord had tried to force the Department of Transport[221] to action by arguing that Captain Lord was not adequately represented in 1912[222]. Harrison drafted a letter, to be agreed by Lord Jr.:"My father had no personal connection with Mr. Dunlop, nor any opportunity to discuss his case with him, or to influence what he chose to say. In the above circumstances would you kindly ask your Department's legal advisors to rule on the formal situation of an aggrieved witness, such as my father, whose case is taken up by a barrister purporting to represent him, but when, in fact, had no authority to do so. In my father's case, he did not knowingly delegate to the Leyland Line, his employers, the authority to make any such arrangement with Mr. Dunlop. If, as I submit, my father was not legally represented at the Inquiry, and received no prior warning of the charges later held proved against him, are the findings of the Inquiry nevertheless to be regarded as irrevocable and completely immune from any subsequent formal challenge?"

    It is not known if the letter was sent or not. The internal Department minutes make no mention of it, and there is no acknowledgement in the legacy of Harrison's papers.

    Two pieces of evidence could conceivably re-open the Inquiry: the actual 1912 positions of the *Titanic* and the *Californian*. The latter seemed to be an impossibility as the only way to determine her location was to work backwards

---

220   One such despatch, which was sent to this author, highlighted Groves' evidence of a ship coming from the south and west, and a sketch showing the *Californian's* heading, and the bearing of Groves' ship; this was contrasted with evidence, again photocopied from the inquiries, showing that the Titanic had been heading almost due west. There is no mention of Captain Lord's sighting of a green light.

221   One of the successors to the original Board of Trade.

222   This was after the Department had tried to argue that, according to Harrison, "the official attitude is that Captain Lord's case was properly put to the 1912 inquiry, and that if it were reopened, there could well be an official endorsement of Lord Mersey's critical finding."

using navigational data gathered on April 15th, but this was subject to personal biases, interpretation of the evidence and an estimation of the strength and direction of the drift that night.

The first of these desirable pieces of data was known, but unavailable. On September 1st, 1985, a Franco-American team had unearthed the location of the *Titanic* wreck with precision. However, these data were not available because of the fear of looting of the wreck by profiteers. But, on 6th October 1987, the positions were published in *"The Discovery of the Titanic"* by Dr. Robert D.Ballard and Rick Archbold. It was felt that, since sufficient people now knew the location of the wreck, it was futile to keep it officially secret. Indeed, in the book, the co-ordinates were revealed in a chapter dedicated to the question of the *Californian*[223]. It turned out that the *Californian's* overnight DR position was some 21 miles to the NNW of the actual wrecksite, and, according to Ballard, rockets could certainly be seen over that distance. Ballard had been critical of Captain Lord and felt that it was a "telling fact" that the men of the *Californian* failed to act when action was needed, even if they could only pluck a few half-dead bodies from the icy waters. He later told Harrison in reply to one of his many letters that he found Walter Lord's *Californian* logic "more persuasive" than that of the ex-M.M.S.A. secretary.

A significant point mentioned many times since the wreck was found was that the bow section (the wreck had broken into two major pieces) pointed just slightly east of north, the stern having turned around 180°. To the opponents of Captain Lord, this was proof that the *Titanic* was pointing in the approximate direction of the *Californian*, but the critics of this stance were unperturbed, one saying that the direction of the bow is no indication of the *Titanic's* heading on the surface, as the stern was headed in the opposite direction. But tests performed by the Discovery TV Channel in the 1990s on a model in a water tank demonstrates that the bow section, being more streamlined and hence susceptible to less drag, would continue to the bottom in the direction in which she was heading on the surface; and Dr. Ballard, in his book, noted that the stern probably rotated as she descended, the same motion being observed in submersibles that fell more or less straight down, as the stern undoubtedly did. Perhaps of more relevance is the *orientation* of the bow from the stern. Drawing a line from the mid-line of the bow to the area of the stern reveals a north-south line; if the bow moved forward as she headed towards the ocean floor, this demonstrates a northward heading ship on the surface.

The Lordites now had a chance; in an article discussing (pro-Lord)

---

223   A mystery exists though, in the strength and direction of the current that existed the night the Titanic went down. The schematics in Ballard's and Archbold's book (reproduced from the December 1985 issue of the National Geographic magazine) and text state that the current was deduced from the Californian's log book, and turned out to be 0.7 knots to the SSE. Not only is this inconsistent with the location of the wreckage on the 15th, but the Californian's log book has been missing for decades.

navigational aspects of the *Titanic* disaster, Harrison wrote, "In 1987, the disclosure of the actual position of the wreck poses a very interesting question: does it constitute 'new and important evidence' within the context of Section 57(1)(a) of the 1970 Merchant Shipping Act, *compelling* [emphasis in original] the Department of Transport to reopen that part of Lord Mersey's Inquiry which censured Captain Lord?"[224]

The answer was "yes" - but the Department would not accede without a fair amount of struggle on their part: for, in the year that Harrison wrote the above paragraph, there seemed to be the first signs that the Political stonewalling was beginning to crumble. On the 3rd August, Peter McClymont, the Private Secretary to Lord Babrazon of Tara, Minister of State for Aviation and Shipping responded to a letter and annotated copy of "*A Titanic Myth*" sent by Harrison two months earlier. McClymont's reply was that, "The Department has carefully considered the evidence, including that provided by the findings of *Titanic's* wreckage, and its conclusion is that you are right in deducing that *Californian* was in all probability substantially further from the *Titanic* than Lord Mersey found. At the same time, the Department consider it inescapable that Captain Lord did merit a degree of censure. When all possible allowances are made for the different circumstances of 76 years ago, including the common use of company identification signals, the fact remains that signals which could have been those of distress were seen in an area which Captain Lord himself considered hazardous enough to require him to stop his ship until daylight. In these circumstances, the Department consider to reopen the Inquiry would serve no useful purpose and might indeed do more harm than good, and so do not propose to do so."

One wonders in vain why such an Inquiry would do more harm than good. Harrison responded by noting his disagreements to this response from McClymont:[225] to his mind, the Department had exposed the absurdity of Lord Mersey's finding that the *Californian* "might have saved many if not all of the lives that were lost." Another point that fuelled Harrison's anger was the mention of distress signals, which are listed in this book, in Appendix B. He listed the four ways, according to law in 1912, that a ship may summon help. However, Harrison was wrong on one crucial point. With regard to "Rockets or shells, throwing stars of any colour or description, fired one at a time, at short intervals," he noted "The eight 'rockets' seen from the *Californian* were not fired 'one at a time, at short intervals,' but irregularly, over a protracted period of time." This is true, but the law did not describe that the rockets or shells should be fired at regular intervals, but only that they should be fired one at a time. The duration of the rocket firing is also irrelevant. The *Californian* saw the eight rockets fired over a possible hour's duration, or an average of one every 7 ½ minutes. What was seen, despite Harrison's interpretation, describes exactly the prescribed method in law for

---

224   *Seaways*, the Journal of the British Nautical Institute, March 1988.
225   Titanic Commutator Volume 12, No.2, 1988

signalling distress at night.

The disclosure of the *Titanic* wrecksite location was causing some furore within the UK Government.[226] Mr. I. Hood, the Treasury Solicitor (Litigation) wrote to Captain James de Coverley (Department of Transport Marine Directorate) on December 22, 1988 saying, "I think it would be a brave man who would say that this Inquiry will be shortly dealt with."

The matter trundled on intermittently. Exactly two months later, Hood wrote back to de Coverley that "Section 6 of the Maritime Convention Act, 1911 [stated that] '...the Master or person in charge of a vessel shall, so far as he can do so without serious danger to his own vessel, render assistance to every person.'" Evidently, some research was being done as to the validity of a possible appeal, or re-appraisal, and what legal arguments could be advanced.

Three months on, de Coverley wrote to Captain Marriott, the Chief Inspector of Marine Accidents at the newly formed Marine Accident Investigation Branch (M.A.I.B.), and Paul Channon, the Secretary of State for Transport. De Coverley stated that "in all probability the *Californian* was, as Captain Lord claimed, much further from the *Titanic* than the Formal Investigation found and could not have assisted her." De Coverley had based this opinion on "a short paper" and the location of the *Titanic's* wreckage[227] but also remarked that "some criticism of Captain Lord remains valid [although] it is very much less severe than that levelled at him in the Report of the Court. It is submitted that it would be difficult and indeed unjust to continue to resist pressure for some action to set the record straight."

"Further," he goes on, "the approaches [i.e. the various letters and appeals regarding Captain Lord] to the Department ... all have to be dealt with, and, as our files show, have occupied a quite significant amount of the time of both nautical and legal staff."

De Coverley saw three possibilities:

The first was to undergo a re-hearing of the relevant part of the Formal Investigation. However, practicalities and costs argued against this.

The second option was a public statement by the Department of Transport, or possibly an answer to an "inspired" question in the house. The disadvantage was that, an unsupported statement might not put the matter to rest. The reader will recall that such an "inspired" question from a Member of Parliament who held no interest in the *Californian* had sounded the first death knell of the 1968 petition.

The third was his preferred option: a re-appraisal of the evidence by the year old M.A.I.B..

But who would perform this re-appraisal? De Coverley favoured "a retired surveyor." This would be someone "outside the branch to ensure that the task is carried out thoroughly and without pressure of other work, yet without taking up

---

226   BT 239/787
227   Perhaps Captain Quick's report; see later

our own time." The cost of this option would be minimal, he further notes, compared to the first option and would "probably be saved in terms of staff time within a very few years."

He signed off his memorandum, "at least we would be seen to be taking action; and once the report was published any further representations could be met by referring to it."

A brief summary of the case was attached to this memo. While it supports the notion of a great distance between the two ships, it ends, "...some criticism of Captain Lord must stand; but the conclusion ... that the grave charge against him of failing to save lives was unjustified – holds good."

Apparently, there was some internal scepticism about de Coverley's favoured option, and. Hood wrote to him that, "I feel that the re-appraisal of the evidence by [the] M.A.I.B. will not put the matter to rest either. That is unless the outcome was a complete exoneration of Captain Lord's, relatively speaking, inactivity in difficult circumstances. That is something which it seems to me is unlikely."

By June 8th 1990, Channon had been replaced by Cecil Parkinson as the Secretary of State for Transport and he had decided that the third option was the best one but he wanted the M.A.I.B. to perform the task, not a retired surveyor. Legal Advisor Geoffrey Beetham tried to convince him that the independent surveyor approach was the best way of proceeding, but Parkinson would not alter his conviction. In a letter to the Secretary of State, Mr. Beetham later wrote that "it seems unlikely that [the location of the *Titanic's* wrecksite] will put an end to all speculation about the relative positions [of the two ships]" as there were many pieces of evidence that needed considering, such as the current at the time of the accident. "All these matters will be open to speculation and opinion, and consequently it is certain that a reappraisal of the existing evidence will not put an end to the questions or speculation. There is therefore a big question mark about the effectiveness of incurring costs on the proposed reappraisal exercise. It is not going to provide definitive answers and put all questions to bed."

"Perhaps of more significance to the Department [of Transport] is the precedent which the reopening of the evidence would provide in other cases. It would not be difficult for interested parties to come up with 'new evidence' in other cases, such as the *Derbyshire* or the *Marques*. In both these cases there are numbers of people who could well benefit financially from a reopening of the investigation. There are parties eager to have these investigations reopened, and it would be difficult to resist their arguments on the basis of new evidence if we have reopened the case of the *Titanic* which is of much more 'academic' interest."

Cecil Parkinson's opinion on the matter changed, and he agreed to de Coverley's suggestion. A suitable "external" assessor was found in Captain Thomas Barnett, a recently retired 60 year old who had been a Principal Nautical Surveyor (Shetland), and was now living in Alderbury. Barnett didn't recall anything about the *Californian's* role in the *Titanic* disaster prior to his appointment, describing himself as a "here and now" person.

The news finally broke. It looked at though nearly three decades of sisyphean propaganda and campaigns for Captain Lord were finally about to produce dividends.

On June 21ˢᵗ 1990, Harrison wrote gleefully to a number of researchers, including Walter Lord and this author. He said that "The Department have already conceded that the *Titanic* and the *Californian* were probably 20 miles apart."[228] Walter Lord was bemused and wrote to Parkinson at the end of August, "I was surprised to read that, 2 weeks before the investigation was announced, the main part at issue had apparently been decided." Walter Lord was concerned, as he wrote to friends, that the new inquiry was simply going to be a case of "putting old wine in new bottles."

The announcement of the re-appraisal was not announced, or at the very least, did not make headlines, until 10ᵗʰ July 1990. The decision was not publicly announced at first, according to Captain Marriott, "to prevent a flood of enquiries and offers to help, many of which would no doubt come from well meaning eccentrics." Almost immediately, newspapers sought interviews with *Titanic* researchers, all of them, as far as this author can determine, on the side of Captain Lord. *The Sunday Telegraph* was typical, the headline bellowing "*Titanic* scapegoat 'victim of clubmen's conspiracy'. Quotes had been elicited from Peter Padfield, who stated that there was an "agreement" that Lord was to be made the scapegoat. "It was not the sort of conspiracy where you have documented evidence, more a case of talks in club chairs. It has every sign of a gentleman's agreement, if you like, that Lord would be got." The paper continues, "To have admitted that the Board of Trade regulations were inadequate would have played into the hands of the Germans who were mounting a strong challenge to the dominance of British liners." Harrison was also widely quoted. In *the Daily Telegraph*, he said, "There is no doubt about it ... they must know they are leading to a vindication of Capt. Lord. He died confident his name would one day be cleared, but we did not know it would take so long."

A few days later, a letter critical of Lord appeared in the same paper. A Capt[229]. A.B.Yarker from Croydon, wrote, "Captain Lord will always remain condemned by his own admission that: He failed to investigate the source of the eight rockets reported to him by members of his crew; he allowed his wireless operator to close down his equipment despite the standing instructions of the Marconi Company that in times of emergency a constant wireless watch was to be kept. Seeing that the *Californian* was surrounded by field ice there could have been little doubt that such an emergency existed. Rockets at sea must always be regarded

---

228   The previous day, Captain de Coverley had written to Leslie Harrison, Peter Padfield and Captain Lord's son informing them of the re-appraisal.
229   An Army Captain, not a Naval one, as he informed Edward de Groot.

as distress signals."

The immediate and overwhelming press and TV coverage resulted in poor Barnett et al. being swamped with letters, the first being from a Mr. Alan Law, forwarded to him from Cecil Parkinson, who claimed that his father, James Law, was the Fourth Engineer of the *Californian* and had bequeathed some interesting tales which he wanted to share with the re-appraisal process. However, the crew list[230] demonstrates that it was actually a Mr. Hooton, and, regrettably, we must conclude that Alan Law was either a victim of a father's tall tales, or that he himself was an attention seeker.

Captain Barnett and his wife took time to visit Captain Lord's son in early July 1990. Stanley Tutton Lord lent two books to Barnett, *"Hands off the Titanic"* (which contained a graphological[231] analysis of the handwriting of Captain Lord) and *"Titanic- Destination Disaster"*; both of these books showed Lord in a favourable light. Stanley T. Lord was able to given Barnett a "vivid" mental picture of his father, somewhat different, as he wrote to Barnett later, "from a heartless murderer and an incompetent drunk" that had percolated through various critics' writings. Leslie Harrison, for his part, deluged Barnett with affidavits and notes collected through the last few decades of his research, in addition to an annotated copy of his book. The only point Harrison wished the inspector to note concerning Captain Lord's 1959 affidavit was that the Captain had been "mistaken" in his sighting of a ship coming from the east, showing a green light, at about 11pm on April 14th. Credence should instead be given, Harrison wrote, to Groves statements of a steamer coming from the south. This is the only concession that Harrison ever made to the 3rd Officer's evidence.

Other correspondents varied in quality, not quantity. One writer, from Western Australia, used the M.A.I.B. Inquiry as a way of publicising his pet theory; that the *Titanic* and the *Californian* saw a unit of the German Navy "practising the deadly night manoeuvres and training in night fighting that would be used to telling effect against the British in the Battle of Jutland some four years later ... the phantom vessel was probably a collier supplying the German units, as no competent seaman would mistake a steamer for a warship." "The *Titanic* and its 1,500 victims along with Captain Stanley Lord," the document concludes, "were the first victims of the 1914-18 Great War that took another 11 million lives."

Unsurprisingly, the author remarked that no papers were interested in buying the story.[232]

One of the most zealous proponents of Lord's case was David L. Eno, the

---

230   *"The Ship That Stood Still"* Appendix J
231   Graphology is hardly an indication of one's personality; it is untested and has yet to be accepted scientifically.
232   This story may be dumped into the same category as the ludicrous *Titanic/Olympic* switch theory and the bizarre tale that the Titanic and its passengers and crew saw an illusory iceberg.

head of "*Titanic* Inquiry III" (or TQ 3), an attempt to uncover evidence to exonerate the late Captain of the *Californian*. Eno offered to present a 4 hour briefing to the M.A.I.B. personnel saying "<u>We think this is critical in your final review</u>" [emphasis in original letter]. Many pieces of data were provided by Eno, most dealing with the *Samson*. Another letter dealt with "Sleeping Condition Number 4", not researched until the 1920s, as a way of explaining Lord's inability to remember Apprentice Gibson's visit to his chart room in the early hours of April 15th, 1912. Eno would later (March 1992) write with the pompous statement, "I am happy to report to you: Capt. Lord is innocent", and tried to organise meetings with Sir Robin Renwick, the British Ambassador to the U.S., or request that a representative of his office attend a "key note" speech to be given in Boston to the remaining survivors of the *Titanic*; this would apparently be part of Eno's quest to approach the U.S. Government to reverse their negative findings against Captain Lord. Embassy staff were open-minded enough not to immediately dismiss the idea of a representative attending this "reunion", but were cautious enough to suggest that it best to stay away if the results of the reappraisal did not match Eno's views. In light of the conclusions reached by the report, this would be a prudent suggestion[233].

Tipped off by Harrison, John Carrothers contacted Barnett, saying that "an exoneration of Captain Lord in England would open the door for us in [the U.S.] to place this matter before the United States Senate in Washington. " The re-appraisal had obviously become the catalyst to initiate political proceedings on both side of the Atlantic.

Barnett soldiered on with his collation of data; he was in correspondence with many researchers, not all of them having a favourable attitude towards the *Californian*. For instance, Walter Lord, obviously stating the critical aspects of the case, pointed out Groves' 1912 evidence and his own experiences with him, the *Virginian's* wireless message (see later), Captain Moore's 1912 evidence placing the *Californian* only 5 or so miles north of the *Carpathia*, and second hand confirmation from Ivan Thompson that officers of that latter ship had seen Captain Lord's vessel early on April 15th. Walter Lord offered to send photocopied copies of his research materials, if needed, and one document was Reade's "Those Inescapable Rockets"[234]. Edward de Groot was also willing to send Barnett copies of material and sketches that would become the basis of his co-authored book the next year, on the proviso that the contents not be divulged and they be returned to him once Barnett had finished with them, which was done.

---

233   On 20th March 1992, Marriott wrote to Mr Foster, Second Secretary (Transport) at the British Embassy in Washington: "The findings of Captain Barnett were not fully accepted by myself and therefore I required further work to be undertaken ... the general outcome of our reappraisal is not too dissimilar to the findings of Mr. Eno, though we are not quite so categorical in removing blame from Captain Lord."

234   This might explain why the final report refers to "scurrilous" arguments

Barnett, for his part, decided also to seek information that, navigationally, would be crucial when determining whether various lights could be seen, and from how far; information such as the power of *Titanic's* masthead lights and how high they would be above the waterline; how powerful her navigation lights were, type of lens and manufacturer's name; details of the Morse signalling lights, and specification of the socket distress signals[235]. He also obtained copies of the M.M.S.A.'s two 1960s petitions.

Perhaps the most interesting document received was written by Captain Quick, the "Professional Officer" at the (then) Board of Trade, on April 14th, 1961. The reasons behind the writing of such a document are unknown, but it was a reasonable attempt to reconstruct the *Californian's* navigation on the 14th/15th April 1912. It also introduced a new hypothesis.

The document starts by discusses the solar sightings taken at 5 and 5.30pm on April 14th to determine the *Californian's* longitude. These sun sights were almost due East, (that is, almost on the Prime Vertical), and "any error in the latitude used in calculating the longitude would not cause an error in the longitude."

Quick was slightly concerned at the altitude of the sun at these times – the first being 17 ½, and next being 11 ½ degrees above the horizon. He writes that "it is not considered good practise to take an observation of the sun when that body is below 10° in altitude [due to refraction effects]. The altitudes in question are above [this value] but are closely approaching it and longitudes obtained from these sights could be two or three miles to the Eastward or Westward of the true longitude."

Captain Quick had no other problems with the navigational details provided by Lord in his testimony: "I have no reason to doubt the latitude of 42° 05'N," although, for the reasons cited above, he feels that the longitude might be slightly off.

With regard to the *Titanic's* distress location, Quick had two positions: the first, "official" (and wrong) location was West of the ice, 20 miles 195° [S15W] from [the *Californian's* 10.21 position]. Lord's estimate of the sinking location, obtained from his observation of the wreckage the following morning was South and East of the ice 26 ½ miles 170° [S 10 E] from [the 10.21 location]. Quick's document refers to a chartlet, which was not included with the rest of his paper; it may be the map created by Foweraker.

"It will be seen that the 6.00 a.m. position is three miles south of the 10.20 [sic] p.m. position of the previous night... the vessel is assumed to have drifted this three miles. I am at a loss to explain how this drift is calculated as there is no

235   Samuel Halpern has followed similar methods of research in his highly recommended series of articles in the Titanic Historical Society Commutator magazine, beginning with issue 177

mention of any sights being taken until noon on the 15th and even that would only give a latitude; it would be necessary to wait until about 3.00 p.m. before obtaining a reasonable sight for longitude," Quick writes. If the map did originate from Foweraker's notebooks, he did go into meticulous detail about a hypothetical direction and speed of drift but it is unlikely that Quick had access to these. However, as Quick points out, none of Foweraker's deductions are backed up by observation. What Quick speculates might have been done – and he admits he would have done too – is work backwards to find out the position at 6.00 a.m. The reader will be familiar with problems with this approach. Firstly, the exact course, speed and duration of the *Californian's* first icefield crossing are speculation. Secondly, Captain Lord never referred to any southerly setting current from 10.21pm onwards; to him, the *Californian's* overnight position was sacrosanct.

Quick had noted several problems in his analysis: "I must point out that a Southerly set is now shown where a few hours previously a set of W.N.W at 1 knot was found. Again, I agree that a W.N.W. current on the surface could be deflected by ice to become a Southerly set[236] but all these little assumptions to make facts fit make it apparent that the position was not as clear cut as the chartlet would indicate and that the 10.20 p.m. [sic] position could be some miles in error."

Quick felt that, taking all this into account, the *Californian* was no closer than 17 miles 199° from the official position, or 24 miles 169° from Lord's stated position of the *Titanic's* wreckage, and he favoured the latter.

"I now quote from the East Coast of the United States Pilot," Quick writes, " under General Navigation is stated:

When the surface (of the sea) is relatively cold and the wind very light so that the density of the air decreases rapidly for a short distance above the surface, light rays from objects low down near the horizon are bent down, the same way in fact as are usually the rays of the sun when entering the earth's atmosphere at low altitude. The effect is to render visible objects that are generally below the horizon e.g. Lights may be 'raised' at night at much greater distances than one would normally expect. This phenomenon is known as 'looming'. "

"'*Titanic*' and '*Californian*' were separated by some 20 miles of sea which was partially covered with ice. The 2nd Officer in his report states that the night was fine and clear with light airs and calms[237]. These conditions are favourable for 'looming' and I suggest this as an explanation for the '*Titanic*' and '*Californian*' each being able to see the lights of each other when other evidence shows them to be some 20 miles apart. There are two items which strengthen this theory, one, the Apprentice saw the masthead lights flickering and thought she was calling up [with

---

236   Captain de Coverley would be criticised for stating that he felt that the effect of the current would only be felt close to the icefield: Quick's report is apparently where he obtained this hypothesis

237   Other observers on the *Titanic* reported that the air was calm, with not a breath of wind.

a Morse hail]; I would expect something like this where a light was abnormally refracted. The other point was that the rockets were 'low lying' and suggest that as these were actually high above the '*Titanic*' they were above the denser refracting belt of air and were not abnormally refracted but were seen by direct vision and were consequently low down[238]."

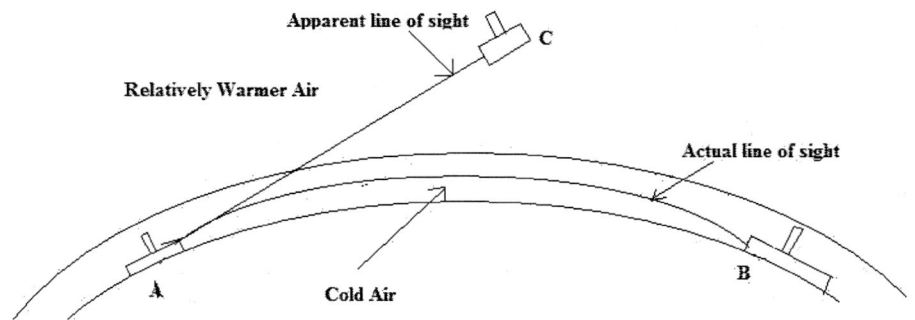

Illustration 37: The phenomenon of "Looming": a ship over the horizon, at point B, can be seen along the line of sight at C, seemingly before the horizon, due to the bending of light rays caused by a layer of warmer area above a colder area. The effect does not seem to be magnifying in nature, and the above diagram is not to scale.

"I do not attempt to explain how the 'strange ship' suddenly changed her bearing from S.S.E to S.W. But I feel that an officer who would see <u>eight</u> rockets go up and not <u>insist</u> on the Master or other senior officer coming to the bridge, might neglect to notice that his own ship was swinging." [emphasis in Quick's report]

"The foregoing confirms that according to the information available regarding the navigation of the '*Californian*' on the 14th and 15th April, 1912, she was some 20 miles away from the '*Titanic*' when that vessel sank. An extract from a letter written to Captain Lord on 21st January 1913 by Lawther Latta and Co., when they were offering him a command which he accepted, reads as follows:-

'the chief point against you was not so much as to whether it was your

---

238   Normally, warmer air is located closer to the Earth's surface, due to the heating of land and sea by the sun, which then re-radiates back. With 'looming', a temperature inversion (or colder air close to the surface) occurs. The strange visual effects that can occur are not just limited to the visible portion of the electromagnetic spectrum. This can lead to radio waves propagating over a greater distance than one would normally expect. Indeed, one correspondent on the <u>www.shipsnostalgia.com</u> website mentions that he saw a coastline on his radar that was over 300 miles away. The range of the radar was 48 miles (!)

command that was nearest the '*Titanic*', but the alleged fact that rockets were seen by your officers, that you were called, but remained callous to the call.'

This fact in this unhappy history remains unchanged."

His research complete, Barnett wrote a draft of his report in March 1991 and sent it to de Coverley for comments. The report is fascinating, and contains a few slight errors; it makes no mention of the "yellow funnel" ship as seen by Stewart at daybreak (Barnett considered this ship to be the *Carpathia*); and that the *Californian* picked up news of the *Titanic* disaster at 6.00a.m. Barnett also was keen for his report to clear up misconceptions. For one, he remarked that many authors had written that, in the findings of the Court, Captain Lord had been blamed for not going to the assistance of '*Titanic*'. "Although Captain Lord is mentioned frequently in Chapter 5 of the Report, it is the '*Californian*' which is found to blame in the findings, not specifically Captain Lord." He also pointed out that the British Inquiry was not operated by the Board of Trade, although it had been ordered by them.

Barnett considered that the times given in evidence, unless those times given in telegrams and log entries, are only accurate to within ten minutes or so. Times given in his report can be taken as approximately New York time plus 1 hour and 50 minutes.

Barnett's reports display the writings of a man who is opposed to Captain Lord, his officers, and their testimony. Through a variety of critical sections of testimony, he considers the *Titanic* and the *Californian* to be extremely close to each other. It is hard to consider his writings as a balanced appraisal. Considering the amount of information that swamped Barnett from pro-Lord sympathisers, it may come as a surprise that he eventually took up a hostile stance.

Additionally, Barnett wrote, "Those persons present at the Inquiry had the benefit of seeing the general reactions of the witnesses, and the tone of their replies ... a much closer insight into the affair can be achieved by reading the minutes of the evidence in full, rather than receiving edited, highlighted selections of evidence selected by various authors. I would therefore recommend that this report is read in conjunction with the full text of the Minutes of Evidence."

"One important and incontrovertible piece of evidence regarding '*Californian's*' movements after Noon April 14th came from her radio message to '*Antillian*' at 19.30 that day, concerning icebergs. The message contained '*Californian's*' d.r. Position at 18.30 – 42°03'N 49°09'W. One of the arguments against the Court's findings was that it would have been impossible for 2nd Officer Stone to have seen '*Titanic*' bearing 135° from True North at 5 miles because, with regard to '*Titanic's*' 'old' position [i.e. The radioed distress location], '*Californian*' would have had to steam 53 miles between 1830 and 2220 [sic] when she stopped; this requires a speed of 13.8 knots. Even to have arrived at the position given by 2nd Officer Stone at the disappearance of '*Titanic*' would have required a speed of 12.5 knots for the 48 miles involved, and '*Californian*' was steaming at 11 ½ knots

302

or less. This argument is disproved by the discovery of 'Titanic'. 2nd Officer Stone's bearing and distance ... from 'Titanic's' 'new' location[i.e. the wrecksite] is only 40 miles from 'Californian's' 1830 d.r position, a speed of only 10.5 knots. The discovery of 'Titanic', therefore provides no argument with which to question the Court's findings that Captain Lord's 2220 position was inaccurate."

"The Court did not find fault, however, with 'Californian's' given position when in vicinity of the 'Titanic's' surface wreckage at 1100 15 April in 41°33'N 50°01'W. From the known position of foundering, 'Titanic's' wreckage position at 1100 15th gives a set and drift of 196°, 11 miles, which is a rate of about 1.3 knots for the period.

Barnett also felt that the 'looming' effect may have been exacerbated "by the masses of billowing steam and debris from the boilers" of the Titanic, but he felt that there were problems in explaining how an object 20 miles away could look to be only 5 miles away. Despite, or perhaps in spite of this, Barnett favoured a 5-7 mile separation between the two ships. He was sceptical of Lord's defence that he could not recall the message about the other ship firing more rockets: "Evidence given by Captain Lord and 2nd Officer Stone gives me the impression that one or both of them are concealing certain facts from the Court." He was also sceptical of the excuse that Lord was asleep, and hence not comprehending when he took messages from Gibson and the voice pipe; as Barnett says, Lord was sufficiently awake to come from the chart room to his cabin next door to speak to Stone via the voice pipe.

"There were attempts to signal the 'other vessel' by Morse lamp. The type of all-round Morse lamp was not satisfactory for use by one person over a long distance, hence the invention today of the 'daylight signalling lamp' which is also put to good use at night." Discussing the flickering seen by the Californian witnesses, Barnett writes "in my opinion, [it] could have been caused by escaping steam whilst 'Titanic' was blowing down her boilers," and considers that the low lying explosions seen by Stone "if true, may have been occasioned by reflections of the rocket flash in the clouds of steam."

This does not seem likely. The rockets would have detonated well above any steam discharge from the boilers via the funnels. If this were the case, two 'flashes' would be seen; the actual detonation and Barnett's 'reflections.'

Barnett considers that the reason the ship seen by Groves put out most of her lights at 11.40p.m was because the vessel had turned to the north, towards the Californian[239]

With reference to the lack of sound from the exploding rockets, Barnett offers the following possibilities;

---

239   De Coverley, in his later hybrid report says that "Evidence of Titanic's change of heading after collision is not absolutely conclusive, but it is known that initially she went to port and the balance of evidence seems to be that afterwards her heading did not much change"

a) The level of ambient sound on '*Californian's*' bridge (probably minimal).

b) The type of clothing worn by Officers on watch on the '*Californian*' (e.g. balaclava helmets)."

c) The direction and strength of the wind [sic – there was no wind!].

d) Echoes (e.g. From icebergs and '*Titanic*' herself) which may lead to prolongation and indistinctness of the sound.

e) The Inverse Square Law (the sound at 5 miles would be around 1% of the intensity at ½ mile).

f) Refraction of sound waves caused by moving through media of different densities (cold air [to] hot steam [to] cold air).

In his reply to Barnett's report, de Coverley agreed with the inspector that the Court's findings could not be regarded as evidence; Barnett regarded them as the "status quo, or equilibrium in this tragedy ... the reversal of the findings with insufficient evidence might produce a 'cause celebre', almost as momentous as the original casualty." De Coverley was concerned about the contradictions in the 1912 evidence but "where there is no contradiction the evidence ought to be accepted unless there is clear reason to the contrary." For one thing, de Coverley saw no grounds for doubting Chief Officer Stewart; the wireless message to the SS *Antillian*, and the observation of Polaris [the Pole Star] supporting his navigation.

Regrettably, the log of the *Californian* was unavailable to Barnett and de Coverley and they had to reconstruct the navigation for the 13th April, leading to speculation about the current affecting Lord and his crew. De Coverley was somewhat sceptical of Barnett's suggestion that a southerly set of 39 miles from noon 13th April to noon the next day was indicative of a massive deflection in the *Californian's* course the next day; based on a knowledge of the currents in that area, he would not have expected a southerly set as early as noon on the 13th, and felt that the *Californian* would have been on course.

De Coverley goes on: "I suggest that the Polaris sight indicates that the southerly set was not in fact encountered until the evening of the 14th ...this would tie in with the presence of the ice, stretching in a north/south direction near the border between the cold southerly current and the Gulf Stream. The sharp division between these two currents cannot be overemphasised: there is a well recorded case of a ship taking simultaneous seawater temperatures at bow and stern as she crossed the boundary between these two currents which were more than 20°F different. I submit that the strong probability is that *Californian* only experienced a southerly current for a very short time before she met the ice. Of course, she will have felt it while she was stopped and therefore I agree that she will have been south of the DR latitude when Stone saw the rockets. I would put her in about 42° 00 minutes North, and accepting that there is no reason to doubt the longitude as at least a fairly good approximation, this as you say ties in well enough with recorded bearings and suggests a distance of the two ships of some 17 miles as you mention."

Barnett had, in his reply to de Coverley, replied that he had approached the controversy over the *Titanic-Californian* distance very carefully. He felt sure that the arguments regarding the *Californian's* possible track up to the evening of April 14th could be included in the re-appraisal. But on other issues, Barnett seems to have decided certain other conclusions, not based on navigational details. He wrote that the ship seen by the *Californian* crew at 4.00a.m. was "the *Carpathia*, to my mind," quoting Captain Moore's U.S. evidence that he saw the *Californian* north of the *Carpathia*. Other evidence supporting a reduced gap between the two vessels comes from a variety of sources, he notes, including 3rd Officer Groves. "Evidence fitting the theory that the '*Californian*' was 17-20 miles away comes only from Captain Lord, Chief Officer Stewart and 2nd Officer Stone – three people who stood to lose their careers, three people whose evidence at the hearing was at variance, one with another."

"Captain Lord, I feel sure, was well aware of the 'looming' phenomenon[240], but there is no evidence to show that he tried to use this in his defence. He seems to have been well aware that the 'other vessel' was 5-7 miles distant, and attempted to base his arguments on the fact that the rockets had been fired from beyond the vessel in view (it sounds as though Captain Lord may have 'got at' 2nd Officer Stone the next day or later, also that Stone did not include this evidence in his written statement ([British Inquiry Question Numbers] 7912-18). However, Captain Lord didn't see the rockets, and 2nd Officer Stone admitted that at least one and most probably all of the rockets were fired from the vessel in sight. Apprentice Gibson was not in any doubt about the fact that the rockets had been fired from the vessel in sight."

In a memo, Captain Marriot wrote to de Coverley reviewing the surveyor's report. He seems to have been disappointed with it as he says, "Perhaps I am wrong but Captain Barnett seems to have concentrated most of his efforts and based his findings on the evidence given at the FI [presumably the First Inquiry]. There seems very few references in his report to other evidence or information which has come to light over the years and when it is referred to it is because it supports the findings of the FI. If I am doing him an injustice and his re-appraisal has covered everything available I think the report should make this clear."

"To have reached his conclusion where [Barnett] considers *Californian* was at 2220 hrs., he appears not to have considered the Chief Officer's latitude by Polaris of 42 05 N at 19.30 hrs. on 14.4.12. Obviously the FI did not consider it as correct but Captain Barnett seems to have ruled it out without even mentioning it. Why should it be disregarded? *Californian* sent a message to *Antillian* at 1930 hrs giving a DR position for 1830 hrs of 42 03 N 49 09 W. I accept that there is two minutes of latitude difference from the Polaris latitude but they must have been

---

240   Or perhaps not. He was in ice for the first time, after all.

confident of that DR. Why send a message to another vessel warning them of ice and purposely giving them a wrong position? This message was sent well before the disaster occurred so they had no possible reason for giving a false position. It seems to me that Captain Barnett's opinion on *Californian's* position is only valid if you assume the Chief Officer was lying about his Polaris sight or that it was a very bad sight <u>and</u> they sent an incorrect DR to *Antillian.*"

"I also have trouble in agreeing completely with Captain Barnett's conclusions concerning the southerly drift. If the evidence of the FI ([questions] 8693-8698) the noon positions for 13.4.12 and 14.4.12 are given which results in a lat of 98 minutes and the Solicitor-General said of that 24 hours "you had made southerly some 39 minutes of latitude?" I do not understand where the Solicitor-General got the 39 minutes from and I cannot recall it being explained or referred to in any other part of the evidence. I do not think it is correct for Captain Barnett to use this figure for calculating possible courses and positions."

Marriott also had difficulties with Barnett's north-easterly course at about 8.00am for the *Californian* to end up at the *Carpathia*, as he could not recall evidence from the *Mount Temple* or *Carpathia* to back up this course, although he did admit that he might be wrong on this point[241].

"If there was not another vessel [in the vicinity] then what did [the *Californian*] see? <u>It must have been *Titanic*</u> [this author's emphasis] but did it have to be as close as either the FI or Captain Barnett says? I am surprised that the question of 'looming' has been put aside so easily. I am not saying that it is an answer but it does leave a question mark over it all. I am no expert on refraction but from my own experiences at sea there were a number of occasions when I saw lights of vessels at some remarkable distances[242]. For this theory to be acceptable it would have to apply for the whole of that night because *Californian* saw *Carpathia* at a fairly good distance but I suppose that cannot be ruled out."

But there was one aspect that both Captains Marriott and Barnett agreed upon: that *Titanic's* rockets had been seen, and that "action should have been taken". Despite their conflicting opinions of the navigation, both de Coverley and Barnett agreed that the *Titanic* and the *Californian* had been in sight at all times, and that the *Californian* and the *Carpathia* were visible to each other[243]. The only

---

241   This was actually contained in Captain Rostron's July 1912 Affidavit in New York: "The first time that I saw the *Californian* was at about eight o'clock on the morning of 15th April. She was then about five to six miles distant, bearing WSW true, and steaming towards the *Carpathia*."

242   Ex-M.A.I.B. Chief Inspector Rear Admiral Lang of the Royal Navy also noted this point at a lecture he gave in Southampton in April 2007. In private communication with this author he noted that one could see lights further away on very cold nights than warm ones.

243   If that is so, how did the ultimate M.A.I.B report contain two separate sets of conclusions?? Was the '17-20' mile distance put into the report simply to appease the Lordites?

point of contention was the mechanism by which the ships had been seen. Barnett considered that navigational matters had brought the vessels into proximity with each other, but de Coverley pondered whether, at a large range, whether 'looming' was the answer.

In conclusion, Marriott wondered how to deal with this. He felt it necessary to invite Barnett to the office so that the contentious points could be discussed. "My own feeling is that at the end of the day we are not going to be able to put up a paper to the Secretary of State which will provide clear answers to all the questions we posed. I think the question of the exact position of *Californian* and her distance from *Titanic* on that night will have to remain with a question mark over it. I know this will not satisfy either the pro-Lord or anti-Lord lobbies but it will have achieved our main objective: a paper which can be used to respond to letters and representations in the future."[244]

Barnett wrote back to Marriott, "I have read the submission [to the Secretary of State on the reappraisal] through and consider that my report has been dealt with fairly. I have no further comments to make."

In October 1991, Barnett wrote that he "hoped everyone would be happy with his report."[245] But not everyone was "happy". Harrison was becoming agitated at the slow progress and pestered the UK Government, newspapers and TV stations to find out what was happening and to keep the story alive in the public eye. It became too much for the BBC who regarded Harrison as a "difficult man to deal with", and had to resort to their legal department to sort things out[246]. On April 11th, Harrison was so confident that Captain Lord would be vindicated that he prepared a statement for Stanley T. Lord to release immediately to the Press Association once this happened: "I am naturally delighted that my father's name has been officially cleared."

The former Secretary of State, Cecil Parkinson wrote to his successor requesting an update of the re-appraisal, and de Coverley wrote back in February 1992 that, although the Surveyor's report was complete, "his work has unfortunately led to the need for further examination by M.A.I.B. staff before a report...can be completed. This has necessarily had a low priority compared with work on current accidents[247]. Nonetheless, the additional work has now been largely completed and the report is being drafted at present."

An advance copy of the re-appraisal was sent by Captain Marriott to Mr. McLoughlin and the Secretary of State on 12th March 1992. It was discussed

244   If a meeting was ever scheduled between Barnett, de Coverley and Marriott, minutes of it have not been provided to this author, probably because they fall under a restrictive section of the UK Freedom of Information Act.

245   Private Information

246   Private Information

247   The other accidents, under analysis at the time, can be found at http://www.M.A.I.B..gov.uk/publications/investigation_reports/1990_to_1998.cfm

whether a copy of the report be sent to Stanley T. Lord, and there were concerns that its confidentiality may be jeopardised if he were to show it to Harrison et al. It was ultimately decided to send a copy of the report to Lord Jr. and Harrison, in confidence, to be received 24 hours in advance of the release date, which was April 2nd, well before its "target" of the *Titanic's* 80th anniversary, and also before the General Election that year.

The resultant report was a peculiar hybrid of both Barnett's and de Coverley's findings, making its key findings on certain aspects of the *Californian* matter valueless; since both sets of results were referenced in the report's finding, both sets had to be discussed. Reading the report makes it seem as if the M.A.I.B. had fallen between two stools; the Lordites and the Anti-Lordites. Inevitably, it would satisfy neither camp as a definitive answer was not given, except in one case.

The report sought to answer four questions:

"To establish so far as is now possible the positions of *Titanic* when she struck an iceberg on 14 April 1912 and when she subsequently foundered; to estimate the positions of *Californian* at the same times; and to deduce the distance apart of the two vessels during the
period between those times.
To consider whether *Titanic* was seen by *Californian* during that period, and if so, when and by whom.
To consider whether distress signals from *Titanic* were seen by *Californian* and if so, whether proper action was taken.
To assess the action taken by Captain Stanley Lord, Master of *Californian*, between about 10.00pm ship's time on 14 April and the time on 15 April when passage was resumed."

The conclusions reached were:-

"*Titanic* was in approximate position 41 47'N 49 55'N [248]when she struck the iceberg at 2345 hrs 14 April, and in position 41°43'.6N 49 56.9'W when she foundered. The position of *Californian* cannot be deduced so accurately; the Inspector [Barnett] considers she may have been in about 41 50'N 50 07'W at the time *Titanic* struck the iceberg, but was probably further East and only 5 to 7 miles off. In [de Coverley's] opinion, *Californian* was in about 42 00'N 50 09'W or a little North of that position, and between 17 and 20 miles from *Titanic* - most likely about 18 miles. A current was setting southerly but is likely to have affected both

---

248   This coordinate was determined merely by drawing a line from the wreckage left by the Californian to the Titanic's wrecksite, and then extending this line until it crossed her path.

vessels similarly until *Titanic* sank, so their distance apart will not have appreciably changed during the period in question.

The Inspector considers that *Titanic* was seen by *Californian*, by her Master and others. I think it possible that she was seen, due to abnormal refraction permitting sight beyond the ordinary visible horizon; but more likely that she was not seen.

The Inspector considers that *Titanic*'s distress signals were seen, and that proper action was not taken. I agree on both counts."

A diagram demonstrating the positional 'findings' were summarised in a chart provided in the report (reproduced here).

The final question – a consideration of Captain Lord's actions – was discussed in the remainder of the report.

De Coverley considered the reason why Lord Mersey had ignored Lord's, Stone's, Stewart's and Gibson's evidence to place the *Titanic* and the *Californian* so close to each other; "No reason for Lord Mersey's opinion is given, but the most reasonable inference to draw seems to be that they agreed that the two ships were in sight of one another but they accepted Captain Lord's position as his genuine estimate; the discrepancy was due to error in reckoning, not deliberate deception, and they did not consider the error likely to be great enough to bring the ships so close to each other as five miles." But de Coverley makes the astonishing claim that, "On the other hand, they would not see each other even on a very clear night at a distance greater than 8 to 10 miles," a claim that the reader will soon learn is untrue, and which contradicts the experience of M.A.I.B. officers.

The crux of the matter is the current on the evening and night of April 14th, 1912. Using the position of the wreckage determined by the *Californian* the next morning and the location of the *Titanic* wreckage, the M.A.I.B. report calculated that the current was setting "a little west of south at rather more than 1 knot." This, of course would be the average current from the time of sinking (11.40pm) and the time that the *Californian* left the flotsam (11.20am, or 10.40am by Groves). What the drift was before then is not known. The vast schism between Barnett's and de Coverley's opinion of the *Californian's* overnight position was due to the deflecting influence of the ocean currents. As related above, Barnett felt that this had influenced Lord's ship since noon on April 14th, and perhaps as early as noon on April 13th, but de Coverley disagreed. He had used the testimony of the Captain of the *Mount Temple* to show that April 1912 had been unusual, in that ice had been seen so far south of its normal boundaries for that time of year, but felt that the current "would have been more unusual for it to have been felt so far east." He further asks, if such a current proposed by Barnett was felt so far east, "why was no ice seen there? There appear to be no reports even of isolated bergs east of 49° W."

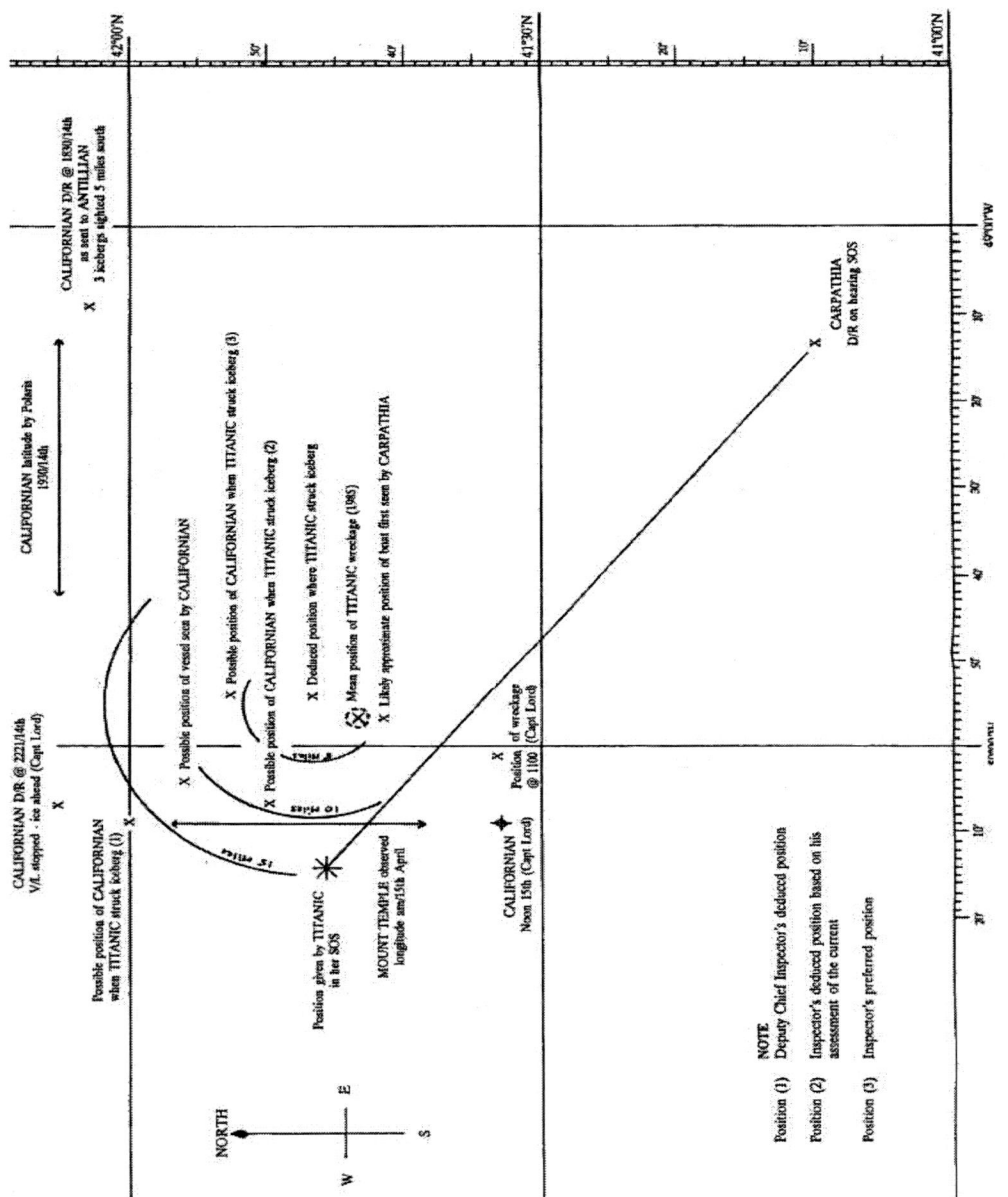

Illustration 38: The relationships between the Titanic, the Californian and the Carpathia as deduced by the M.A.I.B.

The report shows – not for the first, nor the last time - the limits of its historical research. For if one peruses the relevant issues of Lloyd's publications[249] for that time of year, one finds many instances of ice seen well to the east of 49° W. Indeed, one ship, the *Rappahannock*, encountered another ice field on April 11th at 43° 20'N 48° 45'W, and she is claimed to have communicated this information to the *Titanic* two days later by morse lamp. Had some icebergs passed south of the *Titanic's/Californian's* track though? The answer is yes. According to *Lloyd's Weekly Shipping Index* of that era: "On April 5 SS "*Uranium*" which arrived at New York from Rotterdam via Halifax reports having received the following reports by radio: SS "*Bretagne*" bound E, 41°48'N 46°30'W passed last berg; from this position to 41°N 48°W numerous large bergs have been reported ... SS "*Finland*" reported that in 40°46'N 46°35'W and in 40°56'N 47°34'W passed several bergs. SS "Stephen" reported that she saw ice from 41°25'N 46°10'W to 40°40'N 47°W. SS "*Niagara*" reported that she passed 2 bergs in 41°13'N 48°33'W. SS "*Haverford*" reported passing a small berg in 41°21'N 46°16'W and 2 bergs in 41°19'N 46°35'W."

There are also reports of icebergs and yet another ice field in the vicinity of 46°N, 46°W. But was this ice drifting south, and could this drift affect the *Californian*? At noon on April 13th, she was at a latitude of 43°43'N. She saw no ice. Indeed, from a detailed analysis of the ice reports, the ice reports east of 49° W were, for the most part, confined to a segment of the Atlantic north of the *Californian's* track: namely, the 'other' ice field, at 46°N, 46°W which seemed to be remaining static. It seems reasonable to presume that the ice was being carried, at least partially, from the west, and thus from the wrecksite on the easterly flowing North Atlantic Drift, carrying debris and bodies with it. So, de Coverley's conclusions were right – but for the wrong reasons!

For Barnett to have considered that the current had affected the *Californian* so early to bring it within 5 to 7 miles of the *Titanic* at 11.40pm, the Deputy Chief Inspector noted that perhaps the pole star observation by Stewart at 7.30pm was "in error or false evidence was given." But Stewart was sure that his observation was accurate. The only alternative was that the net effect of a southerly current and the steering of the *Californian* was nil as Stewart's latitude was (essentially) the same as the one determined at noon. This displays a lack of knowledge of the navigation of Lord and his officers. Lord's affidavit in 1959 revealed that he had steered a course slightly to the south of due west, and a current to the north west was offsetting his vessel. Lord's evidence was that his course was competing with a claimed north-westerly current, but de Coverley now argues against the

249   Some of these reports can be found at
      http://www.icedata.ca/icedb/ice/ice_charts/1912ap.htm

Californian heading south. If his hypothesis that the "net effect of [the southerly current] was nil," then he implies that the Californian was steering slightly to the north of west!

"One piece of evidence which cannot have been fabricated," writes de Coverley, "is the *Antillian* signal," because this was sent before the *Titanic* accident, and hence before there was any opportunity to doctor evidence. "It adds weight to the statement that the *Californian* was steering westerly." Coupled with the Pole Star sighting, this argues against a southerly current. He then continues, "In fact, the latitude sent to the *Antillian* of 42 03'N which was based on dead reckoning, suggests that the course steered was slightly South of West which, given the subsequent sight, argues a slight northerly set. This is not impossible given the current to be expected; but Captain Lord later recalled the latitude which he wrote out for the Wireless Operator as 42 05'N and it may well be that the figure 5 was misread for 3. But neither figure offers any grounds for deducing a set to the South."

What "current to be expected"? In that area of the Atlantic, the current was either roughly south, or to the east. Lord had claimed a WNW current.

Readers are reminded of our previous discussion of the *Antillian* message.

De Coverley considers the evidence of Captain Rostron to be significant. "After about two hours he sighted a flare from one of the liner's boats about half a point on the port bow. It will be seen that at the time the flare was seen (0240 hrs) the boat which it came from must have been to the north of *Carpathia's* course line and it follows that during the two hours the ship must have been set to the north: otherwise the boat would have been seen on the starboard bow. Bearing in mind that at the time *Carpathia* was eastbound (from New York) it will be appreciated that this argument essentially holds good even if there was some error in her position by dead reckoning."

How did de Coverley reach this conclusion? We do know with *certainty* that the average course of the current (at least after the *Titanic* sank) was to the south, and this is where the lifeboat displaying the flares would have been. If Rostron's course was correct, then he may have been to the east of where he thought he was, perhaps caught in the North Atlantic Drift. If this were the case, then it would have been easy for the *Carpathia* to see the flare on the port bow. There is no need to invoke a northerly current at the latitude of the *Carpathia*. This can be explained in a chart, which the reader will find a few pages hence.

"Clearly none of the arguments are significant if it is the case, as the FI believed that the ships were 8 to 10 miles away," reasons de Coverley. But Barnett's estimate of 5-7 miles is also flawed, as the flares fired from the lifeboat, and having an altitude close to the surface of the sea, would have been seen at this small distance.

The report continues:

"In my opinion, *Titanic* was not seen by *Californian* nor vice versa, except

312

possibly at a range much greater than the ordinarily visible horizon owing to abnormal refraction. This being so, then unlike the Court and the Inspector, I have no need nor cause to discount *Californian's* evidence, and the only adjustment to her position as tendered to the FI which is required is that which follows from what we can now deduce as to the current." For all these reasons, de Coverley did not believe that the *Californian* would have been affected by the southerly set for more than a few hours before reaching the ice field. "She may have met the southerly current before the Chief Officer took the Pole Star sight, the two cancelling each other out." The effect of the current would thus be a difference in latitude of 3 ½ miles at most, and that, while stopped she would have drifted for some 2 miles up to the time *Titanic* hit the berg.

"More likely, taking into account the implication of the *Carpathia's* evidence, the full strength of the current was only felt when close to the ice field."

This would place the *Californian* from 17 to 20 miles from the *Titanic*, bearing about NW by N from the *Titanic*. But then one wonders how the strength of the current was significant only in proximity of the ice? If it were somehow connected with the *Carpathia's* sighting of the *Titanic's* lifeboat flares and a proposed northward current, then one must treat de Coverley's observation – and associated conclusion – with scepticism.

But although the Deputy Chief Inspector considers that the two ships were not in sight of each other, he was, if he reviewed the *Californian's* evidence in isolation, prepared to admit that the ship they saw was the *Titanic*, despite "a good deal of evidence [existing]" that prevents a perfect comparison of events and observations on the two ships. So, apart from the deduced navigation, and his belief that the ships were not visible at extreme range, why did de Coverley think that the *Titanic* evidence did not support the contention of the ships being in proximity?

"The ship thought by the Court to be *Titanic* was in view continuously from *Californian* from 2300 hrs or thereabouts. *Titanic's* speed, maintained until collision at 2340 hrs, suggests that if at that time she was five miles from *Californian*, then at 2300 hrs she will have been nearly 20 miles away, which is a very long way off for her to be seen, but given the possible difference in the two ships' clocks and the imprecision of times, this point is perhaps not very important. What is significant, however, is that no ship was seen by *Titanic* until well after the collision; the exact time is not recorded but seems to have been about 0030 hrs and certainly substantially past midnight. During all this time, although many of the crew were preparing boats or attending to the passengers, watch was maintained with officers on the Bridge and seamen in the Crows Nest, and with their ship in grave danger the lookout for another vessel which could come to their help must have been most anxious and keen. It is in my view inconceivable that *Californian* or any other ship was within the visible horizon of *Titanic* during that period; it equally follows that Titanic cannot have been within *Californian's* horizon. It is no argument to say that *Titanic* was much the more conspicuous vessel of the two: the ship seen by *Californian* was readily noticed, not only from the Bridge but also from the deck, by the casual observation of Mr Gill coming up from the lighted engine room; and the watch officers easily distinguished her individual navigation lights. It is clear therefore that sighting did not depend upon particular conspicuity; and this must equally have been the case in the reverse direction."

A few points deserve to commented upon. First of all, the earliest known sighting of the ship from the *Titanic* was about ten minutes after the collision, according to Buley. Secondly, de Coverley is dismissive of any time difference between the *Titanic* and the *Californian*, which he admits elsewhere in the document, is probably only a few minutes. Barnett's report concurs on this point. Thirdly, de Coverley uses Gill's evidence which is dubious not least because any man coming up from a lighted engine room would be temporarily blinded and thus not able to see any vessel in the distance. Finally, with her lookouts peering ahead, and having their eyes stinging caused by the forward motion of the ship effecting a wind chill of about -11.5°[250], it is likely that the *Titanic's* lookouts were not looking in the direction of the *Californian*, or could not see it. They were concerned with obstructions immediately ahead or on the port or starboard: the *Californian* would be well off to the starboard side and on the horizon. She would not be showing many lights and hence would be very easily missed and at any rate she would not have elicited any attention as she was so far off that she was not a hazard to the Titanic's navigation. The massive White Star Liner, on the other hand, would be showing much more illumination and would be obvious, especially to officers pacing up and down on watch, trying to keep themselves occupied on a ship that was stopped. These officers did not have any "blinkered" view of just the view ahead, but would be observing all horizons.

Back to the M.A.I.B. Report: "There are two possible explanations for what *Californian* saw. The first and most obvious is that a third ship was present which approached from the East, stopped on meeting the field ice, and then after a period steamed away to seek a break in the ice. This is very far from unlikely; the North Atlantic trade was busy in 1912 and a number of other ships are known to have been in the area. A good deal of print has been expended on consideration of the identity of such a ship but the question is not within the remit of the present reappraisal and I do not consider that an attempt to answer it with certainty would be likely to be successful or would be a proper expenditure of public resources."

The other possible explanation was super-refraction ("looming"): "In favour of this theory, the phenomenon is variable in its effect and this might

---

250   Using the *Californian's* log, we now that the air temperature at midnight was -3°c. The wind chill value quoted was for 22.5 knots; recall the *Titanic* was steaming onwards for a few minutes after the collision. Although it is not certain what speed she was moving, this would have generated a wind chill too. This may explain why the lookouts didn't see the *Californian*, and indeed, why she was not seen until the *Titanic* stopped when there would obviously have been no wind chill.

314

explain the apparent movement of each ship as seen by the other when both were in fact stopped. In addition, the rockets seen by *Californian* were described as low-lying (quoted as rising to less than mast-head [sic – half] height) and this could be because they actually rose to a height above the refracting layer and were seen directly. Against the theory, it requires a long period during which *Californian* could see *Titanic* but not vice versa. This is not impossible: the phenomenon does lead to curious results, and further it is possible that *Californian's* lights (though they were electric and could certainly be seen on a night such as this at 5 miles or more range) could not be seen even with super refraction at 17 to 20 miles ... equally, objections [exist] to the general theory that *Titanic* was seen. The first is that, although when he first saw the other ship Captain Lord recalls seeing a green (starboard) sidelight as one would expect with a ship to the south and approaching on a westerly course, later her red (port) light came into view, arguing that after stopping she swung markedly to starboard. Evidence of *Titanic's* change of heading after collision is not absolutely conclusive, but it is known that initially she went to port and the balance of evidence seems to be that afterwards her heading did not much change. Her port sidelight would therefore not be seen. The second is that Mr Stone noticed a change of bearing before the other ship disappeared. I do not place great weight on this, for Mr Stone had no particular reason to take accurate compass bearings of the other ship, and the explanation may have been that his own ship was swinging, leading to a change in relative bearing; but clearly if the compass bearing did change appreciably the vessel cannot have been *Titanic* for she remained stopped; super refraction could not explain a substantial change in bearing. In sum, I do not consider that a definite answer to the question 'was *Titanic* seen' can be given; but if she was, then it was only because of the phenomenon of super refraction for she was well beyond the ordinary visible horizon. More probably, in my view, the ship seen by *Californian* was another, unidentified, vessel. Whether the ship seen during the later stages of the tragedy by *Titanic* was this third ship, becoming visible to her and then disappearing as she sought a break in the ice field, or a fourth vessel is a matter of speculation outside the scope of this reappraisal."

Once more, this paragraph invites comment. De Coverley seems to be unaware of the evidence indicating that the *Titanic* did indeed swing to the north after the collision. Also, Gibson did testify that Stone was taking bearings of the other ship all the time; his own bearings given were absolute, and not relative to his own ship's heading.

But there was one issue that both de Coverley and Barnett agreed on: the rockets. They found that the *Californian* had seen the *Titanic's* rockets: "There is no doubt that some rockets were seen and while it has been suggested that these were Company signals from the other ship seen by *Californian*, I think this possibility is quite unrealistic. Quite apart from the extreme coincidence required, the argument which I advanced in the previous section against *Titanic* and

Californian being in sight of each other equally rules out any vessel other than *Titanic* having fired rockets in the area. It is, if anything, even more certain that rockets would have been seen by *Titanic*, than lights. My opinion that *Titanic* was much further from *Californian* than the FI found or the Inspector considers does not of course rule out her rockets being seen, but it would explain their apparent low altitude. It has been objected that the timings of *Titanic* firing her distress signals do not precisely accord with the times the rockets were seen by *Californian*, but none of the times were recorded precisely and I place no value on that point...Linking the question with the previous one, it will be realised that if the ship seen by *Californian* was a third vessel, she must have been for a considerable period on just the same bearing as *Titanic* for the latter's rockets to be seen apparently coming from her. This may at first glance seem to be stretching credibility, but in fact it is far from impossible. The third ship must have encountered the ice field and, like *Californian*, will have stopped as indeed she was seen to do. Her position will have depended upon the exact configuration of the field which - unlike its general outline - cannot be known, but it is perfectly feasible that it lay on *Titanic's* line of bearing. With all three ships stopped, their only movement will have been with the current and their bearings from each other will not have changed ... rockets were much more used than is now the case for reasons other than indicating distress ... Given the amount of shipping in the area, it must be very probable that *Californian* was not the only ship to see the signals, irrespective of whether the 'third ship' between her and *Titanic* existed."

One will recall that Stone observed rockets coming from, he claimed, a moving ship. The *Titanic* and the *Californian* were stopped. How rockets, which should have been coming on a steady bearing, could be visually deflected so that they followed the path of a moving ship is not explored. This is also ignored by writers sympathetic to Captain Lord.

The situation can be explored in the following sketch map.

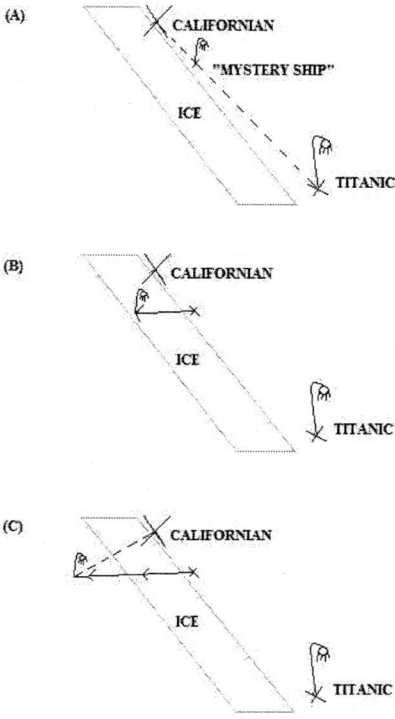

Illustration 39: Diagram showing time evolution of the two rocket firers: in (a), both the Titanic and the mystery ship are firing rockets. Titanic's rockets would reach an altitude whereby they would be seen coming well over the horizon. At (b), the mystery ship is steaming through the ice, still firing rockets. Titanic's rockets should still be seen. (c) The mystery ship fires its last rocket, having cleared the ice. The Titanic, still stopped, also fires its last rocket.

The *Californian, Titanic* and the supposed mystery ship, all (coincidentally) in a line, have stopped close to the eastern edge of the ice field. We know from Captain Rostron at the wrecksite that the ice field ran in a roughly NE-

317

SW direction[251], a fact confirmed by the *Mount Temple* (who hugged the ice field after reaching the distress location and found nothing) and *Frankfurt*, who steamed along the western edge, in a south-easterly direction in the latitude of the wreckage at 11am. The thickness of the ice is taken as approximately 5 miles, in line with the testimony of witnesses. The mystery ship starts to fire rockets, at about the time the *Titanic* was sending up hers. A simple straight-line passage from SE to SW is probably slightly inaccurate, as a ship traversing such a route would be showing her sidelight(s), which Stone insisted was not the case. The "other ship," if it existed, would have manoeuvred in such a way that her coloured lights were shut in.

At the time the 2nd rocket is fired, Stone claims to notice that the other ship is starting to steam away to the south west, from its original location 5 miles to the SE. The *Titanic's* rockets should still have been seen coming over the horizon on the same bearing as before; if Stone is right, looking south, the mystery ship's rockets should be seen coming to the right of the other detonations, coming from over the horizon.

Finally, at about 1.50am (I have used this as Stone provides a bearing of the mystery ship as S.W. x W), the last rocket is fired from the mystery ship. If Captain Lord's later estimate of the distance traversed is right (about 8 miles), the ship would be eight miles away, only its stern light visible, and having travelled almost due west, a distance of 10 miles, if the geometry is correct. And all this time, both sets of rockets would have been visible. And yet Stone and Gibson, and the uncalled *Californian* witnesses, only described seeing one set.

Surprisingly, the hybrid M.A.I.B. report makes mention of the *Samson*: "This does beg the question of why the third vessel - who must also have seen the rockets - did not respond. One possibility is that she was the Norwegian sealer *Samson*; the then Mate of that vessel, many years after the event did indeed state publicly that his ship had been near the scene of the accident and that rockets had been seen. According to his statement *Samson* had been sealing illegally and, fearing that the rockets were from a U.S. Coastguard vessel, she dowsed her lights

---

251   As usual, one can infer conflicting information from the inquiries. If the lay of the ice field was a simple NW-SE configuration, then the location of the wreckage left by the *Californian* would have been in the ice. But, one could argue that the southerly drifting current could allow the location of the wreckage to be in an area uncluttered by ice by the time the *Californian* left the scene. Finally, one must also remember the *Trautenfels* description of the lay of the icefield; less than a day before the Titanic sank, the field was in a NE-SW orientation. Perhaps the North Atlantic Drift/Gulf Stream had altered the direction of the field in the intervening hours? Interestingly, the lay of the icefield as presented in "*The Ship That Stood Still*" page 362, and adapted from *the Daily Telegraph* of April 25th 1912 shows that the southern extremity has a tail that stretches to the south west, from roughly 41°25' N 49° 55' W to 41°20' N 50°25' W; apart from this, the general layout is N-S. Could this southern tail be the *Trautenfels* south-west icefield after over a day's worth of drift?

and made off. There are fairly obvious weaknesses in this account if it is put forward as fully explaining the third ship theory; but one thing it does do is remind us that in those days, before wireless was common at sea, rockets were much more used than is now the case for reasons other than indicating distress."

This is a perfect example of a seeming case of haste in preparing the report before facts could be checked. The weaknesses in the *Samson* story are manifest, and had been known since *"The Night Lives On,"* published 6 years before. Although Barnett had known of Walter Lord's sequel, and did try to obtain a copy of 'Leslie Reed's' [sic] book (though whether he was successful is not known), he had also been furnished with pro-*Samson* material by Eno. Other literature that he had at his disposal, such as '*Titanic – Triumph and Tragedy*' (which does mention the *Samson*) were returned to their original source, and may have not been seen by de Coverley. The only other source material was a copy of the original statement (complete with 'Cape Hatteras') and information that the *Samson* would not have been visible from any other ship as she had shielded lights. De Coverley had presumably written favourably about the *Samson* as a consequence of the only information available to him.

Incidentally, the U.S. Coastguard didn't exist in 1912. And the reader can see in Appendix B that rockets were discouraged, by international convention, from being used for any purpose on the high sea, except for indicating distress.

We now reach the concluding question: "Should *Californian* have taken further action when the rockets were seen; and if so, what action, and why was it not taken?" And on this point, the two inspectors agreed again.

"The Inspector considers that further action should have been taken, and I agree. Although as has been pointed out the use of rockets was much more common 80 years ago than it is today, it was certainly not so ordinary an event that their sighting, especially in an area where ice was about, required anything less than all practicable positive measures to establish the reason for them being fired. Merely attempting to call by Morse lamp fell far short of what was needed. The action which should have been taken by Mr Stone as soon as he was sure that he was indeed seeing rockets
was:

- The Master should have been called and if he did not immediately respond Mr Stone should have reported to him in person;
- Engine Room should have been placed on immediate readiness by ringing 'Stand By Engines';
- The Wireless Operator should have been called; and

- Captain Lord on being called should have at once gone to the Bridge, verified that the Engine Room was at readiness and the Wireless Operator at his post, and then got under way towards the apparent source of the rockets.

It is only possible to speculate why this action was not taken. None of the more picturesque or indeed scurrilous suggestions which have been advanced from time to time - that Captain Lord lay drunk in his cabin, that he was entirely callous or that he was frightened to attempt to manoeuvre in the ice - stand up to even the most cursory examination. On the first, Captain Lord was in fact almost tee-total; and it requires not just that he was incapable but the entire watch on deck as well[252]. That this was not so is patent from the very evidence which leads to criticism of them, namely their admitted sighting of rockets and the degree of correspondence between what they saw and the evidence from *Titanic*. On the second, even if (which I do not for a moment believe) Captain Lord had been devoid of all normal human feelings of compassion, he would still have done his utmost to assist for reasons of personal glory; and of course again it assumes equal callousness or at least extreme pusillanimity on the part of Mr Stone and his watch. As to the third, Captain Lord in fact took his ship through the ice twice once he learnt of *Titanic's* distress: first to head for the reported position, which was west of the ice field, and second to join *Carpathia* in her search. The second passage was made after he had gone to the reported position and found *Mount Temple* there, and it ought to be noted that the latter ship did not attempt to traverse the field to assist *Carpathia*. This is not mentioned in critical spirit; one can well understand the caution of *Mount Temple's* Master with his very large complement of passengers, and he no doubt realised that it was too late for his ship to be of any practical help: but the fact remains that Captain Lord made the effort and he did not. Captain Lord's action may very well have been that of a man who realised that his ship had failed to do what should have been done earlier, and was desperate to make amends; but it is certainly not the action of a coward. Moreover, clearly all these 'explanations' require a high degree of conspiracy in totally fabricating evidence by the witnesses from *Californian* and, quite apart from the inherent improbability of this, the discrepancies which do exist in their evidence argues against it."

With regard to Lord's inability to remember the messages from Stone and Gibson, de Coverley had the following explanation, "This seems to me entirely consistent with a common condition when a man is called while he is sleeping heavily: there is a state of somnambulism quite often experienced in which the subject appears to respond to a call but the message given does not break the barrier between sleep and consciousness. Commonly, when the subject does wake he has no recollection of the call until he is told of it, when there is some memory but only in a very hazy sense. In plain language, I think the message from the Bridge simply did not get through.

This inevitably points to weakness on the part of Mr Stone. Again, I think we need look no further than human fallibility for the cause. There is a natural

---

252   Recall Captain Lord's "certain amount of slackness" statement.

tendency to reject the signals of disaster and to hope that all is well despite the evidence of one's own eyes and senses, Of course, Mr Stone should have gone down himself to the Master when there was no proper response from him, but the impression one gets of Captain Lord is that, far from being slack as has sometimes been suggested, he was in fact something of a martinet, and the young officer may have feared to leave the Bridge (normally a grave dereliction of duty) even though under the circumstances it would have been safe and right to do so[253]. One can readily imagine Mr Stone on the Bridge, knowing in his heart what ought to be done (he is recorded as saying to Mr Gibson that "a ship doesn't fire rockets for nothing") but trying to persuade himself that there was no real cause for alarm - and desperately wishing it was four o'clock and the Mate was there. I sympathise with Mr Stone, but it must be said that he was seriously at fault."

So, what should the *Californian* have done? The situation should, after Stone ensured that the flash in the sky was not a shooting star or visual aberration by waiting for a second occurrence, have seen Lord on the bridge at about 0055 hrs. and then headed his ship for the rockets, "but cautiously at first because of the ice for at that stage the urgency of the situation would not be known and it would be right for him to have regard for the safety of his own ship. Meanwhile, the Wireless Operator would have been called and would shortly receive *Titanic's* SOS with its incorrect position. This would have put Captain Lord in something of a quandary: probably he would have called *Titanic* by wireless giving *Californian's* position, saying what had been seen, and asking *Titanic* to check her position. This would very likely have led to the error in dead reckoning being discovered, after which full speed would be made towards the correct position; but with the time lost *Californian* would arrive well after the sinking"

If de Coverley was right about the 17 mile distance, "the effect of *Californian* taking proper action would have been no more than to place on her the task actually carried out by *Carpathia*, that is the rescue of those who escaped. I do not think any reasonably probable action by Captain Lord could have led to a different outcome of the tragedy. This of course does not alter the fact that the attempt should have been made."

The Deputy Chief Inspector had a number of further points to make: "There is one rather curious point about the distress signals which is worth mentioning. In 1912, under the International Regulations then in force, such signals could be of any colour (*Titanic's* were in fact white) and there was therefore nothing immediately to distinguish them from other rockets. The *Titanic* disaster led to a number of changes improving provisions for emergency at sea, but it was not until 1948 that the rules for distress signals were amended to make the (present) requirement that they be red. Had that rule been in force in 1912, when it was much more needed than now, Mr Stone would surely not have remained

---

253   Groves had earlier left the bridge to report to Lord at a time that could in no
        way be described as "urgent"

passive."

This is bunkum. The Regulations called for rockets of any colour of description fired one at a time, at intervals. This is exactly what was seen. The colour of any such rockets is immaterial as de Coverley notes, and Stone knew it. Stone's only defence against this is his plea in London that "a ship that is in distress does not steam away from you." A defence that was rejected by the court.

"Part of the reason [why no action was taken against Lord after the FI] may have been that, with the weight of a recent FI headed by a very senior and distinguished judge, it was seen as difficult for there to be a completely unprejudiced Inquiry. Be that as it may, it is difficult not to believe that some at least of those responsible at the Board of Trade felt a substantial measure of doubt as to the justice of the findings. It is not surprising if this were so: the case has continued to divide opinion to this day, and has been argued strenuously both on Captain Lord's behalf and against him. Some of the arguments have been well-reasoned but some - on both sides - have been absurd and scurrilous.

Neither party will be entirely satisfied with this Report, but while it does not purport to answer all the questions which have been raised it does attempt to distinguish the essential circumstances and set out reasoned and realistic interpretations. It is for others if they wish to go further into speculation; it is hoped that they will do so rationally and with some regard to the simple fact that there are no villains in this story; just human beings with human characteristics."

So concluded the long awaited M.A.I.B. report. With its report riddled with errors and bizarre reasoning and deductions, this would be theirs – and the UK Government's - last word on 'The *Californian* Incident.' On one point they were proved right. The conjoined conclusions satisfied neither pro- nor Anti-Lord factions.

David Eno gave his own review of the M.A.I.B. re-appraisal[254] in which he complimented Captain Marriott, who "later had his deputy Captain DeCloverly [sic] make alterations to the report based on the new evidence which endorsed the 17 to 20 mile range. Captain Barnett had clung to the original findings of the 1912 inquiries." Eno drastically misinterpreted the law regarding the use of rockets used for distress, viz. "According to existing regulations of 1912, socket distress signals could be any colour or description when fired, rising above the masthead light exploding with a loud report 'used in lieu of cannon' [emphasis in original] which on a clear night at sea could be heard distinctly at a distance of 12 miles." Nowhere does it specify that rockets needed to rise above the masthead light of a vessel, nowhere does it mention that these rockets need to explode with a loud report, nowhere does it refer to a range for the sound to be heard and nowhere does it state that these rockets are 'in lieu of cannon', although Lord Mersey did note that the *Titanic's* rockets were 'in lieu of guns'. This strange hybrid of the use of rockets in 1912 was shared by Captain Robert Meurn, Professor and Chief of Nautical

254   *Titanic Commutator* Volume 16, Number 1 (May-July 1992)

Sciences at the U.S. Merchant Marine Academy at King's Point, New York, who endorsed the bogus "more than half mast height" criterion at the Titanic Historical Society convention in Boston in April 1992 where Eno gave a presentation. Eno was also mistaken in his summary that Captain Marriott had endorsed Captain "DeCloverly's" [sic] report which found that the *Titanic* and the *Californian* were 17-20 miles apart. This is utterly wrong. Marriott endorsed the report submitted by De Coverley, which was a hybrid of his and Barnett's findings. Marriott was therefore endorsing both sets of results.

In an opinion piece for his magazine, "Sea Breezes[255]", C.H. Milsom, who had met Lord some thirty years previously, asked "Capt Stanley Lord: Does it Matter?" It certainly mattered to him. "So, far from being vindicated as many had hoped, Capt. Lord and now one of his officers still stand accused...I am not one to wax romantic about the 'law of the sea' but it is an irrefutable factor in a seafarer's calling that a ship always answers a call for help, regardless of expense or time lost on passage. The accusation that the *Californian* broke that trust was not just a slur on Capt. Lord, it was a slur on the whole of Britain's Merchant Navy. The shame felt in 1912 was bitterly resented: it hurt then and it hurts today. So, yes it does matter for the Merchant Navy will bear the shame of the *Californian* until Capt. Lord, and now 2nd Officer Stone, are totally vindicated of this awful charge. Who, now, will take up the cudgels?"

On the whole, though, UK and International newspapers simply reported on the confusion caused by the two sets of findings. "The more things change, the more they stay the same," reported the largely pro-Lord Titanic Historical Society. Stanley Tutton Lord was disappointed that the report did not fully vindicate his father, but was heartened that he had been cleared of the main charge, that the late Captain could have saved many of the people who died that night.

But a surprising foe to the overwhelming pro-Lord camps was waiting in the wings: Titanic Historical Society member, and later Vice-President, George Behe. To this author, this was a revelation: in 1988, Behe wrote "*Titanic: Psychic Forewarnings of a Tragedy*", and he was seemingly sympathetic to the Lordite cause. But the next year, he seemed to be having misgivings and provided members of the T.H.S. with information at variance with the data used to defend Lord and his ship. Much of this information had been available to researchers for years (for instance, in the transcripts of the 1912 inquiries, and in Bisset's book) but had either been ignored or no-one had cared to look. As Behe wrote in the Commutator volume 14 no.3 (Autumn 1990): "My purpose in playing devil's advocate has been to show that there are at least two sides to every argument. However the scenarios I presented show material can be marshalled to support any theory about the *Californian* that a writer might wish to promote. For both sides to continue filing claims and counterclaims on the same 1912 information, in my opinion, is pointless, since no definitive answer can be arrived at. New information is required

---

255   Vol.66, No.558, June 1992

to break the impasse and solve the mystery ... I've been baffled by the Lordites seeming lack of concern about the identity of the 'mystery ship' which (they contend) lay between the *Titanic* and *Californian* ... They seem content to believe that the *Titanic* saw some vessel other than the *Californian*. A 1981 Commutator Supplement contained my own list of vessels: *Dorothy Baird*, *Kelvindale*, *St.Pierre*, *Eugene Pergeline* and several unnamed vessels[256]. which may have been near the sinking and might be candidates. I thought the Lordites would investigate these vessels to establish the identity rather than rehashing the reasons (in their opinions) the mystery ship could not have been the *Californian*."

Two years later, Behe was still sceptical: "One weakness of the Lordite case is that they must rely on the presence of two unknown ships in order to account for all the events that took place. I've relied on vessels we know were in the area that morning." Behe had spent time examining evidence from Captain Moore, 3rd Officer Groves and Captain Gambell [see the later discussion on the SS *Virginian*'s evidence] and found that not only were their recollections detrimental to Captain Lord's case, but they had never been widely publicised. They would have been, if Leslie Reade's book had been published as planned nearly two decades earlier, but Harrison had seen to it that this didn't occur.

Behe had submitted an article to the T.H.S. about these contrary recollections but despite a little advance publicity that the article would appear in

---

256   *Lloyd's List* for April 15th, reports the following information from the SS *Carmania*: "At least one full rigged ship and one fishing smack are imprisoned in the floes". One of these might be the three-masted barque *Eugene Pergeline*, which was reported on April 10th by the German tanker *Excelsior* to be stuck in the ice 1000 miles east of Sandy Hook. *Lloyd's Weekly Shipping Index* has the following data on the ships: The *Dorothy Baird*, a 199 ton British schooner, until the command of Captain Keeping, left St.John in New Brunswick on April 2nd and docked at Pernambuco on May 11th. According to the *New York Times* on April 17th, the *Etonian* saw the *Dorothy Baird* five nights earlier in the vicinity of 42 N 50 W, drifting in pack ice with sails lowered, apparently waiting for the morning before proceeding. The 2014 ton *Kelvindale* , of the Black Line (a.k.a. The Glasgow Steam Shipping Co.), left Liverpool on April 4th and arrived at Louisburg on April 18. Given that her maximum speed was 12 knots, she may have been somewhere in the vicinity of the Titanic when she sank, although possibly somewhere to the north. The *Eugene Pergeline*, 1953 ton French Barque under the command of Captain Gorgues, departed Dunkirk on April 3rd, passed Ventnor a day later and arrived in New York on May 12th: her possible speed was thus about 6 knots. If this speed was maintained, she could have traversed the distance to witness the death of the *Titanic*: her arrival time in New York indicates a slower speed, which could mean unfavourable wind conditions, or that she was delayed by ice. There are a few vessels named *St. Pierre*; one, of the Nouvelle Societe Navole de l'Ouest fleet was nowhere near the Titanic wrecksite; she was in port, in Marseilles, on April 16th. Another one, a schooner, was seen by the steamer *Atlantian*, who reported after her arrival in Liverpool, that she had seen the *St.Pierre* on March 31st at 48N, 29 W, steering west, or nearly 1000 miles away from the *Titanic*. There is no other surviving documentation on these ship's navigation.

the next Commutator, it was rejected as being "poorly researched and poorly written," something that is hard to believe. Or maybe not, given how close Edward Kamuda, the leading figure in the T.H.S. oligarchy, was with Leslie Harrison. Mr. Kamuda was still repeating the nonsense of the *Samson* story in a TV documentary in 1994, and the society magazine was hostile to any articles that painted Lord and/or Harrison in a bad light. John C. Carrothers had even challenged Walter Lord, via Kamuda, to a debate on the *Californian* issue at a T.H.S. Convention, but Kamuda had thought that their Commutator magazine was 'the proper forum' and he feared that it would be putting a 'guest of honor' on the spot. It is amusing to think how Carrothers and any other Lordites would have reacted to Captain Moore's testimony about seeing the *Californian* and the *Carpathia* in view on April 15th, 1912; a crucial piece of evidence ignored by the Lordites, and possibly unknown to the great number of them.

It is only now, more than ten years after Leslie Harrison's death, that the Titanic Historical Society is now allowing articles that are not so blinkered and gushingly pro-Captain Lord to be published[257]. Other *Titanic* societies would be more tolerant.

Behe's letters rankled Harrison. "Who does Behe think he is?" he grumbled to Stanley T. Lord. Behe's writings may be the reason for the slightly hostile reaction that he received when he wrote to Harrison in 1994[258]

Returning to the aftermath of the M.A.I.B. report, it is indeed a shame that Barnett's analysis of the drift that affected the *Californian* was the major reason for the inability of Captains Marriott and de Coverley to accept his report, for there is evidence that a southerly drift was indeed affecting Lord's vessel. Astonishingly, these data were overlooked until 2006 when Dave Gittins included it in his E-book. Captain Lord provided the data after his interrogation in the United States: on 11th May, Lord wrote to Senator Smith from Liverpool, providing air and water temperatures for the night of 14/15 April that he had been unable to give the Senate Inquiry in Washington during his appearance at the end of April. These numbers show that between Noon and 4pm on the 14th April, the air and water temperature had dropped considerably. The ship was now in the grip of the cold, south-flowing Labrador Current. But this raises a conundrum: if the drift was indeed to the south, then how do we reconcile this with Stewart's 42°05 ½' N Pole Star sighting at

---

257   Perhaps not. The T.H.S./Kamuda combine refused to run a review of the electronic version of this book (ostensibly because they would not be selling it), even after the author offered to allow the society to keep a portion of the proceeds of sales from their website. The T.H.S., of course, sells the pro-Lord "*Titanic and the Mystery Ship*" (see later). So why did the T.H.S. publish Sam Halpern's excellent anti-*Californian* series of articles? Significantly, the articles blame Stone for the *Californian* fiasco, and not Captain Lord – and certainly not Leslie Harrison.

258   Readers are strongly encouraged to read George Behe's website starting at http://ourworld.compuserve.com/homepages/Carpathia/page5.htm and subsequent pages.

7.30pm? One possibility is simple: he was not telling the truth when he gave evidence. The British Inquiry testimony also says that Stewart had the Pole Star at 10.30pm. This seems unlikely for two reasons: firstly, such astronomical sightings are performed with a clear horizon; that is, between sunset and when the sky goes completely black, so that the horizon is visible. The second reason is that Stewart left the deck at 9.30, to get some sleep for his 4am watch. The "ten thirty" mention is probably a mistake in the transcript. If not, it demonstrates that false evidence was given. There is no way to know which is correct.

The air and water temperatures showed the temperature still dropping even during sunlight. It is not known whether this southerly currently affected the *Titanic*. At 7.30pm, her officers took astronomical sights and showed the ship to be exactly on course. However, this is still well to the east of the location of where the *Californian's* 8pm and 4pm temperature readings were taken. It seems likely that, given these facts, the *Titanic* was not influenced by the current until after 7.30pm. Critics on this southerly drift hypothesis may argue that the temperature merely reflects the proximity of the *Californian* to ice. However, she was nowhere near the icefield until close to the time she stopped – 10.21pm. Also, she left the scene of the accident on April 15th, passing through the ice, still being in its locality at noon. The water was actually slightly colder than at 8pm, when she was not near ice.

Time	Air	Water
April 14 - Noon	50° F (10° C)	56° F (13.3° C)
4pm	37° F (2.8° C)	36° F (2.2° C)
8pm	30° F (-1.1° C)	32° F (0° C)
Midnight	27° F (-2.8° C)	28° F (-2.2° C)
April 15 - 4am	29° F (-1.7° C)	29° F (-1.7° C)
6am	-	-
Noon	38° F (3.3° C)	31° F (-0.6° C)

The *Titanic's* water temperature data supports this rapid temperature drop[259]. At 7 p.m. on April 14th, it was 43° F; half an hour later it had dropped to 39° F. But only 30 minutes after that, it had now fallen incredibly to 31-31 ½ ° F, before rising slightly to 33° F at 9 p.m. (perhaps due to interaction with the warmer North Atlantic drift at her much more southern latitude than the *Californian*?)

The *Titanic* would have been in approximate longitude 48 7' W at 8pm, half an hour after a stellar sight had shown her to be on course. The *Californian*

---

259   See *"The Ship That Stood Still"*, page 61 (footnote)

would have reached this longitude at approximately 2.30pm; a time when the water temperature had experienced a drastic drop. Both ships, it would be reasonable to surmise, would be in the grip of the Labrador current in this longitude.

The known positions of the *Titanic* and *Californian*, and the wreckage on April 15th and successive weeks are shown in the chart below. Interestingly, there is evidence of another current, to the ENE, only a few miles south of the *Titanic*: this is the North Atlantic Drift, which feeds into the warm waters of the Gulf Stream; the *Titanic* disaster had occurred in the vicinity of the confluence of this drift and the cold Labrador Current. This can be deduced from the locations of the *Carpathia* when she turned around to provide assistance to the stricken White Star Liner[260]. Captain Rostron thought that his course would take him straight to the SOS location, but, by pure serendipity, he was on an almost perfect track to take him to the actual wrecksite, 13.5 miles away from the radioed distress location. This could only occur if he was slightly east of his anticipated dead reckoning position.

The bodies and wreckage trapped in the Labrador current would eventually find their way into the North Atlantic Drift, and were then carried east and dispersed north and south, where they were reported by passing ships. From a combination of *Lloyd's List* and literature on the *Titanic* disaster, we find the following reports in the first few weeks after the disaster:

On April 20th, the *Portsmouth* was at 41 48N, 49 20 W and "passed through a quantity of wreckage, apparently not long in the water; cabin fittings and white painted woodwork and teak, one cabin sofa, upholstered and one lifebelt, white, hardly discoloured. Dense fog at time" (location "A" on the map)

April 22nd, liner *Cestrian*, at 41 N, 49 12 W to 41 N, 49 34 W, "passed deck fittings, chairs, beddings and other wreckage from *Titanic*" (location "B")

April 25th, the German ship *Graf Waldersee* from Hamburg via Halifax reported, between positions 41 48N, 47 10 W to 41 51N, 49 52W "passed 8 icebergs; also in about same position, passed a quantity of wreckage including life buoys, chairs and pieces of wood believed from sunken *Titanic*" (location "C")

April 27th- the *Sagamore* from Liverpool to Boston, in 41 21N, 49 36W, saw "two dead bodies with life belts on, several deck chairs, racks etc., also a quantity of painted woodwork" (location "D")

"Steamer *Rhein* reports passing wreckage and bodies 42.1 north, 49.13 west, eight miles west of three big icebergs. Now making for that position. Expect to arrive 8 o'clock to-night. (Signed) "*MACKAY-BENNETT.*" (April 20) (location "E").

"Latitude, 41.58; longitude, 49.21. Heavy southwest swell has interfered with operations. Seventy-seven bodies recovered. All not embalmed will be buried at sea at 8 o'clock to-night with divine service. Can bring only embalmed bodies to

260   http://users.senet.com.au/~gittins/Carpathia.html

port." - From *Mackay Bennett*, April 21st (location "F")

New York, April 24 [NB: this is the date of the report, the actual sighting would be about April 20th] - Capt. Wilhelm and passengers of the *Bremen*, which arrived today from Bremen, reported that between 3 and 4 o'clock last Saturday afternoon, while in latitude 42 N, longitude 49.23 W., in the vicinity of where the *Titanic* foundered, his vessel ploughed through fields of bodies of the victims of the disaster. "They were everywhere," the Captain declared, "There were men, women, and children. All had life preservers on. I counted 125, then grew sick of the sight. There may have been as many as 150 or 200 bodies." "A short time before, about fifty or sixty miles north, we passed five icebergs in succession. Our lookout sighted them in time, however, and we had no difficulty in avoiding them." "Why didn't you slow down and take on some of the bodies," he was asked. "It was absolutely useless, for the simple reason that we had no means for caring for them." He said that he knew that the cable steamer *Mackay-Bennett* was searching for bodies and that he had communicated with its commander, informing him of where the bodies were. (location "G"). This is only about 5 or so miles (42 N 49 30 W) from a report from the schooner Banshee, which saw, on April 23rd, "a drawer of a wardrobe with brass knobs on it. Then a part of a cabin door and piece of rail painted white. The wreckage attracted considerable attention on Banshee and all hands viewed it from the deck." Later, two bodies were seen.

Also reported, but not depicted on the map, is a message from the *Paul Paix* from Swansea; on 16th May 1912, at position 41 degrees 51 N, 42 degrees 29 W she "saw a large white painted boat bottom up apparently a ship's lifeboat, not long in the water, very clean and showing no damage about the bottom." This is almost certainly Collapsible lifeboat B, on which some dozen survivors spent the night trembling from the cold; this boat was also seen by the crew of the *Mackay Bennett*, searching for bodies, who saw it at 41.55 N 49.20 W on April 23rd. On May 13th, the *Oceanic* picked up Collapsible A, which had been swamped during the final stages of the *Titanic's* sinking, forcing its occupants to stand in freezing water for hours until they were transferred to other boats. It is a superb demonstration of the unpredictable nature of ocean currents. For, while boats A and B could not have been very far away from each other during the night of April 14th/15th, 'A' was found well to the south east of the wreck site having drifted 7 ¾ nautical miles per day. Boat 'B' was well to the east by this time.

These reports, and accompanying chart, demonstrate the confusing nature that the competing drifts bring to any possible analysis. And the *Titanic* and the *Californian* were only a few miles away from the epicentre of the meeting point of these two great ocean currents, with associated laminar and turbulent flows, and eddies and whorls.

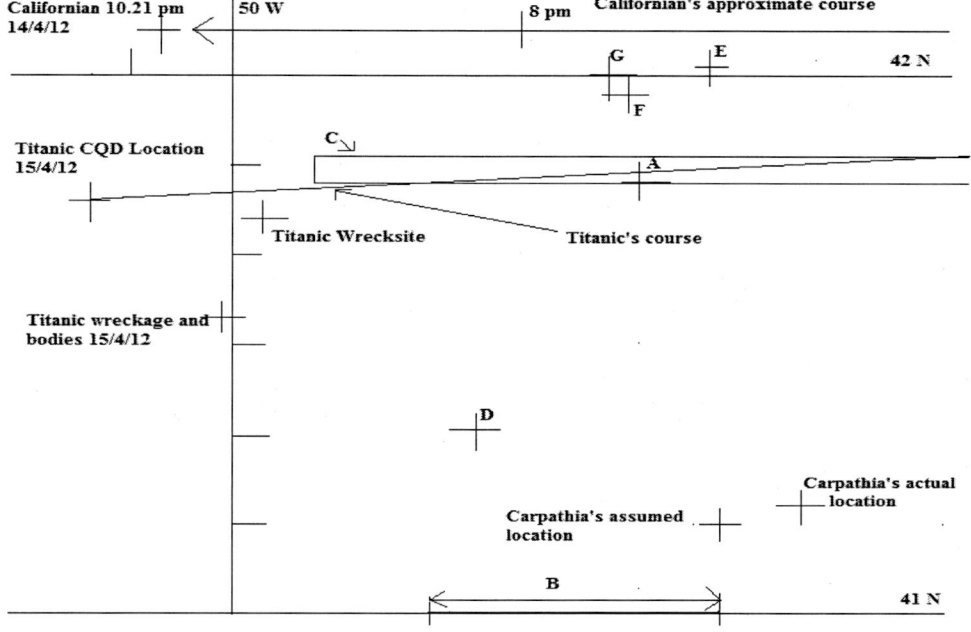

Illustration 40: Drift on April 15th and afterwards. The tick marks represent 10'

Chapter 11. "...nothing overlooked, swept under the rug, or ignored as though it didn't exist[261]."

1992 - present

Of course, now that the results of the re-appraisal had been released to the press, it was prudent for authors to include this new information in their books. One of these was Leslie Harrison, who re-released "*A Titanic Myth*" as a self-published, or 'vanity' edition. This was unveiled to the world at a press conference at the Merseyside Maritime Museum on Harrison's 80th birthday, July 31st 1992.

Harrison must have felt betrayed. He had showered Barnett with information and anecdotes ... Barnett and his wife had the temerity to be cordial to Captain Lord's son ... and now Barnett had produced an adverse finding! At the press conference, Harrison stated that Barnett's report was so bad, it had to be rewritten by de Coverley, but even he had "made fundamental errors too." But during his diatribe to the press, Harrison never once mentioned "rockets", only "detonators". He only used the word "rocket" in informal conversation afterwards, when he decried how the 1958 film '*A Night To Remember*' had used 'rockets on a stick' rather than the more accurate cylindrical socket signal. This is a subject he would return to, first of all in "*A Titanic Myth part 2*" (a damage limitation in the aftermath of Leslie Reade's impending book), and then, in his last literary effort, "*Captain Lord's Plight To Remember*".

Another member of the press conference entourage was Harrison's niece, who in private conversation to the press, said that the *Californian* was her uncle's "life work" and that "both his [late] wife and children had, at one point, felt that he was going too far with it, that it was an obsession of his and that it annoyed, upset and bothered them."[262]

In the epilogue to his re-released book, Harrison sympathised with the "unfortunate Captain de Coverley on being diverted from his already heavy workload ... to try to transform Captain Barnett's findings into something more acceptable to Captain Marriott. In such circumstances it is not surprising that some of his conclusions conflict with the acknowledged facts of the case." The examples offered by Harrison include his reference to the ship stopped near the *Californian*, which he asserts came from the westward, to stop on reaching clear water on the eastern side[263].

"A further and most regrettable omission from Captain de Coverley's report is any supporting evidence for [de Coverley's] assertion that some arguments on

---

261   This is part of Walter Lord's review of Reade and de Groot's work
262   Private Information
263   One can only wonder why a ship would then steam back into an icefield, at
       night, firing rockets.

Captain Lord's behalf have been 'absurd and scurrilous'...as the one who since 1958 has borne primary responsibility for the presentation of Captain Lord's case, I must emphatically deny that any of the arguments I have put forward could possibly justify such a grossly offensive description, nor do I know of any who share my views on Captain Lord's case whose conduct merits such an attack." The only source of scurrilous material in the internal M.A.I.B. files came from Reade's *"Those Inescapable Rockets."*

Great credence is given to Boxhall's evidence, to the exclusion of all else: "[Boxhall] went to the bridge to start firing distress signals in an unsuccessful attempt to summon help from an approaching ship; he abandoned this action when she turned and steamed away." This is untrue: Boxhall only stopped firing when the Captain ordered him to take command of lifeboat 2.

Harrison concludes, "How do matters now rest? Are we to take the M.A.I.B. Report as the final – if inconclusive – official word on the question of Captain Lord's guilt or innocence, or is the report open to amendment in the light of reasoned criticism? The Department of Transport has been presented with a unique opportunity to close a controversial chapter in Britain's maritime history. It would be an unforgivable act for it to be cast aside."

The report was *not* "open to amendment," but Harrison's campaign was far from over. He was interviewed by the *Westcountry Morning News*, and it was published on August 24th that year.

'Why does Harrison bother so many years? "It has become a moral obligation,'" Harrison told the reporter, "The stigma still lies on Lord's name. I promised him I would not let the matter drop."

'Harrison maintains that nobody was lying at the Inquiry."They all told the truth as they saw it" he says'. The reader is reminded of the wide berth between Stewart and Evan's evidence as to why a wireless call was made on 15th April; to establish what the yellow funnelled steamer was to the south, or to find out about a rocket firing ship during the night? And then there is the chasm between Groves' statements and Lord's.

"...Unless the minister acts to absolve Lord, a new book will be published in December based on the papers of an author whose book we managed to kill before it came out," Harrison added, "...the first crack since 1912 in the Establishment's refusal to do anything has appeared. Whitehall must do something – there is still a two foot file on the Minister's desk from people complaining they were unfair to Lord."

The "book we managed to kill" would finally see the light of day the following year. Finally, it was clear; his "moral obligation" had sought to destroy a contrary opinion, not because of copyright infringements, but to protect Captain Lord and his reputation; the last book to do so was *"The Night Lives On"*, and despite his best efforts, Harrison could do nothing about it.

Leslie Reade would at last have his day, 4 years after his death.

"*The Ship That Stood Still*" had been taken up again by Patrick Stephens Limited, the publishers who had originally been approached c.1975, but it was now under the control of Haynes, better known for their car maintenance manuals. The OK to proceed was given in an internal memorandum dated 14th September 1989, with the following background story: "[the manuscript] had many legal problems, chiefly concerning the author's hatred of Leslie Harrison ... there was also the handicap of an exceptionally difficult and dogmatic author, who flatly refused to shorten the book." One member of the committee who agreed the go ahead for the book suggested that the title was slightly inappropriate and that "*The Titanic and the Ship That Stood Still*" perhaps might be more apt. Such a title with the emotive name "*Titanic*" would certainly generate more publicity and hence, sales.

Following legal discussions, the anti-Harrison tone of the original manuscript was considerably toned down[264]. After editing by Reade's friend Edward de Groot, a release date of December 1992 seemed likely, but other factors intervened, and a date of March/April the following year was agreed. Walter Lord wrote a glowing testimonial that appeared on the book's dust jacket, saying that "nothing had been swept under the rug [or] ignored as though it didn't exist." Readers will soon learn how accurate this view is.

The imminent publication of Reade's and de Groot's book invigorated the camps of the pro-*Californian* cause. Leslie Harrison wrote to Captain Lord's son a few week before Reade's posthumous book was released. It is telling in its tactics. "Re: forthcoming publication of de Groot's book... much is being done by supporters of your father's case to make life difficult for him! Much, of course, depends on what the book contains, but I'm pinning my hopes on aspersions on my character which may justify a solicitor's letter comparable with that which destroyed the earlier attempt to publish the book in 1975. Here's hoping!" A few weeks prior to this, he had stated that "should I be libelled in the book (as I am in Leslie Reade's original draft), at the present moment I would be inclined to ignore

---

264   This is also obvious in the single pre- de Groot edited chapter that has survived in the public domain: "The Norwegian Fairy Story", dealing with the Samson story and stored with Walter Lord's material at the National Maritime Museum in Greenwich. This chapter was used as background material in Lord's "*The Night Lives On*," which explains why it has survived. One interesting point is that in "*A Titanic Myth part 2*," Harrison writes (page 140-1), "[About 1991] I made another attempt to ensure that there were no inaccuracies in the manuscript. Through an intermediary, I made an offer to the prospective publishers to read it 'solely to point out any factual errors, and with no intention whatsoever to influence any opinions which it might advance ... my offer was rejected." Haynes comprehensive files on the Reade/de Groot book have no record of this offer.

the fact. Breaches of copyright raise other issues."

One of these supporters was a man from Holland named Rob Kamps. Kamps, who would later inherit a pro-Lord book, had first written to Haynes towards the end of 1992. He alleged that de Groot had performed copyright infringement on a massive scale in a previous work (the Dutch book "*75 jaar Titanic*"); Kamps provided over 80 pages of noted indiscretions, only a couple of which may have been genuine violations. Kamps, who had been keeping an eye on de Groot since 1978 and had held a vendetta ever since, wrote that his compendium of copyright incursions "would have made ample justification to take steps against the man...de Groot should answer for his countless misdeeds and scurrilous remarks." Kamps also accused de Groot of making silent, anonymous phone calls to his home in the early hours of the morning, but refused to allow Haynes to forward his dossier to de Groot for his comments. Haynes were not impressed and thought that "some of his accusations were so bizarre they were simply not credible." With regard to de Groot, they simply noted that, "if Edward has failed to acknowledge the help he obtained from other books, then he can be accused of being an ill-mannered author, but that is all."[265]

Kamps sustained these innuendos for another three years, well after Reade's/de Groot's book was published[266].

David Eno also complained to Haynes, accusing them of ignoring the M.A.I.B. "command finding" [Eno's emphasis] that the *Titanic* and the *Californian* were 17 to 20 miles distant. Again, Eno ignores the other conclusion placing them much closer. He wrote to the Managing Director that "[Haynes] sees the opportunity to ring in fresh cash from old manipulations ... [I have] reviewed the story lines...you're dreadfully lacking in credibility and that of Haynes will follow suit. In fact, Haynes will be aiding and abetting one of the grossest cases of miscarriage [sic] of justice in the 20th century." Eno remarked that he was working on his own book which would explore the "implausibilies [sic]" of the case, but such a manuscript has never materialised.

And so, the long awaited Anti-Lordite book was born, after a previous still-birth and a gestation of nearly three decades. It opened many eyes (particularly this

---

265   This author, and others critical of Captain Lord have also been the target of Mr. Kamps and his smear campaigns. Indeed, Kamps was cordial to this author until he found out my sceptical stance regarding the Californian and his officers. Some of Kamp's comments have been saved and placed on this author's website at http://www.paullee.com/Titanic/articles.html with extra detail added by this current author. Another target of Kamps was none other than Walter Lord, who was the target of a vicious attack sent to the Titanic International Society, a copy of which was forwarded to Lord.

266   In 1992, Kamps claimed to have read a copy of de Groot's manuscript. How did he get hold of it?

author's) about the startling omissions of evidence and tactics of researchers friendly to Lord; nevertheless, the continual barbs against Harrison do become tedious after a while. The major pieces of new evidence uncovered made this book a highly competent antithesis to "*A Titanic Myth*" as the 'case for the prosecution.'

A major revelation in the book was an interview given by Captain Gambell of the SS *Virginian* to *The Times* newspaper when he reached Liverpool, and published on April 22nd 1912: the *Virginian* had been at sea and had only just arrived in port. It is probable that her officers knew nothing of the furore over the *Californian*, currently brewing in Boston, and this is the first opportunity that Gambell had to speak on the matter. Whatever he had to say is then certainly unbiased.

Gambell gives us the following startling piece of news, overlooked for decades: "At 6.10am I sent a Marconigram to the *Californian*:- "Kindly let me know condition of affairs when you get to *Titanic*." She at once replied :- "Can now see *Carpathia* taking passengers on board from small boats. Titanic foundered about 2 a.m." To have seen passengers embarking from the lifeboats and climbing up ladders into the *Carpathia's* open gangway doors, the distance between the two ships would be about 7.8 miles.

Friends of Captain Lord[267] have stated that this "6.10" message was referenced with regard to New York Time, and that the true, local time would be about 8.20am on the *Californian*. Senan Molony (see later) writes that, "If the *Californian* could see the *Carpathia* at 6.10am, then the *Carpathia* should have been seeing the *Californian*". We now know that two people, and maybe more on the *Carpathia* said they saw the *Californian* approach from a close location. And Captain Rostron claimed that he did not identify the *Mount Temple* at the time, even though the *Carpathia* was in view of this latter vessel; this shows that reciprocal sightings at the same time are not always noted.

Lest this analysis be regarded of favouritism, and essential passages edited, or removed, that would help either pro- or anti- camps, let us analyse the relevant sections of Captain Gambells's statement to the press:

"At 12.40 a.m. (ship's time) on the 15th inst. I received the following message by wireless from Cape Race:- '*Titanic* struck iceberg, wants immediate assistance, her position 41.46 N. and 50.14 W." My position then was 42.27 N., 53.37 W., and the *Titanic* bore from me S. 55 ½ E; true distance 178 miles. I at once altered my course to go to her assistance, and advised Cape Race and Messrs. H and A. Allan[268], Montreal to that effect. *Olympic* making all speed towards *Titanic*, but much further off than *Virginian*, her position lat. 40.32 N., long 61.18 W.' At 1.57 a.m. (ship's time), 5.27 (Greenwich time), the *Titanic's* signals ceased abruptly, as if the power had suddenly been cut off. At 3.45 a.m. I was in touch by

---

267   For example, see here:
http://ourworld.compuserve.com/homepages/Carpathia/page7.htm
268   The steamer's owners.

wireless with the Russian steamer *Birma*, and gave her the *Titanic's* position, she was then 55 miles from the *Titanic*, and going to her assistance.

At 5.45 a.m. I was in communication with the Leyland liner *Californian*. She was 17 miles north of the *Titanic*, and had not heard anything official of the disaster. I sent a Marconigram to her as follows :- 'Titanic struck iceberg, wants assistance urgently, ship sinking, passengers in boats, her position lat. 41.46, long. 50.14' Shortly after this I was in communication with the *Carpathia*, the *Frankfurt*, and the *Baltic*, all making for the *Titanic*. At 6.10am I sent a Marconigram to the *Californian* :- 'Kindly let me know condition of affairs when you get to *Titanic*.' She at once replied :- 'Can now see *Carpathia* taking passengers on board from small boats. *Titanic* foundered about 2 a.m.' At 10 a.m. I received the following message from the *Carpathia*:- 'Turn back, everything OK, we have 800 on board, return to your northern track.' At the same time the *Carpathia* sent the following message to the *Baltic* :- 'Am leaving here with all on board, about 800, chiefly third-class, and a lot of stewards, proceed on your voyage to Liverpool, we are proceeding to Halifax or New York under full steam.' I then altered my course to the eastward and proceeded on my voyage."

The *Virginian* did indeed make it to the area of the wrecksite, and her observations in the April 22nd "*Shipping Gazette and Lloyd's List*" puts the ice between 42 3 N, 50 20 W and 41 19 N, 49 50 W where she saw numerous bergs and growlers.

One immediately turns to the PV of the *Virginian* for verification of these statements. Here is a transcript, with explanatory notes, and expansion of acronyms etc. were necessary. All times, according to the PV, are New York Time:

"11.10 Hear MGY calling CQ and giving his position as 41.46 N 50.14 W
11. 12 Call MGY but get no response. MCE then calls me and asked me report to Captain that *Titanic* struck iceberg and require immediate assistance."

This would relate to the distress call as received by the *Virginian*, at 12.40am ship's time.

"11.30 1 to MCE (MSG). MCE informs MGY that we are going to his assistance. Our position 170 miles north of MGY"

MCE is the land station at Cape Race[269]. At 11.25 (New York Time), Cape Race notes in its PV: "Establish communication with *Virginian* here and give him all information re: *Titanic*, telling him to inform Captain immediately. OK. " Thirty minutes later, Cape Race notes: "*Virginian* says he is now going to assistance *Titanic*. *Titanic* meanwhile continues circulating position calling for help. He says weather is calm and clear." Cape Race probably has his timings garbled here, but,

---

269   http://Titanic.gov.ns.ca/wireless.html

if Gambell is right, some time was spent in communication with the owners of his own ship, telling them of his intentions. The time difference with New York would be about 1 hour 30 minutes, or if Gambell's "12.40" time is to be believed, 1 ¼ hours.

The next, incomplete and garbled message is as follows:

11.35 "MKC de [from] MGY --- sinking we are putting passengers and ----- in small boats ---- weather clear. MGY"

MKC is the *Olympic*, and according to her wireless log, at 11.40, the *Titanic* transmitted that passengers were being put off in small boats. At 11.45, the *Titanic* replied to a message from the *Olympic* that the weather was calm and clear. So far, the agreement between all these PVs is extremely good.

11. 50 Cape Race says: "MGN [*Virginian*] Please tell your Captain this; The MKC is making all speed for MGY but his position is 40 32 N 61 18 W You are much nearer to him. He is already putting women off in boats and he says weather is clear and calm. MKC is the only one we have heard say is going to his assistance. The others must be a long way from MGY."

This does not appear in Cape Race's PV (incidentally, Cape Race evidently could not hear the frantic messages from other vessels rushing to the *Titanic's* help). This message is probably the same that Captain Gambell received at 1.20 a.m. ship's time: "I received a further message from Cape Race, which read :- 'Titanic reports ship sinking, and putting women and children in boats. *Olympic* making all speed towards *Titanic*, but much further off than *Virginian*, her position lat. 40.32 N., long 61.18 W.' ", although obviously the wording is different. Again, a time difference with New York of 1 ½ hours is apparent.

12.05 Cape Race says 'we have not heard MGY for about half an hour. His power may be gone
12.10 Hear MGY calling very faintly his power greatly reduced
12.20 Hear two 'V's signalled faintly in spark similar to MGYs. Probably adjusting spark.
12.27 MGY calls CQ unable make out his signal. Ended very abruptly as if power suddenly switched off his spark rather blurred or ragged.

Again, good corroboration with Gambell's "At 1.57 a.m. (ship's time), 5.27 (Greenwich time), the *Titanic's* signals ceased abruptly, as if the power had suddenly been cut off"

00.45 1 [message] from MCE (MSG)

01.15 Exchange signals with *Baltic*. He tries to send us MSG for MGY but his [the *Baltic's*] signals died utterly away.

The *Baltic's* PV confirms this exchange, at 1.10, although she notes that the signal condition was "G" (Good).

02.15 Signals Russian American Liner '*Birma*' says he is 55 miles from *Titanic* but cannot hear anything of him

This exchange does not appear in the *Birma's* PV: the only mention of any conversation was with MGT (British tanker "*Sun*"), asking for news of *Titanic* at 3.20am *Birma* time. Comparing this with Gambell's statement, this implies a 1 ½ hour time difference with New York. At 5.45am, Gambell's told the reporters that he furnished the *Californian* with news of the *Titanic's* position. This would be approximately 4.15am in New York, or 6.05am on the *Californian*. This is in agreement with the findings of the British Inquiry; "4.10am[270] (New York Time) '*Californian*' receives M.S.G. from M.G.N ('*Virginian*')" (*Californian* Marconi Operator Evans said this was about 5.45am when interrogated in London, or, in Washington, a "few minutes" after 3.40 New York Time – or 5.30 *Californian* Time – although interestingly, Evans testified that the *Virginian* told him that the *Titanic* had already sunk).

The next event by Gambell ("Shortly after [5.45] I was in communication with the *Carpathia*, the *Frankfurt*, and the *Baltic*, all making for the *Titanic*") cannot be confirmed in the other PVs. However, the SS *Birma* did communicate with the *Virginian* at 5.00am *Birma* Time, but this cannot be definitively tied to any time on the *Virginian* for reasons that will be discussed presently. The next entry is the contentious "Can now see *Carpathia* ..." entry.

From the *Virginian's* PV:

8.30am Standing by (both operators) all night during which we exchanged signals and compared positions with *Californian, Frankfurt, Parisian* and *Carpathia* all going to   assistance of MGY.

If the timing of Captain Gambell's mention of the *Californian* seeing the *Carpathia* at 6.10am local time is correct, then it should have been mentioned by now, as this would be approximately 4.40am New York Time. Ideally, the PVs of all the ships would be complete records of all messages, but they aren't, probably because the operators were too busy transmitting and relaying traffic. However, it has now been demonstrated that all of Captain Gambell's other statements are in

---

270   The *Virginian's* Marconigram gives the time for this message as "4.00 am" This is in reply to the *Californian's* message saying "Please give MSG on account MGY so as Capt can go off track down to MGY "

chronological order and are given in ship's time, and also corroborate very well with external sources. Why should the message indicating the proximity of the *Carpathia* and *Californian* be any different[271]?

There is one mystery: no other ship refers to the *Titanic* sinking at 2a.m.: regardless of whether the "Can now see *Carpathia*" message was received at 6.10am, or later, how did the *Californian* know[272]? From the accounts of the occupants of lifeboat 4, we know that Captain Rostron would have known the sinking time as soon as he picked up this first boatload at about 4.15am. Did he let his wireless operator, Cottam, know too? And if the *Californian* did see the survivors being picked up, then why did she not head straight for her, rather than the amazing 2 ½ hour long circuitous journey she eventually took? Perhaps Captain Lord, by now well within the ice and heading south-west, realised that he was committed to his voyage and that a quicker passage could be made by maintaining his course, leaving the ice and travelling down the western side at full speed and encountering the *Carpathia* later on? If so, his testimony in London, about stopping his ship at the time he met the *Mount Temple* might make sense: was he deciding what to do next, to force through the ice and risk damage, or was he looking for a comparatively thin patch of field ice to traverse?[273]

Back to the PV:

At 8am *Carpathia* said:- Tell your skipper we are leaving here with all on board - about 800 passengers. Everything OK. Please return your northern course.

This entry from the PV is about right for Gambell's "10am" reference. Indeed, exactly as Gambell says, the *Baltic* heard this message at 7.10am New York Time: "In communication with MPA [*Carpathia*] exchange traffic re passengers and get instructions proceed Liverpool. We turn around at 7.15am" This

---

271   A contradiction exists in the SS *Birma's* PV. At 6.30 local time, it is noted that she had asked the *Californian* for news of the *Titanic*, but none was available. It isn't until 8am that the *Californian* sends a message saying that the *Carpathia* had picked up 20 boats of survivors. These timings are not as clear as they seem.

272   Inspection of many newspaper articles reporting the Gambell interview provide an alternate explanation. In them, some merely report that the Marconigram says "Can now see *Carpathia* taking passengers on board from small boats." Note that the quotation marks close early. The mention of the *Titanic* sinking at 2am could have been tagged on by Gambell, and could have been obtained by other sources.

273   If there was a 1 ½ hour time difference between New York and the *Virginian*, and 1 hour 50 minutes between NYT and the *Californian*, 6.10am on the *Virginian* becomes 6.30am on the *Californian*; by this time, Captain Lord and his crew would have cleared the ice and be trundling down the western side of the icefield. It would make little sense to retrace their path to reach the *Carpathia*. A much more sensible option would be to continue on her course.

338

7.10am message would be 8.40am on the *Virginian*. The *New York Times* reveals that when the *Virginian* received the *Carpathia's* instructions, she had steamed 162 miles. For an 18 knot ship, this equates to 9 hours. 9 hours from 12.40am would be 9.40am, very close to the "10am" time quoted above.

Of course, the one thing that might confirm this is the *Californian's* own PV, but, sadly, or suspiciously, it has been missing for more than 40 years. In the light of the other evidence, the "can now see *Carpathia*" remark is consistent with an early rather than a late sighting of the Cunard vessel. But in the annals of *Titanic* research, nothing is as it seems. One can easily find a piece of evidence to support any claims; but then, other evidence emerges that counters it.

Returning to our discussion of Reade's book, his treatment of the *Samson* story is noteworthy too, for, in addition to the expose of the bogus navigation contained in Naess' 'report', he managed to obtain authenticated copies of a Supplementary Revenue Book of Isafjodhur for 1912. These show that the *Samson* was in port, having seemingly just arrived, on April 6th and 20th, and again on May 9th, as Captain Ring paid his port taxes on these dates. The *Samson*, a 6 knot ship, could not have made it to the *Titanic's* location and back - some 3000 miles - during these dates.

Could a ship using private signals have confused Stone and Gibson? Reade tenaciously tackled this question too. From a list of 190 company signals registered in 1912, he determined that only five shipping lines (Allan, Chargeurs Reunis, Cunard, American and White Star) had rockets in their inventory. The first of these (the Allan Line) had specific instructions *not* to use rockets on the high seas, leaving four (although it seems that the use of rockets on the high seas was discouraged by international agreement, as noted in Appendix B of this book). Of these four, none utilised a white rocket throwing white stars. Three of these were in combination with other coloured pyrotechnic lights. Reade thus eliminated 'company signals containing rockets' from his enquiries. But what of company signals displaying white lights? He found four companies (City of Dublin Steam Packet Co., Norfolk and North American Steam Shipping Company, Siemens Brothers and South Eastern & Chatham Railway) that used white lights alone. An exhaustive research project checking on the whereabouts of all the vessels owned by these lines ensued, with the result that all of those ships are accounted for on the night of April 14th/15th "[This] ends the myth of the *Californian* being deceived by company signals," writes Reade.

Other sections of the book display an impressive amount of attention to many facets of the *Californian* story. For instance, consider the detonation of the rockets. It was a standard ploy amongst Lordite researchers to declare that *Titanic's* signals could be heard up to ten miles away, but with no supporting evidence. This assertion was repeated but never challenged until '*The Night Lives On*', and Reade's book elaborated upon this, where Reade assembled an impressive battery of professional opinion to show that the concept of the sound of rockets propagating over a distance is no more than mere fantasy. Mr. L.G.Reynolds of Trinity House, the General Lighthouse authority for England, Wales, the Channel Islands and Gibraltar told Reade, "Heaven help you if you have to rely on sound for your safety! Sound, as they say, is a last resort." Reynolds spoke of a possible acoustic shadow zone, where sound could be heard closer to, or indeed, further away a source of sound, but a specific area might hear nothing. Dr. V.G.Welsby of the Department of Electronic and Electrical Engineering of the University of Birmingham had this to say: "Sound waves travel faster through cold dense air than through warm light air. Thus, if we happened to have a layer of warmer air over a cold sea[274], there may have been a significant acoustic velocity gradient with respect to height. The effect of this is to tend to refract sound waves upwards, away from the sea, thus forming ... an 'acoustic shadow zone'." This would tend to diminish sound intensity much more rapidly than expected.

Tentative air and water temperatures from the *Titanic* and *Californian* made Dr. R.W.B.Stephens (of the Department of Physics of the Imperial College of Science and Technology) think that the sound of the detonating rockets would tend to turn back towards the sea. And

Mr. D.A.S.Little, Technical Director of Pains-Wessex Ltd., the successors to one of the suppliers of the Cotton Powder Signals who manufactured the signals used by the *Titanic* herself, noted that "...the only sound would be from socket distress signals, and these I would consider to have a range of *3-5 miles*." [Emphasis by Reade.]

There is indeed evidence of abnormal acoustics on the night the *Titanic* went down. With one exception, none of the lifeboats, neither those ones closest nor furthest away from the *Carpathia*, heard the rescue ship's rockets as they detonated. The single exception was boat 13, and Lawrence Beesley took sufficient note of it to mention it in his book, where he describes it as "a faint boom like guns afar off." It was enough to attract the attention of the stoker at the tiller: "That was a cannon!" And yet no-one else heard a thing that night. It is difficult to place where boat 13 was in relation to the *Titanic*; Beesley thought they could be any distance from a mile to two miles away from the wreck when she sank, but that their erratic path led him to think that they could not be very far from the *Titanic*. In an interview in the 1960s with the elderly survivor, Leslie Reade asked Beesley how long the interval was between hearing the rocket and seeing the *Carpathia*. Beesley carefully replied that it was between half and three quarters of an hour. Although Reade accepts a dubious 17 knot speed for the *Carpathia*, the distance was probably at least some 7 to 11 miles, using her maximum speed of 14 ½ knots. Beesley's book remarks that the *Carpathia's* mast lights came into view after the rocket was heard. The height of the aftermost (higher) mast light can be estimated using photographs and the known dimensions of the *Carpathia*, and a height of about 100 feet seems reasonable. From a vantage point in the lifeboats of about 4

---

274   These conditions are ideal for "looming."

feet above the water, this leads to a distance between the *Carpathia* and boat 13 of about 14 miles.

2nd Officer Lightoller, perched along with other survivors atop the upturned collapsible lifeboat 'B' testified that he never heard the rockets. His boat floated off the *Titanic* as she foundered, and was obviously very close to the actual wrecksite, having no motive power and drifting in the current. He could not have been more than a few miles from boat 13, and yet, in those few miles, the sound intensity had gone from cannon-like to silence. Obviously, there was a mechanism at work that attenuated sound far greater than would be expected using conventional physics.

Perhaps this might explain why, in the handbook of the International Mercantile Marine – a combine to which the *Californian* and the *Titanic* belonged, and issued to its officers, it says, "At best, sound signals are but auxiliaries," reinforcing Mr. Reynold's qualified technical opinion above.
The primary method for summoning help, as the I.M.M. tells its crews, is through visual means, which can be detected further than aural means alone.

But Reade contradicts himself on one important matter; in a section describing the *Titanic's* movements after the contretemps with the iceberg, he sees an opportunity to attack Harrison, who had sought to prove that that the White Star liner had not moved, "because obviously there wasn't another ship [nearby] to steam to. This completely disproves that the *Californian* was near the *Titanic*." Harrison's various pronouncements were such that he maintained that the damage to the *Titanic* was "really very limited", that she remained "an effective ship" and that "she could have continued steaming in any direction." After discussing the nature of the iceberg damage, which amounted to only 12 square feet (but spread over a length of some 250 feet), Reade quotes Sir Ivan Thompson, that Harrison's description of the *Titanic* being "an effective ship" was "reckless rubbish ... of course if this suggestion [viz. that the *Titanic* should, or could have steamed on after the collision] was followed ... she would have sunk before any boats could be lowered, and all would have been lost."

Immediately following this quote from Thompson, Reade then discusses evidence that the *Titanic* did indeed commence steaming again, thereby defeating Thompson's own comments on the matter! Reade is quite confident that "during the brief period of steaming ... [Captain Smith must have realised] that to continue [steaming] would have sunk his crippled ship within minutes, rather than hours." Without recourse of some form of psychic communication (necessary since Captain Smith died in the disaster), we can only guess at the reasons for him ordering the ship to move on.

Needless to say, both Reade and Thompson had reasons to make Harrison look as foolish and misguided as possible.

If anything, this shows just how keen Reade was to lap up any information that could damage Leslie Harrison's and/or Captain Lord's case. But there is more evidence that Reade and Thompson were unduly harsh on Harrison's "effective ship" statement: Lawrence Beesley was an especially ardent observer of events, as he was on his first voyage on a ship. He writes in his contemporary book that, while reading in bed, he noticed an extra heave from the engines as they officers tried to dodge the deadly iceberg, and then felt the cessation of movement of the ship. He made two trips to the top deck, each trip ascending and descending four flights of stairs, taking care to compare notes with stewards and other passengers, and also to dress to combat the icy weather. On his second trip aloft, he recalls the cover being thrown off lifeboat 16, on the port rear side of the boat deck. He also noticed that that the *Titanic* was slowly proceeding. As he descended back to his D deck cabin, he met a pair of ladies who were nervous about the state of the ship. Beesley led them along the corridor, where he invited them to put their hands on the side of the bath, to feel the faint vibrations of the massive engines a few decks below them. Satisfied, they retired back to their cabins. *Titanic* was moving, undoubtedly, and Reade's and Thompson's hypothesis is proven false.

Beesley's observations may also help to explain the disparity between Lord's and Groves' London evidence. The former has seen the other ship stop at 11.30; the latter, ten minutes after. Could it be that Lord saw the *Titanic* stop and coast to a halt after hitting the iceberg, and Groves saw her stop – for good – after her engines were restarted? The difference between the accepted time of the collision (11.40) and Lord's evidence could easily be accounted for by a difference in local time aboard the respective ships.

How long were the engines running after the crash? When did the *Titanic* stop? When were her engines restarted, and for how long? Based on surviving crew member's experiences, the lifeboats were readied and swung out between 10 and 20 minutes after the collision: this would be consistent with Beesley's meanderings around the decks after the collision. We do know that 1st Officer Murdoch on the bridge ordered the engines full speed astern at the time he saw the 'berg, but how long would the *Titanic* have coasted on? Evidence is lacking, but we have information that the *Olympic*, while moving at 18 knots (c.f. the *Titanic's* 22 ½), was tested by reversing her engines, and she came to a stop after 3 minutes and 15 seconds. This seems like a reasonable estimate for the time it would take for the *Titanic* to slow to a complete stop, and yet Beesley saw – and felt – the ship proceeding on many minutes after this. The obvious answer is that the engines were restarted at some point. And yet the *Titanic* hadn't sunk immediately, as Thompson had confidently asserted. In fact, Thompson used this "effective ship theory" in yet another tiresome broadside aimed at Harrison: "I have always known that Harrison thought he could just make statements and nobody would question him – e.g. The *Titanic* could have steamed for five miles in any direction after the collision."

A valid criticism is that Reade's book does rely somewhat heavily on the recollections of two people very much opposed to Captain Lord; Sylvia Lightoller and the aforementioned Ivan Thompson. The former was prepared to swear to a false statement and the latter was slightly 'economical with the truth' when he said that he resigned the M.M.S.A. Presidency due to accusations levelled against the *Mount Temple* in 1962. Neither of these 'fibs' are mentioned in '*The Ship That Stood Still*', and under-informed readers may be left with the impression that both of these sources are unimpeachable. Groves is, of course, elevated to the status of 'star witness,' although to his credit, Reade is more circumspect about Gill and his improbable tale.

Returning to Thompson, information that he had provided is both fascinating and credible, such as the letter that he had written to Walter Lord in 1968, which was expanded upon by Reade through his own work. Thompson had written to Walter saying that "I have always been bitter... [Lord] was stopped in ice for the first time and he was determined not [to] move before daylight... that was the right thing to do, as long as nothing happened and of course something did happen... [Lord] would not take any risks in going to a vessel which might have got into trouble [unreadable] proceeding through the ice. Throughout 1912 despite Rostron's heroic dash we, that is Officers of British Ships were given a pretty poor time in the States because of Lord's cowardice. I remember a couple of weeks in the early summer in Mobile, Ala., when nobody wanted to know us," and, during a night's watch serving on the SS *Andania* in 1916[275], Captain Rostron said to Thompson, "You know this is just like the *Titanic* night except that it is not quite as cold" The conversation turned to the *Californian*. [Thompson] said [to Rostron], "Bisset, Dean, Barnish and Rees[276] had all said they watched the *Californian* get underway that morning about 10/12 miles away and they said they had told you." Rostron replied, 'I know they did so did a couple of passengers but I didn't see her until she was only a couple of miles away – I had other things on my mind' ... One of my old friends knew Stone and he told me that by the end of 1912 Stone was telling his friends and shipmates that he <u>did</u> think they were distress signals but they 'couldn't get the old man out of the chart room.' "[emphasis in original letter][277]

Mentioning the pro-Lord campaigns orchestrated by Harrison, Thompson writes, "I have a copy of the M.M.S.A. minutes on all the legal actions taken to suppress any mention of the *Californian* and believe me they are legion!"

Reade's own correspondence with Thompson confirms the account above, and in places, enhances it: "I sailed with Bisset on many ships. Dean, Barnish and Rees ... were all shipmates and friends. They were all adamant that they saw the *Californian* stopped ten miles away when they arrived at the *Titanic's* position. All three watched her approach, while they were busy with the *Titanic's* boats. They told me this. Bisset certainly wasn't the only one who saw her approaching. Rees

---

275   Perhaps a mistake for 1917; Rostron commanded the *Andania* for one voyage only, from Liverpool to New York on its 13th March voyage that year and back again.

276   The other officers on the Carpathia in 1912

277   Compare this with Mainwaring's letter to Walter Lord, referred to earlier.

was an emotional Welshman, and when we were ship mates on the *Laconia*, there were several occasions when he walked out of the wardroom because Lord's name was mentioned ... I sailed under Rostron's command in several ships, including the first *Mauretania*, and we often talked *Titanic*. He was sorry for Lord (weren't we all?), but he used to refer to him as, 'That silly man who wouldn't use his wireless.'"

Readers will recall Rostron's New York affidavit that he did not observe the *Californian* until 8am on the morning of April 15th It seems that Rees, Barnish and Dean had asked Rostron about this. Thompson also questioned Rostron on this matter and he was told, "Dean and others, and some passengers, said they saw the *Californian* and watched her approach. Well, I was mistaken [about seeing her for the first time at 8am]. I had so much to do, I wasn't thinking of the *Californian* and didn't recognise her."

If Thompson (whose low opinion of Captain Lord is self admitted) can be trusted, this discussion with Rostron happened sooner, rather than later, after the *Titanic* disaster when details were still fresh in Rostron's mind. And if true, it "knocks a prop" from beneath Captain Lord's defence, as Reade would later put it.

But Harrison was unconvinced about the contents of Thompson's letters. "From Mr. Reade's book, it appears that Sir Ivan must have acquired this astounding information during his seagoing days, and certainly before his retirement in 1957[278]. If so, why did he keep it a secret from his colleagues at that crucial meeting of the M.M.S.A.'s Finance Committee on 15th July 1958? It was then that Captain Lord's case was brought before the M.M.S.A. Council members for the first time and formal approval given for it to be taken up. The general feeling at that meeting was most uneasy, however, and I am personally quite confident that the merest mention of Sir Ivan's 'inside knowledge' from the *Carpathia* would have tipped the scales and no more would have been heard of Captain Lord's approach," he wrote[279]. "There can only be one credible explanation for Sir Ivan's inaction. The *Carpathia* evidence attributed to him must have been concocted at a relatively late stage ... what is inescapable is the fact that the emphasis placed through Leslie Reade's book on 'evidence' attributed to Sir Ivan Thompson about the *Carpathia's* Captain and officers is completely unreliable and so should be disregarded. In fact, its elimination could well be said to rip the heart out of the book."

A fair comment, one might say. But Harrison's speculation that Reade may have been involved in its 'preparation' is ill-founded, as Sir Ivan had told Walter Lord practically the same information, independently to Reade. Why Sir Ivan did not mention it at the M.M.S.A. Council meeting is unknown, but between then, and his letters to Walter Lord and Reade, Sir James Bisset's book had been published with the same 'close proximity' accusation. Indeed, Sir Ivan had even met Bisset at one point in Australia. Thompson may have been reminded of Rostron's story by

---

278   Obviously, as Rostron was dead when Thompson retired!
279   "*A Titanic Myth part 2*" pages 150-151.

Bisset's recollections.

The *coup de grâce* of the book is Reade's letter from – and subsequent meeting with – Herbert Stone's son, John. Herbert had died some six years previously and Reade was eager to prove a statement oft mentioned in Liverpool[280], but never confirmed, that the old 2nd Officer had known that he was watching distress rockets. John's letter partially reads, "My father never, at any time discussed with me or with my brother and sister his part in the '*Titanic*' story. But my mother tells me (and this is all that she will tell) that, as you say, he was sure that distress rockets were being fired. As you say, he was in a very difficult position, as a very young 2nd Officer, on the threshold of his sea career. But there is no doubt that he felt very deeply about it and was extremely troubled at the time of the Inquiry. Knowing my father, and here I speak of my knowledge of him as a man, not as his son, I am quite sure that he would never do anything dishonourable and he would always do his duty. There is no doubt this unfortunate episode had a great effect upon his career as he never commanded his own ship, although colleagues have praised his seamanship."

Reade then turns to Lawrence Beesley and his 'fathering' of the 1968 M.M.S.A. Petition. Reade has this to say: "With nothing but pity for Captain Lord, and an amiable desire to help his supporters, Mr. Beesley's scientifically trained mind nevertheless would not allow him to lend the support of his name to plain nonsense. It is, therefore, not only relevant, but due to his memory, to state here that only a few months before his death, and more than three years after signing his only statutory declaration dealing with the *Titanic*, Mr. Beesley sent for [Leslie Reade]. While discussing the evidence of Stone and Gibson about the 'queer lights', Captain Lord's [newspaper] statements in Boston, and Herbert Stone's confession, all of which greatly impressed the old man, and the two last of which he had not known, he firmly declared that he had no doubt that the *Californian* had seen the *Titanic* and her rockets. That, and not this posthumous petition ... was Lawrence Beesley's last word on the subject." Reade continues in his summary that Harrison had placed great pressure on Beesley to sign his affidavit; an allegation that would have extremely severe consequences for the book after publication. But, according to the book, Beesley himself does not mention this 'pressure'.

Reade's/de Groot's book was a moderate success, but achieved somewhat limited publicity in *Titanic* circles. The T.H.S., for instance, did not review it, but later gave much publicity to "*A Titanic Myth part 2*," printed to offset Reade's damaging book.. Harrison suggested to a member of the British Titanic Society that he "do something" about Reade's book; the member reacted by telling Harrison that his attempt to stifle the anti-Lord viewpoint was "morally reprehensible."

---

280   Indeed, even Ivan Thompson had heard this story from "a friend" of Stone, who had related it to him in 1912. This was during the Everton-Arsenal football match on October 2nd, 1963.

Some commentators bemoaned the book's reliance on elderly people to provide information to bolster its case against Lord. One of these critics was Leslie Harrison, in his sequel to his previous book, *"A Titanic Myth part 2: Defending Captain Lord"*[281] Other commentators were impressed by the quantity of new information that had been unearthed by Harrison's nemesis.

But criticisms were also levelled at Reade's book for its selective use of evidence; this may be of not matter as the same was also said about Harrison's publications to a larger extent in *Titanic* circles.. An example of Reade's selectivity occurs on page 55 where he says, "Fifth Officer Lowe in his sworn statement before the British Consulate General in New York said: 'As I was putting over the starboard emergency boat (about 1 a.m. [Reade's inclusion]) somebody mentioned something about a ship on the port bow. I glanced in that direction and saw a steamer ... When I had got these boats tied together'[282] – which would have been after 2 a.m. - 'I *still* saw these [lights] *in the same position...*'" [All emphasis by Reade].

Lowe's complete statement in May 1912 states that, when he first glanced over at the boat in the distance, he saw a red light about 5 miles to the northward. However, after seeing the light in the same location, he went on to say that "... and shortly afterwards she seemed to alter her position and open her green [light]. I knew a few minutes afterwards all the lights went out, and I did not see any more lights until I saw the lights of the *Carpathia*."

Obviously, the second section was omitted because it supported the notion of a ship that had moved away, contrary to the *Californian's* motion, or lack thereof. However, lest it be ignored, Boxhall had said that he saw the other ship's green light before the red. Lowe seemed to describe a ship that had turned in the opposite direction to Boxhall's. Of interest is that Lowe placed the light to the north, off the port bow; in other words, he was stating that the *Titanic* was pointing in a northerly direction.

Like Walter Lord, cartography is not one of Reade's strong points. The Reade/de Groot combine misinterpret the maps of the ice fields, which had been shuffled into an appendix, ignoring Captain Moore's testimony which placed the SOS location to the west of the ice field, and also ignoring the myriad observations and data that describe a north-west to south-east configuration of the ice, preferring Captain Knapp's mythical layout. The charts presented in Reade's book "...clearly

---

281   Slightly hypocritical, as Harrison had relied on Captain Lord's affidavit, written when he was about 81, and information obtained from Lawrence Beesley (84) and Californian crewman Benjamin Kirk (78). But then again, Harrison had relied on people who were there, and not on the descendants of witnesses, such as the sons of the uncalled Californian witnesses (Ross and Glenn) and Herbert Stone.

282   As Reade notes, "After leaving the *Titanic* in No.14 at about 1.30 a.m., Lowe had rounded up boats 4, 10, 12 and D, and had them tied up with his own boat and took command of all five."

show the ice field in a north-east to south-west[283] direction with the *Titanic's* position on the eastern side of the ice field, where it logically should be." But of the four maps shown, the scale on one (prepared in 1915) is so large as to be useless, Knapp's map incorrectly shows the icefield, and a sketch by the *Birma's* Captain shows the ice field between the SOS location and the area where the *Carpathia* picked up the lifeboats. '*The Ship That Stood Still*' of course, disses Foweraker's map, with the barbed comment that "...the direction of the icefield on the sketch, which is almost directly north-south, and thus placing the *Titanic's* CQD position to the west of the icefield, whereas she undeniably sank and on the same side where the *Californian* had been during the night." But this is *precisely* what *did* happen! Here Reade constructs, and then destroys a strawman. In fact, the whole book cannot seem to make up its mind about whether the *Titanic's* CQD position is correct or not, and seems to suffer from the editing that occurred between the Reade epoch and the de Groot phase of preparation.

And of course, all the sketch maps of the ice fields and ship movements in the book display a north-south configuration. These maps were prepared by de Groot. So much for consistency in one's statements.

Another lapse of logic[284] occurs in a discussion regarding the departure of the *Carpathia* from the scene of the disaster. The information comes in the form of a Marconigram, sent from the *Carpathia* to New York, which was published in the *New York Times* on 17th April 1912. The message is timed 7.55am:

"Latitude 41 45; longitude 50 20 west – Am proceeding New York unless otherwise ordered, with about 800...."

Reade would want the reader to obtain the impression that Captain Lord's navigation is inaccurate, and that his calculation of 41°33' N 50°01' W (where he

---

283   Other than the *Trautenfels* SW-NE orientation of the icefield, the only other mention of directionality in Lloyd's publications for early/mid April are as follows: "*Empress of India* April 8th – 43 28 N, 49 36 W observed ice field with bergs as far as eye could see from NW to SE"; "*Excelsior* April 10th – lat 41 50 long 50 25 passed a large icefield in a NNE direction, a few hundred feet wide and at least 15 miles in extent"; "*Corby* April 12th – 42 N 49 45 W passed two large icebergs and passed through quantity of field ice extending in a NNE and SSW direction"; "*Rosalind* April 7th – 45 10 N 56 40 W strip field ice 3-4 miles wide extending N & S"; "*Borderer* April 13th – 41 50 N, 50 1 W, ice extending N & S"; "*Kintail* April 12th lat 44 long 46 18 to April 13th lat 44 30 long 49 20 passed field ice. Steamed 40 miles around one pack of field ice shaped like the letter 'S'"; "*Messina* April 11th – lat 44 10 long 48 25 closely packed ice extending for many miles in a NW and SE direction"; "*Minnesota* April 12th – lat 42 long 49 55 passed through field ice about 2 miles wide and extending to the NE and SW as far as the eye could see"; "*Minnesota* April 12th – lat 42 long 49 35 loose field ice extending about 2 miles E & W and to the horizon SW-NE"

284   "*The Ship That Stood Still*" page 134

left the wreckage a few hours later) is wrong, in a dishonest attempt to create as much distance between the *Titanic* and the *Californian* as possible. As Reade says, "It is difficult to believe early on that Monday morning, 15th April, Captain Rostron had begun fabricating evidence against [Lord], for whose misfortune he actually felt and expressed the greatest sympathy. Nevertheless Rostron's latitude was much more north than that found by the *Californian.*"

Let us analyse the position as given by Rostron at this time. The latitude is 1 degree north of the wreck site, and 1 degree south of the CQD/SOS location. It is difficult to know what "7.55am" refers to. If it means New York time, then this would be a local time of approximately 9.55am. The longitude is about 4 ½ miles west of the CQD position, or 17 ½ miles west of the distress position. Obviously, with the *Carpathia* staying at the wreck site until 9.00am, the originator of the Marconigram assumed that the *Carpathia*, having reached the "correct" latitude of 41 45N, simply steamed practically due west. This is simply inaccurate. To do so would have meant steaming through the ice field that the *Californian* had just traversed. Rostron would probably have not exposed his passengers and crew to more peril. Furthermore, we have the recollections of Rostron himself[285] and a few others: all state that the *Carpathia* steamed around the ice, this route taking many hours. Indeed, she passed the SS *Birma* when she rounded the southern tip of the field and started to head back towards New York[286]. Thus, it seems that the latitude and longitude of the *Carpathia* upon leaving the wreck scene is inaccurate and no-one knew for sure exactly where she was. At 9.55am, she would still be to the east of the massive ice field; the "7.55am" message places her well to the west.

So, one more "fact" used to discredit Captain Lord amounts to no more than a grasping attempt to belittle the *Californian*.

"The Ship That Stood Still" labours one point time and again; that, of all the navigators at sea the night the *Titanic* sank, only Captain Lord pushed the White Star giant's position far south, well below 41° 46'N, and thus "proved" that they were too far apart to be seen, at 41° 33' N., 50° 1' W. Lord's opinion was that this was the true collision between the *Titanic* and the iceberg. It was wrong of him to do this, but it does demonstrate that neither Lord nor Harrison never considered the issue of drift, an interesting lapse for so-called 'Master Mariners.'

Corroboration exists for this southerly latitude, in so far as the *Californian* leaving the wreckage on April 15th; this is nowhere mentioned in Reade's book. Captain Knapp compiled a list of known ships movements on the night of 14th-15th April 1912[287] . One of these was the SS *Frankfurt*, bound east for Bremerhaven

285   These can be found in the following sources: *"Home from the Sea"* by Rostron, *"Tramps and Ladies"* by Bisset and *Carpathia* passenger Luke Hoyt 's letter at http://www.numa.net/expeditions/Carpathia_letter.html
286   This was at 12.15pm (local time) according to a statement given by Captain Stulping of the *Birma*, and archived at the UK Public Records Office
287   http://www.titanicinquiry.org/U.S.Inq/AmInq17KnappMemo03.php

from Galveston. Hearing the SOS call, she headed for the radioed distress location and arrived at the uncorrected location (41° 44' N., 50° 24' W) at about 10.50am that morning. She steamed south east, and at 41° 35' N., 50° 15' W, she encountered the *Californian*. This is only 2 miles north of the latitude where Lord and his crew left the *Titanic's* floating debris. Indeed, Lord mentioned this in Washington: "I met [the *Frankfurt*] 5 or 10 minutes past 12, after I was leaving the *Titanic*, the scene of the disaster. He was running along parallel with the ice, apparently trying to find an opening, and he saw me coming through and he headed for the place I was coming out, and as I came out he went in. He went through the same place toward the scene of the disaster.... He was running about south-southeast, when I saw him, coming away from the northwest."

Such corroboration of Lord's navigation is studiously missing from "*The Ship That Stood Still.*"

"The "last, and clinching detail" against Captain Lord is explored in a diagram on page 149 of Reade's book, where the rockets seen from the *Californian*, and the rockets fired from the *Titanic* are compared in a diagram. Most of the comparison is fairly represented and shows that the events on the two ships are arguably consistent with each other, but the text describing the last rocket is misleading. The diagram is depicted below.

From the *Titanic*, it is stated that, "Boxhall later saw the other ship's red sidelight alone. He fired one more rocket, his last. Eight in all, Lightoller said. The last went off about 1.30am" The *Californian's* view of the other ship is given as: "Stone and Gibson saw the other ship fire an 8th rocket, which proved to be the last. Gibson noticed the *Californian* was then heading towards the west, when she must have been showing her red light alone to the other ship. It was then about 1.30am."

This is hardly an accurate statement of what was seen. Gibson said that the last rocket was fired when the other ship was "about one point on the port bow". If the other ship had an initial bearing of S 45 E, and if Stone was wrong about the other ship steaming away, then the *Californian* must have been heading S 33.75 E. However, Reade and de Groot's contention is that there was a simple north-south relationship between the two ships; therefore the *Californian* would have been heading S 22.5 W. Heading "towards the west" is a gross oversimplification. However, the *Californian* would definitely have been showing her red light, and two mastlights.

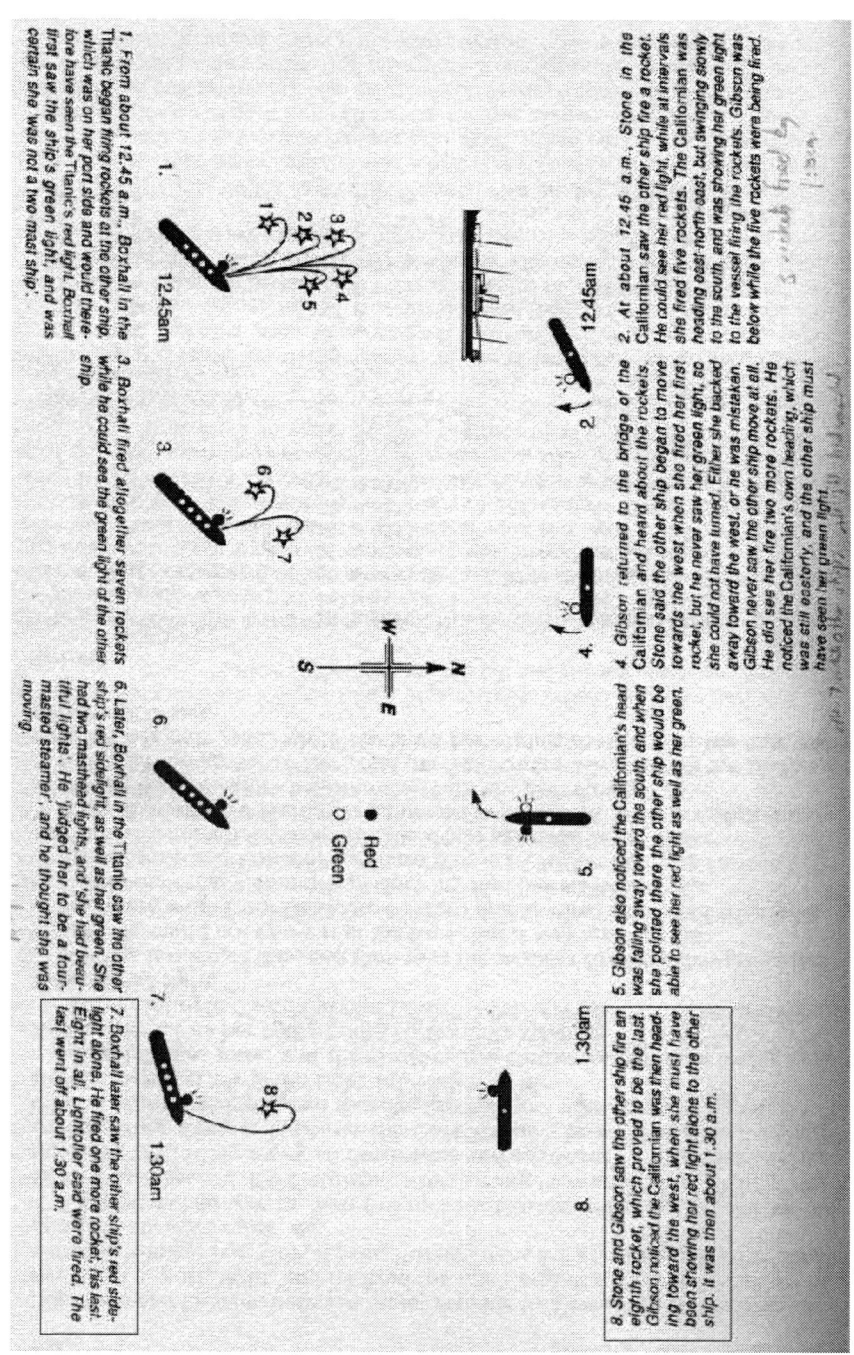

1. From about 12.45 a.m., Boxhall in the Titanic began firing rockets at the other ship, which was on her port side and would therefore have seen the Titanic's red light. Boxhall first saw the ship's green light, and was certain she was not a two-mast ship.

1. 12.45am

2. At about 12.45 a.m. Stone in the Californian saw the other ship fire a rocket. He could see her red light, while at intervals she fired five rockets. The Californian was heading east-north-east, but swinging slowly to the south, and was showing her green light to the vessel firing the rockets. Gibson was below while the five rockets were being fired.

2. 12.45am

3. Boxhall fired altogether seven rockets while he could see the green light of the other ship.

3.

4. Gibson returned to the bridge of the Californian and heard about the rockets. Stone said the other ship began to move towards the west when she fired her first rocket, but he never saw her green light, so she could not have turned. Either she backed away toward the west, or he was mistaken. Gibson never saw the other ship move at all. He did see her fire two more rockets. He noticed the Californian's own heading, which was still easterly, and the other ship must have seen her green light.

4.

5. Gibson also noticed the Californian's head was falling away toward the south, and when she pointed there the other ship would be able to see her red light as well as her green.

5.

● Red
○ Green

6. Later, Boxhall in the Titanic saw the other ship's red sidelight as well as her green. She had two masthead lights, and 'she had beautiful lights'. He 'judged her to be a four-masted steamer', and he thought she was moving.

6. 1.30am

7. Boxhall later saw the other ship's red side-light alone. He fired one more rocket, his last. Eight in all; Lightoller said were fired. The last went off at about 1.30 a.m.

7.

8. Stone and Gibson saw the other ship fire an eighth rocket, which proved to be the last. Gibson noticed the Californian was then heading toward the west, when she must have been showing her red light alone to the other ship. It was then about 1.30 a.m.

8. 1.30am

Illustration 41: From The Ship That Stood Still, this diagram alleges to show the relationship between the Titanic and the Californian. However, the text denoted in the boxes are hardly a fair and accurate description of events that night.

351

Then we must consider Boxhall. While it is true that he saw the red light at one point in the evening, just before he left the *Titanic*, he then says of the other vessel that "[when] I got into the boat she seemed as if she had turned around. I saw just one single bright light then, which I took to be her stern light." He should have seen the red (port) light at this time. This contradiction to his carefully crafted timeline would shatter Reade's hypothesis, but it is not mentioned. How can the observation of the white light be resolved? No attempt is made to do so, but a possible solution is explored in Appendix C.

But these lapses are more than compensated for by the remarkable detective work of the authors in uncovering new leads, and unearthing new sources. Compared to the startling list of omissions from Harrison's works, Reade's few exclusions are but trifles.

Only one day had elapsed since the press conference to release the book; indeed, it was not yet even available to the public[288]. And yet, on April 1st, 1993, Leslie Harrison's solicitors wrote to Haynes publishing, with two sets of instances in the book that had caused offence to the retired M.M.S.A. secretary. These instances were the allegations that Harrison had pressurised Lawrence Beesley into signing a false affidavit; and that Harrison had not only withdrawn permission for Reade to use a photograph of him, but also excerpts from an audio interview with Captain Lord. Reade's/de Groot's book had indicated that this had destroyed the attempted printing of the previous incarnation of *"The Ship That Stood Still"* in 1975.

Haynes replied that there was nothing in the book about which Harrison could complain, but did concede to make a slight change to future reprints, where the word 'unconditionally' would be removed from the description of Reade's use of Harrison's research. But this would only happen if agreeable by Harrison and Stanley Tutton Lord[289], and then, only if this would put an end to any further complaint.

Haynes turned to de Groot for assistance, and he assured them that "... there never was any wording [that the material was for personal use] in Harrison's contact and correspondence with Leslie [Reade]. It was first mentioned when Harrison withdrew his permission to use material, like the tape and his picture."

But this was not the end of it. Later communications between the two side's legal teams revealed that "money means nothing," and that a public apology was

---

288   How did Harrison react so quickly to the contents of the book? Remember that, in his letter to Captain Lord's son only a short time before, he seemed to be oblivious as to what was in the book.

289   Stanley Tutton Lord would die in December 1994, before any agreement between Harrison and Haynes could be reached.

the important thing. Haynes noted that producing evidence that would persuade a court would be expensive and difficult; the process of producing lists of Discovery[290] would be "horrific".

Harrison gave permission to serve the libel case on St. Valentine's day 1994. His solicitor was Miss Heather Rogers[291], "a member of the outstanding team led by Mr. George Carman who recently achieved fame by obtaining record damages for entertainer Elton John," he told Stanley T. Lord. The writ was issued on 27th May and served on June 9th. Such high profile legal advice and representation does not come cheap. Was someone bankrolling Harrison to destroy *"The Ship That Stood Still"*? Haynes thought so, and had a culprit in mind...

Legal discussions between Haynes' and Harrison's legal teams protracted the arguments for the next few years and no "quick settlement" seemed forthcoming. Harrison's side advised Haynes that, "Counsel has advised that should this matter proceed to trial a jury would be likely to award [Harrison] substantial damages. Your delay in sending a defence to the claim confirms our view that there is no defence to Mr. Harrison's claim." Harrison's legal team would later write that, since the book had been on sale for two years, something more than a simple apology in court would have to be conceded, and to "remove any doubt from a reader's mind" regarding Harrison's reputation, a payment of substantial damages must be made. A figure of £25,000 was suggested.

But Haynes were indeed searching for defence material. De Groot has sifted through Reade's letters and research and had found a few examples that demonstrated ill-will by Harrison. It is a matter of conjecture how such material, decades old, would have fared in court against a "live" appearance by Harrison in the witness stand. The main point was the Beesley evidence and the allegation that someone keen to support Captain Lord's cause had influenced the elderly gentleman in his recollections. To Haynes, and de Groot's mind, the 'fanatical person' who had swayed Beesley's mind was none other than Harrison himself; but the retired Master Mariner's lawyers had already used information already contained in *"A Titanic Myth"* to argue that someone else must have obtained an affidavit from Beesley. At about the same time as Harrison. On the same subject. Coincidence?[292]

---

290   In legal terms, Discovery refers to the act of sifting through the opposing claimant's material to find instances of information that may help the client. For instance, Haynes and its lawyers would be granted access to Harrison's research, and Harrison's legal team would be allowed to search through Reade's and de Groot's archives; anything found could be used by either legal teams.

291   Ms. Rogers later served on the legal team that successfully defended Professor Deborah Lipstadt against Holocaust denier David Irving.

292   See http://home.earthlink.net/~dnitzer/3Harrison/Beesley1.html for more information. In a letter to Reade dated 17th August, Mrs. Wade, Beesley's daughter, admitted that she knew little of the *Titanic* matter and that maybe she should be bothered enough to find out more. In this respect, and perhaps knowing that Harrison's

Haynes' lawyers scrutinised the proposed defence material. In addition to the letters from Ivan Thompson, which showed Harrison's fixation with Captain Lord's case, there was a letter from Harrison to Reade (31/7/64) in which a copy of the interview with Lord had been provided "as a guide to Captain Lord's character for your personal use" to the latter author. In all other cases, without exception, whenever Harrison had specified that certain material was for Reade's private use, he always indicated this: the letter in which Harrison provided a picture of himself did not use these exacting words. Reade, when his book was delayed in 1975, tried to argue that he was justified in using extracts from the audio recording in his book because this did not constitute professional use as would an author or journalist. He wrote to Harrison's lawyers, "When stating that the copy tape was to be 'for your personal use', this referred to, and could only refer to, my personal use of it in connexion with the book I was writing." In this respect, it is very hard to understand what Reade was saying, but the tone of his letter was clear: he was furious at the veto. He had to rely on the few snippets that were in the public domain, and he accordingly rewrote huge sections of his manuscript. This was completed by the end of 1975, and a 500 page type set version was even prepared by the U.S. Naval Press for distribution in the United States. It is unclear why the project was not taken up again.

Harrison's photo was not under such restrictions. On 14th June 1971, he was agreeable to providing a picture, as he was told, for Reade's book. On 23rd April 1975, he wrote that "[he] had now changed [his] mind," and formally withdrew permission for his picture to be reproduced.

Beesley's evidence was slightly more complicated. The legal recommendation was that Mrs. Wade's evidence was "apparently unreliable", but why counsel felt this was not made clear; this may be due to the fact that she admitted that she knew nothing about the *Titanic* and that "perhaps for [Reade's] sake, I should know [more about it]." Mr. Beesley's "entirely coherent letters of 14/1/63 to Reade and 3/4/63 to the Plaintiff [made counsel believe that the] defence to the 'statutory declaration allegation' is likely to fail." Presumably, if, as has been claimed, Beesley had wanted to retract his declaration shortly after Harrison's meeting, his letter to Harrison would not have been so cordial. Additionally, it was pointed out that Mr. Harrison wanted the contents of Beesley's book to be confirmed not altered, and that the statutory declaration was in addition to the account in his book. "So far as Mr. Reade was concerned, this modification[293] is immaterial since Beesley's recollection of timing had always been wrong (about 50

---

arguments revolved around the issue of timing, she may have guessed – incorrectly – that Beesley's time of the collision with the iceberg was being questioned.

293   By 'modification', the lawyer meant Beesley seeing eight rockets and stating that all 8 had been fired by the time his lifeboat had left; in his original book, Beesley had only mentioned seeing three rockets.

minutes too early), even in his book of 1912." If only the Haynes team had seen Harrison's "book we managed to kill" quote in the *Westcountry Morning News*, they would have had no doubts at all that his only intention was to suppress Reade's work.

So, what was contained in Mrs. Wade's letters to Reade that would have been used, heaven forbid, in court? On 9th August 1969, Wade wrote to Reade, "I can hardly believe that the silly man Harrison is still at it [i.e. Captain Lord's case]. If he ever really got the Board of Trade to open up the case on anything in my father's wrong declaration, I really would have something to say about undue pressure on a man of 88 [sic]." And, eight days later, she wrote, "...when I say 'oh bother that fool Harrison,' it is because I can see him wearing down an old man with talk, undue pressure, and long past his bedtime until he signed the affidavit. In other words when I said I would go against anything Harrison did it was because I saw for myself that Harrison was unscrupulous in his methods[294]."

Harrison's legal team were unaware of these letters. They sent a copy of a notebook made in December 1962, which listed all Harrison's activities and appointments[295] On the day that he met Beesley, he notes that Mrs. Wade was in attendance, and that he and his companion, Stanley Williamson of the BBC, left Beesley and Wade at 6.30pm, before getting a taxi at Baker Street in London and attending a Royal Ballet performance in Covent Garden (one, or all of a triple bill of 'The Good Humoured Ladies', 'The Invitation' and 'Birthday Offering' if the Royal Ballet archives are correct), which had a probable curtain up time of 7.30pm. Whom should we believe? Wade, who saw pressure exerted on her father, which left her furious with indignation? Or Harrison, who provided 'proof' that he had not kept Beesley up 'past his bedtime' (unless the octogenarian *Titanic* survivor retired remarkably early)?

Haynes were confident that they would win, but should this not be the case, an-out-of-court settlement and an apology would be more palatable that a long legal battle in court and potentially large costs. Nevertheless, the suggested payment of £25,000 was far more than they had been expecting (£5,000). Negotiations followed, and a figure of £17,500 was agreed, which seemed to have devoured more than the profits the book had generated[296]. A statement in open court

---

294   If Mrs. Wade's opinion of her father is correct ("complicated, cold, very charming, clever within the limits of imperseptiveness [sic] and totally without morals" [her emphasis]), Mr. Beesley may have signed anything at all! It must be stated, in fairness, that Wade suffered from a bipolar disorder and her mental state was regarded in disparaging terms by her siblings. Also, Lawrence Beesley had excluded her from his will, so Mrs.Wade's judgement on Beesley may, to put it mildly, be biased!

295   The photocopies sent by Harrison's lawyers were of too poor a quality to assess if "6.30" had been added long after the meeting with Beesley.

296   The statement in open court apologising to Harrison can be found in "*A Titanic Myth part 2*" or at http://www.paullee.com/titanic/articles.html

was read out, apologizing to Leslie Harrison.

The agreement was not to reprint the old book, although a new version with amended versions of the text was permissible, and Haynes were more than happy to apply this retrospectively by recalling unsold copies for alteration and then re-distributing them. The book would ultimately go out of print.

But Harrison's predilection for causing trouble for Haynes was not over yet. During August 1996, Harrison visited his local library in Heswall and complained to a member of staff, upon seeing Reade and de Groot's tome on the shelf that, "It was annoying to be someone who has been so libelled to see the book in question still on display." He asked if there were codes of practise about withdrawing books in which defamatory comments are contained. Harrison had previously visited the library and had "given a copy of the statement in open court" to the library staff; one report says that he "waved it under the nose" of a junior member of staff and told her that she must withdraw from the library shelves "*The Ship That Stood Still.*" Haynes contacted his lawyers and said that this behaviour was in breech of clause 7.2[297] of the Deed (the agreement between Haynes and Harrison). Harrison denied the charge, but agreed to cause no problems for the publishers.

In the summer of 1996, the "Titanic International" society organised a pilgrimage on board ocean liners to rendezvous with RMS Titanic, Inc. (the salvors-in-possession) at the *Titanic's* wreck site. During the various memorials, lectures and events, the (then) CEO of RMS Titanic, Inc., the late George Tulloch, elected to hold an experiment to recreate the firing of rockets to determine how far they could be seen and heard. Although the organisers promised a set of rockets/socket signals made from the original Cotton Powder schematics, these exact recreations proved to be unavailable for reasons of cost and safety, so "off the shelf" fireworks were used. Therefore, an exact comparison between that night and the night of 14th/15th April 1912 was not possible, so only approximate conclusions could be reached. The 1996 rockets lacked the "concussion shell" that created the loud blasts in 1912 and were were set to detonate at 750 feet, comparable to the 600-800 feet mentioned in the literature at which the socket signals would detonate[298].

Two sets of rockets were fired; the first from 8 miles, and the second from 17-18 miles distant[299]. Both sets were clearly seen to detonate, but only the

---

298   "Mr. Harrison undertakes that he will raise no such claim or complaint and that he will neither threaten nor institute proceedings in any jurisdiction anywhere in the world."

298   *Voyage*, the Official Journal of *Titanic International, Inc.*, issue 25.

299   This distance was verified by radar; interestingly, the mastlights of the second

explosions from the first were heard, described as an "insignificant pop".

The decibel (dB) level for firework shells, is typically 88 to 126 dB for a spectator at 800 feet[300] Being generous, and taking the 126 dB value as a maximum value (any louder and damage would result to bystander's ears), we can work out how "loud" the resultant sound waves would be at these distances. We must bear in mind that sound waves propagate in a spherical fashion, unless they were hindered by some mechanism. In scientific parlance, the sound waves obey an inverse square wave law, such that the sound level will drop by half as you double your distance from the source. Also, bearing in mind that the decibel scale is not linear, we find a 6 dB drop every time the source to receiver distance is doubled[301].

At 8 nautical miles, the sound intensity to an observer would be 90 dB, or about the same as a jet aircraft at 300 metres altitude. At 17 miles, the sound would be 84 dB, or not too much different from the value at 8 miles. Clearly these theoretical values do not bear out the observational effects in 1996. So what is different?

Firstly, this is the best case scenario. For an 88 dB airburst, we have 52 and 46 dB respectively at the ranges mentioned above; this is about the sound of a quiet river. Secondly, we must consider the attenuation as the sound front travels through the air[302], and for this we must consider the weather; sonic propagation is highly dependant on humidity, temperature, pressure, sound frequency and wind. The weather during the 1996 experiment was warm and humid (about 80 ° F), with a slight haze. This author has heard fireworks exploding on land under similar weather conditions as the 1996 reconstructions, and, from a distance of 4 statute miles (3.5 nautical miles), the explosions were no more than almost imperceptible distant thuds[303].

How does this compare to the weather the night the *Titanic* went down? It was clear, calm (at least, at surface level) and very cold, teetering about freezing point. Humidity conditions are unknown, except for vague clues, such as

---

ship, much smaller than the *Titanic* were seen, proving that lights at sea can be seen over a great distance.

300   Roger L.Schneider, vice chairman of the International Symposium on Fireworks Society

301   An excellent calculator can be found at http://www.mcsquared.com/dbframe.htm

302   If we take the 126 dB value 'at source' and apply atmospheric attenuation calculation (80 degrees Fahrenheit, 0% humidity) at 8 n.m and 17 n.m, we find, respectively that the sound would be at the same level as 'conversation speech' and 'inaudible'. These would be a lot less if the unknown value of humidity could be factored in.

303   A slightly more accurate observation of the audible range of rockets was later determined on a night much more similar to the one on which the *Titanic* went down; New Years Eve, when celebratory rockets were fired. From a distance of some 3 nautical miles (on land, and in freezing cold conditions), nothing at all was heard.

Quartermaster Rowe seeing "whiskers round the light"; an effect generated by light filtering through ice crystals in the air[304]. Using an atmospheric absorption calculator[305] we can deduce that the dominant effects, when comparing these two extremes of rocket usage in 1912 and 1996, are air temperature, humidity and the frequency range of the sound: the latter two quantities are not known[306]. It may be that the rockets used on 1912 had a reduced range of effectiveness, at least when discussing their explosive effects but all we have are the expert opinions, which put their range at between 2 and 4 miles. But, the atmosphere is a dynamic, turbulent system, and air temperature, wind speed and direction can change as one traverses it. In the case of the 1912 and 1996 situations, we know nothing of the atmospheric effects at altitude. It may therefore be a useless exercise to compare the two time frames[307].

Other than this recreation attempt, matters on the *Californian* front had gone very cold. With more Government action extremely unlikely, there seemed to be nothing more that could be done, except, it would seem, to educate the public about the truth of the *Californian* incident.

Leslie Harrison had one last throw of the die; a small pamphlet published in April 1997, *"Captain Lord's Plight To Remember"*. He died that month, so it is his last word on the matter. In this slim volume, he describes the dialogue in the film version of *"A Night To Remember"*, contrasting it with what actually happened. Or what he says happened. In the section ironically called "The Facts", Groves[308] gets one mention, when the narrative describes Stone relieving him. The rockets seen at 3.15am are not mentioned (but then again, they were not a part of the film, so there was perhaps no need to discuss this; perhaps for the same reason, the discussion between Stone and Gibson as they watched the rockets and the

---

304   Letter from G.T Rowe to Walter Lord, 1955.

305   Again, see http://www.mcsquared.com/dbframe.htm

306   All other things being equal, at the 0% and 100% extremes of humidity, sound propagating through warm air loses more of its energy, and hence its intensity and volume, than through cold air.

307   For another possible mechanism at play that night, see http://www.encyclopedia-titanica.org/articles/rockets_wilkinson.pdf This valuable analysis proves theoretically that sound would be limited to a maximum of 10.8 nautical miles surrounding the source of detonation. Even at 8 n.m. The sound would be little more than a whisper. Note that the human ear would only be able to discern sounds above 0 dB.

308   Ironically, Groves complained about some features in the film. In a letter to Walter Lord, he pointed out that the Captain's cabin on the *Californian* was no "rabbit hutch" and was in fact larger and better furnished than the one on the *Olympic* (*Titanic's* sister ship); that the *Californian's* officer's costumes seemed to be cobbled together, and that he wishes that more attention had been paid to the clockwork detector on the Californian's Marconi apparatus, as this prevented him from hearing the *Titanic's* desperate calls for help.

"queer lights" is nowhere to be found). The rockets from the *Titanic* are again described as going up "200 to 300 feet", which amounts to a maximum visible range of 20 miles, conveniently less than the 21 miles between the *Californian's* 10.21pm DR location and the *Titanic* wrecksite, but with no mention that an observer at altitude can extend this range considerably. The international agreement on rockets as distress signals states that they were to be "fired at intervals of about a minute"[309] [sic]. Boxhall is described as abandoning his attempt to attract the other ship's attention when it was obvious that she was steaming away; there is no mention that Boxhall continued firing until he was ordered to stop and man a lifeboat by Captain Smith. In fact, Boxhall is the only *Titanic* witness mentioned. Gibson's mention that he never saw the *Californian's* other strange ship steaming away is ignored. Great credence is given to Stone's words, even though Harrison had made no attempt to trace him because of the fear of being embroiled in a controversy. Such hypocrisy.

At the end of the volume, Harrison says this: "In October 1996, however, the Minister for Aviation and Shipping formally accepted the point made in his Department's Marine Accident Investigation Branch's report of 1992 to the effect that, given the estimated distance of Captain Lord's ship from the *Titanic*, and the prevailing conditions, she would only have been able to carry out "the tasks actually carried out by the *Carpathia*, that is the rescue of those who escaped."

In conclusion, Harrison had no qualms about "*A Night To Remember*"'s continual screening, although the quote from the UK Government "renders [it] morally indefensible". He suggested a "simple but well displayed" announcement during future showings:

"Since this film was made, it has become officially accepted that Captain

---

309   Harrison was getting confused, or was perhaps confounding the issue, by mixing up two separate ways of signalling distress at night:"A gun or other explosive signal fired at intervals of about a minute" and "Rockets or shells, throwing stars of any colour or description, fired one at a time at short intervals". Of course this latter method was exactly what was being seen on the *Californian*. A further example of confusing this issue can be found at http://www.titanichistoricalsociety.org/articles/rocket.asp where, not only are the regulations regarding rockets misinterpreted and mixed, but we see the introduction of the unverified statement that "The device's report was the sound of distress." Besides, even if Boxhall only considered the use of the socket signals as "guns", which is inconsistent with his testimony, the *Californian* witnesses, unable to hear the explosions, should have regarded them as "rockets or shells", in which case the "fired ... at short intervals" description is an apt one . Ed Kamuda, for the obvious reason of exonerating Captain Lord, would write in an article describing his own communications with QM Rowe, "Attention should be given to Captain Smith's orders to fire rockets. The international code signalling distress is a rocket of any colour fired at short intervals of about a minute. Smith's five to six minute pause between firings was a fatal error and was not the correct description of signal distress!" [sic]

Lord's ship, the *Californian*, could not have been the so far unidentified ship seen from the sinking *Titanic*, and that she was too far away at the time to have played any useful part in the subsequent rescue operations. With this important reservation in mind, and recommended to patrons, the present exhibitors of the film will continue to screen it as a universally acknowledged and outstanding example of the film makers' art."

Harrison had come full circle. The very reason for his introduction to the *Californian* and Captain Lord had elicited his last words on the subject.

With Harrison dead and "*The Ship That Stood Still*" now a deceased project, other researchers came forth with ever more ingenious methods of legerdemain to twist, omit key passages or present information entirely out of context.

A recent book on the *Californian* saga was "*Titanic and the Mystery Ship*" by Senan Molony, an expanded version of "*A Ship Accused*", from a few years before[310]. It received glowing praise from Peter Padfield: "Anyone who can read this book conscientiously and remain a critic of Captain Lord merits condolence." But this is faint praise from a man who edited evidence from his own book that might have damaged the case for Captain Lord, and wavered on several vital points.

To rebut the selected evidence in Molony's book would take too long; as others have also said, to correct some of the more outrageous bald statements takes substantial effort and patience. However some demolition of his theories and statements have already been performed in areas of this current text. There seems to be a significant error, distortion or unwarranted extrapolation of fact on nearly every page. And, indeed, it is not just the text that causes problems. One photograph is captioned, "The Cable ship *Minia* demonstrates how the *Californian* might have looked when stopped in ice." This is a blatantly dishonest description. The *Californian* was surrounded by loose field ice. The photo of the *Minia* shows

---

310   Molony is already known on at least one Titanic forum, where his immature antics, personal vituperations and smug inability to debate politely had forced the foreclosure on many discussions on the Californian subject. For example, http://www.encyclopedia-titanica.org/discus/messages/6584/100461.html?1132189270 and http://www.encyclopedia-titanica.org/discus/messages/6584/100215.html for the infamous "elephants in the living room" thread, http://www.encyclopedia-titanica.org/discus/messages/6584/95010.html and http://www.encyclopedia-titanica.org/discus/messages/6584/94725.html For a "research article" on a non-*Californian* matter, see http://www.encyclopedia-titanica.org/item/5407/ and http://www.encyclopedia-titanica.org/item/5041/ but rebuttals are at http://www.encyclopedia-titanica.org/item/5400/ and http://www.encyclopedia-titanica.org/item/5409/

the ship encased in thick ice; so much so that the crew are seen gambolling around on its surface.

A truly astonishing statement in "*A Ship Accused*" and "*Titanic And The Mystery Ship*" occurs thus: "Three considerations, arguably, ought to guide the reader on the movement issue surrounding the *Titanic's* mystery ship. Firstly, most credibility must be given to those who watched that ship, being tasked to that essential duty if all aboard *Titanic* were to be saved rather than to those who commented on the basis of casual glances or impressions. Essentially that means concentrating on 4th Officer Boxhall. Secondly, weight must be placed where it properly resides for observations at sea at night: with those trained to the task. This means officers of the watch and lookouts. Thirdly, we should favour observations from the boat deck of the *Titanic* with its 70 ft [sic] vantage point above sea level, rather than impressions gained from the hopelessly unreliable sea level viewpoint of a person in a lifeboat ... Let us now examine the evidence of those men to whom we must give the greatest weight in evidence. Not *Titanic* cooks, or bedroom stewards, nor bakers nor greasers, nor even landlubber passengers. But the other officers of the RMS *Titanic*."

One could imagine that, if the above were written on parchment, the author would sign off with a conceited flourish. With three pieces of torturous logic, nearly <u>all</u> the witnesses to the mystery ship are dismissed! One can only be thankful that Courts of Law do not operate in such a way. One shudders to think of the miscarriages of justice that would occur.

The thrust of the above is that Boxhall's "moving ship" observations are the only trustworthy ones. Admittedly passengers untrained in nautical matters may be regarded as useless, but they, collectively, possess the necessary eyesight to view coloured lights at night, or whether a white light was getting fainter as it receded, steaming away. Quite how one's perceptions become "unreliable" close to sea level is never explained: it merely means that an object seen from sea level has a maximum distance closer than one seen from a higher point. One wonders what Molony makes of Boxhall's evidence, that he saw the mystery ship's stern light before the left the *Titanic*, but then lost it after he had reached the water. Does this mean that Boxhall's observations, close to the waterline, have become unreliable? Not at all, as it would cast doubt on his 'moving ship' observation. And then, those people who saw the lights of the other ship well after Boxhall, as they rowed to them as the first glimmerings of sunlight filtered over the sea, must be 'unreliable' and mistaken too, for the mystery ship would have long since left the scene.

"*Titanic and the Mystery Ship*" makes some truly astonishing leaps of logic and possesses severe distortions of evidence. For instance; the reason why Stone and Gibson do not inform Lord of the rockets seen after 3am is "Possible, also, these new rockets were just too much for Stone and Gibson on a very unusual night." Heaven knows how they would have reacted if they had indeed reached the *Titanic* before she went down! It would have yielded paroxysms from the dynamic watchkeeping duo. A more likely explanation is that the two men on the bridge had tried their best to get Lord out of the chartroom (as one of Stone's acquaintances had reported him saying) but had now given up trying to rouse their sleeping master.

Then, Molony described the Captain at the time of Gibson's visit as "Lord with his eyes closed." But Gibson remarked in London that Lord was awake when he saw him!

What of the rockets seen? We have the following: "[Quartermaster Bright's figure of only six rockets fired is] wrong ... because eight were certainly seen [by the *Californian*]. Six from [the port bridge wing] and eight from starboard. But the *Californian* saw just eight. She may have missed a number. Perhaps because she was very distant?" writes Molony. Obviously, no consideration is given to the possibility that witnesses may have been mistaken, and understandably so considering the circumstances, of the number and colour of rockets used; every witness must be correct and their conflicting statements must be merged, somehow. No mention is made of the fact that Bright's recollections are somewhat tainted: indeed, in Washington (the only time he was subjected to questioning) he could not even remember the colour of the rockets that he was helping to fire – and this was less than two weeks after the *Titanic* had gone down! Molony insists that 4th Officer Boxhall was at the starboard side, and Q.M.s Rowe and Bright were on the port side. But this neglects the communication between Rowe and Leslie Harrison (sent via an intermediary contact) for, in a letter sent on 5th March 1963, Rowe clearly states that the rockets were sent up from near lifeboat number 1, on the starboard side. And he should know, as he was helping to fire them!

We do not know exactly where the socket signal firing stations were located, but given the regulations at the time, one firing station would have been forward (starboard side) and one at the stern (at the rear of the ship, at least 500 feet or so astern[311]?) on the port side. When firing the same type of socket signals, reaching the same height, from such a short distance apart, there is no mechanism that would enable one set to be seen and not the other. Signals fired from 21 miles and reaching a minimum height of 660 feet would go above the horizon by 0.3°, or about 3/5ths the width of a full moon, and not "low down on the horizon" as the author remarks.

Molony also pronounces that, listing the four methods of procuring aid at sea at night[312], signals 1 and 4 indicate that "besides visibility, <u>audibility</u> was of prime importance" [Molony's emphasis]. If audibility was of such prime importance, then why did not all four signalling methods include some audible content? Why, for instance, does method 4: "Rockets or shells, throwing stars of

---

311   The location of the aft firing station is not known for certain, but since Q.M. Rowe described how rockets were stored in a locker directly below the aft docking bridge, the firing location may be on the poop, at the extreme stern of the ship.

312   See Appendix B

any colour or description, used one at a time at short intervals" not mention that such rockets or shells must be audible, and perhaps give an estimate of range over which the sound must be heard? The reader is reminded of the statements on sound in the I.M.M. handbook, referred to earlier, as well as expert opinion, from Reade's book.

Outside of these books, Molony's writings had focussed on the *Californian*; one example being the observations by the *Mount Temple*, and his attempts to prove that Captain Moore's statement in London, *viz*:

'And I think shortly before 8 a.m. you came in sight of the *Carpathia* and the <u>Californian</u>?' to which Moore replied, 'Yes[313].'

is correct, but this more detailed testimony in Washington isn't:

Senator SMITH: As I recollect, the Captain of the *Californian*, who was sworn yesterday, and who went to the position given by the *Titanic* in the C. Q. D., also said that he found nothing there, but cruised around this position.
Mr. MOORE: I saw the *Californian* myself cruising around there, sir.
Senator SMITH: She was there when you were there?
Mr. MOORE: She was there shortly after me, because when I came to this great pack of ice, sir, as I remarked, I went to the southeast to try to get around them because I realized that if he was not in that position - I had come from the westward - he must be somewhere to the eastward of me still. Of course, I had no idea that the *Titanic* had sunk. I had not the slightest idea of that
Senator SMITH: How near the *Carpathia* did you get that morning?
Mr. MOORE: This pack of ice between us and the *Carpathia*, it was between 5 and 6 miles. She did not communicate with me at all. When we sighted her she must have sighted us.
Senator SMITH: On which side of the ice pack was the *Californian*?
Mr. MOORE: The *Californian* was to the north, sir. She was to the north of the *Carpathia* and steaming to the westward, because, after I had come away and after giving up my attempt to get through that pack, I came back again and steered back, thinking I might pick up some soft place to the north. As I was going to the north the *Californian* was passing from east to west.
Senator SMITH: And you were also cut off from the *Carpathia* by this ice pack?
Mr. MOORE: Yes, sir; by this ice pack. He was then north of the *Carpathia*, and he must have been, I suppose, about the same distance to the north of the *Carpathia* as I was to the westward of her.

---

313   Why wasn't the reciprocal question asked, namely "At what time did you see the *Californian* and the *Carpathia*"? Captain Moore couldn't possibly know when these two ships had seen the *Mount Temple*, unless he had scrutinised the Inquiry transcripts or newspaper accounts.

Of course, this latter testimony is highly incriminating, as the only time the *Californian* passed westward through the ice with the *Carpathia* in situ at the wreck was between 6 and 6.30am in the morning: if she was in sight of the *Carpathia* then she was certainly in sight of the *Titanic*. If Moore is correct in London, then at about 6am, the *Californian* is only 5 or 6 miles to the north of where the *Titanic* would have been the night before. The word "suppose" in testimony ("He was then north of the *Carpathia*, and he must have been, I suppose, about the same distance to the north of the *Carpathia* as I was to the westward of her") has also been helpfully re-interpreted by pro-Lord authors to mean "I don't know if she was there or not", and not its true meaning, which most rational people would agree was simply used to indicate an estimate of distance. It is argued that Moore, having received the position of the *Californian* earlier would have "known" that the *Californian* had to pass from west to east to eventually head south to meet up with the *Mount Temple*. A little more thought destroys this. Moore was insistent in America that the *Titanic* must have sunk east of her distress position, not south. He knew the *Carpathia* was at the wreck site, and he could see her. Between 6 and 6.30am, the *Californian* must have been approximately 19 or so miles to the north of the *Carpathia* according to Lord's navigation. And yet Moore placed Lord and his crew 5 or 6 miles to the north of his own ship, and the *Carpathia*. How did he arrive at this estimate of distance if he couldn't see the *Californian*?

The above testimony in Washington is reinforced by statements made by Moore in *The New York Times*, on April 25th: "About 6 a.m., on the other side of an immense ice field, we saw the *Carpathia*. We also saw the *Californian*, which was to the northward of us, steaming west, then coming down to the southward, and she met us." Here is confirmation of his Washington testimony, that he saw the *Californian* heading west. Pro-Lord authors may point to the London statements, and say that Moore was mistaken in America, that either he didn't see the *Californian* at 6.30, or that he did, but from a large distance. If Captain Lord's later statements are correct, the meeting between the *Mount Temple* and his ship would be at 7.30am. At 6.30am, the *Californian* would have been about 13.5 miles to the north. At this distance, only the upper superstructure, masts, funnel and smoke would have been visible. However, let us consider this in more detail. At this range, the *Californian's* superstructure would be about the same thickness as a penny held edge-on at arm's length, with no binoculars. Surrounded by ice, and perhaps by eclipsing icebergs, and intermingled with the floes sparkling brightly in the early morning sun, it is doubtful whether anyone on the *Mount Temple* would have seen her.

There are a few other points to consider. Moore gave his interview to the press[314] on April 24th, and he provided testimony on April 27th. Captain Lord gave

---

314   This interview, given by Moore to the press, is easily found using an internet search. Why it was not found is not known. Or, it may have been found but not admitted as it would damage the author's "case".

his version of events to Senator Smith the day before, and he never mentioned his westward passage through the ice and then heading south; in fact, he never mentions seeing the *Mount Temple* at all. The first indication of this was probably his statement to the Receiver of Wrecks upon arrival in Liverpool, and then his testimony in London. If Moore had simply fabricated the movement of Lord's ship, it is astonishing that he could do it so accurately weeks before it was made public. An example of prescience? Or someone who was there and saw it happen?

One other point to consider: neglecting how far the *Mount Temple* was to the southward of the *Californian*, why should the Lordites place the former ship so far away from the *Carpathia*? Moore testified that the *Carpathia* was about 6 miles to the east, but Captain Lord and Foweraker chose to place the *Mount Temple* well to the north-west of the Cunard vessel. A case of nautical musical chairs – or placing ships wherever one's personal biases dictated?

The final points regarding the *Mount Temple* are concerned with the wireless P.V. Much nonsense has been made of an entry made in that log saying "6.0 Much Jamming. M.P.A.+ M.W.L. in sight," MPA and MWL being the *Carpathia* and *Californian* respectively. "6.0[am]" refers to New York Time; local time would be 7.46am. On the face of it, this is confirmation of Moore's London testimony, and refutation of his Washington statements. But a little more thought and analysis would have raised questions. Looking at a copy of the PV, it is obvious that "MPA + MWL in sight" has been added later. This, although in the same hand as the rest of the entries, is different to the remainder of the 6 a.m. entry; the pencilled entry appears sharper, the same as from the 7.15am New York Time entries onwards. Reproduced is a scanned version of a photocopy of the relevant page, although the clarity has suffered in the copying process. An ESDA (Electrostatic Document Analysis) test on the indentations in the page would be interesting to perform to see if such entries are truly contemporaneous; such a test has been used to prove the innocence of people previously convicted of crimes ("The Birmingham 6" in the UK, for instance).

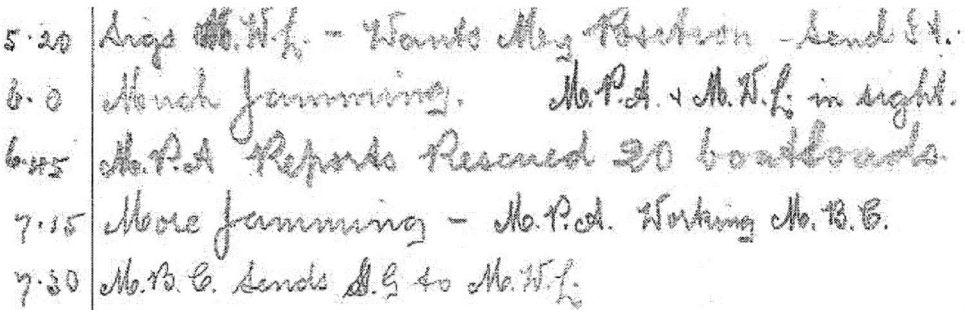

Illustration 42: Section of the Mount Temple's PV demonstrating the change in sharpness of the handwriting for the 6.00am entry, indicating that it was added later.

The copy of the *Mount Temple* PV given to the U.S. Inquiry[315] contains no mention of "MPA + MWL in sight." When, and why the extra detail was added is unknown. When Moore read out his PV in Washington, he omitted this detail about the two ships being in sight, saying simply "6.00. Much jamming." However, this Lord scholar who authored this masterpiece of research writes the following in his article as Moore recites the PV to Smith:

"6.00. Much jamming.
Senator Smith [*Interrupting*] That is, jamming his operators?
Moore: Yes, Sir: 6.45. *Carpathia* reports rescued 20 boatloads."
Moore at 6 a.m. New York time (7.46 a.m.) does not get the chance to finish the line of the actual PV, which notes that MPA (*Carpathia*) and MWL (*Californian*) are 'in sight.' Nor does he return to it after the interruption – but proceeds to the next entry."

Nowhere does the official record say that Smith interrupted Moore. The obvious inference is that Moore forgot to continue the line. It is up to the reader to decide if he did "forget", or, given the difference in the entry in the PV, whether the part about the *Californian* and *Carpathia* being in sight was added much later. Moore was not averse to repeating his testimony. Witness:
Senator SMITH: [The *Olympic*] asked the *Titanic* if he was steering southerly to meet him?
Mr. MOORE: Yes, sir. The *Titanic* says 'We are putting the women off in the boats.'
Senator SMITH. "That is signed Haddock?"[316]
Mr. MOORE: Signed Haddock; yes; and the *Titanic* says: 'We are putting the women off in the boats.'

However, to be fair, the record does say that Senator Smith interposes a reading of a 1.40am communication with the *Carpathia* and Moore never continues with it; it does not say anything about Smith doing so for the 6.00am PV entry. But, and this is the crucial point, the copy of the *Mount Temple* PV that is included in the U.S. Inquiry report does have a complete "1.40am" entry, indicating that the compilers of the report did not rely verbatim on Moore's statements, but on the notes provided by him. These notes also do not include the "MPA + MWL in sight" statement.

Let us also consider the fact that Captain Moore, reading the PV, would have seen the "MPA + MWL in sight" entry as Smith "interrupted" him. Why did he not correct himself? And also, Moore said, "I suppose about 6 o'clock in the morning - that I sighted the *Carpathia* on the other side of this great ice pack".

---

315   http://www.titanicinquiry.org/U.S.Inq/AmInq10PVMT01.php
316   The *Olympic's* Captain

Why isn't the PV note that the *Carpathia* was seen earlier than Moore admitted in London questioned too?

Regarding the timing of the 6.00am entry, Captain Lord claimed he passed the *Mount Temple* at 7.30am; time on the *Californian* was 4 minutes ahead of that of the *Mount Temple*. When Captain Rostron first saw the *Californian*, he claimed, she was 5 or 6 miles to the WSW at 8.00am. Research by Sam Halpern[317] discredits Molony's interpretation of the PV further. Summarising his research, at 7.06 local time on the *Mount Temple* (7.10 on the *Californian*), the former vessel signalled Evans, wanting his position. As Sam writes, "What is [being] claimed from this discovery in the *Mount Temple*'s PV ... is that the hull of the *Californian* was not seen at 7:10 AM. However, by 7:50 AM the *Californian* and the *Carpathia* were both in sight." If Lord is right about the rendezvous time, then at 7.10am, the *Californian* would have been only about 4 or 5 miles away. Before then, the smoke, then funnel and masts, then the superstructure and finally the whole hull, visible at some 8 or so miles, would be seen emerging from over the horizon. The *Californian* then idles past, and at 7.46am, Durrant, tapping away at the Marconi station, casually notices the *Californian* already 4.5 miles to the south, and scribbles in his PV that both that ship and the *Carpathia* are in sight. Let us hope that the officers on the bridge were not so myopic as to miss a ship that had already steamed past them.

Or, as Sam puts it, "It does not mean that they were first sighted at that time or shortly before. " Durrant was in his cabin and had probably just been told by an officer that the ships were in the vicinity." He probably wouldn't have known anything about the location of the *Californian* at 7.06am if he was busy in his cabin. Indeed, a telegram sent from the Acting Premier of Canada to Senator Smith confirms that the *Mount Temple* saw the *Carpathia* at 6.30am, a detail also mentioned in *the Buffalo Courier* on April 25th.

Perhaps there is another way to look at this: Durrant was interviewed by *The New York Times*[318] and his recollections appeared on 26th April 1912. He says, "At 5.11 I had a call from the *Californian*, and told that boat of the disaster, and I gave the position in which it occurred. Shortly after the *Frankfurt* also called me. About forty minutes later we saw the *Carpathia* and *Californian*, with the Russian steamer *Birma*. There was also a tramp steamer cruising round, apparently going in the same direction as us, but as she had no wireless installed and never approached very near[319] we could not find out what she was. As soon as I saw the *Carpathia* I asked for news of the *Titanic* and if she had seen anything but got no reply."

Indeed, the *Mount Temple* PV says this: "3.25. *Californian* calls C. Q. I

---

317   http://www.encyclopedia-titanica.org/discus/messages/6584/113587.html?
       1161124902
318   This also appears in the *Boston Post*, April 26th, 1912.
319   Recall the *Almerian* story, which helpfully got close enough to the *Mount Temple* to partially read her name.

367

answer him and advise of *Titanic* and send him *Titanic*'s position. " 3.25am would be 5.11am on the *Mount Temple*. "Forty minutes later" would be 5.51am, or 5.55 on the *Californian*, extremely close to the time that she started through the ice.

Another piece of research from this author was prompted by a tidbit of information provided by a UK Newspaper. On 16th July 1990, *The Daily Telegraph* published an article by R. Barry O'Brien. Since the M.A.I.B. re-appraisal had recently been announced, the article was relevant. It discussed the long lost PV of a Russian ship, the SS *Birma*. In the resultant article, Molony pounced on one line: "6.0: MWL calls proceeding for Boston informing she is only 15 miles from position given by *Titanic*. *Birma* 22 miles."

With zeal, this was immediately taken as proof that the *Californian* was indeed 15 miles from the wreck site at 6 a.m. It is nothing of the kind. Firstly, if we take the timing of 6a.m. at face value, which Molony did, then what happened to Lord's 19 ½ mile estimate– or any of his other distance calculations on which he was quoted? Of course, one may argue that this was due to the *Californian* drifting during the night (something *The Daily Telegraph* writer did mention, as being "4 miles"). But the concept of the *Californian* drifting from her 10.21pm position was never considered by Captain Lord or by any of his proponents until 1986, although others such as Foweraker attempted to estimate it. At any rate, the *Californian's* overnight position was a DR calculation, the same as the method use to determine the *Titanic's* location. DR positions can only ever be estimates. Therefore, equating the distance between two estimated co-ordinates yields just another estimate, and is quite incorrect to state that this is the actual distance between any ship.

When was the message sent?

The most telling detail of the research article by Molony is its mere acceptance of the facts: it can be used to show that the *Californian*, well to the north at 6am, was not at fault and was too far away to see the *Titanic*.

But a little more care, plus a complete copy of the PV written by De Forest wireless Operator Joseph Cannon would have resulted in different conclusions. Never at any point did Molony consider the time difference between the *Birma*, the *Californian*, New York, or any other ship, though Mr. O'Brien did. He wrote, "*Californian's* time would have been twenty minutes behind because she was some 5 degrees East of the *Birma* when the ships set time by noon observations on April 14th."

The original newspaper article discussing the *Birma's* role in the *Titanic* disaster provides a clue: "*Titanic's* first distress call came in at 11.50 as the Russian ship was receiving a summary of the day's news [press]"[320] The position of the *Titanic* was given as 41°46' 50°14'. We know that this distress location was transmitted for the first time at 10.35p.m. New York Time. So, we have a time

---

320   Question 17181a in London refers to Harold Cottam of the *Carpathia* receiving the first round of press at 10.35pm New York Time at the time of receiving the distress call.

difference of 1 hour and 15 minutes, compared with 1 hour and 50 (or 55) minutes for the *Californian*. If we simply take this and apply it to the 6.00am entry for the Birma, this would give 6.35am *Californian* time.

Other problems become apparent. The SS *Baltic* has a New York Time of 2.15am for the *Birma's* message in which she declares being 55 miles off from the site of the casualty. At 3.45 am local time the *Virginian* refers to this distance. This means a 1 hour 30 minute NYT difference. Given the distance that the *Birma* would have to travel, the *Birma's* local time would be 3.55; 1 hour and 40 minutes ahead of New York.

At 1.30am, the *Birma* reports that *Titanic's* passengers were being put off in boats. This correlates with the SS *Virginian* and SS *Olympic* PV entries at about 11.35pm New York Time, or a time difference of 1 hour 50 minutes. The following messages are niggling: at 6.45 the *Mount Temple* says "Carpathia picked up 20 boat loads". At 6.30 the *Olympic* receives an unofficial message from the *Carpathia* saying 20 boats have been picked up. This would be after the last boat had been picked up (about 8.30 *Titanic/Carpathia* local time). However, the *Birma* has this message coming from the *Californian* at 8.00am local time, which would be 6.10am NYT! A 1 hour 25 minutes time difference would be 6.35am New York Time, which is a nice correlation with the *Olympic/Mount Temple* data.[321]

Other difficulties arise with a modicum of thought. The *Birma* was at 40 48 N 52 13 W upon receipt of the distress call. This is 108 nautical miles from the SOS location. The *Birma's* top speed was 13 knots, but if her radioed messages are to be believed, her officers thought she was doing 14 knots. At the same time as the "*Californian* is only 15 miles away", the Birma is mentioned as being 22 miles away. This would indeed be about 6am in the morning by the *Birma's* clocks. But given the possibility of a change in ship's time, even this must be questioned.

This confusion may sound trivial and confusing, but it is sufficient to prove that, unlike any other existing P.V.s that night, the *Birma* – and the *Birma* alone - was keeping local ship's time. And from the above, one cannot help but feel that the ship's clocks were perhaps altered at midnight. This makes the 6.00am message to the *Birma* hard to place in a chronology. The time difference with New York can be variously taken as being 1 hour 15, 1 hour 25, 1 hour 30, 1 hour 40 or 1 hour 50 minutes. This would place the "15 miles away" message as being literally anything between 6am and 6.35am depending on the whims of researchers. And there is (another!) problem: as demonstrated above, the *Virginian's* "17 miles" distance of the *Californian* from the wrecksite can be timed to be about 6.05am. But here the *Birma* picks up a message saying that the distance was 15 miles! Did the

---

321   If the "15 miles" figure refers to 6.35am local time, then this means that, from a DR distance from the SOS position of 19 ½ miles at 6.00am, the *Californian* would have been moving at nearly 8 knots; hardly consistent with statements about "crawling through the ice" made at the inquiries.

Californian officers not know how far they were away?

Let us try another method to combat this 15 mile conundrum. Lord's affidavit states that at noon on the 14th, he was at 47 25'W, 42 5'N, and steering S 89 W. He claimed that a current of about 1 knot setting to the WNW deflected this anticipated course so that he was heading almost exactly due west. But, without this current, and taking a course of S 89 W and a distance from noon of 120 miles (as he claimed), the *Californian* would be in 42 1' N, 50 7' W. This is 16 miles from the *Titanic's* CQD location, or very close to the "15 mile" as quoted in the *Birma's* message. If Lord was in a hurry to compute distances on the morning of the 15th April, he may have misread numbers, giving us 15 miles; or rounding errors may have crept into the calculations. And of course, this does not allow for the 18 hours of drift between 6.00am and the last observation; this also neglects the 7.30pm Pole Star sight.

As such, this 6.00am message should be treated with caution and not immediately leapt upon as proof of the *Californian's* overnight position. If anything, this demonstrates the lack of consistency in the minds of the pro-Lord camp. But, in this article, the timing of "6.0am" is taken as exact and incontrovertible. It also shows hypocrisy on the part of Molony, who mentions in his book that "Critics of Captain Lord seize on this one strange time of 6.10am ["Can now see *Carpathia*" in the *Virginian's* account]. They act once more as if all times were interchangeable." This is precisely what Molony did with the *Birma's* PV – but then again, he only had one piece of data with which to write a whole "Exclusive Research Article". But one needs such articles to show off irrelevant pictures of Captain Lord surrounded by grinning passengers, or he and his wife going for a drive.

Only having this one major data point with which to work, Molony continues in his article:

"Irrespective of time differences between ships, the *Birma*'s logging of a 6 a.m. message from the *Californian* is absolutely vital to a debate about the latter's distance from the *Titanic* that night.

Now Joseph Cannon's mention of *Californian* being 15 miles away from the SOS position at 6 a.m. corroborates a separate report by the *Virginian* that the *Californian* reported herself 17 miles away as soon as she came on air and learned of the SOS.

Captain G. T. Gambell of the Allan liner *Virginian* told the British press on landfall in Liverpool that he, too, had been forced to steam from the west side of the icefield around to the east.

He declared: "At 3:45 a.m. I was in touch by wireless with the Russian steamer *Birma,* and gave her the *Titanic* 's position. She was then 55 miles from the *Titanic* and going to her assistance.

"At 5.45 a.m. I was in communication with the *Californian,* the Leyland liner. He was 17[322] miles north of the *Titanic* and had not heard anything of the disaster.[323]"

The similarities of the *Virginian* disclosure to the *Birma* log kept by Cannon are profound in their importance. Together they show that the *Californian* wirelessed that she was a massive distance away – with at least two ships hearing and logging the assertion next morning."

A tragedy that this confident bombast omits Captain Gambell's other pronouncement in his statement just a line or two on from the above: "At 6.10am I sent a Marconigram to the *Californian*:- "Kindly let me know condition of affairs when you get to *Titanic*." She at once replied :- "Can now see *Carpathia* taking passengers on board from small boats. *Titanic* foundered about 2 a.m." Regardless of where the *Californian* thought she was, she could now see the *Carpathia*.

The *Birma*'s PV is an interesting report, but it is hardly the panacea that it is claimed to be.

One of Molony's most recent articles[324] argues that the timing of the first lifeboat launching, and that of the first rocket are wrong, based on eyewitness accounts. To this end, Molony proposes that the time that Lord Mersey reported that the first rocket was fired was 12.45am simply because it coincides with 2nd Officer Stone's observation from the bridge of the *Californian*. It is also reasoned that the *Titanic*, based on the testimony of Lightoller, had a time difference of 1 hour and 33 minutes with New York Time. Since the *Californian* had a time difference of 1 hour 50 minutes, when Groves saw 'his passenger steamer' stop at 11.40pm, this would have been 11.23 on the *Titanic*, a time when she was still steaming. Groves is therefore wrong in his identification of this other steamer as being the *Titanic*.

Such acceptance of evidence without analysis, and certainly without discussing contrary data, is quite simply a master-stroke of deceit. *Titanic* Junior Marconi operator Harold Bride mentions in America that the time difference between New York and the *Titanic* was about 2 hours. The *Californian* was keeping 1 hour 50, or 1 hour 55, as told by Evans in America and England respectively.

But let us look at Lightoller's 1 hour 33 minute difference. He told Senator Smith that ship's times were altered at midnight so that, at noon the next day, the

---

322   A curious figure. Captain Lord maintained later that he was 19 ½ miles or so away, and this was before his ship got under way.

323   If the 12.40am (ship's time) notice on the *Virginian* can be equated to the 11.55 New York Time-Cape Race entry, then a 1 hour 15 minute time difference existed. Since a 1 hour 50 minute difference existed between New York and the *Californian*, then the 5.45 "17 miles north" mention becomes 6.20 on the *Californian*, so Captain Lord believes that she had travelled 2 ½ miles in 20 minutes, or 7 ½ knots, and not the "crawling speed" testified to in London.

324   "Titanic International" Society *Voyage* magazine, issue 62

times would approximately be right. 1 hour 33 ahead of New York would equate to a longitude of 51°45' W[325]. This is already about 80 miles to the <u>west</u> of the *Titanic's* wreck[326]! Boxhall's longitude of 50°14'W is 1 hour and 39 minutes ahead of New York. Lightoller's longitude cannot possibly be the noon position on April 14th Could Lightoller have meant that this would be the intended position on 15th April, had not the encounter with ice occurred? Let us examine this. The *Titanic* reached 'The Corner', where her course was changed from south-west to nearly almost due west, at about 5.50pm. This was at about 42° N, 47° W, though there are some indications in the evidence that the turn may have been delayed slightly. Using the *Titanic's* known course, and her speed as being about 22 knots, 51°45' W would have been reached at about 3.20am, and, with the clocks scheduled to be retarded by 47 minutes between 8pm and 4am, this would make on-board time as 2.33am. This is obvious nonsense and doesn't even come close to the longitude that the *Titanic* would reach at noon on 15th April, which would be about 56° 26'W. If 51°45' W was an anticipated noon longitude, it gives an average speed for the noon-to-noon run of just 13.5 knots, well below the 22 knot average on the night of April 14th. Where did Lightoller come up with 1 hour 33 minutes[327]? Whatever its source, it is obviously incorrect, as a little thought would have shown. Bride himself admitted in London that the *Californian's* ice warning, sent at 5.20pm New York Time would be about 7.30 on the *Titanic*; a time difference of over 2 hours, allowing for mistakes in recollections etc.

Can we work out the actual time difference that the *Titanic* had at the time of the collision? We know the approximate location and time of 'The Corner'. 5th Officer Lowe said in Washington that the course beforehand was '60 33½ west', which makes no sense. He probably meant 'south 60 33½ west'. Extrapolating 5 hours and 50 minutes on this course at a speed of 22 knots gives us a longitude of 45°25'. This gives a time difference with New York of about 1 hour 58 minutes, very close not only to Bride's statement, but also to the *Californian's* time difference, whether 1 hour 50, or 55 minutes. Groves' stop time for his ship translates to 11.48, or 11.43 on the *Titanic*; very close to the accepted time of the collision[328]. The noon time longitude is closer to 2 hours than 1 ½ hours.

325   See "*Titanic: Monument and Warning*" by Dave Gittins.

326   All one has to remember when converting time differences to longitude is that the difference between New York and Greenwich is 75°, or 5 hours. There was no adjustment for summer time in 1912.

327   One possibility is that Lightoller assumed that the ship's clocks had retarded. The *Titanic* was due to change her time by 23 minutes before midnight and 24 minutes afterward. If he assumed wrongly that the first of these retardations had taken place, this would place the actual time difference with New York as being 1 hour 57 minutes, close to Bride's evidence. However, there is ample evidence that the clock changes never took place.

328   Bear in mind also that, although the collision was supposed to have taken place at 11.40pm, some witnesses refer to a time of 11.45. Also, the *Titanic* coasted and then

The situation can be demonstrated very ably in the following sketch.

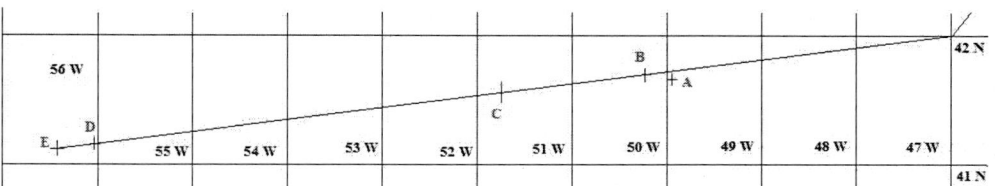

Illustration 43: The Titanic's route after turning towards New York at about 5.50pm on April 14th: (A) indicates the sinking location, (B) the SOS location, (C) is the longitude for a 1 hour 33 minute difference with New York, (D) would have been the Titanic's approximate noontime location at noon on April 15th. A planned, but unperformed, 47 minute clock retardation during the 8pm-4am 14th April/15th April watches would give position (E). Point (C) is nowhere near the noontime positions!

The author of these fine pieces may have proven himself to be a master of selective presentation of information, but it seems that a little thought, and the ability to analyse and interpret what he has written is quite beyond his capacity.

The most recent literary entry in the pro-Lordite catalogue regurgitates yet another old friend: the *Samson*. In this book[329], the April 6th entry in the Supplementary Revenue Book located by Leslie Reade is explained away as a prepayment, but with not one atom of evidence provided to support this claim: conveniently, such evidence was destroyed in a house fire many years ago. Still, how else can one explain the *Samson's* putative presence at the wreck site just eight days later? The book by Kamps and Williams also states that *Lloyd's List* mentions the *Samson* as being in the Icelandic port of Isafjodhur on May 14th. This is true, it does. However, by deliberate omission, or sloppy research, the other entries in Lloyd's publications are ignored. *Lloyd's Weekly Shipping Index* shows that the *Samson* left Tonsberg, Norway on February 2nd [330] for the Arctic, and *not* the North Atlantic as Naess would have us believe If the *Samson* was heading for the Arctic, what on earth was she doing near the Grand Banks of Newfoundland two months later? The *Samson* is next listed as ***arriving*** in Isafjodhur on April 6th . This is the exact day Captain Ring paid his port taxes. The next entry is on May 14th where the entry says "In Port- laid up for repairs – ready in a few days." The *Samson* finally left Isafjodhur on May 31st, arriving in Bergen, Norway on June 6th. The sailing time is consistent with a ship whose engine could produce a 6-knot speed, perhaps

steamed on for a little while after the altercation with the iceberg, meaning that a corrected time of cessation of motion would add a few minutes onto these times too.
329 *"Titanic and the Californian"* by Thomas Williams and edited by Rob Kamps
330 Henrik Naess' statement says this happened on February 8th

supplemented by its sails. The inference of the Lloyd's entries is not clear but they may mean that the *Samson* was damaged, perhaps during its Arctic trip, and was laid up in port for the next 55 days for repairs. The taxes that Captain Ring paid on April 20th could easily be explained as being due to an extended stay in port during the repairs. Without port documents, which were destroyed in a fire in 1924, it is impossible to see definitely.

The book also alleges that the mention of "Hatteras" is a mistranslation for Cape Race, but having seen a typed version of the original Icelandic document, this author can attest that this statement is simply untrue.

Finally, some of the other claims and personal attacks in this tome must be countered; the blurb on the back cover alleges that the author, Thomas B.Williams, uncovered the "new and important" evidence necessary to re-open the case, but the author of this current work has seen the M.A.I.B., and Public Records Office files,and can confidently state that this is categorically untrue: the "evidence" that re-opened the case was the discovery of the location of the *Titanic's* wreckage. It seems at least slightly dishonest for an author and/or publisher to make such bogus claims simply to sell more books.

The claims within the book are ludicrous too. Mr. Kamps caustically states that Reade's book was "rogue" (probably because it contains ideas contrary to his own), and also goes on to say that Harrison was the only one qualified to pronounce on the case: "The truth also is that all [of Captain Lord's critics] are self-appointed experts laying down the law about technical matters on which they are not, in the least, qualified to speak." But, hypocritically, the authors of this book are a journalist and a translator, and yet Kamps[331] is quick to decry his opponents, who he describes as "trash": some of these opponents <u>do</u> have the necessary nautical skills and often post their well-researched analysis and results on internet discussion forums and society journals. We must also add surveyor and mariner Captain Barnett as "someone who is not qualified to speak on the matter" - simply because his opinion differs from Williams' and Kamps; incidentally, Kamps gave "his" book a 5-star recommendation and review on the Amazon on-line retail website, in clear violation of its rules that authors are not allowed to review their own work.

Kamps gloats at *"The Ship That Stood Still"* being 'banned', but this is another untruth. Unsold copies were recalled by the publishers, and, together with items still in stock, pages that were deemed offensive to Harrison were carefully removed and replaced with sanitised versions. The book then went back on sale at a slightly higher price. When these outstanding items had been sold, the book was not reprinted, a far cry from being 'banned'. Ed Kamuda had made the same 'mistake' in his 1997 obituary of Leslie Harrison, published in the largely pro-Lord *Titanic* Historical Society Commutator. Then again, no tears were shed for the maverick Leslie Reade, working on his own, and suspicious of the hidden, pro-

---

331   Private Information

Lord agenda of most of the *Titanic* societies.

Kamps used to write obsequiously to his hero, Leslie Harrison, once a week. So, what was his measured response to those who had caused such an affront to his hero, and his work? We have this inimical response, given to this author; "God how I HATE them" [Kamps' emphasis]. A truly horrid invective for someone who never met or knew Captain Lord, but who had been seduced by the silver tongue of Leslie Harrison.

And so, with new publications, the Lordite camp were jubilant and had seemingly re-asserted themselves as 'the final arbiters' of the *Titanic/Californian* matter by a judicious combination of belittling and suppressing opponent's works, and trumpeting a catalogue of high selective evidence to suit their cause. It is often said that "The winning side writes history," but the Lordite tactics imply a new method: "The winning side has the loudest voice," typified by a flurry of poorly researched articles, accepted as the truth by an unknowing audience.

Epilogue

Could the *Californian* have saved anyone? Lord Mersey and Senator Smith certainly believed so. Leslie Reade and Edward de Groot avoided the question altogether. Walter Lord's arguments revolve around the fact that Captain Lord and his crew did not even attempt a rescue, but in private, he would write that, "The *Californian* could have done a great deal of good."

Let us explore this issue. The *Californian* could attain a maximum speed of 13 ½ knots, which could have been reached within a few minutes. Rockets were first reported to Captain Lord at 1.15am; if 2nd Officer Stone had shown more alacrity, he would have informed the Captain after the second rocket had been sighted and he was sure that he not just viewing shooting stars, perhaps at about 12.50am. What could have been achieved in the next hour, or hour and a half, before the *Titanic* sank? This requires an estimate of the distance; taking a lower limit of 5 miles and a higher one of 21 miles, at top speed, it would take between 22 minutes and 1 hour 33 minutes to reach the *Titanic*. No-one seriously suggests that Lord rush into an ice infested area with such wanton abandon for the safety of his own ship and crew. The argument that Lord should have adopted Rostron's practise by ringing "full speed ahead" down to his engine room is not very compelling. Rostron had received no ice warnings at all; all he knew was that the *Titanic* had hit an iceberg. Captain Lord would almost certainly have been more cautious; not only had he received Marconi reports, but he could see the ice. This would definitely have affected his navigation that night.

What speed would be acceptable in the vicinity of ice? We simply do not know. Sir Ernest Shackleton suggested four to six knots at the British Investigation. With these speeds, the *Californian* would not have arrived in time to pluck anyone from the *Titanic*'s decks. And, with lifeboats rowing towards the mystery steamer on the horizon, Lord would have to have been lucky not to have run over the small craft whilst en route.

Suppose that the *Californian*, by some caprice of good fortune, had arrived at the *Titanic* before she foundered. What then? How could the passengers and crew be transferred (transshipped) safely? How close would Lord have been prepared to take his own ship to the dying giant, without the risk of damaging either vessel?

The boat deck of the *Titanic* was ordinarily 60 feet above the water; at that time on the morning of April 15th, the forward-most end would be lower than this, with the stern end higher. The A deck promenade would be 10 feet lower than the boat deck. The bridge of the *Californian* was 39 feet above the water. How could people lower themselves this distance without injury, given that a separating gap would exist between the two ships? Possibly down the lines ('falls') of departed lifeboats, or by ferrying passengers down in boats to the deck of the *Californian*, raising the boats, and then repeating this process? The absolute earliest that Lord could have arrived at the *Titanic* would be sometime shortly after 1.35 a.m.; at this time, there would only be nine lifeboats left on the *Titanic*, 5 of them being on the port side. To transfer some 1,900 people still on board the ship. With time running out, one can imagine the horrific scrum that would have ensued as people waited for their turn to escape. But with such a huge disparity in the heights of the decks, there could be no other way, short of ladders or gangplanks, which could have provided a point of transfer between these ships. The gangway doors on the *Titanic*, situated on D-deck, were about 20 feet above the waterline, and could have been used, if one fashions a method of transference, but with the *Titanic's* bow dipping ever lower in the water, this would only have been a temporary solution.

There are incidents where passengers and crew have been transshipped[332], the most salient one being three years before the *Titanic* collision; in 1909, the Italian liner *Florida* punctured the hull of another White Star liner, the *Republic*, whilst in dense fog. The *Republic* eventually sank, but its rate of foundering was so slow that all but six people (who were killed in the initial collision) on both ships survived; there was therefore no overwhelming sense of urgency that had been evident during the later stages of the sinking of the *Titanic*. Some 400 passengers were transferred from the *Republic* to the *Florida*, a process that took between 2 ½ to 4 hours (depending on sources) using a single staircase which joined gangway doors on both ships. These passengers – and 900 additional ones from the *Florida* – were then taken again from the heavily overloaded Italian ship to the recently arrived rescue vessel *Baltic*. In rough weather, and using twenty lifeboats from all three vessels, these 1,300 people were transferred the one mile distance from the *Florida* to the *Baltic* in 84 boatloads, in 9 or ten hours. If we consider a hypothetical *Titanic* rescue by the *Californian*, we must remember that weather conditions on April 14th 1912 were perfect, and that Captain Lord may have manoeuvred his ship closer than one mile to the ailing giant. Factored in to a rescue scenario, the "9 or 10" hours quoted for the *Baltic's* rescue may be reduced somewhat, but by no means could the *Californian* have taken everyone on board before the *Titanic* went to the bottom.

A reasonable scenario[333] posits that Lord would have arrived in time simply to rescue some of the people in the water. With a survival time measured in minutes before the onset of hypothermia, it is debatable how many people could have been saved. As with the lifeboats rowing towards his ship, Captain Lord would have to be fortunate not to run over and kill any of the unfortunates in the water, who would have undoubtedly made for this new arrival on the scene.

But there is another matter to consider. In his final report, Lord Mersey writes, "At 12.35 the message from the *Carpathia* was received announcing that she was making for the *Titanic*. This probably became known and may have tended

---

332   For a discussion of these incidents, see http://www.encyclopedia-titanica.org/item/1509/

333   See Dave Gittins' website and e-book.

to make the passengers still more unwilling to leave the ship; and the lights of a ship (the *Californian*) which were seen by many people may have encouraged the passengers to hope that assistance was at hand. These explanations are perhaps sufficient to account for so many of the lifeboats leaving without a full boat load."

If we accept this logic and propagate it further, we can perhaps say that if the *Californian* was underway and was seen by the people on the *Titanic* to be heading towards them, then the sense of security which may have been generated may have actually *hindered* the loading of the lifeboats ("I'm not getting in one of those little row boats. I'm waiting for that ship to arrive!"). More people might have stayed on board the *Titanic*, and the loss of life higher than it eventually was.

Despite its many failings, the Marine Accident Investigation Branch report recognised the futility of the *Californian* effecting a rescue[334]. They stopped short of a full exoneration of Lord and his cohorts. It is a pity that Captain de Coverley did not have the courage of his convictions and agree in writing with the conclusions of Captain Barnett, namely that he felt that the two ships were in sight at all time. Both men, with decades of experience at sea, would then be unanimous, rather than issuing a diluted, useless report issued politically to quell the unending tide of complaints about Captain Lord's treatment.

What of the other aspects of the affair? That Stone saw low lying rockets, that the ship that he had been observing so patiently moved off whilst firing rockets?

Let us deal with the first of these questions. The first description of Stone's rockets comes in his written statement of April 18th: "At about 12:45, I observed a flash of light in the sky just above that steamer. I thought nothing of it as there were several shooting stars about, the night being fine and clear with light airs and calms. Shortly after I observed another distinctly over the steamer which I made out to be a white rocket though I observed no flash on the deck or any indication that it had come from that steamer, in fact, it appeared to come from a good distance beyond her."

Gibson would later refute this, having seen a flash on the deck upon launch of a projectile, and even Stone would later concede that the rockets did indeed come from the other ship. Independent studies of the navigational and observational aspects of the case[335] place the distance between the *Titanic* and the *Californian* as being about 12-14 miles distant. With the *Titanic* pointing nearly at the *Californian*, and not displaying much illumination, and with nothing in the vicinity with which to compare sizes and distances, it would be very easy to confuse a medium sized tramp steamer before the horizon, with a much larger

---

334   Bizarrely, in the 1930s, Lightoller gave his account of the sinking on a radio broadcast and he too said that the two ships could have come alongside and practically everyone rescued. At this time, Lightoller blamed Lord for the loss of life in his autobiography, but did not mention him by name in the radio dispatch.

335   See Appendix C and Sam Halpern's "Lights on the Horizon" series.

vessel beyond the horizon, and partially obscured. For a vessel 12-14 miles distant, and with rockets reaching a maximum height of 860 feet, the rockets would be seen to attain an angle of 0.6° relative to the horizontal. This value changes to 1.6° for a ship only 5 miles away. For Stone, this would have been confusing. He was sure that the ship was only about 5 miles distant, and yet the rockets did not seem to go as high as he would have been expecting. Why? Because he was mistaken about the distance. For rockets seen to reach an angle of 0.6° and fired from only a few miles away, it would *seem* that they would have reached a total height of nearly 400 feet, much less than the altitude he would have been familiar with. Note that Stone's first account of the rocket makes no mention of the half mast-light height he would later cite in London. This picture does help to explain how Stone may have thought that, given his inability to see the flash caused by the launch of the rocket, he would have thought that they seemed to come from a greater distance past the other steamer.

What is the origin of the 'half mast light' height clung to by Stone in London? Let us review his evidence:

7919. Did you ever say to any Officer that you and the Captain had talked about these rockets and had expressed an opinion that they might have come from some other ship? Have you ever said that to anybody till now? You have said it to me, you know?
Yes.
7920. Have you ever said it before to anybody else?
Yes. I think I have said it both to the Chief Officer and to the Third Officer in conversation.

7921. Tell me what you said to the Chief Officer?
I have remarked at different times that these rockets did not appear to go very high; they were very low lying; they were only about half the height of the steamer's masthead light and I thought rockets would go higher than that.

7922. Well, anything else?
But that I could not understand why if the rockets came from a steamer beyond this one, when the steamer altered her bearing the rockets should also alter their bearings.

7923. That pointed to this, that the rockets did come from this steamer?
It does, although I saw no actual evidence of their being fired from the deck of the steamer except in one case.

This disposes of the notion that the rockets were coming from another ship, well beyond the horizon; such a ship would be invisible to Stone and Gibson. Proponents of Lord's case would argue that the distance between the *Californian* and the *Titanic* would be so great that the latter's rockets would appear so low

379

down that they could be mistaken as coming from this other ship, but conveniently 'forgetting' (?) that Stone and Gibson associated the pyrotechnics with the ship that they could see, and not some unknown firework displaying steamer. Since the location of the wreckage of the White Star giant was determined, the overall distance between ships is quoted by friends of Captain Lord as being some 21 miles. But very simple trigonometric calculations (see Appendix E) demonstrate that even rockets fired from that great distance would be seen rising well above the horizon; indeed, the height would be a sizeable fraction of the angular diameter of the full moon. Such rockets would have been obvious and would neither be "low lying" nor reaching "half the height of [a] steamer's masthead light". And if Stone was determined to maintain his "low lying" rockets story, then he should have seen not only them, but the *Titanic*'s own signals in the sky. A truly unforgettable event, if one accepts the extreme coincidence of two sets of rocket firers in that small area of the North Atlantic.

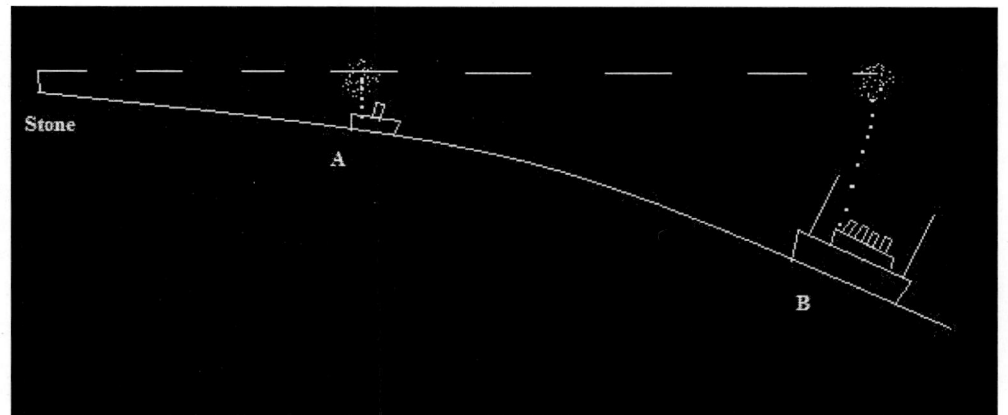

Illustration 44: The confusing situation - a cross-section of the Earth: Stone sees rockets fired, seemingly from a steamer at A, but they are actually being fired from B. From his point of view, the rockets do not seem to go very high. The dashed line indicates Stone's line of sight. The diagram is not to scale.

What if the rockets had come from the *Titanic*? In accordance with the best practises of the Lordite authors, we shall preferentially pick and choose that evidence that suits our theory. The strange ship, seen from the *Californian* stopped by an astonishing coincidence in direct line of the White Star ship. She remains in this exact line-of-sight from 11.40 until 1.45, to allow the rockets to be seen to apparently come from beyond her. Then, somehow knowing that no more rockets are to be detonated, the ship steams off. She may or may not have turned around, but if the latter, this is not seen by Stone or Gibson. Finally, she is last seen about an hour later, having steamed at least eight miles through an ice field. But the simple introduction of troublesome facts scuppers this theory, and yet it has been propagated for decades, and still refuses to die.

We can extend calculations regarding the 'half mast-light flares' even further. We know where the *Californian* was claimed to have stopped. We know the average drift, and its direction, that night. We can therefore work out where Captain Lord and his crew would be at various points that night, if their initial stopping location is right:

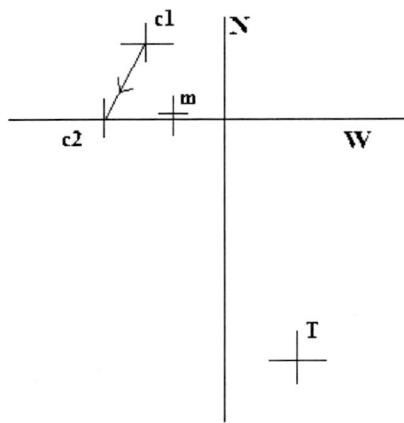

Illustration 45: Diagram displaying the motion of the Californian on the 14th/15th April. The Californian stops at position c1, and by 2.20am, has drifted to point c2. The "mystery ship" would be at point m at 12.45am. The sinking location of the Titanic is at "T". This diagram is highly schematic and is not to scale.

Since both the *Californian* and the *Titanic* were trapped in the same current (a reasonable deduction), both ships would therefore remain in the same position relative to each other. At 2.20am, the distance between the two vessels would be 18.3 nautical miles. At 12.45am, given the "mystery ship" being to the SE and at a distance of 5 miles, according to witnesses, the distance between this unknown stranger and the *Titanic* is some 13.1 miles as the first rocket/flare was ignited. If Stone is correct, we can estimate the height that his flares/rockets would reach, using the *Californian* herself as a template for the mystery ship; after all, Stone, Gibson and Lord all agreed that the ship they saw was the same as themselves. A height, based on the *Californian's* mastlight, of some 40 feet would be a reasonable extrapolation. The height of witnesses' eyes on the boat deck of the *Titanic* is approximately 66 feet. The total distance they could see would thus be 17.3 miles. As any observer who has seen flares, or rockets, exploding at extreme range over a dead calm, flat terrain at night, and with no distracting sources of artificial light, the momentary burst of light would be greater than any other source of illumination. Even when viewed by peripheral vision, the eye would immediately be attracted to this strange flash. So, with so many officers (Boxhall and Smith), crew members (Boxhall at least) and many others, including hundreds of passengers milling around a darkened boat deck, how many saw flares or rockets? Discounting Mrs.Thayer's singular observation detailed in Michael Davie's book, the answer is: none. Flares that should have been seen weren't. So much for Stone.

Given the schisms in the evidence, what can we say about Stone's observations? Charitably, the kindest we can say is that they are 'pure invention.' Whether Stone was coerced, or simply altered his story without prompting, can now never be answered[336]. The 2nd Officer was indeed fortunate that Gibson was never asked how far he saw the rockets reaching.

But why did Stone tell Sydney Gorrell's mother in 1912 that the rockets only attained a low altitude? One must realise that Stone had already given his evidence in London. Lord had probably already lost command of the *Californian*, if not his career in the Leyland Line. For Stone to have now changed his story, and admit to telling lies at the British Investigation, would have left him possibly open to perjury charges, with obvious consequences on his own career. Better to stick to his original story?

Stone's unbelievable rocket observations cast inevitable doubt on his conviction that the other ship was moving. Gibson was certain that she was immobile. Stone had seen the vessel steam off into the ice field, while firing rockets. If Stone had admitted that the ship had not moved, but had still emitted the troublesome pyrotechnic signals, and then had disappeared, one could reach the conclusion that the ship was in distress and had gone to the bottom, exactly like the *Titanic*. But, by introducing the element of motion, Stone could negate the possibility of the ship being in trouble. As he said later, "A ship that is in distress does not steam away from you." Such a well rehearsed line would be ineffective against the hostile countenance of Lord Mersey and his court.

But there is one other matter that should be emphasized. The *Californian* was initially heading north-east at 10.21pm; some 6 hours later, she would be heading westerly. It has always been assumed by many that the swinging motion was in one direction; clockwise. But Gibson's affidavit may tell a different tale. Bear in mind that the initial bearing of the other ship from the *Californian* was to the south-east. The *Carpathia* was heading to the wrecksite on a heading of N52W. The *Californian*, the *Titanic* and the *Carpathia* would therefore be in an almost perfect line. Even if the *Californian* was pointing in a different direction, the rockets seen after 3am would be seen to appear to be coming from the south-east, and on an almost constant bearing. Gibson says this; "I observed a rocket about two points before the beam (Port), which I reported to the Second Officer. About three minutes later I saw another rocket right abeam which was followed later by another one about two points before the beam." If the turn of his ship has been on one direction, he should have seen the first rocket before the beam, the second one abeam, and the third after the beam. If the *Californian* had temporarily swung back

---

336   In London, Captain Lord told the court that companies' signals "do not shoot as high and they do not explode." Did this inspire Stone's story?

the other direction, this may have confused Stone to calculating a wrong bearing of his other rocket-firing ship. To Stone, the ship would have seemed to have moved (relatively speaking) to the right, but in fact, his ship may have swung to the left.

When was the first inkling that the uncommunicative stranger was moving away? Lord later claimed in America and London that Stone had informed him of this fact on the speaking tube at about 1.15am, when he was first told of "a rocket" or "rockets." But this fact is not mentioned in Stone's or Gibson's 18th April statements. The earliest we know of a 'moving' ship is, according to Gibson, after the seventh rocket was fired, when a bearing was taking of the steamer by Stone. Gibson would say in London that this would be after 1.20am[337]

We now enter the realm of speculation. Did Stone make a genuine mistake in taking a bearing? Or did he deliberately decide to concoct a moving ship? A possibility lies, not with the *Titanic*'s rockets, but in the signals sent up after 3am, and which could only have come from the *Carpathia*. The bearing of the other ship from the *Californian* was S 45° E at midnight. The *Carpathia* was on a course of N 52° W to the *Titanic*. The rockets would therefore be seen to the south and east: this is explored further in Appendix D. What did Stone say in his affidavit? "We saw nothing further until about 3:20 when we thought we observed two faint lights in the sky about S.S.W. and a little distance apart." Stone had made a massive mistake of approximately 6 points! This is demonstrated in the sketch below, which makes a mockery of Stone's bearings. The *Californian* would have to have been well to the east, and probably to the south of her 10.21pm DR position! And yet no serious scholar disputes that the *Carpathia's* rockets were indeed seen at this time.

---

337   Stone and Gibson's recollections of time seem to be in disarray. Gibson says he did not return to the bridge until 12.55, but Stone does not place the Apprentice's return to the bridge until after the voice pipe communication with the Captain at 1.15am. If this 20 minute discrepancy is incorporated into Gibson's evidence, this would place the ship moving off at 1.35am. Given that the 8th and last rocket was fired at about 1.45am, 1.35am may be a better placing of this event than 1.20.

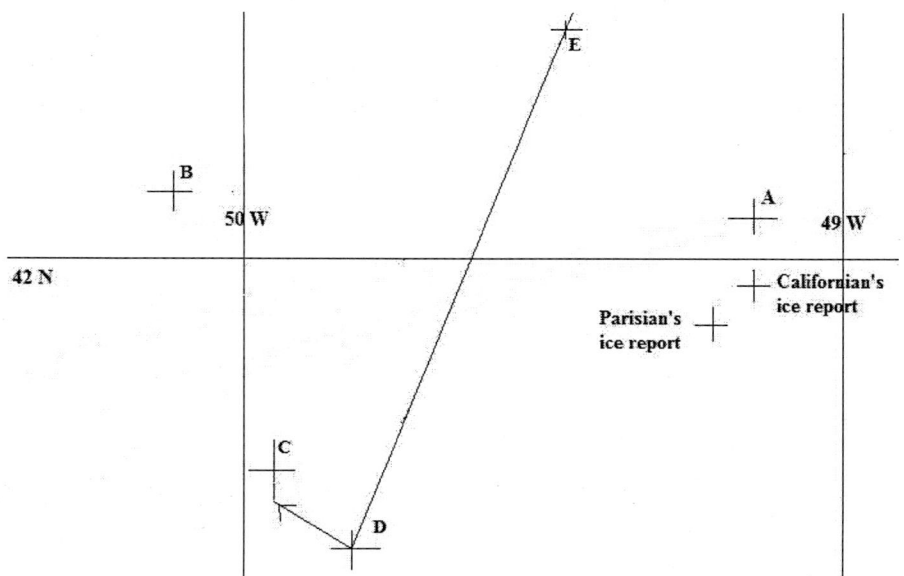

Illustration 46: Chart demonstrating Stone's observations of the rockets at 3.20am; A represents the Californian's DR position in the afternoon, compared to an ice report of three bergs seen by the SS Parisian earlier in the day; B is the DR position at 10.21pm; C is the Titanic's wreck site; D is the approximate location of the Carpathia when she fired her rockets; and E is the maximum theoretical location of the Californian from the Carpathia to enable the latter's rockets to be viewed on a bearing of SSW from Stone.

How could Stone confuse his bearings so badly? A possibility lies in something not considered before: night vision, or the ability to see in the dark. Normally it takes some time for one's eyesight to become adjusted to dark conditions, and until this happens, the vision is impaired.

One would expect the *Californian's* open bridge to have no sources of illumination, except for the occasion use of the morse lamp, from which a beam would be cast outwards, and not inwards, to the bridge. But there was another source of light. Both Leslie Harrison and Leslie Reade reproduce plans of the bridge and the Captain's cabin and chart room in their books. Above the Captain's quarters was a large skylight. The light was on in the chart room, as Captain Lord had pulled his cap down over his eyes to shield them from the illumination. Were the skylights on the chart room closed? We don't know, but Leslie Harrison may supply the answer.

In "*The Night Lives On*", Walter Lord uses Groves' 46 year old memory to state that there wasn't a clock on the upper bridge of the *Californian*. Harrison

385

challenged this in his letter to the T.H.S. Commutator, challenging Walter Lord's research, stating that there was a clock on the rear bulkhead of the chart room, through which the Officer of the Watch could peer, via the skylight (incidentally, Harrison obviously did not realise that he had confirmed Groves' comments about the lack of timepieces on the bridge!). If there was a skylight, Harrison seems to have assumed that it was open, or at least, the blinds were open. For anyone looking into such a light, from a darkened environment, the effect would be instantaneous. The observer would be temporarily dazzled, blinded and unable to see anything for a period of time. Including faint lights of another ship on the horizon, and the markings on the compass in the binnacle.

That Stone was not the most observant watch officer is not in any doubt. He had failed to spot the so-called yellow-funnel steamer at 4am. He had also missed the first of the *Carpathia*'s rockets. Were it not for Gibson, he may not have noticed them at all. He may also have missed the first of the *Titanic*'s rockets, if the research of the uncalled witness by Leslie Reade is any indication. What is not in dispute is that Stone, having seen rockets after 3am, which *could* have been distress signals, didn't bother to report these to the Captain. Perhaps he had just given up trying, but this is a serious lapse for a watch officer.

But why did Stone not write up any of his observations in the scrap log book? He should have been noting the details of the rockets and the strange moving steamer as time progressed. The fact that there was apparently no mention whatsoever of *anything* in the log implies that from a very early time, he had decided not to write anything up on it at all. This seems impossible to believe. If Captain Lord had effected a rescue, no matter how futile, he would have questioned Stone about the lack of written information. And if he didn't, Stewart would have when he copied the scrap log into his fair log. But a rescue *wasn't* effected. Could it be that the rockets were mentioned, but Stewart had neglected to copy them over? With the *Californian* denying seeing rockets or any other signals when she docked in Boston, this at least seems likely. We shall never know for sure.

If we accept the recollections of Mainwaring et al., Stone had indeed tried his best to impress the situation upon his Captain; all to no avail. Now, there was a chance for redemption. A moving ship, steaming away from the *Californian* – a source of assistance - could not be in distress, and hence Lord's inaction was justified. But there was one complication: Gibson. The Apprentice would not agree in London that the other ship was moving, was showing a stern light, and that the red light was shut in. Then there is the problem of Stone and Gibson's conversation about the ship having a list, that it seemed to be in a state of distress, and that a ship does not fire rockets at sea for nothing. Stone would distance himself from these comments when he was sweltering under the pressure in the witness box. But then again, Gibson did not have an Officer's certificate in jeopardy.

What could possibly entice a man like Stone to display so much loyalty to his Captain that he was prepared to fabricate evidence? Leslie Reade expounds a theory in his book, that Stone had found in Captain Lord "an exceptionally dominating and remote skipper", somewhat similar to the "difficult" father that he had sought to escape from by running off to sea, a father who had shaped the mind of Stone for much of his adult life. Reade would write that the "mere presence [of Lord] was enough to arouse in the already insecure Stone a feeling of such inferiority as amounted to actual fear," and that this was "betrayed [as] an almost infantile faith in the infallibility of Lord." Stone did not, according to Reade, find his fellow officers very congenial either. If this thesis is true, Stone identified his father with the cold and callous Captain lying asleep a few feet below him; to have confronted him would be to confront his own dead-rooted fears, inhibiting him from either pulling Lord out of bed, or even venturing the opinion that he was watching distress signals. Stone had told Mersey that he had merely informed Lord of seeing rockets and let him judge. Lord was not satisfied with this report, but did nothing further. The two men were seemingly trapped in a deadlock, with either one unwilling (or in Stone's case, perhaps unable) to capitulate.

It brings this author little pleasure to admit to a workplace situation similar to the one suggested by Reade, albeit without the difficulties that arise in the above 'father-son' situation. In a particular project many years ago, this author was lumbered with a project manager. Unexplainable personality differences existed between us, leading to an awkwardness. Overall, the level of communication was exactly as described above. For Stone it may have been reminisces about his troubled childhood; for this author, it was due to a suspicion and distrust of workplace managers.

This theory is seductive, but it lacks sufficient proof. Groves' interview with Walter Lord gives indications that Stone was so intimidated on board ship, that he took to his cabin between watches. This lacks a certain gravitas when one considers the many problems with Groves' own stories, in 1912 and 1957. We are forced to ask ourselves which version of his tale we believe.

But Reade was not finished with the intricate psychologies of the *Californian* crew. Captain Lord's personality, so warm and genial in his long retirement, was a far cry from the cold and domineering martinet of 1912. Lord had seemingly mellowed, or "gone softly" during his time afloat, as another critic wrote. Reade was later to write to Walter Lord, "Captain Lord was a Caesar in a sailor's suit – not a tyrant, but remote from his own men. Stone, the real 'villain', if there was one, was outwardly a dull lump, but he was afraid of Lord, and at heart a remarkably conscientious and sensitive young man ... When all is said and done, however [Captain Lord's] guilt is more that of Oedipus than Himmler."

But we must question these judgements too. Stone may have been terrified of the Captain, but Groves was so unconcerned by Lord that he disputed his Captain's testimony, and also hinted that Stone had been too lax in his keeping of the Scrap Log while the rockets went aloft. How far can we trust Groves' character assessments during his 'Middle Watch' essay? Captain Lord's pronouncements to the Boston press in the aftermath of the disaster sadly paint him in a very bad light too. Not only did he inaccurately depict the *Californian's* rescue attempt in an overly dramatic way, but he lied when he said that no signals were seen, and then invited his officers to join in his deception. Regardless of whether he and his officers had seen the *Titanic*, or the distress signals, his demeanour is one of a person who suspected that something had happened, but decided it would be best not to mention anything. Two of his indignant crew decided to speak to relatives or the press, and Captain Lord's deceptions were forever demolished.

One last point remains about Groves and his 1912 statements: why did Groves tell despairing tales of his fellow officer's conduct, and Stone defended his companions? There is one reason separate to psychological bullying and hostility: no-one at that stage could have known that Captain Lord would be removed from the *Californian*. For her next voyage, Groves would not sign on. Stone did so. Groves could therefore say whatever he wanted with no fear of him facing his allegedly fearsome master.

Although pro-Lord researchers have huge swathes of letters 'proving' that the Captain was a kind and courteous fellow, this is no indication of reality. Many of these letters are from his time in Lawther Latta; the only exception that we know of was written by Commander John Macnab RNR, an examiner for the Board of Trade. His opinion was reported widely in the press after Mersey's court have dispersed: "Capt. Lord passed all his Board of Trade examinations most brilliantly before me, his testimonials for good conduct and ability at sea being invariably of the highest order. Since then I have ever heard him spoken of as a humane and clever officer and commander as well as a kind husband, a loving father, and a high-principled gentleman. His mental punishment, however, may be assured by the reflection that his sin was one of omission, not commission, and was certainly in no sense intentional. " But generally, we know so very little of the opinion of his fellow mariners during his crucial time with Leyland. As discussed in this book, a semi-anonymous letter written by "J.B." prompted a thorough search through crew agreements for all of Captain Lord's Leyland Line voyages. These show that crew members felt such loyalty to Lord that they signed on for multiple trips with this supposed bully. But we do now know that Lord was prepared to lie, for we have documented evidence on his 1920 application to become a U.S. citizen.

This indicates, to this author anyway, that the rapport between Lord and Stone was perhaps unique[338]. Stone's fragile personality would ultimately lead to

---

338   In his book, Reade writes, "...the fear Stone had for Lord, if not common knowledge, was at least known to persons astonishingly remote from the *Californian*. Charles Burlingham, for instance, counsel in New York for the White Star Line in some

him abandoning his career at sea (see Appendix A). How different history might be if another officer had been on the Middle Watch that night!

Before concluding our discussion of the psychological aspects of Lord, Stone and the others, one other issue remains. If one believes Reade and Groves that Lord's icy demeanour influenced his officers, then what of the Captain's behaviour in Boston? Lord the ice-cold disciplinarian on April 14th had now become Lord the braggart, telling over exaggerated tales of his ship's conduct (*sans* rockets of course) during the rescue operation. What can we make of this? Simply that Lord took advantage of a situation to tell lies about himself and his ship. Ironically, having placed himself near the epicentre of the *Titanic* disaster in 1912, Lord, and his supporters would later make great efforts to remove him from the scene!

What then, do we make of Stewart and his tales? Was Stewart a feeble-minded coward, unable to stand up to his Master, or was he fiercely loyal to Lord? Recall that Stewart and Evans had told different tales of the reason why the Marconi operator had been woken, and one cannot help but feel that Evans' version of events is a lot closer to the truth. And if Stewart lied about this, what else can we also dispute? The 'yellow funnelled steamer', that Stewart denied was the *Carpathia*?

It has been stated that this unidentified yellow funnelled steamer was the *Mount Temple*, a description that matches Stewart's sighting, but Dunlop's closing statements in London, not to mention Lord's 1914 newspaper interview disproves this. The location of this ship was a variable commodity. Initially described as being to the south-west, hinting that it was on the far, western side of the ice field, it eventually moved to more or less due south, on the eastern side (or, in Robertson's address, actually *in* the ice). What on earth was going on with this steamer? A hypothesis can be reasoned. Obviously, Lord, Stone and Stewart couldn't admit that it was the *Carpathia* they were seeing, but they did know that the *Mount Temple* was somewhere near by. Lord could then state that he was seeing Captain Moore's vessel. By the time he gave evidence in Washington, Captain Lord's 'alibi' could be that he saw the *Mount Temple*, to the west of the ice. But the next day, Moore gave evidence that, indeed, corroborated the placing of his ship on the western fringes of the floes. But he also troublesome evidence that the *Mount*

---

of the litigation after the wreck, was aware of the unusual situation." This information is attributed to Private Information, obtained in New York. This author cannot verify these assertions; Reade's collection of *Titanic* material was auctioned off after his death, and attempts to contact his estate have met in failure. The only research material that this author had available were those copied to Walter Lord, and some fragments of information held by Haynes. In conversation with Harrison, Captain Lord's opinion of his shipmates is as follows: "[Stone] was a quiet young fellow, and he wouldn't tell me lies, I'm quite sure of that. And he wouldn't exaggerate. The other fellow [Gibson?] might, but he wouldn't."

Temple was 5 or 6 miles to the west of the *Carpathia*, and the *Californian* was only 5 or 6 miles north of him. The resultant triangle, with a ship at each vertex would show just how close the *Californian* was to the *Carpathia*, then at the wrecksite. Lord may have read about Moore's evidence the next day, as Moore had given more or less the same information in the papers the day of Lord's evidence. Therefore, the *Mount Temple* had to cease to be the unidentified yellow steamer, and its location was quietly shifted to the near side of the ice floe. In his evidence in London, Stewart remarked that this steamer was to the south, as Stone did in his April 18th statement. Only Lord sought to place it to the south-west.

Obviously this is speculation, but it does explain why no one could be sure where the mysterious steamer was[339].

So we now have this stunning triumvirate of witness. Stone, who witnesses low lying rockets and a moving steamer; Lord who would only admit to a 'rocket' in spite of other testimony; and Stewart who gave a false reason for the wireless operator being called. These last two witnesses, of course, dithered a full 45 minutes between the wakening of the Captain and Evans being roused. And Stewart, upon relieving Stone at 4am and being informed of ships and mysterious rockets, turns to the scrap log, and, seeing nothing written down, what does he do? Does he amend the log? Does he confront Stone? He does nothing!

The sighting of the yellow funnelled steamer is not the only instance of evidence being manipulated. The *Mount Temple* had, in American evidence, and in statements to the office of the Canadian Prime Minister, seen the *Californian* and *Carpathia* at about 6.30am. In London, and backed up by the PV, this time was now moved close to 8am local time. What had happened in the meantime between Smith's and Mersey's inquiry? There are indications, described above, that the entry in the PV was added later. How and why did this happen? Did Captain Moore, feeling so sorry for Captain Lord's plight, try to throw him a lifeline by changing

---

339   Leslie Harrison's pronouncements on this mystery steamer are interesting too. In letters to this author, he says that "the ship seen ... could have been one of several bound to the westward who were stopped by the icefield that night. Probably the *Parisian* is the one whose movements (quoted by the U.S. inquiry) conform most with the conclusion that she was that ship." But the data indicate that the *Parisian*, having passed very close to the *Titanic's* wrecksite early in the evening on the 14th, and was well away at the time of the calamity. She would have to have steamed to the north-west <u>and</u> been invisible to all the ships that night for her to be the *Californian's* yellow-funnelled steamship. However, Harrison did relate his impression that this ship, whatever her identity, was to the east of south of the Captain Lord that morning, and that and mystery ship observed from the Titanic could not have been to the north, as "the continuous icefield was too extensive to permit manoeuvring [in this area." This snippet no doubt comes from Lord's description of the ice in London, and featured in Foweraker's map. If this is so, how did the yellow-funnelled ship/"*Parisian*" get to its location at dawn? Incidentally, the *Parisian's* funnel colours were black, white and red!

his story to move the *Californian* further north away from the tragedy? If so (and again, there is no absolute proof) it is a shame that Captain Lord did not reciprocate this kind gesture, for Lord tried to implicate the *Mount Temple* as the mystery ship in the late summer of 1912.

But these are just examples of the wild speculations that can be formed based on the sometimes contradictory evidence given in 1912 and afterwards. The simple truth of the whole saga is the same as provided by Lord Mersey, expunged of his ludicrous statement that "[the *Californian*] might have saved many if not all of the lives that were lost." The conclusions are simple; that the two ships were in sight of each other, rockets were seen and ignored. Arguing about anything else is trivial; as Wyn Craig Wade would write, "[Supporters of Lord] seem to revel in ad-homineum logical fallacies. They say, for example, that Captain Lord was condemned in Washington because Senator Smith was so stupid and that he was condemned in London because Lord Mersey and his panel of marine experts were so clever. If so, it may account for the entrenched popularity of the verdict against Captain Lord: it is a judgement on which fools and wise men agree, and penetrating it with rationality alone leads to the height of absurdity."

In the intervening years, and almost exclusively since 1955, the argument had been sustained by a series of increasingly acrimonious comments and articles on the *Californian – Titanic* affair. A lot has been written on the *Californian* incident, more on the side of Captain Lord than against him, and for this, we thank the zealous Mr. Harrison. His eagerness has only served to stifle criticism and debate on the matter for four decades. A lot of the arguments border on the specious, many are scurrilous and some have little merit. It is fair to say that this aspect of the *Titanic* disaster has generated more unpleasantness than any other single facet of the tragedy. Of the many books and articles written, TV shows broadcast and websites created, some are too readily absorbed by an eager, if ignorant public. It only takes long and tedious research to instil a sense of despair in some of the 'facts' presented.

Readers implicitly place their trust upon authors of books; that they have done sufficient research, which leads to sound and reasonable conclusions. When one finds that this is not the case, or that deductions based on the presented evidence are bogus, one can only feel betrayed. One must ask oneself why such a tactic has been employed, what has been hidden, and why? It must be stressed that this selective use of evidence is not peculiar to the *Titanic* story; the various forms of media are prone to this level of ignorance especially if the subject matter is controversial. It is far easier to ignore or distort evidence that does not support one's hypothesis than it is to explain it; it also takes considerably more time and skill, to analyse the various pieces of testimony and apply the necessary mathematics, physics, personal experience etc. to reach logical conclusions. For some authors, this is too difficult to do. Or perhaps too much effort. Far easier to trump up the necessary pieces of evidence, highlight the inconsistencies, and

391

appeal to faulty logic, ultimately leading the reader to agree with false conclusions. Fortunately, much of the evidence, particularly the Inquiry transcripts, are now available for anyone to peruse, but why should a reader be expected to check on all the claims that a writer asserts? That is the writer's task, surely? This is so, but an independent check would insulate the consumer from the sense of betrayal that one inevitably gets when one discovers that books like "*A Titanic Myth*" are built on foundations of omission, distortion and downright lies.

Mention of this latter book brings a sense of apoplexy to this author; that one author should be able to stymie the efforts of other researchers via legal methods; methods either on his own behalf, or assisted by the considerable clout of a massive seafarer's union. People of seemingly high intelligence, and by this I refer mainly to John C. Carrothers, were bamboozled into believing the supposed 'innocence' of Captain Lord, after being fed carefully selected evidence that failed to impart the full nature of the *Californian* story. There was a 'hard-core' of unbelievers (such as Ivan Thompson, James Bisset, Walter Lord, Robert Ballard, Geoffrey Marcus, Leslie Reade and Edward de Groot) that Leslie Harrison felt a compulsion, or 'duty' in his own words, to educate about his version of the truth of Captain Lord. It is impossible to believe that converts to his cause would have reacted in so restrained and accommodating a manner if they knew only a fraction of what they had *not* been told. How many of these 'friends of Captain Lord' bothered to read the full inquiry transcripts? Not many it is suspected; these transcripts were exceedingly difficult to obtain prior to the advent of the Internet and can be hard to read. Far easier to propagate the same old fables; that the *Titanic* saw a moving ship, that the *Titanic* was an unmistakeable blaze of light etc. etc. Leslie Harrison is no less guilty of seducing readers into believing a bogus fable than his charge, the aged mariner Stanley Lord. And sadly, there is no shortage of gullible believers today, nor is there a dearth of people who write books based on bogus logic or simply because they "love a good fight", and usually bolstered and encouraged by a cabal of sycophants.

The *Californian* saga is a salutary reminder of the dangers inherent when lawyers, journalists, politicians and other advocates, and not historians, try to shape history for their own ends and needs.

Appendix A. Life After Lord

Gibson:

In 1912 Gibson obtained his 2nd masters certificate, and in the same year became a Sub-lieutenant in the Royal Navy Reserves. In 1934, Gibson was the 3rd Officer on the SS *Jonathan Halt*, and a year later, he was described as being a bosun. By 1937, he was an AB and Q.M. with Cunard. Three years later, Gibson had passed the exams necessary for a 1st master's certificate and signed up as 3rd Officer on the *Benedict* and then the *Boniface* of the Booth Line. Gibson left the company after the master of the *Boniface*, Captain F.H.Good, gave him an adverse report. Gibson was described as "a positive menace on the bridge", allowing the ship's only chronometer to run down and having "no interest in cargo or stowage and was no assistance to the Chief Officer". Finally, after lying to the Captain (twice) about a miscalculation in the ship's course, which would have resulted in an imminent grounding, Gibson was ordered from the bridge and relieved[340].

Gibson apparently joined the Holt Line in the Second World War, making voyages to West Africa. However, his misfortunes continued, and, in 1952, he was an AB/Q.M. on the *Reina del Pacifico*, where he received a double DR ("Declined to Report", indicating an adverse report) in his discharge book for two misdemeanors: being drunk on duty, and then later, going AWOL in Kingston, Jamaica. Gibson found employment as an AB on the Hector Whaling Vessel *Powell*, but was discharged from duty after being found twice in a coma, attributed to epilepsy. However, Gibson claimed that his blackouts were due to an injury he suffered after falling on a pipe, and he was allowed to continue his career at sea, working on the *Port Huon*. In 1954, Gibson was discharged from the MN *Neothuma* for misconduct, and he became a shore relief officer in Liverpool[341]. He died in 1963.

In a letter to Leslie Reade following Gibson's death, his widow confirmed that her late husband told her nothing in addition to what he had said at the British Investigation, and that "he was always of the opinion that the ship he saw was not the *Titanic*."

Stone:

Stone served on the ships *Dorelian*, *Huronian* and *Delilian* of the Leyland Line and eventually rose to the rank of Chief Officer. During World War I, Stone was a sub-lieutenant in the RNR in Fleet Auxiliaries in the Dardanelles. He later worked on the *Traveller* and *Wayfarer* for Harrison's shipping line. Following a bad report by the Captain c.1938, Stone went missing in London and was later found

---

340   Information obtained by Leslie Harrison from Gibson's widow, c.1963
341   *The Ship That Stood Still*, Appendix H, page 371

sitting on the wharf of a Devonshire port, near his childhood home after suffering from a breakdown[342]. Stone left Harrison's soon after[343] and worked in the Liverpool docks as a supervisor for the Ellerman lines for the remainder of his life. He had a cerebral haemorrhage on his way to work in September 1959, and died a few hours later leaving his wife and son penniless[344].

Gill:

Ernest Gill left Boston on 5th May 1912 on board the Leyland Line ship *Cestrian[345]* , and arrived in Liverpool on May 15th, in time for his wedding on the 19th to 23 year old Liverpool lass Rose McIver. This was a tragically childless and short-lived marriage. Rose died of tuberculosis and haemoptysis on January 9th, 1914 at the Walton workhouse[346] . On both occasions, the occupation of Gill was listed as "Marine Fireman", destroying the speculation that he left the sea. Also, inexplicably, during the period 1911-4, Gill declared that he lived at quite a few addresses, none of them real. Why he should do so is an intriguing question.

Sadly it is not quite as easy to determine the fate of Ernest Gill. The Central Index Register of Merchant Seamen held by Southampton City Archives do not list him in their records; however, although the Register was started in 1913, the 1913-18 period were destroyed in the 1960s.

There are a number of fatalities in World War 1 with his name or initials, but not all of them carry an age, or any other details, such as parent's details. If Gill died during the Influenza epidemic, he did not leave a death certificate. If one assumes that he did survive World War 1, then a few candidates arise that could match Ernest's details in the first decade or so after he left his companions on the Californian. However, each possibility raises questions. Did he remarry? Did he relocate? Did he change his career, and if so to what? The possibilities include locomotive fireman (possible, as ocean liners were switching from coal to oil at that time), steel worker, or general labourer. Research on this matter continues.

---

342   Stone's family, for obvious reasons, did not seem to be keen for this information be passed down the generation; Herbert's grandson, Robert, knew nothing of this incident.

343   A letter from Captain Penston to Leslie Harrison, 14/2/68. Penston, who served with Stone during this incident as 2nd Officer, noted that Stone's original intention was to be a schoolteacher and was not cut out for sea life. Penston further said that Stone was "ineffective as Chief Officer" and was dismissively known as "Stoney" by the firemen.

344   *The Ship That Stood Still*, page 327. Also information from John Stone to Leslie Reade.

345   Presumably Gill travelled as a passenger as his name does not appear on the crew agreement for that voyage according to Liverpool city records.

346   Despite its formidable name, a workhouse also served as a hospital.

Evans:

For the remainder of his life, Evans was employed by the Marconi Company, and its successor company, Cable and Wireless. He eventually attained the post of Manager Engineer. Between the First and Second World War, Evans worked on the first direct link to Australia. During the 1939-45 fracas, Evans was seconded to the British Army in North Africa, where he took charge of the mobile telecoms unit for the 8th unit. After the war, Evans was based in Bengazi, Palestine, Kuwait and St. Lucia.

For family reasons, he prepended his surname with his middle name and was known as Cyril Furmston Furmston-Evans (indeed, quite a few of Evans siblings and descendants adopted this practise). He retired in 1957 and moved to Boscastle in Cornwall and died of a coronary thrombosis in July 1959.

Groves:

During World War 1, and after he had been granted his extra master's certificate, Groves served in submarines. His vessel beached on the Dutch coast and he and his crew spent the rest of the year in internment in Holland, and Groves spent over a year on parole in England until the war ended. After the war, Groves signed up with W.A. Suter's Sheaf Line, and he became not only their Marine Superintendant but their most trusted advisor too. In World War II, a retired Groves, "having long been in the RNR served with the Admiralty in Southend." He sat on some 25 inquiries as an assessor, and always had the strength of character to maintain his own opinions when he knew he was correct.

Captain Groves died on 4th September 1961.[347]

Stewart:

According to Leslie Reade, in 1940 and at the age of 62, "Stewart, by then a master, but out of a job, signed on as 3rd Officer in the Ernel's Shipping co.'s *Barn Hill*, and was killed in the hold, when the vessel was bombed and sunk, 3 miles SSW of Beachy Head on 29th March 1940."

The Californian:

The SS *Californian* succumbed to the same fate as the *Carpathia* and the *Mount Temple*, when she was torpedoed by a U-Boat in November 1915. Still

---

347   This is a condensed biography of Groves, as found in "*The Ship That Stood Still*" Appendix H. Note that there is at least one opinion of Groves that is contrary to Reade's glowing testament. A Captain J.K. Downey wrote to Leslie Harrison in 1977 that Groves was unpopular with their crew, with the exception of Chief Officer Gill.

under the command of Captain Masters, she had been seconded as a troopship and was on a voyage between Saloniki and Marseille when she was hit. Despite being taken under tow by a French patrol ship, the line between the two vessels parted, and a second torpedo struck the *Californian*. She sank within an hour, 61 miles to the south-east of Cape Matapan. There was one casualty, R.J. Harding.

Appendix B. Distress Signals at Sea

The description of distress signals as used at sea were prescribed by Article 31 of the Rules of the Road[348] which stated that "These signals are made by virtue of the Section 434 of the Merchant Shipping Act, 1894:"

IN THE DAYTIME

1. A gun or other explosive signal fired at intervals of about a minute.
2. The international code of distress indicated by NC;
3. The distant signal, consisting of a square flag, having either above or below it a ball or anything resembling a ball;
4. The distant signal, consisting of a cone, point upward, having either above it or below it, a ball or anything resembling a ball;
5. A continuous sounding with any fog-signal apparatus.

AT NIGHT

1. A gun or other explosive signal fired at intervals of about a minute;
2. Flames on the vessel (as from a burning tar barrel, oil barrel, etc.);
3. Rockets or shells, throwing stars of any colour or description, used one at a time at short intervals;
4. A continuous sounding with any fog-signal apparatus.

In 1900, the above convention was adopted by the following countries in addition to the United Kingdom: the Argentine Republic, Austria-Hungary, Belgium, Brazil, Chile, China (only ships of foreign types), Costa Rica, Denmark, Ecuador, Egypt, France, Germany, Greece, Guatemala, Italy, Japan, Mexico, Netherlands, Norway, Peru, Portugal, Russia, Siam, Spain, Sweden and the United States. In forthcoming years, other countries also used these methods of distress, such as Canada.

A footnote to the Rules of the Road remarks, "The master of a vessel who displays, or allows anybody under his authority to display, the signals when his vessel is not in distress, will be liable to pay compensation for any labour

---

348   *The Rules of the Road At Sea* (3ʳᵈ Edition) by Hubert Stuart Moore, 1900

undertaken, risk incurred, or loss sustained in consequence of the signals having been taken for signals of distress," referring to the Merchant Shipping Act, 1894, section 434, subsection 2.

Obviously, the Rules of the Road prescribed the usage of rockets etc. in an international setting. Ships could use rockets or whatever pyrotechnics they desired in their own countries territorial waters, but the meaning of the footnote is clear: the use of rockets for private meanings in international waters, was discouraged.

Shipping companies were allowed to use rockets, flares, roman candles or combinations of lights to enable identification while away from port. However, the listings of the registered transatlantic private night signals[349] demonstrate that, either rockets were used in areas limited to the vicinity of the UK and Ireland, or that flames, rockets, shells and any of the other methods used for procuring assistance, were not used at all on the high seas. No other signals were used which contradicted the usage of distress signals listed in law: for instance, the only shipping line which explicitly mentioned "white rockets" was the Allan Line, and these were only to be used in passing North of Ireland Signal station, and explicitly not used on the high seas. No "white rockets," either on their own or in combination with other colours are mentioned in the listing of private night signals[350].

The British Government was aware of any ambiguity between "private" and "distress" signals: Section 733 subsection 2 of the Merchant Shipping Act 1894 states that "The Board [of Trade] may refuse to register any signals which in their opinion cannot easily be distinguished from signals of distress or signals for pilots."

To prevent any confusion in the meanings of lights at sea at night, the Board of Trade distributed the registered signals to shipmasters in a pamphlet, which was preceded by the following, "[Note - if these signals are used in any other place, for any other purpose than stated, they may be signals of distress, and should be answered accordingly by passing ships, and claims sent in for payment of salvage.]" This pamphlet would almost certainly have been distributed to Captains and been available on board ship.

Thus, from these internationally agreed items of law, we can only make the following conclusion: Captain Lord and his officers should have treated these white rockets as possible distress signals and investigated them. It also means that Captain Rostron was wrong to use his socket signals, as he did not use them for

---

349   See Appendix K in "*The Ship That Stood Still*" or
http://home.earthlink.net/~dnitzer/4HaasEaton/Compsigstable.html
350   The use of private company signals might have been misstated if Commodore Ivan Thompson is any indication. During a career at sea which spanned five decades, including time before and after the *Titanic* disaster, he had never seen such signals used. Captain Lord had sent up a rocket in his pre-*Californian* days as a greeting to a fellow mariner at sea.

distress purposes; passing ships may have mistaken his signals as distress rockets and may have been diverted away from the important task of heading towards the Titanic's location, and running into the massive ice field between the CQD and actual sinking location, with possible disastrous consequences.. Although the *Carpathia* was sending Marconi messages advising the Titanic and other ships that she was firing rockets, not every ship heard them. Fortunately, Rostron's heroism negated the need for castigation at the inquiries.

Harold Sanderson, a Director of the White Star Line, was asked about the usage of distress signals in his company by Clement Edwards at the British Inquiry. This is the relevant testimony:

19621. In point of fact these Rules which now apply to all the steamers, certainly all the steamers of the White Star Line, and probably to a great many others, are American Rules?

No, My Lord.

19622. They are Rules issued, apparently, by the American Company, because I hold the book In my hand. "The International Mercantile marine Company" - that is the American company?

Those Rules were drafted and prepared here by myself and my colleagues.

19623. That may be. But they are issued by the American company - "International Mercantile marine Company: Ships' Rules and Uniform Regulations." Is not that so?

Their name is on the book, My Lord.

19624. (*Mr. Clement Edwards.*) May I take it that every one of the companies or lines controlled by the International Mercantile marine Company are guided by these Rules?

They are.

19625. Does that apply to the Leyland Line too?

I think they also have adopted the same book.

19626. Do you mind turning to page 23, paragraph 112? Before I read that, however, I should like to ask you a question. You have just said that before this International Company came into existence there were a number of separate Regulations for each of the Companies. You yourself have been for some years attached to the White Star Company, and you have said that you had drawn up these Rules. In regard to assisting vessels in distress do you remember whether this Rule here is at all similar to the old Rule of the White Star Company?

I could not say at this distance of time whether it is identical with it or not.

19627. But this is the Rule to which, as far as its owners are concerned, Captain Lord would be subject?

I believe so.

19628. "Assisting Vessels in Distress - (a.) In the event of falling in with vessels derelict or in distress, Commanders (of the passenger steamers especially.) should bear in mind that by deviating from their courses or from the usual employment of their ships, in order to render assistance to other vessels, otherwise than for the purpose of saving life, questions as to insurance may arise, and responsibility may be incurred to passengers and owners of cargo for detention or risk to which they or their property on board may thereby be exposed. As a general Rule, therefore, Commanders of the passenger steamers in the North Atlantic trade are reminded that it will be better not to interfere in such cases, unless the circumstances be of very special character, or it be for the purpose of protecting or saving life. (b.) In the trans -Pacific and Colonial trades, Commanders of the passenger steamers, in coming to a decision on this point, should bear in mind the great distances involved and the comparatively infrequent opportunities of obtaining assistance which may occur, and that under such circumstances a liberal interpretation of these Rules is permissible." That, of course, is not on the Atlantic. "(c.) In the case of the cargo steamers other considerations apply, and the Commanders of these vessels may, should they consider the circumstances such as to justify their doing so, exercise a wider discretion in carrying out this regulation. (d.) Commanders of all steamers are cautioned that under no circumstances are they, in assisting vessels in distress, to unduly risk their own vessels, or expose the lives of those on board to hazard." So that as far as the Company itself is concerned the thing that is impressed upon their Officers is rather in the direction of not helping than helping?

I do not think that is a fair interpretation of the Rule.

The Commissioner:
Mr. Edwards, are you asking him to interpret what this means?

Mr. Edwards:
Yes.

The Commissioner:
Because, if so, that will not do. I must interpret it.

19629. (*Mr. Clement Edwards.*) Yes, My Lord. With due respect, My Lord, I perhaps ought not to have asked the question.

In addition, Clement Edwards later pointed out to Lord Mersey that page 23 of the Sailing Instructions for I.M.M. Vessels states, "The following signals numbered 1, 2 and 3 when used or displayed together or separately shall be deemed to be signals of distress at night (1.) a gun fired at intervals of about a minute. (2.)

Flames on the ship as from a burning tar barrel, oil barrel, etc. (3.) Rockets or shells of any colour or description fired one at a time at short intervals."

Appendix C. The *Titanic* and the *Californian* – A Possible Solution[351]

Firstly, the standard approximate equation used in this piece is:
distance (in nautical miles) = 1.17 x square root of observer's height above water line in feet

To see the maximum distance that two observers can see each other, just add their respective distances together: this gives a "common horizon". So for instance, two lookouts perched 100 feet above the waterline would just about fail to see a ship's red sidelight 39 feet high, at a maximum distance of 11.7 + 7.3 = 19 miles. The use of this cumbersome equation is due to the curvature of the earth, and doesn't take into account visibility, light brightness, super-refraction etc., which could curtail or extend the range of eyesight.

The key to perhaps understanding the geometry of the *Californian-Titanic* situation is to relate what each other saw. The *Californian* saw the *Titanic*'s red sidelight; and the *Titanic* saw the *Californian*'s sidelights. The *Titanic*'s sidelights were slightly more than 60 feet above the waterline, as seen by Groves, Gibson and Stone, who were 39 feet high (the height of the *Californian*'s flying bridge) + 6 feet (an estimate of their height) above the water. This gives a total distance of 16.9 miles. Similarly, for Boxhall et al. on the stricken liner, we get a value of 16.8 miles. It may be convenient at this stage to accept the smaller of these two values to enable the two ships to be seen. Note that, any further away and the sidelights would be below the horizon, and hence, invisible.

This gives us the maximum distance, but what about the minimum distance? Let me backtrack slightly.

Boxhall's flares, while visible to the *Carpathia*, were invisible to the *Californian*. Dave Gittins has calculated, from a flare held aloft, that the minimum *Californian* to *Titanic* distance was at least 10 miles. The *Californian* witnesses did not see the Cunard company signals, which consisted of blue roman candles firing blue balls to a height of 150 feet (their prescribed height) + 40 feet (the approximate height of the deckhead). The would therefore be seen at a distance of 24 miles. However, we do not know the luminosity of the roman candles. It may be instructive to note that none of the survivors in the *Titanic's* boats saw the candles either, so they must have been comparatively dim.

---

351   This article was originally from the author's website. It has been modified for inclusion here.

Let us now examine what the *Californian* did and what Boxhall saw as he and Rowe were morsing the other ship and firing off socket signals. There is good correlation between Boxhall and Gibson and Stone, with one notable exception. At the time of the last rocket, Boxhall saw the other ship's stern light: the *Californian* was heading nearly WSW and should have been showing her red light and her mastlights. How can we reconcile these two different facts? The human eye's ability to separate closely spaced lighting is rather poor at night, making such lights "fuse" into one glow. About 1 arc minute would be a good basis, based on Wikipedia [352] and internet newsgroup postings. Let us discuss what Boxhall saw and relate it to the *Californian*'s swinging motion. In the following chapter, 'R' and 'G' indicate the red and green sidelights of a vessel.

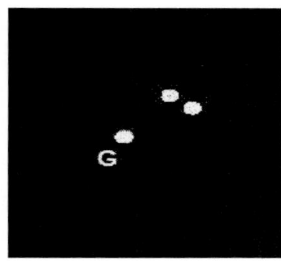

At 12.08 when Stone relieved Groves on the *Californian*, the ship they saw was dead abeam. She would have been showing a green sidelight to the *Titanic*, her two mastlights (on the fore and main mast, the latter being slightly higher than the former, and about 70 feet apart), and perhaps a couple of other lights, not represented here. The *Californian*'s masthead lights would be about 0.04 degrees (2.6 arc minutes) apart.

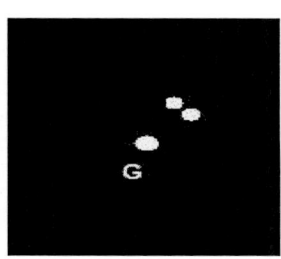

At 12.35, as he goes below to run his chores, Apprentice Gibson notes that the other ship (*Titanic*) is 1.5 points before the *Californian*'s starboard beam. The *Californian*'s mastlights would now be 2.5 arc minutes apart. This is approximately ten minutes before the first rocket was fired, and this therefore represents what Boxhall saw as he was waiting for Rowe and Bright to come to the bridge with detonators for the socket signals. The mast lights are displayed distinctly here as Boxhall would be observing them with binoculars, enabling him to make them out.

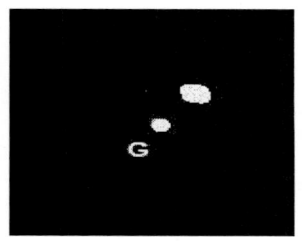

As the 7th rocket was fired, Gibson observes the other ship 2 points on the starboard bow. The mastlights would be separated by 1 arc minute, and would barely be observable as separate lights.

---

352   http://en.wikipedia.org/wiki/Naked_eye

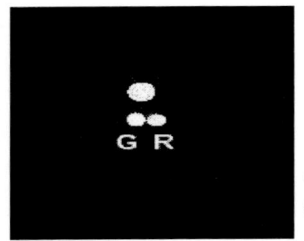

At some point in the evening, the *Californian* would be seen stem-on, showing all her lights.

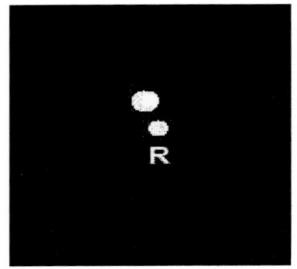

Finally, Boxhall is able to make out the other ship's red sidelight. The two sidelights would be so close as to meld into one glow.

Gibson observes the final rocket at 1.40am, 1 point on his starboard bow. The angular separation between the two mastlights is only 0.5 arc minutes. However, Boxhall doesn't see the *Californian's* red light: to him, it looks like the other ship is only showing her stern light, and he notices that the white light was "bright", exactly what would be expected if the light output of two lamps had fused into one glow. Similarly, Gibson has

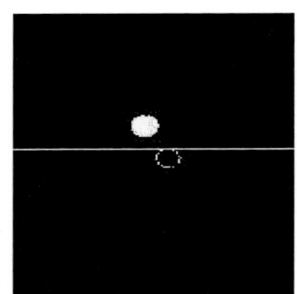

also observed that the other ship's port light has now gone too. The *Californian*, pointing roughly south-west *should* be showing her port light at this point. The thrust of all this is as follows: at this point, their respective red lights are below the horizon (shown as the solid white line). The unfilled circle represents the position of the red light.

So, what happened between 12.35 and 1.40? Simple: the *Titanic* was sinking with her bow down. The line of sight from the bridge was not the same as it was earlier in the evening. The red lights would now be below the horizon. This leads to the following situations:

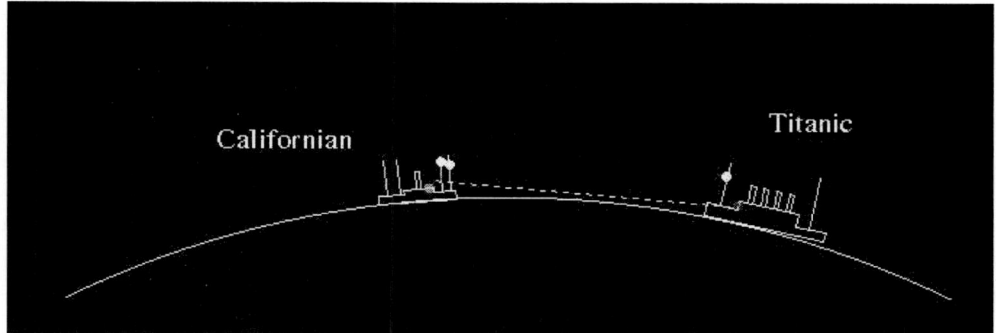

Illustration 47: Titanic - Californian situation at 12.45am

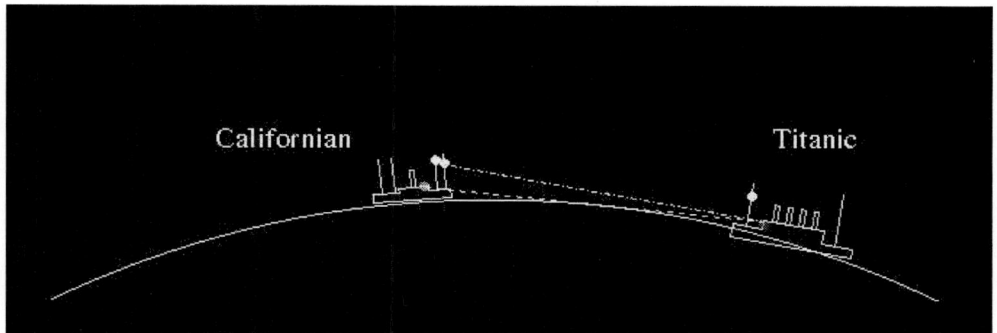

Illustration 48: Titanic - Californian situation at 1.45am

Can we quantify the distance between the two ships by determining how far *Titanic*'s bridge had dipped? It is possible to estimate it, but obviously there are no exact measurements. Shortly after Boxhall left the *Titanic*, Mrs. Thayer noticed that A deck was only 20 feet from the sea. We also have the analysis of Harland and Wolff's marine engineers Bedford and Hackett who give us a value of 5° for the forward list, or "trim". It can be estimated (VERY roughly it should be stressed) that the bridge was only about 35 feet above the waterline at the time Boxhall saw the supposed "stern" light.

How do these observations and findings contribute to this analysis? Let us input the values into the formula. Firstly, let us assume that the red lights were *just about* invisible. Boxhall, whose line of sight was 35 + 6 feet above the sea could not see the *Californian*'s red light (39 feet), which gives a distance of 14.8 miles. Let us do the same for Gibson: this provides a distance of 16.9. Any closer than this, and the red light would be seen. The minimum distance of these two ensures

405

that the red light could not be seen under any circumstance; that is 14.8 miles.

But there is one more element to be considered: analysis by Sam Halpern[353], demonstrates, that, at 1.40am, the *Titanic* suffered from a huge list to port. Sam's calculation, based on the observation that boat 10 was hanging a few feet from the side of the *Titanic* when swung out, is that the ship had a list to port of 10°. This, of course, would have brought the port light closer to the waterline; perhaps only 26 feet or so from the water. If we use this value, and the method described above, then we have a *Titanic-Californian* distance of 13.8 – 13.9 miles.

But how could Boxhall mistake a ship some 14 or so miles for a vessel only 5 miles away? The following diagram illustrates the matter:

On an even keel, and with no trim, the visible distance from the *Titanic*'s bridge to the horizon is some 9.5 miles. Boxhall placed the distance of 'the other ship' at 5 miles, and this is the figure most often quoted for the range of the ship. For symmetry reasons, the left hand diagram shows the placement of the vessel at "A" and "B", 4.5 miles on either side of the horizon limit.

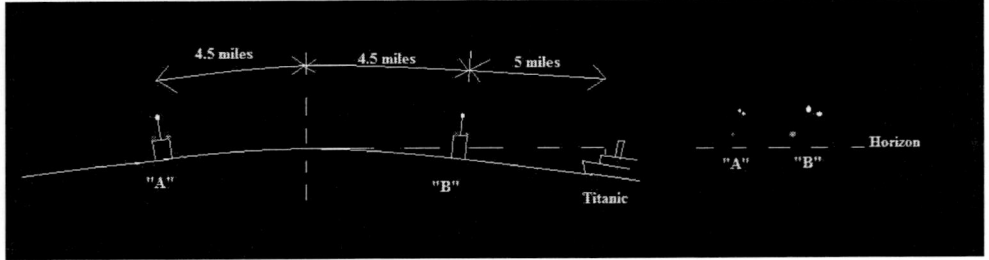

Illustration 49: Diagram showing the curvature of the Earth (not to scale), the Titanic and vessels at 5 and 13.5 miles

How would this have looked? The right diagram describes the situation. Obviously, "B" being closer, would have brighter lights than "A", whose lights would be situated closer together. The dashed line indicates the horizon, which of course, would not be seen unless a star would happen to rise or set. But there would be no points of reference, and nothing with which to compare sizes. Looking at nothing but the lights, there would be no way to determine if a vessel was 5 or 13.5 miles away. There would also be no way to determine if a ship was a larger vessel further away, or a smaller one close by. The *Californian*'s lights would be limited to those in the superstructure; that is, from the vantage of the *Titanic*, very little below this would be seen, as the area below the superstructure would not be lit, these spaces being occupied by engine and boiler rooms, and cargo space. So, looking at "B", there would be no lights on the main body of the ship (that is, "hull up[354]") to

353   http://www.encyclopedia-titanica.org/cgi-bin/discus/show.cgi?5664/78087
354   "Hull down" means that a ship is beyond the range of the visible horizon, and hence only a fraction of the hull would be visible; "Hull up" is the converse situation.

determine on which side of the horizon the lights would be.

Is there anything that can be said about Boxhall's certainty that he was observing a moving ship? Even in the 1960s, he was certain he had seen a vessel underway, and had accused Captain Lord of perjury, such was the level of his certainty. A partial answer is that he may have mistaken a very slowly swinging ship for an approaching steamer, which then turned away. But there may be another explanation, and it lies in the scientific fields of vision and psychology. It is called the 'Auto Kinetic Effect' and manifests itself when an individual observes small, stationary points of light in very dark and/or featureless conditions; exactly the situation on April 14th. Such lights seem to move, and one explanation is that, without any terms of reference to compare locations and movements, the human eye cannot determine a light's exact location[355]. Could the expectation of rescue have 'tricked' Boxhall and others into thinking that the ship was close, rather than distant? It is a fascinating question, but a researcher in the field of psychology has admitted that he did not know the answer as no work had been done in this area. It would be interesting to find out whether the prospect of rescue can colour the judgement of one on the deck of a doomed ship (or any scenario, for that matter).

Just how vigilant was Boxhall? From his testimony, it sounds as if he was watching the strange ship over a protracted period of time, with occasional morse lamp and rocket firing. But QM Rowe provides a different account. He told Leslie Harrison that, after the 2nd rocket has been fired (the first being fired while he was on the poop), he did not see Boxhall again. Where was the errant 4th Officer? A 1962 interview with the BBC provided a hint. He tells us that when he heard the 3 bells from the lookout signifying an obstruction (the iceberg) ahead, he "was sitting in [his] cabin having a cup of tea": quite against the regulations for an officer who should have been on watch and not what he said at the enquiries! Boxhall suffered terribly at the following inquiries, suffering from pleurisy, and the cold during the *Titanic's* voyage would have only exacerbated his condition. Did Boxhall sneak away for a replenishing cup of tea occasionally? In that case, how often did he keep the other ship under observation? Rowe's account makes it sound as if Boxhall was hardly present!

The *Titanic-Californian* distance can be placed between 16.8 and 13.9 miles. I would tend to place it closer to the shorter distance, as Groves watched the ship approaching from an even further distance away after 11.10. For this analysis, I will use the value of 14 miles as this is more convenient to work with.

It should be noted too that these figures may be influenced by the actual, rather than calculated values of the height above the waterline. These pictures of the *Californian* reproduced here, taken the morning after the disaster, show her to be riding slightly high out of the water. However, even an error of 4 feet in this determination only translate to an error of +/- 0.4 miles in determining the distance.

---

355   An excellent demonstration for readers is to look at the small blinking light on a domestic burglar alarm or smoke detector in a pitch black room.

What about the occupants of the lifeboats? Most people who saw the ship off the port bow only report seeing a white light - almost certainly the mastlights "fused" into one. This is logical as, from a lower vantage than the boat deck, they would be unable to see the *Californian's* red and green sidelights. Unfortunately this author is unable to state absolutely just how high above the waterline the line of sight in a lifeboat would be. However, the photo here allows us to estimate this value.

Illustration 50: Californian as seen from the Carpathia

Illustration 51: Another view of the Californian from the Carpathia

From the known length (30 feet) of a standard lifeboat, we can estimate from this picture than an observer would be 5 1/2 feet above the waterline. Note that, in this picture, perhaps because of perspective and maybe because he is standing on a joist, the crewmember at the tiller seems to nearly 9 feet tall! The crewman is standing up obviously, but let us tread carefully. To this author, a value of 5 feet seems reasonable.

Illustration 52: A Titanic Lifeboat, as seen from the Carpathia

To see the masthead lights of the *Californian*, approximately 100 feet above the waterline, the lifeboat would have to be no further than 14.3 miles away. Again, close to the 14 miles distance calculated above. This indicates that, from the waterline, the mastlights would be "right on the edge" of visibility. This may explain why, for instance, Boxhall lost sight of the lights as he rounded the *Titanic's* stern in boat 2, ending up only 200 feet from the starboard beam of the *Titanic*. At such a low height above the waterline, an error of +/- 1 foot equates to 0.3 miles.

Only a few people reported seeing the sidelights of the mystery ship from the water that night. To see them would require a distance of no more than 9.7 miles. Steward Crawford, who gave conflicting evidence on this point in England and America, was in boat 8 and saw them at one point, as did the Countess of Rothes, seated a foot or two above him, managing the tiller. During the night, boat 8 pulled for the light(s) on the horizon for 3 hours, under the instructions of Captain Smith to land the passengers and return with help.

Boat 8 would have had to have rowed about 5 miles: is this possible in the three hours they were underway? The incumbents were pulling diligently, so it may be that they did get close enough to see the sidelights. However, to be fair it should be reported that the lifeboats were rowing into a southerly current which almost certainly would have retarded their progress in fetching help from the uncooperative *Californian* to the north.

(Also, it should be noted that Crawford saw both red and green lights when he turned round to look. Obviously the *Californian* was pointing straight at the *Titanic*, the former of which was slowly swinging clockwise during the night. For Crawford to have seen both lights at such an "early" time after leaving the *Titanic*

409

means that boat 8 must have made much more significant headway than I give them credit for. Allowing for rounding errors etc. in my calculations, it may just be possible).

There are a few other matters of interest, and debate. The *Californian*'s green light was observed by Boxhall and, if his testimony is anything to go by, only through binoculars. Even Fred Fleet, whose eyesight had been tested for responsiveness to colours, only saw a white light.

On the subject of lights, Lowe saw the *Californian*'s red light and mastlights whilst he was preparing lifeboat 1 for lowering. Using the logic as defined above, he should not have been able to see the two white lamps separately, especially as he only give the ship "a glance". If this author may be slightly flippant, it may be that Lowe had eyesight superior to his fellow officers...?

To conclude this section, I propose the following situation, showing that, at 2.20am (in a location that we can be certain that the *Titanic* sank), the two ships were some 14 miles apart.

Sam Halpern, in "Lights on Horizon part 2" calculates the following positions for the *Californian*: at.10.21pm: 41° 56 N 50° 06.5 W At 10.30pm 10.30 41° 55 N 50° 07 W At 2.05am: 41° 52 N 50° 08.5 W. This latter co-ordinate is only 2.3 miles from my deduced co-ordinates in the map.

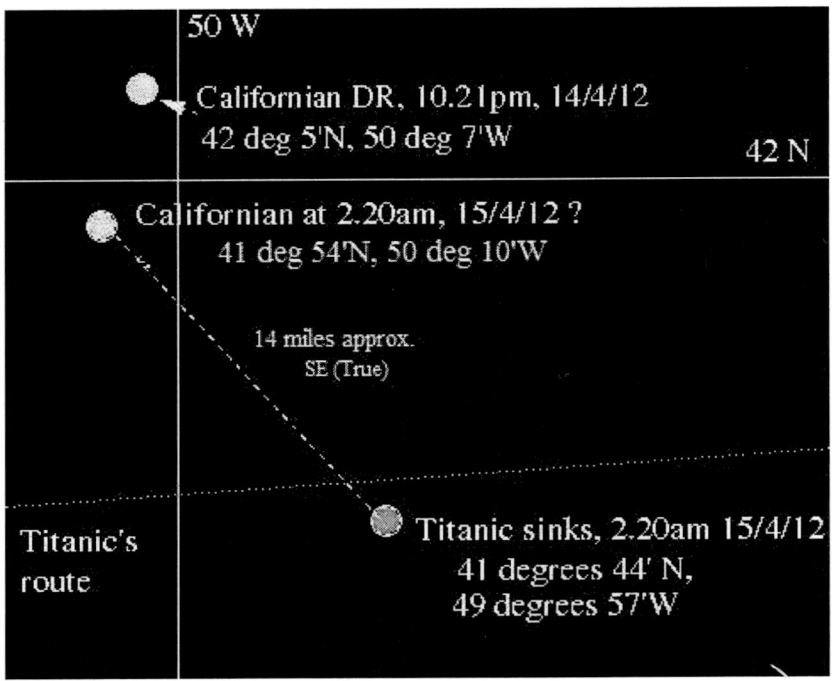

Illustration 53: Possible Titanic - Californian situation

All artist's depictions of the *Titanic* as seen at night show her to be fully lit, every porthole blazing light. The collision is generally accepted to have occurred at 11:40pm, when most passengers would have been asleep. Furthermore the lights for companionways and public rooms would have been extinguished for the night. The lights in the third class public areas would already have been doused as an encouragement to "go to bed", in line with the rules of the White Star Line[356].

Thanks to enlightening discussions on the Encyclopedia-titanica website[357], we can estimate what lights would be seen as the clock neared midnight that Sunday evening. This leads to the following picture:

---

356   The lights in the 3rd class general room, under the poop deck at the extreme stern end of the ship may have been turned on after the collision, as the room started filling with steerage who, by all accounts, played the piano, prayed to God etc. Third class child passenger Marshall Drew noted that, as he entered a lifeboat the aft end of the starboard boat deck, the poop and stern area of the Titanic was completely dark; an impression that stayed with him for the rest of his life.

357   http://www.encyclopedia-titanica.org/discus/messages/5660/86797.html, http://www.encyclopedia-titanica.org//discus/messages/5921/53282.html and http://www.encyclopedia-titanica.org/discus/messages/5660/84172.html

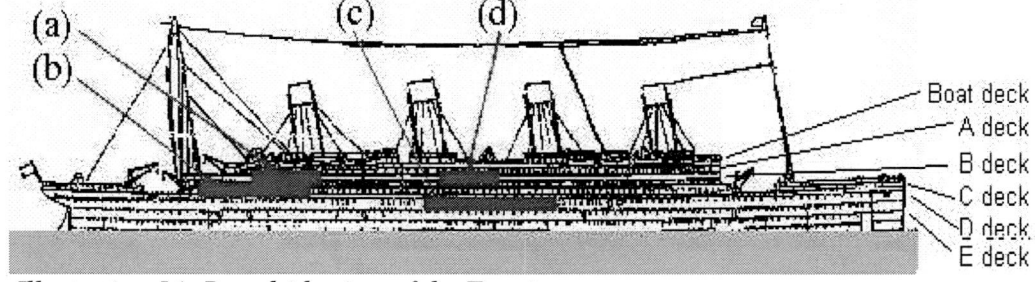
Illustration 54: Broadside view of the Titanic

"a" denotes the 1st class smoking room, "b" denotes the 2nd class smoking room and the Café Parisian, "c" indicates the 1st class dining saloon and "d" is the 1st class lounge. Since they are so close to each other, "a" and "b" would be discerned as one glowing area of light. At a distance, "c" and "d" would also be indistinguishable from "a" and "b." Lawrence Beesley noted a few second class stewards in and near the 2nd class dining saloon shortly after the collision; it is not known if this room's lights were on; but if they were, this would provide a source of illumination slightly below and behind the area "b". Second Class Steward James Witter informed Walter Lord that the 2nd Class Smoking Room was vacated and closed by midnight; this room would therefore cease to be a source of illumination. There would also be navigation lights and a few other cabin lights, but most passengers would presumably be in their cabins asleep at this late hour, their curtains or deadlights closed[358], so lighting from the passenger areas would be at a minimum. It seems unlikely that the lights on promenade deck "A" were lit, because of the inducement for passengers to retire at such a late hour. The lights were on at 2.05am, a quarter of an hour before the final plunge, as passenger Hugh Woolner noted that they were glowing a "devilish red." The power of each lamp on the promenade would be about half that of the mast- and side-lights, and together with the screen that covered the first half of the promenade deck, this would reduce their observability at a distance.

---

358   More discussion on a lit *Titanic* can be found at
        http://home.earthlink.net/~dnitzer/Updates/Glare.html

Illustration 55: The Titanic, approaching the Isle of Wight. The solid outline indicates the A deck promenade: notice how small the windows at the extreme forward end of the deck are. Comparatively little light would be allowed to escape.

How big would such a broadside *Titanic* be? From 5 miles away, she would be seen to be 1.7 degrees across from bow to stern; at 10 miles, this would be 0.8 degrees; and at 15 miles, 0.6 degrees. The amount of space occupied by the saloon lights above would be much less, perhaps about 33% of the total length of the hull.

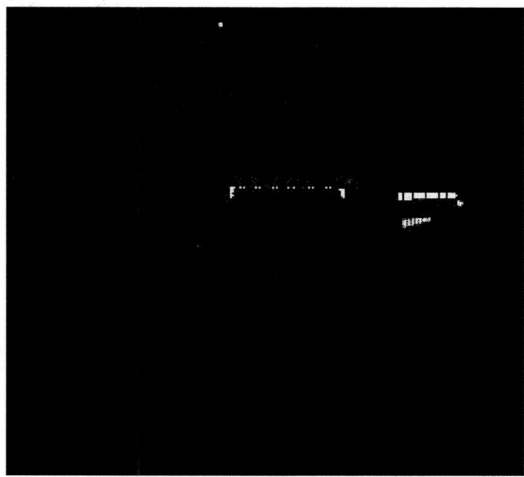

Illustration 56: The Titanic, viewed from 2 points off the port bow. Note that A deck has been illuminated (including the area below the bridge). With the forward end of A deck enclosed, most of the light would come from the comparatively open rear end; "all lit up at the aft end" as Gibson would say.

To make some sense of these numbers, an American, or UK, penny is approximately 19 mm in diameter. Hold it at arms length (about 2 feet). It would cover an angular distance of 1.8 degrees; *Titanic* seen from 5 miles would be 1.7 degrees. At night, with only her lights visible, the angular coverage of the *Titanic* would be dramatically less, as her darkened fore and after decks would not be seen, and nearly everything forward of the 2nd funnel being in darkness, screened by bulwarks etc. And, to give a comparable sense of scale, at a cruising height of 37,000 feet, the distance between the red and green lights on the wing-tips of a 747 "Jumbo" jet as seen from the ground would be just 0.3 degrees.

A northward facing *Titanic* would present little light to an observing vessel, and, at 12-14 miles, would be partially over the horizon, limiting a view of the hull. Stone and Gibson thought that what they were observing was a medium-sized tramp steamer, something like themselves, also pointing somewhere to the north of the *Californian*. The distance would be, in their view, on the order of about 5 miles. This vessel would be before the horizon, but how much of such a ship would be seen? The hull may be used for stowing cargo, and may not have illumination. Crew quarters, either in the forecastle, or the superstructure may show some lights,

415

but it is, of course, impossible to say definitively.

The following sketch may be of some use. It shows what the lights of the *Titanic* would look like, over the horizon. The vessel on the left is a depiction of the *Californian*, headed in the same direction as the *Titanic*'s lights as an example of a medium sized tramp. Note that the superstructure of the *Californian* is above the horizon. If this was the only area that showed any lights (deck lights, red light, engine room skylight etc.), it would be the same as a larger vessel, further away. Although the complete hull of the *Californian*/tramp steamer is much larger than the small area covered by the *Titanic*'s lights, the tramp, when showing lights at night, would appear much smaller.

Also note that, for reasons of clarity, the depiction of the two vessels has been magnified. To give an idea of scale, the apparent length of the *Californian* from this angle would be 0.3 degrees; the same width as a 747 airliner at its cruising altitude. Also note that the *Titanic*'s lights would be very sparse, except for the "faint glare of lights on her after-deck", to quote Gibson.

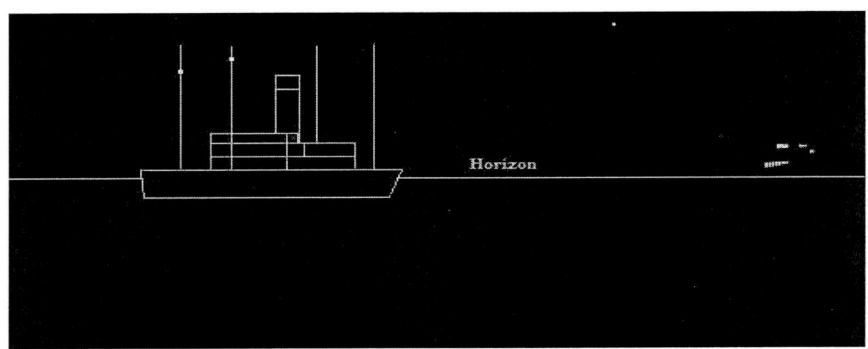

Illustration 57: Lights of the Titanic at night (right) compared with a view of the Californian.

A few other things should be raised. As referred to previously, the angular resolution of the human eye at night is about 1 arc minute. How does this translate into distance?

At 5 miles, any lights within a distance of some 8 feet would not be separable.

At 10 miles, the distance would be 18 feet.

At 15 miles, the distance would be 27 feet.

So, no individual rows of portholes (as Donkeyman Gill on the *Californian* said) would be seen. Another matter is just how much of the *Titanic* could be seen at these distances? At 5 miles, all of the ship would be before the horizon and could be seen; at 10 miles, everything 4 feet above the *Titanic*'s waterline could be

observed; at 15 miles, only those lights 42 feet and above could be seen - that is, the boat deck, and A and B deck lights, from the bridge of the *Californian*. The *Titanic*, hardly a massive blaze of light as depicted in film and paintings, would only be showing isolated spots of light - which would be the smoking rooms and a few other public lounges. There would be nothing else to see.

The *Titanic* would gradually awake from its sleep, lights turning on as stewards awoke passengers, as the situation became apparent..... but viewed from the front, and at distance, lights that would be seen broadside would not be evident.

Titanic researcher George Behe has also written on this subject on his website[359] The only downside is, as George says, the model of the *Titanic* is too brightly lit.

Consulting the following picture of the *Titanic*'s forward starboard boat deck, it should be noted that the deck lights have screens located which prevents any light from being seen, in relative terms, from the forward most portion of the deck. Deck lights seen from forward would be mostly shielded[360].

Illustration 58: Purser McElroy and Captain Smith at the Officers Quarters of the Titanic

Therefore, another interesting piece of evidence that helps to remove the fantasy of a brightly lit *Titanic*, rushing to her doom.

Let us examine what Groves on the *Californian* says about the *Titanic* when he first saw her. At the British Inquiry, he says that at 11.10, he sees a single white light, which he thought might have been a star rising (therefore, he sees it to the east). At 11.25, Groves sees another masthead light; since *Titanic* only carried

359   http://ourworld.compuserve.com/homepages/Carpathia/Page14.htm
360   Another photograph showing the shielded lights can be seen at
   http://www.titanicphotographs.com/galleryB.asp?GalleryID=3&ID=228

one, he must have been mistaken in some way.

By 11.30, Groves reports to the Captain that the "light" was a passenger steamer due to the large amount of light showing. At 11.40, the other ship stopped, or seemed to stop. Later Groves seemed to be mildly confused as to whether the lights he had seen were "put out" or "shut out" for the night - the latter being a common practise by passenger carrying companies as a prompt for the people to "go to bed". However, Groves agrees that the other ship might have turned 2 points to port, as the bright white deck lights were now obscured (or had gone out) enabling him to see the red port light.

From reading the testimony, it seems clear that the court was using the *Titanic*'s movement prior to the collision (a two point deviation to port) and the time of stopping to fix in their mind that the other ship was the *Titanic*. This is seriously flawed. A two point turn to port at the time of the collision would not have shut out the *Titanic's* green light - which Groves never saw. The only way that the red light would be seen is if the Titanic was pointing somewhere between north-west and easterly ... and the former option seems credible as he says that the ship was coming up obliquely to the *Californian*, and was not showing her broadside.

Therefore, it makes this author believe that when the *Titanic* was seen to stop by Groves at 11.40, the White Star liner had already manoeuvred in such a way to be pointing north... the collision must have occurred sometime sooner than this, and the "11:40" timing must be a coincidence due to the differences in ship's times. If the *Californian* had seen the *Titanic* before it started moving in an arc, then heading northward, then she would have been moving slightly south of west - in other words, getting further and further away, and hence making her lights even more indistinct, rather than brighter and clearer. If we take the computer simulation (from the Encyclopedia-titanica website, as will be discussed shortly), then it would take about 6 minutes for the *Titanic* to come heading North.

When Stone came on the bridge at 12.08 to relieve Groves, he saw the other ship and checked its bearing with the compass - which he saw to be SSE, directly on the starboard beam. The compass deviation that night was 2 points, so the bearing would be SE (true).

I would direct the reader to the previous section of this piece discussing the amount of light visible to Groves, and later, Stone and Gibson. At 14 miles, only the lights of the boat deck (that is, very few), A deck and B deck would be observable. The bridge would be dark.

Regarding the *Titanic*'s movements post-collision, an excellent discussion on a computer simulation can be found[361]. It is apparent that, when the *Titanic* performed her big arc, and came to be heading North, her latitude was roughly what it was before the collision. After this, she steamed on at half speed. Unfortunately, there is no consensus on how long this occurred. For the sake of

---

361   http://www.encyclopedia-titanica.org/discus/messages/5664/85047.html

discussion, let us assume 10 minutes. At half speed, this amounts to a distance of about 2 miles. Again, these figures are rough, but illustrative. The main point is that, just after the collision, but before steaming on, more of the *Titanic* would be hull down (below the horizon), and hence less light would be displayed. An extra 2 miles south would obscure everything 67 feet above the waterline... which means only the mastlight would be seen. It may be that Groves saw nothing of the collision and its immediate aftermath.

Once she had come to a stop, the passengers would be roused to prepare for the evacuation. But, because the ship is facing north and is so far away, very few of her lights would be seen. The lights on the A-deck promenade below the bridge etc. may be lit, which would provide some little illumination. The forward facing cabins on A and B deck were mostly unoccupied, so the only light would be from the deck lights which were mounted on the roof, not on the forward bulkhead. A speculative article on cabin allocations[362] lists only two occupied cabins on B deck forward (the similar area on A deck had no occupants):

B3 - Robert, Mrs. Edward Scott and Maid
B5 - Allen, Ms. Elizabeth Walton and Madill, Ms. Georgette Alexandra

It now seems likely that Mrs. Roberts' maid was on E-deck. A further hypothesised occupant on these B-deck cabins (the famous Margaret "Molly" Brown) could also have been located on E deck too[363]

Of these two cabins, B3 and B5, information is sketchy, but thanks to the generous help of George Behe, the following may be said: Mrs. Roberts may have been trying to get some sleep - in various accounts, she had either "just dropped off to sleep", "was awakened by the crash" or "was awake in her cabin when the crash came". It may be that she was dozing in her cabin with the lights off. Miss Allen had either just retired to her cabin (where Ms. Madill had already gone) or was in the library. It seems possible that, at the time of the collision, this cabin's lights were on, although it is not known whether their curtains were drawn. Even so, it provides more credible evidence that the Titanic must have been showing very little light forward of her bows.

With regards to other areas of the forward superstructure, the bridge would be in a darkened state too, to prevent extraneous lighting ruining the "night vision" of the officers of the watch. Furthermore, as discussed, Lloyd's publications highly recommended that lights in the vicinity of the Morse lamps (on top of the wing cabs either side of the bridge) should be doused. To summarise this discussion, the *Titanic* would appear to be poorly lit, with most, if not all the lights, coming from the right, of the port lamp - as Gibson said later.

---

362   http://www.encyclopedia-titanica.org/cabins.html
363   http://www.encyclopedia-titanica.org/articles/molly-brown_klistorner.pdf

This leads us to the heading of the *Titanic*, as she ultimately "finished with engines". Today, the bow section of the wreck lies facing "slightly east of North", as Dr. Ballard said shortly after her discovery.

This leads to a conundrum. George Behe places the *Titanic* heading slightly north of NNW; in line with Gibson's statement at the British Inquiry. This is quite true, and survivors' accounts place the "white light" anywhere between 1/2 point and 4 points off the starboard bow. Of course, it may be advisable to use Boxhall's testimony, since he was observing the other ship for the longest period of time. He says that, at first the other ship was 1/2 point away, and when he last saw her, she was 2 points away. Of course, both ships were stopped, but the Titanic may have been turning in the drift, giving the impression to Boxhall that the ship he was seeing was steaming off. Q.M. Rowe on the *Titanic* says that the stern was swinging making the bow face North. However, Pitman, lying close to the ship off the starboard side didn't see the *Titanic* turning. It should be noted that Pitman was evidently not the most observant of witnesses as he failed to see the ship breaking up as she sank!

One more point: Lawrence Beesley, for one, reported that his boat (13) rowed forwards in the direction that the Titanic was heading before she sank - and this turned out to be North-West.

Can we determine where the *Californian* was when she stopped? If we take a proposed 14 mile *Titanic-Californian* distance, at a bearing of SE/NW to be accurate at all times that night, we can come up with some more co-ordinates, if we say that the *Californian* was at 41°55'N at 2.20am. We know the *Titanic* was at a latitude of 41°47'N when she struck, if she was on track[364]. She steamed northwards for some time, to end up at some location: given the times and speed, this may have been about 2 miles. When the *Titanic* struck, the Californian would have been at a latitude of 41°57'N. When *Californian* stopped at 10.21, this would put her at about 41°59'N. At 6.00am, she would be at 41°51'N... 7 miles north of the wrecksite.

Captain Lord estimated that he was at 42°5'N, 50°7'W when he stopped for the night. This author would put him at about 42°N, 50°10'W, a difference of 6.3 miles. All these numbers assume a southerly current with no east/west component. However, Stewart's Pole Star sighting at 7.30pm (giving a latitude of 42°5.5' N) excepted, the agreement between these numbers is satisfactory. The distance between my 2.20am position and the 10.21pm DR position of Captain Lord is 11.4 miles, and a bearing of 191.5°. Some estimate of the current can be attempted: from 10.21 to 2.20, we get a drift of 2.85 knots. This seems quite high. Let us try another tactic: if we assume that Stewart's Pole Star sight was correct, and that the current started to affect the *Californian* immediately afterwards, we can get a minimum drift. 11.4 miles over nearly 7 hours gives us 1.6 knots. Let us compare this with

---

364   Sam Halpern's excellent analysis can be found at
    http://www.glts.org/articles/halpern/collision_point.html

the average drift that the *Titanic*'s wreckage were subjected to between 2.20 and 11.20am on April 15th. The distance would be 11.6 miles and a bearing of 195.2° : the bearings are extremely close, as is the drift rate (1.3 knots).

For too long now, the positioning of the *Californian* with respect to the *Titanic* has been like a game of "pin-the-tail-on-the-donkey". Find the *Titanic*. Draw a line in whatever direction you want and there is the *Californian*. Very little attempt has been made to explain the locations, based on what was seen. The "5 mile", or "10 mile" mantra has been repeated with very little thought by the opponents of Captain Lord. On the other hand, the arguments of Senan Molony, Leslie Harrison et al., although weak, do provide one strong point of discussion. For the *Californian* to have wound up so far south, this would mean a massive error on the part of the stellar observations, steering and/or drift that night. This, to my mind is impossible. I suspect that the *Californian* stopped roughly where she said she was, so I was surprised, and delighted to have this confirmed during this analysis.

Were it not for various conflicting pieces of testimony, the "mystery" would not have endured for as long as it has. With the bulk of the evidence supporting the hypothesis that the two ships were in sight of each other, there are bound to be pieces of the story that don't fit in (such as Groves first seeing the ship well aft of the starboard beam, seemingly putting its motion eastward, and Stone seeing a moving ship whose rockets only went up to half the height of the mastlight). In actual fact, the socket signals from the *Titanic* went up to 600-800 feet according to available literature from the period. If we take the lower of these two values, then it means that an observer at sea level 28.7 miles from the point of detonation (along the surface of the sea) could see the rockets, depending on the brightness of the explosion. For Captain Lord's supporters to insist that none of the *Titanic*'s rockets were seen means that she must have been this distance away from the *Titanic* - in fact, if we take the height of Stone and Gibson above the water line, then the distance becomes over 36 miles! Compare this with the distance from the wreck site to Captain Lord's claimed location - approximately 21 miles. It is impossible to imagine anything that would cause such a huge error in navigation to enable the *Californian* to be outside the range of the rockets.

In fact, this whole point of the brightness of the detonating rockets being more of a deciding factor in their visibility can be qualified by some basic conjectures. Readers are invited to read Dave Gittins website; as a navigator, he approaches various practical *Titanic* problems from a novel point of view.

Let us not forget the *Carpathia* either. Traditional *Titanic*-lore suggests that she was racing at 17.5 knots during her dash to the north. This is a physical impossibility. Her true speed may have been 14-15 knots. She was about ten miles away from the wreck site when her officers saw Boxhall's green flares, sighted at approx. 3.15am. This was about 1.5 hours after the last *Titanic* rocket was fired.

This gives a rough distance from the wreck site of 1.5*(15) + 10 = 32.5 miles at 1.45am. Rockets fired, and reaching a height of 600 feet could be visible for up to 36 miles. Every officer on the bridge of the *Carpathia* was scanning their direction of travel, looking for icebergs - and they saw no rocket detonations from the *Titanic*. The *Californian's* watch officers saw rockets fired at about 3.15am, which can only have come from the *Carpathia*. If the above essay is correct, then the distance between the *Carpathia* and the *Californian* must have been 15 + 10 = 25 miles. These rockets were seen, but at the limit of visibility. So, from this, the observable range of the rockets was between 25 and 32.5 miles. Readers may wish to read about the inverse square law to explain how the intensity of light diminishes with distance.

Putting these details aside, the only mystery is one of psychology: the relationship between Lord and Stone, and why information just wasn't getting through from the bridge. Why wasn't enough urgency placed on the sighting of rockets? In an interview with Walter Lord, when writing "*A Night to Remember*", Groves recalled Stone as being lazy, and taken to snoozing in his cabins between watches - a man who wasted life, as Groves said. He also said that Stone was afraid of Captain Lord. In such circumstances, Stone may have been the sort of person who didn't want to press the issue, as Groves said to Walter Lord. As Stone said, he simply informed the master of the situation and left him to judge. Lord relied on Stone, the Officer of the Watch. Stone relied on Lord for guidance. And so, the information just didn't get through. And if Ivan Thompson was correct in his letter to Walter Lord, this caused frustration to the men on the bridge: they tried and tried to get the Captain out of the chart room where he was sleeping, as Thompson said.

Readers will note that Gill's information, whom this author has never trusted, is not regarded here as his story is very flimsy.

Regarding the navigational aspects of the case, the two ships were certainly more than 10 miles apart. Had they been any closer, then the green flares[365] would have been seen by the *Californian* crew. Therefore, if this author is right, this would make Lord Mersey's 5-10 mile distance estimate very wrong indeed.

The only untested part of this theory is whether the ships could see each over such a distance: this author has no data on the power output of either ship's navigational lamps, but a magnificent theoretical treatment does exist[366]. As discussed in the main text of this book, an attempt was made to replicate the *Titanic-Californian* situation in 1996, during the RMS Titanic Inc./Titanic International memorial cruise. Two ships, of intermediate size between that of the *Titanic* and the *Californian* were placed 16-19 miles apart and rockets were fired, which reached a height of 750 feet. The rockets were seen, as expected, but so were

---

365   http://users.senet.com.au/~gittins/calpos.html
366   http://www.glts.org/articles/halpern/masthead_light.html Note that the mast and sidelights were equipped with dioptric lenses, which would have concentrated the emitted light output.

the mastlights of the other ship, albeit very faint. The cruise liner *Royal Majesty* observed the proceedings while the research vessel *Ocean Voyager* (ex-*Pandora II*) fired the rockets. I was intrigued to know how the *Ocean Voyager*, which sank in 2002, compared to the *Titanic*. The *Ocean Voyager* was 186 feet long and the height from waterline to the **top** of the mast is about 76 feet. Of course, the mast light would be affixed some distance below this. It is also estimated that the height from water line to the bridge would be approximately 38 feet. Remember that only the mastlight was seen, faintly. The estimated distance from the top deck of the *Royal Majesty* (the ship "doing" the observing) was about 80 feet above the water. Applying the usual formula for maximum observing distances, it can be found that the furthest an observer on the top deck of the *Royal Majesty* could see the top of the *Ocean Voyager*'s mast would be some 21 miles. So, it would seem that, the lights are visible for quite a fraction of the distance to the observable horizon. And of course, observing conditions on the 14th and 15th April 1912 were extremely clear. On the night that the recreation was performed, the atmosphere was described as slightly hazy.

Sam Halpern's analysis of the *Titanic*'s mastlight, as described in the reference above shows that, at 17 miles, the light would be as bright as a star with an apparent magnitude of 1. To give an indication as to how bright this is, the two lower left stars in Orion's belt, Alnitak and Alnilam, are magnitude 1.7. Magnitude 1 is twice as bright as 1.7 and would be very noticeable, especially if one considers that the only other star of comparable brightness as seen from the *Californian* in the south-east would be Antares - also magnitude 1. *Titanic*'s lights would therefore be noticeable and obvious. In fact, Antares would be on the horizon and rising at about the same time that Groves saw the other ship's light at 11.10pm; Antares is in the same direction as this light and would naturally have drawn one's eyes to the ESE.

To summarise, the physics and geometry of the *Titanic-Californian* are, for the most part, quite simple, and the two ships could be seen. But the bigger mystery is that of the inaction of the *Californian*. What we can't do is psychoanalyse the men on the *Californian*, their relationships with each other, and their ability to take the initiative in unusual situations. If we could, we would finally know just why the whole mess was allowed to happen. Of course, clues exist in the evidence and from other correspondents, but dead men can tell no tales.

Appendix D. The Mystery Lights[367]

In addition to the unidentified ships seen on the western side of the icefield, another possible mystery ship was seen to its east, the side that the *Carpathia* was approaching from, and the side on which the *Californian* lay stopped for the night.

At 12.30am, the *Carpathia* started her dash to the north-west. By 3.00am, she noticed green flares in the distance, 1/2 point off his bow - flares fired by Boxhall. At the same time, Captain Rostron and his officers noticed two masthead lights and a red port light of a ship 2 points off his starboard bow. To reassure *Titanic*'s passengers that help was on the way, he ordered rockets and Cunard company signals to be fired. At exactly this time, somewhere to the north of the wreck site, the *Californian* noticed rockets right on the horizon, at "such a distance that if it had been much further I should have seen no light at all," as 2nd Officer Stone said later. Three rockets were seen, separated by a few minutes.

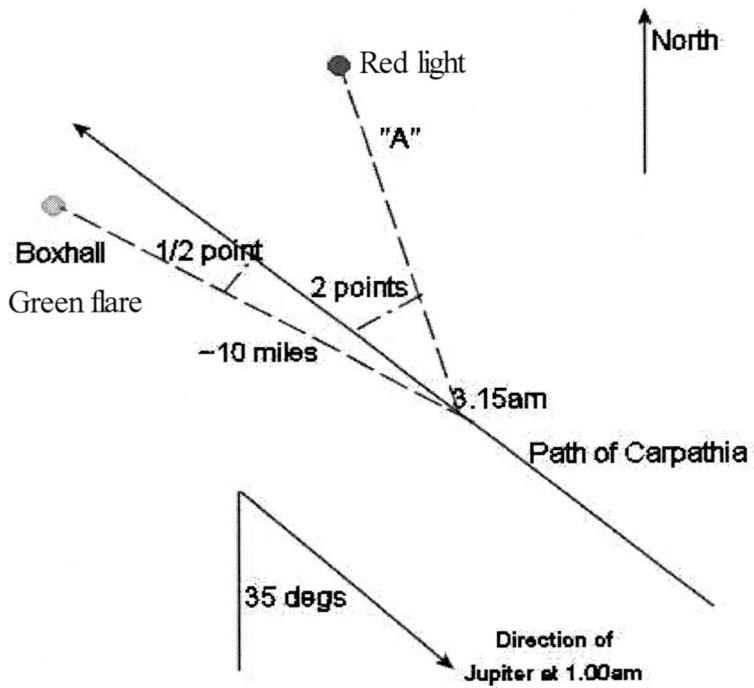

Illustration 59: The path of the Carpathia, en route to the Titanic

Neither Stone, nor Apprentice Gibson who standing beside him, saw

367   Adapted from the author's website.

anything of the ship firing these rockets. If they could see the *Carpathia*, they would have seen the mastlights, the blue Cunard recognition signals, comprising of roman candles firing balls to a height of 150 feet, the green starboard light and perhaps some lights on the superstructure.

It has been suggested that the *Californian*, heading roughly west, saw the *Carpathia*'s rockets (which is plausible) and the *Carpathia* saw the *Californian*'s red sidelight. If the *Californian* was only ten miles due north of the *Titanic*, it meant that the distance between the two ships would be about 17 miles - theoretically, within viewing distance of each other; however, the lights would be right on the edge of the visible horizon. It does seem odd that two ships looking at each other should see different things. Also, although most witnesses on the *Titanic* reported seeing the lights of a ship off the port bow (that is, to the North), one witness did report seeing a red and a white light on the starboard beam - roughly in the direction that the *Carpathia* saw "her" red lights.

However, we do know that the bearing of the *Californian*'s mystery ship was S45E (True), and not due south. Thus, the map as shown in "*The Ship That Stood Still*" seriously misrepresents the locations of the vessels in the area.

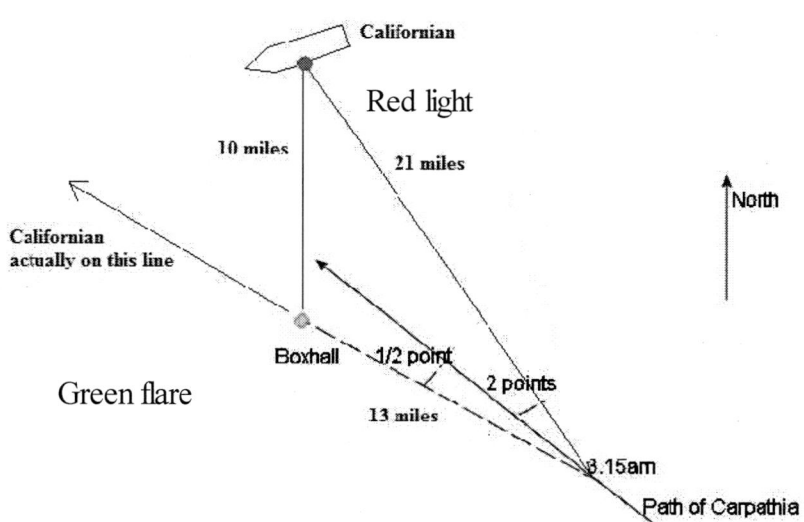

Illustration 60: The relation between the Carpathia, Californian and the Green Flares as depicted in "The Ship That Stood Still."

Although the geometry seems reasonable, except for the north-south bearing of the *Californian* from the *Titanic* wrecksite, the quoted distance from the *Carpathia* to the *Californian* is an astonishing 21 miles. At such a range, the

Californian's mastlights might be seen, although perhaps too faint to be seen as artificial lights, but her red light would be well below the horizon. Stone and Gibson saw nothing of the *Carpathia*. One possible solution is to invoke "super refraction" to allow lights to be visible from beyond the horizon, but the editor of *"The Ship That Stood Still"* is sceptical of this explanation. Thus, the situation has been accepted simply as more "evidence" against Captain Lord.

If the "13 mile" estimate between the *Carpathia* and Boxhall at 3.15am is correct, then the *Californian* would have been almost on the same line of bearing – but at least ten miles beyond, otherwise the green flares would have been seen by Stone and Gibson. The distance between the *Carpathia* and the *Californian* would be about 23 miles, and Captain Lord's ship would be seen almost dead ahead of the Cunarder. A 23 mile distance would negate any possibility of the *Californian* being seen by Rostron and his officers.

Using such logic, it seems clear that the red light and mastlights did not belong to the *Californian*. The bearings are completely wrong!

One must also consider Quartermaster Rowe. As recounted previously, Rowe was convinced he saw a ship's stern light on the *Titanic's* starboard quarter some time after 1.00am, heading away from them. Although Captain Smith thought that it was a planet, astronomical programs show that the only visible planet in the sky was Jupiter. It was, however, sufficiently high in the sky for it to have been impossible to have been mistaken for a ship's light on the horizon. Rowe was sure that the light he saw was a ship's light. At this time, the *Carpathia* was too far away to have been responsible for this light, even though the bearings from the *Titanic* are extremely similar.

The situation is summarised in the diagram below. On the *Carpathia*, the red lights of the ship were seen at roughly the time that Boxhall's flares were seen (at 3.15am, with about ten miles to go to the wreck site). If the *Titanic* was pointing roughly North, and a *Carpathia* to "red light" distance ("A" on the first map) was less than the maximum visible distance, then this would put the unknown red light ship much closer to the *Carpathia's* track - i.e. further to the south and east. Thus, this red light could correspond to Rowe's observation of a light on the *Titanic's* starboard quarter (i.e. right rear). This does not unfortunately give us the heading of the unknown ship as the sidelights cover a range of angles. Admittedly, this does rely on the above sequence of events being correct, but it would mean that, after 1.00am, Rowe saw his ship's light. At 3.15am, Rostron sees the red light of (perhaps) this same ship, in very roughly the same location as Rowe. If these observations relate to the same ship, the following situation becomes possible (note that the drift is denoted in a southerly direction for simplicity)

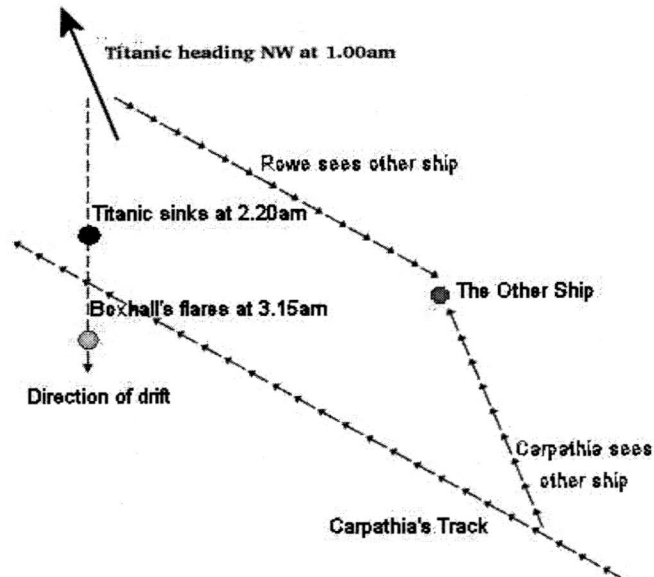

Illustration 61: Possible location of a mystery ship seen from the Carpathia and (possibly) the Titanic

The identity of this ship has never been established. As Dave Gittins says, "The great mystery of *Carpathia's* ship is that none of her crew later appeared to tell of sighting the Cunarder rushing through the night, firing a mixture of socket signals and Roman candles. Given the propensity of seamen to tell good yarns, this silence is remarkable[368]." As he says, the *Californian* crewmen couldn't keep quiet!

---

368   http://users.senet.com.au/~gittins/Carpathia.html In his e-book, Dave remarks that these lights are not mentioned in Rostron's or Bisset's memoirs. Incidentally, despite mentioning it to Ivan Thompson a few years after the Titanic disaster, Rostron does not mention seeing the *Californian* early in the morning in his recollections. Human memory is a wonderful – and fallible thing.

Appendix E. The Rockets Above The Horizon

This appendix deals with the necessarily mathematical treatment of the trigonometry of the rockets, the height they attained, and how far above the horizon they would be seen. In the following sketch, 'C' represents the *Californian,* 'T' the *Titanic* and 'R' the height at which the rockets detonated.

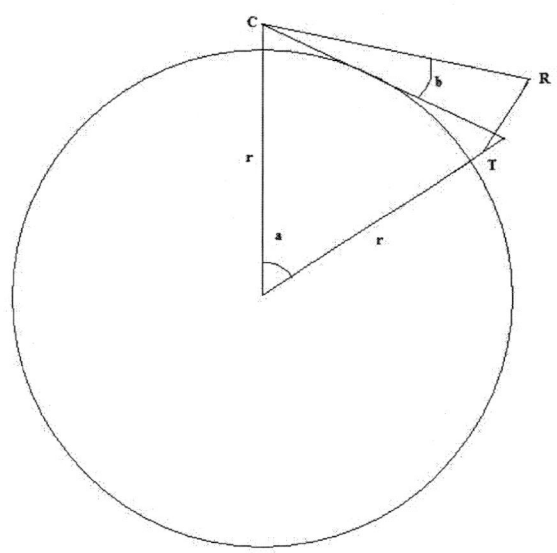

Illustration 62: Cross-section of the Earth (not to scale)

The first step is to calculate the angle 'a' between the position of the *Californian* ('C') and the *Titanic* ('T'). The frequently quoted value for the distance between them is some 21 miles; this would be the arc length, along the perimeter of the Earth, not the 'straight-line' distance. The standard formula that relates these variables is:

s = ra, where 'r' is the Earth's radius, 's' is the arc length, and 'a' is given in radians. Despite the fact that geodesic studies have determined that the radius varies slightly with latitude, over the comparatively small distances mentioned here, it can be taken as a constant value.

'a' thus becomes 0.006 radians.

We can elaborate on the triangle above the Earth's circumference.

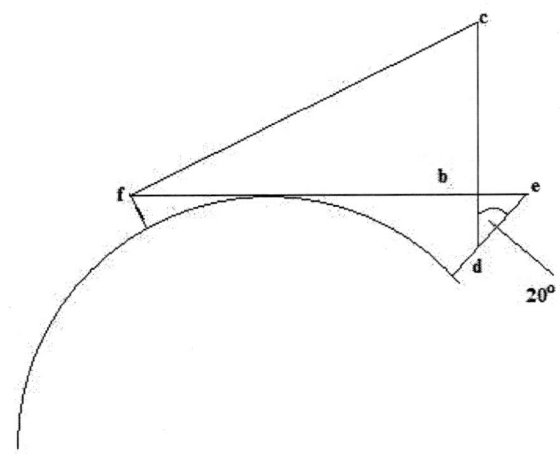

Illustration 63: Elaboration of the Titanic-Californian-Rocket geometry

How high above the surface of the water would the rockets – or a ship for that matter, have to be for it to be observed at 21 miles? This is given by the familiar equation:

21 miles = 1.17(square root of *Californian* observer's height above the sea ('f) + square root of 'e').

Solving this, we find that 'e' is 126 feet. Rockets would reach a height of about 860 feet maximum, so obviously they would rise well above the horizon, but from an observer at 'f', how far? This is complicated by the fact that the rockets were not discharged vertically, but at angle of 20°. What we need is to calculate the distance 'b – c'. The height of the *Titanic's* boat deck was 60.5 feet; this is the distance from the surface to 'd' on the diagram above. What is the distance 'd - b' ? This is (126 – 60.5) cos 20 = 61.5 feet. The distance 'b – c' is therefore 800-61.5 = 738.5 feet.

We need to know a few more parameters before we can work out the angle that rockets would be seen to rise, relative to the horizontal. We need to know the distance 'f – b' and the angle at 'b'. Let us deal with the first of these.

We can use the cosine rule to determine 'f – b'; this can be found as follows:

'f-b'^{2} = r ^{2} + r ^{2} – 2r ^{2} cos a

Technically, the values of 'r' (radius of the Earth) should really be, respectively, the radius plus 'f' and 'e'; however, these heights above the surface are so small compared to 'r' that they are of negligible significance.

The distance 'f – b' is 125553 feet or 20.7 nautical miles. Compared to this, the value 'e – b' is sufficiently small to be negligible.

Modifying the above diagram somewhat, we find the following:

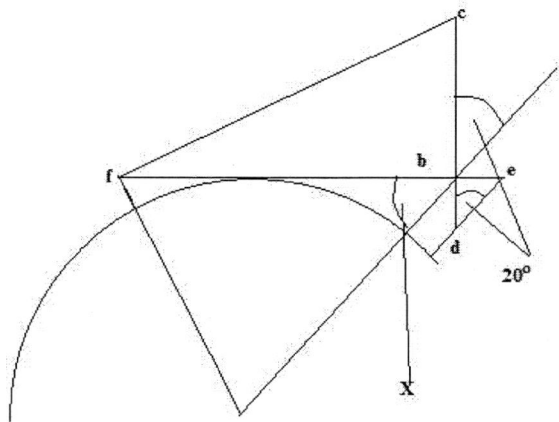

Illustration 64: Determination of angles

The diagram includes a few assumptions; mainly that, when drawing a radial line from the centre of the Earth to points 'e' and 'b', that these are sufficiently parallel that the angle between these radii and the rocket trajectory is still 20°. Given the small angles and distances involved, compared with the Earth's radius, these tiny approximations are reasonable.

Since they are on a straight line, $180° =$ angle X + angle b + $20°$

We use the cosine rule again:

$r^2 = {}'f - b'^2 + r^2 - 2('f-b')(r) \cos X$

Which yields X = arccos ('f – b'/2r)

Thus X gives us 89.8°. Angle b is therefore 70.2°. Finally, this gives us the following picture:

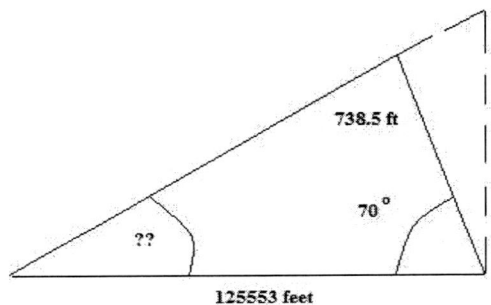

Illustration 65: Final trigonometric deduction

This unfortunately presents a minor problem. To determine the unknown angle, we need a right-angled triangle. However, we can determine the height of the triangle (the dashed vertical line) by projecting the 738.5 feet line onto a vertical. Thus, the unknown height is given by

Height = 738.5/cos (20°) = 786 feet

The unknown angle is therefore arctan (785/125553) = 0.36°, or, rounding up, we deduce a value of 0.4° ; this is reasonable since we have made some assumptions and approximations in our reasoning. A rocket reaching 660 feet would yield a value of 0.29°

This should be compared with the angular width of a full moon, of 0.5°.

Bibliography

Ballard, Dr. Robert D. Ballard and Rick Archbold *"The Discovery of the Titanic"*, Hodder and Stoughton, 1987
Behe, George *"Titanic: Psychic Forewarnings of a Tragedy"*, Patrick Stephens 1988
Butler, Daniel Allen, *"The Other Side of the Night"*, Casemate 2009
Bryceson, Dave *"The Titanic Disaster"* Patrick Stephens 1997
Davie, Michael *"The Titanic – The Full Story of a Tragedy"*, Bodley Head 1986
Gittins, Dave *"Titanic: Monument and Warning"*, self published e-book, 2005
Harrison, Leslie *"The Californian Incident: An Echo of the Titanic Disaster"*, M.M.S.A., 1962
Harrison, Leslie - 1965 and 1968 petitions issued to the Board of Trade, M.M.S.A.
Harrison, Leslie *"A Titanic Myth"*, William Kimber, 1986
Harrison, Leslie *"A Titanic Myth Part 2: Defending Captain Lord"*
Harrison, Leslie *"Captain Lord's Plight To Remember"* self-published, 1997
Lord, Walter *"A Night To Remember"*, Penguin, 1975
Lord, Walter *"The Night Lives On"*, Morrow, 1986
MacQuitty, William *"Titanic Memories – the making of 'A Night To Remember'"*
Marcus, Geoffrey *"The Maiden Voyage"*, George Allen and Unwin, 1969
Molony, Senan *"A Ship Accused"*, Cedric Information Services, 2002
Molony, Senan *"Mount Temple and Titanic: Murmurs and Misadventure"*, published by the author, 2003
Molony, Senan *"The Titanic and the Mystery Ship"*, Tempus publishing, 2006
Moore, Hubert Stuart *"The Rules of the Road At Sea* (3rd Edition)" J.D.Potter, 1900
Padfield, Peter *"The Titanic and the Californian"*, Hodder and Stoughton, 1965
Reade, Leslie and de Groot, Edward (editor) *"The Ship That Stood Still"*, Patrick Stephens, 1993
Wade, Wyn Craig *"The Titanic – End of a dream"*, Weidenfeld, 1986
Williams, Thomas and Kamps, Rob (editor) *"Titanic and the Californian"*, Tempus publishing, 2007
Winocour, Jack (Editor) *"The Story of the Titanic As Told By Its Survivors"*, Dover, 1960

Periodicals consulted include; The Titanic [Historical Society] Commutator, [The Titanic International Society Journal] Voyage, United States Naval Institute Proceedings, the London and New York *Times*, Sea Breezes, National Geographic and Lloyds publications.

Websites:

Dave Billnitzer - http://home.earthlink.net/~dnitzer/titanic.html

Dave Gittins - http://users.senet.com.au/~gittins/index.html
George Behe - http://ourworld.compuserve.com/homepages/Carpathia/
Sam Halpern - http://www.geocities.com/samuel_halpern/mypage.html
Great Lakes Titanic Society - http://www.glts.org/
Titanic Inquiry Project - http://titanicinquiry.org/
Titanic Research and Modelling Association - http://www.titanicmodel.com
Encyclopedia Titanica - http://www.encyclopedia-titanica.org

Index

Note to readers: frequently occurring indexed terms (for instance, *"Californian"*, *"Captain Lord"* and *"Titanic"*) have been omitted from this compilation. In some instances, where a first name, initials, or title of a person is not known, this has resulted in that person simply being known by his/her surname, sadly.

440

441